THE SPLENDID TABLE

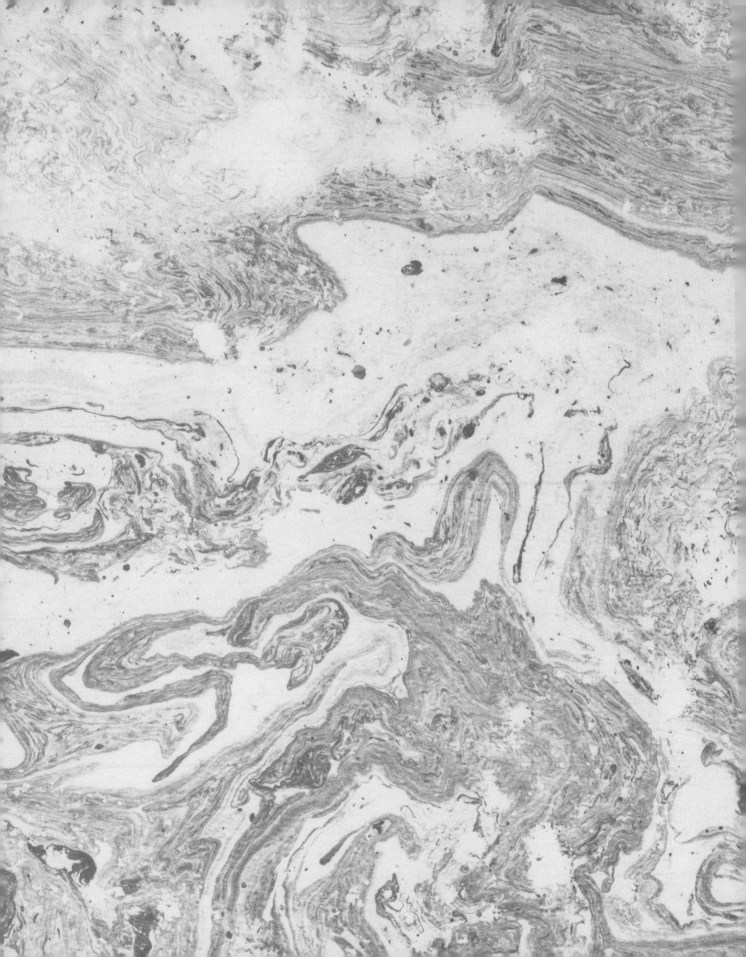

THE SPLENDID TABLE

Recipes from Emilia-Romagna, the Heartland of Northern Italian Food

Lynne Rossetto Kasper

Art direction by Richard Oriolo
Design concept by Stephanie Tevonian
Color photographs by Louis Wallach
Line drawings by Laura Hartman Maestro

William Morrow and Company, Inc.
New York

It is the policy of William Morrow and Company,
Inc., and its imprints and affiliates, recognizing the
importance of preserving what has been written, to
print the books we publish on acid-free paper, and we
exert our best efforts to that end.

Library of Congress Cataloging-in-Publication Data
Kasper, Lynne Rossetto.
    The splendid table: recipes from Emilia-
Romagna, the heartland of Northern Italian food /
    by Lynne Rossetto Kasper.
        p. cm.
    ISBN 0-688-08963-1
        1. Cookery, Italian—Northern style.   I. Title.
TX723.2.N65K37 1992
    641.5945'4—dc20   91-23512
                                                     CIP

Printed in the United States of America

First Edition

9 10

To Frank, Cara and Marjorie with love and thanks

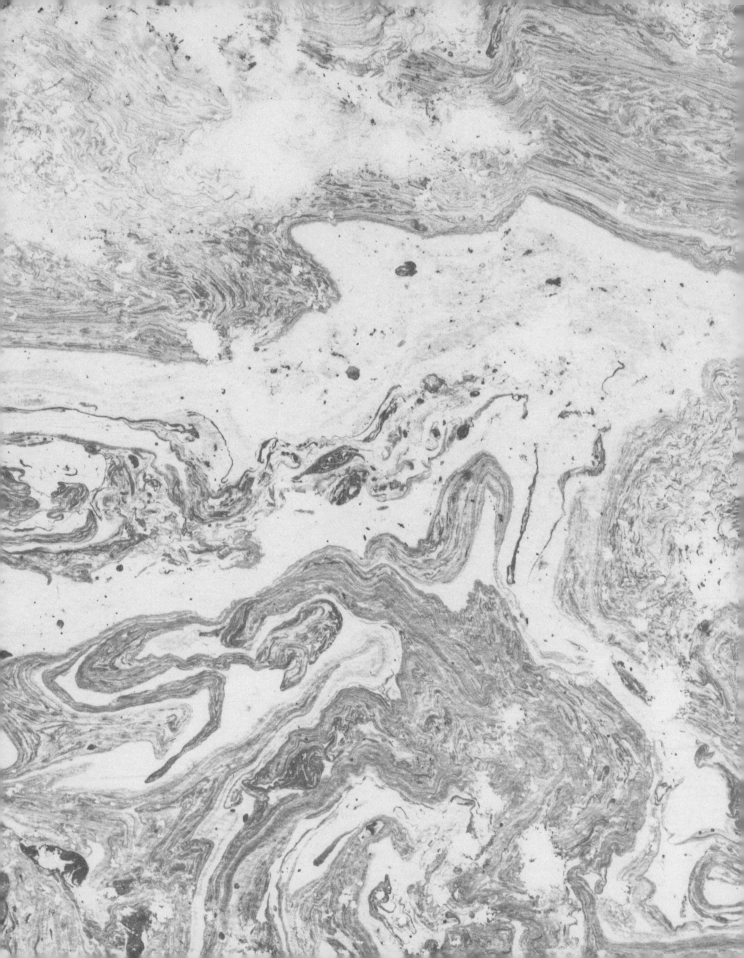

Acknowledgments

The greatest joy in this book has been the people who made it possible. I want to wrap my arms around the entire region of Emilia-Romagna in appreciation. She and her people shared so much, not only in tangible information, but in the intangibles: the spirit of her hospitality, the way light moves across her plain and her deep passion for her own culinary heritage.

There are so many to thank. But I begin with four people who have shared, supported, helped, and urged me on. So many times they literally lived and breathed Emilia-Romagna with me. Without them there would have been a book, but not this one.

My husband, Frank, heard and critiqued endless drafts of this book. He supported, encouraged, and cheered me on even when it meant my total distraction from anything to do with our life. He made me laugh at those times when laughter was the furthest thing from my mind.

Cara De Silva may well be the only other person in America who cares as deeply about Emilia-Romagna as I do. We have shared so many voyages there. Weeping over extraordinary tortellini, searching for an elusive bread, asking endless questions (and recalling ones I had forgotten), Cara is not only the sister I never had, but also part of the heart and soul of this book.

Marjorie Cater defines the word *friend.* When I could no longer see forests for trees, Marjorie said, "Let me help." For six weeks Marjorie and her husband, Fred, stopped their lives and opened their home to my computer and library. Together we sorted through the grain and chaff of the manuscript. No friend or writer could be blessed with more.

Maria Guarnaschelli is a writer's dream of an editor, bringing every bit of her remarkable intelligence, passion, objectivity, wonderful humor and incredible energy to this project. She is the midwife and second mother of this book. I can never fully express my thanks for her deep commitment and friendship.

Jane Dystel has been agent par excellence—always there and always savvy. She is everything an author could ask for in an agent.

Mario Zannoni of the Consorzio del Formaggio Parmigiano-Reggiano and Parma scholar shared his passion for Parma and Parmigiano-Reggiano, answered nine years' worth of questions, and urged my thinking and my research in the directions that formed much of this book. My debt to him is boundless.

Photographer Lou Wallach and food stylist Rick Ellis translated my vision and the food of Emilia-Romagna into superb pictures. Thanks to them and their crews. Special appreciation to Richard Oriolo for his help with the photos and the sensitive layout of the book. Food historian and friend Alice Ross unhesitantly opened her home and fabulous 18th-century cooking studio to us, making possible photographs that would have been otherwise impossible.

So much gratitude to my mother and stepfather, Elda and Arthur Fulvini, for their love and encouragement. They joined forces with my aunt and uncle, Rita and Edward Buonaccorsi, in an emergency grapevine run so our tortellini pie could be photographed in a proper setting. Anna Teresa Callen is an Italian fairy godmother who insisted on my readopting my Italian maiden name, loaned her treasures for photographs, then patiently checked over my Italian throughout the manuscript. Thank you, dear lady. Alice Fixx is this book's great-aunt, leading me to so many people, hosting so many voyages of adventure, while encouraging and advising.

Lin Lacy and Barbara Greenspon listened and urged me on with *unfailing belief. Designer Stephanie Tevonian brought her flair to the book, creating a thing of beauty. Francesca Lo Baido brought her warm and tireless support to the book, as did all the entire Modena/St. Paul Sister City Committee. Kit Rogers lent his talent and wonderful humor. My thanks to Colleen Herrick and her husband, Michael, who worked unstintingly testing recipes with me. Denise Landis gave perceptive and thoughtful notes on the first drafts of these dishes, helping me rethink and rework where necessary. Thanks, too, to Janice Cole, Hally Herron and Lois Lee, who generously helped with the last of the tests, and to everyone at Cook's of Crocus Hill.*

Maureen Walker helped with proofing, giving her time with such generosity. Andrea Grover, Mary Beth Clark and Gisella Isadori shared contacts and information.

Pat Brown, as editor of Cuisine, *sent me to Emilia-Romagna on assignment. That article planted the seeds for this book. My gratitude to her is not only for that, but for the lunches of enthusiasm and support. And to everyone at* Bon Appétit*—Bill Garry, Barbara Fairchild and former editor Marilou Vaughan—my thanks for the encouragement and for the years of working with some of the nicest people in the business.*

Anyone writing about Italy owes much to Marcella Hazan. She is the doyenne. My introduction to Emilia-Romagna was through her classes in Bologna in 1977. My appreciation to the Italian Trade Commission in New York for so much help, especially Dr. Giorgio Lulli and Michele Jones.

Bologna was opened to me through the years by Anna Maria and Paolo Penzo, who shared so much. The tourist board there orchestrated much of the beginnings of my research and stepped in with assistance whenever I asked. Special thanks to Aldo d'Alfonso and Dr. Gianna Spezia. These are some of the Bolognese who offered so much information and assistance: Giancarlo Roversi, Bruno Tasselli, Giovanni Tamburini, Franco Rossi, Romano Fornasari, Anna Maria and Romano Bonaga, Athos Conti, Eligio Grasselli, Renato Gualandi, Ivo Salsini, Franco Cazzola, Piero Bondi and Ivo Galletti.

Paola Bini and the farm women at Villa Gaidello shared Modena's and Bologna's farm traditions as well as friendship and recipes. My deep appreciation to Dr. Guidotti-Bentivoglio, Mario Costanzini, Professor Renato Bergonzini and members of the Consorzio Produttori Aceto Balsamico Tradizionale di Modena for their years of help. Bergonzini unfailingly shared contacts, history, and his vast knowledge. Gran Maestro Benedetto Benedetti, Florindo Sirotti, Giuseppe Giusti, Giuseppe Cattani, Italo Pedroni and other members of Spilamberto's vinegar consortium first introduced me to the artisanship of balsamic vinegar. The Leonelli family of Rodiano introduced me to Tigelle; Eugenio Gollini graciously shared everything about Torta Barozzi except the recipe, and Mauro Cappi and Vasco Bagni brought alive so many Modena hill traditions.

The consortium of Parmigiano-Reggiano cheese has been a mainstay for almost a decade. So much has been shared far beyond cheese, an entire chapter could be written on their contributions. My special thanks to Senator Giampaolo Mora, Renzo Cattabiani, and Dr. Leo Bertozzi. Doors have opened and people have welcomed me because of their help. Ettore Grisendi, Signore Fanti and Massimo Montuschi of the Consortium of Prosciutto di Parma deserve so much thanks. Ettore's knowledge of Parma foods is encyclopedic. Thanks also to Guglielmo Capacchi, Ugo Falavigna, Dino Piani, Paola Cavazinni, Elia Fanti, Maurizio Rossi, Sergio Ravazzoni, everyone at Salumeria Garibaldi, Eletta Violi, Erminia Marasi, Anna Bertolazzi, Barilla Pasta, Dr. Luigi and Elsa Zannoni, Miriam and Elena Leonardi, Giancarlo Grassi, the staff of Due Foscari, and Giovanni Ballarini.

In Reggio my thanks to Pier Paolo and Stefano Veroni, who patiently responded to faxes and phone calls of endless questions, to the Dallari pasta makers, and erbazzoni maker Leonardo Righi.

So much of Piacenza was shared by my stepfather, Arthur Fulvini, and his family there—Delphina Fulvini, Dr. Ugo Gazzola, and his wife, Cesarina. Through them I met Giorgio Cogni and Maria Bertuzzi.

Ferrara's Nicola Gigli and the tourist board always were on the spot with responses, assistance, and fine good humor. Riccardo Rimondi helped shape the essence of this book with his recipes and information. Thanks also to Sergio Ferrarini, Michele Bonino, Ida Bonfiglioli Ascoli, the Perdonati bakers, Aldo Brando, Lanfranco Viola and Giovanni Battista Panatta.

Gianni Quondomatteo and his family brought alive the folklore of Romagna. I can never repay their instant kindness and generosity. Franco Casalboni gave a whole new dimension to <u>cucina povera</u> with his "poor" lunch. Thanks also to Elettiziana Bernardini, Fabiano Bernardini, Antonio Monti, Rosa Severi Grazia, Elionore Dallaro, Annapia Bertoni and Primo Grassi.

Contents

llazione, che si da più ò meno copiosa ogni due mesi alla Guardia de Suizzeri dal Confaloniero di Bologna il giorno avanti ..... ingresso   G. M. Mitelli fece ..

THE SPLENDID TABLE

SWITZERLAND

AUSTRIA

FRANCE

VAL
D'AOSTA

ALTO ADIGE

TRENTINO

FRIULI-
VENEZIA
GIULIA

SLOVENIJA

•Milan

LOMBARDY

PIEDMONT

VENETO

LIGURIA

EMILIA-ROMAGNA

Genoa

Bologna

Venice

Ligurian
Sea

Adriatic Sea

TUSCANY

•Firenze

MARCHE

UMBRIA

ABRUZZI

LAZIO

•Rome

MOLISE

SARDINIA

CAMPAGNA

APULIA

Tyrrhenian
Sea

Naples

BASILICATA

ITALY

CALABRIA

SICILY

INTRODUCING EMILIA-ROMAGNA

Ask an Italian where to eat only one meal in Italy and, after recommending his mother's house, it is more than likely he will send you to the region of Emilia-Romagna. Few foreigners know the region by name, but even those people with only a passing interest in food recognize its products. By law, Parmesan (Parmigiano-Reggiano) cheese and Prosciutto di Parma (one of Italy's two most admired prosciutti) can be produced only in Emilia-Romagna. And its wealth of handmade pastas, including the famed tortellini, are admired far beyond its borders.

Balsamic vinegar originated here over a thousand years ago. Even though imitations are now made from Naples to Milan, the great balsamics—the ones that are aged for decades and are luscious enough to be sipped like liqueurs—are made only in the region.

The region's cuisine is as complex as an intricately woven tapestry. There is a peasant kitchen, a thriving middle-class cuisine, and the highly refined traditions of the region's nobility. This book is about five centuries of that culinary heritage.

If only one word could describe Emilia-Romagna, it would have to be rich. Not rich in the sense of fat, but rich in dishes of deep, layered tastes. Even at its simplest, Emilia-Romagna's food tastes as if it has evolved from a long tradition. Yet there is always a spontaneity to what you eat.

Emilia-Romagna sits between Florence and Venice, to the south of Milan. The wedge-shaped region nudges its way into northern Italy from the Adriatic Sea. Its borders are formed by the Adriatic coast, the Po River and the peaks of the Apennines. The region is half mountains and half plains. Its geography is crucial to its cuisine.

If this book were a novel, two of its main characters would be the Po River plain and the road called the Via Emilia. A large section of the plain, Italy's largest and most fertile expanse of land, lies within Emilia-Romagna's borders. That plain (the Padano) has made the region a major agricultural force. Its rich grazing and good land produces Parmigiano-Reggiano (Parmesan) cheese, Parma ham and the wheat for an extraordinary variety of handmade pastas.

When the Romans built Italy's main north-south trade route, the Via Emilia, they ran it up the entire length of Emilia-Romagna. That road, along with the east-west routes that crossed it, made Emilia-Romagna a crossroads for all of northern Italy—including her two major ports, Genoa and Venice, and their links to the worlds of the East and West. It tied the region to northern, central and eastern Europe, and to Rome and the south. Each link brought traders, visitors, and conquerors with their new foods, dining traditions and ideas. Today a superhighway parallels the Via Emilia.

The original road is Main Street to six of Emilia-Romagna's eight provincial capitals: Piacenza, Parma, Reggio, Modena, Bologna and Forlì. Each of these cities grew up on the Via Emilia at a point where it was crossed by a major trade road out of the Apennines. The two remaining provincial capitals lie out on the Po plain. Ravenna, the ancient Roman seaport and later the western capital of the Byzantine Empire, sits on the old route from Rome to Venice. Ferrara is farther inland, on the road connecting Florence, Bologna and Ferrara with Venice.

Ferrara's strategic placement on the banks of the Po not far from the Adriatic gave her control of northern Italy's most important river and delta. That piece of geography helped Ferrara's Este family create and sustain one of the most powerful and long-lived dynasties of the Renaissance. Among the legacies of the Este are invaluable written records of their feasts and foods, dishes that are still a vital part of Ferrara's cooking today.

Food changes subtly and sometimes dramatically from one part of Emilia-Romagna to another. Once you are inside, you discover that each area has its own style—the elegant restraint of Parma's cooking, the medieval flavors still dominating Ferrara's foods, Bologna's lustiness and complexity, the richness and slightly countrified quality of Modena's dishes, Reggio's refinements, Piacenza's blending of the three regions pressing at her borders, and the underlying simplicity of Forlì's and Ravenna's specialties.

Emilia and Romagna were created by warring Romans and Gauls. The first Etruscan and Greek settlers gradually gave way to the Gauls from the north, who were attracted by the area's rich land and vineyards. Expanding their empire north from Rome, the Romans challenged the Gauls for possession of the region. The Gauls stopped the advancing legions south and east of Bologna. That area remained Roman, or Romagna, while the plains and mountains to the west and north eventually became Emilia. Finally Rome gained all of Emilia-Romagna and the region's Roman settlers went on to create some of the earliest written records of the region's foods.

Today the border between Romagna and Emilia is still elusive—I have yet to see it marked on a regional map. Everyone agrees that Romagna encompasses all of the region's Adriatic coast, including the provinces of Forlì and Ravenna. Part of Ferrara province falls under Romagna, but not Ferrara city. Romagna also includes part of Bologna province, but stops somewhere (few agree precisely where) short of the city of Bologna. Emilia includes the provinces of Piacenza, Parma, Reggio, Modena and part of Ferrara. A portion of Bologna province and, technically, all of Bologna city are Emilian. But Bologna is the region's capital, and the Bolognese make a strong point of being neither of Emilia nor Romagna but an entity unto themselves.

Through the centuries, Romagna generally remained under the control of forces outside the region. First it was under the rule of the Roman Empire, then of the Byzantine Empire, and finally of the church as part of the Papal State, which joined Romagna with central Italy. Local noble families periodically wrested away land and gained power, but usually they lost it again, and Romagna remained of Rome and the papacy.

As a result, today Romagna's food is more unified than Emilia's, tasting more of central Italy than of the north. Certainly each area of

Romagna has its specialties and its own character, but provincial distinctions and the elaborate dishes of old court life are less prominent here than in Emilia. Food in Romagna tends to be more direct and assertive—the everyday and feast-day dishes of townspeople, farmers, and fishermen.

Emilia's destiny was different. After the Roman Empire crumbled and local lords jousted for rule of the plains and mountains during the Dark Ages, Emilia was divided among a handful of Renaissance families.

All of Ferrara, Modena and Reggio were ruled by the Este family from 1208 to 1598. Then Ferrara passed to the Pope, and the Este packed up six hundred wagons with three hundred years' worth of possessions and caravanned across the Po plain to make Modena their new capital. They ruled Modena and Reggio until the mid-1800s, when their alliances with Austria took the last Este duke to Vienna and Modena and Reggio became part of unified Italy.

Parma and Piacenza went from papal possession to a duchy ruled between 1545 and 1732 by the Farnese dukes originally from Rome. They then passed to France, Austria, and finally joined the Italian unification movement. Those centuries as a center of court for some of the mightiest powers in Europe—as an annex to the 18th-century court of Louis XV, it was known as "the Athens of Italy"—gave Parma's food its foundations of refinement and finesse.

Bologna, like Romagna, was part of the Papal State. It became a sophisticated trade center and second only to Rome in power. As the seat of Europe's first university, founded in 1080, Bologna attracted the offspring of the continent's nobility. Those young students came with their own retainers, bringing to Bologna new dining habits, food preferences, cooking styles and wealth. The university thrives today, and the city still bustles as an important trade center.

Bologna has three titles in Italy. She is called Bologna the Wise for her fame as a seat of learning. Bologna the Red for her red tiled roofs, russet-colored buildings and, some say, her years of Communist government. Finally, the title every Italian knows is Bologna the Fat, for the wealth of her land and table since the days of the Romans.

Aside from Emilia-Romagna's geography and history, intangibles formed her character and are at the heart of the development of her gastronomy. Perhaps because of those thousands of years of trade, the *people of the region have an openness to the outside world and a winning graciousness with strangers. Both the Romagnoli and the Emiliani seem to have had the rare ability to take whatever was offered by their rulers, conquerors and visitors and then refashion it into something that worked for them. Frequently what was offered was meager indeed, yet the region not only survived, it thrived.*

To this keen sense of survival add an even keener sense of excellence. In Emilia-Romagna there is real joy in creating something extraordinary, whether it be a sheet of pasta dough, a vinegar, a ham or a cheese.

In embracing five hundred years of cooking in the region, this book includes dishes from every level of Emilia-Romagna's culture. The range is broad and deep, from the stews of pasta and beans that sustained field hands and laborers to the grand gilded pies that crowded the tables of counts, dukes and princes. You will find dishes created centuries ago and modern innovations on those old themes. Famous regional specialties known throughout the world are collected here, along with rare dishes unheard-of away from their home villages. All make superb eating.

This portrait of Emilia-Romagna begins with the Renaissance, an era that is still a vital and immediate part of the region's food. People here talk of dining in the 1500s the way Americans mention going out to dinner last week.

The Renaissance had as its status symbols spices and sugar that were used in its banquets of many dishes. The style lingered through the 1600s. But by the mid-1700s meals in Emilia-Romagna had changed. Spices were toned down. Sweet and savory flavors that had mingled in dishes from first courses to last at Renaissance banquets parted company in the 18th century and took their places in specific parts of the menu. The foundations of modern cooking begun during the Renaissance were taking recognizable shape by the late 1700s. Meat ragù sauce over pasta, now one of Emilia-Romagna's most typical dishes, first appears at this time. The tomato gradually loses its status as a curiosity and is accepted as an ingredient. When Napoleon conquers all of Italy for France, French influence strengthens in Emilia-Romagna.

By the early 1800s, the scores of dishes that had made up 16th-century banquet menus for the region's aristocrats had diminished to a mere twenty or thirty. If you were rich you ate foods with French,

Austrian, Spanish and Middle European, as well as Italian, names, and you ate meat with abandon. If you were an artisan, professor, landowner, winemaker or merchant, you ate more modest versions of those dishes, with less meat. If you were a field hand, tenant farmer or laborer, the foods of the rich were as distant and exotic as the foods of China. The mainstays of your diet were stews of beans, polenta and seasonal vegetables, with small bits of the cheapest pork cuts flavoring the pot. Meat marked the celebrations of Christmas, Easter and special occasions. Bread was of dark flours. White flour for pasta and bread was attainable for all only with the arrival of the Industrial Revolution in the mid-19th century.

In spite of the harsh lines drawn between the classes, the region endured. It has come through centuries of invasions and occupations, internal political upheaval and social rebellion. Today everyone eats, and eats well. Today Emilia-Romagna prospers. And today, perhaps more than ever, she reaches out to strangers with her irresistible openhanded hospitality. "Come join us, come and feast," she always seems to be saying. In that spirit, and on her behalf, with this cookbook I extend that same invitation to you all.

A NOTE ON THE RECIPES

My goal was to keep tastes, character and traditions intact, bringing you the flavors of Emilia-Romagna in all their glory. Keeping recipes authentic and their tastes true brought the inevitable difficulties encountered whenever you take the regional food of one place to another part of the world. Often products are unavailable. For instance, the young, artisan-made balsamic vinegars used by families in Reggio and Modena for salads and for cooking <u>into</u> dishes (as opposed to the older, artisan-made vinegars used to flavor finished dishes) are not to be had in the United States. To come close to their rich yet acidic character, I borrow a trick from a talented Modenese cook. She adds a tiny amount of brown sugar to good quality commercially produced balsamic.

When I translated recipes from Emilia-Romagna to America, often products that seemed the same were not. For example, Emilia-Romagna's salt pork is sweeter, rounder in flavor, and far less salty than the salt pork of the United States. And it is often cured to be eaten raw. It is not exported to the U.S.A. So here in America, I substitute domestically produced pancetta for salt pork. Its slow-cure and round sweet flavor comes close to the character of Emilia-Romagna's salt pork.

As regional cooks now do, I use olive oil as the actual cooking medium, with reduced quantities of pancetta, prosciutto, and mortadella as flavorings. Although this changes some old recipes, with their generous quantities of pork and butter, it makes them available to a whole new public both in Emilia-Romagna and here.

In recipes where generous amounts of fat were called for, I recommend discarding it after browning or skimming it off after the final cooking, leaving behind only flavor. My thanks to Paula Wolfert and her work with fats for pointing out this technique. If dietary and health concerns require that you eliminate even small amounts of pork or butter, do not omit the dish from your repertoire. Substituting olive oil for all the fats will alter the dish's character, but not its goodness.

Wherever I felt a dish's authenticity and quality would be lost with these changes, I left it in its original state, just as it is preserved in Emilia-Romagna.

Cream is almost nonexistent in Emilia-Romagna's dishes. Bolognese food expert Giancarlo Roversi said recently, "Whoever introduced cream into our cooking should be guillotined." You will find cream in desserts, but rarely in savory foods.

It is very tempting to say that there is only one way to cook a dish. But the most important thing I learned in my years in Emilia-Romagna is one way of preparing a dish was always countered with varying renditions from down the block, down the road, or across the province. So what you will find in these pages are the dishes, and the methods of making them that are the most typical of Emilia-Romagna.

Vital to keeping tastes as authentic as possible is understanding the foundation ingredients of Emilia-Romagna's foods, knowing what to seek out and how to use it. "A Guide to Ingredients" (page 467) provides this information. Note that each recipe has a "Working Ahead" section, so you can anticipate the recipe's rhythm. Menu suggestions are extensive. They illustrate not only how a dish fits into Emilia-Romagna's cuisine but also how it translates into American dining.

Wine suggestions offer regional wines that may be available here. They also include wines from other parts of Italy, more readily found in the United States. While drinking a wine from the same origin as the dish is a wonderful experience, Emilia-Romagna's wines are not broadly distributed in the United States at this time. Other Italian wines make fine stand-ins.

Since recipes tell only half the story of what makes this cuisine so special, I have accompanied many of them with notes that share the legends, histories, origins, and people that shape this place and its foods.

Giuseppe Giusti Salumeria, Modena

THE ANTIPASTO COURSE

In Emilia-Romagna the antipasto is usually savored as a single dish presented at the table before the first course. It can be as simple as a few slices of prosciutto or as elaborate as a mousse of chicken and duck livers. The richer the dish, the smaller the portion. There is a fine balance here; rarely are antipasti overdone. These first tastes are meant to remind us just how hungry we are for what is to come and to keep us that way.

Occasionally confusing to non-Italians is the fact that the antipasto is not a first course. In Italy first courses are pastas, risotti, soups and important vegetable dishes. The antipasto is the optional introduction to a menu, sometimes offered before the first course.

I have included menu suggestions with each antipasto recipe, but enjoy these dishes as your mood dictates. Emilia-Romagna's most important culinary tradition is taking pleasure on your own terms.

Platter of Cured Meats in the Style of Emilia-Romagna
Antipasto di Salumi

No matter where you dine, from Ferrara to Piacenza, in homes, remote <u>trattorie</u> in the country or in city restaurants, a platter of cured meats is the most frequently served antipasto. On it you will always find oval slices of locally made salami, thin rounds of coppa and even thinner pieces of prosciutto. Occasionally pancetta or mortadella appear, depending on where you happen to be. These platters testify to the skill of Emilia-Romagna's artisans. Endless variations in artisans' styles assert themselves: one adds some red wine to his salami, another cinnamon or garlic or cloves.

Sometimes baskets of fritters and small dishes of marinated vegetables are added for a more substantial first course or a whole meal. Most of the time, the platter stands alone, with everyone taking just enough to work up an appetite. Cured meats are usually eaten at the table with a knife and fork. Breads like Ferrara's <u>Coppia,</u> Romagna's <u>Piadina</u> or Modena Mountain Bread are offered. Butter is often set out, but few use it.

Parma ham and cooked prosciutto (much like boiled ham) are the only Italian pork products imported into the United States at this time. But you can assemble your own platter by finding the best source in your area for domestically made cured meats. Count on $\frac{1}{2}$ to 1 ounce of meat per person.

Emilia-Romagna's most classical and elegant antipasto is three or four sheer slices of Prosciutto di Parma served only with a bread like Ferrara's Coppia. In this country, use a crusty baguette. No fruit or other embellishments are needed. For a more informal platter, set out short links of cacciatore salami (hunter's-style salami), thinly sliced, with Modena Mountain Bread and Marinated Baby Onions. Cubes of mortadella on long bamboo skewers are traditional before a meal of Bolognese dishes. Good coppa, sliced thin, is the classic starter for a Piacenza menu. Mix coppa, salami and a robust, slightly salty prosciutto to go with a Modena meal.

When it is difficult to find meats cured in the style of Emilia-Romagna, I serve several types of salami inspired by other northern regions—Genoa-style, Tuscan and Venetian, for instance. Paper-thin slices of pancetta and coppa are another favorite combination. If I come across a superb salami, I serve it by itself. The key is to present the best meats you can buy. Better one excellent example than three lesser ones.

Method **Working Ahead:** *Slices of meats can be arranged on the platter up to 4 hours before serving, covered tightly with plastic wrap, and refrigerated. Bring them to room temperature, covered, before serving.*

Suggestions **Wine:** In the region, drink Parma's own sparkling Malvasia with Prosciutto di Parma. Here, try a Casal Garcia Vinho Verde from Portugal, an unexpected success discovered by wine expert David Rosengarten. With other cured meats drink Lambrusco in Italy; or a fresh young red like Valpolicella Classico, Sangiovese di Romagna, a fizzy Freisa d'Asti, "La Monella" Braida di Giacomo Bologna, or Barbera di Rocchetta Tanaro from the Piedmont, all available here.

Menu: Serve cured meats before pastas, risotti, and soups offered as first courses, or before simple main dishes that do not contain cured meats. Always serve in small quantities.

Nineteenth-century New Year engraving

Antipasto Castelvetro
Antipasto Castelvetro

I *first tasted the combination of sweet/tart marinated onions, cured meats and puffed bread fritters at the medieval castle restaurant Al Castello, in the Modenese hill town of Castelvetro. Since then I have often eaten this classic country antipasto in much of Emilia. For lighter appetites, the trio makes a fine meal by itself. Modenese trenchermen, however, regard it as an overture to several courses, including soup, pasta and meats.*

Marinated Baby Onions
Cipolline sott'Aceto

B*urnished a deep burgundy by their robust marinade, at Al Castello these onions were pierced with long bamboo skewers and presented on a white platter. They are a perfect contrast for cured meats, as well as for roasted or grilled beef, lamb, duck and pork. Although not part of any Italian tradition I know of, the onions are superb with roast Christmas goose instead of the traditional sweet/sour red cabbage.*

[Serves 8]

4 quarts water

2 pounds red onions, 1¼ to 1½ inches in diameter (yellow onions can be substituted)

1½ cups sugar

½ cup water

½ cup full-bodied dry red wine

½ cup extra-virgin olive oil

2 cups red wine vinegar

⅛ teaspoon salt

About ⅛ teaspoon freshly ground black pepper

¼ cup commercial balsamic vinegar

Long bamboo skewers

Method   **Working Ahead:** *For the best flavor, prepare these at least 3 days in advance. Onions can be peeled a day before cooking; keep them covered and refrigerated. The marinated onions will hold for 3 weeks in the refrigerator.*

Peeling the Onions: Bring the 4 quarts of water to a boil in a 5- to 6-quart pot. Cut a cross into the root end of each onion. Drop them into the water, boil 1 minute, and drain in a colander. Stop the cooking by rinsing under cold water. Trim away the very top of each onion, and the skin will slip off easily.

Making the Marinade: Combine the sugar and ½ cup water in a 5- to 6-quart nonaluminum pot. Have a cup of cold water and a brush on hand. Boil the mixture over medium heat until the sugar has dissolved and the syrup is clear; then boil over high heat 2 minutes, or until pale caramel colored. As the syrup bubbles, brush down the sides of the pot with the brush dipped in cold water. Take care not to let it go beyond pale caramel. Standing back, pour in the red wine (the syrup will erupt and seethe). Once the mixture has calmed down, stir in the olive oil, wine vinegar, salt, and pepper. Boil the marinade, uncovered, 2 minutes over high heat. If you are not cooking the onions right away, remove from the heat.

Cooking the Onions: Add the onions to the marinade and bring the liquid to a slow bubble. Cover the pot and cook the onions over medium to medium-low heat, unattended, 10 to 15 minutes. The onions should be tender but a little resistant when pierced with a knife. Remove the pan from the heat and stir in the balsamic vinegar. Cool to room temperature. Taste for a pleasing balance of sweet to tart, adding a little more vinegar or sugar if needed.

Marinating the Onions: Pour the onions and their liquid into a glass storage container. Refrigerate, covered, at least 3 days and no more than 3 weeks.

Serving: Lift the onions from their liquid. (Refrigerate any onions you are not using in their liquid.) Let them come to room temperature. Stand the onions upright on a platter and spear them with the long skewers. Serve with thinly sliced prosciutto, salami, and coppa and a napkin-lined basket filled with hot, freshly made bread fritters (page 382). In true Modena style, the meats are eaten with forks and knives, accompanied by torn-off pieces of fritter and bites of onion.

Suggestions   **Wine:** In Modena a local crisp, dry Lambrusco is always taken with cured meats. The wine's fresh fizz lightens the impact of rich salami, coppa, and prosciutto. Imported Lambruscos seem too sweet, so try a chilled white Trebbiano di Romagna or di Lazio instead, or a red "La Monella" Braida di Giacomo Bologna or Barbera di Rocchetta Tanaro from Piemonte.

Menu: This three-dish antipasto is excellent on its own for lunch or supper, serving six. As a first course it is best before a light main dish, such as Herbed Seafood Grill (page 254), Giovanna's Wine-Basted Rabbit (page 284), or Grilled Winter Endives (page 337).

Cook's Notes   Although a surprise to most Modenese, caramelizing sugar syrup helps broaden and deepen the flavors of commercial balsamic vinegars available in the United States, bringing them closer to the rich, deep character of the local artisan-made vinegars. For information on balsamic vinegars, see page 467.

Balsamic Vegetables
Verdure sott'Aceto

Every year when vegetables are harvested in the Modena area families put up jars of marinated peppers, cauliflower, and onions. Traditionally served as a first course with bread fritters, these can also be an unusual condiment with ham, roast pork, or any cured meat. Mix them into salads for a great boost in flavor. They are a refreshing alternative to the jarred versions sold in Italian grocery stores.

[Makes 2 quarts]

1 quart white wine vinegar	3 medium red bell peppers, cut
2⅔ cups water	into ½-inch-wide strips
½ cup extra-virgin olive oil	3 medium yellow bell peppers, cut
1 tablespoon coarse salt	into ½-inch-wide strips
¼ cup sugar	½ medium-size cauliflower, cut
½ teaspoon freshly ground black	into bite-size flowerettes
pepper	8 to 10 pearl onions, peeled
1½ teaspoons chopped fresh basil,	⅓ cup commercial balsamic
or ½ teaspoon dried basil	vinegar

Method

Working Ahead: *Make this at least 3 days before you intend to serve it. Cooked vegetables will keep, covered, in the refrigerator up to 3 weeks; make sure they are covered with their cooking liquid.*

Making the Marinade: In a 4-quart heavy nonaluminum saucepan, combine the white wine vinegar, water, olive oil, salt, sugar, pepper, and basil. Bring to a boil and simmer 2 to 3 minutes.

Cooking the Vegetables: Drop the peppers and cauliflower into the marinade, and bring back to a boil. Cook, uncovered, 2 to 3 minutes. Remove with a slotted spoon, leaving the marinade in the saucepan. Put the vegetables into two 1-quart glass jars. Add the onions to the hot marinade and cook 5 minutes, or until barely tender. Remove with a slotted spoon and add to the vegetables. Now boil the marinade, uncovered, 5 minutes. Remove from the heat, add the balsamic vinegar, and pour the marinade over the vegetables, making sure it completely covers all the pieces, adding a little more white wine vinegar, if necessary. Cool, cover tightly, and refrigerate.

Suggestions

Wine: The vinegar in this recipe overwhelms most wines.

Menu: Serve the vegetables as part of an antipasto, accompanying a Platter of Cured Meats (page 14) and Crispy Fritters (page 373) or with Garlic Crostini with Pancetta (page 28). They are excellent on a buffet table with roasted turkey or game.

Although created less than a decade ago, this antipasto called Salad of Tart Greens with Prosciutto and Warm Balsamic Dressing *(page 26)* plays on ancient themes.

A trio of Emilia-Romagna's pastas in broth: *(from top to bottom)* Anolini of Parma *(page 149)*, Garganelli *(page 86)*, and Tortellini in Broth Villa Gaidello *(page 134)*.

One of Bologna's (and Emilia-Romagna's) most famous dishes: Tagliatelle with Classic Ragù Bolognese *(page 44).*

An autumn lunch before the fire: Ferrara's Couple bread *(page 364)*, Maccheroni with Baked Grilled Vegetables *(page 126)*, and homemade wine.

Ferrara's most famous pasta, Cappellacci with Sweet Squash *(page 145),* set atop hand-printed cloth from the village of Gambettola.

A favorite spring dish, Risotto of Baby Artichokes and Peas *(page 209),* joins two of Emilia-Romagna's most popular vegetables.

Linguine with Braised Garlic and Balsamic Vinegar *(page 110)* cooks on an old wood-burning stove.

From the time of Lucrezia Borgia, Lasagne Dukes of Ferrara *(page 168)* has been served on silver dishes at a 16th-century banquet table of the Este court.

An Unusual Tortellini Pie *(page 175)* descends from the lavish gilded pies of Renaissance banquets. It is still an important part of Emilia-Romagna celebrations today.

The credenza of a Renaissance banquet with Christmas Capon *(page 281)* on a bed of Tagliatelle with Caramelized Oranges and Almonds *(page 188)* about to be presented at the duke's table.

Romagna Grilled Veal Chops *(page 297)* cook over an open fire as the region's *Piadina* flatbread *(page 384)* bakes in the old way, on a terra-cotta griddle set over hot coals.

The Adriatic seafood stew, *Brodetto (page 259),* is a favorite one-dish supper of Romagna's fishing families. Which fish to use and in what proportion is debated up and down the coast.

Fresh Tuna Adriatic Style *(page 256)* tastes of summer on the Romagna coast.

On Emilia-Romagna's plain, Rabbit Roasted with Sweet Fennel *(page 289)* often becomes a one-dish country dinner.

For Bologna and Modena, Pan-Fried Veal Chops with Tomato Marsala Sauce *(page 292)* is the local version of Italy's famous veal and tomato dish.

Grilled Winter Endives *(page 337)*, hot from the wood-fired grill and ready to be eaten as a main dish or accompaniment.

A Modena country house dinner with Balsamic Roast Chicken *(page 279)*, Modena Mountain Bread *(page 388)*, and Asparagus in the Style of Parma *(page 341)* waiting to be served from the sideboard. Guests will use the precious artisan-made balsamic vinegar in the small bottle to season their chicken at the table.

Three polenta dishes: *(from top left to right)* A Baked Pie of Polenta and Country Ragù *(page 311),* Braised Pork Ribs and Polenta *(page 309),* and Grilled Polenta *(page 354)* with Piacenza Peppers Country Style *(page 244).*

Chestnut Ricotta Cheesecake *(page 452)* is a farmhouse dessert of unexpected elegance.

The "Keeping Cakes" of winter celebrate Christmas in Emilia-Romagna: *(from top left to right)* Ferrara's Chocolate Christmas Spice Cake *(page 458),* Spiced Christmas Cake of Bologna *(page 460),* and Honeyed Christmas Cake *(page 462)* of the Parma and Reggio area.

Baked Pears with Fresh Grape Syrup *(page 442)* and Sweet Cornmeal Biscuits *(page 422)* mean harvest and robust winter eating for Emilia-Romagna's winemaking families.

Set before a Parma yellow wall, Marie Louise's Crescents *(page 426)* are especially memorable with their filling of candied citron, almonds, and a secret ingredient.

The mystery chocolate cake of Vignola, Torta Barozzi *(page 395)*.

There is no mistaking that this is a 19th-century sideboard in Parma. The enticing Frozen Zuppa Inglese *(page 430)* was a favorite dessert of Parma's ducal court in the early 1800s. Amid the family pictures and mementos are Parma's famed violets, an etching of her opera house, and photographs of the province's two most admired personages, Marie Louise, Duchess of Parma, and the charismatic composer Giuseppi Verdi.

Paola Bini's Potato Salad
Insalata di Patate Paola Bini

Potatoes dressed with olive oil, vinegar, and seasonings are relished in Italy, especially as a summer antipasto. Paola Bini of the Villa Gaidello in Modena gives her potato salad a distinctive touch with Modena's homemade marinated vegetables with balsamic vinegar, and with the unexpected addition (in Italy) of mayonnaise.

2⅓ pounds small red-skinned potatoes (Red Bliss if available)

Cold water (for potatoes)

2 small leeks (white part only), cleaned and chopped into ¼-inch dice

3 medium stalks celery, cut into ¼-inch dice

1¾ cups diced (¼ to ½ inch) Balsamic Vegetables (page 18), plus ¼ cup liquid from vegetables

3½ tablespoons commercial balsamic vinegar

½ teaspoon sugar

1 to 2 teaspoons fresh lemon juice

1 teaspoon Dijon mustard

1 cup mayonnaise

Salt and pepper to taste

Garnish

4 to 5 clusters of attractive fresh celery leaves

Method
Working Ahead: *The finished salad can be prepared up to 24 hours before serving; keep it covered and refrigerated. Serve lightly chilled.*

Cooking the Potatoes: Cook potatoes in simmering water to cover 10 minutes, or until tender but not mushy.

Making the Dressing: In a large bowl stir together the leeks, celery, pickled vegetables (set aside about ½ cup of the red and yellow peppers for garnish), marinating liquid, balsamic vinegar, sugar, lemon juice, and mustard.

Making the Salad: Drain, peel, and cut the cooked potatoes into ½-inch dice. As they are cut, add them to the dressing, but do not stir. Once all the potatoes are diced, use a spatula to gently fold them into the dressing. Cool to room temperature. Gently fold in the mayonnaise. Season with salt and pepper. Cover and refrigerate.

Serving: Potatoes absorb and mute flavors as they sit, so taste the salad for salt, pepper, and acidity before bringing it to the table. If necessary, add a little more lemon juice or balsamic vinegar. Mound on a platter and scatter reserved peppers over the salad. Garnish with clusters of celery leaves.

Suggestions **Wine:** A crisp Sauvignon Blanc from Emilia-Romagna. More widely available in the United States is Sauvignon Blanc or Pinot Grigio from Friuli.

Menu: Serve as part of an antipasto with cured meats or as part of a buffet with Garlic Crostini with Pancetta (page 28), Valentino's Pizza (page 29), cold turkey, *Erbazzone* (page 247), and Tart of Fresh Artichokes (page 245). Paola Bini serves it with Giovanna's Wine-Basted Rabbit (page 284).

Paola Bini and Villa Gaidello

In the countryside of Castelfranco, near Modena, is Villa Gaidello, a guest farm where you can eat food prepared by local farm women and stay in one of three simple apartments. Villa Gaidello is also where local traditions of family cooking and handcraft are revitalized by the villa's owner, Paola Bini. For me, Paola touches at the heart of Emilia-Romagna's culinary identity in her work with the land and the local peasant women. Paola speaks of sowing what naturally grows best in a way that gives nourishment back to the soil. Her beliefs have made Villa Gaidello an organic farm. They have also brought a new life to the women who had been the property's tenant farmers for years.

After inheriting the family farm, Paola needed a way of keeping it alive. Taking in guests and serving meals prepared by the farm women seemed the answer. Then she discovered the women found more status in earning money as sales help in Castelfranco's equivilant of the five-and-ten than in continuing the old crafts learned from childhood— handmade pastas, preserving fruits and vegetables, baking bread, curing meats, and cooking traditional dishes. Letting those skills slip away meant not only possibly losing the farm, but also losing crafts accumulated over centuries. By hiring the women at generous salaries and encouraging them to cook as they always had, Paola helped revive their pride in local food traditions. At the same time, visitors could experience the closest thing to real home cooking short of being invited to a family Sunday dinner.

Paola stresses that Villa Gaidello is neither a restaurant nor a hotel. The Villa continues an old Italian tradition, *soggiorno in campagna,* or the holiday in the country. Years ago, families often vacationed on farms, going back, if even for a few weeks, to their rural roots. Every Sunday you can share the tradition in miniature at Villa Gaidello. Families come from as far away as Milan to feast, stroll through the fields and refresh themselves after weeks of city living. In the converted hay barn, you sit down to eat before a stack of thick white pottery plates. The top plate is filled with the course being served and then removed to make way for the next dish. There will be at least five courses, but never a printed menu. Paola explains a local saying, "Here we eat as in the convent, meaning we use what comes along." What comes along is good home food, and a sense that local traditions are not stopped in time and preserved under glass, but continuing to evolve and flourish.

Spring Salad with Hazelnuts
Insalata d'Asparagi, Parmigiano e Nocciole

An unusual combination that makes a fresh and crisp beginning to almost any menu.

[Serves 6]

1 pound pencil-slim asparagus, trimmed of tough ends

12 cups (12 to 14 ounces) tiny dandelion greens (harvested before there is any sign of flower stalks), or a blend of young curly endive, leaf lettuce, and corn salad (mâche)

3 ounces Italian Parmigiano-Reggiano cheese

¾ cup toasted hazelnuts, skinned and coarsely chopped

Dressing

¾ cup extra-virgin olive oil

¼ to ⅓ cup red wine vinegar

Salt and freshly ground black pepper to taste

Method

Working Ahead: *The asparagus can be cooked and then assembled with the greens early in the day; cover with plastic wrap and refrigerate until about 20 minutes ahead. Shred the cheese, chop the nuts, and make the dressing several hours ahead. Sprinkle the cheese, nuts, and dressing over the salad just before presenting.*

Cooking the Asparagus: Steam the asparagus until tender but still crisp, about 3 to 4 minutes. Rinse under cold water to stop the cooking and set the color. Cut each stalk in half on the diagonal.

Assembling the Salad: Divide the dandelion greens or mixed salads among six salad plates. Scatter the asparagus pieces over the greens.

Coarsely shred the cheese (the coarse shredding helps it stand up to the assertive dandelion). Place a portion of the cheese in the center of each salad. Sprinkle the chopped nuts around the cheese.

Making the Dressing: Blend the dressing ingredients in a bowl. Taste for acid/oil balance. Season with salt and pepper. Just before serving, lightly drizzle the dressing over salads.

Suggestions

Wine: Because of the dressing's vinegar and the asparagus, wine does not shine with this dish.

Menu: Carry out the spring theme with Risotto of Baby Artichokes and Peas (page 209) or Pan-Roasted Quail (page 283). Serve the salad before any roasted or braised dish, especially rich pasta and rice dishes like Lasagne Dukes of Ferrara (page 168) and Dome of Rice Stuffed with Braised Pigeon (page 216).

Mousse of Mortadella
Spuma di Mortadella

I *first tasted this mousse at Ristorante Diana in Bologna. There it is presented in crocks alongside toasted triangles of fine-grain bread. As each silken mouthful melts on your tongue, it is hard to save room for what is to come. This lighter version, inspired by Bolognese chef Renato Gualandi, substitutes velouté sauce for whipped butter. For guaranteed success, use a top-quality mortadella.*

[Serves 8]

1 tablespoon unsalted butter

1 tablespoon all-purpose unbleached flour (organic stone-ground preferred)

⅓ cup Poultry/Meat Stock (page 66) or Quick Stock (page 68)

¼ cup heavy cream

¾ teaspoon plain gelatin soaked in 3 tablespoons stock

⅛ teaspoon freshly ground nutmeg

Freshly ground black pepper to taste

8 ounces mortadella

½ cup heavy cream, whipped and chilled

¼ cup finely minced onion

Garnish

10 slices good-quality white bread

24 small Boston lettuce leaves

Method

Working Ahead: *The mousse can be prepared up to 24 hours ahead. It must chill at least 4 hours. The bread can be toasted up to 8 hours ahead, cooled, wrapped, and stored at room temperature.*

Making the Velouté: Melt the butter in a small heavy saucepan over medium-low heat. Stir in the flour with a wooden spatula until smooth. Cook several minutes, until bubbly. Keeping the heat at medium-low, slowly blend in the stock and ¼ cup cream with a wire whisk. Stir until the mixture is smooth. Then whisk constantly 5 minutes, or until the sauce is bubbling, thickened, and all raw flour taste has cooked away. Thoroughly blend in the gelatin, and let simmer 1 minute. Season with the nutmeg and pepper. Pour the sauce through a strainer into a bowl, and cool to room temperature.

Assembling the Mousse: Dice 1 ounce of the mortadella into ¼-inch cubes and set aside. Purée the rest to a smooth paste in a food processor. Turn the purée into a bowl, and blend in the velouté. Using a spatula, fold in the whipped cream, onion, and the reserved mortadella cubes, keeping the mixture as light as possible. Once the mousse is blended, stop folding.

Pour into eight small crocks or a large bowl. Cover and chill.

Making Toast Points: Trim the crusts from the bread slices, and cut each slice into six triangles. Toast the triangles on a baking sheet in a 400°F oven 5 minutes, or until golden brown. Cool, and store in a plastic bag at room temperature.

To Serve: The mousse should be lightly chilled but not ice cold. Remove it from the refrigerator about 40 minutes before serving. Present in individual crocks with toast points. Or arrange clusters of lettuce leaves on individual plates, scoop out small balls of mousse (about 1½ inches in diameter), and nest them into the leaves. Tuck toast points around the lettuce, and serve.

Suggestions   **Wine:** In Bologna, Lambrusco and mortadella are inseparable. In the United States, occasionally you can find "La Monella" from the Piemontese vineyard Braida di Giacomo Bologna. This wine is an ideal stand-in for high-quality Lambrusco. Otherwise, drink a sparkling white Brut di Venegazzù, Brut di Pinot, or Pinot di Pinot. For a still wine, have a young white Tocai from the Friuli region.

Menu: Serve the mousse before Lemon Roast Veal with Rosemary (page 294), Christmas Capon (page 281), or Balsamic Roast Chicken (page 279). The mousse also works well before a main-dish pasta, such as Tagliatelle with Ragù Bolognese (page 93), Linguine with Braised Garlic and Balsamic Vinegar (page 110), or Tagliatelle with Caramelized Onions and Fresh Herbs (page 101).

The mortadella of Bologna from the 17th-century board game "The Game of Cucagna where no one loses and everyone wins," by Bolognese artist Giuseppe Maria Mitelli

Chicken and Duck Liver Mousse with White Truffles

Spuma di Fegato con Tartufi

Although thought of as French, mousses, pâtés, and terrines of meat, poultry, and seafood have been prepared for centuries all over Italy. Some Italian food authorities believe the technique originated on the long peninsula, a point debated with zeal by the French. This recipe is adapted from one created years ago by Valentino Marcattilii, chef of Imola's Ristorante San Domenico. His inspiration came from Nino Bergese, his teacher, private cook to Italian nobility, and the man he calls the Escoffier of Italy. Perfect at an elegant dinner, it is delicious even if you cannot get duck livers or white truffles.

[Serves 8 to 10]

8 ounces chicken livers, preferably from free-range, organically fed chickens

8 ounces free-range duck livers (or substitute chicken livers)

4 California bay laurel leaves

1 clove garlic, lightly crushed

5 tablespoons brandy

¾ cup dry Marsala

4 tablespoons (2 ounces) unsalted butter

2 tablespoons Poultry/Meat Stock (page 66) or Quick Stock (page 68)

Salt and freshly ground white pepper to taste

10 tablespoons (5 ounces) unsalted butter, at room temperature

1 small fresh white truffle (1 to 2 ounces), shaved into very thin slices, or 6 sprigs Italian parsley

Good-quality crusty bread

Method   **Working Ahead:** *The livers must be marinated a day ahead, and the mousse can be finished a day before serving. Keep it covered and refrigerated. Once it has been whipped the second time, it can be refrigerated an hour or two. Serve it only lightly chilled.*

Marinating the Livers: Trim the livers of all connective tissues and cut away any greenish areas. In a glass or stainless steel bowl, combine the bay leaves, garlic, brandy, and Marsala. Toss with the livers. Cover, and refrigerate overnight.

Cooking the Livers: Drain the livers, reserving the marinade. Pat them dry with paper towels. In a large heavy skillet, heat the 4 tablespoons butter over medium-high heat. Add the livers, the reserved bay leaves, and garlic, and toss 20 seconds or until the livers lose their red color. Pour in the marinade and boil about 2 minutes. The livers should be firm but still pink inside. Scoop them out of the pan with a slotted spoon, and set aside. Continue boiling down the liquid until all of it has evaporated and the butter sputters. Add the 2 tablespoons of stock to the pan, and scrape the contents over the livers. Cool to room temperature. Purée the livers in a food processor until smooth. Season with salt and freshly ground white pepper. (Overseason a bit, as the mousse is served lightly chilled, which mutes flavors.)

Making the Mousse: Have a large bowl of ice handy. In a medium bowl, whip the 10 tablespoons butter with a portable beater at medium speed until fluffy. Gradually beat in the liver purée. Then set the bowl over ice and continue beating at medium speed 8 to 10 minutes, or until the mixture has lightened in color and is very fluffy. Cover and refrigerate 1 to 2 hours.

To Serve: Bring the mousse close to room temperature. Spoon it into individual 3-inch ramekins or crocks, or mound it in a 3-cup terrine. Sprinkle generously with the shaved truffle or parsley leaves. Accompany with bite-size pieces of crusty bread.

Suggestions   **Wine:** A soft, fruity white like a Müller-Thurgau or Riesling Renano from the Trentino–Alto Adige.

Menu: Serve before Almond Spice Broth (page 237) or "Little" Spring Soup from the 17th Century (page 232), followed by Rabbit Dukes of Modena (page 286), Pan-Roasted Quail (page 283), or Porcini Veal Chops (page 290). Finish with Ugo Falavigna's Apple Cream Tart (page 411). For a simple menu, after the mousse serve Tagliarini with Fresh Figs Franco Rossi (page 107), a green salad, chunks of Parmigiano-Reggiano cheese, and chocolate Torta Barozzi (page 395).

Cook's Notes   Use free-range organically raised poultry. Its taste is reminiscent of the farm chickens in Emilia-Romagna. Many health experts claim free-range organic poultry livers do not contain harmful substances that collect in that part of the bird's anatomy.

Salad of Tart Greens with Prosciutto and Warm Balsamic Dressing
Insalata di Prosciutto e Aceto Balsamico

The good tastes of Emilia-Romagna meet in this unusual salad. Inspired by the improvisations of several regional cooks, it becomes a light one-dish supper when not served as antipasto.

[Serves 6 to 8 generously as an antipasto, 6 as a light supper]

1 medium red onion, sliced into thin rings

½ cup red wine vinegar

1 small head each romaine, radicchio, red-leaf lettuce, and curly endive

½ cup (2 ounces) pine nuts, toasted

3 to 4 whole scallions, thinly sliced on the diagonal

3 ounces Italian Parmigiano-Reggiano cheese, shaved with a vegetable peeler into thin curls

3 ounces thinly sliced Prosciutto di Parma, cut into bite-size squares

1 cup lightly packed fresh basil leaves

1 cup lightly packed fresh Italian parsley leaves

8 large cloves garlic, cut into ¼-inch dice

About ⅔ cup extra-virgin olive oil

3 to 6 tablespoons commercial balsamic vinegar

3 tablespoons red wine vinegar

About 1 tablespoon dark brown sugar

Salt and freshly ground black pepper to taste

Method

Working Ahead: *The salad can be assembled several hours ahead; cover it with plastic wrap and refrigerate. Serve it lightly chilled. The dressing can be cooked up to several hours ahead. Cover and set aside at room temperature. Reheat just before serving.*

Assembling the Salad: Rid the onions of their sharpness by soaking them in the ½ cup vinegar about 30 minutes. Meanwhile, wash and dry the lettuces, throwing away any coarse or bruised leaves. Tear the leaves into bite-size pieces. In a large bowl, toss the greens with all but 3 tablespoons of the pine nuts, most of the scallions, half the cheese, half the prosciutto, and all the basil and parsley. Arrange on a large platter.

Making the Dressing: In a medium skillet, slowly cook the garlic in the olive oil over very low heat 8 minutes, or until barely colored. Remove with a slotted spoon and reserve. Turn the heat to medium-high, and add the vinegars to the oil. Cook a few moments, or until the acid has diffused slightly. Add brown sugar to taste (this gives some depth to commercial balsamics), and let the mixture bubble slowly 1 minute. Taste for sweet/tart balance (take care to cool the sample, as the hot oil makes this *scorching* hot). Stir in extra brown sugar or balsamic vinegar to taste. If the dressing is too sharp, simmer for a few moments to boil off some of the vinegar's acid. Stir in the reserved garlic, and season with salt and pepper. Set aside until ready to serve.

To Serve: Top with drained red onion, and scatter the rest of the scallions, pine nuts, cheese, and prosciutto over the salad. Reheat the dressing, stir vigorously to blend, and spoon over the salad. Serve immediately.

Suggestions **Wine:** A simple young red, such as a Sangiovese di Romagna from Emilia-Romagna or a Bardolino of the Veneto.

Menu: The salad on its own is a fine one-dish supper. For a full menu, offer small servings before Tagliatelle with Caramelized Onions and Fresh Herbs (page 101) or the Risotto of Baby Artichokes and Peas (page 209), followed by roasted chicken or lamb. For dessert, the Espresso and Mascarpone Semi-Freddo (page 428). For a lighter meal, serve before Tagliatelle with Ragù Bolognese (page 93), Spaghetti with Shrimps and Black Olives (page 132), or Maccheroni with Baked Grilled Vegetables (page 126). Dessert could be homey Modena Crumbling Cake (page 400) or Nonna's Jam Tart (page 413).

Cook's Notes The commercial balsamics available in the United States vary greatly in quality. See page 469 for information on a high-quality commercial vinegar.

A Saracen Invention?

Italy comes quite rightly by her antipasto salads, even though many consider them a hallmark of France's nouvelle cuisine. Composed salads of all kinds were very much a part of the elaborate first courses (the forerunner of the antipasto) at Italian Renaissance banquets, when Italy defined much of the dining fashion for all of Europe. Scholars speculate that the first-course salad originated in Italy during the 1400s. I have wondered if the Saracens (Moslems from the Middle East) introduced the concept long before the Renaissance. During their occupation of Sicily in the 9th and 10th centuries, their influence spread far beyond the southernmost portion of Italy. Perhaps then they were serving salads at the opening of meals just as is typical today in North Africa and the Middle East. Perhaps the idea was adopted by Italy's nobles, just as they eagerly took spices, hard wheat, pastry, and confectionery from the Saracens.

Garlic Crostini with Pancetta
Crostini con Pancetta

Popular in Emilia-Romagna's countryside, thin slices of coarse-grained bread are rubbed with garlic, lightly toasted, then topped with pancetta and run under the broiler. On a lazy Sunday afternoon with friends, set out the antipasto and invite everyone to help themselves.

[Serves 6 to 8]

1 loaf Modena Mountain Bread (page 388), or 1 baguette crusty whole-wheat or multi-grain bread

2 large cloves garlic, halved

About ⅓ cup extra-virgin olive oil

About 12 ounces pancetta, thinly sliced

Method

Working Ahead: *The bread can be toasted several hours ahead. Let it cool and then wrap it. Store at room temperature. Top the bread with pancetta and broil just before serving.*

Toasting the Crostini: Preheat the oven to 400°F. Cut the baguette into ½-inch-thick diagonal slices. If you are using Modena Mountain Bread, slice the loaf about ¼ to ½ inch thick, and divide each slice into thirds. Rub the slices with the split garlic cloves and brush lightly with olive oil. Arrange on a baking sheet, and bake about 8 minutes, or until they are starting to crisp but not brown. Remove and set aside.

Finishing the Crostini: Shortly before serving, preheat the broiler. Top each piece of bread with a thin slice of pancetta, and arrange them on the baking sheet. Run it under the broiler, keeping the slices about 3 inches from the flame. Broil until the pancetta begins to seethe and soften, 3 to 4 minutes. Serve hot.

Suggestions

Wine: A young red Sangiovese di Romagna, a Valpolicella Classico from the Veneto, or the Piedmont's Barbera.

Menu: This is rustic food, perfect before Riccardo Rimondi's Chicken Cacciatora (page 275) or Grilled Beef with Balsamic Glaze (page 303). The crostini become a first course when pasta is the main dish. Serve Baked Maccheroni with Winter Tomato Sauce (page 173), Linguine with Braised Garlic and Balsamic Vinegar (page 110), Tagliarini with Lemon Anchovy Sauce (page 112), or Spaghetti with Shrimps and Black Olives (page 132).

Valentino's Pizza
Pizza di Valentino

An unexpected rendition of a pizza, first created years ago by Valentino Marcattilii, chef at Imola's Ristorante San Domenico. The puff pastry crust and untraditional filling make this elegant finger food to serve with drinks.

[Serves 8 to 10]

12 ounces puff pastry
  (store-bought)
1 tablespoon unsalted butter
1 tablespoon extra-virgin olive oil
3 medium onions, thinly sliced
3 medium carrots, shredded
3 tablespoons half-and-half

⅔ cup (2 ounces) shredded
  imported Italian Fontina cheese
½ cup (2 ounces) freshly grated
  Italian Parmigiano-Reggiano
  cheese
Salt and freshly ground black
  pepper to taste
Garnish
⅓ cup fresh Italian parsley leaves

Method

Working Ahead: *The pastry can be rolled out and frozen 1 week ahead. The crust can be baked and the filling prepared up to 8 hours ahead. Store them, covered, separately. The cooked pizza holds well about 6 hours; reheat 10 minutes in a 350°F oven.*

Preparing the Pastry: Roll out the sheet of puff pastry very thin, and fit into a greased 11½ by 17½-inch jelly roll pan. Prick the entire surface with a fork, and freeze at least 2 hours. Preheat the oven to 400°F, setting the rack in the lowest possible position. Bake the frozen pastry 5 minutes, prick again, and continue baking another 10 minutes, or until pale gold. Remove and allow to cool. (Keep the oven on.)

Making the Filling: While the pastry is baking, heat the butter and oil in a large skillet over medium-high heat. Add the onions and cook over high heat, stirring often, 10 minutes or until golden. Stir in the carrots and cook another 3 minutes, scraping up any brown glaze at the bottom of the pan. Remove from the heat and stir in the half-and-half. Cool slightly, and then stir add half the Fontina and half the Parmigiano-Reggiano. Season with salt and pepper.

Baking and Serving: Spread the vegetable mixture evenly over the crust. Top with the remaining cheeses, and bake at 400°F 15 to 20 minutes, or until the cheeses have melted but not browned. Sprinkle with the parsley leaves and cut into small squares. Serve hot.

Suggestions

Wine: A dry sparkling Piemontese Pinot di Pinot or Pinot Brut, or a still Pinot Bianco from Trentino–Alto Adige or Friuli–Venezia Giulia.

continued

Menu: For a traditional menu, follow with "Little" Spring Soup from the 17th Century (page 232) or Soup of Porcini Mushrooms (page 226). Afterward serve Lemon Roast Veal with Rosemary (page 294), Giovanna's Wine-Basted Rabbit (page 284), or Pan-Roasted Quail (page 283). Finish with Baked Pears with Fresh Grape Syrup (page 442) or Strawberries in Red Wine (page 445).

Fresh Pears with Parmigiano-Reggiano and Balsamic Vinegar
Antipasto di Reggio

This appetizer from Reggio shows off two of Emilia-Romagna's most renowned foods, a stunning Parmigiano-Reggiano cheese and the lushest of artisan-made balsamic vinegars. There is no cooking, and the dish is assembled effortlessly.

[Serves 6]

3 ripe Anjou or Comice pears
Juice of 1 small lemon
3 to 4 ounces Italian
  Parmigiano-Reggiano cheese,
  in 1 piece

About 1 tablespoon artisan-made
  balsamic vinegar ("Aceto
  Balsamico Tradizionale di
  Modena" or "di Reggio")

Method

Working Ahead: *The antipasto is best assembled and then eaten right away.*

Assembling and Serving: Shortly before dining, halve and core the pears, leaving their skins intact. Then slice each half into long thin slivers. Drizzle with a little lemon juice to keep from turning brown. Fan out four or five pieces of pear on each of six salad plates. At the base of the fan place a knob of cheese. Moisten each chunk with a few drops of balsamic vinegar, and serve.

Suggestions

Wine: A white Sauvignon Blanc from the Bolognese hills or one from Friuli.

Menu: Serve before any pasta, rice, or meat dish not containing balsamic vinegar or fruit. It is especially good before Rabbit Roasted with Sweet Fennel (page 289), Herbed Seafood Grill (page 254), Lasagne Dukes of Ferrara (page 168), Christmas Capon (page 281), or January Pork (page 312).

Cook's Notes If you are using a commercial balsamic vinegar, blend ¼ teaspoon dark brown sugar with 1 tablespoon vinegar. See page 469 for information on balsamics.

Hot Caramelized Pears with Prosciutto
Antipasto di Pere e Prosciutto

Caramelizing pears in a little sugar and butter gives just the right accent to a robust but salty prosciutto. Make sure the pears are packed with flavor and the prosciutto is at room temperature.

[Serves 4]

2 large ripe, flavorful Bosc pears
½ lemon
3 tablespoons unsalted butter
About ½ teaspoon sugar
Generous pinch freshly ground
   black pepper

8 thin slices robust but salty
   prosciutto, at room temperature
4 sprigs fresh mint

Method

Working Ahead: *This dish comes together quickly and is best made just before serving.*

Preparing the Pears: Warm four salad plates in a low oven. Peel the pears vertically with a vegetable peeler, trimming away the stem. Halve them, and then core and cut into each pear into eight wedges. Rub with the lemon to keep from discoloring. Heat the butter in a heavy 12-inch sauté pan over medium-high heat. Add the pears in one layer, and sprinkle lightly with the sugar. Cook over high heat, about 3 minutes, to brown lightly on both sides, turning gently with two wooden spatulas so the pieces don't break.

To Assemble: Fan out four pear wedges on each heated plate. Sprinkle lightly with pepper. Drape two prosciutto slices over each pear serving so it looks like two or three waves undulating up from the plate. (The ham could also be woven under and over the pears.) Garnish each serving with a sprig of mint.

Suggestions

Wine: In the region, drink a soft white from Bologna's hills, Bianco dei Colli Bolognesi. More readily available in the United States is a fruity Tocai from Friuli or a Müller-Thurgau of the Trentino–Alto Adige area.

Menu: Serve before Risotto of Red Wine and Rosemary (page 205), Tagliatelle with Balsamic Radicchio (page 98), or tagliatelle with Piacenza's Porcini Tomato Sauce (page 64). Second dishes could be Artusi's Delight (page 300), Maria Bertuzzi's Lemon Chicken (page 273), or Rabbit Dukes of Modena (page 286).

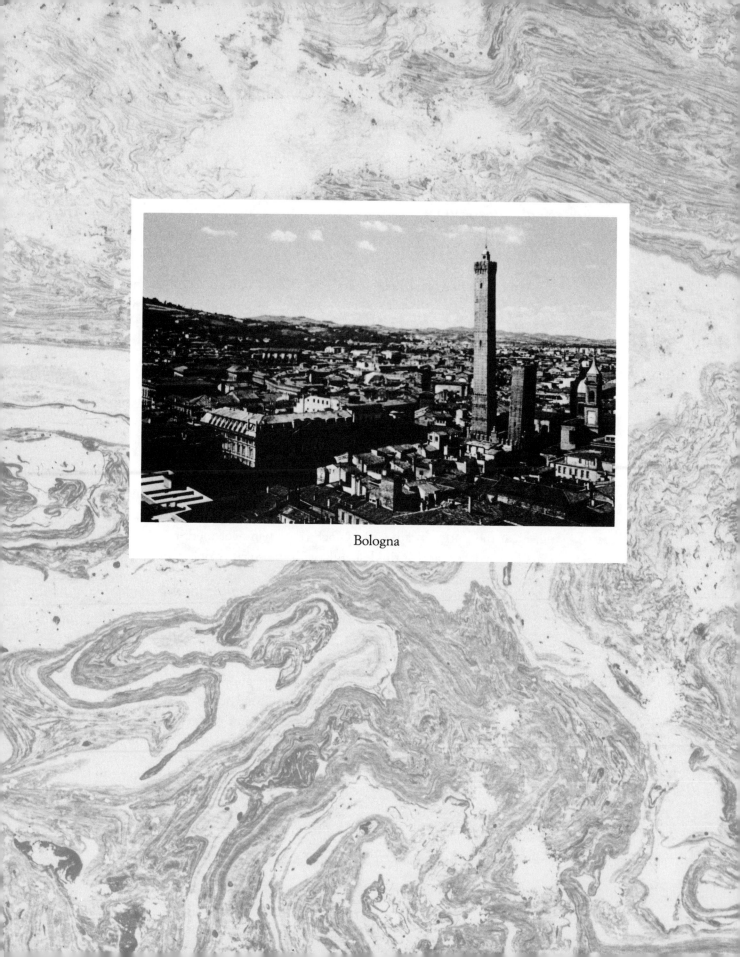

Bologna

RAGÙS

In Emilia-Romagna, where pasta reigns as queen, the ragù sauce is king. Although meat ragùs are made throughout Italy, I know of no other region where the sauce has gained such importance. Hardly a restaurant in Emilia-Romagna omits Tagliatelle with Ragù from its menu, and it is a rare home where some form of pasta sauced with some kind of ragù is not eaten at least once a week.

Ragù is a sauce of chopped meat(s) and sautéed vegetables cooked in liquid. The liquid can be stock, wine, water, tomato, milk or cream, or a combination of several of these. What a ragù is _not_ is a tomato sauce with meat. It is a meat sauce sometimes flavored with tomato. In Emilia-Romagna and much of northern Italy, the meat is chopped into the sauce, while in southern Italy chunks of meat are frequently cooked into a ragù and served separately from it.

Such attention is lavished on ragùs in Emilia-Romagna, with each cook creating yet another interpretation, that their scope could never be reflected in only one recipe. I have gathered a diverse collection of favorites, each expressing another dimension of ragù or an important part of the sauce's past. But was ragù always a sauce? Where did it begin and how did it evolve? Researchers in Bologna came to one conclusion, which, in turn, led me to another.

The most famous ragù in Emilia-Romagna is <u>Ragù Bolognese.</u> For the people of Bologna, their meat sauce is a vital part of their culinary identity. They believe Bologna is a center of discerning taste, where the best of raw materials are combined to perfection by gifted cooks.

When Bologna's chapter of one of Italy's preeminent gastronomic societies, L'Accademia Italiana della Cucina, chose one recipe as the most typical example of <u>Ragù Bolognese,</u> it raised a furor of debate. For weeks afterward, the city's newspapers documented heated exchanges over the validity of the sauce. Almost everyone had an opinion. Home cooks questioned every ingredient, its quantity, its tradition, its inclusion or exclusion. Bolognese restaurant cooks, who saw themselves as the keepers of Bologna's culinary traditions, were angered over not being consulted. Historians and food experts argued over the origins of the ragù, and its legitimacy as an expression of Bologna's kitchen.

The Academy stood its ground. For them, the recipe found on page 44 embodied the most important characteristics of the ragù. It verified their belief that <u>Ragù Bolognese</u> began as a humble dish in Bologna's farm kitchens a century ago.

According to Academy members, meat was expensive then, even for farmers. The beef in this sauce often came from a milk cow grown too old for milking. Skirt steak was a cut few people wanted because, in spite of its good flavor, it was lean and tough. Slow cooking tenderized the meat. The quantity of the sauce was stretched with generous amounts of vegetables and salt pork. Because the salt pork was the cheapest of meats and always available, often there was as much of it in the pot as beef.

The recipe's reduced cream may appear an affectation, but in fact it nearly duplicates an original ingredient, cream skimmed from cooked milk. New milk, fresh from the cow, was preserved by long heating. Gradually the cream separated and coagulated on the milk's surface. As the cooled milk stood by the kitchen door in a covered can, the cook would reach out with a shallow cup and skim off the top cream as it was needed.

That cream, full of flavor, went a long way in enriching the sauce and eliminating the need for large quantities of broth. Although made from bones and scraps, broth was still a meat product and treasured.

Using cream created a sauce so rich and filling that only a little was needed for saucing enough tagliatelle to feed a large family.

With this explanation, the Academy's _Ragù Bolognese_ became official by decree. After receiving more government seals, ribbons and stamps than an international peace treaty, the recipe was deposited in the town hall to stand for all time as the typical ragù of Bologna.

My own research into the ragùs of Emilia-Romagna turned me in another direction. Much evidence points toward the oldest ancestors of today's sauces being stews created in palaces, not on farms. I believe country-style ragùs came from working people emulating the sauces of the aristocracy. Since the mid-1800s ragù has been women's food—the food of the home cook. But its birth could have been under the hands of men—the court cooks of the 16th and 17th centuries.

The region's Renaissance cookbooks make no mention of ragù, nor of meat sauces for pasta. But they do give recipes for stews that sound like ragùs done in the fashion of the day, with an emphasis on spices and sugar. During the early 1500s, cookbook author Christofaro di Messisbugo served up ragù-like dishes to his master at Ferrara's court banquets. Exotic, savory and sweet, these were chunky stews composed of cut-up meats. Sometimes fruits and nuts were added. Usually the stews were cooked in a strong broth and a tart or sweet wine. Seasonings seemed more Middle Eastern than Italian—rosewater, saffron, cinnamon, ginger, coriander, plenty of black pepper, and always sugar. These creations were eaten on their own or filled elaborate pies. They were not served over pasta, at least not yet. Through the 17th and 18th centuries the stews continued evolving. The quantities of sugar diminished and the spices were toned down.

Italy's stews shared many characteristics with France's ragoûts of the same period. (_Ragoût_ was and is a stewlike dish of cut-up ingredients, cooked in liquid and eaten on its own. Italy's _ragù_ is always a sauce.) Considering the centuries of exchanges between the two countries, Italy's stews and France's ragoûts probably influenced each other. The important questions are: When did Italy's stew become ragù? Did the name come from France? And when did Italian ragù first sauce pasta?

A combination of forces came into play toward the end of the 18th century that no doubt helped the word _ragoût_ become _ragù_ as it emigrated from France to Italy, and to Emilia-Romagna.

In the 1700s ragoûts became fashionable food for the well-to-do

French, and contained everything from meats to vegetables to nuts and even olives. At the same time, Emilia-Romagna's affluent citizens were captivated by all things French. The French were everywhere. Parma was annexed to the court of Louis XV, and 10 percent of her population was French. Modenese nobility took French husbands and wives. Each wedding brought large entourages of French relatives and servants. Bologna traded and politicked with France. Finally, Napoleon took possession of northern Italy for France in 1796. Why not bow to the fashion of the day and call those stews ragù?

The first record of someone doing just that was in the late 18th century when Alberto Alvisi, cook to the Cardinal of Imola, near Bologna, made a sauce called "ragù for maccheroni." It tastes like a cross between classic Ragù Bolognese and a 20th-century French brown sauce. There were still remnants of those Renaissance flavorings. The sugar is gone, but the sauce's flavors of deeply browned meat are set off by cinnamon and black pepper.

After 1830, ragùs appear frequently in Emilia and Romagna cookbooks. By 1832, Napoleon's widow, Marie Louise, the Duchess of Parma, was dining on a ragù of chicken and prosciutto cooked in wine and lemon. Another ragù of chicken cooked with sausage, beef and giblets was saucing a Bolognese tortellini pie (see page 175). Merchants and landowners in Romagna were eating a variety of ragùs on their own as well as over pastas, including one much like the giblet ragù on page 54. In mid-century, Romagna cookbook author Pellegrino Artusi was eating maccheroni with a ragù of veal filet in a Bolognese tavern while his companions plotted the unification of Italy. Interestingly, only a few of these ragùs contain tomato.

During the late 1800s, as white flour for pasta making became more affordable because of the Industrial Revolution, ragù crossed over class lines. The less affluent imitated the wealthy but used smaller portions of less expensive meats to make their ragù. Serving it over pasta stretched the sauce. An old saying states that tagliatelle with ragù becomes two courses in one: the pasta is the first and the ragù's meat makes the second. Tagliatelle with ragù became a popular one-dish meal.

The recipes collected here are not historical curiosities. Each is a memorable dining experience in its own right. Ragù is still alive and well, and these recipes represent the best of the living tradition.

Building a Ragù

The following technique creates ragùs full of flavor, rich without being heavy. It can do the same for stews, braisings, and non-ragù sauces. Making a ragù involves three simple steps: browning the vegetables and meats, reducing flavorful liquids over the browned foods to build up layers of taste, then covering them with liquid and simmering gently until the flavors have blended and the meats are tender.

Browning: This is the taste foundation for the ragù. Browning slowly or quickly determines whether the foundation is mellow and sweet or robust and full-bodied. Slow browning over low heat brings out the sweetness of onion and carrot, while fast browning over high heat yields punchier, more robust flavors. Browning on medium heat strikes a balance between the two. I favor medium heat for most ragùs. Once the onion begins to color, the meats are added. After throwing off liquid, they begin browning. Some cooks like meats taken to a dark crisp brown, while others prefer lighter browning. Using a saucepan instead of a sauté pan ensures leisurely browning, building up rich caramelized flavors. As the foods cook, a brown glaze, packed with flavor, develops on the bottom of the pan. Protect it from burning by lowering the heat. Nonstick cookware discourages glazing and should not be used for ragùs, sauces, sautés, braisings, or stews.

Reductions: Repeatedly pouring wine, stock, and/or water over the browned base and simmering down each addition to an essence achieves two things: First, the reductions blend the highly flavored brown glaze into the sauce. Without it, ragùs lack depth. Second, each reduction builds another stratum of flavor, giving the sauce more complexity. Adding all the liquids at the same time produces a one-dimensional ragù. Wine creates a·round and tangy taste layer, providing a needed contrast to the big flavors of browned vegetables and meat. Stock reduced to almost nothing imparts more full meat flavor. Repeat the stock reduction again and again, and see how intensely aromatic the sauce becomes. Always add any tomatoes *after* the reductions, as they will make the ragù acid-tasting.

Simmering: Flavors mellow and the ragù's meats cook to tenderness when they are covered with liquid and left to bubble gently for an hour or more. Remove the sauce from the heat, let it settle a few moments, and then skim off all possible fat.

Ingredients

Beef: Often used by itself in Bologna, and blended with other meats in other parts of the region. The more flavorful the cut, the tastier the ragù. Best-tasting for ragù is the hanging tender, a small cut that literally hangs off the kidney inside the left hindquarter of the steer. Hanging tenders are not easy to come by (there is only one per steer) and must be ordered from a butcher. Skirt steak is my second choice. Cut from inside the rib cage in the forequarter, this, too, must be specially ordered and is worth seeking out. More readily available and almost as good are cuts from the chuck, such as blade-cut chuck, center-cut chuck, and seven-bone chuck steak or roast.

Capon Breast: Italy's favorite domestic poultry gives the rich character to red meats and lightens ragùs. It is worth special ordering, but if unavailable, turkey breast comes close.

Chicken Giblets: Chicken or turkey giblets are frequently the mystery ingredients used with other meats in a ragù. Although almost impossible to detect, they impart body and character to the sauce. Ragùs composed only of giblets are often balanced with the addition of porcini mushrooms.

Pork: Cuts from the shoulder and sirloin are used in ragùs throughout Emilia-Romagna. Pork sweetens the sauce and balances particularly well in combination with veal.

Sausage: Often used in the ragùs of Modena, much of Romagna, and occasionally in Reggio, the sausage is never seasoned with hot pepper. Blending small quantities of sausage with other meats adds zest and character. A ragù of only sausage (page 114) is traditional with gramigna pasta.

Veal: Usually blended with other meats for lightness. One exception is the Light Veal Ragù with Tomato (page 52), where the veal and tomato combination makes for a particularly fresh-tasting sauce. Seek out "kind" veal, from calves raised organically with space to move about.

Butter: Gives sweet, rich undertones.

Pancetta and Prosciutto: Their meat and fat are so suave that they give ragùs an elegance unequaled by butter or olive oil. Even when the fat is skimmed from the finished sauce, their flavors remain.

Lard: This has always been the cheapest and most accessible fat, used in the ragùs of the less affluent. Fine lard tastes of good pork meat. Cholesterol concerns have removed it from favor.

Olive Oil: Adds subtle fruitiness to ragùs. Traditionally Bologna and Romagna used more olive oil than the rest of Emilia-Romagna. Today, health concerns are causing its popularity to spread rapidly.

Wine: Wine's roundness and acidity bring balance to full-bodied ragùs. Always add it after the meat has browned, and slowly cook the wine away to nothing. Do not use cooking wine. Instead, cook with a wine you would drink, using either red or white—the choice is up to the cook. Red Sangiovese di Romagna and white Trebbiano are most favored in Emilia-Romagna.

Stock/Broth: Heightens meatiness. Since reductions intensify the stock's flavor, make sure it is saltless and, ideally, homemade.

Water: Used for clear, neutral flavor, letting other ingredients shine.

Milk: For an especially mellow and sweet sauce with tender meats, use milk as the main cooking liquid, adding it after the reductions. For more subtle sweetness, add milk in small quantities during cooking. Skim milk does an admirable job.

Porcini Mushrooms: Dried mushrooms used in small quantities give a wild, woodsy flavor to a ragù. For greater intensity, include their soaking liquid in the reductions. Do not overdo; porcini can easily dominate a sauce.

Herbs and Spices: Used infrequently in ragùs and always with a careful hand.

A Little History

The Cardinal's Ragù (page 40) is one of the earliest of Emilia-Romagna's ragùs to be served with pasta. The recipe was found in a small manuscript of fifty or so written by Alberto Alvisi. Between 1785 and 1800 Alvisi cooked for the Cardinal of Imola, Gregorio Chiaramonti. The cardinal went on to become Pope Pio VII, while Alvisi dropped into obscurity. Food historians Aureliano Bassani and Giancarlo Roversi discovered his manuscript in Bologna's archives, and published it 180 years after the cardinal dined on this ragù.

The Cardinal's Ragù
Ragù per li Maccheroni Appasticciati

This ragù from the late 18th century tastes rich, brown, and velvety, with the surprise of cinnamon and black pepper. The sauce blends well with tagliatelle, pappardelle, and garganelli pastas. Experience it as it was first made centuries ago by combining the ragù with hollow maccheroni and baking it.

[Makes enough sauce for 1 recipe fresh pasta (pages 80 to 82) or 1 pound dried pasta]

2 tablespoons fat rendered from salt pork

2 tablespoons unsalted butter

1 medium onion, minced

1¼ pounds beef skirt steak or boneless chuck blade steak, trimmed of fat and cut into ¼-inch dice

¼ teaspoon ground cinnamon

Salt and freshly ground black pepper

4⅓ cups Poultry/Meat Stock (page 66) or Quick Stock (page 68)

2 tablespoons all-purpose unbleached flour (organic stone-ground preferred)

Method

Working Ahead: *The ragù holds well, covered, in the refrigerator 2 days and freezes 1 month. Skim off the fat and reheat before serving. Taste for cinnamon and pepper before tossing with the pasta. There should be a sparkle of pepper and a soft backtaste of cinnamon.*

Browning the Ragù Base: Heat the pork fat and butter in a heavy 4-quart saucepan over medium-high heat. Stir in the onions and meat, turning the heat up to high. Use a wooden spatula to push apart the pieces of meat as they throw off moisture and begin to brown. Lower the heat if the meat threatens to burn, or if the brown glaze on the bottom of the pan turns very dark. Cook until the beef browns.

Reducing and Simmering: Sprinkle the ¼ teaspoon cinnamon and a little salt and pepper over the meat, and stir in ½ cup of the stock. Scrape up the brown glaze with a wooden spatula as the stock bubbles slowly over medium heat. Once the stock has cooked down to nothing, add another ½ cup of stock. Repeat the reduction once more, using another ½ cup. Blend in the flour. Then pour in the remaining stock and bring it to a very slow bubble. Partially cover the pot and cook 2½ hours, or until the meat is tender. The sauce should have the consistency of heavy cream. Add water if it thickens too much or threatens to stick and burn.

Finishing and Serving: Sprinkle the sauce with generous pinches of cinnamon and pepper. There should be a whisper of discernible cinnamon and a gentle tingle from the pepper. Serve over garganelli (page 86), tagliatelle (page 90), dried boxed pappardelle, or baked with maccheroni as described in His Eminence's Baked Penne (page 170).

Suggestions　**Wine:** From Emilia-Romagna, a red Barbera or Merlot from Colli Bolognesi; or Piedmont's Dolcetto d'Alba, or a Merlot from Friuli. All are sometimes available here.

Menu: Serve as a main dish after Fresh Pears with Parmigiano-Reggiano and Balsamic Vinegar (page 30). Ugo Falavigna's Apple Cream Tart (page 411) makes a fine finish. If you are offering the ragù as a first course, begin with the pears, serve the ragù, and then have Christmas Capon (page 281), Pan-Roasted Quail (page 283), or Rabbit Roasted with Sweet Fennel (page 289). For dessert, have Frozen Zuppa Inglese (page 430) from early 19th-century Parma.

Cook's Notes　The original recipe offered the cook a choice of beef, veal shoulder, pork loin, or poultry giblets. Any of these could be substituted in equal amounts for the beef. Adding Parmigiano-Reggiano cheese overwhelms the sauce's cinnamon and pepper, and its texture alters the ragù's silkiness.

A Remarkable Thigh

Chunks of boned chicken thigh are an important aspect of Baroque Ragù (page 42). They became part of the recipe one day when veal was not to be had. They stayed in the dish because of their succulence and absence of fat. Thigh meat loses none of its moist goodness through long sautés and simmerings. When excellent veal is not available for stews or braisings, substitute chicken thigh. Yes, its taste is different, but it unfailingly complements the flavorings and ingredients usually cooked with veal.

Baroque Ragù
Ragù de' Nobili

Succulent and chunky, the taste of this ragù is dominated by chicken. Although adapted from a modern recipe, its ancestry can be traced back to the aristocratic meat stews of the Renaissance, when sauces like this one were layered into elaborate pies. Today this ragù is still baked into a pie, the memorable Unusual Tortellini Pie. Another dish inspired by the Renaissance, Lasagne Dukes of Ferrara, combines the ragù with pasta, pine nuts, raisins, and spices. Enjoy the ragù, too, on ribbon-style pastas, especially tagliatelle or pappardelle, either fresh or dried and boxed.

[Makes enough sauce for 1 recipe fresh pasta (pages 80 to 82)
or 1 pound dried pasta]

1½ tablespoons extra-virgin
   olive oil

1 tablespoon unsalted butter

½ medium carrot, minced

½ medium stalk celery, minced

½ medium onion, minced

2 ounces pancetta, minced

4 ounces mild Italian sausage
   (made without fennel)

12 ounces chicken thighs, skinned,
   boned, and cut into ¼- to
   ½-inch dice

4 ounces turkey or chicken giblets,
   trimmed and finely chopped, or
   4 ounces lean ground pork

4 ounces lean beef chuck, finely
   chopped

1 California bay laurel leaf

½ cup dry white wine

Generous pinch of ground cloves

1¼ cups Poultry/Meat Stock
   (page 66) or Quick Stock
   (page 68)

1 clove garlic, crushed

1½ tablespoons imported Italian
   tomato paste

¼ cup heavy cream

Salt and freshly ground black
   pepper to taste

Method

Working Ahead: *The ragù can be refrigerated, covered, up to 3 days, and frozen up to 1 month. Skim any fat from the sauce before using. If you freeze it, add the cream when reheating.*

Browning the Ragù Base: Mincing the meats by hand makes for better browning and gives a silkier texture to the sauce. In a 12-inch sauté pan, heat the oil and butter over medium heat. Add the vegetables and pancetta. Leisurely sauté, stirring often, until they begin to color, about 8 minutes. Add the sausage, chicken, giblets, beef, and bay leaf. Cook over high heat 8 more minutes, or until they begin to brown. Lower the heat to medium, and continue sautéing, stirring often with a wooden spatula, 10 minutes, or until the meat is rich dark brown. It should sizzle quietly in the pan, not violently pop and sputter. Slow browning protects the brown glaze forming on the bottom of the pan.

Simmering and Finishing: Drain off fat by tipping the browned meat into a large sieve and shaking it. Put the meat back into the pan, placing it over medium-high heat. Add the wine and cloves. Cook at a lively bubble 3 minutes, or until the wine has evaporated. As the wine bubbles, use a wooden spatula to scrape up the brown glaze from the bottom of the pan. Reduce the heat to medium and add ¼ cup of the stock. Take about 3 minutes to cook it down to nothing. Stir in the garlic, tomato paste, and another ¼ cup of stock; bubble it down to nothing again. Turn the mixture into a 2½- to 3-quart saucepan.

Add the remaining stock to the saucepan and let it bubble slowly, uncovered, 30 to 45 minutes, or until the stock has reduced by about one third and the sauce is moist but not loose. Add the cream, and simmer 3 to 5 minutes. Season to taste. Allow the ragù to cool; cover and refrigerate. Defat the ragù when it is cold.

Serving: Toss the reheated ragù with cooked pasta as suggested above. Serve in heated bowls, passing freshly grated Parmigiano-Reggiano cheese separately.

Suggestions **Wine:** A soft red like a Sangiovese di Romagna Riserva, a young Merlot from the Veneto region's Pramaggiore or Colli Berici, Tuscany's young Chianti Montalbano, or Chianti Classico. Or accent the delicacy of the sauce with a big white Gavi dei Gavi of the Piedmont.

Menu: Serve the ragù over tagliatelle or pappardelle as a main dish after an antipasto of Hot Caramelized Pears with Prosciutto (page 31) or Spring Salad with Hazelnuts (page 21). Follow the pasta with a green salad and then Caramelized Almond Tart (page 409) or Strawberries in Red Wine (page 445). Offer it in small portions as a first course before Giovanna's Wine-Basted Rabbit (page 284) or Pan-Roasted Quail (page 283). Have Nonna's Jam Tart (page 413) for dessert.

Cook's Notes **The Ragù in a Pie:** This ragù is vital to An Unusual Tortellini Pie (page 175). Double the ragù recipe, cooking the sauce in a 3½- to 4-quart pot instead of the 2½- to 3-quart size mentioned above. Browning the meats will take a little longer, but a 12-inch skillet still works best.

Ragù with Polenta: For an excellent main dish, spoon a single recipe of the ragù over hot Creamy Polenta (page 354).

In Bologna's marketplace, engraving by Giovanni M. Tamburini, from a picture by Francesco Curti, circa 1640

A Classic Ragù Bolognese
Ragù Bolognese

Bologna's ragù is the most famous in Italy. According to the Bologna chapter of Italy's gastronomic society, L'Accademia Italiana della Cucina, this is the most typical and authentic-tasting rendition of the city's famed sauce. Cara De Silva, dear friend and authority on ethnic foods, researched and developed this recipe from the Academy's Bolognese original.

For our modern tastes this ragù is reserved for times of special indulgence because of its generous amounts of fat. Although a fine lower-fat version follows, I urge you to sample this recipe, if only in very small portions to experience what home cooking was like a hundred years ago in northern Italy's countryside.

[Makes enough sauce for 1½ recipes fresh pasta (pages 80 to 82) or 1½ pounds dried pasta]

½ cup heavy cream

10 ounces fresh unsalted fatback or lean salt pork, cut into small dice

About 1 quart water

1 cup diced carrot (⅛- to ¼-inch dice)

⅔ cup diced celery (same dimensions)

½ cup diced onion (same dimensions)

1¼ pounds beef skirt steak or boneless chuck blade roast, coarsely ground

½ cup dry Italian white wine, preferably Trebbiano or Albana

2 tablespoons double or triple-concentrated imported Italian tomato paste, diluted in 10 tablespoons Poultry/Meat Stock (page 66) or Quick Stock (page 68)

1 cup whole milk

Salt and freshly ground black pepper to taste

Method **Working Ahead:** *The ragù is best kept warm and eaten within about 30 minutes after it has finished cooking.*

Cooking the Cream: Simmer the cream in a tiny saucepan until reduced by one-third. There should be about 6 tablespoons. Set aside.

Blanching the Salt Pork: Fresh fatback needs no blanching. If you are using salt pork, bring the water to boiling, add the salt pork, and cook for 3 minutes. Drain and pat dry.

Browning the Ragù Base: Sauté the salt pork or fatback in a 3- to 4-quart heavy saucepan over medium-low heat. Sauté 8 minutes, or until almost all its fat is rendered. Stir in the chopped vegetables. Sauté for 3 minutes over medium-low heat, or until the onion is translucent. Raise the heat to medium and stir in the beef. Brown 5 minutes, or until the meat is medium brown in color and almost, but not quite, crisp. Take care not to let the meat become overly brown or hard.

Simmering and Serving: Stir in the wine and diluted tomato paste, and reduce the heat to very low. It is critical that the mixture reduce as slowly as possible. Cook, partially covered, 2 hours. From time to time stir in a tablespoon or so of the milk. By the end of 2 hours, all the milk should be used up and the ragù should be only slightly liquid. Stir in the reduced cream. Toss the hot ragù with freshly cooked tagliatelle and serve.

Suggestions   **Wine:** A young red Sangue di Giuda from Lombardy's Oltrepo Pavese area, the Piedmont's "La Monella" from Braida di Giacomo Bologna, a light-bodied Merlot from the Veneto, or a young Valpolicella Classico.

Menu: Serve ragù and pasta as a main dish after a light antipasto of wedges of fresh fennel for dipping into tiny bowls of balsamic vinegar, or small portions of Spring Salad with Hazelnuts (page 21). For dessert, arrange apples, pears, and grapes on a platter, along with handfuls of unshelled nuts. Tucking clusters of glossy lemon leaves, fresh bay laurel, or evergreens around the fruit and nuts makes an appealing presentation.

Old engraving of Bologna

A Lighter Contemporary Ragù Bolognese

Tasting like a hearty beef and wine stew with lots of browned onion, this ragù is one of the simplest in Emilia-Romagna. Eliminating most of the fat from Classic Ragù Bolognese creates a sauce much to the modern tastes of Americans—and to the people of Bologna. Three tablespoons of olive oil and an ounce of pancetta replace ten ounces of salt pork and half a cup of cream in the original recipe. Cooking and attitudes toward food evolve and change slowly, but constantly. This ragù could well represent the next generation of food in Emilia-Romagna.

[Makes enough sauce for 1 recipe fresh pasta (pages 80 to 82)
or 1 pound dried pasta]

3 tablespoons extra-virgin olive oil

1 ounce pancetta, finely chopped

1 large carrot, finely chopped

2 small stalks celery, finely chopped

½ medium onion, finely chopped

1¼ pound beef skirt steak, or boneless chuck blade roast, coarsely ground

½ cup dry white Trebbiano or Albana wine

2 tablespoons double- or triple-concentrated Italian tomato paste, diluted with 10 tablespoons Poultry/Meat Stock (page 66) or Quick Stock (page 68)

Salt and freshly ground black pepper to taste

1½ cups milk

Method

Working Ahead: *This ragù is at its best eaten within 24 hours after it is cooked. Cover and refrigerate it. Skim off the fat before reheating. The sauce can be frozen up to 1 month.*

Browning the Ragù Base: Heat the oil and pancetta in a 3- to 4-quart saucepan over medium-low heat. Cook 8 minutes, or until the pancetta has rendered much of its fat but has not browned. Raise the heat to medium, stir in the chopped vegetables, and sauté 3 minutes, or until the onion is translucent. Keeping the heat at medium, add the beef. Cook, stirring frequently, 5 to 7 minutes, or until the meat is medium brown and almost, but not quite, crisp. Take care not to let the meat become overly brown or hard.

Simmering and Finishing: Add the wine and the diluted tomato paste. Stir to combine. Keep the heat very low. It is critical that the mixture reduce as slowly as possible. Cook, partially covered, 2 hours. From time to time stir in 2 tablespoons of the milk. By the end of 2 hours all the milk should be absorbed and the ragù the consistency of a thick soup.

Serving: Toss the hot ragù with freshly cooked tagliatelle, garganelli, or dried boxed casareccia or sedani maccheroni. Pass freshly grated Parmigiano-Reggiano cheese.

Suggestions **Wine:** In keeping with its rural origins, wine for the ragù should be simple and direct: a young red Sangiovese di Romagna or from Umbria, a Barbera of the Bolognese hills (Colli Bolognesi) or a Piemontese Barbera.

Menu: Serve the ragù and pasta in small portions before Balsamic Roast Chicken (page 279), Lemon Roast Veal with Rosemary (page 294), or Porcini Veal Chops (page 290). For lighter dining, have the ragù as a main dish after a few slices of coppa (page 474) as antipasto. Make dessert Baked Pears with Fresh Grape Syrup (page 442).

Bologna's marketplace, engraving by Giovanni M. Tamburini, from a picture by Francesco Curti, circa 1640

Country-Style Ragù
Ragù alla Contadina

This ragù is homey and suave at the same time, with a pleasing lightness. Milk is its secret ingredient, mellowing, tenderizing and sweetening the ragù. Sunday dinners throughout Emilia-Romagna's countryside, especially in Modena and Romagna, begin with tagliatelle or maccheroni tossed with some variation of this ragù. Not only is it one of my favorite recipes, it is a fine example of the home-style ragùs prepared with a variety of meats.

[Makes enough sauce for 1 recipe fresh pasta (pages 80 to 82) or 1 pound dried pasta]

3 tablespoons extra-virgin olive oil

2 ounces pancetta, finely chopped

1 medium onion, minced

1 medium stalk celery with leaves, minced

1 small carrot, minced

4 ounces boneless veal shoulder or round

4 ounces boneless pork loin, trimmed of fat, or 4 ounces mild Italian sausage (made without fennel)

8 ounces beef skirt steak, hanging tender, or boneless chuck blade or chuck center cut (in order of preference)

1 ounce thinly sliced Prosciutto di Parma

⅔ cup dry red wine

1½ cups Poultry/Meat Stock (page 66), or ⅔ cup Meat Essences (page 61), or 1½ cups Quick Stock (page 68) (in order of preference)

2 cups milk

3 canned plum tomatoes, drained

Salt and freshly ground black pepper to taste

Method

Working Ahead: *The ragù can be made 3 days ahead. Cover and refrigerate. It also freezes well for up to 1 month. Skim the fat from the ragù before using it.*

Browning the Ragù Base: Heat the olive oil in a 12-inch skillet over medium-high heat. (Have a 4- to 5-quart saucepan handy to use once browning is completed.) Add the pancetta and minced vegetables and sauté, stirring frequently with a wooden spatula, 10 minutes, or until the onions barely begin to color. Coarsely grind all the meats together, including the prosciutto, in a food processor or meat grinder. Stir into the pan and slowly brown over medium heat. First the meats will give off liquid and turn dull gray, but as the liquid evaporates, browning will begin. Stir often, scooping under the meats with the wooden spatula. Protect the brown glaze forming on the bottom of the pan by turning the heat down. Cook 15 minutes, or until the meats are a deep brown. Turn the contents of the skillet into a strainer and shake out the fat. Turn them into the 4- to 5-quart saucepan and set over medium heat.

Reducing and Simmering: Add the wine to the skillet, lowering the heat so the sauce bubbles quietly. Stir occasionally until the wine has reduced by half, about 3 minutes. Scrape up the brown glaze as the wine bubbles. Then pour the reduced wine into the saucepan and set the skillet aside.

If you are using stock, stir ½ cup into the saucepan and let it bubble slowly, 10 minutes, or until totally evaporated. Repeat with another ½ cup stock. Stir in the last ½ cup stock along with the milk. (If using Meat Essences, add it and the milk to the browned meats, and do not boil it off.) Adjust heat so the liquid bubbles very slowly. Partially cover the pot, and cook 1 hour. Stir frequently to check for sticking.

Add the tomatoes, crushing them as they go into the pot. Cook, uncovered, at a very slow bubble another 45 minutes, or until the sauce resembles a thick, meaty stew. Season with salt and pepper.

Serving: Toss with freshly cooked pasta and serve immediately. Pass freshly grated Parmigiano-Reggiano cheese.

Suggestions **Wine:** A red Bresciano Chiaretto from Lombardy's Riviera del Garda, Sicily's Cerasuolo di Vittoria, or Apulia's velvety, full Salice Salentino Rosso.

Menu: Offer as a main dish after Fresh Pears with Parmigiano-Reggiano and Balsamic Vinegar (page 30). Follow with Salad of Mixed Greens and Fennel (page 349), and Home-Style Jam Cake (page 401). Serve in small quantities as a first course before Balsamic Roast Chicken (page 279), Giovanna's Wine-Basted Rabbit (page 284), or a lighter dish of Grilled Winter Endives (page 337). End the meal with Meringues of the Dark Lake (page 421) and espresso.

Game Ragù
Ragù degli Appennini

As leaves start falling in the high Apennine mountains, family kitchens fill with the aromas of this big sauce. Everyone has their own rendition. The ragù is fine over tagliatelle and small hollow pastas like penne rigate, but it is at its best on wide ribbons of pappardelle. Try it, too, spooned over squares of grilled polenta. Although delicious made with beef, this ragù traditionally features game. If you can get venison, hare, wild rabbit, wild boar, or elk, do use them. The sauce mellows nicely if made several days ahead.

[Makes enough sauce for 1½ recipes fresh pasta (pages 80 to 82) or 1½ pounds dried pasta]

2½ to 3 tablespoons extra-virgin olive oil

1 medium onion, minced

1 small carrot, minced

2 pounds boneless venison, hare, wild boar, wild rabbit, elk, or beef, trimmed of excess fat and cut into ¼- to ½-inch cubes

Salt and freshly ground black pepper

1 large clove garlic, crushed

2½- to 3-inch sprig fresh rosemary, or 1 teaspoon dried whole rosemary leaves

3 large leaves fresh sage, or 3 large dried sage leaves

1 tablespoon imported Italian tomato paste

¼ teaspoon ground cloves

¼ teaspoon ground cinnamon

3 to 4 tablespoons wine vinegar

1 cup dry red wine, Barolo or California Zinfandel

2 cups Poultry/Meat Stock (page 66) or Quick Stock (page 68)

Method

Working Ahead: *The ragù holds well in the refrigerator 4 days and freezes up to 1 month. Remove any hardened fat from its surface before serving or freezing.*

Browning the Ragù Base: Heat the olive oil in a 12-inch sauté pan over medium-high heat, and add the onion and carrot. Turn the heat down to medium, and cook 3 minutes, or until the onion is slightly softened but not browned. Add the meat to the pan so the pieces do not touch, and sprinkle lightly with salt and pepper. Take about 20 minutes to brown the meat on all sides, turning the pieces with a wooden spatula. Adjust the heat so as not to blacken the brown glaze forming on the bottom of the pan, and to protect the onion and carrot from burning. A leisurely browning builds up deep brown flavors.

Adding the Seasonings and Reducing: Once the meat has reached a rich dark brown color, sprinkle it with the garlic and herbs, and cook another few seconds. Stir in the tomato paste, cloves, cinnamon, and vinegar. Cook 1 minute, still over medium heat. Add ½ cup of the red wine and simmer, uncovered, over medium heat, 5 minutes, or until all the liquid has evaporated. As the wine cooks down, scrape up the brown bits on the pan's bottom with a wooden spatula. Turn into a 4-quart saucepan, and add the rest of the wine. Concentrate the sauce's flavor base even more by simmering it 10 minutes, or until all the liquid has cooked off. Stir frequently.

Simmering the Sauce: Add the stock, partially cover the pot, and lower the heat so it cooks with an occasional bubble. Cook, stirring now and then, 1½ to 2 hours, adding water or stock as needed to keep the meat barely covered with liquid. The cooking time varies according to the meat being used. It should be tender but not falling apart, generously moistened but not soupy. If necessary, uncover and simmer off some of the liquid. Aim for deep, robust flavors, with a suggestion of the vinegar's tang. Add a teaspoon of vinegar if needed. Season with salt and pepper.

Serving: Defat the sauce. Toss with freshly cooked pasta and serve immediately. Pass freshly grated Parmigiano-Reggiano cheese.

Suggestions   **Wine:** Romagna's Barbarossa di Bertinoro, Sangiovese di Romagna Riserva, or Bologna's Barbera dei Colli Bolognesi di Monte San Pietro. From other parts of Italy: Tuscany's Rosso di Montalcino (Brunello of young vines), Carmignano, or Chianti Classico. When cooked with strong game like hare, an aged Barbaresco or Barolo from the Piedmont.

Menu: Serve as a one-dish meal followed by a Salad of Mixed Greens and Fennel (page 349) and chunks of Parmigiano-Reggiano cheese for a savory finish.

In the tradition of feast days and special occasions, serve over pappardelle in small portions before Pan-Roasted Quail (page 283), Balsamic Roast Chicken (page 279), or Christmas Capon (page 281).

Cook's Notes   **Game Cuts:** The best game cuts to use here would be shoulder, rump, shank, neck, or leg.

Polenta Variation: Cook Polenta (page 352) and pour it onto a heated platter. Spoon hot ragù over the polenta, and serve accompanied by freshly grated Parmigiano-Reggiano cheese.

Grilled Polenta Variation: Slice cooled or leftover Polenta (page 352) about ½ inch thick. Brush lightly with olive oil on both sides, and grill in a ribbed skillet or in a heavy frying pan until golden brown on both sides (the polenta is especially good cooked over a wood or real-wood-charcoal fire). Arrange on a heated platter and spoon the simmering ragù over the slices.

Light Veal Ragù with Tomato
Ragù Vecchio Molinetto

This ragù is my tribute to Parma's trattoria Il Vecchio Molinetto, where chef Erminia Marasi maintains the traditions of Parmesan home cooking. Hers is a very different interpretation of Emilia-Romagna's popular ragù, perhaps the lightest of them all. Rarely is veal the only meat cooked into a ragù but when properly browned, it has fine character. Tomatoes plump out the sauce, while water instead of stock keeps the flavors clear and light. Elegant enough to open almost any type of menu, the ragù is at its best over tagliatelle.

[Makes enough sauce for 1 recipe fresh pasta (pages 80 to 82)
or 1 pound dried pasta]

4 tablespoons extra-virgin olive oil

1 medium carrot, finely chopped

1 large stalk celery, finely chopped

1 medium onion, finely chopped

1 pound boneless veal sirloin or shoulder, trimmed of fat and connective tissue, diced into ¼-inch pieces

Salt and freshly ground black pepper

2-inch sprig fresh rosemary, or ½ teaspoon dried whole rosemary leaves

½ cup dry white wine

2 teaspoons imported Italian tomato paste

1 cup water

1½ pounds canned tomatoes with their juice or full-flavored fresh tomatoes, peeled, seeded, and chopped

Method

Working Ahead: *The ragù's flavors are best the same day it is cooked. But it can be partially cooked 1 day ahead, with the tomatoes added the day it is served. Take care in reheating. If the veal overcooks, the flavors will flatten.*

Browning the Ragù Base: Heat the oil over medium heat in a heavy 3½- to 4-quart saucepan. Drop in the carrot, celery, and onion. Sauté 10 minutes over medium to medium-low heat, or until the onion is very soft and beginning to color. Turn the heat to medium-high and add the meat. Stir the veal with a wooden spatula, scooping under it to keep the meat from sticking. Allow 8 to 10 minutes for the veal's liquid to evaporate, then adjust the heat so that it is cooking slowly, taking about 20 minutes to reach deep golden brown. Stir frequently. Sprinkle the meat lightly with salt and a few grindings of pepper. Add the rosemary sprig, cook another 5 minutes, then discard it.

Reducing: Stir in the wine. Let it bubble down to nothing while you scrape up the brown glaze from the bottom of the pan. This takes 3 to 4 minutes. Blend in the tomato paste and water. Bring the ragù to a slow bubble over low heat.

Simmering: Partially cover and cook 1 to 1¼ hours, or until the meat is tender and the sauce is richly flavored. The consistency should be thick but still moist. If necessary, add a little more water during cooking. (If you are preparing the sauce ahead, stop at this point and allow it to cool; then cover and refrigerate. One of the keys to its fresh flavor is cooking the tomatoes only a short time.)

Finishing and Serving: Stir in the tomatoes and cook slowly, uncovered, 5 to 10 minutes. The meat and tomato flavors will blend, but the tomato must retain its fresh, distinctive character. Toss the ragù with fresh or boxed tagliatelle. As befits a sauce from Parma, Parmigiano-Reggiano cheese is delicious with the ragù.

Suggestions   **Wine:** A young red Merlot del Piave of the Veneto, a Sangiovese di Umbria, or a red Rincione of Sicily.

Menu: Serve in small quantities before Erminia's Pan-Crisped Chicken (page 270) (also from Il Vecchio Molinetto), Giovanna's Wine-Basted Rabbit (page 284), or any other dish made without tomato. Serve as a main dish, beginning the meal with Salad of Tart Greens with Prosciutto and Warm Balsamic Dressing (page 26). Ugo Falavigna's Apple Cream Tart (page 411) from Parma is an ideal finale.

"Stretching the Pot"

"Stretching the pot" is a phrase I often heard from the Tuscan side of my family. This expression came to life for me years ago in the mountains above Reggio and Modena. After talking with a farmer about his crops, I was invited to join his family and friends for dinner. A sauce very similar to Game Ragù (page 50) had been made to dress pasta. With the arrival of five unexpected guests, stock and water were blended into the ragù. After about 20 minutes of simmering it appeared on the table as a filling and satisfying soup, with plenty for all.

Try adding 2 quarts of stock to this sauce (after refrigerating and defatting). Serve with a bowl of Parmigiano-Reggiano cheese for sprinkling over the soup and either Modena Mountain Bread (page 388) or *Spianata* (page 367).

Ragù of Giblets
Ragù di Rigaglie di Pollo

One of my favorite ragùs, this sauce has an ancient lineage, dating back at least 400 years. Giblets are the last thing most of us expect to taste like a blend of well-aged beef, fine old Barolo wine, and mature prosciutto. But they do, and this sauce is one of the most distinctive I know. Its character is full-blown and robust, yet elegant and perfectly balanced on the palate. There are several interpretations within Emilia-Romagna and many more in neighboring regions, where it is sometimes called "false game sauce." Tagliatelle bring out the ragù's elegant side, while small hollow macaroni like penne or sedani emphasize its earthiness.

[Makes enough sauce for 1 recipe fresh pasta (pages 80 to 82)
or 1 pound dried pasta]

¼ cup (¼ ounce) crumbled dried porcini mushrooms

1 cup hot water

4 tablespoons extra-virgin olive oil

2 ounces lean pancetta, finely chopped

1 large onion, minced

1 small carrot, minced

1 small stalk celery, minced

2 pounds chicken or turkey hearts and gizzards, trimmed of tough tissue and cut into ¼-inch dice

2 tablespoons minced Italian parsley

1 large clove garlic, crushed

1 large California bay laurel leaf

2 large fresh sage leaves, or 2 whole dried sage leaves

1½ cups dry white wine

2 tablespoons imported Italian tomato paste

3 cups Poultry/Meat Stock (page 66) or Quick Stock (68)

1 cup drained canned tomatoes, crushed

Salt and freshly ground black pepper to taste

Method

Working Ahead: *The ragù can be made up to 4 days before serving. Store it, covered, in the refrigerator. It freezes successfully 1 month. Remove any hardened fat from its surface before freezing or reheating.*

Preparing the Porcini: Stir the mushroom pieces into a bowl of cold water, let the particles settle, and lift out the mushrooms. Repeat with fresh water until there is no sign of grit or debris. Soak the rinsed mushrooms in the hot water while the meat is browning. Line a small sieve with a paper towel to strain the liquid.

Browning the Ragù Base: Heat the oil in a heavy 6-quart pot over medium-low heat. Add the pancetta and minced vegetables. Stir them occasionally as they cook, about 8 minutes, or until the onions are soft and clear. Raising the heat to medium-high, sauté the vegetables another 5 minutes, or until they begin to color. Turn the heat down to medium or medium-low, and add the gizzards and hearts. Brown them very slowly, taking 30 to 40 minutes. Use a wooden spatula to scoop under the meat and turn it, keeping it from sticking.

Reducing: Lift the mushrooms out of their liquid, reserving the liquid. Stir the mushrooms, parsley, garlic, bay leaf, and sage into the pot. Sauté 2 to 3 minutes over medium-low heat. Strain the mushroom liquid into the pot. Let it bubble slowly over medium-low, about 5 minutes, scraping up the brown bits clinging to the bottom of the pan. Cook until the liquid has evaporated. Blend in the wine and tomato paste. Keeping the wine at a slow bubble, reduce it to nothing. Repeat the process with 1 cup of the stock. Stir in the remaining 2 cups of stock and tomatoes. Bring to a very slow bubble.

Simmering: Partially cover the pot. Cook 1 hour, or until the gizzards are tender and the sauce is thick but not dry. Add water or more stock if necessary. Season with salt and pepper. Let the sauce cool a short while off the heat sauce, then skim off the fat.

Serving: Bring the sauce to a simmer, toss with freshly cooked pasta, and serve accompanied by freshly grated Parmigiano-Reggiano cheese.

Suggestions   **Wine:** A red Barbera from the region or from the Piedmont, a Sangiovese di Romagna Riserva, or a lighter-styled Barolo from the Piedmont.

Menu: Have small portions of the ragù over penne before Erminia's Pan-Crisped Chicken (page 270), Grilled Beef with Balsamic Glaze (page 303), or Lemon Roast Veal with Rosemary (page 294). Serve as a main dish after Hot Caramelized Pears with Prosciutto (page 31). Finish with Strawberries in Red Wine (page 445).

Cook's Notes   **Risotto Variation:** Follow the recipe for the Classic White Risotto (page 201), adding a half recipe of Giblet Ragù once the rice is sautéed. Reduce the stock in the risotto by 2 to 3 cups. Proceed with the recipe as directed.

Meat Ragù with Marsala
Ragù di Carne e Marsala

*This ragù grew out of a taste
memory and two old Ferrara family recipes. In test after test, trying to
duplicate my favorite Domed Maccheroni Pie of Ferrara, I was haunted
by an elusive element, a taste I could not quite single out. Finally
Ferrarese linguist Riccardo Rimondi shared his family's recipes, and there
it was: a little Marsala, reduced into the pie's ragù sauce to make the
subtlest, but all-important, difference. Emerging from this ragù of several
meats and savory liquids are flavors that constantly change on the
palate. Certainly use this ragù in the domed pie, but savor it to the full
all by itself over pasta—tagliatelle is my preference. The recipe doubles
easily.*

[Makes enough sauce for ¾ recipe fresh pasta (pages 80 to 82)
or 12 ounces dried pasta]

12 ounces turkey or chicken
giblets, trimmed of tough
membrane and cut into large
chunks

8 ounces veal loin chop, boned
and cut into large chunks

3 tablespoons unsalted butter

1 small to medium onion, minced

½ stalk celery, minced

½ medium carrot, minced

1 ounce Prosciutto di Parma,
minced

3 ounces lean ground beef chuck

2 ounces prosciutto cotto or boiled
ham, chopped

6 tablespoons dry Marsala

⅔ cup dry white wine

⅔ cup strained porcini mushroom
soaking liquid (see Note)

1½ tablespoons imported Italian
tomato paste

⅔ cup Poultry/Meat Stock (page
66) or Quick Stock (page 68)

Method   **Working Ahead:** *The ragù can be made up to 3 days ahead. Store, covered, in the
refrigerator. It freezes well up to 1 month. Skim off any fat from the surface before
rewarming or freezing. Reheat the sauce gently.*

Browning the Ragù Base: Coarsely grind the giblets and veal together in a food
processor fitted with the steel blade, or in a meat grinder. Heat the butter in a 12-inch
heavy skillet over medium-high heat. Drop in the minced vegetables and Prosciutto
di Parma. Sauté, stirring often with a wooden spatula, 3 minutes, or until the onion

begins to pick up color. Add the ground meats, including the beef and the prosciutto cotto. Turn the heat up to high, breaking up the chunks and stirring to encourage even browning. A brown glaze should develop on the pan's bottom. Take care not to burn it, as the glaze contributes important flavor to the sauce. The browning takes 8 to 10 minutes.

Reducing: Add the Marsala, reduce heat to medium, and bubble slowly, until all the liquid has evaporated. Keeping the heat at medium, add the white wine and cook it off as you scrape up the brown glaze. This should take about 15 minutes. Reduce the mushroom liquid and tomato paste down to nothing.

Simmering: Turn the ragù into a 3- to 4-quart saucepan. Stir in the stock, and adjust the heat so that the ragù is bubbling very slowly. Partially cover, and cook 30 to 40 minutes, until it resembles a thick soup.

Serving: Toss with freshly cooked pasta, and serve at once. Freshly grated Parmigiano-Reggiano cheese is delicious with this ragù.

Suggestions   **Wine:** A soft light-bodied red, like a young Santa Maddalena Classico from the Trentino–Alto Adige region or a young Valpolicella Classico of the Veneto.

Menu: Use the ragù in Domed Maccheroni Pie of Ferrara (page 180). Serve the ragù over tagliatelle or any small hollow pasta before a Salad of Mixed Greens and Fennel (page 349) and a dessert of Sweet Tagliarini Tart of Ferrara (page 194). Or as a first course before Balsamic Roast Chicken (page 279) or Rabbit Roasted with Sweet Fennel (page 289). Have Riccardo Rimondi's Spanish Sponge Cake (page 433) filled with raspberry jam or Espresso and Mascarpone Semi-Freddo (page 428) for dessert.

Cook's Notes   **Porcini Mushroom Liquid:** Whenever the mushroom's liquid is not called for in a recipe, strain it and freeze it for dishes like this one. If unavailable, substitute another ⅔ cup stock.

The pine nuts of Ravenna, from a 17th-century board game, by Bolognese artist Giuseppe Maria Mitelli

Behind the scenes at Ristorante San Domenico in Imola

ESSENTIAL SAUCES AND STOCKS

auces in Emilia-Romagna's cooking fall into three categories. There are the sauces created for a specific pasta, like those found in the pasta chapter. There is the sauce yielded in the cooking of a dish, like the sauce that comes from the slow braising of a chicken in wine and tomato. A third type is the sauce made to enrich, or to be the sole garnish of, a dish—these sauces are included in this chapter. Of these, Meat Essences is the ultimate enrichment. It is very much a creation of the last century, when mere spoonfuls of this concentration of meat juices and wine added character to many dishes. I have revived this old sauce base because it works the same magic on modern recipes. It plays a role in many pastas and main dishes in this book, and it is indispensable in Nino Bergese's extraordinary risotto.

Tomato sauces play several roles in Emilia-Romagna's cuisine, but the most important is as a dressing for pasta. Winter Tomato Sauce is full and deep-flavored, meant to make the most of canned tomatoes. The sauce of porcini mushrooms and tomato can be traced to Piacenza. Each of these recipes offers specific recommendations for the pastas and other foods that work best with them.

Good stock is essential to much of Emilia-Romagna's cooking. The renowned Tortellini in Broth is one prime example, and most ragù sauces call for homemade stock. Boiling stock down to a rich but fat-free concentrate produces a fine stand-in for butter in the simple sauces for Emilia-Romagna's filled pastas like Cappellacci of Sweet Squash or Tortelli of Cabbage and Potatoes. A really full-flavored stock creates effortless pan sauces from roasts and sautés, as illustrated in Basil and Balsamic Veal Scallops and Lemon Roast Veal with Rosemary.

While French cooking may call for veal stock in one dish and chicken in another, Emilia-Romagna usually requires only one. But what a luscious stock it is. Traditionally the region's brodo, or stock, comes from simmering capon and beef. Capon (substitutions are suggested in the recipe) makes a sweet delicate stock, while beef adds resonance and body. My own version requires almost no effort and achieves good flavor with the aid of a few simple tricks. Quick Stock is a bow to convenience, using a quick and easy method to improve on canned broth.

The recipes are extremely versatile. Don't think of them solely for the dishes of Emilia-Romagna. Enjoy them as part of other recipes too.

Meat Essences
Il Sugo di Carne

Literally translated as *"juice of the meat,"* <u>Il Sugo di Carne</u> is an old sauce base that was developed in the wealthy kitchens of the last century. With the disappearance of servants and hired cooks, it fell into disuse. I think it deserves revival, and agree with the few cooks still making <u>Sugo di Carne</u> that it brings a special elegance to foods. A hundred years ago, when a soup, sauce, stew, or sauté lacked depth or character, the cook often stirred in a few tablespoons of Meat Essences. It was a flavor booster then, and it does the same today. Think of it as a concentrate bursting with the flavor of meat but low in fat. A few spoonfuls can cause a dish to taste as if it has been cooking for hours, when in reality it was on the stove for only a few minutes. This is splendid on its own over pasta, making an elegant meat sauce with surprising lightness. A full recipe sauces four pounds of tagliatelle. A quarter to a half cup brings new dimension to Classic White Risotto and Risotto with Red Wine and Rosemary. Since the essence freezes well and a little goes such a long way, make a batch every few months. Just the aroma is worth the effort of cooking it.

[Makes 4 cups]

1 tablespoon unsalted butter

3 tablespoons extra-virgin olive oil

2 ounces lean pancetta, chopped

6 thin slices prosciutto, chopped

1 large onion, thinly sliced

1 small carrot, thinly sliced

1 small stalk celery with leaves, thinly sliced

1 pound meaty veal neck bones or chopped breast of veal, trimmed of fat

1 pound chicken wings, chopped into small pieces

1½ to 2 pounds meaty beef neck bones, trimmed of excess fat

2 large California bay laurel leaves

6 whole cloves

1 cup dry red wine

3½ quarts Poultry/Meat Stock (page 66)

⅔ cup drained canned tomatoes, crushed

2 small cloves garlic, crushed

Method   **Working Ahead:** *Meat Essences holds well 5 days, covered, in the refrigerator. It freezes up to 3 months.*

continued

Browning the Sauce: Divide the butter and oil between two large, heavy sauté pans. Spread a layer of half the pancetta and prosciutto in each pan. Then divide the onion, carrot, celery, veal, chicken wings, and beef between the pans. Set the pans over medium-high heat. Do not stir or cover until you can smell the onion browning and hear sizzling in each pan. This takes about 8 minutes. Lower the heat to medium.

Using a wooden spatula, turn the meats over and continue cooking 20 minutes, or until the pieces are deeply browned on all sides. Lower the heat if necessary to avoid burning the onion or the brown glaze forming on the bottoms of the pans.

Reducing: Stir in the bay leaves and cloves. Divide the wine between the two pans and let it bubble slowly, scraping up the brown glaze as the wine cooks down. Cook 8 to 10 minutes over medium heat until the wine has disappeared. Add 1 cup of the stock to each pan, and let it bubble slowly another 8 to 10 minutes, or until reduced to nothing. Stir frequently. Repeat twice more with 1 cup of stock each time for each pan. Make sure the stock is totally evaporated before adding the next cup.

Simmering and Finishing: Turn the contents of both pans into a 6- to 8-quart heavy pot. Stir in the remaining stock, along with the tomatoes and garlic. Adjust heat so the liquid is bubbling only occasionally. Partially cover. Cook 6 hours, stirring occasionally and adding more stock or water to keep the meat and bones barely covered. Strain the essences into a bowl, firmly pressing on the meat and vegetables to extract as much liquid as possible. Allow to cool; then cover and refrigerate overnight. The next day, skim off all the fat from the surface, and refrigerate or freeze.

Cook's Notes Do not substitute Quick Stock here or any other stock based on canned broth. Having the salt-free Poultry/Meat Stock enriched from its own long cooking as the base of the essence ensures the fullest, deepest flavor possible.

Winter Tomato Sauce
Salsa di Pomodoro Invernale

A simple and basic sauce to toss with pasta, fold into a risotto, layer in a lasagne or anywhere you want a meatless sauce. Play with the sauce's flavorings as Emilia-Romagna cooks do. Sauté in a little butter, pancetta, or prosciutto instead of olive oil. Season with basil, rosemary, marjoram, or sage. The recipe doubles easily.

[Makes enough sauce for 1 recipe fresh pasta (pages 80 to 82)
or 1 pound dried pasta]

3 tablespoons fruity extra-virgin
   olive oil
1 medium onion, minced
1 small carrot, minced
1 small stalk celery with leaves,
   minced
3 tablespoons minced Italian
   parsley
1 large clove garlic, minced
3 tablespoons chopped fresh basil
   leaves, or 2 fresh sage leaves and
   ½-inch sprig fresh rosemary

1 tablespoon imported Italian
   tomato paste
2 pounds canned tomatoes with
   their liquid, or fresh tomatoes,
   peeled, seeded, and chopped
Pinch of sugar (optional)
Salt and freshly ground black
   pepper to taste

Method   **Working Ahead:** *The sauce can be made up to 4 days before serving. Cool, cover, and store in the refrigerator. Freeze the sauce up to 3 months.*

Making the Sauce: Heat the oil over medium heat in a 3- to 4-quart heavy saucepan. Drop in the minced vegetables and parsley. Slowly sauté, stirring often, 10 minutes, or until they are golden brown.

Add the garlic and herbs, and cook only 30 seconds. Blend in the tomato paste and the tomatoes, crushing them as they go into the pot. Bring the sauce to a lively bubble and keep it uncovered as you cook it over medium-high heat 8 minutes, or until thickened. Taste for seasoning.

Serving: Toss with freshly cooked pasta, and serve immediately with freshly grated Parmigiano-Reggiano cheese. savoriness.

Suggestions   **Wine:** A simple red like a young Sangiovese di Romagna, a red Corvo from Sicily, or a young Chianti Classico.

Menu: Serve over almost any pasta as a light main dish after the Salad of Tart Greens with Prosciutto and Warm Balsamic Dressing (page 26). Dessert could be Marie Louise Crescents (page 426) or Baked Pears with Fresh Grape Syrup (page 442). When serving it with pasta as a first course, follow with Rabbit Roasted with Sweet Fennel (page 289) or Porcini Veal Chops (page 290). Have Zabaione Jam Tart (page 415) for dessert.

Cook's Notes **Tomatoes:** Tomatoes vary greatly in quality. See page 505 for information.

Piacenza's Porcini Tomato Sauce
Salsa di Porcini con Pomodori

This is the best kind of home cooking: utterly satisfying and quick and easy to make. A lavish amount of dried porcini mushrooms creates a sauce tasting of meat where no meat exists. Toss the sauce with any number of pastas, whether homemade or store-bought. I like it especially on homemade or dried imported tagliatelle. It is excellent over simple risotti, like the Classic White Risotto. Or you can add a quart of stock to the sauce and create a fine soup.

[Makes enough sauce for 1 recipe fresh pasta (pages 80 to 82)
or 1 pound dried pasta]

2 cups (2 ounces) dried porcini mushrooms

2 cups hot water

3 tablespoons extra-virgin olive oil

2 tablespoons unsalted butter

2 medium onions, minced

1 clove garlic, minced

6 to 7 medium to large full-flavored, vine-ripened fresh tomatoes, peeled, seeded, and chopped, or 13 drained canned plum tomatoes, crushed

1¾ cups water

Salt and freshly ground black pepper to taste

Method

Working Ahead: *The sauce can be made up to 5 days ahead. Store it, covered, in the refrigerator.*

Preparing the Porcini: Clean the mushrooms either by rinsing large pieces under cold running water or by dropping smaller pieces into a medium-size bowl filled with cold water. Swish them around vigorously for a few seconds. Then let the particles settle and remove the mushrooms. Repeat two more times, or until very few particles appear. Do not let the mushrooms soak in the cold water for more than about 20 seconds, or they will lose some of their flavor.

Cover the rinsed porcini with the hot water, and let them soak about 30 minutes. Lift them out of the liquid, squeezing not too vigorously to remove excess liquid. Chop and reserve. (The liquid can be strained through paper towels and frozen for later use.)

Making the Sauce: Heat the oil and butter in a 5- to 6-quart heavy saucepan over medium heat. Add the onion, lower the heat to medium-low, and sauté 10 to 15 minutes, or until the onions are soft and clear. Stir in the garlic, porcini, tomatoes, and water. Bring to a gentle bubble. Partially cover, and cook 25 minutes, or until the mushrooms are very tender, the flavors have melded, and the sauce has thickened a little. If the sauce tastes weak, uncover and simmer another 5 to 10 minutes to intensify flavors. Season with salt and pepper.

Serving: Toss the hot sauce with freshly cooked pasta, and serve immediately with freshly grated Parmigiano-Reggiano cheese.

Suggestions   **Wine:** A soft, light red like a young Merlot from Friuli, Lombardy's Groppello, or the Veneto's Bardolino Classico.

Menu: Begin with Spring Salad with Hazelnuts (page 21) or Hot Caramelized Pears with Prosciutto (page 31), serve the sauce with pasta as a light main dish, and finish with Cinnamon and Clove Custard (page 440). Also use the sauce over Piacenza's Tortelli with Tails (page 162) and Tortelli of Cabbage and Potato (page 160).

Cook's Notes   **Variation:** In the Apennine mountains above Parma, Borgotaro is famous for its porcini. There this sauce makes a Christmas Eve specialty, Pappardelle of the Vigil: 1 pound of cooked pappardelle is baked in a casserole with the porcini sauce and 4 ounces of Parmigiano-Reggiano or a mild, young sheep cheese.

Poultry/Meat Stock
Brodo

Although this is the foundation of many dishes in Emilia-Romagna's cuisine, the stock is terrific on its own. Drink it first as a restorative from steaming mugs on an icy winter night. It is one of the most flavorful and satisfying stocks I know, and I doubt I could recover from a cold without it. The stock also creates the most elegant of openings to a dinner party when served in deep soup cups, accompanied only by spoonfuls of freshly grated Parmigiano-Reggiano cheese. Of course ladles of it bring depth and character to soups, stews, sautés, and sauces. Make Poultry/Meat Stock in large quantities every few months, as it freezes with great success.

[Makes about 8 quarts]

2 to 3 pounds meaty beef shank or "soup" bones, trimmed of fat

8 to 9 pounds whole capon or turkey wings (or a combination), chopped into 3-inch pieces

3 stalks celery with leaves, chopped

3 large carrots, chopped

4 very large onions, unpeeled (trim away root ends), chopped

2 large California bay laurel leaves, broken

3 sprigs Italian parsley

2 large cloves garlic, unpeeled, crushed

Method

Working Ahead: *The stock holds, covered, in the refrigerator 3 to 4 days. Freeze it up to 4 months in different-size containers, from 2-tablespoon ice cubes to quart jars.*

Starting the Stock: In one 20-quart or two 10-quart stockpots, combine the beef and poultry. Cover it with cold water by about 4 inches, and set over medium heat. Let the water come to a slow bubble. Skim off all foam rising to the surface.

Simmering: Add the vegetables, bay leaves, parsley, and garlic. Regulate the heat so the broth bubbles only occasionally (so you can say "one hundred" between bubbles). Partially cover, and cook 12 to 14 hours, skimming the fat from the surface every so often. If necessary, add boiling water to keep the solids covered.

The long cooking time surprises many. This extended simmering draws all the flavor from the meat and bones, producing a stock with exceptionally deep taste. You can start the stock after dinner and let it cook all night, partially covered, at a slow bubble. Make sure it is bubbling slowly, because leaving it below a bubble will cause spoilage. The next morning turn off the heat and strain the stock.

Finishing: Refrigerate the strained stock until fat hardens on the surface. Discard all but 2 tablespoons of the fat. (In Emilia-Romagna one sign of a proper broth is luminous pin dots of fat called the "eyes" of the broth. Although never greasy, that tiny amount of fat gives flavor.) Pour into storage containers and refrigerate or freeze.

Cook's Notes **Garganelli in Broth:** Serve 8 to 10 people a memorable first course by cooking a half recipe of garganelli pasta (page 86) in 3 quarts Poultry/Meat Stock until it is tender but still firm to the bite. Ladle into heated soup dishes. Season with spoonfuls of freshly grated Parmigiano-Reggiano cheese.

Porcini Tomato Soup: Made an easy soup by diluting Piacenza's Porcini Tomato Sauce (page 64) with 8 cups Poultry/Meat Stock. Simmer about 5 minutes, then serve in heated soup dishes. Pass a bowl of freshly grated Parmigiano-Reggiano cheese.

Pan Sauces: Because it is salt-free and so intensely flavored, Poultry/Meat Stock boils down into a fine pan sauce, as in Basil and Balsamic Veal Scallops (page 296) and Lemon Roast Veal with Rosemary (page 294).

Capon and Turkey Wings

This stock has many variations within Emilia-Romagna, but almost all call for capon with beef, or occasionally capon with veal. I worried about providing a recipe calling for capon, which is difficult to find in some parts of the United States. But when admiring the robust stock of Imola chef Valentino Marcattilii, I discovered that he used turkey wings instead of capon, and the problem was solved. In any recipe, poultry wings make fine stock as they are neither dark nor light meat but a blend of the two and particularly flavorful. So I offer you the choice. The stock is richer with the capon, and I like to use that version when making Tortellini in Broth Villa Gaidello (page 134) or Anolini of Parma (page 149). But the turkey wing version is not a compromise; it is equally delicious.

Quick Stock
Brodo Rapido

A *practical solution for those days when you do not have time to make the long-simmered Poultry/Meat Stock. This quick version uses canned broth, blunting its canned taste with aromatic vegetables and herbs. Although it is no match for the lusty Poultry/Meat stock, it does work well in most dishes, with the exception of pastas cooked and served in broth.*

[Makes about 6 cups]

1 medium onion
Four 14½-ounce cans low-salt
   chicken broth, chilled
1 large stalk celery with leaves,
   coarsely chopped
½ large carrot, coarsely chopped

2 medium onions, unpeeled (trim
   away root ends), coarsely
   chopped
2 sprigs Italian parsley
1 large clove garlic, crushed
Generous pinch of dried basil

Method

Working Ahead: *You can hold Quick Stock, covered, in the refrigerator 3 to 4 days, or freeze it up to 3 months.*

Making the Stock: Preheat the broiler, setting the oven rack as close as possible to the flame. Trim the root end from the first onion, but do not peel it. Cut it into 4 thick slices. Arrange them on a sheet of aluminum foil and slip it under the broiler. Broil 15 minutes, or until browned on both sides, turning once. Pour the broth into a 6-quart pot, and skim off the hardened fat. Add the broiled onion and all the remaining ingredients, and bring to a boil. Adjust the heat so the broth is bubbling slowly, cover tightly, and cook 30 minutes. Remove the pot from the heat, and strain the stock. Use it right away, or allow it to cool, and then cover and refrigerate or freeze.

Store-Bought Wonders

Stock is the food writer's nightmare. Good homemade stock makes dishes sing, but most readers have little time to prepare it. Canned stocks are always a compromise, even when enriched with vegetables and seasonings as in my Quick Stock. Bouillon cubes and sauce base pastes have no place in good cooking. Occasionally supermarkets and specialty food shops carry commercially made salt-free stocks of high quality. One such brand is Perfect Addition, a California-based company. Their Rich Stock—which comes in beef, veal, chicken, vegetable, and fish versions—is found in frozen food cases throughout the United States. For availability in your area, write to Perfect Addition, P.O. Box 8976, Newport Beach, CA 92658-8976, or telephone (714) 640-0220.

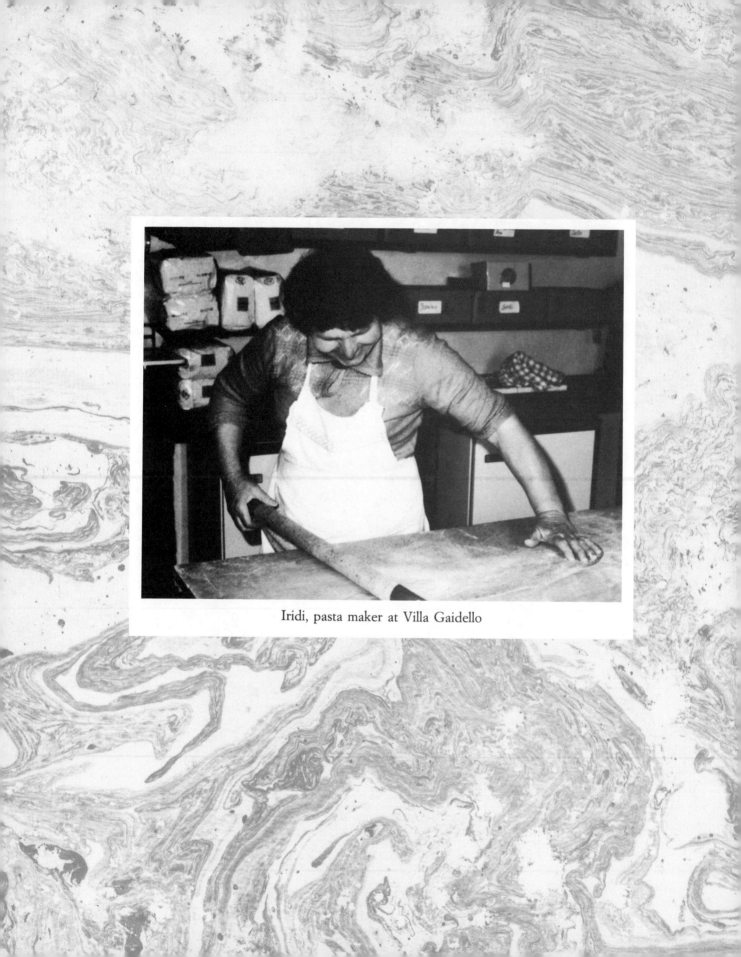

Iridi, pasta maker at Villa Gaidello

PASTAS

Of Sacred Navels, Priest Stranglers, and the Paradise of the Poor

A s early as the 14th century, trade, agriculture and strategic geographic placement made Emilia-Romagna one of Italy's wealthiest regions. For the area's aristocracy food was status and creativity was encouraged. Pasta became more than a single food; it became the region's most celebrated first course.

Although each region of Italy takes pride in its own special pastas, Emilia-Romagna's, made solely of flour and egg, are admired throughout the country. For many cooks all over Italy, they set a standard of excellence.

That excellence was no accident. It was born of wheat, trade and wealth. The region's fertile Po River plain nourished a particularly soft and fine wheat. When blended with the area's abundance of eggs, it became a tender pasta, best eaten fresh. Its moderate protein and starch content separated this pasta from its counterpart in southern Italy. There, wheat high in protein and low in starch produced a pasta that dried and stored well. Emilia-Romagna's wheat yielded pasta too brittle for successful drying and storing. Hence the region's tradition of fresh pasta began.

Pasta in Emilia-Romagna speaks of many things—traditions of birth, marriage and even death; centuries of Christmases, Easters and saints' days, each celebrated with its special dish. Pasta speaks of geographic origin and even of a family's social status. Pasta wittily expresses anticlerical sentiments without a word being spoken. It is steeped in legend, sometimes quite sensuous legend at that. And pasta often is so entrenched in tradition that one misstep in its preparation or presentation can outrage the most accommodating diners.

Those traditions have passed from hands to hands, through centuries of daughters watching mothers make pasta. Pasta is the food of women. Until very recently, while a woman in Emilia-Romagna could command accolades for many achievements, making superb pasta headed the list.

Almost every restaurant in the region, no matter how small or simple, has its _sfoglina,_ a woman who comes in every morning, pours out a mountain of flour onto her work board, blends in eggs, kneads, and then hand-rolls _la sfoglia,_ the sheet or "leaf" of golden dough. From this she fashions all the pasta served that day. She often creates enough to feed hundreds. If you showed her a food processor or a pasta machine, she would think you were mad.

The sfoglina tradition may be approaching its twilight. For years shops selling handmade pastas have supplemented the efforts of busy home cooks. As elderly sfoglinas retire and fewer young women take their places, those shops are beginning to supply restaurants. Certainly the pasta is still fresh and made by talented craftswomen; nothing less is acceptable in Emilia-Romagna. But with waning interest in the craft among young people, the region's great culinary heritage is threatened. Handmade pasta could become a curiosity tasted only on holidays.

To celebrate the past, if not the future, this chapter reflects 500 years of Emilia-Romagna's pasta making. You will find both classic and modern dishes. But to savor them fully, you need to understand the lively culture they evolved from.

Myth has it that pasta was poor man's food, implying that for centuries Italian peasants survived on plates of spaghetti. Sadly that was not so in much of Emilia-Romagna. During the all-too-frequent poor harvests and famines, wheat became the exclusive property of the wealthy. The poor could get wheat only when it was abundant. Wheat pastas stretched with ground chestnuts and cornmeal still survive from those times. *Polenta and beans, now eaten more out of nostalgia than necessity, were what much of Emilia-Romagna's peasantry survived on. Pasta was really the food of the affluent until the Industrial Revolution.*

Bologna's first pasta factory was chartered by the city council on November 20, 1586. Shortly after New Year's Day, 1587, Giovanni dall'Aglio started making "Vermicellos, Lasagnas, Macarones as they are made in Rome, Naples and Venice."

Cookbooks of the time document court banquets where pastas with the same names were served. Recipes from those books describe doughs often flavored with rosewater, sugar, saffron and/or butter. Maccheroni "in the style of" Naples or Rome seemed to be especially chic.

Renaissance pastas often accompanied meat dishes. In Italy today, serving pasta as a side dish is culinary heresy. With very few exceptions, pasta is always a separate course. But during the 16th and 17th centuries, filled and ribbon pastas often garnished roasts and stews. Then, most pasta dishes were topped with a blend of sugar, cinnamon, and grated Parmesan-style cheese. Believe it or not, the mixture can be quite delicious, as the chapter on Renaissance pastas proves.

Sugar was a prime status symbol, displayed and used with abandon by the aristocracy. Sweet and savory flavorings were intermixed from the first courses to the last on Medieval and Renaissance menus, and were often combined in pasta fillings. Some of these still survive, like Ferrara's cappellacci filled with sweet squash and Parmigiano-Reggiano and Parma's old recipe for pillowlike tortelli filled with spiced fruits and chestnuts. The spirit of sweet/savory dishes lives on in the many elaborate pies of the region, pies that are seen in those magnificent still-life paintings of the 16th and 17th centuries. With their sweet crusts and fillings of savory pastas, sauces and meats, they might have been handed straight out of those old picture frames.

In the 18th century, savory and sweet parted company, with most sugared dishes presented at the end of the meal. By the early 19th century, pasta had its own place on the menu. Marie Louise, the Duchess of Parma and wife of the exiled Napoleon, prized elegant renditions of baked maccheroni cooked in the style of Naples and Spanish Aragon and served in fancy molded shapes.

Another dish favored by Marie Louise was <u>Tortellini alla Bolognese.</u> This is possibly the most famous and remarkable of Emilia-Romagna's filled pastas, the centerpiece of Bolognese cuisine. First made to be served

A wreath of tortellini surrounds pig and mortadella in this early 20th-century magazine cartoon of Bologna the Fat.

in broth, the doughnut shape allows flavorings not only to surround the tortellino, but also to flow through it for a perfectly even distribution of tastes. The meat and cheese filling needs little embellishment. Good homemade broth or a simple tossing with butter and Parmigiano-Reggiano cheese is more than sufficient. Some Bolognese prefer tortellini tossed with their meaty ragù; others claim the ragù overwhelms the pasta. But if pasta as a side dish is heresy in Italy, for the Bolognese tortellini salad, so common in the United States, is barbarism.

Although tortellini are eaten in other parts of Italy, Bologna claims them as her own. An old Bolognese legend tells of the days when the gods walked the earth, and Venus and Zeus paused for the night at a small inn near Bologna. The innkeeper was so enchanted by the goddess that just before dawn, he peeked into her bedroom. There she lay on the bed, with sheets tossed aside, sprawled in exquisite disarray. The humble man wondered how he, an illiterate, a mere cook and innkeeper, could pay compliment to such beauty. He went to his kitchen, and shortly after sunrise he emerged with a tribute to the goddess. He had modeled the little tortellino after Venus's navel. Even now in Bologna, the pasta's nickname is "sacred navels" (umbilichi sacri).

To this day, Bologna honors outstanding achievement in tortellini making with the Golden Tortellino, the pasta maker's Oscar. Tortellini are stuffed with a varying blend of sautéed pork, veal, beef, and/or capon, along with prosciutto, mortadella, and Parmigiano-Reggiano cheese. Their delicacy is easily overpowered by complicated or highly seasoned sauces. One exception is Bologna's tortellini pie. This holdover from the most baroque era of the Renaissance combines the pasta with an array of sauces and meats, all enclosed in a decorated sweet crust. The result brings alive an extraordinary taste of the past. Grand pies like these are reserved for holidays and special occasions.

The intricacy of the tortellino's shape and the rich ingredients of its filling suggest the pasta began as court food. Eventually tortellini filtered down the economic scale to the middle class of merchants, land owners and professionals, and finally to the tables of laborers and peasants. Until roughly 50 years ago, the poor ate tortellini only during holiday celebrations. They usually saw meat (other than pancetta, salt pork and salami) only at Christmas and Easter. Even then, quantities were small, the meat was tough, and it needed long simmering. For these people who had so little, tortellini were a way of stretching limited amounts of precious meat. A half pound of boiled meat fills enough tortellini to feed twelve, and the meat's broth is a delicious cooking medium for the pastas. The combination must have been more than merely filling and satisfying, it must have tasted of pure luxury.

Some Italian writers claim tortellini existed as far back as the early 10th century, but actual evidence is hard to come by. Cookbooks of the 16th and 17th centuries mention filled pastas called tortelletti and other variations on the word torta, which means cake or turnover. But thus far none of the early recipes describe its unusual shape. Tortellini shaped as we know them today were definitely eaten in Bologna by the 1830s. Vincenzo Agnollotti, Marie Louise's cook, gives a recipe for tortellini alla Bolognese in his 1834 cookbook. Late-19th-century cookbook author Pellegrino Artusi describes three different tortellini in detail ("all' Italiana," "alla Bolognese," and a last one stuffed with pigeon) in his Science of Cooking and the Art of Eating Well. He even supplies an illustration of the pasta's actual size: the pasta was cut into discs $1^1/_2$ inches in diameter before stuffing.

Tortellini's much larger cousins are called tortelloni. Traditionally they are meatless, stuffed with ricotta, parsley, Parmesan, egg, and nutmeg. But greater liberties are taken with this filling. Tortelloni lend themselves to imaginative treatments inspired by a cook's mood and inclination.

Mood and inclination combine with strong local tradition to confound anyone set on standardizing pasta in Emilia-Romagna. For the past 2,000 years so much of the region was broken up into separate and ever-changing political entities. Every province, often every town, has its own history and its own renditions of the region's pastas. Sometimes the name changes while the pasta stays the same. Or the pasta and its filling, shape, or sauce change while the name remains the same. Hopeless but delicious confusion takes hold for anyone trying to decipher all the local subleties.

For example, tortellini and tortelloni keep their names as you go north to Modena. To the east of Bologna in Ferrara, big tortelloni become cappellacci ("big hats"), always filled with sweet squash, nutmeg, and Parmigiano-Reggiano cheese.

South of Bologna, in Romagna, the same shape becomes cappelletti ("little hats"—even though, confusingly, the pasta may be large or small). The filling changes with location. There are at least four versions of cappelletti between the Romagna towns of Ravenna, Rimini, Forlì and Faenza, a distance of 37 miles. Some are totally meatless; others blend several meats with cheese. Each is supported by strong local tradition. Never tell a Riminese that his meatless cappelletti remind you of Bologna's meat-filled tortellini. By regional reasoning they are two entirely different pastas.

No matter what the local variations are, however, making tortellini or cappelletti on Christmas Eve is a rite that has united women from Modena to Rimini for at least 150 years. The ritual begins when the entire family gathers for an afternoon of stretching, filling, and shaping pasta. The finished pastas are then spread on a cloth-covered table where they will rest—as though on an altar, as one chronicler of regional folkways put it. On Christmas afternoon they "die nobly" in capon broth. When the big tureen of tortellini/cappelletti is brought forth from the kitchen, the feast of Christmas officially begins.

Tortellini are not found north of Modena. In Parma rectangular tortelli have some of the significance of Bologna's tortellini. They can be filled with sweet squash, cabbage, potato, spiced fruit or chestnuts, but Tortelli d'Erbette, rectangles of pasta stuffed with ricotta, Parmigiano-Reggiano, and mild greens, are the most popular.

Anolini are Parma's other specialty. These small discs or half moons are filled with the braising juices of a beef pot roast cooked up to three days, butter-toasted bread crumbs, and Parmigiano-Reggiano cheese. Anolini are always served in broth.

When anolini move north to neighboring Piacenza, they pass through several mutations. Out on the banks of the Po in Piacenza province, they are stuffed with roast veal, pork and brains, cut with zigzag edges instead of smooth ones, and called by a new name, marubei.

Reggio adds chicken giblets to Piacenza's filling and calls the same disc shape cappelletti. These look nothing like Romagna's cappelletti, but they too have always been holiday food. An old saying indicates how special meat-filled pastas were: "Making love and cappelletti are the paradise of the poor." Along Reggio's Po embankment paradise includes a little local Lambrusco added to a deep soup plate before the hot broth and cappelletti are ladled in. The dish now tastes like an entire meal.

Strozzapreti look like thick, twisted tagliatelle. They were first made in Romagna long ago, when the village priest always ate for free at the local trattorie. A thick, heavy pasta was served to fill him up so he could not devour too much of the next course, which was a far more expensive commodity—meat. Strozzapreti translates as "priest stranglers." They have different dialect names and slightly different shapes all the way from Romagna down to southern Italy.

Gramigna ("little weeds") are small wiry cords of pasta with a narrow hole running through them. The process of making them by pressing dough through a hand-operated extruder has not changed in 200 years. Braised sausage is the traditional accompaniment.

It has been said that garganelli makes slaves of women. The first time I made them, I understood why. An egg pasta flavored with Parmigiano-Reggiano and nutmeg is cut into small squares. Each square is shaped into a ribbed hollow tube with points at either end by rolling two opposing corners of the square over each other around a dowel. The ribs are pressed into the dough by rolling the dowel over a small grooved board. The result resembles a ribbed quill (penne) pasta. Garganelli are delicious, but imagine a woman rolling one or two at a time when hundreds are needed for family dinner!

Garganelli owe their creation to hemp. They were first made near Castel Bolognese, about 25 miles south of Bologna, and are rarely eaten much farther south. Hemp flourished on that particular part of the Po plain, and every house had its hemp loom. Originally, the ribs were pressed into garganelli by rolling the pasta over the loom's comb.

Modena, to the north, had hemp too. There garganelli are called _maccheroni al pettine_ ("maccheroni of the comb"). Sometimes the comb was replaced by a little square frame with rough hemp cording stretched across it. Today small plastic washboards are sold to achieve the same result.

Stricchettoni are rectangles of pasta pinched in the center to make bows. Like garganelli, they are made with egg, nutmeg, and Parmigiano-Reggiano, along with pepper, and in some parts of Romagna, lemon zest. Near Modena parsley is used instead.

In Romagna stringhetti are made the same way, with the addition of lemon zest, and are cut on the diagonal before pinching.

Although not native to the region, _spaghetti_ are well liked in Romagna. The people of Emilia rarely eat them. The pasta will always be purchased dried and boxed, made only with durum wheat and water.

Although maccheroni (today defined as dried commercial pasta made of flour and water, often in hollow shapes) have never approached the popularity of fresh egg pasta, they have been used in the region since at least the 16th century.

Tagliatelle are cut into long ribbonlike strips from rolled and thinned sheets of dough. They are one of the few pastas that retain the same name throughout the region. This golden egg pasta was supposedly first created in the 16th century by Bolognese cook Maestro Zefiramo, who was inspired by Lucrezia Borgia's blond tresses. The infamous beauty was entertained in Bologna to honor her marriage into Ferrara's illustrious Este family. The most versatile of pastas, tagliatelle (from _tagliare,_ to cut) are the traditional partner to meat ragùs. One of the earliest mentions I have found of them is in 1557, but no doubt they existed before then. When sheets of egg pasta are cut very thin they become _tagliarini, taglioline_ and other diminutives of _tagliare._

In the early 1970s, Bologna's chapter of Italy's gastronomic society, the Italian Academy of the Kitchen (Accademia Italiana della Cucina), attempted to define and standardize tagliatelle's dimensions. No two cooks cut them the same size, and Italy's pasta manufacturers have sidestepped standardization of shapes for centuries. After much research and debate, the Academy declared to the world that tagliatelle are 8 mm wide and .6 mm thick ($^5/_{16}$ inch wide and $^1/_{32}$ inch thick). To ensure that there could be no doubt about its proper measurements, the official *tagliatelle was cast in solid gold. On April 16, 1972, pasta's "golden rule" was given a place of honor in Bologna's city hall.*

But this is only half the story. Eight millimeters wide is the easy expression of the real measurement. Bologna's symbol to the world is her two leaning Medieval towers. Out of respect for the early origins of the tagliatelle, its true measure is $^{1}/_{12,270}$ the height of the tallest of the two towers, La Torre degli Asinelli.

Exacting measurements or no, pasta in Emilia-Romagna is pure pleasure. I can think of no more enticing way of sharing the region's culinary heritage than by inviting you to enjoy these recipes.

Bologna's leaning medieval towers, the taller Asinelli and the shorter Garisenda

Homemade Pasta in the Style of Emilia-Romagna

Making pasta by hand is simplicity itself—blend flour with eggs, knead the dough, stretch it or roll it into thin sheets, and then cut it into any shape you want. Pasta is also the most forgiving of doughs. You can easily correct most problems that arise as you go along.

The mystique of fresh pasta has been exaggerated to the point that many cooks feel it must be made at the very last moment. Pasta is far better made an hour or more ahead, as it settles and collects itself with standing, resulting in a better texture.

In Emilia-Romagna pasta is often made in the morning, to be eaten later in the day. I prefer using filled pastas the same day they are made, but when pressed I have found that refrigerating them for 12 to 24 hours did no harm, except with very moist fillings that can make the pasta gummy. Unfilled pastas taste freshest when eaten within 6 to 8 hours of being rolled and cut, but are still delicious and light after drying for a week at room temperature.

Since each of the following recipes is made with the same method, I have given four lists of ingredients and one set of instructions. You can find more information on flour on page 479, and advice about store-bought pasta on page 92.

Egg Pasta
Pasta all' Uovo

Use this for ribbon pastas—that is, pastas rolled or thinned into flat sheets and cut, like tagliatelle or tagliarini; or for flat pastas, like maltagliati and lasagne. Also use it for filled pastas like tortellini, tortelli, and cappellacci.

[Makes enough for 6 to 8 first-course servings or 4 to 6 main-course servings, equivalent to 1 pound dried boxed pasta]

4 jumbo eggs

3½ cups (14 ounces) all-purpose unbleached flour (organic stone-ground preferred)

Spinach Egg Pasta
Pasta Verde

Use wherever spinach pasta is called for or desired.

[Makes enough for 6 to 8 first-course servings or 4 to 6 main-course servings, equivalent to 1 pound dried boxed pasta]

2 jumbo eggs
10 ounces fresh spinach, rinsed, stemmed, cooked, squeezed dry, and finely chopped; or 6 ounces frozen chopped spinach, defrosted and squeezed dry

3 ½ cups (14 ounces) all-purpose unbleached flour (organic stone-ground preferred)

Egg Pasta with Parmigiano-Reggiano Cheese and Nutmeg Villa Gaidello
Pasta Villa Gaidello

This recipe comes from the Villa Gaidello guest farm outside Modena. Use it when a recipe calls for garganelli, stringhetti—and for the Villa Gaidello version of tortellini (page 134).

[Makes enough for 6 to 8 first-course servings or 4 to 6 main-course servings, equivalent to 1 pound dried boxed pasta]

4 jumbo eggs
¼ teaspoon salt
¼ teaspoon each freshly ground black pepper and nutmeg, or 1½ teaspoon grated lemon zest
1½ cups (6 ounces) freshly grated Italian Parmigiano-Reggiano cheese

3 cups (12 ounces) all-purpose unbleached flour (organic stone-ground preferred)

Wine Pasta
Pasta al Vino

Replacing half the eggs with wine creates a lean and supple pasta, strong enough to hold soft, moist fillings and delicious on its own with simple sauces. The pasta is found in Romagna and in the Liguria region. It is the secret of the balance in Tortelloni of Artichokes and Mascarpone (page 141); an all-egg pasta would be too heavy with such a rich filling. Make it whenever you want a light yet resilient pasta.

[Makes enough for 6 to 8 first-course servings or 4 to 6 main-course servings, equivalent to 1 pound dried boxed pasta]

2 jumbo eggs
½ cup dry white wine

3½ cups (14 ounces) all-purpose unbleached flour (organic stone-ground is best)

Making the Dough

Light, delicate pasta comes from working the dough as much as possible to develop the elasticity of the flour's protein, or gluten. Kneading and then gradually rolling, stretching, and thinning the dough lengthens the gluten strands, producing tender and resilient pasta. Shortcutting the process results in heavy noodles. There is nothing difficult here, but like any craft the pleasure of achievement comes from learning a few basics and then practicing. Take time to work the dough well and it will pay you back tenfold in dining pleasure.

Measuring the Flour: Weighing flour on a scale is easier and more accurate than measuring by cups. Pour the flour onto the scale and you are done. If your scale is too small to neatly hold all the flour, set a medium-size paper bag on it and pour flour into the bag. There is no mess, and the bag can be used again and again.

If measuring flour by the cup is the only method available, keep in mind the following: Spoon it from the flour sack into your measuring cup and then level with the flat side of a knife blade. Resist the temptation to tamp or tap the cup before you level. A leveled cup of untamped flour weighs 4 ounces, the measure used in these recipes.

On wet and humid days a little more flour may be needed; on dry days a little less. Judge this by the feel of the dough: it should be pliable, elastic, and not too stiff.

It is better to err on the side of too much liquid than too much flour. Kneading extra flour into an overly moistened dough is much easier than working in more liquid. If you think your flour is particularly dry because of the climate or time of year, add an additional tablespoon or two of beaten egg.

Working by Hand

Equipment:

♦ *A roomy work surface,* 24 to 30 inches deep by 30 to 36 inches wide. Any smooth surface will do, but marble cools dough slightly, making it less flexible than desired.

♦ A *pastry scraper* and a *small wooden spoon* for blending the dough.

♦ A *wooden dowel-style rolling pin.* In Italy, pasta makers use one about 35 inches long and 2 inches thick. The shorter American-style pin with handles at either end can be used, but the longer it is, the easier it is to roll the pasta. Long dowel pins and long American-style rolling pins can be found or ordered at kitchenware shops.

♦ *Plastic wrap* to wrap the resting dough and to cover rolled-out pasta waiting to be filled. It protects the pasta from drying out too quickly.

♦ *A sharp chef's knife* for cutting pasta sheets, or whatever cutter or equipment is specified for special shapes.

♦ *Cloth-covered chair backs,* broom handles, or specially designed pasta racks found in cookware shops for draping the ribbon pastas. Ribbon or filled pastas can be spread on *large flat baskets* (inexpensive, and usually sold as cheese servers) that have been covered with a single layer of kitchen towel. The porosity of the basket and cloth helps the pasta dry evenly and protects pastas with moist fillings from becoming gummy.

Mixing the Dough: Mound the flour in the center of your work surface. Make a well in the middle. Add the eggs, along with any liquids and flavorings. Using a wooden spoon, beat together the eggs and any flavorings. Then gradually start incorporating shallow scrapings of flour from the sides of the well into the liquid. As you work more and more flour into the liquid, the well's sides may collapse. Use a pastry scraper to keep the liquids from running off and to incorporate the last bits of flour into the dough. Do not worry if it looks like a hopelessly rough and messy lump.

continued

Kneading: With the aid of the scraper to scoop up unruly pieces, start kneading the dough. Once it becomes a cohesive mass, use the scraper to remove any bits of hard flour on the work surface—these will make the dough lumpy. Then knead the dough about 3 minutes. Its consistency should be elastic and a little sticky. If it is too sticky to move easily, knead in a few more tablespoons of flour. Continue kneading 10 minutes, or until the dough has become satiny, smooth, and very elastic. It will feel alive under your hands. Do not shortcut this step. Wrap the dough in plastic wrap, and let it relax at room temperature 30 minutes to 3 hours (when I am rushed I skip this step, with no ill effect on the pasta).

Stretching and Thinning: If using an extra-long rolling pin work with half the dough at a time. With a regular-length rolling pin, roll out a quarter of the dough at a time. Keep the rest of the dough wrapped. Lightly sprinkle a large work surface with flour. The idea is to stretch the dough rather than press down and push it. Shape it into a ball and begin rolling out to form a circle, frequently turning the disc of dough a quarter turn. As it thins out, start rolling the disc back on the pin a quarter of the way toward the center and stretching it gently sideways by running the palms of your hands over the rolled-up dough from the center of the pin outward. Unroll, turn the disc a quarter turn, and repeat. Do twice more.

Stretch and even out the center of the disc by rolling the dough a quarter of the way back on the pin. Then gently push the rolling pin away from you with one hand while holding the dough sheet in place on the work surface with the other hand. Repeat three more times, turning the dough a quarter turn each time.

Repeat the two processes as the disc becomes larger and thinner. (If you make pasta frequently, your body will develop a rhythm with the dough. You'll find that your instincts will take over, with your hands and the pasta leading the way while your mind is freed for relaxation. It is a calming experience, and for some as soothing as meditation.)

The goal is a sheet of even thickness. For lasagne and filled pastas such as tortellini, anolini, and Tortelli of Cabbage and Potato the sheet should be so thin that you can clearly see your hand through it and can see colors, for instance a bright photograph. For tagliatelle, tagliarini, and other flat ribbon pastas, the dough can be a little thicker. Do not take too long in thinning and stretching as the dough starts drying out. Too-dry dough stiffens, stretches poorly, becomes lumpy, and cooks unevenly.

Cutting: Once the dough destined for tagliatelle or other ribbon-style pastas reaches its desired thickness, spread it out on a flat surface and dry 20 minutes, or until leathery in texture (turn it over several times to encourage even drying). To cut, roll up the pasta jelly roll fashion and slice it to the desired width. For special shapes, see page 86. Instructions for filled pastas can be found in their respective recipes.

A Reliable Old Formula: An "Egg of Pasta"

Many old regional recipes simply refer to so many "eggs of pasta," meaning 1 egg and the flour it absorbs, enough for a very generous serving of ribbon pasta. The most commonly used formula is 100 grams, or 3½ ounces (¾ cup plus 2 tablespoons), flour per egg. Of course this varies slightly with the flour's moisture, the climate, the size of the egg, and its absorption capabilities.

I use 1 jumbo egg, instead of the more usual "large," per 3½ ounces of flour. This moister dough builds up greater elasticity, making lighter pasta. One "egg" of my dough makes 1½ to 2 servings of ribbon pasta and much more of filled ones.

Working with Machines

Using a food processor to mix the dough and a pasta machine to thin and stretch it shortens the work time by about 30 percent. I am referring to the type of pasta machine, made of stainless steel, that has two parallel rollers with adjustable settings for thinning the dough, a hand crank (that can be fitted with an electric attachment if desired), and cutters for making wide or thin pastas.

It is true that the pebbly texture of hand-rolled pasta combines beautifully with sauces. For example, a juicy ragù melts into and joins with hand-rolled tagliatelle but slips off the slicker surface of machine-thinned noodles. Pasta purists in Emilia-Romagna consider it heresy to use a machine for stretching and thinning. But my goal is to coax you into making fresh pasta. If you find rolling by hand tedious or daunting, by all means use the pasta machine.

Note: Please do not use machines that take the dough ingredients in at one end, blend them, and then extrude finished pasta out the other end. The dough is rarely worked enough to form light, supple pasta.

Equipment: You will need the same tools as outlined in Working by Hand (page 83), with the exception of the blending implements and the rolling pin. In selecting a pasta machine, look for a sturdy one whose narrowest setting produces a very sheer pasta. Some machines' thinnest settings still yield pasta that is too thick (Atlas brand is one). Two brands I have had success with are Altea and Imperia.

More pasta can be thinned at one time in a pasta machine equipped with extra-wide rollers. These machines are expensive and often must be ordered through commercial kitchenware suppliers. But if you make pasta often and want to cut work time, the wider rollers are handy to have.

Mixing the Dough in a Food Processor: Make sure the ingredients are cool, because a processor can overheat the eggs and the flour. Place the liquids and any seasonings in a food processor fitted with the steel blade. With the machine running, add the flour through the feed tube. Process until the dough forms a ball on the blade. It should be a bit sticky. (If it is too sticky, break it up into small clumps, sprinkle it with flour, and process again.) Now process 30 seconds, wait about 1 minute so the dough can cool, and process another 30 seconds. Remove the dough from the processor and knead it by hand a few moments to check the consistency. It should be satiny, smooth, and very elastic. At this point the dough can be stretched and thinned immediately, or covered in plastic wrap and left at room temperature up to 3 hours.

Stretching and Thinning with a Pasta Machine: Work with a quarter of the dough at a time, keeping the rest wrapped. Lightly flour the machine rollers and the work surface around the machine. Set the rollers at the widest setting. Flatten the dough into a thick patty. Guide it through the rollers by inserting one end into the space between the two rollers. Turn the crank handle with one hand while holding the upturned palm of your other hand under the sheet emerging from the rollers. Keep your palm flat to protect the dough from punctures by your fingers.

As the emerging sheet lengthens, guide it away from the machine with your palm. Pass the dough through the rollers five to six times, folding it in thirds each time. Then set the rollers at the next, narrower setting and pass the dough through three times, folding it in half each time. Repeat, passing it through three times at each successively narrower setting. Repeated stretching and thinning builds up elasticity making especially light pasta. If the sheet becomes too long to handle comfortably, cut it in half or thirds and work the pieces in tandem.

Don't worry if at first the dough tears, has holes, is lumpy, or is very moist. Just lightly flour it by pulling the dough over the floured work surface. (Take care not to overdo the flouring, or the dough may get too stiff.) As you keep putting it through the rollers, it will be transformed from slightly lumpy and possibly torn to a smooth, satiny sheet with fine elasticity.

How Thin?: Different machines have different numbers of settings. Tagliatelle and ribbon pastas should be a bit thicker than lasagne and pastas for fillings. Usually the thinnest setting on a machine will be thin enough for you to see color and shape through it; this is perfect for lasagne and filled pastas. If it is so thin that the dough tears easily, however, stop at the next to last setting. The setting above the one for filled pastas is fine for tagliatelle and tagliarini.

Making the Shapes

Whether you have made the pasta by hand or with machines, do cut it by hand for a more authentic finish.

Garganelli: Hollow ribbed cylinders resembling quill pen points.

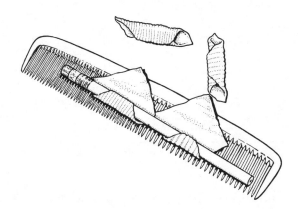

Use Villa Gaidello pasta (page 81), thinned until you can see color through the sheet. Have on hand a dowel about ⅜ to ⅝ inch in diameter (a round pencil works well), and a sterilized comb or the bottom of a flat woven basket. Work with a quarter of the dough at a time. Keep all but a small portion covered with plastic wrap. Cut the pasta into 1½- to 1¾-inch squares.

Make two garganelli at a time by setting two pieces close together with a corner of each square pointing toward you. Flour the dowel, and lay it across the two pieces. Roll it so the opposite corners overlap and seal, forming hollow tubes with quill-like points at both ends. Then roll the dowel over the comb or basket to make grooves in the dough. Slip the garganelli from the dowel, and arrange them in a single layer on towel-covered flat baskets to wait for cooking. Continue until all the dough is used.

Make garganelli with friends. Equip everyone with dowels or pencils, and combs or baskets, and you will have piles of pasta in no time.

Serve them in Poultry/Meat Stock (page 66), or with sauces like roasted peppers, peas, and cream (page 116), Winter Tomato Sauce (page 62), or The Cardinal's Ragù (page 40).

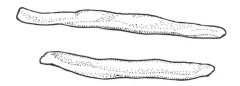

Gramigna ("Little Weeds"): Wiggly cords of egg pasta made by forcing the dough through a special hand-operated press that pierces a narrow hole down their centers. Short of having your own gramigna press, this form can be simulated by rolling Egg Pasta (page 80) to about ⅛ inch thick and then cutting strands about 3/16 inch wide by about 2½ inches long.

Lasagne: Large rectangles made from Egg Pasta (page 80) for Lasagne Dukes of Ferrara (page 168), Lasagne of Wild and Fresh Mushrooms (page 171) or from Spinach Egg Pasta (page 81) for Lasagne of Emilia-Romagna (page 165). Roll thin

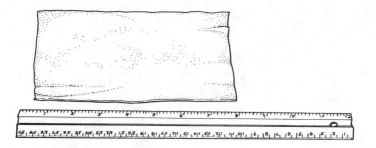

enough for color and form to be seen through the dough, and cut into rectangles about 4 by 8 inches.

Maltagliati ("Badly Cut"): Cut rolled-up Egg Pasta (page 80) at an angle to form uneven triangles and diamonds. Often used for bean soups and other country dishes.

Quadretti ("Little Squares"): Egg Pasta (page 80) cut into ½-inch squares and used in broths and soups.

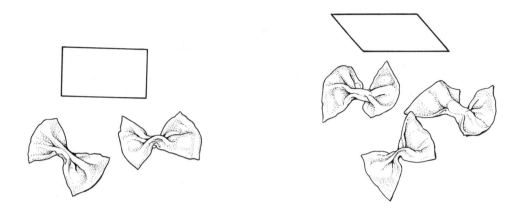

Stricchettoni: Bow ties in the style of Villa Gaidello. Use Egg Pasta Villa Gaidello (page 81) with nutmeg, adding ½ cup chopped Italian parsley to the dough. There should be flecks of parsley, not a purée, in the pasta. If you are mixing the dough with a food processor, knead the parsley in by hand after the machine blending is finished. Cut thinned pasta sheets into rectangles about 1 by 1½ inches. Firmly pinch each rectangle in the center to make a bow shape.

Stringhetti: Bow ties in the style of Romagna. Use Egg Pasta Villa Gaidello (page 81), substituting lemon zest for the nutmeg. Cut as for stricchettoni (above), but on the diagonal forming trapezoids. Pinch in the center. Try these instead of spaghetti in Spaghetti with Shrimps and Black Olives (page 132) or to replace maccheroni in Maccheroni with Baked Grilled Vegetables (page 126).

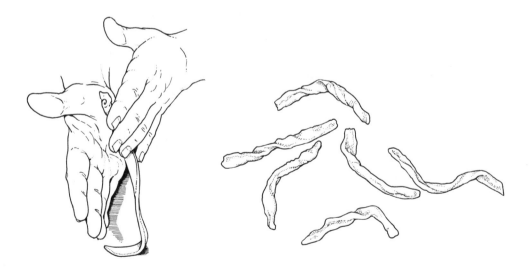

Strozzapreti ("Priest Stranglers"): These look like twisted strands of tagliatelle. Use Wine Pasta (page 82), made with water instead of wine. Roll the pasta a bit thicker than usual. Cut it into strips about ⅜ inch wide. Gently hold the top of a long strip between your palms. Slide the palms past each other, allowing the pasta to coil in opposite directions, so in profile it forms the letter "S." Break off the coiled portion by slipping one hand down and twisting the pasta. Repeat the movement with the next portion of the strand. Do this until the strand is finished, and repeat the process with the rest of the dough. Strozzapreti are seldom perfectly neat, so do not be concerned if they appear haphazard. Spread them on a towel-lined basket.

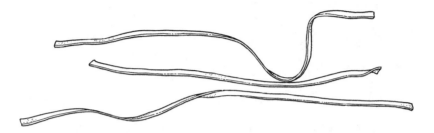

Tagliarini: The narrowest of flat ribbon pastas. Egg Pasta (page 80) is cut 1/16 inch wide and used for delicate sauces, in soups, and in the Sweet Tagliarini Tart of Ferrara (page 194).

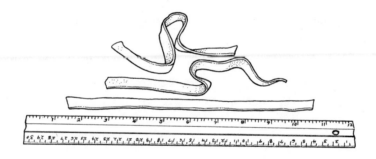

Tagliatelle: Long flat ribbons cut just under 3/8 inch wide. That is, if you are following the "golden rule" of Bologna (page 79). In contrast to Bologna's attempt at standardizing tagliatelle, recipes in Romagna often call for them to be cut to different widths for different sauces. This is the most versatile of pastas, substantial enough for chunky sauces, yet delicate enough for lighter ones.

Directions for shaping filled pastas appear in their respective recipes.

Storing

To Freeze or Not to Freeze: Freezing ribbon pasta does nothing to improve it. Better to dry it at room temperature and then store it in a sealed tin or plastic bag for about 2 weeks. Many filled pastas freeze well, such as tortellini, anolini, and Tortelli of Cabbage and Potato (page 160). Those with moist fillings become soggy when frozen—Chestnut Tortelli (page 155), Tortelloni of Artichokes and Mascarpone (page 141), or Cappellacci with Sweet Squash (page 145).

Cooking the Pasta

For each recipe of fresh pasta or pound of dried boxed pasta, you will need 6 to 8 quarts of boiling water seasoned with about 2 tablespoons salt (if salt is a health concern, omit it). Make sure the water is bubbling fiercely. Drop in the pasta and boil, stirring frequently, about 30 seconds to 2 minutes for fresh pastas and anywhere from 5 to 15 minutes for dried boxed examples. Taste for doneness. Perfectly cooked pasta is called *al dente,* meaning "to the tooth," or still a little firm to the bite—never soft and mushy.

Once the pasta is done, drain it immediately in a large colander. Toss to rid it of excess liquid, and then blend with the sauce. Pasta, other than lasagne or others destined for baking, should never be rinsed, nor should it be partially or fully cooked ahead.

Oil in the Water?: Adding oil to the water does not protect large pastas from breaking or sticking. Rather than clinging to the pasta and making it slippery so pieces slide past each other, the oil remains on the boiling water's surface. The best way to protect delicate pastas from breaking or big ones from sticking is to cook them in generous amounts of water, about 6 quarts per 8 ounces. Individual recipes provide specific cooking instructions.

Serving Pasta

In Emilia-Romagna today pasta is always a course unto itself, never a side dish. Even at its simplest, its texture and flavor are too complex for pairing with another dish. Whether you decide on pasta as a first course, as is traditional in Italy, or as a main dish, which is often done there as a light lunch or supper, let it stand on its own. Celebrate the pure pleasure of eating pasta with these simple guidelines:

First and foremost, pasta must be hot, so heat the dishes. The pasta will keep hot longer in shallow soup dishes than on flat plates. That traditional soup dish also makes eating the often singleminded noodles easier. Ribbon or string pastas are twirled, a few strands at a time, on the fork into neat bite-size bundles. Bracing the fork against the side of a soup dish instead of on a flat plate makes for neater dining and more elegant twirling.

If you are serving more than one pasta (as is so often done in Emilia-Romagna), offer them one after another in separate plates. Restaurants' penchant for serving three or more pastas in tiny portions on the same plate is dining overkill. Textures and flavors become a meaningless blur.

A succession of small portions of pasta presented at a leisurely pace lets you savor each one to the full. And the cook need not be imitating an acrobatic act in the kitchen in an attempt to get several pastas out at once. Decide on the order by going from simple to complex and light to robust. For instance, start with small bowls of garganelli in Poultry/Meat Stock (page 66), then Tagliarini with Fresh Figs Franco Rossi (page 107), and finish with small portions of Pappardelle with Game Ragù (page 123).

Buying Pasta

Although logic says store-bought fresh pasta (or pasta made locally and dried) should be next best to homemade, often it is not. Do some trial tasting of fresh pastas available in your area. You may find, as I have, that some are good, but many disappoint. Doughs are often insufficiently kneaded and the stretching is done with such speed that the pasta never develops body and spring. Fresh extruded pastas like spaghetti and linguine are often heavy, as most machines in stores seem unable to work the dough with enough time and vigor to fully develop the gluten. When buying ready-made filled pastas, the dough should be sheer enough to detect the filling inside, and fillings should be delicious.

Boxed dried pasta from Italy is often preferable to commercially made fresh noodles. In Italy, dried commercial pasta and fresh pasta are not compared as better or worse, they are simply different. Having high-quality dried pasta on the pantry shelf ensures good eating when there is no time to make fresh.

The finest dried pastas are made from durum wheat (semolina is ground durum). Durum in the pasta is not the whole story, however. High-quality durum makes a springy, lively pasta, but low-quality durum produces a slack noodle.

The roughened surfaces of many dried commercial Italian pastas help hold the sauce, a characteristic much admired. When eating a good pasta, the noodle is lively and resilient in the mouth, with no sense of starchiness or heaviness. The best examples exude a wheaten flavor and are fragrant while cooking.

Flour-and-water commercial pastas are usually associated with southern Italy, while egg-and-flour pastas more strongly suggest the north. Emilia-Romagna's dried commercial pastas are made solely with durum flour and egg.

Several excellent brands come to America from the region and can be found in specialty food stores or ordered by mail (see page 509). Barilla of Parma is one of Italy's largest manufacturers, making a wide range of shapes in a resilient, flavorful pasta. Dallari makes rough-textured, very thin, light tagliatelle, lasagne, and linguine (which, in this case, is really a tagliarini). Fini and Armando Scapinelli & Figli are two Modena companies creating pastas a bit bolder in substance, pebbly in texture, and with excellent "spring." Although not from Emilia-Romagna, Delverde, Rusticella, Cara Nonna, and De Cecco are all good pastas. More exports should be available as our country's interest in all things Italian keeps burgeoning. Sample new brands as you discover them to decide which are the most satisfying.

Tagliatelle with Ragù Bolognese
Tagliatelle con Ragù Bolognese

"Bolognese" ragù usually means a meat sauce simmered with milk or cream, and often made with only beef. For a rich, old-style ragù, have Classic Ragù Bolognese. For a sauce in modern Bologna style, try the Lighter Contemporary Ragù Bolognese.

[Serves 8 to 12 as a first course, 6 to 8 as a main dish]

1 recipe Classic Ragù Bolognese (page 44) or Lighter Contemporary Ragù Bolognese (page 46)
10 quarts salted water
1½ recipes Egg Pasta (page 80) cut into tagliatelle (page 90), or

1½ pounds imported dried tagliatelle
2 cups (8 ounces) freshly grated Italian Parmigiano-Reggiano cheese

Method

Working Ahead: *Make the ragù up to 30 minutes ahead. The pasta must be cooked at the last moment and tossed with the ragù just before serving.*

Making the Dish: Have a serving bowl and shallow soup dishes heating in a warm oven. Have a colander set in the sink for draining the pasta. Heat the ragù to a simmer. Bring the salted water to a fierce boil. Drop the pasta into the water and cook until tender but still a little firm to the bite. Take care with fresh pasta, as it can cook in less than a minute; dried pasta will take about 8 minutes.

Serving: Drain the pasta and toss with the hot sauce. Serve in heated soup dishes, passing the cheese separately.

Suggestion

Wine: Sangiovese di Romagna is the traditional partner to Tagliatelle with Ragù Bolognese. A Sangiovese Riserva adds extra elegance. From other regions, drink a Piemontese Barbera d'Alba; or a soft and fruity Tuscan Chianti Classico or Chianti Montalbano; or a Brunello wine from young vines, the Rosso di Montalcino.

Menu: Serve in small quantities as a first course before simple roasted meats or poultry, such as Balsamic Roast Chicken (page 279). It is also often served at the beginning of elaborate holiday dinners following bowls of Tortellini in Broth Villa Gaidello (page 134) and before Christmas Capon (page 281). To suit contemporary American tastes, start with a light antipasto like the Spring Salad with Hazelnuts (page 21) or the Salad of Tart Greens with Prosciutto and Warm Balsamic Dressing (page 26), and then serve the Tagliatelle with Ragù Bolognese. Have fresh fruit and Sweet Cornmeal Biscuits (page 422) for dessert.

Tagliatelle with Prosciutto di Parma
Tagliatelle al Prosciutto di Parma

The people of Parma have been eating their famous ham with homemade pasta and the local sweet butter for centuries. Lightening this classic combination by substituting reduced stock and a little wine for most of the butter brings out the prosciutto's deep meaty taste. Its natural sweetness is enhanced by whisking a little unsalted butter into the sauce at the last moment. Here butter becomes a flavoring rather than a cooking medium, with fine results.

[Serves 6 to 8 as a first course, 4 to 6 as a main dish]

5 ounces Prosciutto di Parma, sliced very thin

2 tablespoons unsalted butter

2 medium onions, finely chopped

6 tablespoons dry white wine

3 cups Poultry/Meat Stock (page 66), reduced to 1 cup, or 4 cups Quick Stock (page 68), reduced to 1 cup

6 to 8 quarts salted water

1 recipe Egg Pasta (page 80) cut into tagliatelle (page 90) or 1 pound imported dried tagliatelle

3 tablespoons unsalted butter

Freshly ground black pepper to taste

1½ cups (6 ounces) freshly grated Italian Parmigiano-Reggiano cheese

Method

Working Ahead: *The sauce can be cooked up to the point of adding the stock, and then set aside up to 1½ hours (cover once the sauce has cooled). Allow about 10 minutes just before serving to cook the pasta and finish the sauce.*

Making the Sauce: Trim the white fat from the edges of the prosciutto slices; chop and reserve the fat. Cut the meat into bite-size squares (do not stack the slices to cut them, as they'll stick together), and set aside. In a large heavy skillet set over medium heat, swirl the 2 tablespoons of butter until melted and bubbly. Add the chopped prosciutto fat and the onions. Sauté the onions 10 to 15 minutes over medium heat, or until the onions are a deep golden brown. Stir often with a wooden spatula. Stir in half the prosciutto and cook 1 minute. Add the wine and simmer, uncovered, 3 minutes, or until it has totally evaporated, scraping up the brown glaze from the bottom of the skillet. Stir in the stock and heat to bubbling. Remove the pan from the heat.

Cooking the Pasta and Finishing the Sauce: Warm a serving bowl and shallow soup dishes in a low oven. Bring the salted water to a boil. Drop in the pasta and cook until tender but it still has some bite. Taste for doneness. Fresh pasta will cook in 30 seconds or more. Dried pasta takes up to 8 minutes or so. Turn the pasta into a large colander, and drain. Once the pasta is draining, quickly reheat the sauce to bubbling. Stir in the remaining 3 tablespoons butter until creamy but not fully melted (30 to 45 seconds). Add the pasta to the skillet, tossing over medium heat until thoroughly coated with sauce. Blend in the remaining prosciutto, season with pepper (salt should not be necessary), and immediately turn into the heated serving bowl. Serve, passing the cheese with the pasta.

Suggestions   **Wine:** In Parma only one wine is sipped with prosciutto: fresh white Colli di Parma Malvasia Secco from Parma's hills. It is low in alcohol, with some fizz, lots of fruit, and a hint of sweetness. The wine rarely leaves Parma province, and no doubt would prove too fragile to cross an ocean. Drink it there and enjoy. In the United States pair this dish with a nutty white with enough substance to back the onion sauté and stock reduction. Try a Pinot Bianco or Chardonnay from the Trentino—Alto Adige or Friuli regions.

   Menu: Serve before Pan-Roasted Quail (page 283), Balsamic and Basil Veal Scallops (page 296), or any roasted or grilled meat or poultry dish not made with prosciutto. When using as a main course, either the Spring Salad with Hazelnuts (page 21) or Fresh Pears with Parmigiano-Reggiano and Balsamic Vinegar (page 30) makes a fine starter.

Cook's Notes   **Prosciutto di Parma:** See page 497 for information on selecting a fine ham.

   Tomato Variation: Tomatoes and peas are often added to this dish. Their flavors emerge best with older hams full of big, ripe flavors or with salty prosciutti. Add 2 cups of peeled and seeded fresh tomatoes, or well-drained canned tomatoes, to the onion sauté after the prosciutto has cooked for 1 minute. Omit the wine and stock. Let the tomatoes boil 3 minutes, or until thick. Heat 1 cup cooked sweet peas in the sauce just before adding the butter. Finish the recipe as described above.

Prosciutto coach, 19th-century wood engraving

Tagliatelle with Fresh Porcini Mushrooms
Tagliatelle con Funghi Porcini

In spring and fall, when porcini mushrooms are literally cropping up after almost every rain, this easily-put-together pasta is found throughout Emilia-Romagna. Sautéing the porcini in butter and seasoning with only Parmigiano-Reggiano and a little salt and pepper makes a fine sauce for pasta.

Fresh porcini are appearing more and more at specialty food markets on this side of the Atlantic. Most plentiful in autumn and spring, the mushrooms are usually imported from Italy, and are often shipped whole and frozen. My personal preference is for unfrozen porcini, with their firm, velvety texture intact. But even though defrosted mushrooms tend to be spongy, they are still delicious in this dish. Save this recipe for a time when you need a fast but elegant supper.

[Serves 6 to 8 as a first course, 4 to 6 as a main dish]

6 quarts salted water
1 to 1½ pounds fresh porcini mushrooms (smaller size preferred)
4 tablespoons (2 ounces) unsalted butter

1 recipe Egg Pasta (page 80) cut for tagliatelle (page 90), or 1 pound imported dried tagliatelle
Salt and freshly ground black pepper to taste
About ⅔ cup freshly grated Italian Parmigiano-Reggiano cheese

Method

Working Ahead: *This dish goes together in about 15 minutes and is best cooked and eaten immediately.*

Sautéing the Porcini and Cooking the Pasta: Bring the salted water to a full rolling boil. Warm a serving bowl and shallow soup dishes in a low oven.

Use a damp towel to wipe away any sand and debris clinging to the mushrooms. Pay special attention to the underside of their caps. Do not immerse them in water. Cut the mushrooms into ½-inch dice. Heat the butter in a 12-inch skillet over medium heat. Raise the heat to medium-high, add the mushrooms, and sauté 3 to 5 minutes, or until browned. Lower the heat to medium and cook another 6 to 7 minutes, or until tender.

While the mushrooms are cooking, drop the pasta into the water. Boil fiercely until pasta is tender but still a little firm to the bite. Fresh pasta can cook in a matter of seconds; dried pasta can take about 8 minutes. Drain immediately in a colander. Once the mushrooms are tender, season them with salt and pepper. Add the hot pasta to the skillet and toss to blend. Add the cheese and toss to thoroughly coat the pasta.

Serving: Turn the pasta into the heated bowl, and serve immediately.

Suggestions   **Wine:** Drink a full white like Arneis from Piemonte, Lugana of Lombardy, or Tuscany's Montecarlo.

Menu: Serve before Erminia's Pan-Crisped Chicken (page 270), Giovanna's Wine-Basted Rabbit (page 284), Christmas Capon (page 281), or Rabbit Dukes of Modena (page 286). Offer as a main dish after the Salad of Tart Greens with Prosciutto and Warm Balsamic Dressing (page 26), Fresh Pears with Parmigiano-Reggiano and Balsamic Vinegar (page 30), "Little" Spring Soup from the 17th Century (page 232), or Modena's Spiced Soup of Spinach and Cheese (page 234). Have Ugo Falavigna's Apple Cream Tart (page 411) for dessert.

Cook's Notes   **Porcini Mushrooms:** See page 494 for information on porcini.

Using Olive Oil: A delicate extra-virgin olive oil from Liguria, the Veneto, or Sicily can be substituted for the butter. See page 485 for information on olive oils.

Only Tagliatelle Will Do

I wish I had a nickel for every pound of fresh tagliatelle made in Bologna to go with Ragù Bolognese (page 93). Although ragùs are eaten with maccheroni, pappardelle, garganelli, and lasagne, tagliatelle is its most popular partner. These ribbons of egg pasta are just the right width to hold the nubbins of meat and vegetable, absorb the ragù's juices, yet not be overwhelmed by it. In the mouth, tagliatelle and ragù taste right together; they occupy equal space on the palate and blend perfectly. Chunkier sauces often balance better with bigger maccheroni or pappardelle, and in other parts of Emilia-Romagna such choices are not questioned. But when dining in the style of Bologna, where tagliatelle was first created, only this pasta will do.

Tagliatelle with Balsamic Radicchio
Tagliatelle con Radicchio e Aceto Balsamico

In Modena and Reggio, braised or grilled radicchio has long been seasoned with the balsamic vinegar. Adding fresh pasta to the vegetable creates a dish that is delicate, light, and substantial all at the same time, rather like a fresh hot salad. Sprinkling shreds of raw radicchio over the finished dish lets you taste the two dimensions of this distinctive green. Since radicchio's prices can soar into the stratosphere, treat this pasta as you would fine veal or a rare seafood. There is one difference, however: tagliatelle with radicchio will be an elegant surprise for everyone you share it with.

[Serves 6 to 8 as a first course, 4 or 5 as a main dish]

1½ pounds radicchio (4 to 5 heads)

3 tablespoons extra-virgin olive oil

2 ounces thinly sliced pancetta, minced

1 large red onion, minced

2 large cloves garlic, minced

20 large fresh basil leaves, chopped, or 2 teaspoons dried basil

⅔ cup Poultry/Meat Stock (page 66) or Quick Stock (page 68), or ⅓ cup Meat Essences (page 61)

14- to 16-ounce can tomatoes, thoroughly drained, or 1 pound fresh tomatoes, peeled, seeded, and chopped

1 generous pinch freshly ground black pepper

Salt to taste

6 to 8 quarts salted water

1 recipe Egg Pasta (page 80) cut into tagliatelle (page 90), or 1 pound imported dried tagliatelle

4 to 6 tablespoons commercial balsamic vinegar

1½ cups (6 ounces) freshly grated Italian Parmigiano-Reggiano cheese

Method

Working Ahead: *The radicchio can be cooked up to 8 hours before serving; cool, cover, and refrigerate until ready to reheat. Finish the sauce and cook the pasta just before serving.*

Braising the Radicchio: Cut the radicchio heads in half, core them, and then cut each half into six wedges. Slice into wide shreds, yielding about 12 cups. Set aside

2½ to 3 cups for finishing the sauce. Cover and refrigerate the radicchio if held more than an hour or so.

Heat the olive oil in a large sauté pan (the bigger the better, as the radicchio needs plenty of room), and cook the pancetta over medium to low heat. Stir occasionally, and adjust the heat so the pancetta slowly gives off its fat while barely browning. After about 10 minutes the pancetta will be tinged with gold and almost transparent. Turn the heat to high. Add the onion and radicchio (except the reserved portion), and cook, uncovered, stirring occasionally, until the radicchio has wilted and a dark brown glaze has formed on the bottom of the pan. Stir in the garlic and basil, and cook a few seconds. Keep the heat high and add the stock or meat essences. As the liquid comes to a boil, scrape up the brown bits from the bottom of the sauté pan but do not boil down the liquid. Crush the tomatoes as you add them to the pan. Sprinkle with black pepper. Stir the braising radicchio while it boils over high heat. After about 3 minutes it should be thick, with most of the liquid from the tomatoes cooked off. If it is still watery, cook another minute or two. Then remove from the heat, and season to taste with salt.

Cooking the Pasta: Have a serving dish and shallow soup dishes warming in a low oven. Bring the salted water to a vigorous boil. Drop in the tagliatelle, wait a few seconds for them to soften, and stir with a wooden spoon to keep the pieces from sticking. Boil about 30 seconds to 1 minute for fresh pasta and up to 8 minutes for dried, stirring frequently. Taste for doneness. When it is tender but still firm to the bite, drain immediately in a large colander.

Finishing and Serving: While the pasta cooks, quickly reheat the braised radicchio over high heat. Add the drained pasta to the pan along with the balsamic vinegar, and toss over medium heat to blend. Start with 4 tablespooons of the balsamic, adding more to taste. The vinegar should give sweet/tart flavor to the radicchio but not dominate the dish with too much acid. Toss in about half the reserved radicchio, and then turn the pasta into the serving dish. Sprinkle with the remaining raw radicchio, and serve. Pass the cheese separately.

Suggestions   **Wine:** The tangy quality of this dish calls for a red that is all fruit and youth, like a young Sangiovese di Romagna, or a young Merlot from the Veneto or Friuli regions.

Menu: I like the Tagliatelle with Radicchio as a supper main dish. Start with a few slices of good salami and coppa (pages 501 and 474) or Mousse of Mortadella (page 22), serve the pasta, then offer shales of Parmigiano-Reggiano cheese with the last of the wine. Dessert could be pears or clusters of grapes. Serve as a first course before Giovanna's Wine-Basted Rabbit (page 284), Pan-Roasted Quail (page 283), or almost any grilled or roasted meat or poultry not seasoned with basil or balsamic vinegar.

continued

Cook's Notes **Radicchio:** Check radicchio for bitterness by tasting near the center of a leaf. Counteract bitterness by increasing the stock to 1 cup (or Meat Essences by 2 tablespoons) and adding an additional ½ cup well-drained tomatoes.

Balsamic Vinegar: A rich, well-balanced balsamic vinegar makes this dish sing. See page 467 for selecting vinegars.

Tagliatelle with Light Veal Ragù
Tagliatelle con Ragù Vecchio Molinetto

Veal is usually too delicate for ragù. But in this sauce slow browning gives it depth and character. Serve when you want a meat sauce that isn't heavy.

[Serves 6 to 8 as a first course, 4 to 6 as a main dish]

1 recipe Light Veal Ragù with Tomato (page 52)

6 to 8 quarts salted water

1 recipe Egg Pasta (page 80) cut for tagliatelle (page 90), or 1 pound imported dried tagliatelle

2 cups (8 ounces) freshly grated Italian Parmigiano-Reggiano cheese

Method   **Working Ahead:** *The sauce is best eaten the same day it is cooked. Cook the pasta and toss it with the ragù just before serving.*

Making the Dish: Have a serving bowl and shallow soup dishes warming in a low oven. Reheat the ragù, adding the tomatoes only 5 to 10 minutes before the sauce is tossed with the pasta.

Bring the salted water to a full boil. Drop in the pasta, and boil fiercely until tender but still pleasantly firm to the bite. Fresh pasta will take 30 seconds to several minutes. Dried pasta needs about 8 minutes. Do taste for doneness. Drain immediately in a colander, and toss with the hot ragù.

Serving: Present at the table, passing the cheese separately.

Suggestions   **Wine:** See recommendations in the ragù recipe, page 52.

Menu: In addition to the menu suggestions in the ragù recipe (page 52), offer the ragù as a main dish after "Little" Spring Soup from the 17th Century (page 232), and follow with the Salad of Spring Greens (page 350). Have Frozen Hazelnut Zabaione with Chocolate Marsala Sauce (page 436) as dessert.

Tagliatelle with Caramelized Onions and Fresh Herbs
Tagliatelle con Cipolle e Erbucce

My passion for fresh herbs reaches fever pitch in high summer. Turn me loose in a farmers' market, and within minutes I am embracing armloads of basil, sage, rosemary, thyme, marjoram and anything else that is aromatic and good to eat. All this in spite of the fact that I have a thriving herb garden at home. Give me another half hour and I will have arranged bouquets of herbs all over the house, invited friends for an impromptu lunch, and begun to sauté the onions for this dish.

Few pasta recipes celebrate fresh herbs quite like this one. The blending of sautéed onion, cream and lively herbs is adapted from a recipe by Ido Migliari, who with his family runs Trattoria da Ido, tucked away along the canals of Ferrara's countryside. Ido and his son gather wild salad greens from neighboring fields, then sauté them with fresh herbs to sauce tagliatelle. This version captures the fresh, bright quality of his own.

[Serves 6 to 8 as a first course, 4 to 6 as a main dish]

3 tablespoons extra-virgin olive oil

4 medium to large onions, chopped

Salt and freshly ground black pepper

2 large cloves garlic, minced

1½ cups Poultry/Meat Stock (page 66) or Quick Stock (page 68)

1 recipe Egg Pasta (page 80) cut into tagliatelle (page 90), or 1 pound imported dried tagliatelle

6 to 8 quarts salted water

1⅔ cups tightly packed fresh herbs (basil, marjoram, rosemary, sage, and thyme)

⅔ cup heavy cream

1 to 2 ounces thinly sliced Prosciutto di Parma, chopped

3 tablespoons minced Italian parsley

8 large whole scallions (green and white parts), chopped

Salt and freshly ground black pepper to taste

2 cups (8 ounces) freshly grated Italian Parmigiano-Reggiano cheese

continued

Method   **Working Ahead:** *Once stock is in the sauce, the sauce can be set aside, covered, 2 to 3 hours.*

Making the Sauce: Heat the oil in a large heavy sauté pan over medium heat. Add the onions and a light sprinkling of salt and pepper. Stir them to lightly coat with the oil, then cover the pan, and lower the heat to the lowest possible setting. Cook 25 to 30 minutes, or until the onions are soft and almost transparent. Once the onions' natural sweetness has been accentuated by slow cooking, you can bring out their rich, savory side with browning. Uncover and raise the heat to medium-high or high. Sauté the onions to deep golden brown, stirring often with a wooden spatula and scraping up the brown glaze collecting on the bottom of the pan. Take care not to let the glaze burn. If necessary, lower the heat slightly. Onions will resemble a thick, amber marmalade.

Turn the heat to low and blend in the garlic. Cook, stirring often, about 5 minutes. Add the stock and simmer until reduced by about one quarter. As the stock bubbles, scrape up the brown glaze from the bottom of the pan with a wooden spatula.

Finishing the Sauce and Cooking the Pasta: Roughly chop the herbs before starting to cook the pasta (see Cook's Notes). Bring the pasta water to a fierce boil. If using fresh pasta that cooks in almost no time, reheat the sauce as the water is heating. If using dried pasta, the sauce can be reheated while the pasta is cooking. Drop the pasta into the water, stir once it softens, and continue boiling, stirring occasionally, until a tasted piece is tender but still firm enough to have a little bite. Drain in a colander.

To finish the sauce, reheat the onion mixture over medium-high to high heat and add the cream. Stir until the cream begins to bubble. Before going to the next step, have the cooked pasta draining and hot. Warm soup dishes and a serving bowl. Stir the prosciutto, parsley, scallions, and herbs into the sauce. Cook only long enough to heat through—the fresh, uncooked taste of the herbs is important here. Season to taste with salt and pepper, and then quickly toss the sauce with the pasta and about 2/3 cup of the cheese. Serve immediately in the warmed dishes, passing the remaining cheese separately.

Suggestions   **Wine:** An Albana Secco from Romagna, Trebbiano del Lazio from near Rome, or Tocai dei Colli Orientali del Friuli from northeastern Italy.

Menu: This stands on its own as a light main dish. Start with Garlic Crostini with Pancetta (page 28), or thin slices of salami and Balsamic Vegetables (page 18). In summer iced melon with mint, or fresh peaches sprinkled with a rich balsamic vinegar (page 467) make superb endings. In cooler weather try Zabaione Jam Tart (page 415). Offer as a first course before Lamb with Black Olives (page 305), Mardi Gras Chicken (page 277), or Rabbit Roasted with Sweet Fennel (page 289).

Cook's Notes **Olive Oil:** A flowery oil like those from the Imperia area of Liguria make a backdrop for the herbs and cream. See page 485 for information.

Fresh Herb Blend: Make the major part of the mixture fresh basil and marjoram accented by small amounts of fresh rosemary, sage and thyme. When harvesting your own herbs for this dish, remember most herbs (especially basil) peak in flavor just before flowering. Before roughly chopping the herbs, finely chop the rosemary and sage. Their assertive flavors could overwhelm the palate if eaten in larger pieces.

Tagliatelle with Radicchio and Two Beans
Tagliatelle e Fagioli con Radicchio

Radicchio imparts a tangy kick to the ancient pairing of pasta and beans. This blend of browned onions, radicchio, chick-peas, and borlotti beans enriched with Meat Essences was created from leftovers. Valentino Marcattilii, chef of Ristorante San Domenico in Romagna, improvised it one evening for the restaurant staff with trimmings from radicchio destined for roasting, beans left from the previous day's soup, a few ladles of Meat Essences, and fresh pasta . For those who grow their own radicchio, this is excellent on the first cool days of fall.

[Serves 6 to 8 as a first course, 4 to 6 as a main dish]

1 pound radicchio (3 to 4 heads)

5 tablespoons extra-virgin olive oil

1 large and 1 medium onion, cut into thin strips

15-ounce can chick-peas, rinsed and drained

1¼ cups cooked borlotti, bolita, or pinto beans (16-ounce can, rinsed and drained) (see Note)

2 large cloves garlic, minced

1 cup Poultry/Meat Stock (page 66) or Quick Stock (page 68)

⅓ cup Meat Essences (page 61), or ½ cup Poultry/Meat Stock (see Note)

2 teaspoons imported Italian tomato paste

Salt and freshly ground black pepper to taste

6 to 8 quarts salted water

1 recipe Egg Pasta (page 80) cut into tagliatelle (page 90), or 1 pound dried imported tagliatelle

1½ cups (6 ounces) freshly grated Italian Parmigiano-Reggiano cheese

continued

Method   **Working Ahead:** *The sauce can be completed several hours ahead. Cool and cover it until you are ready to cook the pasta.*

Preparing the Radicchio: Tear away any spoiled areas on the outer leaves. Quarter the heads vertically, core them, and then cut them horizontally into thick shreds.

Making the Sauce: Heat the oil in a 12-inch sauté pan over high heat. Add the onions and cook, tossing with two wooden spatulas, 4 to 5 minutes, or until medium gold. Push the onions to the side of the pan and add the radicchio. Cook over high heat, uncovered, 5 to 8 minutes, stirring often, until a brown glaze has formed on the bottom of the pan and the radicchio has wilted.

Turn the heat down to medium, add the chick-peas and the beans, and cook, stirring, for about 5 minutes. Add the garlic and stir about 1 minute. Blend in the stock, Meat Essences (or additional stock), and the tomato paste. Turn the heat to high, and boil 3 minutes, stirring often, to concentrate the flavors. Season the sauce to taste and keep it warm over low heat.

Cooking the Pasta and Serving: Bring the salted water to a fierce boil, drop in the pasta, and cook until tender but still a little firm to the bite. Fresh pasta will cook in 30 seconds to several minutes; dried pasta will take about 8 minutes. Drain the pasta in a colander, and toss with the hot sauce and 4 tablespoons of the cheese. Pass the remaining cheese separately.

Variation: Triangles of maltagliati pasta (page 88) can be substituted for the tagliatelle.

Suggestions   **Wine:** A young Sangiovese di Romagna, or a Salice Salentino Rosso from Apulia.

Menu: This substantial dish stands on its own as a simple main dish. If you are using it as a first course, follow with Lemon Roast Veal with Rosemary (page 294) or Erminia's Pan-Crisped Chicken (page 270).

Cook's Notes   **Stock:** If you are using 1½ cups stock and no Meat Essences, boil the stock in a separate pot until it is reduced by about one third before adding it to the sauce.

Meat Essences: Using Meat Essences in such a typically peasant dish like pasta and beans gives away the elegant restaurant origins of this recipe. Pasta and beans are the foods of survival; Meat Essences is the food of affluence.

Radicchio: Taste a little raw leaf near the core before cooking. If bitter, soften its impact with another 3 tablespoons Meat Essences or ⅓ cup Poultry/Meat Stock.

Radicchio is often ridiculously expensive. Save this dish for the season when less expensive radicchio is coming from local sources. Also the amount could be halved with no change to the cooking instructions. The dish will be less robust and tart, but still very good.

Borlotti Beans: These dried Italian beans are plump and colored a pink-beige with maroon to black streaks and speckles. They taste meaty and full-bodied. Find them, dried and canned, in Italian groceries and specialty food markets. The pink/brown bolita bean or the speckled pinto bean from the United States's Southwest can be substituted when borlotti are not to be found.

Tagliatelle with Fresh Tomatoes and Balsamic Vinegar
Tagliatelle con Pomodori e Aceto Balsamico

There is almost no effort to putting together this fat-free dish, created several years ago in Modena. But there are two qualifiers: the tomatoes must be vine-ripened and succulent, and the vinegar must be richly sweet/tart and full of woodsy character. A fine pasta for hot summer evenings.

[Serves 6 to 8 as a first course, 4 to 6 as a main dish]

¾ cup commercial balsamic
   vinegar

2 large cloves garlic, minced

1 medium to large red onion, cut
   into ½-inch dice

6 to 8 quarts salted water

8 large vine-ripened tomatoes
   (about 3½ pounds), cored and
   cut into bite-size pieces

⅔ cup tightly packed fresh basil
   leaves, minced

Generous amount freshly ground
   black pepper

1 recipe Egg Pasta (page 80) cut
   for tagliatelle (page 90), or 1
   pound dried imported tagliatelle

Salt to taste

1¼ cups (5 ounces) Italian
   Parmigiano-Reggiano cheese,
   shaved with a vegetable peeler

Method

Working Ahead: *This dish is made in almost no time. It does not benefit from being prepared ahead.*

Marinating the Tomatoes: Measure the vinegar into a medium-size glass or pottery bowl. Add the garlic and onion. Marinate about 15 minutes. Set the salted water on to boil. Fold the tomatoes, basil, and pepper into the vinegar mixture and let stand 10 to 15 minutes to blend flavors.

continued

Cooking the Pasta and Serving: Drop the pasta into the boiling salted water. Cook at a fierce rolling boil 30 seconds to several minutes for fresh pasta, and up to 6 or 7 minutes for dried. Taste to make sure the pasta is tender but still a little firm to the bite. Drain the pasta in a colander, and toss it with the tomato mixture. Season to taste, and serve topped with the shaved cheese.

Suggestions   **Wine:** Even though balsamic vinegar can be smooth and sweet, it is acidic. The quantity used here discourages most wines. Save the wine for sipping with Parmigiano-Reggiano after the pasta.

Menu: Serve before grilled or roasted main dishes not prepared with tomatoes or balsamic vinegar, such as Herbed Seafood Grill (page 254) or Erminia's Pan-Crisped Chicken (page 270). On hot summer nights enjoy it as they do in Modena—outdoors, served as a main dish, followed by shales of Parmigiano-Reggiano and then fresh peaches.

Cook's Notes   **Balsamic Vinegar:** I have adapted this dish from its Modena original using a fine commercial balsamic vinegar, the sort available throughout the United States. For information see page 469. If good fortune brings you a generous amount of artisan-made balsamic vinegar from Modena or Reggio, savor the dish in all its authenticity: Reduce the quantity of vinegar to ½ cup; halve the amount of garlic, onion, and basil; and use only 2 ounces of Parmigiano-Reggiano.

Tagliarini with Fresh Figs Franco Rossi
Tagliarini ai Fichi Ristorante Franco Rossi

A *Renaissance-inspired dish created at Bologna's Ristorante Franco Rossi, here sweet figs play against the savoriness of Parmigiano-Reggiano. The whole thing is then accented by pepper and lemon zest. Fruit and pasta makes an unusual combination for most of us. Discover how good it can be in this dish.*

[Serves 6 to 8 as a first course]

6 to 8 quarts salted water
1 recipe Egg Pasta (page 80) cut for tagliarini (page 90), or 1 pound imported dried tagliarini
8 tablespoons (4 ounces) unsalted butter
Shredded zest of 1 large lemon
12 large ripe figs, peeled and coarsely chopped

Generous pinch of red pepper flakes
Heaping ¼ teaspoon freshly ground black pepper
1 cup heavy cream
1¼ cups (about 5 ounces) freshly grated Italian Parmigiano-Reggiano cheese
Salt to taste

Method

Working Ahead: *This dish comes together in a matter of minutes. The trick is not overcooking the figs. You must be cooking and draining the pasta just as the sauce is ready to be blended with it. If this seems too much of a juggle, first give your full attention to cooking the pasta. Just before draining it, start heating the butter. Then drain the pasta and quickly cook the sauce. Warm a serving bowl and shallow soup dishes in a low oven about 20 minutes ahead so they are waiting when you are ready to serve.*

Cooking the Pasta: Bring the salted water to a fierce boil. If you are using dried pasta, cook it about halfway, 4 minutes. Meanwhile, melt the butter in a 12-inch heavy skillet over medium heat. If you are using fresh pasta, drop it into the water once the butter has melted.

Making the Sauce: Just before starting to cook the sauce, taste the pasta for doneness. If you feel it might be ready within a few moments, keep your eye on it and wait to cook the figs. Better to have the pasta draining a few extra minutes than to have overcooked, mushy figs.

Raise the heat under the skillet to high, add the lemon zest, and cook about 30 seconds. Add the figs and both peppers. Cook over high heat 1 minute, searing on all sides by turning them gently with two wooden spatulas.

continued

The letter "H," 17th-century engraving, by Bolognese artist Giuseppe Maria Mitelli

Assembling and Serving: Once the figs are seared, quickly drain the pasta (if you have not already done so) and add it to the skillet with the cream. Toss the pasta with the figs and cream no more than 30 seconds. Add the cheese and toss until blended. Taste for salt. Turn the pasta from the skillet into a heated serving bowl or individual soup dishes, and serve immediately.

Suggestions **Wine:** A soft flowery white with some fruit and spice is needed here. In Bologna it would be a Pinot Bianco dei Colli Bolognesi. On this side of the ocean, Tocai from Italy's Friuli region is found more easily. A well-made Chenin Blanc also works well.

Menu: In a simple menu, figs with tagliatelle are a fine prelude to Pan-Roasted Quail (page 283) or Porcini Veal Chops (page 290). Create a menu echoing the Renaissance ("echo" because a typical period menu had between 30 and 100 dishes)

by beginning with a few slices of Prosciutto di Parma (page 14), then offering small bowls of "Little" Spring Soup from the 17th Century (page 232), then pasta with figs, followed by Christmas Capon (page 281). Make the dessert either Paola Bini's Sweet Ravioli (page 424) or Capacchi's Blazing Chestnuts (page 450).

Variation with Dried Figs: The fresh fig season is fleeting, especially in the middle of the United States. My dried fig variation of Franco Rossi's dish has become a favorite supper around the Christmas holidays.

[Serves 6 to 8 as a first course]

8 tablespoons (4 ounces) unsalted butter

1 pound dried California Calimyrna figs, trimmed of stems and cut into eighths

Shredded zest of 1 large lemon

Generous pinch of red pepper flakes

Generous ¼ teaspoon freshly ground black pepper

¼ cup dry white wine

1 cup heavy cream

6 to 8 quarts salted water

1 recipe Egg Pasta (page 80) cut into tagliarini (page 90), or 1 pound imported dried tagliarini

1½ cups (6 ounces) freshly grated Italian Parmigiano-Reggiano cheese

Salt to taste

Follow the directions as above, but add the figs and zest to the hot butter together. Cook the figs until their skin is golden brown. Then add the wine and boil it off. Add the cream, bring to a simmer, and then add the drained pasta and toss with sauce and cheese. Serve immediately.

Linguine with Braised Garlic and Balsamic Vinegar
Linguine con Aglio e Balsamico

This dish is a garlic lover's paradise, taking Italy's popular pasta with garlic and oil into a new realm. Balsamic vinegar spooned over the finished pasta is the all-important refinement. The dish comes together in almost no time.

[Serves 6 to 8 as a first course, 4 to 6 as a main dish]

3 tablespoons extra-virgin olive oil or unsalted butter

8 large cloves garlic, cut into ¼-inch dice

6 quarts salted water

1 pound imported dried linguine, or 1 recipe Egg Pasta (page 80) cut into tagliarini (page 90)

3 tablespoons extra-virgin olive oil or unsalted butter

Salt and freshly ground black pepper to taste

1 to 1½ cups (4 to 6 ounces) freshly grated Italian Parmigiano-Reggiano cheese

8 to 10 teaspoons artisan-made or high-quality commercial balsamic vinegar (if using commercial, blend in 1 teaspoon brown sugar)

Method

Working Ahead: *The garlic can be braised up to 8 hours ahead. Set it aside, covered, at room temperature. The dish is best finished and eaten right away.*

Braising the Garlic: In a large heavy skillet, heat the 3 tablespoons oil or butter over medium-low heat. Add the garlic, and lower the heat to the lowest possible setting. Cook, covered, 5 minutes. Uncover and continue cooking over the lowest possible heat 8 minutes, or until the garlic is barely colored to pale blond and very tender. Stir it frequently with a wooden spatula. Do not let the garlic turn medium to dark brown, as it will be bitter.

Cooking the Pasta: Warm a serving bowl and shallow soup dishes in a low oven. As the garlic braises, bring the salted water to a fierce boil, and drop in the pasta. Stir occasionally. Cook only a few moments for fresh pasta, and up to 10 minutes for dried pasta. Taste for doneness, making sure the pasta is tender but still firm to the bite. Spoon about 3 tablespoons of the cooking water into the cooked garlic just before draining the pasta. Drain in a colander.

Finishing and Serving: Remove the garlic from the heat and add the hot drained pasta. Add the additional 3 tablespoons of oil or butter (the fresh taste of uncooked oil or butter brightens the dish), and toss with two wooden spatulas. Season with salt and pepper. Now toss with all of the cheese. Turn into the heated serving bowl. As you serve the pasta, sprinkle each plateful with a teaspoon or so of the vinegar.

Suggestions **Wine:** A simple but fruity white, like Trebbiano del Lazio or Frascati.

Menu: Serve before simple or complex dishes: Herbed Seafood Grill (page 254), Braised Eel with Peas (page 261), Christmas Capon (page 281), Beef-Wrapped Sausage (page 314), Lamb with Black Olives (page 305), or Rabbit Roasted with Sweet Fennel (page 289). Offer as a main dish after Prosciutto di Parma (page 14), Mousse of Mortadella (page 22), Garlic Crostini with Pancetta (page 28), Chicken and Duck Liver Mousse with White Truffles (page 24), or Valentino's Pizza (page 29). Have Riccardo Rimondi's Spanish Sponge Cake (page 433) for dessert.

Cook's Notes **Balsamic Vinegar:** See page 467 for information on selecting balsamic vinegars.

Variation with Fresh Basil: In summer add 1 cup coarsely chopped fresh basil leaves to the braised garlic a few seconds before tossing with the pasta. Let the basil warm and its aromas blossom, then add the pasta to the pan.

Tagliarini with Lemon Anchovy Sauce
Tagliarini con Bagnabrusca

The unusual but winning combination of lemon and tomato come together in this sauté of garlic, parsley, and anchovy. After a few minutes of cooking, you have a light and fresh-tasting first course. Served as a main dish, it makes a fast and satisfying weekday supper. This recipe comes from the cooks of Modena's and Ferrara's Jewish communities.

[Serves 6 to 8 as a first course, 4 to 6 as a main dish]

Sauce

10 whole salted anchovies, or two 2-ounce cans anchovy filets

1 cup cold water

6 tablespoons extra-virgin olive oil

6 tablespoons minced Italian parsley

1 large clove garlic, minced

½ cup water

2 large fresh tomatoes, cored, peeled, and chopped, or 6 canned plum tomatoes, drained and crushed

3 tablespoons fresh lemon juice

Freshly ground black pepper to taste

Pasta

6 quarts salted water

1 recipe Egg Pasta (page 80) cut into tagliarini (page 90), or 1 pound imported dried tagliarini, linguine, or spaghetti

1 tablespoon minced Italian parsley

Method

Working Ahead: *The sauce cooks in no time and is best made just before serving.*

Preparing the Anchovies: If you are using salted anchovies, rinse off the salt. Then open each up like a book, and gently pull away the backbone running down the center. Soak the anchovies 10 minutes in the cold water; then drain and coarsely chop.

If using canned anchovies in oil, rinse them and soak in cold water 10 minutes. Drain and coarsely chop.

Making the Sauce: In a 12-inch heavy skillet, heat the oil over medium heat. Add the parsley and cook slowly, lowering the heat so it sizzles gently. Cook only 1 minute, or until the green herb darkens. Stir in the drained anchovies and cook over medium-low heat for 30 seconds. Add the garlic and sauté, stirring frequently, 2 minutes or until the small pieces turn golden, taking care not to burn it. Immediately stir in the ½ cup water and cook over low heat about 2 minutes, or until the anchovies are melted. The goal is not to evaporate the water, but simply to melt down the anchovies. Blend in the tomatoes and lemon juice, raise the heat to medium, and cook 1 minute. Generously season the sauce with black pepper. Remove the skillet from the heat.

Cooking the Pasta: Have a serving bowl and shallow soup dishes warming in a low oven. Bring the salted water to a fierce boil. Drop in the pasta, stir to separate the strands, and cook only 1 minute or so for fresh pasta, up to 8 minutes for dried. Taste a strand for tender texture with some firmness or bite. Drain immediately in a colander.

Serving: Return the sauce to high heat and quickly bring it to a boil. Immediately add the cooked pasta, and toss to coat it with the sauce. Turn out into the serving bowl, sprinkle with the tablespoon of parsley, and serve. (No cheese accompanies this dish.)

Suggestions   **Wine:** In the region drink a full, crisp white Sauvignon from the Bolognese hills (Colli Bolognesi). From other parts of Italy pour a white Vespaiolo from the Veneto or Friuli's Sauvignon.

Menu: The bright tastes of this pasta work well before Mardi Gras Chicken (page 277), Herbed Seafood Grill (page 254), or Beef-Wrapped Sausage (page 314). The pasta makes a fine main dish. Have Modena's Spiced Soup of Spinach and Cheese (page 234) beforehand. End the meal with Nonna's Jam Tart (page 413) or Sweet Cornmeal Biscuits (page 422).

Cook's Notes **Salted Anchovies:** Although these have a richer flavor than oil-packed anchovies, they can be difficult to find. Check with local shops carrying foods from Mediterranean countries. Wrap them in plastic wrap and store in the refrigerator up to 3 days.

An Ancient Seasoning

In Italian this sauce is *bagnabrusca,* meaning tart marinade or seasoning. Dating back to the Middle Ages, the sauce came to Ferrara and Modena with Jews who were fleeing persecution in other parts of Italy and in Spain. They sought the protection of the Este dukes, who had petitioned the Pope, requesting freedom for the Jews living in their duchy. Eventually Ferrara's Jewish community became one of the largest in northern Italy, bringing a wealth of new dishes to Emilia-Romagna and changing the face of Ferrara's cooking. Proof of the recipe's Medieval origins is found in old renditions requiring not tomatoes but *agresto* (the juice of unripe grapes), a favorite seasoning of the Middle Ages. Then *bagnabrusca* was spooned over poached meats and seafood rather than pasta. Try it today over poached or baked bluefish, mullet, or cod and over grilled chicken and lamb.

Gramigna with Wine-Braised Sausage
Gramigna alla Salsiccia e Vino

This is Emilian coming-home-to-mother food. The combination of gramigna (curly pasta) and sausage almost always appears on the menus of local restaurants in Bologna's countryside. This sauce lends itself to being prepared in advance and reheated just before serving. Take care not to overcook the tomatoes.

[Serves 6 to 8 as a first course, 4 to 6 as a main dish]

1 to 1½ pounds mild Italian sausage (made without fennel), sliced into ½-inch rounds

2 tablespoons extra-virgin olive oil

1 medium onion, minced

6 tablespoons minced Italian parsley

3 tablespoons minced carrot

1 large clove garlic, minced

3 large fresh sage leaves

Generous pinch ground cloves

1 tablespoon imported Italian tomato paste

1 cup dry white wine

6 to 8 quarts salted water

1 recipe Egg Pasta (page 80) cut into gramigna (page 87), or 1 pound imported dried cavatappi

1 pound vine-ripened tomatoes, peeled and chopped, or 14- to 16-ounce can tomatoes with their liquid

1½ cups (6 ounces) freshly grated Italian Parmigiano-Reggiano cheese

Method   **Working Ahead:** *Prepare up to 1 hour ahead, to the point of adding the tomatoes. Cover lightly and hold at room temperature.*

Making the Sauce: In a large heavy skillet, slowly sauté the sausage over medium to medium-low heat 15 minutes, or until most of its fat is released and the pieces are browned. Turn often with a wooden spatula. Scoop up the browned sausage with a slotted spoon and transfer to a platter. Set aside. Pour out all but 1 tablespoon of the drippings. Add the olive oil to the skillet, keeping the heat at medium. Stir in the onion, parsley, and carrot. Cook 10 minutes, or until golden, taking care not to burn the brown crusty bits on the bottom of the pan.

Add the sausage, garlic, and sage, and cook about 2 minutes. Add the cloves, tomato paste, and half the wine. Bring to a gentle bubble, scraping up the brown bits on the bottom of the pan, and cook 8 minutes, or until the wine is totally evaporated.

Add the remaining wine and simmer so it bubbles very slowly until the sauce has a rich, deep aroma, about 10 minutes.

Cooking the Pasta and Assembling the Dish: Have a serving bowl and shallow soup dishes warming in a low oven. While the sauce is simmering, bring the salted water to a fierce boil. Drop in the pasta. If you are using fresh gramigna, check for doneness after about 1 minute. Dried pasta will take longer, about 10 minutes. Taste for a pleasing chewiness without any suggestion of a raw taste. Drain in a colander. While the pasta cooks, quickly bring the sauce to a gentle simmer over high heat. Stir in the tomatoes, reduce the heat to medium, and let it bubble with some liveliness 5 minutes, or until thickened. Stir often to keep from sticking. Toss the sauce with the pasta and about one third of the cheese. Turn into the serving bowl or individual soup dishes. Serve hot, passing the additional cheese.

Suggestions   **Wine:** An uncomplicated red like a young Barbera or Sangiovese from Emilia-Romagna, the Piedmont's Barbera, or a young Chianti Classico from Tuscany.

Menu: In the countryside gramigna and sausages are served in the traditional way, following an antipasto of local salami and coppa (pages 501 and 474) with Balsamic Vegetables (page 18) and perhaps bread fritters (page 373). If meat is served after the pasta, it is simply grilled or roasted. A lighter, more contemporary menu is an antipasto of Salad of Tart Greens with Prosciutto and Warm Balsamic Dressing (page 26), followed by the pasta, and then fruit for dessert.

Cook's Notes **Regional Variations:** In the provinces of Modena, Reggio, and Parma, this sauce is tossed with dried boxed maccheroni such as ziti, penne rigate, or sedani. ◆ In Romagna, "Priest Stranglers" (page 89) replace the gramigna. ◆ Old recipes use high-quality lard instead of olive oil. ◆ The cooks of Bologna, Modena, Reggio, and Parma often mellow and sweeten the sauce with cream: Cut the tomato quantity in half. Stir in 1 cup heavy cream just before adding the tomatoes. Cook as described above.

The sausage of Modena from the 17th-century board game "The Game of Cucagna where no one loses and everyone wins," by Bolognese artist Giuseppe Maria Mitelli

Garganelli with Roasted Peppers, Peas, and Cream

Garganelli con Peperoncini Dolci, Piselli, e Crema

There is a lovely play of sweet flavors here—roasted peppers, peas, cream and prosciutto. The dish is made in almost no time. By not reducing the cream, but merely heating it, the pasta maintains an unexpected lightness. Cooks around Imola and Castel Bolognese, where garganelli pastas were first made, sometimes add tomato or pancetta to the sauce.

[Serves 6 to 8 as a first course, 4 to 6 as a main dish]

4 medium red bell peppers
1½ tablespoons unsalted butter
2½ ounces thinly sliced Prosciutto di Parma, coarsely chopped
1 cup heavy cream
6 to 8 quarts salted water
1 recipe Egg Pasta Villa Gaidello (page 81), shaped into garganelli (page 86), or 1 pound imported dried penne rigate

2⅓ cups very sweet fresh peas, lightly steamed, or frozen tiny peas, defrosted
1 cup (4 ounces) freshly grated Italian Parmigiano-Reggiano cheese
Salt to taste
¼ to ½ teaspoon freshly ground black pepper

Method

Working Ahead: *The peppers can be roasted a day in advance, and stored in a sealed container in the refrigerator. The sauce cooks in almost no time and is best made at the last minute.*

Roasting the Peppers: Roast the peppers by searing and blistering them all over on an outdoor grill, or on a sheet of aluminum foil on an oven rack set about 3 to 4 inches below the preheated broiler. Keep turning until their surfaces are well seared. Then tuck them into a plastic or paper bag, seal, and let stand about 30 minutes. Slip off the skins, core, and seed. Cut into ½- to ¾-inch dice.

Making the Sauce: In a 12-inch skillet, melt the butter over medium-high heat and sauté the prosciutto 30 seconds. Add the peppers and cook another 30 seconds. Add the cream, and set aside off the heat.

Cooking the Pasta and Assembling the Dish: Have a serving bowl and shallow soup dishes warming in a low oven. Bring the salted water to a vigorous boil. Drop in the pasta and cook until tender but still firm to the bite. Watch carefully; fresh pasta could cook in about 30 seconds. Dried pasta will take 10 to 12 minutes. Drain in a large colander. Quickly bring the sauce to a boil, stirring in the peas. Immediately add the hot pasta, and toss over high heat until the sauce has totally covered the garganelli. Add the cheese, and toss to coat and penetrate. Add salt to taste, and lots of freshly ground pepper. Serve in the heated serving bowl.

Suggestions   **Wine:** From the region, drink a dry Albana di Romagna, Terre Rosse Malvasia, or a Pinot Bianco from the Bologna area. Or try a white Pinot Bianco or Pinot Grigio from the hills of Friuli (Colli Orientali del Friuli).

Menu: In early summer, when the last of the peas and the first of the peppers appear in the market at the same time, enjoy the garganelli as a main dish. Serve a green salad or a few slices of salami (page 501) first. As part of a larger menu, serve the pasta before Herbed Seafood Grill (page 254), Romagna Grilled Veal Chops (page 297), Lamb with Black Olives (page 305), or Balsamic Roast Chicken (page 279).

Cook's Notes   **Prosciutto:** This dish needs a ham that is earthy, salty, and has a big meaty flavor. Ask for Prosciutto di Parma cut from the narrower shank end, where flavors are riper and fuller than in the thicker parts of the ham.

Pasta of the Loom

Garganelli originated on Romagna's plain. Most homes had a hemp loom for working the coarse fiber that flourished in the thick clay soil north of Cesena. Around Castel Bolognese and neighboring Imola, women used the loom for hemp, and the loom comb, or little plaques of hemp woven on a frame, to fashion garganelli. They made the hollow ribbed pasta by rolling small squares of pasta around a dowel and over the comb or woven hemp plaque at the same time.

I think about those women's hands, coarsened and thickened over years of working with the wiry hemp, that then shaped such delicate pastas. Now the looms are all but gone. But the combs remain, and today regional women gather to gossip, laugh, and make great piles of garganelli for special occasions.

Parsley Pasta with Tomato and Peas Villa Gaidello

Stricchettoni Villa Gaidello

This pasta is a specialty of the local women who cook at Villa Gaidello, a guest farm outside Modena. They work parsley, Parmigiano-Reggiano cheese, nutmeg, and pepper into a pasta dough similar to the dough for garganelli. It is then cut and pinched into bow ties. After cooking, the colorful noodles are sauced with sautéed tomato, onion, peas, and prosciutto. My husband and I like to mark special moments with this pasta, sharing it as a main dish. It also doubles easily.

[Serves 4 as a first course, 2 to 3 as a main dish]

½ recipe Egg Pasta Villa Gaidello (page 81), made with nutmeg and ½ cup chopped Italian parsley

½ cup fresh sweet peas or frozen tiny peas

4 quarts salted water

6 tablespoons (3 ounces) unsalted butter

2 ounces Prosciutto di Parma, thinly sliced and cut into matchsticks

½ medium onion, minced

1 small clove garlic, minced

1 cup halved cherry tomatoes, or 1 large vine-ripened tomato, peeled, seeded, and diced

½ teaspoon imported Italian tomato paste

Generous pinch of sugar (optional)

Salt and freshly ground black pepper to taste

1 cup (4 ounces) freshly grated Italian Parmigiano-Reggiano cheese

Method   **Working Ahead:** *The dough can be made and the fresh peas cooked 1 day in advance. The sauce is cooked as the pasta water comes to a boil.*

Making the Dough and Preparing the Peas: Make the pasta dough as directed in the recipe, blending in the ½ cup of parsley. Cut and pinch into bow ties (stricchettoni, page 89). Cook fresh peas in a steamer over boiling water until barely tender, about 5 minutes. Turn them into a strainer and rinse under cold running water to stop the cooking and set the color. If you are using frozen peas, simply defrost them.

Making the Sauce: About 20 minutes before dining, place shallow soup dishes in a warm oven to heat. Bring the salted water to a fierce boil. While the water is coming to a boil, melt the butter in a large heavy nonaluminum skillet over medium-low heat. Add about one third of the prosciutto and all the onion. Slowly cook 8 minutes, or until the onions are soft and clear, stirring frequently with a wooden spatula. Take care not to brown them. Stir in the garlic and remove the skillet from the heat.

Cooking the Pasta: Drop the pasta into the vigorously boiling water. Stir to separate the pieces, and cook only about 30 seconds to 1 minute. Taste for doneness. The pasta should be tender but still slightly firm to the bite. Drain the pasta in a colander and immediately finish making the sauce.

Finishing the Sauce: Turn the heat to medium-high under the onions, and stir in the tomatoes and tomato paste. Heat 1 minute, or until the tomato skins are seared, taking care not to break up the tomato pieces. Don't cook the tomato; you are simply heating it through, keeping its fresh flavor intact. Stir in the sugar and the peas, cooking only until the peas are heated through, about 30 seconds. Taste for seasoning. Turn the drained pasta into the skillet, and add the remaining prosciutto. Turn gently with two wooden spatulas, coating the bow ties with the sauce. Spoon them into the heated soup dishes, and serve immediately. Pass the cheese separately.

Suggestions   **Wine:** A Bolognese Chardonnay, or a round, full one from Friuli or the Piedmont.

Menu: Serve as a main dish after Fresh Pears with Parmigiano-Reggiano and Balsamic Vinegar (page 30). Marie Louise's Crescents (page 426) served with sweet wine are an ideal dessert. For a more elaborate spring dinner, have Spring Salad with Hazelnuts (page 21) before the pasta. Follow the pasta with Balsamic Roast Chicken (page 279) or Pan-Roasted Quail (page 283). If using the quail, a dessert of strawberries sprinkled with rich balsamic vinegar makes a memorable finale. If not, serve Marie Louise's Crescents (page 426).

Cook's Notes   **Substituting Store-Bought Pasta:** Replacing the flavored homemade pasta with boxed pasta changes the dish but still makes for good eating. Commercially produced bow ties are too large and thick for this dish. Wide ribbons of thin-rolled pappardelle come close to the light, delicate quality of Villa Gaidello's pasta. Break 8 ounces dried boxed pappardelle into 3-inch pieces. Cook in 4 quarts of boiling salted water until tender but still firm to the bite. Drain, and toss with the sauce.

Tomatoes: Our own cherry tomatoes are similar to Villa Gaidello's home-canned tomatoes. If possible, taste the tomatoes before buying.

Pappardelle with Lentils and Parmigiano-Reggiano
Pappardelle alle Lenticchie

A *recipe from the farm kitchens of Modena that raises pasta and legumes to a new elegance, this is a perfect dish for those seeking good food with little meat. Traditionally lentils and pasta are a one-dish meal. The lentils are so aromatic and satisfying, you may want to eat them on their own. They get their special taste from browned bits of pancetta (the fat is poured off). Before serving, add a generous amount of Parmigiano-Reggiano to round out all the flavors.*

[Serves 6 as a main dish]

Lentils

1¼ cups (8 ounces) green or brown lentils

½ stalk celery with leaves

½ medium onion, coarsely chopped

8 large fresh sage leaves, chopped, or 8 whole dried sage leaves

1 large clove garlic, minced

½ cup dry white wine

Salt and freshly ground black pepper to taste

Aromatics and Pasta

4 ounces lean pancetta, thickly sliced

3 tablespoons extra-virgin olive oil

2½ medium onions, finely chopped

10 whole fresh sage leaves, chopped, or 10 whole dried sage leaves

1 large clove garlic, minced

Salt and freshly ground black pepper to taste

6 to 8 quarts salted water

1 pound dried imported pappardelle

1¾ cups (7 ounces) freshly grated Italian Parmigiano-Reggiano cheese

Method   **Working Ahead:** *The lentils can be cooked and combined with the aromatics 1 day ahead. The pancetta can be cooked at the same time, but store it separately. Cool, cover, and refrigerate. Reheat the lentils and add the pancetta before blending with the pasta.*

Cooking the Lentils: Combine the lentils, celery, onion, sage, garlic, and wine in a heavy 2-quart saucepan. Add enough water to cover by about 2 inches, and bring to a boil. Turn the heat down so the water bubbles very slowly. Stir the lentils with a wooden spatula and partially cover the pan. Cook 15 to 18 minutes, or until the lentils are tender enough to eat but still have some firmness; they should not be falling apart. Remove the pan from the heat, uncover the lentils and let them cool in their liquid while you prepare the aromatics. Season the lentils with salt and pepper.

Cooking the Aromatics: Coarsely chop the pancetta into pieces about ½-inch square. Cook it in a large skillet set over medium-low heat. Once most of the fat has melted away from the pancetta, raise the heat just a little and slowly cook to golden brown. Have several layers of paper towels laid out on a plate, ready to drain the browned pancetta. Lift out with a slotted spoon and spread them on the towels.

Pour off the fat from the skillet, leaving only about 2 teaspoons. Add the olive oil to the skillet, and set over medium heat. Once it is hot (about 1 minute), add the onion and sage. Cook over medium heat 15 minutes, or until the onion is a deep golden brown. Stir frequently with a wooden spatula. Once the onion is browned, stir in the garlic and cook about 1 minute.

Drain the cooled lentils in a colander, discarding the larger pieces of onion and celery. Turn the lentils into the skillet, and cook over medium-low heat about 10 minutes so they absorb some of the rich flavor from the onion. Keep running the wooden spatula under the lentils to keep them from sticking. Stir in the reserved pancetta, and season with salt and pepper. Remove the lentils from the heat.

Cooking the Pasta and Assembling the Dish: Have a serving bowl and shallow soup dishes warming in a low oven. Bring the salted water to a vigorous boil. Break the pappardelle into 3-inch pieces. Drop them into the water and cook at a fierce boil, stirring frequently, 7 minutes, or until tender but still a bit firm to the bite.

As the pasta cooks, rewarm the lentils over medium heat. Add about ⅔ cup of the pasta water to the lentils, carefully stirring it in so as not to break them up. The lentils should be moistened but not soupy. A little liquid should cover the bottom of the skillet, so you are be able to scrape up any brown bits there. If necessary, add another ⅓ cup water. When the pasta is done, drain it in a colander and then toss with the lentils. Blend in the Parmigiano-Reggiano cheese, and taste for seasoning. Turn the pasta and lentils into the heated bowl, and serve immediately.

Suggestions **Wine:** A red wine that fills the mouth with fruit, such as a Sangiovese di Romagna Riserva from Emilia-Romagna, a Piemontese Dolcetto d'Alba, Alto Adige's Pinot Nero, or a Merlot from the Veneto.

Menu: Serve an antipasto of Balsamic Vegetables (page 18) with a few slices of salami (page 501), then the pasta and lentils. Following the country theme, dessert can be fresh fruit, Nonna's Jam Tart (page 413), or Cinnamon and Clove Custard (page 440). To serve lentils with sausages, see the zampone recipe on page 315.

Cook's Notes **Breaking Pasta:** Breaking pasta before cooking it is frowned upon. The exception is when substituting pieces of pappardelle for the handmade bow tie pasta sometimes used in this dish. Commercial bow tie pasta is too heavy to properly balance with the lentils, whereas 2- to 3-inch lengths of pappardelle work well.

Lentils: France's green lentils from the Puy area are exceptionally flavorful in this dish. Find them in specialty food stores.

Is It in the Pasta?

Tallying the musical talent that has come out of Emilia-Romagna in just the last two centuries could easily have you speculating over whether there may be some secret ingredient in the pasta. Parma has been especially gifted. Its opera house is said to be one of the most challenging in Italy. Arturo Toscanini, the fiery and perfectionistic conductor, was born in Parma. Soprano Renata Tebaldi did not have the good luck of being born in the region, but she did have the good sense to begin her musical training in Parma. Most famous is composer Giuseppe Verdi, born on the Parma plain in 1813 in the tiny village of Roncole, near Busseto. Strongly linked with Italy's unification movement, Verdi created his name from the initials of the freedom movement's hoped-for king, Vittorio Emmanuele, Re d'Italia. In his later life Verdi settled near Busseto, at his beloved farm estate of Sant'Agata. With him was another musicial great, the diva Giuseppina Strepponi. You can still feel the power of Verdi's charisma in Busseto, where even the butcher shop has a corner devoted to the composer. Yet another native son, tenor Carlo Bergonzi, runs Busseto's Il Due Foscari, the hotel named for a Verdi opera.

Composer Gioacchino Rossini began life in the neighboring Marche region during 1792, but he studied and lived in Bologna for many years. There, while writing comic operas, he nurtured a passion for Emilia-Romagna's foods. When he moved to Paris, Rossini's longings constantly surfaced in his prolific correspondence with Italian friends. He spoke of the tranquility induced by balsamic vinegar, the succulence of zampone and the rest of Emilia-Romagna's *salume,* and how the French knew nothing of making pasta. Of course, good food and Luciano Pavarotti are synonymous. In his beloved hometown of Modena, the singer's passion for local dishes is as much admired as his voice. One afternoon a neighborhood *salumeria* became the site of an impromptu opera history lesson as shoppers discussed Pavarotti's career. Critiquing twenty years of performances drove one woman to dash out for her cassette player. Clicking on a recent Pavarotti recording, she defied anyone to prove his voice was not richer than ever. The response was the silence of ardent listening. That same recording featured another Modenese, soprano Mirella Freni. She and Pavarotti share years of friendship and of performing together throughout the world.

Pappardelle with Game Ragù
Pappardelle con Ragù degli Appennini

Wide ribbons of pappardelle pasta are just right for this ragù, with its big flavors of red wine, wild game, and spices. In the Apennine mountains hunters make the ragù with whatever game is available. Now that venison and other game meats are found in more and more shops across the United States, try this sauce as it is done in Emilia-Romagna.

[Serves 8 to 10 as a first course, 6 to 8 as a main dish]

1 recipe Game Ragù (page 50)
8 to 10 quarts salted water
1½ pounds dried imported pappardelle, or 1½ recipes Egg Pasta (page 80) cut into ⅝-inch-wide strips

2 cups (8 ounces) freshly grated Italian Parmigiano-Reggiano cheese

Method   **Working Ahead:** *The sauce can be made up to 1 month ahead. Have it warming before you cook the pasta.*

Making the Dish: Warm a serving bowl and soup dishes in a low oven. Gently heat the ragù over medium heat. Keep partially covered. Bring the salted water to a full rolling boil. Drop in the pasta and cook at a full boil until tender but still firm to the bite. Fresh pasta can cook in a matter of a few minutes, so watch it carefully; taste for doneness after about 1½ minutes. Dried pasta will take 5 minutes or more. Drain the pasta thoroughly in a colander. Toss the hot pasta with the ragù, and turn into a serving bowl. Present the dish at the table, passing the cheese separately.

Suggestions   **Wine:** See recommendations in the Game Ragù recipe (page 50).

Menu: In addition to the suggestions found with Game Ragù, serve the pasta and sauce as a one-dish main course after Hot Caramelized Pears with Prosciutto (page 31). Follow it with fresh roasted chestnuts, peeled at the table and dunked in a sweet wine like the red of Sardegna, Anghelu Ruju, or the simpler white Recioto di Soave from the Veneto. An alternative dessert is Marie Louise's Crescents (page 426) served with the Recioto di Soave.

"Priest Stranglers" with Fresh Clams and Squid
Strozzapreti con Poveracce e le Seppie

In this Romagna recipe inspired by regional food historian Gianni Quondamatteo, squid is braised with tomatoes, basil, and wine to melting tenderness, then tossed with steamed clams and served over pasta. The combination makes a good supper in itself, or a prelude to any dish not made with tomato or basil. Of course, the "Priest Strangler" pasta is a delightful conversation piece. See page 89 for its story. Many people are put off by squid, when in fact its flavor is extremely delicate. The trick with squid is to either cook it in a flash or simmer it long and slow. This recipe takes the long and slow approach. Try it, especially since much of it can be prepared in advance.

[Serves 6 to 8 as a first course, 4 to 6 as a main dish]

Clams

18 to 24 (1½ to 2 pounds) small to medium clams

4 quarts cold water

¼ cup salt

¼ cup cornmeal

Squid and Sauce

4 tablespoons extra-virgin olive oil

1 large onion, minced

4 tablespoons minced Italian parsley

1 pound cleaned squid, rinsed, dried, and chopped into bite-size pieces

1 large clove garlic, minced

¼ to ½ teaspoon freshly ground black pepper

3 tablespoons minced fresh basil leaves, or 2 teaspoons dried basil

½ cup dry white wine

½ cup Poultry/Meat Stock (page 66) or Quick Stock (page 68)

1 pound fresh tomatoes, seeded and chopped, or 14- to 16-ounce can plum tomatoes with their liquid

6 to 8 quarts salted water

¾ recipe Wine Pasta (page 82) made into strozzapreti (page 89), or 1 pound imported dried spaghetti

About 5 sprigs fresh basil for garnish

Method

Working Ahead: *The clams and squid can be prepared 24 hours in advance; cover and refrigerate separately. Combine them just before serving.*

Preparing and Cooking the Clams: Purge the clams of sand by first scrubbing them with a stiff brush under cold running water. Then put them in a large glass or stainless steel bowl, cover them with the cold water, and sprinkle with the salt and cornmeal. Refrigerate about 1 hour. Drain the clams and arrange them in a single layer in a large skillet. Cover with a lid or aluminum foil, and cook over medium heat 5 minutes, or until they open (discard any that do not open). Saving the pan liquid, remove the meat from the clams and set it aside in a small bowl.

Strain the cooking liquid into a saucepan through a sieve lined with paper towels. Boil down 2 minutes, or until reduced by half (do not worry if the quantity is small). Reserve the clam meat and reduced liquor separately in covered glass or stainless steel bowls. Refrigerate if holding more than an hour or so.

Braising the Squid: In a medium-size skillet, heat the olive oil over medium-high heat. Add the onion and parsley, and sauté until the onion begins to color. Turn the heat to high, add the squid, and toss for 1 minute. Then stir in the garlic, the pepper, and half of the basil. Cook a few seconds. Add the wine and boil down to almost nothing.

Turn the mixture into a 3- to 4-quart saucepan. Add ¼ cup of the stock and all the tomatoes. Partially cover, bring to a very slow bubble, and cook 1 hour, or until the squid is tender and the sauce is rich in flavor. Keep the pan partially covered and stir occasionally, checking for sticking. If you are working ahead, let the mixture cool, then refrigerate in a covered glass or stainless steel container.

Cooking the Pasta and Finishing the Sauce: Have a serving bowl and shallow soup dishes warming in a low oven. When you are ready to serve, bring the salted water to a vigorous boil. Drop in the pasta. Blend the reserved clam liquor and the remaining ¼ cup stock into the squid, cover tightly, and simmer very slowly while you cook the pasta. Fresh "Priest Stranglers" take about 4 minutes to cook, while dried spaghetti needs 7 to 9 minutes. Test the pasta for doneness. It should be tender but still a little firm to the bite. Drain in a colander. Add the remaining basil and the reserved clams to the sauce. Turn the drained pasta back into its pot, pour in the sauce, and toss. Taste for seasoning; add enough pepper to make the sauce piquant. Serve at once in the heated bowl and soup dishes, garnishing the pasta with sprigs of basil.

Suggestions   **Wine:** In the region, a local dry white Albana di Romagna or Trebbiano di Romagna is served with this dish. More readily available here are a Piemontese Arneis or a Chardonnay from Umbria, Trentino–Alto Adige, or Friuli.

Menu: In warm weather, make a supper of the pasta preceded by Balsamic Vegetables (page 18) and a platter of sliced salami and coppa (pages 501 and 474). If you are offering it as a first course, follow with Herbed Seafood Grill (page 254) and then Frozen Chocolate Pistachio Cream with Hot Chocolate Marsala Sauce (page 438).

Cook's Notes **Olive Oil:** For authentic flavoring, use an oil packed with fruity taste from Tuscany or Umbria.

continued

On Buying Clams and Squid: Clams should be shut tight, smell of the sea with no fishiness, and not sound hollow when tapped. Any open clam shells should close when handled. If not, pass them by. Fresh squid exudes sweet, pleasing aromas and glistens attractively. If cleaned, the squid body is white. A dusky dappling indicates that its camouflage film is still intact. The film is easily pulled off. Squid freezes well, so if fresh is not available, buy frozen. Defrost overnight in the refrigerator in a pottery or glass bowl.

Variation: Mussels can be substituted for the clams without any other change in the recipe.

Maccheroni with Baked Grilled Vegetables
Maccheroni, Peperoncini e Zucchini alla Pescatore

This dish represents Romagna's home cooking at its best. Originally the vegetables were prepared by Adriatic fishermen's wives to eat with the day's catch. Many cooks transform them into a first course by tossing the vegetables with maccheroni. My favorite version sears the vegetables over a wood fire. They are then layered in a casserole, sprinkled with olive oil, and seasoned with a <u>battuto</u> ("fine mincing") of parsley, garlic, and anchovy. Just before serving, they are tossed with pasta and cheese.

[Serves 6 to 8 as a first course, 4 to 5 as a main dish]

4 medium red bell peppers

⅔ cup loosely packed Italian parsley leaves

2 large cloves garlic

½ cup loosely packed fresh basil leaves

2-ounce can anchovy filets in oil, rinsed

Extra-virgin olive oil

Salt and freshly ground black pepper

5 small onions (about 1 pound), sliced vertically about ¼ inch thick

3 medium zucchini, cut horizontally into long strips about ¼ inch thick

6 to 8 quarts salted water

1 pound dried imported penne rigati (ribbed penne pasta)

12 ounces young pecorino (sheep cheese), shredded (see Note)

Method   **Working Ahead:** *The vegetable casserole can be assembled early in the day; cover and refrigerate until 1 hour before serving.*

Roasting the Peppers: Roast the peppers until well seared on all sides over a wood or charcoal fire or under the broiler. Seal them in a plastic or paper bag, and let rest about 30 minutes. Peel, seed, and cut into ½-inch or 1-inch dice. Set aside.

Preparing the Battuto: Mince together the parsley, garlic, basil, and anchovies until they are almost a paste. Set aside, covered, in a small bowl.

Grilling the Vegetables: Lightly oil the vegetables with olive oil to encourage browning, and as they cook season them with a little salt and generous amounts of pepper. Either use an outdoor grill fired with real wood charcoal, or work indoors with a heavy gridded or flat skillet. Have a shallow 2½-quart baking dish handy. Quickly brown the onions, and then the zucchini pieces, on both sides over high heat so they stay crisp. As they are done, remove the onions and spread them over the bottom of the glass baking dish. Top with the zucchini. Using a fork to steady the vegetables, cut them into small pieces. Sprinkle the *battuto* over all, and top with the roasted peppers.

Finishing the Vegetables and Serving: Preheat the oven to 375°F. About 20 minutes before serving, sprinkle the vegetables with 3 to 4 tablespoons olive oil. Bake 20 minutes, or until the oil around the edge of the dish is bubbling.

Meanwhile bring the salted water to a fierce boil. Warm a serving bowl and shallow soup dishes in the oven. Drop the maccheroni into the water and boil vigorously, stirring often, 12 to 15 minutes or until tender but still pleasingly firm to the bite. Drain thoroughly and turn it into the warmed serving bowl. Add the baked vegetables and about one third of the cheese, and toss to blend. Taste for seasoning, adding salt and freshly ground pepper if necessary. Present the dish at the table, passing the remaining cheese separately.

Suggestions   **Wine:** Roasted peppers tend to fight elegant or complex wines. Pour a young red Sangiovese di Romagna, Dolcetto d'Alba, or a simple, fruity Merlot.

Menu: On hot summer nights, the pasta makes light eating when followed by a simple green salad and then fresh melon. In cooler weather have an antipasto of Garlic Crostini with Pancetta (page 28). After the pasta serve Balsamic Roast Chicken (page 279) or Maria Bertuzzi's Lemon Chicken (page 273).

Cook's Notes   **Young Pecorino Cheese:** In Romagna the pecorino, or sheep cheese, flavoring the pasta is young and nutty in flavor with a hint of pleasant gaminess. Pecorinos from other parts of Italy work well here too—Lago Monate's pecorino, young Pecorino Sardo, or even a salted ricotta of pecorino. Do not substitute sharp and salty pecorino Romano. If none of these is available, use California Dry Jack.

Variations: On their own these vegetables are a traditional accompaniment to grilled seafoods, and they make a fine antipasto served at room temperature.

A Little History

In the days before hollow pastas were extruded by forcing dough through a pierced plate, as they are now, making tubes of maccheroni was a tedious business. Renaissance chronicles tell of cooks wrapping pasta doughs around iron dowels, sealing them, and then cutting the long hollow tubes into stubby pieces. After pulling the dowel out, the pasta was left to dry. Imagine heaps of maccheroni drying in Renaissance castle kitchens throughout Emilia-Romagna, and hundreds of hands endlessly rolling and sealing sheets of dough to form a kind of pasta that today we think of as labor-saving. In those times the dough might have been flavored with rosewater, saffron, sugar, or even butter, like the Rosewater Maccheroni Romanesca found on page 192. The Renaissance passed, but making maccheroni by hand continued, especially in southern Italy. Maccheroni traditions are part of local lore, with shapes and names changing from one town to the next. In those settings—usually rural—old-time cooks are often insulted by a box of pasta. They continue winding thick strands of pasta around rods for corkscrews of *fusilli;* wrapping dowels in dough for all sorts of hollow pastas; and dimpling pea-size lumps of dough to produce discs of *orecchiette,* or "little ears."

Penne with Ragù of Giblets
Penne con Ragù di Rigaglie di Pollo

Few ragùs combine elegance and heartiness quite the way this one does. And few diners detect the secret of its goodness: the browned giblets and sautéed porcini mushrooms. This sauce, in many subtle variations, is found throughout Emilia-Romagna.

[Serves 6 to 8 as a first course, 4 to 6 as a main dish]

1 recipe Ragù of Giblets
(page 54)
6 to 8 quarts salted water
1 pound imported penne rigate or
sedani pasta (see Note)

2 cups (8 ounces) freshly grated
Italian Parmigiano-Reggiano
cheese

Method   **Working Ahead:** *The ragù can be made and frozen up to 1 month before serving. But the pasta must be cooked and tossed with the hot ragù just before presenting the dish at table.*

Making the Dish: Have a serving bowl and shallow soup dishes warming in a low oven. Reheat the ragù to a gentle bubble before cooking the pasta. Keep partially covered. Bring the salted water to a fierce boil. Drop in the pasta and boil, stirring frequently, 8 to 10 minutes, or until tender but still pleasantly firm to the bite. Drain immediately in a colander.

Serving: Toss the ragù with the pasta in the warm serving bowl. Bring to the table immediately, passing the cheese separately.

Suggestions   **Wine:** See the recommendations with the Ragù of Giblets recipe (page 54).

Menu: In addition to those offered in the ragù recipe, serve the pasta and ragù as a main dish after small tastes of a Platter of Cured Meats in the Style of Emilia-Romagna (page 14) and Marinated Baby Onions (page 16). Follow the ragù with the Salad of Mixed Greens and Fennel (page 349), and then a dessert of Baked Pears with Fresh Grape Syrup (page 442).

Cook's Notes   **Penne Rigate and Sedani Maccheroni:** *Penne rigate* are narrow tubes of pasta with points at their ends, like the quilled pens that are their namesakes. *Rigate* pasta, meaning grooved, is etched with ribs that hold sauce even better than its smooth counterparts. *Sedani* (celery) is a tube of pasta with ribs. Although it is harder to find than penne, I prefer it with the Ragù of Giblets.

Spaghetti with Anchovies and Melting Onions
Spaghetti con Alici e Crema di Cipolle

From Ferrara's Po delta, this is one of those easily-put-together dishes, a typical Sunday-night supper of the area. I have found that even those who claim to dislike anchovies enjoy their mild flavor in this dish, where their assertiveness is tamed by the sweet caramelized onions.

Traditionally pastas with fish are served without cheese. In this dish, a few spoonfuls of olive oil season the hot pasta just before serving.

[Serves 6 to 8 as a first course, 4 to 6 as a main dish]

Three 2-ounce cans anchovies in oil

About ¾ cup cold water

5 tablespoons extra-virgin olive oil

1 tablespoon unsalted butter

3 medium onions, finely chopped

½ cup minced Italian parsley

1 to 2 cloves garlic, minced

6 to 8 quarts salted water

1 pound imported dried spaghetti

Freshly ground black pepper to taste

Method

Working Ahead: *The sauce can be prepared several hours in advance, up to the point of adding the pasta water. Cover and keep at room temperature.*

Preparing the Anchovies: Drain the anchovies of their oil and place them in a small bowl. Cover with the cold water, and let soak 20 to 30 minutes. Drain and set aside.

Making the Caramelized Onions: In a large heavy skillet, heat 3 tablespoons of the olive oil and the butter over medium heat. Stir in the onion and parsley. Cover the skillet, turn the heat to low, and cook 30 minutes, or until the onions are clear, soft, and seem to be melting. Uncover the skillet and turn the heat to medium. Sauté the onions 20 to 30 minutes, until they are caramelized. (Their liquid cooks off first and then the browning begins.) Avoid scorching by stirring with a wooden spatula, scraping up the brown glaze forming on the skillet bottom. Take care not to burn the glaze; it is the secret of the dish's deep flavor. After 20 to 30 minutes the onions will be golden brown, the consistency of marmalade, and sweet-tasting.

Adding the Anchovies and Garlic: Add the anchovies and the garlic, stirring to break up the anchovies. Reduce the heat to medium-low, and cook 8 minutes, or until the anchovies break down and dissolve into the onions. Stir frequently. Once the anchovies are done, turn off the heat.

Cooking the Pasta and Assembling the Dish: Slip a serving bowl and shallow soup dishes into a warm oven to heat up. Bring the salted water to a fierce boil. Drop in the spaghetti and stir to keep it from sticking. Cook at a full boil 7 to 8 minutes, or until tender but pleasingly firm to the bite. Just before draining, add about ¾ cup pasta water to the sauce. Drain the cooked pasta in a colander. As it is draining, quickly turn the heat to high under the sauce. When the sauce comes to a boil, scrape up the brown glaze from the bottom of the skillet with a wooden spatula. Add the pasta to the skillet and toss over medium heat until it is coated with the sauce. Season generously with black pepper. Turn into the warmed serving bowl, sprinkle with the remaining 2 tablespoons olive oil, and serve right away.

Suggestions   **Wine:** From the region, pour a Trebbiano di Romagna. From elsewhere in Italy, drink a young Tuscan Vernaccia di San Gimignano.

Menu: Serve as a light supper after Salad of Tart Greens with Prosciutto and Warm Balsamic Dressing (page 26). For a more substantial menu, follow the pasta with Herbed Seafood Grill (page 254) and Sweet Cornmeal Biscuits (page 422) with fresh fruit for dessert.

Cook's Notes   **Olive Oil:** Use a fruity olive oil from Tuscany, the Veneto, or Umbria. For information on selecting oils, see page 485.

Butter: For a more authentic taste of old-style Ferrara cooking, substitute unsalted butter for all the olive oil in the recipe. The last 2 tablespoons are melted in as the hot pasta is tossed with the onion mixture.

Spaghetti with Shrimps and Black Olives

Spaghetti con Gamberoni e Olive Nere

On the Adriatic coast of Romagna, sautéing fresh seafood with a few herbs, tomato, and a handful of olives is as complicated as any fish dish gets. The shrimps could stand on their own as a good main dish—just eliminate the pasta and leave them whole. You can do most of the preparation in advance. The dish comes together in minutes just before serving, making it a fine first course or main dish for company.

[Serves 6 to 8 as a first course, 4 to 6 as a main dish]

3 cups Poultry/Meat Stock (page 66) or Quick Stock (page 68)

1½ pounds jumbo shrimps (about 12 to the pound), shelled and cut into thirds or quarters (reserve the shells)

⅔ cup dry white wine

6 tablespoons extra-virgin olive oil

2 large cloves garlic, lightly crushed

1 medium to large onion, minced

¼ cup minced Italian parsley

1 sprig (about 3 to 4 inches) fresh rosemary, or ½ teaspoon dried rosemary

2 fresh sage leaves, or 2 dried whole sage leaves

1 teaspoon fresh marjoram leaves, or ¼ teaspoon dried marjoram

6 to 8 quarts salted water

1 pound imported spaghetti or freshly made stringhetti (page 89)

Generous pinch of red pepper flakes

4 medium vine-ripened tomatoes, seeded, cored, and chopped, or 6 canned plum tomatoes, crushed, with a little of their juice

30 Italian oil-cured black olives, pitted and chopped

Generous amount of freshly ground black pepper

Juice of ½ to 1 lemon

Salt to taste

Method

Working Ahead: *The sauce can be made early in the day to the point of cooking the shrimps. Cover and refrigerate until 20 minutes before serving. Cook the spaghetti and shrimps at the last moment, and serve.*

Making the Sauce: Combine the stock, shrimp shells, and wine in a saucepan. Boil, uncovered, 10 to 15 minutes, or until reduced to about 1 cup. Strain, cover, and chill until needed. Heat the oil in a 12-inch heavy sauté pan over medium heat. Cook the garlic, rubbing the cloves over the bottom of the pan with a wooden spatula, until they begin to color. Discard the garlic. Turn the heat up to medium-high to high, and quickly cook the onion, parsley, and herbs 5 minutes, or until the onion is pale gold. Remove the pan from the heat, and discard the rosemary and sage. Cover and set aside.

Cooking the Pasta and Shrimps: Slip a serving bowl and shallow soup dishes into a warm oven to heat. Bring the salted water to a boil. Drop in the spaghetti, let it soften a few moments, and then stir to separate the strands. Cook at a vigorous boil, stirring frequently, 7 to 8 minutes, or until tender but still firm to the bite. Drain in a colander. As soon as the pasta is in the colander, place the sauté pan over medium-high heat. Add the shrimps and red pepper flakes, and toss quickly until the shrimps begin to turn pink, about 30 seconds. Add the reserved shrimp stock, and cook 30 seconds. Add the tomatoes, olives, and black pepper, and cook over high heat another 30 seconds. Watch the shrimps carefully; they should be tender and succulent, not rubbery. If you have any doubt, stop the cooking by quickly adding the pasta. Turn the heat down to medium. Add the drained hot pasta to the skillet, and toss with lemon juice to taste. Add salt as needed. Turn the pasta into the warmed bowl, and serve in heated soup dishes. (Cheese is not used with seafood sauces.)

Suggestions   **Wine:** Pour a dry Albana or Trebbiano from Emilia-Romagna. From outside the region, drink a Pinot Grigio or Chardonnay from the Veneto or Friuli regions.

Menu: Serve Garlic Crostini with Pancetta (page 28) as an antipasto, then the pasta as a light supper dish; or follow the pasta with Giovanna's Wine-Basted Rabbit (page 284) and Caramelized Almond Tart (page 409).

Cook's Notes **Olive Oil:** A delicate, flowery oil from Liguria blends well with the sauce. See page 485 for more information.

Using Stock: Using a poultry-based stock is an old trick to bring out the natural sweetness of shrimps and other shellfish.

Bolognese tavern sign, "The Two Crayfish," 17th century, by Giuseppe Maria Mitelli

Tortellini in Broth Villa Gaidello
Tortellini in Brodo Villa Gaidello

The tortellino (singular of tortellini) is the most famous and distinctively shaped pasta of Emilia-Romagna. Tortellini in broth mark Sunday dinners, holidays and special occasions. They evoke memories of mothers and grandmothers who cooked like angels.

Today in America commercially produced tortellini are so commonplace, you might think I exaggerate in telling you how marvelous homemade ones can be. But pure ambrosia is a bowl of your own handmade tortellini floating in homemade broth.

This recipe from the farm women of Villa Gaidello is especially fine. The filling is simple and exceptionally flavorful. Enveloping it in Villa Gaidello's pasta, flavored with Parmigiano-Reggiano, nutmeg, and pepper, makes these tortellini even more distinctive. Serve them in the classic manner, in broth, as described below, or tossed with a little butter and Parmigiano-Reggiano cheese. Tortellini are overwhelmed by complicated sauces and heavy seasonings. This recipe can be halved.

[Makes about 140 pieces; serves 8 to 10 as a first course]

Filling

5 to 6 ounces boneless top loin beef steak, trimmed of fat

4 ounces mortadella

4 ounces Prosciutto di Parma, thinly sliced

1 cup (4 ounces) freshly grated Italian Parmigiano-Reggiano cheese

Pasta and Broth

1 recipe Egg Pasta Villa Gaidello (page 81)

5 quarts Poultry/Meat Stock (page 66) or Quick Stock (page 68)

Salt and freshly ground black pepper to taste

2 to 3 cups (8 to 12 ounces) freshly grated Italian Parmigiano-Reggiano cheese

Method

Working Ahead: *The filling can be made a day ahead; cover and refrigerate. Filled tortellini can be refrigerated, covered with a towel, up to 12 hours. They freeze successfully up to 3 months. Freeze the pastas spread out on baking sheets. Then turn them into rigid plastic storage containers and return to the freezer. Boil them while still frozen, allowing a few extra moments of cooking.*

Making the Filling: In a food processor fitted with the steel blade, grind the steak very fine. Transfer it to a medium-size glass or stainless steel bowl. Place the mortadella and prosciutto in the processor, and grind very fine. Add to the bowl along with the 1 cup of Parmigiano-Reggiano. Blend the ingredients into a stiff paste, cover, and refrigerate until ready to use.

If working by hand, finely chop the meats until they are almost a paste. Blend in the cheese, cover, and refrigerate.

Shaping the Tortellini: Work with a quarter of the dough at a time, keeping the remainder loosely wrapped in plastic. Stretch and thin, by hand or by machine, until you can detect the color of a ball of the filling through the dough (see pages 83 to 86). Divide the sheet in half, and cover both halves with plastic wrap to keep them from drying out.

Cut one sheet into 1¾-inch rounds, using a small glass or a biscuit cutter. Cover the rounds to keep them from drying out. Make little crescents with ¼ teaspoon of the filling. Place a crescent in the center of each round, fold the dough over, and tightly pinch the edges together to seal thoroughly. Then bring the tails of the crescent together, overlapping them, and twist one over the other. Seal well so that you have tiny doughnut shapes, with the sealed edges curving over the filling. Spread the finished tortellini on flat baskets or baking sheets covered with kitchen towels, taking care to not let them touch. Continue working until the sheets of dough are used up. Leave the tortellini uncovered as you work. Turn them over after an hour or so to keep them from getting soggy. Dry any dough scraps to use in soups and where maltgliati (page 88) are called for.

Roll out the remaining dough (still working with only a quarter at a time), and repeat the process until all the dough is used up. Any leftover filling could be frozen for future use and is delicious stuffed into flattened chicken breasts.

Cooking and Serving: Have a tureen and soup dishes warming in a low oven. Turn the stock into an 8- to 10-quart pot and bring to a boil. Season with salt and pepper. Drop in the tortellini and cook a minute or two. Then taste one. Fresh tortellini will cook in 2 to 5 minutes. They should be tender but still have some "bite," or firmness. Drier or frozen tortellini will take a little longer. Ladle the broth and tortellini into the warmed tureen. Pass the extra Parmigiano-Reggiano cheese for sprinkling over the soup as a final and vital seasoning.

continued

Suggestions   **Wine:** The meaty flavors of Tortellini in Broth are too complex for anything but a fresh, bright, grapy red. In Emilia-Romagna, Lambrusco is the wine of choice for tortellini. Here, seek out a dry red Freisa d'Asti or "La Monella" of Braida di Giacomo Bologna from Piemonte, a fruity white Piemontese Arneis, or Sicily's white Rapitalà.

Menu: In Romagna and southern Emilia, Christmas, weddings, and feast days begin with Tortellini in Broth; then two or three other pastas are served in progression. After a pause, Christmas Capon (page 281) and vegetables come to the table. Desserts are likely to be Paola Bini's Sweet Ravioli (page 424) or an assortment of baked tartlets, Home-Style Jam Cake (page 401), turnovers, and "Keeping Cakes" like the ones found on pages 456 to 464. For a simpler elegant menu have the tortellini, then Balsamic Roast Chicken (page 279), Sweet Fennel Jewish Style (page 335), and Torta Barozzi (page 395) for dessert.

Cook's Notes   **Beef:** Steaks cut from the top loin blithely change names from one part of the United States to another. New York steak, Delmonico steak, club steak, Kansas City strip, and shell steak all come from the tender top loin and are ideal for this recipe.

Prosciutto: Taste prosciutto before buying. If it is salty, reduce the quantity in half and increase the beef by 2 ounces.

Stock: For the most authentic flavor, cook the tortellini in Poultry/Meat Stock. Quick Stock comes together more quickly, but it lacks the depth and fullness of flavor that sets apart Poultry/Meat Stock.

Variation with Butter and Cheese: This is the other classic presentation of tortellini. Cook the tortellini in stock if possible (it could be saved and frozen for later use) drain, and toss with a little butter and Parmigiano-Reggiano cheese. Serve in heated soup dishes.

Variation with Leftovers (La Tardura): In Emilia, leftover Tortellini in Broth from Sunday dinner is made into a Monday night supper, or *la tardura* (meaning late, belated or left back), by beating 1 egg into about 1¼ cups grated Parmigiano-Reggiano for every 10 cups of leftovers. Reheat the soup to a simmer and stir in the egg mixture. Keep stirring until the cheese and egg firms, forming threads. Serve hot. These measurements are flexible.

Regional Tortellini Variations

Travel from one small province to the next within Emilia-Romagna, and you will discover tortellini-type pastas taking on different names, varied fillings, and even slightly different shapes.

To compound the geographic variations, no two cooks in any one place will make tortellini/cappelletti exactly the same way. So even though these recipes are etched by tradition, their color and verve are determined by the cooks who make them.

Each filling recipe uses 1 recipe Egg Pasta (page 80).

"Little Hats" Faenza Style
Cappelletti Faentini

From Romagna's ceramic center, famed since the 1300s for its pottery, comes these meatless cappelletti. Their individuality comes from the flavoring of lemon and the tangy fresh cheeses that abound in Faenza. Luckily we can approximate two of those cheeses, squaquerone and ricotta, in our own kitchens. Cut the pasta into 2-inch squares with a crenelated pasta wheel (instead of the rounds described in the tortellini recipe). Cappelletti Faentini are modeled after the tricornered hats of Napoleon's army.

[Makes about 85 pieces]

¾ cup (6 ounces) creamy fresh whole-milk ricotta cheese (see Note)

½ cup Fresh Squaquerone Cheese (page 386)

1¾ cups (7 ounces) freshly grated Italian Parmigiano-Reggiano cheese

½ teaspoon freshly grated lemon zest

⅛ teaspoon freshly ground black pepper

⅛ teaspoon freshly grated nutmeg

Salt to taste

1 egg yolk

Blend all the ingredients together except the egg. Taste for salt, stir in the egg yolk, cover, and chill 2 hours or overnight before using.

Fill, shape, and cook in broth as described in the main recipe (page 134).

Cook's Notes **Ricotta Cheese:** If creamy, sweet ricotta is unavailable, make your own from the recipe on page 454.

Folklore: Honoring the oldest in the family with a single giant cappelletti in broth is an old Faenza custom. In dialect the big pasta was *caplett d'e nunen* or *caplett a e vecc d'la ca'* (cappelletti of nonno, or grandfather; or cappelletti for the old one of the house).

Christmas Cappelletti
Cappelletti Ferraresi

Until about 40 years ago, these were eaten in Ferrara only at Christmas. Even in the humblest homes, cooking and serving these cappelletti was treated with all the anticipation and ceremony befitting a royal banquet. Old recipes like this one, scented with cinnamon and originally flavored with cured pork collar, descend directly from 16th-century pasta fillings. Today's stuffings closely resemble Bologna's or Modena's formulas, using salami and salt pork instead of prosciutto and mortadella. Make the cappelletti by cutting 1½-inch squares instead of rounds.

[Makes about 150 pieces]

6 ounces boneless pork loin

4 ounces very lean salt pork, cooked 5 minutes in boiling water

Salt and freshly ground black pepper

6 ounces boneless turkey breast

¼ cup dry white wine

2 ounces salami (made without fennel and hot pepper)

About ¼ cup water

1 cup (4 ounces) freshly grated Italian Parmigiano-Reggiano cheese

⅛ teaspoon ground cinnamon

⅛ teaspoon freshly grated nutmeg

1 egg, beaten

Preheat the oven to 350°F. Place the pork and salt pork in a shallow pan, sprinkle lightly with salt and pepper, and roast about 20 minutes. Add the turkey breast and white wine, and roast another 20 minutes, or until the breast is firm. Baste the meats often with the pan juices. Remove the meats with a slotted spoon, cool, and cut into cubes. Grind the meats, including the salami, in a food processor or meat grinder until finely ground but not puréed. Turn into a bowl.

Spoon off all but about 1 tablespoon fat from the pan juices. Liquefy the delicious brown glaze on the pan bottom by swishing in the water and simmering over medium heat, scraping up any brown bits clinging to the pan. Boil down to about 2 tablespoons and add to the meats. Fold in the cheese, spices, and egg. Cover and refrigerate up to 24 hours.

Fill, shape, and cook as described in the main recipe (page 134).

Cappelletti Imola Style
Cappelletti Imolesi

According to Imola historian Aureliano Bassani, these cappelletti imitate the hats of the Spanish soldiers who invaded Italy in the 17th century. Imola lies between Bologna and Faenza, and interestingly, her filling seems to be a combination of Bologna's meats and Faenza's fresh cheeses. Make the cappelletti by cutting the pasta into 1½-inch squares instead of rounds.

[Makes about 150 pieces]

2 ounces mild Italian sausage (made without fennel), cooked
6 ounces roasted pork loin
4 ounces mortadella
1½ cups (6 ounces) freshly grated Italian Parmigiano-Reggiano cheese

¼ cup creamy fresh ricotta cheese (see Note)
Large pinch of freshly grated nutmeg
1 egg

In a food processor fitted with the steel blade, blend all the ingredients until finely ground but not puréed. Turn into a bowl, cover, and refrigerate 3 hours to overnight.

Fill, shape, and cook as described in the main recipe (page 134).

Cook's Notes **Ricotta Cheese:** If creamy ricotta is not available, make your own from the recipe on page 454.

Tortellini Bologna Style
Tortellini alla Bolognese

No two Bolognese cooks agree on the filling of their most famous pasta. Constants are breast of turkey or capon, prosciutto, fresh pork, and Parmigiano-Reggiano cheese; the rest is passionately debated. This particular blend meets with more agreement than most. Modena's tortellini are similar, but often include about two ounces of veal loin and double the amount of Parmigiano-Reggiano cheese. And they are flatter in shape. Serve these tortellini in broth or with butter and cheese as outlined in the Villa Gaidello recipe.

[Makes about 140 pieces]

2 tablespoons unsalted butter

5 ounces boneless pork loin

3 ounces boneless turkey breast

1 large California bay laurel leaf, broken

4 ounces mortadella

4 ounces Prosciutto di Parma

½ cup (2 ounces) freshly grated Italian Parmigiano-Reggiano cheese

Large pinch of freshly grated nutmeg

1 egg, beaten

Melt the butter in a 12-inch skillet over medium-high heat. While the butter is melting, thinly slice the pork and turkey breast. Add the pork, turkey, and bay laurel to the skillet. Cook over medium-high heat, turning often, until the turkey pieces and pork pick up color. Reduce the heat to medium-low, cover, and cook 15 minutes, or until both meats are firm when pressed with the finger. Discard the bay leaf and cool the meats in the skillet about 10 minutes.

Scrape the contents of the pan into a food processor fitted with the steel blade. Add the mortadella and prosciutto, and process until finely ground but not puréed. Turn into a bowl, and fold in the cheese, nutmeg, and egg. Cover and refrigerate 3 hours or overnight.

Fill, shape, and cook as described in the main recipe (page 134).

Liberty-style advertisement for Bolognese maker's Tortellini and Zuppa Imperiale, circa 1900. The Atti shop still hand-makes and sells Tortellini and Zuppa Imperiale today.

Tortelloni of Artichokes and Mascarpone
Tortelloni di Carciofi e Mascarpone

Sautéing artichoke bottoms with basil, garlic, and lemon, then finishing the blend with Parmigiano-Reggiano and mascarpone, creates a sumptuous filling. Encase it in silky pasta, shape it into big tortelloni, and you have the fantasy dish first created by Tamburini in Bologna (see box).

[Makes about 45 pieces; serves 4 to 6]

Filling
3 large lemons
2 cups water
7 medium or 6 large artichokes
1 tablespoon unsalted butter
1 tablespoon extra-virgin olive oil
6 tablespoons minced onion
1 tablespoon minced carrot
Salt and freshly ground black
    pepper
2 large cloves garlic, minced
3 tablespoons minced fresh basil
    leaves, or 2 teaspoons dried basil
½ cup Poultry/Meat Stock (page
    66) or Quick Stock (page 68)
8 ounces mascarpone cheese
    (see Note)

¼ cup (1 ounce) freshly grated
    Italian Parmigiano-Reggiano
    cheese
Pasta and Sauce
¾ recipe Wine Pasta (1 jumbo
    egg, ⅓ cup wine, and about 11
    ounces flour; page 82)
1½ cups Poultry/Meat Stock
    (page 66) or Quick Stock (page
    68), reduced to ½ cup
4 tablespoons (2 ounces) unsalted
    butter
Salt and freshly ground black
    pepper to taste
8 quarts salted water
1 cup (4 ounces) freshly grated
    Parmigiano-Reggiano cheese

Method

Working Ahead: *This is not the sort of dish you whip together after coming home from work. The stuffing can be made a day ahead. The finished tortelloni will hold, lightly covered, 12 hours in the refrigerator; turn twice to keep them from getting soggy. They do not freeze well.*

Preparing the Artichokes: Remove the zest from 1½ lemons using a zester that cuts it into thin strips. Set it aside. Halve the remaining lemon and squeeze the juice from 5 halves into a medium-size stainless steel or glass bowl. Add the 2 cups water, and set aside.

continued

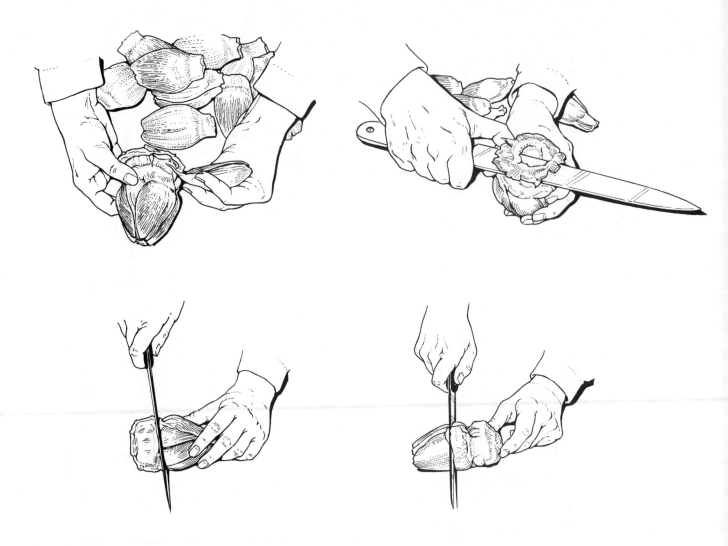

Create artichoke bottoms by cutting away the stem of each artichoke. Then, with a sharp, narrow-bladed knife trim away all the dark green leaves from the bottom of the artichoke and from the sides around its base. As the side leaves are cut away, the solid pale green bottom will be revealed. Frequently rub the cut areas with the remaining lemon half to keep them from darkening. Lay the artichoke on its side and slice away the top two thirds with all the leaves. Now you have the bottom with its fuzzy choke. Scrape out the choke with a spoon. Immediately immerse the finished bottom in the prepared lemon water. Repeat with the remaining artichokes.

Making the Filling: Drain the artichoke bottoms, pat dry, and cut into eighths. Heat the butter and oil in a 12-inch skillet over medium-high to high heat. Add the artichoke bottoms and cook until they begin to color. Add the onion, carrot, and a light sprinkling of salt and pepper. Cook over medium-high to high heat, stirring frequently, 8 minutes, or until the onion is browned and the artichokes are golden. Turn the heat down to medium, add the garlic, basil, and the reserved lemon zest, and cook 30 seconds. Add the stock and bring to a boil, scraping up any brown bits from the bottom of the skillet.

Cover and simmer over low heat 2 to 3 minutes, or until the bottoms are still a bit firm when pierced with the tip of a knife. Uncover, and take a minute or two to cook down the juices to a moist glaze on the bottom of the skillet. The artichokes should be cooked through but still have some crispness. Cool to room temperature, and transfer to a food processor. Use the on/off pulse until finely chopped; do not purée. Turn into a bowl and blend with the cheeses. Cover and chill until ready to use.

Preparing the Tortelloni: Prepare the dough as directed on pages 83 to 86, and roll out about a third at a time. Cut it into rounds with a 3½-inch biscuit cutter or glass. Moisten the edges of each round with water, and place a generous teaspoon of the filling in the center of each round. Fold in half, sealing the edges well. Then bring both ends of the half-moon pasta together, overlapping them, and twist one over the other. Seal together by pinching. Lay the tortelloni on flat baskets lined with kitchen towels, making sure they do not touch. Refrigerate if holding more than 1 hour.

Cooking and Saucing the Tortelloni: Warm a serving bowl and shallow soup dishes in a low oven. Bring the reduced stock to a simmer, and whisk in the butter until it is creamy but not entirely melted. Season with salt and pepper. Keep warm. Bring the salted water to a vigorous boil. Drop in the tortelloni. If very fresh they will be ready after boiling no more than 1 minute or so. If they have waited several hours, they could boil up to 4 minutes. Taste one to be sure that their edges still have a little resistance or "bite." Lift the pastas from the water with a large skimmer, and place them in the heated serving bowl or individual dishes. Sprinkle each layer or serving with a little sauce and about 2 tablespoons cheese. Serve at once.

Suggestions   **Wine:** A dry Albana di Romagna Secco, or a Tocai from Friuli.

Menu: Follow the tortelloni with a simple but equally festive main course, such as Giovanna's Wine-Basted Rabbit (page 284), Porcini Veal Chops (page 290), or Erminia's Pan-Crisped Chicken (page 270).

continued

Cook's Notes **Mascarpone:** This creamy fresh cheese is made in two styles: as a compressed, sliceable loaf and as a spoonable cheese with the consistency of thick whipped cream. The tortellini filling needs the thick cream type. Mascarpone spoils quickly, so always taste before buying, and do not plan on keeping it more than a few days.

An Unorthodox Variation: Thin the filling with a little broth for an excellent sauce for tagliatelle.

A Bolognese Fantasy

In Italy, an improvised dish not following any established tradition is called a *fantasia,* or fantasy. These tortelloni were the fantasy of Tamburini, Bologna's fancy food emporium. Tamburini's windows are always crammed with the kind of home-style dishes that make you consider giving up on your own cooking altogether. While walking past the shop one autumn morning, I eyed a platter of big tortelloni stuffed with artichokes, mascarpone, and fresh white truffles. It looked too good to resist. I bought several and carefully peeled back the fresh pasta to taste the filling. It was splendid. Italy's white truffles are pungent with scents of garlic and earth. Combining them with artichokes, creamy mascarpone, the flintiness of Parmigiano, and a hint of lemon was pure genius. The combination stayed with me. After toying with all sorts of formulas, I finally came close to reproducing the one I tasted from Tamburini. Some adjustments were necessary. Fresh white truffles are not easy to come by on this side of the Atlantic, hence the hint of garlic. Basil softens the garlic's edge, sparks the artichokes, and accentuates the mascarpone's natural sweetness.

Cappellacci with Sweet Squash
Cappellacci con la Zucca

*T*he Bolognese call the people of Ferrara "squash eaters" because of their love for the sweet orange squash that fills these cappellacci. The pastas themselves step straight out of the Renaissance. Filling them with squash and Parmigiano-Reggiano cheese perpetuates that period's passion for sweet/savory flavors. Cappellacci with Sweet Squash are bold and undainty, shaped like oversized cartoons of tortelloni. They taste best when coated only with melted sage-scented butter and crumbles of Parmesan.

[Makes about 80 pieces; serves 6 to 8]

Filling

1 tablespoon vegetable oil

1½ pounds butternut squash

12 ounces sweet potatoes or yams

1 tablespoon sugar (optional)

1 cup (4 ounces) freshly grated Italian Parmigiano-Reggiano cheese

Freshly grated nutmeg to taste

Freshly ground black pepper to taste

Pasta and Sauce

1¼ recipes Egg Pasta (page 80)

5 to 7 tablespoons (2½ to 3½ ounces) unsalted butter

5 large fresh sage leaves, or 5 whole dried sage leaves

8 to 10 quarts salted water

⅔ to 1 cup freshly grated Italian Parmigiano-Reggiano cheese

Freshly ground black pepper (optional)

Method

Working Ahead: *The filling will hold 24 hours, covered, in the refrigerator. The cappellacci can be filled and shaped up to 1 day ahead. Once shaped, cover them with a cloth and refrigerate; turn them several times to protect the pasta from becoming gummy. Cook straight from the refrigerator. These do not freeze well.*

Making the Filling: Preheat the oven to 375°F. Cover a baking sheet with foil, and lightly oil the foil. Cut the squash in half vertically, scoop out the seeds, and turn them cut side down on the foil. Scrub the potatoes, and make a 2-inch slit in the skin. Bake the squash and the potatoes 1 hour, or until the potatoes feel soft when squeezed and the squash are easily pierced with a knife. Allow to cool.

Scoop out the flesh of both vegetables. Put it through a food mill, or purée for a few seconds in a food processor. Taste for sweetness. The squash/potato mixture should be quite sweet but not sugary. If necessary, add the tablespoon of sugar. Then

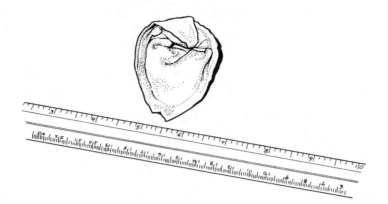

stir in the cheese. Grate in enough nutmeg to give just a soft taste of it to the filling. Add enough pepper to give sparkle, but do not overwhelm the filling.

Shaping the Cappellacci: Follow the directions (pages 83 to 86) for rolling out the pasta dough, making it thin enough to detect color through the sheet. Once it is rolled out, keep all but about one third of the sheet covered with plastic wrap. Using a knife, cut 3½- to 4-inch squares. Cut no more than about five at a time to keep the dough from drying out.

Place a generous spoonful of filling (a ball about 1¼ to 1½ inches in diameter) in the center of each square. Fold the squares in half, forming triangles, and forcing out the air as you seal the edges together (moisten the edges with a little water if necessary). Then form an oversize tortellino by bringing the two ends together, folding one over the other, and sealing them. Place them on towel-lined baskets or baking sheets without touching. Pull back the plastic wrap on another third of the pasta, and cut more squares. Continue filling and shaping until done.

Cooking and Serving: Melt the butter with the sage leaves in a small saucepan. Set aside and keep warm. Warm a serving bowl and shallow soup dishes in a low oven. Bring the salted water to a vigorous boil. Drop in the cappellacci, and cook about 3 minutes at a full boil, or until the edges of the pasta are tender but still firm to the bite. These are too fragile to drain in a colander. Instead, turn off the heat, and use a big skimmer or large flat slotted spoon to gently scoop out the cappellacci, pulling about a third from the water. Work quickly so as not to overcook the pasta. Drain the water from the pastas by holding the skimmer over the pot a few seconds. Then slip them into the warmed serving bowl. Quickly sprinkle with about a third of the melted butter and a third of the Parmigiano-Reggiano. Repeat the process, making another two layers. Season lightly with pepper if desired, and serve immediately. (The dish could be garnished with a few fresh sage leaves.)

Suggestions   **Wine:** From the region, a soft, fruity white wine like Bianco del Bosco, or an Albana Secco. From other parts of Italy drink a Tocai from Friuli, or a Müller-Thurgau from Terlano or Valle Isarco, both in the Trentino–Alto Adige region.

Menu: Serve before January Pork (page 312), Erminia's Pan-Crisped Chicken (page 270), Basil and Balsamic Veal Scallops (page 296), a Thanksgiving turkey, or glazed American-style baked ham.

Cook's Notes **The Parma Version:** Make Parma's *tortelli di zucca* by trimming sheets of rolled-out dough to about 5 inches wide and 18 inches long. Dot with two rows of small dabs of filling, 1½ inches in from the long edges. Fold over the edges and seal around the filling. Using a crenelated pastry cutter, cut into rectangles about 2 inches by 1½ inches. Serve with melted butter (not flavored with sage) and cheese.

Being There

Butternut squash (or fresh pumpkin) blended with sweet potato approximates the flavor of the squashes from Ferrara and Parma, which have a spicy sweetness and a moist texture. When exploring the open markets in either city, you will often see bright orange slices of these big squashes, whose shape resembles a violin or an elongated figure eight. Take a moment to inhale their bouquet; it suggests flowers, cinnamon, and sugar all at the same time.

One True Recipe?

The word *cappellacci* comes from *cappello* (hat), supposedly inspired by the tricornered hats of Napoleon's time. I think they more closely resemble men's hats of the 15th and 16th centuries, when plumped crowns and soft-turned brims were fashionable. Certainly their play of sweet against savory is straight out of that time—such a perfect dish for Ferrara, where it often feels as if the town clock stopped somewhere in the mid-1500s. The first written recipe for cappellacci with sweet squash appeared around 1584, but historians think the dish had already existed for many years. Possibly true, as illustrations of squashes resembling the ones used today are found in northern Italian medical handbooks of the 14th century.

The idea of a sweet/savory squash filling spread from Ferrara to her neighbors. Just across the Po River, squash-filled pastas are eaten in the city of Mantua. There, square-shaped pastas served as a first course are stuffed with squash, Parmigiano-Reggiano, crumbled amaretti cookies, and sometimes *mostarda di Cremona* (whole candied fruits in spiced syrup). Modena, Ferrara's Emilian neighbor to the west and long under her rule, eats squash-filled pastas only on Christmas Eve. Parma has almost the same filling as Ferrara, but in a tamer casing—rectangular *tortelli di zucca*. Reggio's filling resembles Parma's, sometimes adding amaretti—an ingredient not worried over in Mantua, but whose validity is heatedly debated by Emilians. As you roam Emilia and Romagna, you will find raisins added here, pine nuts there, and even tart/sweet grape syrup stirred into some renditions. Only two constants prevail: the pastas are always served as a first course, and dispute never ceases over the one "true" recipe.

Anolini of Parma
Anolini di Parma in Brodo

Joyous occasions in Parma are marked with these coin-shaped pastas, whether they be homecomings, anniversaries, Christmas or Easter. Parma is the only place I know of in Italy where the meat usually stuffed into a pasta is cooked for hours or even days, then tossed away, and only its cooking juices are kept.

But the stuffing of these little pastas is not as extravagant as it might seem. A pot roast (stracotto) is cooked from 12 hours to 3 days, giving its all to a braising liquid of wine, broth, and vegetables. Every bit of flavor is pressed from the meat before its concentrated sauce is blended with toasted bread crumbs, Parmigiano-Reggiano cheese, and nutmeg, and then stuffed into small discs of fresh pasta. Anolini are always served in homemade broth. Considering that the filling is almost a meal in itself, even butter and cheese seem excessive.

This recipe is based on one by Professor Guglielmo Capacchi, from his book, The Home Cooking of Parma (La Cucina Popolare Parmigiana).

[Makes about 120 pieces; serves 8 to 12]

Filling

7 tablespoons (3½ ounces) unsalted butter

1 small to medium onion, minced

1 small carrot, minced

1 small stalk celery with leaves, minced

2-pound beef rump roast, trimmed of fat

Salt and freshly ground black pepper

3 whole cloves

2 teaspoons imported Italian tomato paste

2 tablespoons water

7 to 9 cups Poultry/Meat Stock (page 66) or Quick Stock (page 68)

2 cups dry red wine (see Note)

1½ tablespoons unsalted butter

2 cups fresh bread crumbs

1½ cups (6 ounces) freshly grated Italian Parmigiano-Reggiano cheese

Pinch of freshly grated nutmeg

1 egg, beaten

Pasta and Broth

1½ recipes Egg Pasta (page 80)

2½ quarts Poultry/Meat Stock

2 cups (8 ounces) freshly grated Italian Parmigiano-Reggiano cheese

continued

Method   **Working Ahead:** *The pot roast* (stracotto) *can be cooked up to 3 days before you make the pastas. I usually cook it on a weekend when I am working around the house and can occasionally check its progress. Cover and refrigerate the resulting sauce. The toasted bread crumbs hold well in the refrigerator, in a sealed container, 2 days.*

Of course, shaping the filled pastas is speeded up when done with friends. They can be filled up to 12 hours before cooking. Store, covered with a cloth, in the refrigerator. Because of the pot roast's long cooking time, the filling must be started at least 20 hours before serving the anolini.

Cooking the Stracotto: Please see "The Old Way" in the Cook's Notes before beginning.

Melt the 7 tablespoons butter in a heavy 3½- to 4-quart saucepan over medium heat. Add the onion, carrot, and celery, and then the beef. Lightly salt and pepper the meat. Slowly brown the beef on all sides over medium to medium-low heat about 30 minutes, building a foundation of deep flavors. The meat should be a deep, crusty brown. Add the cloves, the tomato paste, water, and enough stock to barely cover the meat (more will be needed later). Heat until the broth bubbles very, very slowly. Cover with a doubled piece of parchment paper that has a slit about 3 inches long cut in the center. Then partially cover the pan with the lid.

Pour ¼ cup of the wine over the slit every hour or so until the 2 cups are used up. Keep the heat low so the liquids bubble very slowly. Cook about 9 hours, turning the meat two or three times. Then remove the lid, but leave the parchment, and simmer another 3 hours, spooning in more stock to keep the meat barely covered with liquid. At this point the meat can be refrigerated overnight. The next day, continue cooking with only the slitted parchment on top 4 to 6 hours, or until the meat literally falls apart when touched with a fork.

Turn the contents of the pan into a strainer, and press on the meat with the back of a large spoon, extracting as much of its juices as possible. Then discard the meat, as all its flavor is now in the cooking juices. Turn the juices back into the saucepan and boil down, 10 to 15 minutes, to about 1 to 1¼ cups. This sauce should be richly flavored. Turn it into a bowl and allow to cool.

Toasting the Bread Crumbs: While the beef is cooking, dot a baking sheet with thin slices of the 1½ tablespoons butter. Spread the crumbs over the sheet, and bake at 350°F, stirring often, 8 to 10 minutes, or until golden. Cool.

Finishing the Filling: Combine the sauce, crumbs, Parmigiano-Reggiano, and nutmeg. Taste for salt. Add the egg, blend well, cover, and refrigerate until needed.

Preparing the Pasta: Have handy several large flat baskets or baking sheets covered with kitchen towels. Working with a quarter of the dough at a time, use a pasta machine or rolling pin to thin and stretch the dough until it is so sheer that you can see color through it (see pages 83 to 86).

Cut the dough into strips about 3½ inches wide. Protect the strips from drying by covering them with plastic wrap. Pull back the wrap on about 6 to 8 inches of a strip, and dot the dough about 1 inch in from the edge with a row of ½-teaspoon mounds of filling. Space them about 1 inch apart. Fold the dough over and seal around each mound, pressing out air pockets as you go. If the dough seems dry, dip your finger in water and moisten around each mound before folding the pasta over. Use a 1½-inch diameter glass or round cutter to cut out each anolino. (They can also be cut as half moons.) Spread them out on the baskets without touching. Repeat the process until the pasta and filling are used up.

Cooking and Serving: Have a tureen and shallow soup dishes heating in a low oven. Bring the 2½ quarts stock to a vigorous boil, tasting to see if it needs salt and pepper. Add the anolini to the broth and boil 3 to 10 minutes, depending upon how dry they are. Taste for doneness; the edges should be a little chewy. Serve in the warmed tureen or ladle into soup dishes. Pass the remaining cheese as the final and vital seasoning—a generous teaspoon should be sprinkled over each serving.

Suggestions **Wine:** In Parma drink a fresh fizzy red Rosso di Colli di Parma. From other parts of Italy try a full white Chardonnay from Trentino–Alto Adige, or a Pinot Bianco from Friuli.

Menu: Before anolini serve Prosciutto di Parma (page 14). Christmas Capon (page 281) is the traditional holiday main dish after anolini. Less festive second courses are Pan-Roasted Quail (page 283), Maria Bertuzzi's Lemon Chicken (page 273), or Porcini Veal Chops (page 290).

Cook's Notes **The Old Way:** In Parma *stracotto* is cooked in a terracotta *stracottiera,* a pot whose form has not changed in several hundred years. Just large enough to hold the pot roast snugly, it has a porous concave lid where the wine is placed so that it may slowly seep over the meat. Professor Capacchi describes his mother covering the meat with a cracked plate that served the same purpose, allowing wine to seep through the crack, slowly basting the meat. If you have a plate that has a crack in the middle, do wash it well and use it.

My improvised *stracottiera* is done with a heavy saucepan large enough to hold the meat snugly and a double thickness of parchment paper with a slit in the middle. This may be fanaticism on my part, but the fragrance of the wine slowly evaporating on the warm paper and over the meat, mixed with the meat's aromas, fills the house with such wonderful smells that the little extra effort is highly worthwhile—a lovely bonus from an exceptional dish.

Red Wine: Cook the *stracotto* in a Barolo, Barbaresco, or a big Zinfandel.

Piacenza Variation: Marubei: Make a quarter of the *stracotto* recipe, cooking it only 4 hours. Grind the meat along with 8 ounces each roasted veal and pork. Finely chop 8 ounces calf's or lamb's brains that have been gently poached until firm. Boil down the *stracotto* sauce until rich (about ⅓ cup) and blend with the meats, brains, bread crumbs, Parmigiano, and 2 eggs. Fill pastas as described above.

A Little History

It is intriguing to think that this luxurious pasta may have been born of crusts of bread discarded after Medieval banquets. Once the trenchers, or "plates," of crisp bread were soaked with meat juices, they were thrown away, to be gathered by peasants who waited eagerly for any leftovers. Imagine an economical housewife stretching the discarded trenchers by using them to fill pastas, making a one-dish meal for her family. It is a logical explanation, if a little too tidy.

According to Guglielmo Capacchi, authority on all things Parmesan, the first mention of anolini was in 1570. That year Bartolomeo Scappi, Bolognese cook to Pope Pius V, published a recipe, "To make Tortelletti with Pork Belly or Other Material that in (Common or) Vulgar Language are Called Annolini." The dish contained spices, raisins, and meats and had a sauce of cheese, sugar, and cinnamon.

By the early 19th century anolini had lost their sweet ingredients and were firmly ensconced in Parma's culinary repertoire as a first course. Every family had special cutters for the round or half-moon-shaped pastas. Smooth discs are typical of Parma province. Along the Po River in neighboring Piacenza, crenelated cutters are used, actual meats (not only cooking juices) are added to the filling, and anolini become *marubei*. To the south of Parma in Reggio, anolini remain round, are called *cappelletti,* and have chicken giblets added to Piacenza's recipe. In Parma, almost everyone agrees that anolini are made with beef—although some old-timers insist that donkey, which was popular for many years, gives even better flavor. There are two different forms of the pasta, depending upon who is the cook. Half moons are less wasteful and appear often, but coin-size discs are more traditional. Anolini's coin shape actually comes from a coin, the Marie Louise silver piece of over 150 years ago. The 1½-inch size fits nicely into a large soup spoon and is easily cut out with a liqueur or shot glass.

Tortelli of Ricotta and Fresh Greens
Tortelli d'Erbette

Tortelli d'Erbette is Parma's version of the ubiquitous cheese-stuffed pasta and is all but sacred within its borders. The simple filling exudes a natural sweetness and freshness. Mild local greens (the erbette), closely resembling Swiss chard, are mixed with fresh ricotta, Parmigiano-Reggiano cheese and a suggestion of nutmeg.

There is a trick to the pasta. It has to be substantial enough to hold the soft, moist filling, yet sheer enough to make light tortelli. Many old recipes suggest decreasing the number of eggs and adding more water for a lighter, more resilient pasta. Tortelli d'Erbette are always dressed with nothing more than butter and Parmigiano-Reggiano cheese.

[Makes 120 pieces; serves 10 to 12 as a first course, 8 as a main dish]

Filling

1½ cups water

1½ pounds Swiss chard

1 pound fresh whole-milk or homemade ricotta cheese (see Note)

2 cups (8 ounces) freshly grated Italian Parmigiano-Reggiano cheese

Freshly grated nutmeg

Salt and freshly ground black pepper

2 eggs, beaten

Pasta and Sauce

1 recipe Wine Pasta (page 82), using 3 jumbo eggs, ½ cup water instead of wine, and 4¼ cups plus 2 tablespoons flour (17 ounces)

8 tablespoons (4 ounces) unsalted butter

12 quarts salted water

About 1½ cups freshly grated Italian Parmigiano-Reggiano cheese

Method

Working Ahead: *The filling can be made the day before you fill the pasta. You can fill and shape the tortelli up to 12 hours before serving, though they are best eaten within about 4 hours. Store them in the refrigerator on towel-lined baskets or baking sheets, making sure the pieces do not touch; cover with another towel, and turn every 2 hours to ensure even drying. These do not freeze well.*

Making the Filling: Bring the 1½ cups water to a boil in a medium saucepan. While it is heating, trim away the Swiss chard's stalks (reserve them for another use). Wash the leaves under cold running water. Drop them into the boiling water and cook, covered, until wilted, about 5 minutes. Drain in a sieve, let cool briefly, and then squeeze out as much liquid as possible. Chop the leaves very fine.

continued

In a medium-size bowl, blend the chard with the ricotta, Parmigiano-Reggiano, and a generous pinch of nutmeg. Add salt and pepper to taste. Stir in the eggs until thoroughly blended. Turn the mixture into a stainless steel or glass container, cover, and chill until ready to use.

Shaping the Tortelli: Have handy several large flat baskets or baking sheets covered with kitchen towels. Stretch and thin the pasta as directed on pages 83 to 86, working a quarter of the dough at a time. You should be able to see color and form through the dough. Cut it into sheets 5½ inches wide, covering them with plastic wrap to keep them from drying out.

Make a row of small spoonfuls of filling along each of the two long edges of a pasta strip. Place the filling about 1 inch in from the edge, and space the spoonfuls about 1½ inches apart. Fold the two long edges over, toward the strip's center, so they cover the filling. Seal the dough around the filling, eliminating air pockets as you work. Then, using a pasta wheel, cut rectangular tortelli, about 1½ by 2 inches, around each mound of filling. Arrange in single layers, without touching, on the baskets.

Cooking and Serving the Tortelli: Warm a serving bowl and shallow soup dishes in a low oven. Melt the butter in a small pan and keep warm. Bring the pasta water to a fierce boil (in two pots if necessary). Slip the tortelli into the boiling water and cook 4 to 10 minutes, depending upon how dry they are. If very fresh, they'll cook in even less time. Taste for doneness, testing sooner rather than later. The edges should be tender but still have some resistance or "bite."

Lift about half the tortelli from the boiling water with a large skimmer, letting the water drain back into the pot. Spread the pastas in a layer in the heated serving bowl. Quickly spoon some of the butter and a generous sprinkling of Parmigiano-Reggiano over the tortelli. Skim out the rest of the pastas, moisten them with butter, and sprinkle with cheese. Serve at once. Pass the rest of the Parmigiano-Reggiano.

Suggestions   **Wine:** In Parma white Sauvignon Blanc of Parma's hill country is served with *Tortelli d'Erbette.* It echoes the soft herbal quality of the filling's greens. More available in the United States are Sauvignon dei Colli Berici of the Veneto, and from the Friuli region, Sauvignon del Collio or Sauvignon dei Colli Orientali del Friuli.

Menu: A light menu with the tortelli as its main dish could begin with Spring Salad with Hazelnuts (page 21) and end with Frozen Chocolate Pistachio Cream with Hot Chocolate Marsala Sauce (page 438). More traditionally the tortelli are served after a few slices of Prosciutto di Parma or fine salami (pages 497 and 501), and before simple grilled or roasted meats like Lemon Roast Veal with Rosemary (page 294), January Pork (page 312), or Maria Bertuzzi's Lemon Chicken (page 273).

Cook's Notes   **Fresh Ricotta:** Ricotta with a fresh, sweet character gives the filling authenticity and sets off its flavors. Buy it at cheese shops, specialty food stores, and Italian groceries. Or make your own (page 454).

Chestnut Tortelli
Tortelli di Mostarda e Castagne

This dish captures all the exuberance of Parma's countryside at harvest time. In the 19th century these tortelli celebrated the autumn harvest with their filling of preserved fruits, roasted chestnuts, and the syrupy juice, or must, of freshly pressed grapes. Moistened with reduced stock and butter, and finished with Parmigiano-Reggiano cheese, the filled pastas were—and still are—an unusual first course.

In the farm kitchens of Parma's hills, bathing them with extra grape syrup instead of butter and cheese transformed the tortelli into an old-style dessert.

The tortelli deserve revival. Their filling satisfies as few do, tasting of good country food with lots of chunk and bite. Save this recipe for when the first fresh chestnuts appear during November and December. Then build a dinner around the unusual pastas, using the menu suggestions below. This recipe is adapted from <u>The Home Cooking of Parma</u> <u>(La Cucina Popolare Parmigiana)</u> by Guglielmo Capacchi.

[Makes 144 pieces; serves 12 as a first course, 8 as a main dish]

Filling

½ cup raisins

½ cup dry white wine

1½ pounds fresh chestnuts, rinsed

½ small Granny Smith apple

½ small underripe Bosc pear

1½ tablespoons unsalted butter

Grated zest of 1 large lemon

Generous ¼ teaspoon ground cinnamon

2 generous pinches of freshly ground black pepper

½ cup Fresh Grape Syrup (recipe follows)

¼ cup water

Pasta and Sauce

1 recipe Wine Pasta (page 82), using 21 ounces flour (5¼ cups spooned and leveled), 4 jumbo eggs, and ½ cup dry white wine or water

2 cups Poultry/Meat Stock (page 66) or Quick Stock (page 68)

4 tablespoons (2 ounces) unsalted butter

12 quarts salted water

Salt and freshly ground black pepper to taste

2 cups (8 ounces) freshly grated Italian Parmigiano-Reggiano cheese

continued

Method   **Working Ahead:** *The filling can be made a day ahead; cover and refrigerate. Filled tortelli hold well in the refrigerator about 12 hours; spread them on a towel-lined basket or baking sheet, and cover with a towel. You can freeze the tortelli up to 3 months.*

Soaking the Raisins: Combine the raisins and wine in a small bowl and soak, uncovered, about 2 hours.

Roasting the Chestnuts: While the raisins are soaking, prepare the chestnuts. Cut a slit two thirds of the way around each nut with a small sharp knife. To cook the chestnuts over an open fire (which gives them a fine smokey flavor and was the method used in Italy until about 40 years ago), use a long-handled perforated skillet or chestnut roaster. Set the pan on a rack about 6 inches above the hot coals. Roast 30 to 45 minutes, or until the chestnuts' interior is mealy and tender. Shake and stir the nuts often.

To cook the chestnuts in the oven, preheat to 400°F. Spread the chestnuts in a large shallow baking pan, and roast them 1 hour, or until the interior of the chestnuts is mealy and tender. Cool the roasted chestnuts about 15 minutes. Then pull away their shells and inner skin. (Pull away all the inner skin, as it can be bitter.) Pass through the coarsest blade of a food mill, or finely chop them in a food processor (do not purée). Transfer them to a medium-size bowl.

Making the Filling: Peel and core both the apple and the pear. Cut the fruit into ¼- to ½-inch dice. Heat the 1½ tablespoons butter in a medium skillet over high heat, taking care that it does not burn. Add the pear, apple, and lemon zest. Cook quickly, scooping the fruits up with a wooden spatula and turning them so they brown evenly. This takes 3 to 5 minutes. Watch carefully; their sugar content encourages burning.

Once the pieces are a rich golden brown, add the cinnamon and pepper and cook for a few seconds or until you can smell the cinnamon. Add the raisins and their liquid, and continue cooking over high heat, about 3 minutes, while scraping up the brown glaze in the bottom of the skillet. Add 6 tablespoons of the grape syrup, and boil for a few seconds until thick. Remove from the heat and allow to cool. Using a spatula, fold the sautéed fruit, the remaining 2 tablespoons grape syrup, and the ¼ cup water into the chestnuts. Blend well.

Preparing the Tortelli: Have handy several large flat baskets covered with kitchen towels. Stretch and thin the pasta as directed in the recipe, working with about a quarter of the dough at a time. Cut it into sheets about 5½ inches wide, keeping them covered with plastic wrap to prevent their drying out.

Dot a row of small spoonfuls of filling along the two long edges of the strips, spacing the spoonfuls about 1½ inches apart and 1 inch in from the edge. Fold the edges over the filling and toward the strip's center. Seal the dough around the fillings, eliminating air pockets as you work. Then, using a pasta wheel, cut rectangular tortelli (about 1½ by 2 inches) around each mound of filling. Arrange the tortelli in single layers, without touching, on the baskets.

Cooking and Serving: Have a serving bowl and shallow soup dishes warming in a low oven. Take about 8 minutes to boil the stock down to about ¾ cup. Then whisk in the 4 tablespoons butter, not letting it melt entirely. Keep warm.

Bring the salted water to a fierce boil (use two pots if necessary). Slip the tortelli into the water and cook 3 to 10 minutes, depending upon how dry they are. Taste the edge of one for doneness. It should be tender but still have some resistance or "bite." Turn off the heat and, using a big skimmer, quickly lift batches of tortelli from the pot, let them drain a few seconds, and then transfer them to the warm serving bowl. Moisten each batch with the butter sauce. Season with a little salt and pepper, and sprinkle generously with Parmigiano-Reggiano. Pass the rest of the cheese separately.

Suggestions   **Wine:** Pour a young red Sangue di Giuda from Lombardy, a young Freisa d'Asti from Piedmont, or a Valpolicella Classico from the Veneto.

Menu: The tortelli are substantial enough to be a main dish. Have a few slices of salami and coppa (pages 501 and 474) before, or a Salad of Mixed Greens and Fennel (page 349). For dessert serve Riccardo Rimondi's Spanish Sponge Cake (page 433). If you are serving them as a first course, make the portions small and follow with a simple dish like Grilled Beef with Balsamic Glaze (page 303), Balsamic Roast Chicken (page 279), or Erminia's Pan-Crisped Chicken (page 270). Even though balsamic-flavored dishes are not eaten in Parma, the vinegar's sweet/tart quality is a good complement to the fruit-and-chestnut-filled tortelli.

Cook's Notes   **Fruits:** The sautéed and spiced fruits here are a substitute for the preserve called *mostarda,* in which autumn fruits cook with spices and one of the oldest of sugar substitutes, reduced grape juice.

Sweet Variation: To make the dessert version, heat 2 to 3 cups Fresh Grape Syrup (page 158) and keep it warm while the tortelli cook. Drain the tortelli, and moisten them with the grape syrup instead of the butter and cheese. Serve hot.

Fresh Grape Syrup
Sapa

Depending upon where you are in Italy, Sapa's name changes with local dialect and tradition. No matter what it is called, this boiled-down juice of freshly pressed wine grapes (also known as "must") has sweetened and flavored dishes as far back as biblical times. When sugar was the property of the rich, peasants used Sapa and honey. Many makers of balsamic vinegar in Emilia-Romagna's Modena and Reggio provinces believe the unique vinegar was born over a millennium ago of Sapa left to age in wooden vinegar barrels.

Today Sapa is either stored in sterilized bottles or cooked into fruit conserves called by many names, among them savor and mostarda. The plain syrup becomes a sweet/tart dessert known as mosto once it is cooked down even more, thickened with arrowroot, cooled, and cut into squares about the size of a brownie. On Emilia-Romagna farms, the syrup becomes a winter treat for children when it is mixed with new snow.

For those seeking a natural sugar-free sweetener, Sapa is an answer. Use it instead of sweetened fruit purées in saucing desserts, spoon it, instead of jam, onto muffins and breads, pour it over pancakes, or bake fruits with it.

Ideally, red wine grapes are used. But table grapes work too, whether they be Flame Tokay, Red Malaga, Exotic, Ribier, Red Emperor, Muscadine, Catawba, Concord, or described simply as "red." Taste for those that are not only sweet but complex in flavor. Adding a little red wine to the syrup gives depth to American table grapes.

Start making the Sapa 2 days before you want to use it. This recipe doubles easily.

[Makes 2½ to 2¾ cups]

4½ pounds flavorful red grapes, with or without seeds

1 cup dry red wine

Method

Working Ahead: *Fresh Grape Syrup keeps 5 days in the refrigerator, or several months if stored in sterilized bottles or frozen.*

Crushing the Grapes: Wash and stem the grapes. Fit a food processor with the steel blade and process the grapes in a couple of batches until finely chopped. Turn the crushed grapes into a glass or stainless steel container, cover, and refrigerate 48 hours.

Strain the grapes through a sieve set over a heavy 5-quart casserole. Press as much liquid as possible out of the grapes, and allow some of the pulp to be blended into the liquid by scraping the underside of the strainer.

Cooking the Grapes: Boil the strained grape juice, uncovered, over medium-high heat 20 to 30 minutes, or until thickened and reduced to about $2\frac{1}{4}$ to $2\frac{3}{4}$ cups. The syrup will foam with large bubbles as it approaches proper thickness. Stir occasionally and check for burning. Blend in the wine, boil 1 minute, and allow to cool.

Cook's Notes In addition to Chestnut Tortelli, use Fresh Grape Syrup in Paola Bini's Sweet Ravioli (page 424), with Baked Pears with Fresh Grape Syrup (page 442), or over Cinnamon and Clove Custard (page 440).

Tortelli of Cabbage and Potato
Tortelli di Verza e Patate

This is simple food from the farmlands of Parma and Piacenza, originally created to enhance a limited winter pantry. Cabbages and potatoes, as easy to grow as they are to store, were always plentiful to all. The idea of enclosing them in pasta made them special.

[Makes 70 pieces; serves 6 to 8 as a first course, 4 to 6 as a main dish]

Filling

2½ tablespoons extra-virgin olive oil

2 ounces pancetta, minced

8 to 10 ounces green cabbage, chopped into ½-inch dice (4 cups)

1 medium to large onion, minced

1 large clove garlic, minced

About ½ cup chicken stock or water

2½ pounds small red-skinned potatoes, baked until tender

⅓ to ½ cup (about 2 ounces) freshly grated Italian Parmigiano-Reggiano cheese

Salt and freshly ground black pepper to taste

Freshly grated nutmeg to taste

Pasta

1 recipe Wine Pasta (page 82), made with water instead of wine

10 quarts salted water

Sauce

3½ cups Poultry/Meat Stock (page 66) or Quick Stock (page 68)

4 tablespoons (2 ounces) unsalted butter

1 cup (4 ounces) freshly grated Italian Parmigiano-Reggiano cheese

Method

Working Ahead: *The filling holds well 24 hours; cover and refrigerate. The filled pastas can be refrigerated, covered with a cloth, up to 12 hours before cooking and serving; turn three or four times to keep them from becoming gummy.*

Making the Filling: In a 12-inch sauté pan, heat the olive oil and pancetta over medium-high heat. Cook 3 minutes, or until the pancetta begins to melt and looks transparent. Turn the heat to high. Add the cabbage and sauté, stirring frequently, 5 minutes or until it begins to brown. Add the onion and continue stirring frequently over high heat another 5 minutes or until the onion and cabbage are deep golden brown. Lower the heat if the brown glaze at the bottom of the pan threatens to burn. That glaze is the key to the filling's big flavors. Stir in the garlic, and cook just a few seconds.

Turn the cabbage and onion into a bowl. Put the sauté pan back over high heat, and immediately add the ½ cup stock or water. Boil it down as you scrape up the brown glaze with a wooden spatula. When nearly all the liquid has evaporated, add it to the cabbage mixture. If the potatoes are still hot, cool them about 20 minutes. Then split them and spoon the pulp into the bowl with the cabbage. Toss the cabbage mixture with the ⅓ to ½ cup Parmigiano-Reggiano cheese, salt and pepper, and nutmeg. Avoid mashing the potatoes. Instead crush them, keeping the mixture chunky. There should be more than a suggestion of nutmeg and pepper.

Preparing the Tortelli: Follow the directions on page 82. Fill the pasta as for Tortelli of Ricotta and Fresh Greens (page 153), being a little more generous with the stuffing, resulting in tortelli about 2½ by 2½ inches. Spread them on flat cloth-lined baskets, making sure the pieces do not touch.

Cooking the Tortelli and Sauce: Have a serving bowl and shallow soup dishes warming in a low oven. Bring the salted water to a fierce boil. While the water is heating, take about 5 minutes to boil down the stock to about 1¼ cups. Stir in the butter, and heat until creamy but not totally melted. Keep warm.

Drop the tortelli into the boiling water and boil 3 to 10 minutes, depending upon how dry they are. Taste for doneness; the edges should be tender but still have some resistance or "bite." Quickly lift half the pastas from the water with a large skimmer. Drain them for a few seconds over the pot, and slip them into the heated serving bowl. Spoon some of the sauce and Parmigiano-Reggiano cheese over them. Lift out the remaining tortelli, and top with the remaining sauce and cheese.

Suggestions   **Wine:** Serve a young red, a Sangiovese di Romagna, or a Merlot from the Veneto or Friuli.

Menu: The tortelli are substantial enough to be a main course, preceded by Garlic Crostini with Pancetta (page 28) or a simple salad. A more traditional menu has the pasta as a first course before Rabbit Roasted with Sweet Fennel (page 289), Lamb with Black Olives (page 305), or January Pork (page 312).

Cook's Notes   **Variation with Tomatoes:** Use 1 recipe Piacenza's Porcini Tomato Sauce (page 64) instead of the stock and butter sauce.

Baked Variation: Serve the filling without its pasta casing as a first course or side dish. Spread it in a lightly oiled baking dish, cover with foil, and bake at 350°F 30 minutes, or until heated through. Uncover, sprinkle with another few tablespoons of cheese, and serve hot.

Piacenza's Tortelli with Tails
Tortelli con la Coda alla Piacentina

Looking like long sticks of hard candy in cellophane wrapping, with twisted tails at either end, these pastas are made even more unusual by the evenly tucked and pleated closure down their length. Called <u>turtei</u> in Piacenza dialect, their simple filling of cheese and greens is light and fragrant. Although time-consuming to make, they can be shaped well ahead of time and need only to be tossed with butter and cheese before serving.

My favorite Piacenza cook happens also to be my step-aunt, Delphina Fulvini Ozera. Her turtei are legendary—sweet with the freshest ricotta and young chard, and so light they levitate off the plate. Sitting in Delphina's kitchen, watching her rhythmically fold, pleat, and twist piece after piece, is both mesmerizing and intimidating. Would that I could equal her skill. Some comfort comes from knowing that Delphina was making turtei before I was ever dreamt of. In her girlhood no Piacenza woman was considered properly brought up unless she could make perfect turtei.

Although you may lack a Piacenza childhood, a little practice and patience produce reasonable facsimiles of Delphina's elegant pastas. Count on the first ten or so being "for the family," as is said in Italy. After that they will start to look quite good. Serve to friends who truly love pasta, and who will applaud your accomplishment.

[Makes about 85 pieces; serves 6 to 8 as a first course, 4 to 6 as a main dish]

Filling

10 to 12 ounces Swiss chard, or 5 ounces fresh spinach leaves

⅓ cup water

1½ cups (12 ounces) creamy fresh whole-milk ricotta cheese (see Note)

¾ cup (3 ounces) freshly grated Italian Parmigiano-Reggiano cheese

Salt and freshly ground black pepper pepper to taste

Freshly grated nutmeg to taste

1 egg, beaten

Pasta

1 recipe Wine Pasta (page 82), made with water instead of wine

10 quarts salted water

Sauce

6 tablespoons (3 ounces) unsalted butter

1½ cups (6 ounces) freshly grated Italian Parmigiano-Reggiano cheese

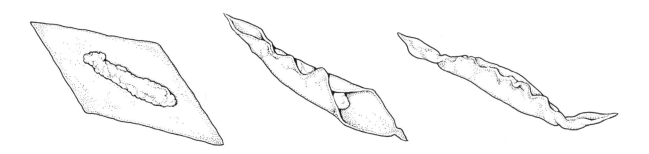

Method **Working Ahead:** *The filling will hold, covered, in the refrigerator 24 hours before stuffing the tortelli. The pastas can then be filled 24 hours ahead and stored, covered with a kitchen towel, in the refrigerator. Turn them three or four times. They do not freeze well.*

Making the Filling: Trim away the Swiss chard's white stalks and reserve them for another use. (If you are using spinach, trim away the tough stems.) Wash the leaves well, and without shaking off the water clinging to them, tuck the leaves into a 4-quart saucepan. Add the ⅓ cup water, cover, and cook over medium heat until wilted, 3 to 5 minutes. Drain and allow to cool. Squeeze the leaves as dry as possible, finely chop, and transfer to a medium-size bowl.

Push the ricotta through a strainer, or purée it in a food processor. Stir it into the chard or spinach. Blend in the ¾ cup Parmigiano-Reggiano, salt and pepper, and nutmeg. Taste for balance; the nutmeg should be only a whisper of flavor. Then beat in the egg. Cover and refrigerate until ready to use.

Filling the Pasta: Stretch and thin the pasta until you can see color through it, as described on pages 83 to 86. Work with only a quarter of the dough at a time, thinning and filling before going on to the next portion.

Now the fun begins. Settle back and enjoy making these tortelli. Don't try to rush the experience. Sharing the adventure with like-minded friends makes shorter work of it. Have handy several large flat baskets covered with kitchen towels.

Cut the pasta into long strips about 4½ inches wide. Cut each strip in half lengthwise. Keep the strips of pasta covered with plastic wrap until you are ready to work with them. Create diamond shapes by cutting each of the strips on the diagonal, spacing the cuts every 2¼ inches, so that each diamond's sides measure about 2¼ inches. Keep the cut pieces covered while you work with one or two. Put a narrow row (about 1 teaspoon) of filling in the center of a diamond.

Place the pasta with the long strip of filling perpendicular to you. Fold the two points of the diamond on the left and right of the row of filling over each other, covering the filling. Pinch together the two overlapping pieces of pasta, using your thumb and forefinger to make a row of pinched closures down the length of the pasta. As you pinch together the pasta, twist it slightly to create an undulating ridge. This pleating will form a rippling scalloped appearance.

continued

Twist and seal the ends, creating the "tails." Place them in a single layer, without touching, on the towel-lined baskets. Uncover more of the cut pasta and repeat the process. Once the first batch is done, stretch and thin the next portion of the dough, and continue.

Cooking and Serving the Turtei: Have a serving bowl and soup dishes warming in a low oven. Have a large colander ready for draining the tortelli. Bring the salted water to a strong boil. Drop in the pastas and cook until their tails are pleasingly firm to the bite yet tender enough to eat. If freshly made, they will take about 3 to 4 minutes. If they have been done up to 24 hours ahead, they may need 8 or 10 minutes. While the pasta cooks, melt the butter in a small saucepan.

Gently pour the cooked tortelli into the colander, taking care not to break them. Carefully pour about one third of the pastas into the heated serving bowl. Spoon a third of the butter over them, and then a generous sprinkling of the cheese. Top with another third, and more butter and cheese. Finally pour in the last portion, top it with the remaining butter and some more cheese, and serve immediately. Pass any leftover cheese separately.

Suggestions **Wine:** A white Pinot Grigio dei Colli Piacentini from the region, a Pinot Grigio from Friuli or the Veneto, or a young fresh white Lugana from Lombardy.

Menu: Tortelli with Tails are excellent before roasted meats or poultry, as well as Maria Bertuzzi's Lemon Chicken (page 273) or Porcini Veal Chops (page 290). I often hold back a few servings of turtei for a light supper the next day. A salad, some fruit, and white wine makes a fine meal.

Cook's Notes **Ricotta:** A creamy ricotta with sweet flavor makes an important difference here. If high-quality ricotta is not available, consider making your own (page 454).

Variation: Tortelli with Tails are often served with Piacenza's Porcini Tomato Sauce (page 64)

Early 20th-century advertisement for Parma's Barilla pasta

Lasagne of Emilia-Romagna
Lasagne Verdi al Forno

    This is one of the most sumptuous yet restrained dishes found in Emilia-Romagna's repertoire. Yes, the lasagne is rich. But for all its richness, the dish maintains an elegance rarely surpassed by any other lasagne in Italy.

    Although strongly identified with Bologna, this lasagne is found throughout the region. Its ragù sauce may change slightly from one area to another, but the dish is always a vivid expression of the "less is more" philosophy of cooking. Mere films of béchamel sauce and meat ragù coat the sheerest spinach pasta. Parmigiano-Reggiano cheese dusts each layer. There is nothing more; no ricotta, no piling on of meats, vegetables, or cheeses; little tomato, and no hot spice. Baking performs the final marriage of flavors. The results are splendid.

[Serves 8 to 10 as a first course, 6 to 8 as a main dish]

4 tablespoons (2 ounces) unsalted butter

4 tablespoons all-purpose unbleached flour (organic stone-ground preferred)

2⅔ cups milk

Salt and freshly ground black pepper to taste

Freshly grated nutmeg to taste

10 quarts salted water

1 recipe Spinach Pasta (page 81) cut for lasagne (page 87), or 1 pound imported dried lasagne

1 recipe Country-Style Ragù (page 48)

1 cup (4 ounces) freshly grated Italian Parmigiano-Reggiano cheese

Method

    Working Ahead: *The ragù and béchamel sauces can be made 3 days ahead; cover and refrigerate. The ragù also freezes well up to 1 month. The pasta can be rolled out, cut, and dried up to 24 hours before cooking. The assembled lasagne can wait at room temperature about 1 hour before baking. Do not refrigerate it before baking, as the topping of béchamel and cheese will overcook by the time the center is hot.*

    Making the Béchamel: Melt the butter in a 3- to 4-quart saucepan over medium-low heat. Sprinkle with the flour and whisk until smooth. Stir without stopping about 3 minutes. Then whisk in the milk a little at a time, keeping the mixture smooth. Bring to a slow bubble, and stir 3 to 4 minutes, or until the sauce thickens. Cook, stirring, 5 minutes, or until all raw flour taste has disappeared. Season with salt, pepper, and a hint of nutmeg.

Assembling the Ingredients: Have the pasta, ragù sauce, béchamel, and cheese at hand. Have a large perforated skimmer and a large bowl of cold water next to the stove. Spread a double thickness of paper towels over a large counter space. Rewarm the sauces gently over medium heat. Preheat the oven to 350°F. Oil or butter a 3-quart shallow baking dish.

Cooking the Pasta: Bring the salted water to boil. Drop about four pieces of pasta in the water at a time. Cook about 2 minutes. If you are using dried pasta, cook about 4 minutes, taste, and cook longer if necessary. The pasta will continue cooking during baking, so make sure it is only barely tender. Lift the lasagne from the water with a skimmer, drain, and then slip into the bowl of cold water to stop cooking. When cool, lift out and dry on the paper towels. Repeat until all the pasta is cooked.

Assembling the Lasagne: Spread a thin film of béchamel over the bottom of the baking dish. Arrange a layer of about four overlapping sheets of pasta over the béchamel. Spread a thin film of béchamel (about 3 or 4 spoonfuls) over the pasta, and then an equally thin film of the ragù. Sprinkle with about 1½ tablespoons of the cheese. Top with another layer and repeat the process. Reserve about ⅓ cup of the béchamel and about ⅓ cup of the cheese for the top of the lasagne. Spread the sauce to completely cover the last layer of pasta. Then top with a generous dusting of cheese.

Baking and Serving the Lasagne: Cover the baking dish lightly with foil, taking care not to let it touch the top of the lasagne. Bake 40 minutes, or until almost heated through. Remove the foil and bake another 10 minutes, or until hot in the center. Test by inserting a knife in the center. If it comes out very warm, the dish is ready. Take care not to brown the cheese topping. It should be melted, creamy-looking, and barely tinged with a little gold. Let the lasagne rest in the turned-off oven with the door ajar about 10 minutes. Then serve. This is not a solid lasagne, but a moist one that slips a bit when it is cut and placed on a dinner plate.

Suggestions   **Wine:** From Emilia-Romagna, a full and generous red Cabernet Sauvignon Colli Bolognesi, a Sangiovese di Romagna Riserva, or a Barbarossa. From other parts of Italy, drink a round and rich Piemontese Barbera d'Alba, or a Tuscan Chianti Classico.

Menu: In Emilia-Romagna it is offered in small portions as a first course. I find it complex and interesting enough to also hold its own as a main dish. Keep the other dishes simple and direct. Everything should be a prelude or aftermath to the lasagne. Start with a few slices of salami or coppa (pages 501 and 474) and Balsamic Vegetables (page 18), or Spring Salad with Hazelnuts (page 21). Finish the meal with Baked Pears with Fresh Grape Syrup (page 442) and Sweet Cornmeal Biscuits (page 422).

Variations: Other ragùs are also excellent in the lasagne. Try The Cardinal's Ragù (page 40), A Lighter Contemporary Ragù Bolognese (page 46), or Baroque Ragù (page 42). For a meatless lasagne, Winter Tomato Sauce (page 62) or Piacenza's Porcini Tomato Sauce (page 64) can stand in for the meat ragùs. Egg Pasta (page 80) can be substituted for Spinach Pasta.

Cook's Notes **Dried Pasta:** Boxed lasagne pasta should be as sheer as possible. See page 92 for guidelines.

It's a Girl!

According to Emilia-Romagna folklorist Piero Camporesi, for many families in Emilia-Romagna a lasagne celebrated the birth of a girl.

Lasagne Dukes of Ferrara
Lasagne Duchi di Ferrara

Inspired by a 16th-century banquet dish, sheets of sheer pasta are layered with a ragù of chicken and sprinklings of nuts, raisins, spices, cheese, and a touch of cream. What emerges is a lasagne hinting at the extravagance and exotica of <u>The Arabian Nights.</u> Serve it whenever you want an uncommon dish that pasta lovers will applaud, yet one easily done in advance.

[Serves 6 to 8 as a first course, 4 to 6 as a main dish]

6 tablespoons golden raisins

1 cup hot water

10 quarts salted water

1 recipe Rosewater Maccheroni Romanesca (page 192) cut for lasagne (page 87), or 1 pound imported dried lasagne

2 tablespoons unsalted butter

1 recipe Baroque Ragù (page 42)

¾ cup heavy cream

6 thin slices Prosciutto di Parma, cut into finger-size strips

1¼ cups (5 ounces) freshly grated Italian Parmigiano-Reggiano cheese

6 tablespoons pine nuts, toasted

Ground cinnamon

Method

Working Ahead: *The ragù can be made up to 3 days ahead; cover and refrigerate. Or it can be frozen up to 1 month. The fresh pasta can be made early in the day and dried at room temperature. The lasagne can be assembled hours before baking. I prefer not to refrigerate lasagne before baking as the topping usually dries out before the interior is heated through.*

Soaking the Raisins: Soak the raisins in the hot water about 30 minutes while you prepare the other ingredients.

Cooking the Pasta: Spread a double thickness of paper towels over a large counter space. Have a large perforated skimmer handy, and a large bowl of cold water near the pasta cooking pot. Bring the salted water to a fierce boil. Drop in about four pieces of pasta. Cook fresh pasta about 2 minutes, and dried pasta a bit longer. Taste the pasta, making sure it is only barely tender, as it will cook again in baking. Lift the sheets from the water with the skimmer, and drop them into the cold water to stop cooking. Lift out the cooled pasta sheets and dry them on paper towels. Keep repeating the process until all the pasta is cooked.

Assembling the Lasagne: Preheat the oven to 350°F. Use the 2 tablespoons butter to slather a shallow 3-quart baking dish. Drain the raisins, discarding their liquid. Spread 3 or 4 tablespoons of ragù over the bottom of the baking dish. Cover the ragù with sheets of cooked pasta, butting them side by side. Spread about a third of the ragù over the pasta. Top with another layer of pasta. Spread the sheets with 3 tablespoons of the cream. Sprinkle with half the prosciutto, 6 tablespoons of the cheese, 2 tablespoons of the raisins, and 3 tablespoons of the pine nuts. Sprinkle very lightly with a pinch of cinnamon.

Cover with another layer of pasta. Spread another third of the ragù over the pasta sheets, and cover the ragù with pasta. Again spread on 3 tablespoons cream, the rest of the prosciutto, 6 tablespoons cheese, 2 tablespoons raisins, and the rest of the pine nuts. Dust with a pinch of cinnamon. Cover with a final layer of pasta, and cover it with the remaining ragù. (Do not be concerned if there are some pasta sheets left over. Cut them up into bite-size pieces and use them in soup or bean dishes.) In a medium bowl blend together the remaining cream, cheese, and raisins. Stir in a pinch of cinnamon. Spoon this sauce over the ragù, making parallel diagonal stripes atop the lasagne.

Baking and Serving: Cover the dish with foil, taking care not to let it touch the top of the lasagne. Slip it into the oven and bake 45 to 50 minutes, or until a knife inserted in the center comes out very warm or hot. Uncover and bake another 5 minutes. The top should be bubbly and creamy, not dried out or browned. Let the lasagne rest in the turned-off oven with the door ajar about 10 minutes. Serve it cut in squares, lifting the pieces out with a spatula. This is not a solid lasagne; it slips a bit as it is cut and placed on a dinner plate.

Suggestions   **Wine:** A soft fruity red: the Piedmont's Barbera d'Asti, Tuscany's Rosso di Montalcino, or an elegant Chianti Classico Riserva.

Menu: Serve in small portions before Giovanna's Wine-Basted Rabbit (page 284), Lemon Roast Veal with Rosemary (page 294), or Balsamic Roast Chicken (page 279). End the meal with Meringues of the Dark Lake (page 421), served with espresso. Offer as a main dish after Fresh Pears with Parmigiano-Reggiano and Balsamic Vinegar (page 30). Follow the lasagne with a simple green salad. Have the Strawberries in Red Wine (page 445) for dessert.

Cook's Notes   **Dried Pasta:** Dried boxed lasagne should be as sheer as possible. See page 92 for guidelines.

Bolognese tavern sign, "The Rooster," 17th century, by Giuseppe Maria Mitelli

His Eminence's Baked Penne
Maccheroni al Forno Cardinale Chiaramonti

It was the end of the 18th century
when Imola's Cardinal Chiaramonti enjoyed this meat ragù seasoned
with cinnamon and pepper. Serve the penne at the start of a special
dinner or as a main dish. This is a rare example of a meat and pasta
dish that is *not* complemented by Parmigiano-Reggiano cheese.

[Serves 6 to 8 as a first course, 4 to 6 as a main dish]

1 recipe The Cardinal's Ragù
  (page 40)
6 quarts salted water

1 pound imported dried penne
  maccheroni, or 1 recipe
  Rosewater Maccheroni
  Romanesca (page 192)
1 tablespoon unsalted butter

Method

Working Ahead: *The ragù and pasta can be combined and put in the baking dish 24 hours before serving. Keep the dish covered and refrigerated. Remove it from the refrigerator about 1 hour before baking.*

Cooking the Pasta: Have the ragù ready. Set a large colander in the sink. Bring the salted water to a vigorous boil. Cook the penne until it is just tender enough to be edible. It should be slightly undercooked, as it still has to be baked. Drain immediately.

Assembling and Baking: Preheat the oven to 350°F. Use the tablespoon of butter to grease a 2½-quart shallow baking dish. Taste the ragù for seasoning; it may need a pinch more cinnamon and/or pepper. Turn the pasta and ragù into a deep bowl, and toss to combine. Transfer the mixture to the baking dish and cover with foil. Bake 30 to 40 minutes, or until a knife inserted into the center of the casserole comes out warm.

Serving: Spoon the maccheroni into preheated soup dishes, and serve hot.

Suggestions

Wine: A red Barbera from Emilia-Romagna, a Barbera d'Asti from the Piedmont, or a soft red Merlot of Friuli.

Menu: Serve the casserole, as either a first course or a main dish, after Spring Salad with Hazelnuts (page 21) or Fresh Pears with Parmigiano-Reggiano and Balsamic Vinegar (page 30). If it is a first course, hold to the 18th-century theme with Christmas Capon (page 281). Make dessert Frozen Zuppa Inglese (page 430).

Lasagne of Wild and Fresh Mushrooms
Lasagne ai Funghi

During wild mushroom season in Emilia-Romagna, fresh porcini are sautéed, cooked with herbs and tomato or cream, and baked between hand-size sheets of fresh pasta. They make the simplest of lasagnes. Most contain very little meat. This is a melding of three recipes from the Bologna area, with dried porcini and fresh cultivated mushrooms replacing hard-to-find fresh porcini.

[Serves 8 to 10 as a first course, 6 to 8 as a main dish]

Porcini

1½ cups (1½ ounces) dried porcini mushrooms

2 cups hot water

Sauce

3 tablespoons extra-virgin olive oil

1 large onion, minced

1 ounce Prosciutto di Parma, finely chopped (optional)

¼ cup minced Italian parsley

1 pound fresh button mushrooms, sliced

1 large clove garlic, minced

2-inch branch fresh rosemary, or ½ teaspoon dried whole-leaf rosemary

4 fresh sage leaves, or 4 dried whole sage leaves

⅔ cup dry white wine

1½ to 2 pounds canned tomatoes, drained of most of their liquid and crushed

Pasta and Topping

6 quarts salted water

¾ recipe Egg Pasta (page 80) cut for lasagne (page 87), or 12 ounces imported dried lasagne

1½ cups (6 ounces) freshly grated Italian Parmigiano-Reggiano cheese

½ cup heavy cream blended with ¼ cup milk

Method

Working Ahead: *The sauce can be made 2 days ahead; cover and refrigerate. The lasagne can be assembled several hours before baking. I prefer not to refrigerate lasagne before cooking, as the topping usually overcooks before the interior is heated through.*

Preparing the Porcini: Rinse the dried mushroom pieces under cold running water to rid them of sand and particles. If mushroom pieces are small, rid them of sand by swishing them in a bowl of cold water. Pause for a moment, allowing the sand and particles to settle to the bottom of the bowl, then quickly scoop out the mushrooms with your hands. Repeat if necessary. Then place them in a medium-size bowl and cover with the hot water. Let stand 30 minutes, or until softened. Lift the mushrooms from the soaking liquid, squeeze out excess moisture, and coarsely chop. Line a small sieve with a paper towel for straining the liquid into the mushroom sauce.

Making the Sauce: Heat the oil in a large skillet. Add the onion, prosciutto, and parsley. Sauté over medium heat, stirring frequently, 5 minutes, or until the onion is barely tinged with gold. Add the fresh mushrooms and cook over high heat 10 minutes, or until they are golden brown. Stir in the chopped porcini, reduce the heat to medium-high, and cook 2 minutes. Cook in the garlic and herbs 1 minute.

Strain the mushroom soaking liquid into the skillet. Let it bubble down over medium heat, 5 minutes, or until it forms a thin film on the bottom of the skillet. As the liquid simmers, use a wooden spatula to scrape up the brown glaze on the bottom of the pan. Add the wine and reduce it in the same manner, about 3 minutes. Once the wine has cooked down to a sheer film, add the tomatoes. Cook, uncovered, over medium-high heat 10 minutes, or until the sauce is richly flavored. If it is at all watery or lacking body, keep it bubbling over medium-high heat until reduced and intensified.

Cooking the Pasta and Assembling the Lasagne: Spread a double thickness of paper towels on a large counter space. Have a large bowl of cold water handy. Bring the salted water to a vigorous boil. Drop three or four sheets of lasagne into the boiling water, and cook until tender but still pleasingly firm to the bite. This will take about 2 minutes for fresh pasta, 4 or more for dried. Remove the sheets with a large skimmer or flat slotted spoon, and drop them in the cold water to stop the cooking. Then lift the sheets from the water and drain on the paper towels. Repeat with all the lasagne sheets. Lightly oil or butter a shallow 2½- to 3-quart baking dish. Have the sauce, cheese, pasta, and cream mixture close at hand. Film the bottom of the baking dish with a little of the sauce. Cover the sauce with overlapping sheets of pasta. Spread about ¼ to ⅓ cup of the sauce over the pasta, just enough to moisten the sheets. Sprinkle the sauce with 2 to 3 tablespoons Parmigiano-Reggiano. Repeat the layering, saucing, and sprinkling with cheese until you reach the top of the dish. All the mushroom sauce should be used up, and about 8 tablespoons of cheese will be left over. Blend the remaining cheese with the cream mixture, and spread it over the last layer of pasta. Lightly cover the lasagne with foil.

Baking and Serving: Preheat the oven to 350°F. Bake the lasagne 30 minutes. Uncover and bake another 10 to 15 minutes, or until bubbly. Turn off the oven, leave the door slightly ajar, and let the lasagne rest about 10 minutes. Cut the lasagne into squares, slipping a spatula under each portion to lift it to a dinner plate.

Suggestions   **Wine:** A young Sangiovese di Romagna, a red Corvo of Sicily, or a light-bodied Chianti from Colline Pisane.

Menu: Serve the lasagne in small portions before Balsamic Roast Chicken (page 279), Giovanna's Wine-Basted Rabbit (page 284), or Lemon Roast Veal with Rosemary (page 294). Serve as a main dish after "Little" Spring Soup from the 17th

Century (page 232) or Modena's Spiced Soup of Spinach and Cheese (page 234). Have fresh fruit and Sweet Cornmeal Biscuits (page 422) for dessert.

Cook's Notes **Fresh Wild Mushrooms:** Fresh wild mushrooms are appearing frequently in American markets. Substitute one or a blend of the following for all or part of the 1 pound button mushrooms: porcini, cremini, parasol, grisette, Portobello, oyster, angel trumpets, lobster, or butter mushrooms. Wipe the mushrooms clean with a damp cloth, and trim away stems. Oriental mushrooms, such as straw, shiitake, wood-ear, and enoki, are not appropriate in this dish.

Baked Maccheroni with Winter Tomato Sauce
Maccheroni al Forno

This is typical of baked maccheroni casseroles found throughout Emilia-Romagna, where each cook creates his or her own personal recipe. Mine improvises on several versions of the dish tasted in Ferrara and Correggio. Layers of sautéed mushrooms, tomato sauce, and sweet peas are sprinkled with nutty sheep cheese. Keep a few batches of Winter Tomato Sauce in the freezer to make quick work of putting this dish together. Assemble it one evening, and serve it the next as a one-dish dinner. The casserole is ideal for those seeking robust and satisfying dining without meat.

[Serves 6 to 8 as a first course, 4 to 6 as a main dish]

Mushrooms
3 tablespoons extra-virgin olive oil
1 pound small fresh button mushrooms, halved or quartered
3 tablespoons minced Italian parsley
Salt and freshly ground black pepper
1 large clove garlic, minced
Sauce and Pasta
1 recipe Winter Tomato Sauce (page 62)
½ cup heavy cream

1⅓ cups fresh peas, cooked, or tiny frozen peas, defrosted
6 quarts salted water
1 pound dried imported penne, sedani, or fusilli maccheroni
½ cup (2 ounces) freshly grated Italian Parmigiano-Reggiano cheese
1 tablespoon extra-virgin olive oil
6 ounces mild Italian sheep cheese (Lago Monate Pecorino, Fiore Sardo, Pecorino Crotonese)

continued

Method **Working Ahead:** *The casserole can be assembled up to 24 hours before serving. Cover it and refrigerate. Let the casserole stand 1 hour at room temperature before baking.*

Sautéeing the Mushrooms: Heat the 3 tablespoons olive oil in a 12-inch skillet over high heat. Add the mushrooms and parsley, and cook over high heat, uncovered, stirring frequently, 3 minutes, or until they start giving off a little liquid. Sprinkle lightly with salt and pepper, then add the garlic. Continue sautéing, turning often 8 minutes, or until the mushrooms are golden brown and all their liquid has evaporated. Allow to cool, and taste for seasoning.

Preparing the Sauce and Pasta: In a large bowl, combine the Winter Tomato Sauce, cream, and peas. Bring the salted water to a hard rolling boil. Drop in maccheroni and stir to separate the pieces. Cook at a fierce boil 12 minutes, or until the pasta is barely tender enough to eat, still a little underdone. Drain thoroughly in a colander. Fold the pasta into the sauce, along with the Parmigiano-Reggiano cheese.

Assembling and Baking: Use the 1 tablespoon olive oil to grease a 2½-quart shallow baking dish. Preheat the oven to 350°F. Spread half the pasta in the baking dish. Spoon all of the mushrooms over the pasta. Using a vegetable peeler, shave half the sheep cheese over the mushrooms. Cover with the remaining pasta, then top with shavings of the rest of the cheese.

Cover the dish lightly with foil, and bake 40 to 45 minutes, or until a knife inserted in the center comes out warm. Uncover the dish and bake another 5 to 10 minutes, or until the cheese is melted but not browned. Serve hot in warmed soup dishes.

Suggestions **Wine:** An uncomplicated Sangiovese di Romagna, a young Dolcetto d'Alba or Barbera d'Asti from the Piedmont, or a young Merlot from Friuli.

Menu: Have a few slices of coppa and salami (pages 474 and 501) with Balsamic Vegetables (page 18), or Spring Salad with Hazelnuts (page 21), before serving the maccheroni as a main dish. If you are serving it as a first course, follow with the Herbed Seafood Grill (page 254), Grilled Winter Endives (page 337), or Balsamic Roast Chicken (page 279).

Cook's Notes **Variation:** Bring another dimension to the mushrooms by substituting Piacenza's Porcini Tomato Sauce (page 64) for the Winter Tomato Sauce.

It's a Boy!

According to Emilia-Romagna folklorist Piero Camporesi, hollow maccheroni like penne were served to celebrate the birth of a male child.

An Unusual Tortellini Pie
Pasticcio di Tortellini con Crema di Cannella

A *lavish piece of the past, this tall pie with its sweet crust and layering of tortellini, ragù, and tiny meatballs is well-known feasting food in Emilia-Romagna, especially in Bologna and Romagna. What sets this recipe apart is the sweet, cinnamon-scented custard that is added just before the top crust is put in place. It accents the meaty flavors of the pie's filling.*

Save tortellini pie for the most important of occasions. Although time-consuming to make, it is fully worth the effort. Prepare in easy stages. Each component can be done days ahead, and the pie is assembled and in the oven before guests arrive. The meatballs, ragù, and custard also stand on their own, as a fine antipasto, a dressing for pasta, and a sauce for desserts.

[Serves 12 as a first course, 8 to 10 as a main dish]

Pastry

3½ cups (14 ounces) all-purpose unbleached flour (organic stone-ground preferred)

1 cup (4 ounces) cake flour

¼ teaspoon salt

¾ cup (5 ounces) sugar

½ teaspoon baking powder

1 teaspoon grated lemon zest

11 tablespoons (5½ ounces) unsalted butter, chilled, cut into chunks

3 large egg yolks

5 to 8 tablespoons dry white wine

Method   **Working Ahead:** *The pastry can be made 2 days ahead; wrap and refrigerate. Or freeze it up to 3 months. The custard keeps, covered, in the refrigerator 3 days, but it cannot be frozen. The meatballs can be made a day ahead and refrigerated overnight. Do not freeze them. The Baroque Ragù can be refrigerated, covered, up to 3 days, and frozen up to 1 month. Skim the fat from it before using.*

Food Processor Method: Combine the dry ingredients and the lemon zest in a food processor fitted with the steel blade. Blend 10 seconds. Add the butter, and process with the on/off pulse until the mixture looks like coarse meal. Turn off the machine. In a small bowl, beat together the yolks and 5 tablespoons of the wine. Add the mixture to the processor. Process with the on/off pulse until the dry ingredients are moistened and the dough begins to collect in clumps. If the dough seems dry, sprinkle with 2 or more tablespoons of wine, and process a second or two. Turn the pastry out onto a counter, gather it into a ball, wrap in plastic wrap, and chill at least 1 hour. Remove from the refrigerator about 30 minutes before rolling it out.

Hand Method: Using a fork, mix together the dry ingredients and the lemon zest in a large bowl. Add the butter. Use your fingertips to rub together the flour and butter until the mixture resembles coarse meal. Do not worry if there are a few larger pieces of butter. Make a well in the center; add the yolks and 5 tablespoons of wine. Beat the liquids with the fork to thoroughly blend. Toss with the dry ingredients. Avoid stirring or beating, which toughens the dough. If the dough is dry, sprinkle with another 2 or more tablespoons of wine, and toss to moisten. Once the dough is moist enough to be gathered into a ball, wrap in plastic wrap and refrigerate at least 1 hour. Remove from the refrigerator 30 minutes before rolling it out.

Cinnamon Custard

4 egg yolks

5 tablespoons sugar

2 tablespoons plus 2½ teaspoons all-purpose unbleached flour (organic stone-ground preferred)

Dash of salt

2 cups milk, scalded

2 tablespoons unsalted butter

2 generous pinches of ground cinnamon

Cooking the Custard: In a heavy nonaluminum 3- to 4-quart saucepan, whisk together the yolks and sugar until light in color. Beat in the flour and salt. Slowly whisk in the hot milk until the custard is smooth. Set the saucepan over medium heat, and stir constantly with a wooden spatula to make sure nothing sticks to the bottom of the pan. Cook 3 minutes, or until the custard comes to a bubble. Then stir continuously at a slow bubble another 5 minutes, or until the custard is thick enough to coat the spatula with a sheet of custard that does not slip off easily. Check for doneness by tasting and making sure there is no flavor of raw flour. Pour the custard through a strainer into a bowl, stir in the butter and cinnamon, and cool. Lay a film of plastic wrap over the surface of the custard, and refrigerate it.

Meatballs

2 to 3 ounces Italian Parmigiano-Reggiano cheese, cut in chunks

7 tablespoons minced Italian parsley

1 large clove garlic

1 medium onion, coarsely chopped

10 ounces chicken thighs, boned, skinned, and cut into chunks

6 ounces pancetta, chopped

10 ounces ground lean beef round

1 tablespoon imported Italian tomato paste

¼ cup dried bread crumbs

1 egg, beaten

¼ teaspoon salt

⅛ teaspoon freshly ground black pepper

4 tablespoons vegetable oil

About ½ cup water

Preparing the Meatballs: Grate the cheese in a food processor fitted with the steel blade. Add the parsley, garlic, and onion. Run the processor about 3 seconds to mince but not purée the ingredients. Drop in the chicken pieces and pancetta. Use the on/off pulse to grind quite fine. Add the beef and process only a second or two. Turn everything into a bowl, and blend in the tomato paste, bread crumbs, egg, salt, and pepper. Shape into 1-inch balls.

Cooking the Meatballs: Line a baking sheet with a triple thickness of paper towels. Heat the oil in a large sauté pan over medium-high heat. Cook half the meatballs 7 to 8 minutes, or until dark brown and crusty on all sides. Lift out the browned meatballs with a slotted spoon, and drain on the paper towels. Repeat with the second batch. Once they are cooked and drained, place in a bowl. Pour all the fat out of the pan, and add the water. Bring to a boil, scraping up the brown bits in the pan, and boil down to about 4 tablespoons. Pour this over the meatballs, and cool. Cover and refrigerate.

Assembling and Baking the Pie

Unsalted butter
Sweet Pastry
1 recipe Tortellini (page 134), or
    2½ pounds store-bought
    meat-filled tortellini
8 quarts Quick Stock (page 68)
    or water
Salt
Double recipe Baroque Ragù
    (page 42)

1½ cups (6 ounces) freshly grated
    Italian Parmigiano-Reggiano
    cheese
2 eggs, beaten
Meatballs
Cinnamon Custard
Lemon leaves, spruce sprigs,
    grapes, or sprigs of bay leaves
    for garnish

Method

Working Ahead: *The pastry dough must be rolled out 1 hour before assembling the pie. Although the pie cannot be assembled far in advance, it requires about 1½ hours of unattended baking and resting before serving. This allows plenty of time for conversation, drinks, and a first course.*

Preparing the Pastry: Butter the bottom, sides, and rim of a 10½- to 11-inch springform pan. On a floured surface, roll out two thirds of the pastry to form a ⅛-inch-thick round. Fit it into the springform pan, covering the bottom and sides. Trim the edges at the rim so there is a 1-inch overhang. Save the scraps for decorations. Roll out the remaining dough to about ⅛ inch thick, and trim it to form a 13-inch round. Cover a cookie sheet with foil, and lift the pastry onto it. Arrange the scraps around the pastry. Chill both pastries about 30 minutes.

continued

Cooking the Tortellini: Stock is the traditional cooking medium here. It can be saved for future use once the tortellini are drained. If you are using water instead of stock, add 2 tablespoons salt. Bring the stock or water to a fierce boil. Drop in the tortellini and cook 3 to 8 minutes, or until tender but firm enough to have resilience or "bite." Drain well and turn into a large bowl.

Assembling: Gently warm the ragù. Wrap the meatballs in foil and warm them 10 minutes in a 350°F oven. Remove the meatballs and turn the heat to 400°F. Add two thirds of the ragù (save the rest for another use) to the tortellini, along with half the Parmigiano-Reggiano cheese and about two thirds of the beaten egg. Gently fold together until well blended.

Take the springform pan and cookie sheet out of the refrigerator. Spoon half the meatballs over the bottom of the crust, and sprinkle with 1 tablespoon of cheese. Spread half the tortellini over the meatballs pressing them down gently with the back of a large spoon. Top with the remaining meatballs and another spoonful of cheese. Add the remaining tortellini, gently pressing them into the filling with the back of the large spoon. Dust with the rest of the Parmigiano-Reggiano. Spread the cinnamon custard over all. Brush the overhanging crust with beaten egg. Seal the reserved pastry round to the rim of the pie by pinching the two pieces together. Form a thick upstanding rim by rolling the edge in toward the center of the pie. Crimp or flute all around the crust. Brush the entire surface with more beaten egg.

Decorating the Crust: Roll out the leftover dough. Cut 4-inch-long ovals of dough to resemble long California bay leaves. Cut a 1-inch-diameter steam hole in the center of the crust, and arrange the leaves in a sunburst pattern around it, overlapping them slightly toward the center. Small leaves could be arranged in clusters around the pie's rim. Brush all the decorations with beaten egg, and set the pie on a baking sheet.

Baking: Place the baking sheet in the lower third of the oven, and bake 40 minutes. Lower the heat to 350°F and bake another 40 minutes. Let the pie stand in the turned-off oven with the door open halfway 10 to 20 minutes before serving.

The Presentation: Unmold by setting the springform pan on three large cans. Release the springform and let it drop down to the counter. Place the pie on a large silver tray or china platter garnished with clusters of lemon leaves, spruce sprigs, grapes, or bouquets of fresh bay leaves. Cut the pie at the table.

Suggestions   **Wine:** The sweet undertones of this dish present challenges in selecting a wine. An aged red Recioto della Valpolicella Amarone from the Veneto is ideal with the pie.

Menu: Although traditionally a first course at festive meals, the pie is a spectacular main dish for buffets and special dinners. In keeping with the pie's lineage, start with Almond Spice Broth (page 237). Afterward pass platters of fresh fennel and chunks of Parmigiano-Reggiano to eat with the last of the red wine. Dessert could be Strawberries in Red Wine (page 445) or Meringues of the Dark Lake (page 421).

Cook's Notes **Store-Bought Tortellini:** Look for fresh or frozen tortellini made with pasta sheer enough to detect the filling through it. Dried tortellini sold in boxes and needing no refrigeration are unacceptable.

A Little Renaissance Dinner

It was a cold afternoon in January, 1529. The turreted Este Castle in Ferrara's main square appeared and disappeared in billows of fog. Outside all was gray and icy. Inside, one of Ferrara's state banquets was about to begin. On the surface it was Don Ercole d'Este honoring his father, Alfonso, the Duke of Ferrara. But the banquet was really about the power of the Este family, about displaying Ferrara's wealth to the important guests—ambassadors of the Venetian Senate and the Archbishop of Milan among them. One hundred and four sat down to a dinner that expressed every bit of the magnificence the Este court was famous for. Leonardo da Vinci had stated that Ferrara possessed "the most brilliant and enlightened court in Europe."

Over 120 dishes were served in ten courses. Specially composed music marked each service. Ariosto, the poet and playwright of the day, presented a new comedy. The main table was decorated with tall-sided pies, whose fancy crusts were gilded in golden egg yolk. Few dishes surviving today so vividly express the grandeur and glamour of those times. Records of Italian court life during the Medieval and Renaissance eras tell of many types of elaborate and savory pies. The legacy of pastry, sugar, and spice from the Arab world gave birth to these fantastical creations. Sugar was a status symbol. It was used with abandon. Sweet crusts enclosing savory/sweet fillings were the fashion of the day. Many were designed to be show-stoppers: when their lids were lifted, flocks of live birds flew out. Some fillings contained 3 pounds each of butter and salt pork, four roast pigeons, juice of sour grapes, saffron, nutmeg, cloves, and handfuls of cinnamon and pepper. Others still sound feasible to modern palates, like the simplicity of veal sautéed with lemon and pistachios.

Savory pies still mark important occasions in Emilia-Romagna. Sweet crusts have survived, but the fillings generally center on pasta; stuffed ones in Bologna and Romagna; hollow maccheroni in the rest of the region. The recipe for this Unusual Tortellini Pie is adapted from one handed down through a Bolognese family. The pie illustrates the evolution of these dishes from the Renaissance to today. The custard's sweetness and spice keeps that Arab legacy intact, while the meat ragù reflects the 18th and 19th centuries, with its wine, broth, and tomato instead of sour grape juice and spices. The cream in the ragù sauce marks the 20th century by replacing the traditional béchamel.

Domed Maccheroni Pie of Ferrara
Pasticcio di Maccheroni

From the tables of Ferrara's 18th-century nobility, this domed pie is still popular today. Under a sweet crust is maccheroni in a creamy sauce, studded with porcini mushrooms and a chunky ragù.

The pie was created in 1700, when a papal legation arrived in Ferrara with much pomp and feasting. Its dome shape, inspired by the priests' hats, was a tribute to the churchmen. It is still the traditional first course of Ferrara's weddings and holiday dinners, and Pasticcio di Maccheroni always marks Fat Tuesday and the last Sunday of Carnival before Lent. Some cooks use fresh local white truffles instead of the wild mushrooms. This particular recipe is a melding of two family versions shared by Ferrarese linguist Riccardo Rimondi.

[Serves 10 as a first course, 6 to 8 as a main dish]

Mushrooms

2 cups (2 ounces) dried porcini mushrooms

1½ cups hot water

1 tablespoon unsalted butter

1 small onion, minced

Salt and freshly ground black pepper

Béchamel

3 cups milk

1 medium onion, sliced

½ teaspoon white peppercorns, crushed

½ teaspoon whole cloves, crushed

2 California bay laurel leaves

5 tablespoons (2½ ounces) unsalted butter

5 tablespoons all-purpose unbleached flour (organic stone-ground preferred)

Salt and freshly grated white pepper to taste

Freshly grated nutmeg to taste

Pastry

3½ cups (14 ounces) all-purpose unbleached flour (organic stone-ground preferred)

1 cup (4 ounces) cake flour

½ cup (3½ ounces) sugar

Pinch of salt

10 tablespoons (5 ounces) unsalted butter, chilled

2 eggs

2 egg yolks

Pasta, Ragù, and Cheese

1 tablespoon unsalted butter

6 quarts salted water

1 pound dried imported penne rigate (ribbed narrow tubular maccheroni)

1 cup (4 ounces) freshly grated
Italian Parmigiano-Reggiano
cheese
1 recipe Meat Ragù with Marsala
(page 56)

Garnish
1 egg, beaten
Fresh lemon leaves, bay leaves,
laurel leaves, or ivy

Method   **Working Ahead:** *Prepare each part of the dish well ahead, and then assemble it shortly before baking. The mushrooms, béchamel, and ragù will hold, covered, in the refrigerator up to 3 days. (The ragù can be frozen up to 1 month.) The pastry dough can be made 3 days ahead; wrap and refrigerate.*

Preparing the Mushrooms: Porcini can be sandy, so first swish them in a bowl of cold water. Pause for a moment, allowing the particles to settle to the bottom of the bowl, then quickly scoop out the mushrooms with your hands. Repeat two times. Put the mushrooms in another bowl and cover with the hot water. Soak 30 minutes, or until softened. Lift out the mushrooms, squeezing them to release as much liquid as possible. Reserve the soaking water. Coarsely chop. Heat the 1 tablespoon butter in a small skillet over medium-high heat. Add the mushrooms and small onion, and sauté 3 minutes. Season lightly with salt and pepper. Cool, cover, and refrigerate. Strain the soaking liquid through a paper-towel-lined sieve, measuring out the 2/3 cup needed for the ragù.

Making the Béchamel: This old-style recipe produces an especially aromatic version of béchamel. Combine the milk with the onion, white peppercorns, cloves, and bay leaves in a 4-quart pot. Simmer, uncovered, 10 minutes, and remove from the heat. In another 3- to 4-quart pot, melt the butter over medium-low heat. Stir in the flour and cook about 5 minutes, stirring, adjusting the heat so the flour does not color. Strain the milk into the flour mixture and raise the heat to medium. Whisk continuously, 3 to 4 minutes, or until the sauce comes to a gentle bubble. Keep whisking as the sauce bubbles, 5 to 8 minutes. The béchamel is ready when any raw flour taste has disappeared and the sauce is thick enough to generously coat a spoon. Season with salt, white pepper, and nutmeg. If you are not using the béchamel soon, allow it to cool, cover the surface with a sheet of plastic wrap, and refrigerate.

Making the Dough by Hand: Stir the dry ingredients together in a large bowl. Using only your fingertips, rub in the butter until the mixture resembles coarse meal with occasional shales of flour-coated butter. Hollow out a well in the flour, and add the eggs and yolks. Beat the eggs with a fork to blend them. Then gradually toss them with the flour/butter mixture until the dough is moistened. Do not stir or beat, and don't worry if the dough looks rough. Gather it into a ball, wrap, and chill at least 30 minutes.

continued

Making the Dough in a Food Processor: Combine the dry ingredients in the processor, add the butter, and process with the on/off pulse until the mixture looks like coarse meal. Add the eggs and yolks, and blend with the on/off pulse until the mixture starts to gather in clumps. Turn it out onto a sheet of plastic wrap, gather into a ball, wrap, and chill at least 30 minutes.

Assembling the Pie: Preheat the oven to 425°F. Allow the mushrooms, ragù and béchamel to come to room temperature if they were chilled. Grease the bottom and sides of a 10-inch springform pan with the tablespoon of butter. Roll out one third of the pastry to form a round about ¼ to ⅛ inch thick. Trim it to a 13-inch circle. Fit it into the bottom of the pan, forming a 1½-inch border up the sides (the dough is fragile, so do not hesitate to press it into the pan if it breaks). Chill about 30 minutes. Line the chilled pastry with foil, weight it with dried beans or rice, and bake 10 minutes. Remove the liner and weights, prick the crust with a fork, and bake 5 more minutes. Allow it to cool. Leave the oven on.

Bring the salted water to a fierce boil. Drop in the pasta and cook, stirring frequently, about 2 minutes, or until barely tender (it still has to bake inside the pie). Drain thoroughly in a colander, and turn into a large bowl. Blend the béchamel and half the cheese into the pasta. Fold in the mushrooms, but do not blend them in totally. Spread half the pasta mixture over the bottom crust (still in the springform pan). Top it with half the ragù, and sprinkle with half the remaining cheese. Top the ragù with half the remaining pasta, forming a domed mound. Spread the rest of the ragù and cheese over the pasta. Then top everything with the pasta that is left. Use the back of a large spoon to gently compress the layers into a tall dome shape.

Roll out the remaining pastry to form a large round. Set the springform pan on several large cans. Release and slip off the sides. Then transfer the *pasticcio,* still on the springform bottom, to a baking sheet. Brush the outside of the pastry base with beaten egg. Lay the rolled-out pastry over the mound, sealing it to the egg-covered base. Trim the top pastry so there is a 1-inch border around the pie. Roll it up to form a crimped rim around the base of the dome. This decorative rim should almost entirely cover any sign of the springform pan base.

Brush the crust with beaten egg. Using a fluted biscuit cutter, cut out several different-size rounds from leftover dough, and arrange them in a geometric pattern over the top of the pie (if the dough broke while it was being laid over the pie, pinch the breaks together and cover them with decoration). Make four slits near the top of the pie, and brush it again with egg. Slip the baking sheet onto the middle rack of the oven.

Bake 20 minutes at 425°F. Lower the heat to 375°F and bake 35 to 40 minutes more, or until the pastry is deep golden brown. Turn the oven off, leave the door ajar, and let the pie rest in the oven 10 minutes (not much longer, as it will dry out). Set it on a large round platter, and garnish with clusters of fresh lemon leaves, bay leaves, laurel leaves, or ivy. Serve hot.

Suggestions   **Wine:** From Emilia-Romagna, pour a white Albana di Romagna Secco or a red Sangiovese di Romagna Riserva. From other parts of Italy, drink a white Tocai from Friuli, or a soft red Merlot from Friuli or the Veneto's Colli Berici.

Menu: Serve the *pasticcio* after Modena's Spiced Soup of Spinach and Cheese (page 234), following it with a green salad of lettuces and fresh herbs, and a dessert of Meringues of the Dark Lake (page 421), served with fresh fruit. The pie also is an attractive buffet centerpiece. Instead of soup, offer Marinated Baby Onions (page 16), Mousse of Mortadella (page 22), and Salad of Tart Greens with Prosciutto and Warm Balsamic Dressing (page 26).

Scale di palmi Romani

Banquet tables arranged around a free-standing centerpiece

THE SWEET
PASTAS
OF THE
RENAISSANCE

uring the Renaissance, Italian pasta was seasoned by spices of every description—spices long used in the cuisines of ancient Persia and Arabia, Southeast Asia and China. The affluent Italian's taste for sweetness and spice was heightened by Medieval trade links with the East and Arab occupations of southern Italy. So many old Italian court recipes seem influenced by the Middle East. Sweet spices like cinnamon, nutmeg, clove and ginger were accented by pepper, perfumed with rosewater, or their sweetness took on arid/herbal overtones from generous doses of saffron. These blends, in turn, were mixed into dishes with nuts, fruits, meats and cheeses.

The ancestors of today's filled pastas were stuffed with these combinations and then sprinkled with grated cheese, sugar, and cinnamon. On the religious calendar's many meatless days, when one ate magro, or lean, pasta was cooked in milk or water. Broth of game or meat was the cooking medium on meat-eating, or fat (grasso) days. Those forerunners of present-day pastas evolved in remarkable settings. The Renaissance was a time of lavish banquets, a time when the foundations of modern cuisine were gradually taking shape in the noble kitchens of Italy. Her foods and manners were emulated, debated, and often envied throughout the Western world.

A typical menu of the period had a minimum of three courses, each with five to twenty or more dishes. Basic banquet etiquette called for covering tables in silky linen and changing the tablecloths up to three times during a meal. Fashion dictated centerpieces of Greek gods romping through mythical settings, the sculptures carved from sugar paste, then gilded with sheets of gold and silver and painted in bright enamels. Each place setting was marked by napkins folded to resemble sailing ships, fanciful beasts, or flowers. Washing hands with scented waters between courses was accepted ritual. Music, short plays, and dancing supplied a change of pace between courses.

Sweet and savory flavors dominated dishes throughout the meal. Sugar was expensive, a status symbol, and used lavishly. Pasta had not yet taken its place as solely a first course. It appeared from first dishes to last.

The first course always came from the credenza, or sideboard. Imagine a Welsh cupboard–like arrangement, a flat serving table backed by shelves. On those shelves your host displayed his best silver, gold, and pottery. Below, the tabletop was covered with a mosaic of room-temperature dishes arranged in perfect symmetry. Once the guests were ready, the entire collection of dishes was carried to the dining tables. There the multiple servings—green salads, bright fruits, cured meats, cold roasts, cheeses, marzipan, sweet tartlets, and perhaps pasta sprinkled with sugar, cheese, and cinnamon—were set out again in a symmetrical display.

After the first course was carried away by servants, a second service came hot from the kitchen. Great pies covered with decorated crusts and filled with meats and/or pastas were paraded before the guests. Platters of hammered silver were mounded with roasts and stews, often nested into beds of filled or ribbon pasta. At an elaborate feast there would be two, three, four, and even five of these courses from the kitchen.

The last course came again from the sideboard: vegetables dressed in vinegar and pepper, candied and fresh fruits, little cakes and pastries gilded with sugared seeds of melon or anise, savory tarts, fresh fennel to sweeten the breath, and perhaps squares of pasta filled with sugar, spices, fresh cheese and rosewater.

Descriptions of these feasts and foods of Emilia-Romagna are preserved in books and chronicles of the period. Four of them are especially useful. Two were written in the region, the other two were created by cooks native to the region, but working elsewhere.

Christofaro di Messisbugo was the scalco or major duomo to the Cardinal Hippolito d'Este at the 16th-century court of Ferrara. His two books, Banquets (Banchetti) and New Book (Libro Novo), published in 1549 and 1552, record banquets, recipes and details of kitchens and pantries. One hundred years later Carlo Nascia was cooking for the Duke of Parma, Ranuccio II, and writing his Four Banquets Destined for the Four Seasons of the Year (Li Quatro Banchetti Destinati per le Quatro Stagioni dell'Anno). Nascia's eye for detail is limited to the kitchen. Interestingly, there are few recipes for pasta. At about the same time Bartolomeo Stefani traveled from his native Bologna across the Po River to cook for the Gonzaga family, rulers of Mantua. His small book, The Art of Cooking Well (L'Arte di Ben Cucinare), was published in 1662 with not one pasta dish. Writing a few decades after Messisbugo, Bolognese Bartolomeo Scappi chronicled the banquets of nobles and churchmen. He cooked in Rome for Pope Pius V and wrote one of the period's most complete and extensively illustrated cookbooks containing many pasta recipes.

These records present pasta as court food, rather than food of the commoner. The white flour that produced the lightest pasta was the exclusive property of the wealthy. Today these sweet and savory recipes stand on their own as new and interesting pasta dishes. Certainly they speak of that glamorous era, but their exotic and unusual flavors fit very much into the world of the 20th century, where new tastes are embraced with such enthusiasm.

Christofaro di Messisbugo, 16th-century Ferrara cookbook author. Engraving from 1547.

Tagliatelle with Caramelized Oranges and Almonds

Tagliatelle con Arance e Mandorle

At 16th-century banquets this pasta accompanied poultry and meats. Try the combination with Christmas Capon for an important dinner. The sweet pasta makes an unexpected and very good dessert.

[Serves 10 to 12 as dessert or as a side dish with Christmas capon]

1 quart water

3 large Valencia or navel oranges

8 tablespoons (4 ounces) unsalted butter

1½ cups orange juice

⅔ cup sugar

Generous ⅛ teaspoon freshly ground black pepper

6 quarts salted water

1 recipe Wine Pasta (page 82), or 1 pound imported dried tagliatelle

3 to 4 tablespoons sugar

½ to 1 teaspoon ground cinnamon

⅔ cup (5 ounces) freshly grated Italian Parmigiano-Reggiano cheese

1 cup whole blanched almonds, toasted and coarsely chopped

Method

Working Ahead: *The sauce can be made several hours ahead; cover and set it aside at room temperature. Reheat to bubbling before adding the pasta.*

Preparing the Orange Zest: Bring the 1 quart water to a boil. Using a zester, remove the zest from the oranges in thin, long strips. Boil 3 minutes. Drain in a colander, rinse with cold water, and set aside.

Making the Sauce: Melt the butter in a large skillet over medium heat. Using a wooden spatula, stir in about ¼ cup of the orange juice and the ⅔ cup sugar. Melt the sugar in the butter over medium heat, frequently stirring in more spoonfuls of orange juice to keep the sauce from crystallizing (reserve about ⅓ cup for finishing the sauce). Once the sugar has dissolved, turn the heat to medium-high and stir occasionally as the mixture slowly turns amber, about 2 minutes. Once it reaches deep golden amber, blend in the pepper and two thirds of the orange zest. Cook only a second or two, to protect the zest from burning. Step back from the skillet and, at arm's length, pour in the last ⅓ cup of orange juice. It will bubble up and possibly spatter, then will thin the sauce to the ideal consistency. Turn off the heat.

Cooking the Pasta: Have a large platter and dessert dishes warming in a low oven. (If you are serving this with the capon, the bird should be ready. Bring the salted water to a boil. Drop in the pasta, and cook until tender but still a little resistant to the bite. Drain in a colander. Reheat the sauce to a lively bubble. Add the pasta to the skillet, and toss to coat thoroughly. Turn it onto the heated platter, and sprinkle with the sugar, cinnamon, cheese, almonds, and lastly, the remaining orange zest. Mound small portions on heated dessert plates, and serve hot. Or place the capon atop the pasta, and serve.

Suggestions   **Wine:** From Emilia-Romagna, a fruity and softly sweet Albana di Romagna Amabile (*amabile* is sweet), or Sicily's white Malvasia delle Lipari. With the capon and pasta a red Recioto della Valpolicella Classico Amarone.

Menu: Offer as dessert after a meal that evokes the 16th century: Start with Modena's Spiced Soup of Spinach and Cheese (page 234), then serve Rabbit Dukes of Modena (page 286), and a simple salad. Serve the tagliatelle and capon after "Little" Spring Soup from the 17th Century (page 232). For dessert, Marie Louise's Crescents (page 426).

Sweet Vermicelli Pancake
Torta di Vermicelli Carlo Nascia

Straight from the ducal banquet tables of 17th-century Parma, this thick pasta "pancake" is crisp and golden on the outside, spicy and crumbly on the inside. It is served hot, with a sugar syrup. In the time of Carlo Nascia, cook to the Duke of Parma, it accompanied savory dishes. Although for modern tastes the vermicelli cake makes a good dessert, try it too, cut into wedges and served alongside slices of roast venison, wild duck, hare, pork, or veal as they used to eat it in Parma.

[Serves 8 to 10 as dessert or side dish]

Sugar Syrup
½ cup sugar
1 cup water

Spiced Bread Crumbs and Pasta
2 tablespoons extra-virgin olive oil
1 cup fresh bread crumbs made
   from half-stale bread
¾ teaspoon ground cinnamon
⅛ teaspoon freshly grated nutmeg

Generous pinch of freshly ground
   black pepper
6 quarts salted water
10 ounces imported dried
   vermicelli or cappellini
6 tablespoons vegetable oil
5 tablespoons (2½ ounces)
   unsalted butter

Method

Working Ahead: *The sugar syrup can be made 1 week ahead; cover and refrigerate until needed. Prepare the bread crumbs up to several hours ahead. Let them stand, covered, at room temperature until needed.*

Making the Sugar Syrup: Combine the sugar and water in a small saucepan, and boil 3 minutes, or until the sugar has completely dissolved. Set aside.

Toasting and Spicing the Bread Crumbs: In a 10-inch heavy skillet, heat the olive oil over medium heat. Add the bread crumbs and cook, stirring frequently, 4 minutes, or until golden. Take care not to burn them. Turn them into a small bowl and add the cinnamon, nutmeg, and pepper. Taste for balance. The spices should blend with no one taste standing out, except a tingle from the pepper. Wipe the skillet out with a thick wad of paper towels.

Cooking the Pasta: Bring the salted water to a boil. Add the pasta and cook 2 minutes, or until slightly underdone. Drain it in a colander, tossing to rid it of excess liquid.

Cooking the Pancake: Have a serving platter warming in a low oven. Heat half the vegetable oil and half the butter in the skillet over high heat, swirling to coat the sides of the pan. Take care not to let it smoke. Add half the pasta, arranging it a nest. Reduce the heat to medium. Spread the bread crumbs over the center of the pasta nest to within 1½ inches of the edge. Top with the rest of the pasta, completely covering the first layer and enclosing the bread crumbs. Press with the back of a spatula to gently compact the pancake.

Cook over medium to medium-low heat 10 to 13 minutes (checking occasionally for burning), or until the bottom is a deep golden brown. Place a large plate on top of the pancake, and flip it over. Now quickly heat the remaining oil and butter in the pan over high heat, taking care not to let it smoke. Slip the pancake back into the pan, lower the heat to medium, and cook as for the first side. Meanwhile, warm the sugar syrup over medium-low heat.

Serving: Slide the pancake onto the warmed serving platter, and pour the warm sugar syrup over it. Serve hot, cut into small wedges.

Suggestions **Wine:** A young sweet white: Moscato d'Asti, Asti Spumanti, or Moscato del Trentino.

Menu: Serve after roasted meats, poultry, or game. A Parma-inspired menu begins with small servings of Paola Cavazzini's Eggplant Torte (page 241) as a first course, then Erminia's Pan-Crisped Chicken (page 270), a Salad of Mixed Greens and Fennel (page 349), and then the *torta*. As a side dish, have the pancake with January Pork (page 312), Lemon Roast Veal with Rosemary (page 294), or Christmas Capon (page 281).

A Chinese Pancake?

Although the idea of pan-fried pasta was not new in Nascia's time, it was nonexistent in Emilia-Romagna. Nascia was a Neapolitan. Then (as now) Naples had an omelette filled with leftover pasta. The vermicelli in this recipe suggests that he might have brought this dish with him from his home. Although vermicelli had become known throughout Italy by Nascia's time (and was often a generic name for string pastas), they represent southern cooking rather than that of Parma in the north. The fact that no eggs are used in Nascia's *torta* sets loose another thread of speculation. Pan-fried noodles—sometimes stuffed, sometimes not—are frequently made in China. Considering that China possessed a sophisticated pasta culture before Christ, pan-cooked noodle cakes might have been common for centuries before Nascia's *torta.* Is it possible that Nascia heard of such a dish from the traders and travelers who crossed his path at the port of Naples, or in Parma's court? Did he then reinterpret it to suit the tastes of his employers?

Rosewater Maccheroni Romanesca
"A Fare Dieci Piatti di Maccheroni Romaneschi"

This pasta made with rosewater, bread, and sugar, in addition to flour and egg, is a 16-century recipe from Ferrara's majordomo Christofaro di Messisbugo. More of a curiosity than a dish for our 20th-century palates, the recipe shows how pasta doughs were often flavored at the time. These are the ancestors of today's pastas of saffron, herbs, and spices. Serve with The Cardinal's Ragù, or sprinkle on crushed pistachio or toasted almonds along with the cheese, sugar, and spices called for below.

Romanesca, or pasta in the Roman style, is one of the many predecessors of today's hollow maccheroni. The dough was rolled around batons and cut into short lengths to make one of the earliest recorded tubular pastas in Emilia-Romagna. This variation is an alternative offered by Messisbugo, suggesting the pasta be cut into wide strands.

[Serves 4 as a first course, or garnishes a roast serving 6]

Pasta

1 small white roll (about 2 inches in diameter), trimmed of crust and crumbled

⅓ cup rosewater

2¼ cups plus 6 tablespoons (10 ounces) all-purpose unbleached flour (organic stone-ground is preferred), plus extra as needed

3 tablespoons sugar

Pinch of salt

3 eggs, beaten

6 quarts Poultry/Meat Stock (page 66), Quick Stock (page 68), or milk

Sauce

6 to 7 tablespoons (3 to 3½ ounces) unsalted butter, at room temperature

1 teaspoon rosewater

¼ cup sugar

⅔ cup (2½ ounces) freshly grated Italian Parmigiano-Reggiano cheese

Generous sprinkling of ground cinnamon

¼ teaspoon coarsely ground black pepper, or more to taste

¼ cup shelled pistachio nuts, lightly crushed (optional)

Method   **Working Ahead:** *The pasta can be made 1 day ahead. Spread it on towel-lined baskets or baking sheets, and let dry at room temperature.*

Making the Dough by Hand: Soak the crumbled roll in the rosewater about 20 minutes. Mound the flour on a work surface, sprinkle it with the sugar and salt, and make a well in the center. Add the eggs and the crumbled roll with its liquid. Working with a fork, stir the eggs and roll together to blend. Then gradually stir flour into the mixture. Use a pastry scraper to mass the dough together. Once a rough dough has formed, knead it 10 minutes, or until smooth and elastic. Wrap it in plastic wrap, and let it rest at room temperature 20 minutes.

Making the Dough in a Food Processor: Combine all the ingredients in the processor and process until smooth. Knead the dough by hand about 10 minutes. Wrap in plastic wrap, and let rest at room temperature 20 minutes.

Shaping the Pasta: Line several large flat baskets with kitchen towels. Thin and stretch the dough by hand or pass it through a pasta machine, as described on pages 83 to 86. The dough should be thin enough to clearly see the outline of your hand through it. Cut it into ³⁄₈-inch strips, and spread them on the baskets to dry.

Or, to make the maccheroni as done in Messisbugo's day, collect some knitting needles or chopsticks to use as dowels. Cut the thinned dough into strips about ³⁄₄ inch wide and as long as the dowels. Flour the dowels and wrap the dough strips around them, pinching the edges together. Let dry about 20 minutes, and then make cuts around the dowels, creating hollow pastas about 2 inches long. Dry another 3 to 4 hours, then slip the maccheroni off the dowels. The maccheroni can be dried at room temperature several days.

Cooking the Pasta: Bring the stock or milk to a boil. Drop in the pasta and cook 1 to 5 minutes, depending upon how dry it is. Taste for doneness; it should be firm but tender enough to eat. Drain, and toss the hot pasta with the butter, rosewater, sugar, cheese, cinnamon, and pepper. Sprinkle with the nuts if desired. Serve hot.

Suggestions   **Wine:** A sweet Albana di Romagna Amabile or Moscato d'Asti if you are serving the pasta as a first course. With meats, drink a dry red wine like Sangiovese di Romagna Riserva or Dolcetto d'Alba.

Menu: Serve as in Messisbugo's day by spreading the sauced maccheroni on a large heated platter. Then set Lemon Roast Veal with Rosemary (page 294) or Christmas Capon (page 281) on the pasta. Balsamic Roast Chicken (page 279) is also good with it. Carve the meats on the platter so the juices flavor the pasta. Top with The Cardinal's Ragù (page 40) instead of butter, rosewater and spices. Or serve it with the topping described above as a first course before Artusi's Delight (page 300), Rabbit Dukes of Modena (page 286), or Giovanna's Wine-Basted Rabbit (page 284).

Sweet Tagliarini Tart of Ferrara
Torta di Tagliarini Ferrarese

From the time when pasta with sugar was a sign of high status, this tart combines them with toasted almonds in a sweet crust. It often appeared as small tartlets at the beginning of a Renaissance banquet or with the last course. Serve it today as everyone does in Modena and Ferrara—as a dessert presented to special guests and on important family occasions.

[Serves 8 to 10 as dessert]

Sweet Pastry

1 cup (4 ounces) all-purpose unbleached flour (organic stone-ground preferred)

½ cup plus 2 tablespoons (2½ ounces) cake flour

½ cup (3½ ounces) sugar

Pinch of salt

½ teaspoon grated lemon zest

8 tablespoons (4 ounces) unsalted butter, chilled, cut into chunks

3 egg yolks, chilled

1 to 2 tablespoons cold water

1 tablespoon unsalted butter (for greasing pan)

Filling

2 quarts salted water

2 ounces fresh tagliarini, cut as thin as possible (page 90), or 3 ounces imported dried fidelini or cappellini

1½ cups (6 ounces) blanched almonds, toasted

1 cup (7 ounces) sugar

3 tablespoons all-purpose unbleached flour

9 tablespoons (4½ ounces) unsalted butter, melted

½ teaspoon almond extract (see Note)

2 tablespoons Strega, Galliano, or liqueur of Moscato

3 tablespoons water

3 egg yolks

6 egg whites

Garnish

⅓ cup powdered sugar

Method　　**Working Ahead:** *The pastry can be mixed 1 day ahead; wrap it and store in the refrigerator. Bake the tart 8 hours before serving. Tightly wrapped, the tart keeps in the refrigerator several days.*

Making the Dough by Hand: Stir the dry ingredients together in a large bowl. Using your fingertips, rub in the butter until the mixture looks like coarse meal with a few large shales of flour-coated butter still intact.

Make a well in the center and add the egg yolks and 1 tablespoon water. Beat the egg yolks and water with a fork until smooth. Then toss with the dry ingredients until everything is moistened. Do not stir or knead because the dough can toughen. Gather the dough into a ball. If it is too dry, sprinkle with the remaining tablespoon of water, toss for a few seconds, and then gather into a ball, wrap, and chill at least 30 minutes.

Making the Dough in a Food Processor: Put the dry ingredients and the lemon zest in a food processor fitted with the steel blade, and blend for a few seconds. Add the butter and process until the mixture resembles coarse meal. Add the egg and 1 tablespoon of the cold water, and process with the on/off pulse until the dough barely gathers into small clumps. Turn the dough out onto a sheet of plastic wrap, gather it into a ball, wrap, and chill at least 30 minutes.

Making the Crust: Sprinkle a work surface with flour. Thoroughly grease a 9-inch layer cake pan with removable bottom and 1¾-inch sides with the tablespoon of butter. Roll out the dough to form a large round about ⅛ inch thick. Make sure the pastry is all of even thickness. Fit into the cake pan, bringing the dough up its sides and neatly trimming it around the pan's rim. Because of its high sugar content, this pastry breaks easily. Just press it into the pan a piece at a time. Chill about 1 hour.

Preheat the oven to 400°F. Line the crust with foil and weight it with dried beans or rice. Bake 12 minutes. Then remove the liner and weights, prick the bottom of the crust with a fork, and bake another 8 to 10 minutes, or until it is barely beginning to color. Remove from the oven and allow to cool.

Making the Filling: Preheat the oven to 375°F. Have a 10-inch round of parchment paper handy. Bring the salted water to a vigorous boil. Drop in the pasta. Cook fresh pasta only about 10 seconds. Allow 1 minute for dried pasta. It should be tender enough to eat but still quite firm. Drain, rinse under cold water, and shake dry. Spread the pasta out on paper towels.

Coarsely chop one quarter of the almonds. Set aside. Combine the remaining almonds with the sugar and flour in a food processor, and grind to a powder (or use a hand-operated nut grater). Add 6 tablespoons of the melted butter, the almond extract, liqueur, water, and egg yolks to the food processor. Blend thoroughly. Turn into a large bowl. Beat the egg whites to form soft peaks. Lighten the almond mixture by stirring in a quarter of the whites. Then gently fold the rest of the whites in, blending thoroughly but keeping the mixture light. Slather half the filling over the bottom of the crust. Spread half the pasta over it. Then top with the remaining filling.

continued

Sprinkle the reserved almonds over the filling, top with the rest of the pasta, and drizzle with the remaining melted butter.

Baking the Tart: Lightly cover the tart with a round of parchment paper, and bake 20 minutes. Uncover and bake another 30 to 35 minutes, or until a knife inserted about 2 inches from the edge comes out clean. Cool the tart on a rack.

Serving: Slip off the side of the pan, and serve at room temperature. Sift a generous dusting of powdered sugar over the tart just before presenting.

Suggestions   **Wine:** From Emilia-Romagna, a sweet white Bianco di Scandiano. From other parts of Italy, the Piedmont's Caluso Passito or Malvasia delle Lipari from Sicily. Although heresy to Italian purists, France's Château d'Yquem Sauternes complements the tart splendidly when fine Italian dessert wines are not available.

Menu: Serve after dishes from the Modena/Ferrara area, such as Balsamic Roast Chicken (page 279), Rabbit Dukes of Modena (page 286), Artusi's Delight (page 300), Rabbit Roasted with Sweet Fennel (page 289), or Riccardo Rimondi's Chicken Cacciatora (page 275). For a lighter menu, serve a main dish of tagliatelle with Meat Ragù with Marsala (page 56), Risotto of Baby Artichokes and Peas (page 209), or Risotto of Red Wine and Rosemary (page 205), then the tart.

Cook's Notes   **Almond Extract:** Almond extract replaces the traditional bitter almonds, used for centuries to accent almond dishes. Bitter almonds, which can form harmful prussic acid, are banned in the United States. If available, the kernel found inside a peach or apricot pit can be toasted and ground with the almonds to attain a bitter almond flavor.

Idealized portrait of Lucrezia Borgia by Bartolomeo Veneto

The Misunderstood Borgia

The infamous Lucrezia Borgia is inseparable from the Sweet Tagliarini Tarts found in every Ferrara pastry shop. The Ferrarese speak of the woman as though she has just left the room. Affection for her has not diminished in the four and a half centuries since her death. Few believe she murdered her first two husbands. Everyone, from the lady waiting on you in the pastry shop to the town's leading businessmen, explains how misunderstood she was, how her father and brother were the evil ones. Besides, even if some suspicion might have clouded her earlier marriage, once she settled down in Ferrara with her third husband, Alfonso d'Este, heir to the Este dukedom, all was well. As Duchess of Ferrara, she became a patroness of the arts, famous for her gentleness, beauty, and keen intelligence.

In 1502, the about-to-be-married Lucrezia entered Ferrara with such a lavish show of wealth that even the Este, masters of appearing richer than they actually were, were impressed. Five years were needed to calculate the value of her dowry, which included whole towns as well as jewels, furnishings, artworks and gold. Ferrara lore claims that Sweet Tagliarini Tart was created by Este court cooks for Lucrezia's wedding feast, its tangled topping of golden pasta strands a tribute to Lucrezia's blond hair. Different versions of the tart are found in Modena and across the Po River in Mantua, which shared much with Ferrara during the centuries of Este rule.

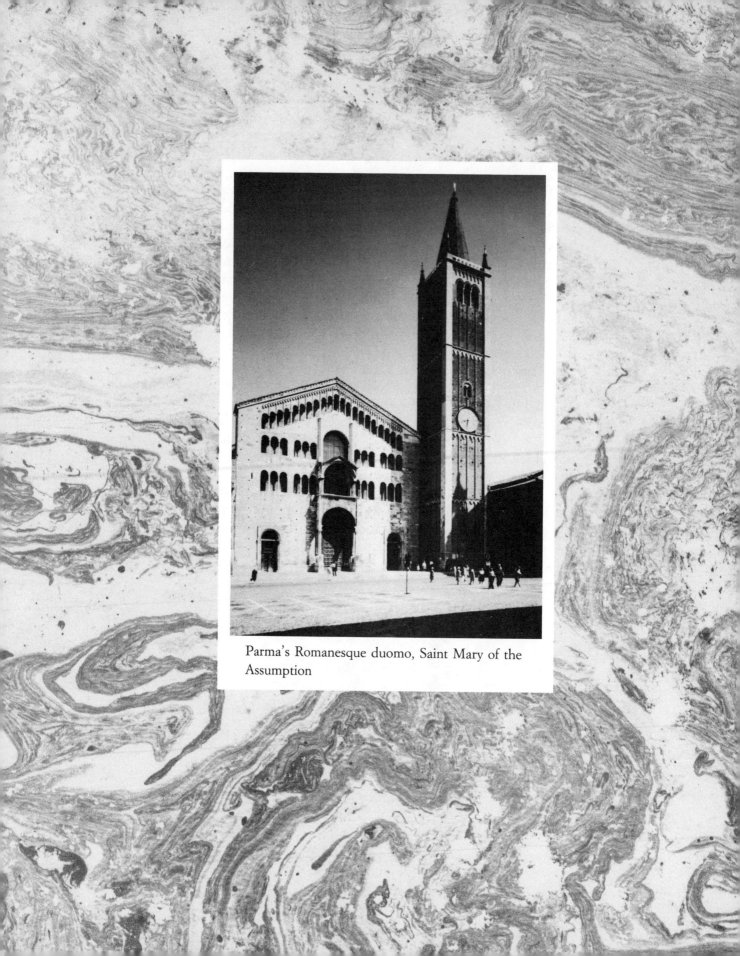

Parma's Romanesque duomo, Saint Mary of the
Assumption

RISOTTO, SOUP, AND VEGETABLE FIRST COURSES

*I*n Emilia-Romagna the first course is the one not-to-be-missed part of a meal. When not eating pasta, everyone has soup, risotto or a vegetable dish. Italians sometimes skip an antipasto or forego a second dish, but rarely will they give up their first course.

Many of these dishes make much of little and come from peasant beginnings. For instance, Reggio has a tart made with greens gathered from the hillsides. Modenese laborers had a soup of beans, potatoes and cabbage to celebrate Christmas Eve. Out on the Po plain a risotto of locally grown rice was cooked with more local red wine than meat-based broth.

Today in Emilia-Romagna these dishes often become meals unto themselves because of hectic lives and lighter eating. A century ago for the poor, many of these dishes were one-dish meals because there was nothing more to eat.

At the other end of the spectrum are the first courses of the wealthy. These were and still are taste-teasers. Light soups like Almond Spice Broth and "Little" Spring Soup from the 17th Century were the palate fresheners on tables laden with more elaborate banquet food than anyone could finish. Rice of the Princes, Domed Rice with Pigeon, and Nino Bergese's Risotto all began on those same banquet tables.

For the farmers of the time a feast was a bowl of beans and pasta. Today these crosses between soups and stews are still enthusiastically eaten in the region. They are included in this chapter because they are more about vegetables than pasta. Flour for pasta was expensive and used sparingly. Beans and legumes grew in the garden and could be cooked any number of ways.

Another outgrowth of the peasant tradition are dishes centering on one vegetable. Oven-Glazed Porcini and Paola Cavazzini's Eggplant Torte are elegant dishes today, but they come from a time when a single vegetable in its seasonal prime was used not only for its good taste, but because it was easily had.

Eat these dishes as in Emilia-Romagna, serving several, one after the other. Or let them stand on their own, eaten after an antipasto and followed by fruit or dessert.

Three hungry gentlemen wearing wigs of state eye a wedge of Parmigiano-Reggiano cheese in this mid–20th century advertisement. Coating the cheese in black ash and crushed grape seed was discontinued in the 1950s and 1960s.

Classic White Risotto
Risotto in Bianco

It is mesmerizing to watch women create this risotto with the instincts that come from years of practice. The finish is the best part, when big handfuls of grated Parmigiano-Reggiano cheese are folded into the risotto. Nothing happens for a few moments. Then, as the cheese warms, its fragrance fills the room.

The white in the title comes not only from the color of the rice but also from the dish's classic simplicity. No saffron, tomatoes, vegetables, or meats are used. The risotto depends on a homemade stock and a good Parmigiano-Reggiano cheese. Renditions of this risotto are made throughout Emilia-Romagna. They illustrate the innate restraint of the region's foods, in the seamless blending of subtle but distinctive ingredients.

[Serves 6 to 8 as a first course, 4 to 6 as a main dish]

2 tablespoons unsalted butter

1 medium onion, minced

8 cups Poultry/Meat Stock (page 66) or Quick Stock (page 68)

2 cups (14 ounces) imported Superfino Arborio or Roma rice (see Note)

⅓ cup dry white wine

Salt and freshly ground black pepper to taste

1 tablespoon unsalted butter, or ¼ cup heavy cream

⅔ to 1 cup (3 to 4 ounces) freshly grated Italian Parmigiano-Reggiano cheese

Method

Working Ahead: *Risotto is best cooked just before serving. The cooking time can be cut slightly by sautéing the onion several hours ahead. Cool, cover, and set aside at room temperature. Once the onion is reheated and the stock is bubbling, cooking the rice takes no more than 15 to 20 minutes.*

Making the Onion Base: Melt the 2 tablespoons butter in a heavy 5- to 6-quart casserole over medium heat. Stir in the onion and cook slowly 8 minutes, or until very soft and clear, but not browned.

Cooking the Risotto: Warm shallow soup plates in a low oven. Bring the stock to a gentle bubble over medium heat. Using a wooden spatula, stir the rice into the onions over medium heat. Use broad strokes, sweeping the rice up from the bottom of the pot. Cook 3 minutes, or until it looks chalky and you can see a white dot in the center of each grain. Keeping the heat at medium, stir in the wine and keep stirring as it is absorbed by the rice. Then start stirring in the stock, 1 cup at a time.

continued

Each cup must be absorbed before the next is added. Stir the risotto to prevent sticking, pulling it down from the pot's sides and folding the top to the bottom as you go.

Once 6 cups have been absorbed, add the stock in ½-cup portions and start tasting the rice. A good risotto is tender but still a little firm to the bite—never mushy. Some prefer risotto creamier than others, but it is never soupy or dry. Risotto has flow and movement, yet enough substance to be mounded on a soupspoon.

Finishing and Serving: Take the risotto off the heat when the rice still has a little more resistance than you would like. Season with salt and pepper. The next step not only finishes seasoning the rice but completes its cooking. Fold in the butter or cream and the cheese, keeping the mixture light. Taste again for salt and pepper, adding more if necessary. Once everything is blended in, let the risotto rest a moment or two. The rice will swell a little as it absorbs the final flavorings. Spoon the risotto into heated soup dishes, and serve immediately.

Suggestions   **Wine:** A white Gavi dei Gavi from the Piedmont or Tuscany's Montecarlo.

Menu: If the risotto is a main dish, the Salad of Tart Greens with Prosciutto and Warm Balsamic Dressing (page 26) is a fine prelude. For dessert, Ugo Falavigna's Apple Cream Tart (page 411) is ideal. For a rich and elegant finish, have Frozen Chocolate Pistachio Cream with Hot Chocolate Marsala Sauce (page 438). A fuller menu has the risotto followed by Pan-Roasted Quail (page 283), Lemon Roast Veal with Rosemary (page 294), or Maria Bertuzzi's Lemon Chicken (page 273).

Cook's Notes   **Parmigiano-Reggiano:** See page 488 for information on selecting a fine cheese.

Arborio and Roma Rice: Find these imported Italian rices in Italian grocery and specialty foods stores. Arborio will be more available than Roma.

Rice in Parma

Many believe Emilia-Romagna's rice dishes were always made with rice imported from neighboring Lombardy and the Piedmont. But Parma food historian Guglielmo Capacchi explains that rice was grown in what is now Parma province as far back as the 1400s. After city dwellers claimed their water supply was ruined by the rice's standing water, and local millers objected to the diversion of water from their mills to the rice fields, rice growing was banned on Parma's plain in 1542.

Rice's availability from nearby areas and the strong Spanish connections of the Farnese dukes (Parma's ruling family from 1545 to 1731), made rice dishes a permanent part of Parma's repertoire. Rice still grows in Emilia-Romagna around the village of Rolo in Reggio province, with the fields stretching into neighboring Modena province. The baked Modena Rice Pudding found on page 398 is from that area. In Parma, the Superfino Roma rice of Reggio and Modena is often used in risottos instead of Arborio.

Nino Bergese's Risotto
Risotto Mantecato

Risotto Mantecato is an unforgettable dish. Its big golden and brown tastes meld into each other like the colors of an old Italian still-life. Rich sweet onion and meaty stock flavor the rice, which in turn is gilded with spoonfuls of a Marsala-flavored sauce. This dish is a cook's reward for having Meat Essences and Poultry/Meat Stock on hand. The risotto was created by the now-deceased Nino Bergese, chef to Italian nobility and co-founder of Imola's Ristorante San Domenico. Although it requires some advance preparation, the final dish needs only a few extra minutes more than a usual risotto.

[Serves 8 as a first course, 4 to 6 as a main dish.]

Onion Base

2 tablespoons unsalted butter
1 tablespoon extra-virgin olive oil
2 large onions, thinly sliced
Salt to taste
Water as needed

Sauce and Risotto

2 cups Meat Essences (page 61)
¼ cup dry red wine
¼ to ⅓ cup dry Marsala
7 to 9 cups Poultry/Meat Stock
(page 66)

1½ tablespoons unsalted butter
2½ cups (17 ounces) imported
  Superfino Arborio or Roma rice
⅔ cup dry white wine
2 tablespoons unsalted butter
About ½ cup freshly grated Italian
  Parmigiano-Reggiano cheese
Salt and freshly ground black
  pepper to taste

Method

Working Ahead: *The onion base can be cooked and puréed up to 3 days ahead; cool, cover, and refrigerate. Season the Meat Essences about 1 hour before serving; set aside, covered, at room temperature.*

Making the Onion Base: This slow cooking must be done over very low heat. Use a flame-tamer if necessary. Combine the butter, olive oil, onion, and salt in a heavy medium-size skillet. Cover and cook over low heat 3 hours, stirring occasionally and making sure the onions are not coloring. They go from white and crisp to moist and almost transparent. Do not rush or shortcut this step; it gives the onions the deep sweetness important to the risotto's foundation.

Uncover and continue cooking the onions over low heat another 2 hours, or until caramelized to the color of a copper penny. They will have a rich aroma and taste almost sugary. Run a wooden spatula under the onions frequently to keep them from sticking and to bring up the brown glaze from the bottom of the skillet. Let the onions cool. Then transfer them to a blender or food processor, and purée until smooth. Add a few spoonfuls of water if necessary.

Making the Sauce: Combine the Meat Essences and red wine in a 1½-quart heavy nonaluminum saucepan. Simmer, uncovered, 10 minutes, or until reduced to about ¾ cup. Add ¼ cup Marsala, and simmer 3 to 4 minutes. The sauce should be deeply flavored, robust, with a touch of sweetness. Add more Marsala if necessary. Set aside.

Cooking the Risotto: Have shallow soup dishes heating in a low oven. Heat the 7 to 9 cups of stock to a gentle simmer. Heat the 1½ tablespoons butter in a 5-quart heavy casserole over medium heat. Stir in the onion base and heat through. Stir in the rice with a wooden spatula, and cook a few minutes, or until it looks chalky. Keeping the heat at medium, stir in the wine. Keep stirring to prevent sticking as it is absorbed. Then start blending in the stock, 1 cup at a time. Each cup must be absorbed before the next is added. Stir the risotto to keep it from sticking, pulling it down from the pot's sides and folding the top to the bottom as you go. Once 6 cups have been absorbed, add the stock in ½-cup portions and start tasting the rice. Risotto is tender but still firm to the bite, never mushy. The ideal consistency differs slightly from one cook to the next—some prefer their risotto creamier than others— but it always has flow and movement. It is never soupy or dry. Bergese's risotto needs enough substance to be mounded on a soupspoon.

Finishing and Serving: Take the risotto off the heat when the rice still has a little more resistance than you would like. Fold in the 2 tablespoons butter and the cheese, keeping the mixture light. Taste for salt and pepper. Once everything is blended in, let the risotto rest a moment or two. Meanwhile, reheat the sauce. Mound the risotto in the center of the heated soup plates. Using the side of a wooden spoon, make five grooves, like the spokes of a wheel, down the sides of each mound. Drizzle each serving with about 1½ tablespoons of the sauce. Serve immediately.

Suggestions   **Wine:** A Sangiovese di Romagna Riserva, a Tuscan Carmignano, or a Barbera d'Asti.

Menu: For a full menu, serve before Giovanna's Wine-Basted Rabbit (page 284), Lemon Roast Veal with Rosemary (page 294), or Erminia's Pan-Crisped Chicken (page 270). As a first course, a lighter menu, begin with Fresh Pears with Parmigiano-Reggiano and Balsamic Vinegar (page 30) and close the meal with Strawberries in Red Wine (page 445) or Capacchi's Blazing Chestnuts (page 450).

Cook's Notes   Although the success of this dish depends on two time-consuming recipes, both Meat Essences and Poultry/Meat Stock freeze well.

Risotto of Red Wine and Rosemary
Risotto al Barbera

This simple risotto often begins winter game dinners in Emilia-Romagna. Use a Barbera, a Barolo, or a big Zinfandel for cooking and drinking.

[Serves 4 to 5 as a first course, 3 as a main dish]

2 tablespoons unsalted butter or extra-virgin olive oil

1 small to medium onion, minced

1 large California bay laurel leaf

Two 2-inch sprigs fresh rosemary, or 1½ teaspoons dried rosemary leaves

5 to 6 cups Poultry/Meat Stock (page 66) or Quick Stock (page 68)

2 cups (14 ounces) imported Superfino Arborio or Roma rice

2½ cups dry red wine

2 tablespoons unsalted butter

2 cups (8 ounces) freshly grated Italian Parmigiano-Reggiano cheese

Salt and freshly ground black pepper to taste

Method   **Working Ahead:** *Although the rice should be cooked just before dining, the onion and herbs can be sautéed several hours in advance. Set them aside, covered, until ready to cook the rice. Allow yourself about 20 to 25 minutes to finish the risotto.*

continued

Making the Flavor Base: Heat the butter or oil in a heavy 5-quart pot over medium-high heat. Add the onion, bay leaf, and rosemary. Turn the heat to low, cover the pot tightly, and cook 15 minutes, or until the onion is soft and clear, not browned. Stir occasionally and check for browning.

Cooking the Rice: Have soup dishes warming in a low oven. Bring the stock to a gentle bubble. Uncover the onions and raise the heat to medium. Add the rice and sauté, stirring frequently with a wooden spatula, 3 minutes, or until it looks chalky and a white dot appears in the center of each kernel. Stir 1 cup of the wine into the rice. Keep stirring as the wine bubbles and is slowly absorbed by the rice. Sweep the spatula over the bottom and sides of the pot to keep the rice from sticking. Add the rest of the wine and stir until it is absorbed.

Now blend in 1 cup of the stock until it is absorbed. Keep adding cupfuls of stock, stirring and folding in each addition, until you have used about 4 cups. Taste the rice. It should have a suggestion of tenderness but still some crunch. Now add stock in ½-cup portions, cooking until the rice is just a shade too firm. If it is very thick and stiff, thin it to a creamy consistency with another ¼ cup of stock. Take it off the heat.

Finishing and Serving: Fold the 2 tablespoons of butter and ½ cup of the cheese into the risotto with a big folding motion that protects the grains from being crushed. Keep folding until the butter has melted. Season the rice with salt and pepper. Spoon the risotto into the heated soup dishes, and serve immediately. Pass the rest of the cheese separately.

Suggestions   **Wine:** Serve the same wine used to make the risotto: a Barbera or Barolo from the Piedmont, or a big California Zinfandel.

Menu: Have the risotto in small quantities before Pan-Roasted Quail (page 283), Christmas Capon (page 281), or Rabbit Dukes of Modena (page 286). Serve it as a main course after Spring Salad with Hazelnuts (page 21). Fresh pears and Sweet Cornmeal Biscuits (page 422) make a fine finish.

Piacenza's Risotto with Ragù
Risotto alla Piacenza

We rarely think of ragù with risotto, yet it is a favorite combination throughout much of northern Italy. Often the ragù is prepared as the flavor base of the risotto and cooked into it. But in this Piacenza dish the ragù is made separately and layered into the finished risotto on its serving platter. I prefer this approach, since the ragù can be prepared well in advance. And it is particularly colorful, with the rice tinted golden by saffron and set off by the deep russets of the ragù. No doubt the saffron is evidence of influence from Piacenza's neighbor to the north, Milan. Saffron is one of the hallmarks of the famous Risotto alla Milanese.

[Serves 8 to 10 as a first course, 6 to 8 as a main dish]

1 recipe Country-Style Ragù
  (page 48)
About 10 cups Poultry/Meat Stock
  (page 66) or Quick Stock
  (page 68)
½ teaspoon saffron threads
3 tablespoons unsalted butter
1 medium onion, minced

3½ cups (1½ pounds) imported
  Superfino Arborio or Roma rice
¾ cup dry white wine
Salt and freshly ground black
  pepper to taste
2 cups (8 ounces) freshly grated
  Italian Parmigiano-Reggiano
  cheese

Method

Working Ahead: *The ragù can be stored, covered, 3 days in the refrigerator, and freezes well up to 1 month. The risotto is best cooked and eaten right away. But the onion can be sautéed several hours in advance; cover and keep at room temperature. The risotto will take about 20 minutes to cook.*

Making the Base: Place a large platter and soup dishes in a low oven to warm. Have the ragù heating up in a saucepan over medium heat; keep covered. Pour all but 1 cup of the stock into a saucepan, and bring it to a gentle bubble. Dissolve the saffron in the reserved cup of stock. Heat the butter in a heavy 5- to 6-quart casserole over medium heat. Add the onion and slowly sauté until it is soft and clear, about 10 minutes.

Cooking the Risotto: Add the rice and stir over medium heat 3 minutes, or until a small white dot appears in the center of the kernels. Stir in the wine and simmer, stirring constantly, until it is absorbed by the rice. Blend in the saffron-flavored stock, stirring frequently until it is absorbed by the rice. Add the remaining stock, 1 cup at a time, stirring each addition until it is absorbed. Never cover the pot.

After about 6 cups of stock have been added, taste the rice. The risotto is ready when the rice is tender but still has a pleasant firmness that slightly resists the bite. As the risotto gets close to this stage, add the stock in ½-cup amounts. Keep tasting. Finally, make sure the risotto is creamy, not dry. If necessary, stir in another ½ cup of stock once the rice is done. Remove the pot from the heat and fold in ½ cup of the cheese. Taste for salt and pepper. Let the risotto rest 2 or 3 minutes as you remove the serving platter and soup dishes from the oven. Make sure the ragù is hot.

Serving: Spread half the risotto on the platter. Top it with half the ragù and a sprinkling of about 3 tablespoons of cheese. Then add the remaining risotto, ragù, and another 3 tablespoons cheese. Serve hot. Pass the remaining cheese separately.

Suggestions   **Wine:** Pour a Gutturnio from Piacenza or a Sangiovese di Romagna Riserva. From other parts of Italy, drink a Tuscan Chianti Classico, a Barbera from Lombardy, or the Piedmont's Barbera d'Asti or d'Alba.

Menu: Serve the risotto as a main dish, beginning with the Platter of Cured Meats (page 14) and Marinated Baby Onions (page 16) or Spring Salad with Hazelnuts (page 21). Following a Piacenza theme, the cured meats could be solely a fine coppa (page 474). Serve Salad of Mixed Greens and Fennel (page 349) after the risotto if you are not having a salad antipasto. Nonna's Jam Tart (page 413) or Capacchi's Blazing Chestnuts (page 450) is a typical family-style dessert.

Risotto of Baby Artichokes and Peas
Risotto Carciofi e Piselli

Artichokes and peas are a favorite springtime combination throughout Italy. They make this risotto substantial enough to be a main dish. Sometimes no bigger than a Brussels sprout, the artichokes for this recipe come from the bottom of the plant and have no coarse choke in their centers. New peas have such fresh flavors that cooks in Emilia-Romagna often sweeten spring risotti with the pods as well as the pea.

[Serves 6 to 8 as a first course, 4 to 6 as a main dish]

2½ pounds (24 to 35) baby artichokes (see Note)
½ lemon
Juice of 2 large lemons
1½ quarts cold water
3 tablespoons unsalted butter
1 medium onion, minced
2½ cups freshly shelled sweet peas or frozen tiny peas, defrosted
Salt and freshly ground black pepper to taste
1 large clove garlic, minced

7 to 8 cups Poultry/Meat Stock (page 66) or Quick Stock (page 68)
2 cups (14 ounces) imported Superfino Arborio or Roma rice
Handful of pea pods (optional)
Salt and freshly ground black pepper to taste
1½ tablespoons unsalted butter
1 to 1½ cups (4 to 6 ounces) freshly grated Italian Parmigiano-Reggiano cheese

Method

Working Ahead: *Although the risotto is best made just before serving, its base can be prepared several hours ahead. Cool, cover, and refrigerate until ready to use. Allow about 20 minutes to finish the risotto.*

Preparing the Artichokes: Break off the dark green outer leaves until you reach leaves that are yellow-green at their base. With a small sharp knife, trim away any dark green stubs around the base of the artichokes. Keep rubbing the cut areas with the lemon half to avoid darkening. Then cut off and discard the top half of the remaining leaves. You now have artichoke hearts. Cut half the artichoke hearts into quarters. Thinly slice the other half. Drop both into separate bowls of lemon water created by combining the lemon juice and cold water.

Making the Base: In a heavy 5- to 6-quart pot, heat the 3 tablespoons butter over medium heat. Stir in the onions with a wooden spatula. Soften and sweeten them by turning the heat to medium-low, covering the pot, and cooking 10 minutes. Meanwhile, pat dry the sliced artichokes. Uncover the pot and add the sliced artichoke hearts. If you are using fresh peas, add 1 cup now. Sprinkle the mixture lightly with salt and pepper, turn the heat up to medium, and cook about 5 minutes, stirring frequently with the wooden spatula. The artichoke pieces will be tinged with gold.

If you are using frozen peas, add 1 cup now. Then stir in the garlic and ½ cup of the stock. Bring to a simmer, cover the pot securely, and cook over medium-low heat 10 minutes, or until the artichokes are soft. Stir to keep from sticking. While the artichokes are cooking, bring the remaining stock to a boil over high heat. Turn the heat to medium-low so the stock bubbles occasionally, and keep partially covered.

Cooking the Risotto: Warm soup plates in a low oven. Pat dry the quartered artichokes. Once the artichokes have softened, stir in the quartered pieces and cook 1 to 2 minutes. Stir in the rice and cook over medium heat, stirring constantly, 2 minutes, or until it looks chalky and you can see a white dot in the center of each grain. Now add about 1 cup of the simmering stock to the pot, along with the pea pods if you are using them. Stir over medium heat until the stock is absorbed. The stock should bubble gently once it has settled into the rice. Add another cup of stock and repeat the process, stirring with the spatula to prevent sticking. Lower the heat if necessary.

If you are using fresh peas, stir in the remaining 1½ cups after you have added about 3 or 4 cups of stock. Once the rice has absorbed about 6 cups of stock, start adding the stock in ½-cup increments. Perfect risotto is moist, creamy, and pleasantly tender, but is still firm enough to resist a little when bitten. A dry risotto can be moistened with a little extra stock.

Finishing and Serving: When the rice is tender but still a little firm, fold in the remaining frozen peas if you are using them. Taste the rice for salt and pepper. Then remove the pot from the heat (pluck out the pea pods at this point), and fold in the 1½ tablespoons butter and the cheese. Keep the risotto light and avoid crushing the rice by scooping down to the bottom of the pot and up with a big circular motion. Keep folding until the butter has melted and is thoroughly blended, about 1 minute. Spoon the creamy risotto into the heated soup dishes, and serve immediately.

Suggestions   **Wine:** A white Trebbiano Val Trebbia from Piacenza or a Trebbiano d'Abruzzo.

Menu: Serve in small quantities followed by Erminia's Pan-Crisped Chicken (page 270), Green Beans Bolognese (page 327), and Ugo Falavigna's Apple Cream Tart (page 411). For lighter dining, begin with Fresh Pears with Parmigiano-Reggiano and Balsamic Vinegar (page 30). Serve the risotto as a main course, and finish with the tart.

Cook's Notes   **Using Large Artichokes:** Follow the same procedure of breaking off the dark green leaves until you reach the pale green inner leaves. Trim away the top two thirds of the inner leaves. Quarter the hearts and cut away the fuzzy choke. Then cut half the artichoke hearts into eighths and thinly slice the remainder. Keep in lemon water as described.

Peas: One 10-ounce package of frozen tiny peas yields 2½ cups.

Traditional Variation: Stir 2 ounces chopped Prosciutto di Parma into the risotto with the butter and cheese.

Rice of the Princes
Riso Mantecato al Mascarpone, Uvetta, Pinoli, e Cannella

Technically this is not a risotto, as all the liquid is added at once and the rice is cooked covered. A blend of past and present created by Ferrara chef Sergio Ferrarini, this rice, with its nuts and spice, is served on a bed of roasted greens and topped with marscapone. Tart and sweet, crunchy and smooth, cool and hot play on the palate with wonderful sensuality. Dolloping a little mascarpone on each serving gives a rich and satiny finish to the dish.

[Serves 6 to 8 as a first course]

16 escarole or curly endive lettuce leaves, rinsed and dried

8 Boston lettuce leaves, rinsed and dried

Olive oil

Salt and freshly ground black pepper

½ cup raisins

½ cup dry white wine

3 tablespoons unsalted butter

1 medium onion, minced

2 generous cups (1 pound) imported Superfino Arborio or Roma rice

1 scant cup (4 ounces) pine nuts, toasted

Pinch of ground cloves

1 quart Poultry/Meat Stock (page 66) or Quick Stock (page 68)

1 cup (about 4 ounces) freshly grated Italian Parmigiano-Reggiano cheese

Generous pinch of ground cinnamon

1 cup (about 4 ounces) mascarpone cheese

Method   **Working Ahead:** *Although the rice is best made just before serving, the sautéed onion base and roasted lettuce can be prepared several hours ahead and held at room temperature. Allow the lettuce to cool, and keep at room temperature.*

continued

Roasting the Lettuce: Preheat the oven to 450°F. Cover a baking sheet with aluminum foil and arrange half the lettuce leaves on it without overlapping. Sprinkle lightly with olive oil, salt, and pepper. Roast 10 or 15 minutes, or until the edges are crisp and golden brown. Carefully lift the foil off the baking sheet without disturbing the leaves. Set it aside. Spread another sheet of foil on the baking sheet and repeat with the remaining leaves.

Making the Flavor Base: Soak the raisins in the wine about 30 minutes. In a heavy 5-quart pot, heat the butter over medium heat. Add the onion and sauté 8 minutes, or until soft and golden.

Cooking the Rice: Have dinner plates warming in the oven. Stir the rice into the pot and sauté 3 minutes, or until it looks chalky. Drain the wine from the raisins into the rice (reserve the raisins). Stir over medium heat, 5 minutes, or until the rice has absorbed the wine. Stir in the raisins, pine nuts, ground cloves, generous sprinklings of salt and pepper, and all of the stock. Bring to a simmer over medium heat and then turn it to low. Cover the pot tightly, and cook 18 to 20 minutes, or until the rice is tender but still has a little bite in the center.

Serving: When the rice is done, remove it from the heat and fold in the Parmigiano and cinnamon. Season with salt and pepper. Fan out a cluster of three roasted lettuce leaves (two escarole or curly endive and one Boston) on each heated plate, with the leaf bases in the center of the dish. Cover the bases with mounds of rice. Top each serving with generous spoonfuls of the mascarpone, and serve immediately.

Suggestions   **Wine:** A dry Albana di Romagna, Trebbiano from Emilia-Romagna, or Tocai from Friuli's Colli Goriziano or Colli Orientali.

Menu: Weave through the region's culinary history by following the rice with Rabbit Dukes of Modena (page 286) or Christmas Capon (page 281). Offer a dessert of Marie Louise's Crescents (page 426) served with Romagna's dessert wine, Albana Amabile, or Malvasia delle Lipari from Sicily.

Cook's Notes   **Pine Nuts:** Pine nuts spoil easily, so always taste for a sweet fresh flavor before buying. Store them in the freezer.

At Table with the Princes

In 1988 Ferrara celebrated her golden age in an exposition, "At Table with the Princes," which centered on the court of the Este dukes from the 14th through the 16th centuries. Chef Sergio Ferrarini re-created the foods of the period in a restaurant set up within the walls of the Este Castle. Most of the dishes were inspired by Christofaro di Messisbugo, the 16th-century cookbook author. This was not simply a matter of developing recipes with modern ingredients. Ferrarini worked with a team of scholars. Agricultural historians, botanists, and farmers strived to re-create foodstuffs of the 16th century. Researchers discovered how food was cooked, served, and eaten in the period, detailing the original utensils, table settings, and decorations.

Thanks to their work, it is now possible to stand in the frescoed halls of Ferrara's Este Castle and bring to life a court banquet of the era. At the head table, the Este and honored guests could have been scooping up a rice dish similar to this one, with spoons made of lapis lazuli and mother-of-pearl. Sweet wine was sipped from tall Venetian glasses, so fragile and blown into such delicate shapes, it is remarkable how the ones exhibited at the exposition could have survived to this day. Everyone probably remarked on the novelty of rice, this exotic food from Spain and the East.

Messisbugo's many recipes reveal few rice dishes. Most of them suggest using rice or *farro* (spelt or emmer), a word used to describe the several ancient wheat grains known to the Romans and still used in central Italy. No doubt these dishes were made with farro until the Arab invasion of Sicily and Spain introduced the cultivation of rice to Europe during the Middle Ages. By the mid-15th century, rice paddies were flooding the Po plain northwest of Ferrara. Still, rice seems to have been more an exotic than a staple in the dukes' kitchens. This recipe blends ingredients and techniques from three of Messisbugo's dishes: Turkish Rice, Sicilian Rice, and Rice with Egg Yolks and Cheese. He never mentions risotto, nor the risotto technique of cooking rice by first sautéing it and then stirring in small quantities of liquid until the rice is creamy and tender. Instead, rice is added to a sauté of flavorings along with all the liquid. Chef Ferrarini's touch of roasted greens gives a tart balance to the rice's sweet overtones and stays true to the flavor combinations of the period. However, he eliminated the pound or more of sugar required by the original recipes (even though these were savory, not dessert dishes). Duplicating the cultures and airborne microbes that produced the cheeses of centuries ago is a study in frustration, but mascarpone may come close to the fresh fat cheese Messisbugo calls for.

Imola's Risotto of the Vigil
Risotto della Vigilia di Natale

A *sauté of beef and cabbage simmers in a risotto of tomato and wine. Carrot and onion browned with fresh sage and a hint of garlic boost the flavors of this country dish. Breaking Christmas Eve's meatless vigil with this one-dish feast was the tradition in the farmhouses of Imola's countryside.*

[Serves 6 to 8 as a first course, 4 to 6 as a main dish]

About 4 cups water

3 ounces lean salt pork, cut into small dice

2 tablespoons extra-virgin olive oil

6 ounces lean beef chuck, cut into ¼- to ½-inch pieces

1 small carrot, coarsely chopped

1 small stalk celery with leaves, coarsely chopped

1 medium to large onion, coarsely chopped

3 large fresh sage leaves, or 3 large dried sage leaves

1 medium head Savoy cabbage (about 1 pound), halved, cored, and coarsely chopped

3 cups Poultry/Meat Stock (page 66) or Quick Stock (page 68)

2 cups water

1¼ cups (8½ ounces) imported Superfino Arborio or Roma rice

⅓ cup dry white wine

1 large clove garlic, minced

1 cup Winter Tomato Sauce (page 62), or 1 cup canned tomatoes with their liquid and 1 tablespoon chopped fresh basil leaves

2 cups (8 ounces) freshly grated Italian Parmigiano-Reggiano cheese

Salt and freshly ground black pepper to taste

Method   **Working Ahead:** *The risotto is best cooked just before serving, but its base can be prepared several hours ahead. Refrigerate the browned beef. The sautéed vegetables can be held up to 3 hours at room temperature in their covered pot.*

Blanching the Salt Pork: Bring the water to a boil, drop in the salt pork, and boil about 4 minutes. Drain, rinse, and pat dry.

Making the Base: In a heavy 5-quart pot, heat the olive oil over medium heat. Add the salt pork and cook slowly 8 minutes, or until it has given up much of its fat and turned golden brown. Remove the pork bits with a slotted spoon, and reserve. Pour off and discard all but 3 tablespoons of the fat. Turn the heat to high and add the beef. Quickly brown 8 minutes, or until dark and crusty on all sides. Remove with a slotted spoon, and reserve. Stir the carrot, celery, onion, and sage into the pot, and cook over medium heat, 5 to 7 minutes, or until the onion is golden brown. Add the cabbage, and stir frequently over medium-high heat, about 10 minutes, or until wilted.

Cooking the Rice: Warm shallow soup dishes in a low oven. Bring the stock and 2 cups of water to a simmer in a saucepan. Add the rice to the vegetable mixture, and stir over medium heat about 2 minutes. Blend in the wine and garlic and cook at a gentle simmer, stirring frequently, 5 minutes, or until the wine has been absorbed. Then add the tomato sauce or canned tomatoes and basil, along with the reserved salt pork and beef, and cook another 5 minutes, stirring to keep from sticking.

Keep the heat at about medium so the mixture simmers. Add 1 cup of the stock mixture and stir until it has been absorbed by the rice. Repeat, stirring in 1 cup at a time, until the rice is still a little too firm to be eaten. Then start adding the liquid in ¼-cup quantities until the rice has only slightly more bite than you would like.

Finishing and Serving: The risotto's consistency should be like a thick soup. Fold in about ⅔ cup of the cheese, remove from the heat, and season with salt and pepper. Let the risotto rest, uncovered, 5 minutes. Mound the risotto in the heated soup dishes and serve, passing the remaining cheese separately.

Suggestions   **Wine:** A young Sangiovese di Romagna, a soft Dolcetto d'Alba from the Piedmont, or a Salice Salentino Rosso of Apulia.

Menu: The risotto makes a substantial main dish after the Salad of Tart Greens with Prosciutto and Warm Balsamic Dressing (page 26). Finish the meal with Baked Pears with Fresh Grape Syrup (page 442) and a platter of Sweet Cornmeal Biscuits (page 422).

Dome of Rice Stuffed with Braised Pigeon
Bomba di Riso

Both Piacenza and Parma claim this dish as their own, dating back to the 16th and 17th centuries when both provinces were a single duchy ruled by the Farnese family. <u>Bomba di Riso</u> was a favorite ducal dish. Eaten as a first course on festive occasions, it is especially popular during Advent and after Christmas. In the United States, serve it as a main dish on New Year's Eve or for special dinners. If pigeon or squab is unavailable, duck makes a good substitute.

[Serves 8 to 10 as a first course, 6 to 8 as a main dish]

Braised Pigeon

2½ to 3 pounds pigeon or squab (4 to 5 birds), or one 5- to 6-pound duckling

1 large California bay laurel leaf

1½ cups dry white wine

1 clove garlic, crushed

3 tablespoons extra-virgin olive oil

2 tablespoons minced Italian parsley

Salt and freshly ground black pepper to taste

1 medium onion, minced

1 small carrot, minced

1 small stalk celery with leaves, minced

1 cup canned tomatoes with their liquid

2 cups Poultry/Meat Stock (page 66) or Quick Stock (page 68)

Rice

9 cups Poultry/Meat Stock or Quick Stock

¼ cup dry white wine

Salt and freshly ground black pepper

3 cups (21 ounces) imported Superfino Arborio or Roma rice

3 eggs, beaten

1½ cups (6 ounces) freshly grated Italian Parmigiano-Reggiano cheese

2 tablespoons salted butter

1 cup dried bread crumbs

Garnish

Lemon leaves or sprigs of fresh bay leaves (optional)

Method   **Working Ahead:** *Braising the pigeon, squab, or duck 2 days ahead allows the flavors to mellow. Once the meat is tender, take it from the bones, combine it with the defatted sauce, cover, and refrigerate. The bones could be frozen for use in stock later. Assemble the dish 8 to 10 hours ahead; cover and refrigerate. Bring it close to room temperature before baking.*

Marinating the Pigeon: The night before cooking them, quarter each bird, discarding the skin and any fat in the cavities. In a glass or stainless steel bowl, toss the pieces with the bay leaf, 1½ cups wine, and the garlic. Cover and refrigerate overnight. If you are using duck, trim away all skin and fat, and discard. Cut the duck into eight pieces and combine with the marinade as described above.

Braising the Pigeon: The next day, drain the birds, reserving the marinade. Pat the pieces dry. Heat the olive oil in a large heavy casserole over medium heat. Add the poultry pieces, sprinkle with the parsley, salt, and pepper, and take about 30 minutes to brown them on all sides over medium to medium-low heat. Transfer the browned poultry pieces to a platter, and add the minced vegetables to the pot. (If you are cooking duck, pour off all but 2 tablespoons of fat from the pot before adding the vegetables.) Brown them over medium heat, taking care not to burn the brown glaze forming on the bottom of the pot. Return the poultry pieces to the pot, and add half the reserved marinade with the crushed garlic. Bring it to a slow bubble and cook, uncovered, 15 minutes, or until the wine has totally evaporated. Turn the pieces occasionally as the wine cooks away. Repeat with the remaining wine and cook another 15 minutes, or until it is gone.

Stir in the tomatoes and cook another 10 minutes, stirring often. Then add the stock. Bring it to a very gentle bubble, partially cover the pot, and cook about 40 minutes for squab, 1¼ hours for pigeon, and 1½ hours for duck. Whichever poultry is used, the meat must be tender and succulent, but not overcooked or stringy. Cool the poultry in its sauce and discard the bay leaf. Remove the meat from the bones.

Skim as much fat as possible from the sauce, and taste for intensity. Boil the sauce down until it is deeply flavored, 3 to 5 minutes. Add the meat pieces, cool, cover, and refrigerate. Reheat before filling the rice mold.

Cooking the Rice: Set a strainer over a large bowl. Bring the stock and the ¼ cup wine to a boil in a 4-quart heavy saucepan over high heat. Season with salt and pepper. Pour in the rice, cover, and cook 10 minutes over high heat. Strain the rice, reserving the stock for another use. Turn the rice into a bowl, and once it has cooled to warm, blend in the eggs and cheese.

Assembling the Bomba: Slather a 9½-cup stainless steel bowl or dome mold with the 2 tablespoons butter, and then coat it with the bread crumbs. Pat a ½-inch-thick layer of rice over the bottom and about 2 inches up the sides of the bowl. Add half the warmed pigeon meat and its sauce. Cover with enough rice so you cannot see the meat. Build the rice up to the bowl's edge. Spoon in the remaining pigeon. Cover it with the rest of the rice, sealing and patting it with the back of a large spoon or metal spatula so that the rice is compact. Cover the top with a piece of aluminum foil.

Baking and Serving: Preheat the oven to 375°F. Bake the mold 45 minutes to 1 hour, or until heated through. Test by inserting a tester or knife into the center and checking it for warmth. Unmold the rice by setting a large round platter atop the bowl and then, using pot holders, flipping it over so the mold rests on the plate. Tap the bowl's sides and top, and gently lift it off the rice. Garnish the mold with shiny lemon leaves or small clusters of fresh bay leaves, if desired. Cut into wedges at the table.

Suggestions   **Wine:** A young red Gutturnio from Piacenza, Parma's Colli di Parma Rosso, a Bolognese Merlot, or a Tuscan Monte Antico, Morellino di Scansano, or Chianti Montalbano.

Menu: For a festive menu, serve in small portions before Christmas Capon (page 281), finishing the meal with a green salad and for dessert, Frozen Chocolate Pistachio Cream with Hot Chocolate Marsala Sauce (page 438). Serve as a main dish after Priest's Soup (page 227). Have a green salad afterward, and then Marie Louise's Crescents (page 426).

Cook's Notes **Squab and Pigeon:** Squab is young pigeon specially raised for the table. Its flesh is lighter colored and milder in flavor than wild pigeon's. For this dish I prefer wild pigeon, the bird of choice in Piacenza and Parma, because of its bolder character. Both are available through mail-order sources (page 509).

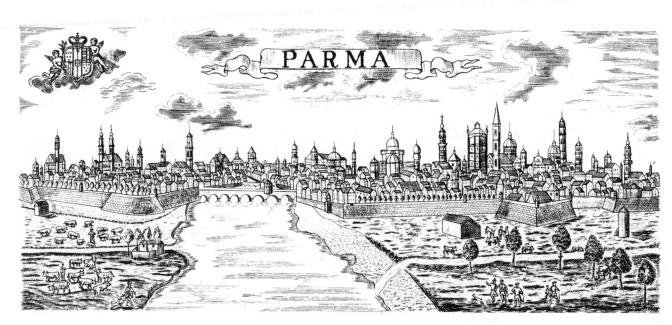

Old engraving of Parma

Parma Consulates and the Bomb Scare

Parma is more than a geographic location; it is a state of being. To be a Parmesan is to know you live in the best possible place on earth. Other parts of Italy and even the world may attract, but only Parma nourishes your soul. You are a Parmesan first, then an Italian. Other Italians concede that Parma's reputation for elegance and refinement, won over the centuries as a center of court, is well founded. Strong links with the courts of Spain, France, and Austria during their respective heydays only add luster to Parma's aura. With this powerful provincial identity, it is not surprising to discover that Parmesans felt displaced when, after unification, they took up official positions in Italy's central government in Rome.

According to Dr. Mario Zannoni, Parma scholar and Parmigiano-Reggiano cheese expert, it was during the 1890s that the homesick Parmesans in Rome made an important decision: They would create a permanent meeting place where their countrymen could gather, carry on Parma traditions, and share their love of homeland—a Parma consulate. Today Parma consulates exist in many foreign places, among them Romagna and Bologna, both no more than 3 hours away, as well as London and Caracas. A short time after the first Parma consulate opened in Rome, its members found themselves longing for one of their favorite dishes, the *Bomba di Riso*. This savory rice dish molded into a dome and stuffed with braised pigeon is traditional winter food. By good luck, a friend coming to Rome from Parma was delighted to bring the dish. It was agreed that he would telegraph just before he stepped onto the train so that all the necessary preparations for the feast would be completed when he arrived.

As the train pulled out of the Parma station a message was wired to Rome: "The bomb is on the train. Stop." Rome's telegraph office immediately relayed the message to the police. They, in turn, telegraphed Parma's police: "Stop train, find out what bomb. Stop." While they waited for a reply, other trains were cleared from the Parma train's route, Rome's station was surrounded, and incoming tracks were cordoned off. Armed police waited for the order to close in.

Finally a message came from the Parma police: "Bomb: A typical Parma dish of rice and pigeon. Stop." I do not know if they ever got to eat the *Bomba di Riso* that year.

Ferrara's Soup of the Monastery
Zuppa dei Frati Cappuccini

An old recipe with a fresh contemporary feel. Stories tell of the Capuchin friars of Ferrara creating this tomato and cauliflower soup. The secret of its success is a final sprinkling of fresh rosemary, parsley, and crisp pancetta bits. Cooking away most of the pancetta's fat keeps the soup light.

[Serves 6 to 8 as a first course, 4 to 6 as a main dish]

1½ tablespoons extra-virgin olive oil

1 ounce pancetta, minced

1 large onion, finely chopped

1 large cauliflower, cored and cut into bite-size pieces

3 tablespoons minced Italian parsley

3 fresh sage leaves, or 3 dried whole sage leaves

3-inch sprig of fresh rosemary, or 1 teaspoon dried rosemary leaves

1 large clove garlic, minced

2 cups drained canned tomatoes, or 2 medium vine-ripened tomatoes, peeled, seeded, and chopped

Salt and freshly ground black pepper to taste

8 cups Poultry/Meat Stock (page 66) or Quick Stock (page 68)

2 tablespoons red wine vinegar

Garnish

2 tablespoons minced Italian parsley

1 teaspoon chopped fresh rosemary leaves, or ½ teaspoon dried rosemary leaves

1 cup (4 ounces) freshly grated Italian Parmigiano-Reggiano cheese

Method   **Working Ahead:** *The soup can be made 1 day in advance. Take care not to overcook the cauliflower so that it keeps some of its crispness in reheating. Cool the cooked soup to room temperature, cover, and refrigerate. Garnish just before serving.*

Making the Flavor Base: Heat the olive oil and pancetta in a large pot. Cook over medium heat, 8 minutes, or until the pancetta is golden. Using a slotted spoon, remove and reserve the pancetta. Spoon off all but about 2 tablespoons oil from the pot. Turn the heat to medium-high and add the onion, cauliflower, parsley, and herbs. Cook, stirring frequently with a wooden spatula, 8 to 10 minutes, or until the onion is a deep golden brown and the cauliflower has browned too. Remove the herbs if they threaten to burn. Stir in the garlic and tomatoes, and boil about 5 minutes.

Cooking and Serving: Have soup dishes and a tureen warming in a low oven. Pour the stock into the pot and simmer 15 minutes, or until the cauliflower is tender-crisp. Sprinkle the soup with the vinegar. Transfer it to the tureen, and sprinkle with the garnish of parsley, chopped rosemary, and the reserved pancetta. Serve, passing the Parmigiano-Reggiano separately.

Suggestions   **Wine:** In Ferrara a red Rosso del Bosco is the choice. Otherwise, serve a simple red Refosco from the Friuli region's Colli Orientali, or a Merlot d'Aprilia from Latium.

        Menu: Serve in small quantities before Balsamic Roast Chicken (page 279), Artusi's Delight (page 300), or Herbed Seafood Grill (page 254). Finish the meal with Meringues of the Dark Lake (page 421) from Ferrara's countryside, or Home-Style Jam Cake (page 401). Present the soup as a main dish after Spring Salad with Hazelnuts (page 21). Make dessert Espresso and Mascarpone Semi-Freddo (page 428).

A Ferrara court kitchen in the 16th century, from *Libro Novo,* by Christofaro di Messisbugo

Fresh Garlic Soup Brisighella
Zuppa di Aglio Fresco

*T*his *cross between a soup and a creamy purée is as healthful as it is delicious. An old Romagna cure for colds, the soup has been fed to babies and the elderly for generations, especially in the hills of Brisighella, the spa town above Faenza.*

Don't be put off by the amount of garlic. The soup is mellow and mild, yet full-flavored. It is one of my favorite dishes—easy to do and substantial enough to make a light supper main dish on its own. (The recipe doubles easily.) If possible, use the fresh garlic of spring and early summer, still green and moist. Special thanks to Gianni Quondamatteo, who shared the traditions of this recipe.

[Serves 4 as a first course or light supper]

Soup

2 heads large-cloved garlic

4 cups water

2 small to medium onions, finely
  chopped

½ cup extra-virgin olive oil

6 medium fresh sage leaves, or 6
  small dried sage leaves

3½ cups Poultry/Meat Stock
  (page 66) or Quick Stock
  (page 68)

Salt and freshly ground black
  pepper to taste

Croutons

Four ½-inch-thick slices
  good-quality Italian baguette-style
  bread

⅔ cup (about 3 ounces) shredded
  Italian Parmigiano-Reggiano
  cheese

Method

Working Ahead: *The soup comes together quickly once the garlic has been peeled and boiled 10 minutes. This could be done 1 day ahead and the garlic refrigerated in a sealed container. The croutons can be prepared at the same time, then wrapped and stored at room temperature. Rewarm them in a 300°F oven 5 minutes. Make the soup itself, without puréeing, within 2 hours of serving. Reheat to a boil, purée and serve.*

Preparing the Garlic: Separate the cloves from each head of garlic, but do not peel them. Bring the water to a rolling boil in a 2-quart saucepan. Drop in the garlic cloves and boil 10 minutes. Drain them in a sieve and peel. If you are using fresh green garlic, do not peel the cloves.

Making the Soup: Return the garlic cloves to the saucepan, and add the onion, olive oil, sage, and stock. Bring to a lively bubble over medium-high heat. Partially cover and cook 5 minutes. Uncover, adjust the heat so the liquid bubbles slowly, and cook another 5 minutes.

Making the Croutons: Preheat the broiler. While the soup is simmering, arrange the bread slices on a baking sheet. Toast them under the broiler 1 to 2 minutes per side, or until the slices are crisp and golden. Set aside a few spoonfuls of the cheese to top the soup. Sprinkle the rest over the bread slices. Slip the baking sheet back under the broiler only a second or two, to melt the cheese but not brown it. Keep warm.

Finishing and Serving: Have four soup dishes warming in a low oven. The garlic cloves will be meltingly soft when the soup finishes cooking. Remove all but 1 sage leaf, and purée the soup in a blender or food processor. Season to taste. Arrange the croutons in the soup dishes, and pour the purée over them. Sprinkle each serving with a few shreds of cheese, and serve immediately.

Suggestions   **Wine:** A crisp white Sauvignon from Romagna, Emilia, Alto Adige, or Friuli.

Menu: For a simple supper, have Marinated Baby Onions (page 16) with the Platter of Cured Meats (page 14) before the soup, and a green salad afterward. Make dessert Paola Bini's Sweet Ravioli (page 424) or fresh pears with homemade squacquerone cheese (page 386). A more elaborate menu has the soup served in half portions before Lamb with Black Olives (page 305). It is also particularly elegant as a prelude to Balsamic Roast Chicken (page 279). Finish the menu with Caramelized Almond Tart (page 409).

Cornmeal Pasta with Braised Beans
I Gnuchétt

*T*his *is lusty winter food from Romagna, best eaten around a fire on an icy evening after a day out-of-doors. The beans are fragrant with a sauce of browned vegetables, sage, and rosemary, while the unusual cornmeal pasta gives a chewy counterpoint.*

Today gnuchétt *is enjoyed as delicious nostalgia by many Romagnoli. Before World War II it was peasant food. Then, cornmeal stretched expensive wheat flour in the pasta. Sausage and pancetta meant times were good.*

[Serves 6 to 7 as a one-dish meal]

continued

Pasta

1½ cups water

2 cups organic stone-ground cornmeal

¼ teaspoon salt

2½ to 3 cups (10 to 12 ounces) all-purpose unbleached flour (organic stone-ground preferred), or more as needed

2 eggs, beaten

Beans

2 cups dried borlotti, pinto, or bolita beans

3 tablespoons extra-virgin olive oil

2 ounces pancetta, finely chopped

1 large onion, finely chopped

1 medium carrot, finely chopped

1 large stalk celery with leaves, finely chopped

4 tablespoons minced Italian parsley

3-inch sprig of fresh rosemary, or 1 teaspoon dried whole rosemary leaves

4 large fresh sage leaves, or 4 large dried sage leaves

1 large clove garlic, crushed

1 cup water

1 cup well-drained canned tomatoes

2 tablespoons red wine vinegar

Salt and freshly ground black pepper to taste

1 pound mild Italian sausage (without fennel), cooked (optional)

8 quarts salted water

2 cups (8 ounces) shredded young pecorino (sheep) cheese, such as Canestrato, Lago Monate Pecorino, or Fiore Sardo

Method

Working Ahead: *The pasta can be made up to 3 days ahead. Dry it at room temperature, turning the pieces several times. The beans can be cooked 1 day before serving. Let them cool before covering and refrigerating.*

Making the Dough by Hand: Bring the 1½ cups water to a boil. Combine the cornmeal and salt in a deep bowl. Stir the cornmeal with a long-handled spoon while pouring in the boiling water. Stir 1 minute, then blend in 2½ cups of the flour and the beaten eggs. Turn the dough out onto a floured work surface and knead it for a few moments. Work in enough additional flour to make an elastic, but not very sticky, dough. Knead 10 minutes, adding another few spoonfuls of flour if needed. Wrap the dough in plastic wrap and let it rest at room temperature 30 minutes.

Making the Dough in a Food Processor: Pour the cornmeal and salt into a processor fitted with the steel blade. With it running, add the boiling water and process 30 seconds. Add 2½ cups flour and the beaten eggs. Process until smooth and elastic, adding the remaining ½ cup flour if the dough is too soft or sticky. With or without the additional flour, process 30 seconds, turn the machine off for a minute, then process another 30 seconds. If the dough is still sticky, process in a few extra tablespoons of flour. Wrap the dough in plastic wrap and let it rest 30 minutes at room temperature.

Rolling and Cutting: Have handy several large flat baskets covered with kitchen towels (baking sheets can stand in for the baskets if necessary). Generously flour a large work surface. Roll out all the dough until it is a little less than ⅛ inch thick (gnuchétt is rolled thicker than wheat-flour pasta). Let it dry 15 minutes, and then cut into 1-inch squares. Spread the squares out on the baskets and let them dry at room temperature at least 3 hours. Turn them over after about 12 hours.

Cooking the Beans: Cover the beans with cold water and let them soak overnight in the refrigerator. Or if time is short, cover them with boiling water and let stand 2 hours at room temperature. Either way, drain and rinse the beans before cooking. Then pour them into a 4-quart saucepan and cover with 2 inches of fresh water. Heat until the water bubbles slowly, then partially cover and cook 1½ to 2 hours.

As soon as the beans are cooking, heat the olive oil and pancetta in a large skillet over medium-high heat. Using a wooden spatula, stir in the onion, carrot, celery, parsley, rosemary, and sage. Take 8 to 10 minutes to cook the onions to golden brown, stirring often. Add the garlic, cook 30 seconds, and then stir in the 1 cup water. Bring it to a boil and scrape up the brown glaze from the bottom of the pan. Scrape the contents of the skillet into the bean pot, stir in the tomatoes and vinegar, and sprinkle with salt and pepper. Stir the beans frequently, checking for sticking, as they cook at a slow bubble. Keep partially covered.

If you are using the cooked sausage, slice it into ¼-inch-thick rounds and stir them into the beans when they are barely tender (after about 1¼ hours). Continue cooking until the beans are tender, another 15 to 45 minutes. They should have the consistency of a thick soup. Add a little water to the pot if too thick.

Cooking the Pasta and Serving: Have bowls heating in a warm oven, and make sure the beans are hot. Bring the salted water to a fierce boil. Drop in the pasta. If it has dried for several days, count on 23 to 28 minutes of cooking. If fresher, 8 to 13 minutes. It must have bite but not be too hard. Just before draining, spoon about ⅓ cup of the pasta water into the beans. Drain the pasta in a large colander and stir it into the beans. Serve in the bowls, topping each serving with a generous spoonful of cheese. Pass the rest of the cheese separately.

Suggestions   **Wine:** In Romagna *I Gnuchétt* is accompanied by a simple local red Sangiovese di Romagna. A young Chianti, a Merlot from Lombardy, or a Valpolicella Classico is a good stand-in.

Menu: *Gnuchétt* needs only a green salad served before or after. Roasted chestnuts or fresh fruit is a traditional dessert. (Romagna custom has everyone dipping hot peeled chestnuts into the red wine.)

Soup of Porcini Mushrooms
Zuppa di Funghi Porcini

This is a big, full-flavored soup, yet it is amazingly light. Dried porcini and cultivated mushrooms replace the fresh porcini used in Parma hill country.

[Serves 6 to 8 as a first course, 3 to 4 as a main dish]

½ to ⅔ cup (½ ounce) dried porcini mushrooms

1½ cups hot water

1 tablespoon extra-virgin olive oil

1 medium onion, minced

1 large clove garlic, minced

6 large fresh basil leaves, or ¾ teaspoon dried basil

2 tablespoons minced Italian parsley

8 ounces white button mushrooms, thinly sliced

½ cup dry white wine

1 tablespoon imported Italian tomato paste

7 cups Poultry/Meat Stock (page 66) or Quick Stock (page 68)

3 tablespoons dry white wine

6 tablespoons dry Marsala

2 tablespoons heavy cream

Method

Working Ahead: *The soup can be prepared 1 day ahead, but do not add the Marsala and cream. Cool, cover, and refrigerate. Bring it to a gentle bubble before serving, stir in the Marsala and cream, and ladle into bowls.*

Preparing the Porcini: If the mushroom pieces are large, rinse them under cold running water to rid them of sand and grit. If the pieces are small, drop them into a bowl of cold water and quickly swish them around; then allow a few seconds for the particles to settle, and scoop the mushrooms out of the water. Repeat several times if the mushrooms are still sandy. Put the rinsed mushrooms in a small bowl and cover with the hot water. Let stand 20 to 30 minutes. Then scoop them out of the water and finely chop. Reserve the soaking liquid.

Preparing the Base: Heat the olive oil in a 6-quart pot over medium-high heat. Stir in the onion, garlic, basil, parsley, and both mushrooms. Turn the heat to low, cover the pot, and cook the mixture 30 minutes, stirring occasionally. The vegetables will be wilted and aromatic.

Cooking and Serving: Have soup dishes warming in a low oven. Line a strainer with paper towels, and strain the reserved mushroom soaking liquid over the vegetables. Add the ½ cup wine and the tomato paste. Bring the liquid to a boil and cook down, uncovered, 5 minutes, or until reduced by about half. Stir in the stock, and adjust the heat so the soup bubbles very slowly. Cover and cook 30 minutes. Then add the 3 tablespoons wine and simmer for 1 minute.

Stir in the Marsala and cream. Serve right away.

Suggestions   **Wine:** A still, dry Colli di Parma Malvasia or the Friuli region's Pinot Bianco or Riesling Italico.

Menu: Serve the soup before Christmas Capon (page 281) or Erminia's Pan-Crisped Chicken (page 270). Hold to the Parma theme with a dessert of Frozen Chocolate Pistachio Cream with Hot Chocolate Marsala Sauce (page 438) or Marie Louise's Crescents (page 426). For lighter dining, serve Spring Salad with Hazelnuts (page 21) before having the soup as a main dish.

Cook's Notes For information on buying porcini, see page 494.

Priest's Soup
Minestra del Prete

Savory croutons are cut from a baked pudding of cheese, butter, and egg. They float in this simple and genteel soup, the mainstay of a century's worth of special dinners in Bologna, Ferrara and Modena. Imperial Soup is the soup's most common name. You will see the label on the big baked squares of golden croutons ready-made and displayed in the windows of Bologna's food shops. My friend Riccardo Rimondi shared this recipe. He thinks it is more delicious than the Imperial version—certainly worthy of a priest's dinner.

[Serves 6 to 8 as a first course]

1 tablespoon unsalted butter

3 eggs

¾ cup (3 ounces) freshly grated Italian Parmigiano-Reggiano cheese

6 tablespoons (3 ounces) unsalted butter, melted

¾ cup all-purpose unbleached flour (organic stone-ground preferred)

Generous pinch of salt and freshly ground black pepper

Generous pinch of freshly grated nutmeg

8 cups Poultry/Meat Stock (page 66) or Quick Stock (page 68)

1½ cups (6 ounces) freshly grated Italian Parmigiano-Reggiano cheese

continued

Method   **Working Ahead:** *The croutons can be baked and diced up to 3 months ahead. Dry the diced croutons at room temperature 3 days, then freeze them in a well-sealed plastic bag. Drop the defrosted croutons into the boiling stock just before bringing the soup to the table.*

Making the Croutons: Preheat the oven to 375°F. Grease an 8-inch square or round cake pan with the 1 tablespoon butter. In a bowl, whisk the eggs into a froth. Beat in the ¾ cup cheese and the melted butter. Using a spatula, lightly fold in the flour and seasonings until just blended. Spread the batter in the baking pan, and bake 15 to 18 minutes, or until a tester inserted near the middle comes out clean. A film of bubbly butter forms over the cake and is absorbed as the cake cools. Once the cake has cooled, cut it into ½-inch dice, and spread the croutons out on a platter to dry.

Serving the Soup: Have soup dishes, and a tureen if desired, warming in a low oven. Bring the stock to a lively bubble in a 4-quart saucepan. Season with salt and pepper. Drop in the croutons, and turn the soup into a tureen or ladle it into the soup dishes. Pass the Parmigiano-Reggiano separately.

Suggestions   **Wine:** A young white Pinot Bianco Colli Bolognesi or a Pinot Bianco from Friuli.

Menu: Small bowls of the soup are excellent before roasted, grilled, or braised meats and poultry, such as Maria Bertuzzi's Lemon Chicken (page 273) or Rabbit Roasted with Sweet Fennel (page 289). For dessert, have fresh pears and grapes with Sweet Cornmeal Biscuits (page 422).

Cook's Notes   **Variation with Mortadella:** Mortadella and extra cheese baked into the croutons takes the soup from delicate to robust. Whisk 4 eggs to a froth. Beat in 1¼ cups Parmigiano-Reggiano cheese, 4 tablespoons melted unsalted butter, and 2 ounces ground mortadella. Finally, fold in 3 tablespoons semolina flour. Bake, cool, and finish the recipe as described above.

Thumb Pasta and Tomato Braised Beans Piacenza Style
Pisaréi e Fasô

Pisaréi e Fasô is a proud peasant tradition in Piacenza. Pisaréi are little coils of chewy pasta made by a press and flick of the thumb. The bread crumbs in the pasta give it a pleasant graininess. Stirred into the braised beans (the fasô), the pisaréi become a one-dish meal. On fast days, the stew is made meatless with an extra spoonful of olive oil standing in for the pancetta. Pisaréi e fasô is good party food. Double this recipe and serve it at a buffet.

[Serves 6 to 8 as a first course, 4 to 6 as a main dish]

Pasta

1 cup water

2 cups dried bread crumbs

4 cups (16 ounces) all-purpose unbleached flour (organic stone-ground preferred)

2 eggs

10 tablespoons water

Beans

2 cups dried borlotti, bolita, pinto, or Great Northern beans

8 fresh sage leaves, or 8 dried whole sage leaves

Two 3-inch sprigs of fresh rosemary, or 1 1/4 teaspoons dried rosemary

Sauce

4 tablespoons extra-virgin olive oil

2 ounces pancetta or fat from Prosciutto di Parma, chopped

1 medium and 1 large onion, minced

4 tablespoons minced Italian parsley

1 large clove garlic, minced

3 tablespoons minced fresh basil, or 2 teaspoons dried basil

2 tablespoons imported Italian tomato paste

Two 14- to 16-ounce cans tomatoes with their liquid

Salt and freshly ground black pepper to taste

3 cups water

Assembly

8 quarts salted water

2 cups (8 ounces) freshly grated Italian Parmigiano-Reggiano cheese

Method   **Working Ahead:** *This dish comes together very easily, especially if each of its components is prepared ahead. The tomato sauce can be made 2 days ahead. Store it, covered, in the refrigerator. The pasta can be blended and shaped 24 hours before cooking.*

continued

Turn the pieces over after 8 to 12 hours of drying. The beans can also be cooked 1 day ahead. After cooling them, cover and store in the refrigerator. Allow about 30 minutes before serving for cooking the pasta, reheating the sauce and beans, and combining them all together. Leftover Pisaréi e Fasô *reheats successfully.*

Making the Dough by Hand: Bring the 1 cup water to a boil. Pour the bread crumbs into a bowl and add the boiling water. Let stand 10 minutes. Mound the flour on a work surface. Using a wooden spoon, make a well in the mound that looks like a volcano crater. Add the eggs, 10 tablespoons water, and soaked bread crumbs to the well. Blend them together with a wooden spoon. Then gradually stir in the flour by making shallow scrapings along the walls of the well and incorporating the flour into the liquids. Use a pastry scraper to catch any liquids that might escape from the flour crater. Once the mixture becomes a rough dough, knead it by hand 10 minutes, or until elastic. It should be quite stiff and not very sticky. Wrap the dough in plastic wrap and let it stand at room temperature 30 minutes to 2 hours.

Making the Dough in a Food Processor: Bring the 1 cup water to a boil. Pour the bread crumbs into a bowl and add the boiling water. Let stand 10 minutes.

In a food processor fitted with the steel blade, combine the eggs, 10 tablespoons water, and the soaked bread crumbs. Blend about 10 seconds. With the machine running, pour in the flour through the feed tube. Process about 30 seconds. The dough should be stiff and just a little sticky. Let the dough rest about 30 seconds, and then process again 30 seconds. Turn the dough out onto a board and knead 5 minutes, or until elastic. Wrap it in plastic wrap, and let it rest 30 minutes to 2 hours at room temperature.

Shaping the Pisaréi: These little pasta curls are shaped by taking a pea-size piece of dough, pressing it with the tip of the thumb, then pulling the thumb back and up in a quick motion. The dough thins and curls, forming a "C" shape in profile. After you've made several pieces, a rhythm will develop and shaping the pisaréi will become automatic. Have handy several large flat baskets lined with kitchen towels for drying the pasta. Take one quarter of the dough (keep the rest wrapped in plastic wrap) and divide it into 10 pieces. Roll out each piece with the flat of your palms to form a long cord ¼ to ½ inch in diameter. Keep the cords covered with plastic wrap. Take out one cord and cut it into pea-size pieces. Use the tip of your thumb to press each piece into the work surface and then pull back and up. It is a flicking motion. Some cooks prefer pushing forward and up. Either way, the pasta will curl. Pisaréi are not elegant-looking. Although every piece should be about the same thickness, they look handmade, with slightly uneven shapes and rough edges. They should be about the same size as the beans they are to be served with. Continue making pisaréi with the remaining dough. Spread them on the baskets without letting the pieces touch.

Cooking the Beans: Bring a pot of water to a boil. Pour the dried beans into a bowl, cover them with boiling water, and let stand about 2 hours. Drain the beans and turn them into a 5-quart pot. Sprinkle with the sage and rosemary. Add enough cold water to cover by about 3 inches. Cover and bring to a very slow bubble over medium heat. Adjust the heat so the water bubbles slowly. Cook, covered, 1 hour, or until the beans are just tender enough to eat but not at all mushy. Drain the beans in a colander, and return them to the pot.

Making the Tomato Sauce: While the beans are cooking, heat the olive oil and pancetta or prosciutto fat in a heavy 4-quart saucepan over medium-high heat. Add the onion and parsley. Sauté the onions to a rich golden brown, about 10 minutes. Stir often. Blend in the garlic, basil, and tomato paste, and cook about 30 seconds. Add the tomatoes and their liquid, breaking them up as they go into the pan. Bring to a lively bubble and cook, uncovered, 5 minutes. Season with salt and pepper.

Finishing the Beans: Add the tomato sauce and the 3 cups water, and bring the bean/tomato mixture to a gentle bubble. The mixture should bubble very slowly. Partially cover and cook 1½ hours, or until the beans are very tender (but not falling apart), and have the consistency of a thick soup. Stir frequently to check for sticking. Add more water if the mixture threatens to burn.

Cooking the Pasta and Serving: Have a serving bowl and soup dishes warming in a low oven. If necessary, reheat the beans to a slow bubble. Bring the salted water to a boil. Drop in the dried pisaréi and boil 5 to 15 minutes, depending upon how dry they are. Taste for tender yet firm texture with no suggestion of raw flour. Drain in a colander. Pour the beans into the heated serving bowl. Turn the colander full of pisaréi into the bowl and fold the two together, taking care not to break up the pasta. Sprinkle with a few spoonfuls of the cheese, and serve. Pass the rest of the Parmigiano-Reggiano separately.

Suggestions   **Wine:** In Piacenza, local reds like Barbera Colli Piacentini or Gutturnio are served with this dish. From other parts of Italy, try a Piemontese Barbera, Friuli's Santa Maddalena, or the Valtellina's Sassella or Inferno.

Menu: Traditionally *Pisaréi e Fasô* is a one-dish meal, and it works best that way today. Serve with salad, and offer Baked Pears with Fresh Grape Syrup (page 442) for dessert. Make a buffet dinner with a double recipe. Serve a Platter of Cured Meats (page 14) and perhaps Balsamic Vegetables (page 18). Have the Salad of Mixed Greens and Fennel (page 349). Offer fresh fruit, roasted chestnuts, and wedges of Nonna's Jam Tart (page 413) for dessert.

Cook's Notes **Variation:** Spoon the braised beans over platters of hot Polenta (page 352).

"Little" Spring Soup from the 17th Century

Minestrina di Latecchi, Punte di Sparagi, Fondi d'Artichiochi, et Agro di Limoni

This soup comes straight through three centuries from the dining table of Ranuccio Farnese II, Duke of Parma. His cook, Carlo Nascia, combined slivers of asparagus, artichoke bottoms, and spring lettuces in a "good broth of substance." Beaten egg yolk makes golden threads in the soup. The broth and greens are seasoned with tart lemon juice and sweet pistachios. In all, the soup takes about 10 minutes to cook.

[Serves 4 as a first course]

4½ cups Poultry/Meat Stock
  (page 66)
Salt and freshly ground black
  pepper to taste
Freshly grated nutmeg to taste
6 ounces thin asparagus
2 large artichokes

1 large lemon, halved
2 egg yolks, beaten
¾ cup chopped heart of Boston
  lettuce or leaf lettuce
3 tablespoons coarsely chopped
  pistachio nuts

Method

Working Ahead: *The soup loses its fresh taste and appearance if cooked ahead. But seasoning the stock and preparing the vegetables can be done several hours in advance. Set them aside, covered, at room temperature.*

Seasoning the Stock: Pour the stock into a 3-quart saucepan and bring to a slow bubble. Season with salt and pepper, and grate in enough nutmeg to give a hint of its taste. Keep the stock at a slow bubble.

Preparing the Vegetables: While the broth is heating, trim the tough ends from the asparagus. Cut off the tips on the diagonal, then continue cutting the stalks on the diagonal into ¼-inch-thick slices. Prepare one of the artichokes by trimming away any part of the stem that seems tough. Peel the rest of the stem and rub it with one of the lemon halves. Break off all the outer leaves around the base of the artichoke. Using a sharp thin-bladed knife, trim away the dark green leaf stubs until you can see the pale green of the artichoke bottom. Now hold the artichoke upside down, and cut away any dark green around the base. Rub the surface with the lemon. Cut away the top two thirds of the leaves, and scoop out the choke with a spoon. Rub every surface with the lemon. Repeat with the second artichoke. Then cut each bottom into quarters and thinly slice into small chips. Toss with the juice from the lemon half you've been using.

Making the Soup: Warm soup dishes, and a tureen if desired, in a low oven. Extract 1 to 1½ tablespoons juice from the other lemon half. Bring the stock to a boil, drop in the artichoke slices, and boil, uncovered, 1½ minutes, or until barely tender. Add the asparagus and boil, uncovered, 2 to 3 minutes, or until barely tender. Turn down the heat so the soup simmers gently. Add the yolks to the stock and stir slowly until firm threads are formed. This happens in a matter of seconds. Season with the lemon juice. There should be a distinctive lemony flavor. Ladle the soup into the soup dishes or tureen. Sprinkle with the lettuce and pistachios, and serve immediately.

Suggestions   **Wine:** Wines are defeated by the soup's fresh lemon.

Menu: Because of its lightness, the soup successfully introduces any main dish not flavored with lemon. Serve it as the beginning to a meal built around the Domed Maccheroni Pie of Ferrara (page 180) or An Unusual Tortellini Pie (page 175). It matches the period of both these dishes, and its light body and tartness prepares the palate perfectly for the creamy richness of what is to come.

Cook's Notes   **Variation with Cheese:** Although Nascia does not suggest it, the addition of freshly grated Parmigiano-Reggiano cheese is excellent here. The cheese is a magical addition to soups, especially broth-based ones. Stir the cheese into a bowl of plain broth, and you will experience an explosion of taste. In soups like Nascia's, Parmigiano-Reggiano accentuates each ingredient without overwhelming any of them. Add 1 tablespoon to each serving.

From the fantasy land of plenty, Cucagna, the Palace of Delicious Tastes, by Bolognese artist Giuseppe Maria Mitelli, 1703

Modena's Spiced Soup of Spinach and Cheese
Minestrina di Spinaci alla Modenese

Fresh spinach, Parmigiano-Reggiano cheese, and prosciutto are an unbeatable combination. In this dish they meet in a homemade broth scented with cinnamon and nutmeg. Strong similarities to the 17th-century soups of Parma's chef Carlo Nascia suggest that this may have been Modenese court food years ago. Made without eggs, it is a fine opening for elegant but simple menus. You can make the soup in only 10 minutes, with or without egg.

[Serves 6 to 8 as a first course, 4 to 6 as a main dish]

8 cups Poultry/Meat Stock (page 66) or Quick Stock (page 68)

3 eggs (optional)

2 generous pinches of ground cinnamon

2 generous pinches of freshly ground black pepper

2 generous pinches of freshly grated nutmeg

½ cup (2 ounces) freshly grated Italian Parmigiano-Reggiano cheese

4 ounces fresh spinach, well rinsed and cut into thin shreds

1 to 2 ounces Prosciutto di Parma, cut into thin shreds

Salt to taste

Method

Working Ahead: *Although the soup must be cooked at the last moment, it takes no more than 10 minutes and little effort. You can prepare all the ingredients hours ahead; cover and refrigerate them. The stock could be made months ahead and frozen.*

Cooking the Soup with Eggs: Have soup dishes, and a tureen if desired, warming in a low oven. Bring the stock to a slow bubble in a 3-quart saucepan. In a medium bowl, beat the eggs with the spices and cheese. Stir the mixture into the bubbling stock with a fork, making lacy threads. Taste the soup for seasoning. Drop in the spinach and prosciutto, and immediately pour the soup into the tureen or ladle it into soup dishes, and serve while the spinach is still bright green.

Cooking the Soup Without Eggs: Have soup dishes, and a tureen if desired, warming in a low oven. Bring the stock to a slow bubble in a 3-quart saucepan. Add the spices to the stock, and cook for a few moments. Taste for seasoning. Then stir in the spinach, cheese, and prosciutto, and immediately serve in the soup dishes or tureen, while the spinach is still bright green.

Suggestions   **Wine:** A soft white Trebbiano from the Modena area, Sicily's young Corvo Colombia Platino, or Müller-Thurgau from Lombardy.

Menu: Do a menu from Modena by following the eggless soup with Giovanna's Wine-Basted Rabbit (page 284) or Zampone of the Aristocrats (page 315). Make dessert Modena Crumbling Cake (page 400) with sweet wine. If you are serving the soup as a light main dish, begin with Modena's Antipasto Castelvetro (page 16).

Cook's Notes   **Prosciutto:** Prosciutto di Parma (see page 497) replaces the robust hams from Modena's mountains, not yet available in the United States.

Bolognese tavern sign, "The Garden," 17th century, by Giuseppe Maria Mitelli

Mountain Soup with Garlic Croutons
Zuppa di Cavolo Nero

I *first heard of this from Modenese Americans originally from the Modena mountains, now living in Highwood, Illinois. According to Maria Picchietti, Anna Mardini and Sue Bernardi, the soup, a cross between a soup of winter greens and a stew thickened with garlic-scented country bread, had to contain at least seven vegetables. On Christmas Eve there was no meat in the pot, but at other times a little pancetta, some meat broth or a prosciutto bone would find its way into this recipe.*

The croutons and olive oil seasoning come from an old recipe from Modena, and hint at Tuscan origins (Tuscany lies on the other side of those high mountains). The region's unusual black cabbage originally gave the soup its name. Tuscans love sprinkling thick soups with olive oil instead of cheese as a final seasoning at the table, just as this one is seasoned. And thickening dishes with bread is another hallmark of the Tuscan kitchen.

When I asked the Highwood women if they thought the soup might come from Tuscany, they were puzzled. One replied, "It is our cooking, of our home. My mother and her mother made the soup this way, and now I do." Perhaps only outlanders need labels and borders.

[Serves 6 to 8 as a first course, 4 to 6 as a main dish]

continued

3 tablespoons extra-virgin olive oil

1 large onion, minced

1 medium carrot, minced

1 stalk celery, minced

3-inch sprig of fresh rosemary, or
   1 teaspoon dried whole rosemary
   leaves

1 large baking potato, peeled and
   cut into bite-size dice

1 large clove garlic, minced

½ small green cabbage, chopped

Leaves of 1 bunch Swiss chard, or
   14 large Romaine lettuce leaves,
   chopped

½ head black cabbage, or 24
   stalks curly endive lettuce,
   chopped

3⅓ cups canned borlotti or pinto
   beans, rinsed and drained

2 tablespoons imported Italian
   tomato paste

9½ cups water

Salt and freshly ground black
   pepper to taste

Croutons

4 large slices Modena Mountain Bread
   (page 388) or other country bread
   (see Note)

1 large clove garlic, halved

About 1 cup extra-virgin olive oil

Freshly ground black pepper to
   taste

Method **Working Ahead:** *The soup mellows nicely if done 2 or 3 days ahead. Make sure it is cool before covering and refrigerating. Croutons hold well for several hours after they are toasted. Reheat them in a 300°F oven before serving with the soup.*

Cooking the Soup: In 6- to 8-quart pot heat 3 tablespoons of oil over medium heat. Sauté the onion, carrot, celery, and rosemary 15 to 20 minutes, or until golden brown. Blend in the potato, garlic, and greens. Let them melt into the browned vegetables, cooking over medium heat, uncovered, 10 minutes. The greens will wilt and start to sauté. Stir in the beans, tomato paste, and water. Bring to a gentle bubble, partially cover, and cook 40 minutes, or until thick. Season with salt and pepper.

Making the Croutons: Preheat the oven to 450°F. Cut each bread slice into four pieces. Brush with olive oil, and toast on a cookie sheet, about 3 minutes per side. Remove, cool, and rub both sides of each slice with the split garlic. Rewarm before adding to the soup.

Serving the Soup: Have soup dishes warming in a low oven. Make sure the soup is bubbling. Taste for seasoning. Have about a cup of olive oil in a small pitcher at the table, along with a peppermill. Put two croutons in the bottom of each soup bowl. Ladle the soup over them and serve hot. Encourage everyone to drizzle about ½ tablespoon of olive oil into their soup, and sprinkle with freshly ground pepper.

Suggestions **Wine:** A young red Sangiovese di Romagna or from Umbria, a Cabernet Franc from Friuli's Collio Goriziano or Grave del Friuli areas.

Menu: Make the soup a main dish. A few slices of salami (page 501) could be its prelude. Follow the soup with Paola Bini's Sweet Ravioli (page 424) or Baked Pears with Fresh Grape Syrup (page 442).

Cook's Notes **Bread:** If Mountain Bread of Modena is unavailable, use a country-style bread, dense and crusty, made without sugar but with enough bran and whole wheat flour to give it a full, nutty flavor. Farmers' markets, health food stores and local bakeries are good sources.

Almond Spice Broth
Minestrina di Mandorle

An unusual opening to menus from the past or special dinners of today, this delicate infusion of almonds, stock, and spices was inspired by Carlo Nascia, 17th-century cook to the Duke of Parma. This recipe doubles easily.

[Serves 5 to 6 as a first course]

7 cups Poultry/Meat Stock (page 66) or Quick Stock (page 68)

1½ cups (6 ounces) blanched almonds

1 large clove garlic

½ teaspoon cracked black pepper

2 generous pinches of freshly grated nutmeg or ground cinnamon

Salt to taste

½ to 1 tablespoon fresh lemon juice

2 whole scallions, cut into 1-inch julienne

3 large thin slices Prosciutto di Parma, cut into 1-inch julienne

Method **Working Ahead:** *Start steeping the ground almonds and spices in the stock 1 day ahead. Store, covered, in the refrigerator. If time is short, steep the stock unrefrigerated, at least 45 minutes. Strain it before finishing the recipe.*

Making the Infusion: Bring the stock to a lively bubble in a 3- to 4-quart saucepan. Meanwhile combine the nuts, garlic, pepper, and nutmeg or cinnamon in a food processor fitted with the steel blade. Grind to a powder. Stir the almond mixture into the bubbling stock, cover, and remove from the heat. Let steep at room temperature at least 45 minutes.

Finishing and Serving: Strain the stock into a bowl, and then pour it back into the cleaned saucepan. Have small soup bowls, and a tureen if desired, warming in a low oven. Just before serving, bring the stock to a gentle bubble. Add enough salt and lemon juice to satisfy your taste. Sprinkle with the scallions and prosciutto, and ladle into the tureen or soup bowls. Serve immediately.

Suggestions   **Wine:** A flowery white Trebbiano dei Lazio or a delicate Riesling from Bologna or Friuli.

Menu: Serve small bowls of the soup before period dishes such as Christmas Capon (page 281), Domed Maccheroni Pie of Ferrara (page 180), or An Unusual Tortellini Pie (page 175). Finish the menu with chunks of Parmigiano-Reggiano and raw fennel, then Strawberries in Red Wine (page 445) or Frozen Hazelnut Zabaione with Chocolate Marsala Sauce (page 438). For a more contemporary menu, have as a prelude to Porcini Veal Chops (page 290), Pan-Roasted Quail (page 283), or Rabbit Dukes of Modena (page 286).

Almond Milk

The foundation of this soup used to be called almond milk. Medieval and Renaissance recipes called for the ground almonds to be infused in hot broth, water, or milk. The naturally sweet liquid held its popularity in many court kitchens well into the 18th century, saucing meats, moistening stews, becoming desserts, or, as in this dish, standing on its own as soup. In Italy during the mid-1600s, soup was not served as it is today. It often appeared in the middle of the meal, presented at the same time as the meats, savory/sweet pies, and sweet tidbits. In recording the banquets he prepared for the Duke of Parma, Carlo Nascia reports menus where soups like this one follow two other courses of over fifteen dishes each.

Oven-Glazed Porcini
Porcini al Forno Franco Casalboni

Franco Casalboni, of Ristorante Belvedere in Romagna's Bertinoro, created this dish at the height of porcini season. Balsamic vinegar, minced radicchio and arugula give this easy gratin great taste.

[Serves 4 as a first course, 2 as a main dish]

½ cup (½ ounce) dried porcini mushrooms

1½ cups hot water

2 large leaves arugula, finely chopped

4 small leaves radicchio, finely chopped

3 tablespoons minced onion

4 to 5 tablespoons (2 to 2½ ounces) unsalted butter

10 to 11 ounces fresh cremini or white button mushrooms, sliced vertically ⅛ to ¼ inch thick

Salt and freshly ground black pepper to taste

2 ounces Italian Parmigiano-Reggiano cheese

2 tablespoons extra-virgin olive oil

1½ to 2 tablespoons balsamic vinegar (artisan-made *tradizionale* if possible, see Note)

Method

Working Ahead: *This dish comes together and cooks in almost no time. The mushrooms must be served right after cooking, but the dish can be assembled up to the point of broiling 1½ hours ahead.*

Preparing the Porcini: If they are large, rinse the porcini pieces under cold running water to rid them of sand. If the pieces are small, drop them into a bowl of cold water and immediately swish them around. Let any particles settle a few seconds, and then scoop the mushrooms out of the water. Repeat if they seem very sandy. Place the rinsed porcini in a small bowl, and cover with the hot water. The mushrooms will be softened in 20 to 30 minutes.

Assembling the Dish: Combine the arugula, radicchio, and onion in a bowl. Use one third of the butter to slather the bottom and sides of two 13- to 14-inch oval gratin dishes or one large rectangular shallow baking dish made of enameled cast iron. Remove the soaked porcini from their liquid, and coarsely chop. Scatter half the sliced fresh mushrooms over the bottom of the dishes. The mushrooms should *not* entirely cover the bottom of the dish. Sprinkle them with half the chopped porcini, onion, arugula, and radicchio. Dot with half the remaining butter, and sprinkle with salt and pepper. Make another layer of mushrooms, and top as you did the first.

Broiling and Serving: Preheat the broiler, setting the oven rack so the baking dishes will be as close as possible to the flame. Shave the cheese into large furls with a vegetable peeler. Have the olive oil in one ramekin and the balsamic vinegar in another. Set out the ramekins on the table, along with two serving spoons and heat protectors for the baking dishes. (You present the hot baking dishes at the table, toss the mushrooms with the oil and vinegar, and serve.)

Slip the baking dishes under the broiler and cook 5 minutes, or until the mushrooms are sizzling and browning at the edges. During the last minute, spread the cheese shavings over the mushrooms. Broil only until the cheese has melted but is not browned. Immediately present at the table. Sprinkle the mushrooms with the olive oil and balsamic vinegar, and toss. Spoon onto individual dishes. The mushrooms could be served over small triangles of Grilled or Baked Polenta (pages 354 and 353).

Suggestions   **Wine:** A red Sangiovese di Romagna Riserva, or Tuscany's Monte Antico, or Chianti Montalbano.

Menu: The mushrooms make a fine main course after Chicken and Duck Liver Mousse with White Truffles (page 24) or Tagliatelle with Caramelized Onions and Fresh Herbs (page 101).

Cook's Notes   **Balsamic Vinegar:** If using commercial balsamic, add a generous pinch of dark brown sugar before sprinkling it over the mushrooms. For information on balsamic vinegar, see page 467.

Bertinoro Hospitality

Franco Casalboni and his restaurant carry on a Bertinoro tradition of hospitality. The town crowns a hilltop, and a tall column stands in front of the Renaissance palace that is now Bertinoro's town hall. Large iron rings attached near its base are the key to its name, the Hospitality Column. Until the last century, each ring was the charge of a Bertinoro family. When a stranger arrived and tied his or her horse to a ring, that family became responsible for the stranger's care and well-being. Today restaurateurs and local vintners carry out Bertinoro's tradition to the extent of making guests feel especially welcome and never sending anyone on their way without some form of sustenance.

Paola Cavazzini's Eggplant Torte
Tortino di Melanzane La Greppia

This is a dish worthy of culinary canonization. Chef Paola Cavazzini of Parma's Ristorante La Greppia layers rounds of crisp-fried eggplant with two cream sauces, slices of nutty Fontina, a tomato sauce (excellent eaten on its own), and Parma's famous namesake cheese, Parmigiano-Reggiano. From an American point of view, this is the ultimate eggplant Parmesan. Yet that southern Italian dish is unknown in Parma. For Parmesans this tortino, *or little cake, is enjoyed as an original, available only at La Greppia. The torte is versatile; serve it hot or warm, as a starter or a main dish.*

[Serves 8 to 10 as a first course, 6 as a main dish]

Cheese-and-Egg Cream

3 eggs

¾ cup (3 ounces) freshly grated Italian Parmigiano-Reggiano cheese

½ cup heavy cream

Cooked Cream

1 tablespoon all-purpose unbleached flour (organic stone-ground preferred)

1 cup milk

⅔ cup heavy cream

Salt and freshly ground black pepper to taste

Freshly grated nutmeg to taste

Assembly

Salt

2½ pounds eggplant, unpeeled, sliced into ¼-inch-thick rounds

About 2 cups extra-virgin olive oil

2 cups all-purpose unbleached flour (organic stone-ground preferred)

2½ cups Winter Tomato Sauce (page 62), puréed

6 ounces imported Italian Fontina cheese, thinly sliced

¼ cup (1 ounce) freshly grated Parmigiano-Reggiano cheese

Method

Working Ahead: *The components of the torte can be prepared several days ahead, but the dish is at its best assembled no more than about 1 hour before baking. Winter Tomato Sauce can be made months in advance and frozen. Up to 3 days ahead, prepare the two cream sauces, storing them, covered, in the refrigerator. Up to 8 hours before assembling the dish, fry the eggplant, and keep it uncovered at room temperature.*

Preparing the Cheese-and-Egg Cream: In a bowl, blend together the 3 eggs, ¾ cup Parmigiano cheese, and ½ cup cream. Cover and refrigerate.

Preparing the Cooked Cream: In a small saucepan, whisk together the 1 tablespoon flour with ¼ cup of the milk until smooth. Use a wooden spatula to stir in the rest of the milk and the ⅔ cup cream. Heat over medium-high heat until the sauce bubbles gently. Keep stirring while it bubbles, 5 minutes, or until thick enough for you to see the bottom of the pan as you pull the spatula across it. Cool, and season to taste.

Cooking the Eggplant: Early on the day you will be serving the torte, lightly salt the eggplant slices, and arrange them between several layers of paper towels. Weight them with a heavy cutting board at least 4 hours or up to 10 hours. Heat about 1½ inches of olive oil in a large heavy skillet over medium-high heat. The oil should be hot but not smoking. Dredge the eggplant in the flour, shaking off any excess. Fry several slices at a time, 1½ minutes per side, or until golden. Drain on paper towels, gently pressing with additional paper towels to absorb excess oil.

Assembling the Torte: Preheat the oven to 350°F. Lightly oil a 2½-quart shallow glass baking dish. Have the tomato sauce, cream sauces, and two cheeses handy. Cover the bottom of the dish with a thin layer of cooked cream. Arrange half the eggplant slices in a single layer over the cream. Scatter half the Fontina over the eggplant, and slather with half the tomato sauce. Spread half the cheese-and-egg cream over the tomato sauce. Lay the rest of the eggplant over the sauce. Spread it with the remaining Fontina, cheese-and-egg cream, tomato sauce, and finally the remaining cooked cream. Sprinkle with the Parmigiano-Reggiano cheese and bake 35 to 40 minutes. Let the torte stand at room temperature 10 to 15 minutes before cutting it into small squares. Serve on heated plates.

Suggestions   **Wine:** A soft white like an Arneis from the Piedmont, a Chardonnay from Bologna, the Trentino, or Friuli, or Tuscany's white Montecarlo.

Menu: Offer in small quantities before Parma dishes like Porcini Veal Chops (page 290) or Erminia's Pan-Crisped Chicken (page 270). Finish the meal with chunks of Parmigiano-Reggiano cheese followed by fresh pears. If serving as a main dish, begin with "Little" Spring Soup from the 17th Century (page 232). Serve a green salad after the torte, and finish with either fruit and Parmigiano-Reggiano cheese or Marie Louise's Crescents (page 426).

Will the Real Eggplant Parmesan Please Stand?

No, that great Italian standby, known to most Americans, did not originate in Parma. The casserole of fried eggplant slices baked with tomato sauce, mozzarella, and Parmesan was born in the southern Italian region of Campania. There it is called *Parmigiana di Melanzane* (Parmesan of Eggplant), no doubt because expensive Parmigiano-Reggiano cheese imported from the north figures so importantly in its flavorings. I say "no doubt" but must include a fascinating note from Mary Taylor Simeti. In *Pomp and Sustenance: 25 Centuries of Sicilian Food,* she explains *melanzane alla parmigiana* is really a mispronunciation. Most Sicilians believe their dish of sliced eggplant layered with tomato sauce and local caciocavallo cheese was originally *Melanzane alla Palmigiana. Palmigiana* means shutter in Sicilian, and reflects the layered louver-like pattern of eggplant slices. Sicilians have difficulty pronouncing "*l,*" and so the dish became *alla parmigiana.*

The Parma dish is *Melanzane alla Parmigiana* (Eggplant Parmesan), but in the four renditions I have found from Parma, only one calls for the area's famous cheese. Obviously the name means eggplant as cooked in Parma, not eggplant with Parmesan cheese. Parma food historian Guglielmo Capacchi dashes a local theory that eggplant made its debut in Parma during the 1600s, when ducal cook Carlo Nascia brought it from southern Italy. According to Capacchi, old records tell of eggplant being eaten in Emilia during the 13th century. But the proof gets even better, claims Capacchi. It was recorded in the 14th century that a medical teacher in Bologna, Master Taddeo, stated emphatically to his students the accepted medical fact of the day: Eat eggplant for nine days straight and you will go mad. (Some etymologists believe *melanzane* derives from "apple [*mela*] of madness [*insano*].") True to the spirit of inquiry, one student performed the experiment. At the end of the ninth day, convinced Taddeo would be amazed, he announced to his teacher and fellow students that he was not mad. Taddeo remained unperturbed, simply commanding his class to write down a new margin note: "The eggplant theory has been tested and is not true."

One last note on origins: Many assume the purple vegetable came by its English name solely because of shape. But in India, where many historians believe eggplant originated, one species grows as a small oval white vegetable. Small white eggplants are found in Southeast Asian markets, and large white eggplants are often seen in the vegetable stalls of Emilia-Romagna.

Piacenza Peppers Country Style
Rustisana Piacentina

A dish of late summer from the farmhouses of Piacenza, Rustisana was often communal family food, eaten from a shallow pot set in the middle of the table. Some spooned the braising of sweet peppers and tomatoes over toasted bread; others ladled it onto slabs of baked or grilled polenta. Rustisana became a more substantial dish when topped with poached eggs and shavings of local grana cheese. Enjoy it hot or at room temperature.

[Serves 6 to 8 as a first course, 4 to 5 as a main dish]

2 tablespoons extra-virgin olive oil

1 tablespoon unsalted butter

2 medium onions, sliced into strips

2 large red bell peppers, cut into 1-inch triangles

2 large yellow bell peppers, cut into 1-inch triangles

1 small clove garlic, minced

8 fresh basil leaves, or 2-inch sprig fresh rosemary, chopped

3 vine-ripened tomatoes, cored, seeded, and chopped, or 6 canned plum tomatoes, drained and crushed

Salt and freshly ground black pepper to taste

Optional Accompaniments

3 ounces Parmigiano-Reggiano cheese, shaved with a vegetable peeler

8 slices Modena Mountain Bread (page 388) or other bread, toasted and rubbed with garlic

½ recipe Polenta (page 352), baked and sliced

Method

Working Ahead: Rustisana *can be cooked ahead and held, covered, up to 3 hours at room temperature or as long as 4 days in the refrigerator. It is fine at room temperature or briefly reheated.*

Cooking the Peppers: Heat the oil and butter in a large skillet over medium-high heat. Add the onions and peppers and cook quickly, tossing with two wooden spatulas, 4 minutes, or until the onions are golden brown. Turn the heat up to high if necessary. Stir in the garlic and basil or rosemary, cook a few seconds, and then add the tomatoes. Simmer 3 minutes, or until thickened. Remove from the heat and season to taste.

Serving: Spoon into a shallow bowl, and pass with any of the desired accompaniments.

Suggestions   **Wine:** Piacenza's fresh white Monterosso Val d'Arda, Sicily's white Rapitalà, or a Pinot Bianco from the Veneto's Breganze area.

Menu: This is fine outdoor food. Serve before almost any grilled or roasted dish not containing tomatoes, such as Herbed Seafood Grill (page 254), Grilled Beef with Balsamic Glaze (page 303), or Erminia's Pan-Crisped Chicken (page 270). Follow with Paola Bini's Potato Salad (page 19), and fruit for dessert.

Tart of Fresh Artichokes
Torta di Carciofi

A melt-in-the-mouth pastry encloses chunks of sautéed artichoke made even more savory by additions of onion, carrot, garlic, basil, and Parmigiano-Reggiano cheese. You will discover many renditions of this tart in pastry shop windows throughout the region.

[Serves 8 to 10 as a first course, 6 as a main dish]

Pastry

1½ cups (6 ounces) all-purpose unbleached flour (organic stone-ground preferred)

½ cup (2 ounces) cake flour

¼ teaspoon salt

¼ teaspoon freshly ground black pepper

10 tablespoons (5 ounces) unsalted butter, or half butter and half lard, chilled

6 to 8 tablespoons cold water

Filling

6 large artichokes

2 large lemons

1½ cups water

1 ounce thinly sliced pancetta, chopped

2 tablespoons extra-virgin olive oil

1 small to medium onion, minced

3 tablespoons minced carrot

Salt and freshly ground black pepper to taste

1 tablespoon shredded lemon zest

1 large clove garlic, minced

6 tablespoons minced fresh basil leaves, or 2½ teaspoons dried basil

½ cup water

1 to 2 teaspoons fresh lemon juice

¾ to 1 cup (3 to 4 ounces) freshly grated Italian Parmigiano-Reggiano cheese

Glaze

1 egg, beaten

continued

Method   **Working Ahead:** *The pastry can be made up to 3 months ahead and frozen. It can be rolled out 24 hours before baking the tart. The filling keeps, covered, in the refrigerator 2 days, but the tart is at its prime when baked and eaten within a day. Rewarm it before serving if possible.*

Making the Pastry: Grease a 9- to 10-inch fluted tart pan with removable bottom. Combine the flours, salt, and pepper in a food processor or mixing bowl and blend. Cut in the butter until the mixture resembles small peas. Either process a few seconds in the machine, or use a hand-held pastry cutter or two knives. Sprinkle the cold water over the dough. In a processor, use the on/off pulse to blend the dough just until it forms clumps. By hand, toss with a fork to moisten. Do not mix so much that the dough forms a ball—that will toughen it. Using your hands, gather the dough into a ball, wrap in plastic wrap, and chill about 30 minutes. Roll out half the dough to less than ⅛ inch thick, and fit it into the tart pan, leaving a 1-inch border. Roll out the remaining dough to form a large circle of the same thickness. Spread it on a foil-covered baking sheet. Chill both pastry pieces 30 minutes or up to 24 hours.

Preparing Artichoke Bottoms: Halve both lemons and squeeze the juice of three halves into a medium bowl. Add the water. As you cut the artichokes, keep rubbing the surface with the remaining lemon half to keep them from darkening. Begin by cutting away the stem. Then pull off the leaves, starting at the base and going up halfway. Trim away the leaf stubs around the base until you see the pale green bottom. Turn the artichoke upside down and cut away the dark green from its base. Then cut away the leaves from the top of the artichoke, and scoop out the fuzzy choke with a spoon. Immediately immerse the bottom in the lemon water.

Cooking the Filling: Drain the artichoke bottoms, pat them dry, and cut into bite-size chunks. Heat the pancetta and oil in a 12-inch skillet over medium heat. Sauté pancetta 2 to 3 minutes to give up its fat. Then turn the heat to medium-high. Add the artichoke pieces and sauté, uncovered, 4 minutes, or until they begin to color. Stir in the onion, carrot, and a light sprinkling of salt and pepper. Cook, stirring frequently with a wooden spatula, 4 minutes, or until the onion has browned and the artichokes are golden.

Reduce the heat to medium, add the lemon zest, garlic, and basil, and cook 30 seconds. Add the water and bring to a boil, scraping up the brown bits from the bottom of the skillet. Cover and simmer over low heat 3 to 4 minutes, or until the artichokes are slightly softened. Uncover and cook down the juices 1 minute, or until they form a moist glaze on the bottom of the skillet. The artichokes should still be a bit crisp. Remove from the heat and allow to cool. When they are cool, season them to taste with lemon juice.

Assembling and Baking the Tart: Preheat the oven to 425°F. Remove the pastry from the refrigerator. Spread the filling in the tart pan. Sprinkle it liberally with the cheese, and top with the sheet of dough, pressing the edges together. Fold the overhanging pastry over toward the tart's center, and crimp into a zigzag shape. Brush the crust with the beaten egg, and pierce with a fork. Bake in the lower third of the oven 15 minutes. Lower the heat to 375°F and bake another 25 minutes, or until golden brown. Serve hot or warm.

Suggestions   **Wine:** Artichokes and wine are not a happy marriage.

Menu: For a light menu, have as a main dish after Salad of Tart Greens with Prosciutto and Warm Balsamic Dressing (page 26). Follow it with Espresso and Mascarpone Semi-Freddo (page 428) or Strawberries in Red Wine (page 445). For picnics, serve the tart, then pieces of cold Erminia's Pan-Crisped Chicken (page 270) with Paola Bini's Potato Salad (page 19). Fresh berries make a fine dessert.

Reggio's Tart of Garden Greens
Erbazzone Reggiano

This big round tart of crisp pastry and sautéed greens is a favorite snack in Reggio. There you will see shoppers eating <u>Erbazzone</u> as street food from folded paper napkins. This version is tastier than most because a little of the onion, pancetta, and garlic are held back from the filling sauté and added just before baking.

Years ago, <u>Erbazzone</u> was an entire meal for a peasant family, marking the first green leaves of spring and the last signs of green before winter set in. When the filling is wrapped in big turnovers of pastry and deep-fried, it becomes <u>Erbazzone Fritto.</u> Many Reggiani claim the true <u>Erbazzone</u> must contain ricotta. When made without ricotta, some call the tart <u>Scarpazzoun.</u>

[Serves 10 to 12 as a first course or snack, 6 to 8 as a main dish]

continued

Crazy Dough

2 cups (8 ounces) all-purpose unbleached flour (organic stone-ground preferred)

½ cup (2 ounces) cake flour

¼ teaspoon salt

5 tablespoons high-quality lard, or 2 tablespoons (1 ounce) butter and 3 tablespoons extra-virgin olive oil, chilled

7 to 10 tablespoons cold water

1 tablespoon olive oil for pan

Filling

5 ounces thinly sliced pancetta, minced

3 large cloves garlic, minced

3 medium-large onions, chopped

Freshly ground black pepper to taste

2 tablespoons extra-virgin olive oil

2½ pounds fresh spinach, beet greens, or Swiss chard leaves, or a blend, cooked until barely wilted, squeezed dry, and chopped

1½ to 2 cups (6 to 8 ounces) freshly grated Italian Parmigiano-Reggiano cheese

Salt to taste

2 eggs, beaten

2 tablespoons high-quality lard or olive oil

1 clove garlic, minced

Method   **Working Ahead:** *The pastry can be made up to 3 months ahead and frozen. Or roll it out and chill overnight if convenient. The filling can be made 1 day ahead. The Erbazzone is at its best when eaten the same day it is baked. Serve it hot, warm, or at room temperature.*

Making the Pastry by Hand: Combine the flours and salt in a bowl. Make a well in the center and add the cold lard or butter and oil. Working with your fingertips or a pastry cutter, blend the fat and flour until the mixture resembles coarse meal. Sprinkle with 7 tablespoons of the water, and toss with a fork until the dough begins to form clumps. If it is dry, add more water. Gather the bits of dough into a ball, wrap, and chill at least 30 minutes.

Making the Dough with a Food Processor: Combine the dry ingredients in a processor fitted with the steel blade. Blend a few seconds. Then add the fat(s), processing until the pastry looks like coarse meal. Sprinkle about 7 tablespoons of the cold water over the dough, and process just until the mixture begins to gather into clumps (add more water if necessary). Wrap and chill 30 minutes. Roll out a generous half of the dough very thin, and lay it over a greased 14-inch pizza pan, leaving about a 1-inch overhang. Roll out the remaining dough to form a 15-inch round, and set it on a foil-covered baking sheet. Refrigerate both pieces at least 30 minutes.

Making the Filling: Combine about ¼ cup of the minced pancetta with a little of the garlic, about ¼ cup of the onion, and a generous amount of black pepper. Set aside. Heat the remaining pancetta with the oil in a large skillet over medium-low heat. Cook about 5 minutes, or until the pancetta has given off much of its fat. Add the remaining onion and cook, covered, 15 minutes, or until softened. Uncover, raise the heat to high, and cook another 6 minutes, or until a rich golden brown. Add the spinach or chard, and sauté 3 to 5 minutes, adjusting the heat to prevent burning.

Stir in the remainder of the 3 garlic cloves, and cook another 30 seconds or so. If a brown glaze forms on the skillet bottom, add a little water and simmer, scraping it up with a spatula to incorporate the glaze into the filling. Cook a minute or so until the liquid evaporates. Turn the filling into a bowl and cool. Blend in 1½ cups of the cheese and reserved pancetta mixture. Taste for seasoning and for enough cheese, and then blend in the eggs.

Baking the Erbazzone: Preheat the oven to about 400°F. Set the rack as close to the bottom of the oven as possible. Combine the lard and garlic in a small pan, and heat over medium heat only 2 minutes, or until the lard is melted.

Spread the filling over the pastry-lined pizza pan, leaving about a 2-inch border. Dampen the edges with water, top with the remaining dough, and pinch the edges together. Fold the edges over toward the center of the tart, and crimp. Make slashes in the top of the crust. Bake 20 minutes. Then brush the crust with the melted lard and garlic mixture, and bake another 20 minutes, or until pale gold and very crisp. The edges of the tart will be golden brown. Cut in narrow wedges to serve.

Suggestions   **Wine:** In Reggio a local Lambrusco is ideal. Outside the region drink a Gamay della Valle d'Aosta, Umbria's Castel Grifone, or a Merlot from Friuli's Aquilea or Collio Goriziano areas.

Menu: Serve as a main dish after a Platter of Cured Meats (page 14) with Balsamic Vegetables (page 18) or Spring Salad with Hazelnuts (page 21). Finish with Capacchi's Blazing Chestnuts (page 450) or pears and Parmigiano-Reggiano cheese. Have *Erbazzone* as a first course before country dishes like Maria Bertuzzi's Lemon Chicken (page 273) or Grilled Beef with Balsamic Glaze (page 303).

Cook's Notes   **Lard:** For information on lard, see page 483.

Crazy Dough

This dough is found in old peasant recipes. Rather than tender and melting, this pastry is lean, thin, and crisp. Nothing but flour, water, and a little lard makes the crazy dough *(pasta matta),* as it was called years ago. Even lard (called the butter of the poor) must have been scarce for many, because the trick in this dish was to stretch the lard's goodness. The melted lard brushed on the crust (an amount too small to have any effect as an ingredient *in* the crust) makes it very crisp. Without this finishing touch, the crust's lean qualities are all too evident. Today many cooks gentrify and tenderize the crust with generous amounts of butter and olive oil. But I am still in awe of the skill of those grandmothers and great-grandmothers who could create such elegantly satisfying food from so little.

Villa Gaidello

SECOND COURSES

Seafood, Poultry, and Meats

*I*t is often said that Italy's second courses are more austere than her first dishes. Not in Emilia-Romagna. Yes, second courses are often simple affairs of grilled or roasted meats, poultry, or fish. But "austere" hardly does justice to their deep brown flavors or the bold tastes imparted by fresh herbs and bastings of wine. The region's stews and sautés are even more bountiful, with their multi-step cooking technique creating complex layerings of tastes. Emilia-Romagna is the land of plenty, and her second courses are as much a testament to her heritage of good eating and consummate cooking skills as is the rest of her regional menu.

But the second course of decades ago had a very different meaning than it does today. Until post–World War II prosperity made meat available to almost everyone, the second course was the economic dividing line between the peasant and the middle class. Before World War II most of the recipes in this section were the dishes of the prosperous. To have meat was to have status. For the farm laborer and city factory worker, dishes like January Pork, Lamb with Black Olives, or Maria Bertuzzi's Lemon Chicken meant holidays, harvest parties, or special family celebrations. The staples of the peasant diet were the foods of first courses: polenta, beans, vegetables, soups, rice and pasta, and of *course bread. For day-to-day eating, especially in the late 19th century and later, small amounts of meat fed many by becoming ragùs for pasta. Before that, even ragùs were regularly eaten only by the more prosperous.*

Each area of Emilia-Romagna has its specialties, whether they are relegated to occasional feasts or eaten every day.

Veal is used more than beef throughout the region. Along the coast, seafoods are eaten—usually simply grilled, fried, or stewed.

Especially in Romagna, chops of veal, pork, and lamb are rubbed with olive oil and herbs and grilled over a wood fire. One of Romagna's most favored meats is the neutered young ram (castrato).

Rabbit is eaten everywhere, but Reggio's rabbit gained a particularly fine reputation decades ago. And Modena would not dream of letting a holiday go by without its stuffed pig's foot sausage, zampone.

For the entire region, Christmas means capon, either poached so its broth can welcome tortellini or cappelletti, or roasted with its skin burnished to edible gold.

Guinea hen, pigeon, and quail are always available, but autumn and winter bring game from the mountains and the plain—especially pheasant, hare, wild duck, partridge, and wild boar. Early summer is marked with signs at snack stands and restaurants offering frogs.

Chicken is perhaps the most popular meat of all, easy to raise almost anywhere.

Emilia-Romagna's pork defines succulence, but traditionally almost every part of the pig went for curing. When the pig met its demise, whole families spent days preserving it for a year's sustenance. On those evenings they feasted on fresh pork ribs and loin, the rare treats of winter.

Re-creating an Italian meal in the United States is a matter of subtly adjusting the menu's balance. America's main course is often merely Italy's second dish—another element on the menu, not a dish the entire meal revolves around. In Italy second dishes frequently hold equal weight with first courses. And no matter how many pastas, risottos, or soups begin a meal, or how substantial they may seem, they are always considered first courses.

When first courses are intricate or plentiful, second dishes are simple, like grilled or roasted meats or fish. More elaborate second dishes, such as Rabbit Dukes of Modena or Zampone of the Aristocrats, demand

THE SPLENDID TABLE

center stage. The dishes that precede them should be direct and uncomplicated, not distracting from the grandeur of what is to come.

The "Menu Suggestions" section of each recipe gives guidelines for serving these dishes as they are eaten in Italy, as well as ideas for weaving them into lifestyles on this side of the Atlantic. For instance, in Parma, Erminia's Pan-Crisped Chicken is eaten hot at the table with a knife and fork. But in America I enjoy it also as cold finger food on summer picnics. For those of us who cannot spend hours cooking just before a dinner party, there is the blessing of dishes that are better for being made ahead, like Mardi Gras Chicken, Rabbit Dukes of Modena, and Beef-Wrapped Sausage. Notice, too, that most of the recipes are prepared in stages, so the cooking can be adjusted to individual schedules.

Many of these dishes are about celebration and about firsts. In Emilia-Romagna they mark the birth of a new baby, the summer's first harvests of wheat and hay, the rigging of a new boat, a marriage, or the beginning of spring and rebirth. Herald the coming of spring with Mardi Gras Chicken. Feast on the first peppers from the garden with Riccardo Rimondi's Chicken Cacciatora. Enjoy the first summer cookout with Herbed Seafood Grill or Grilled Beef with Balsamic Glaze. Celebrate a first Sunday with the entire family with Balsamic Roast Chicken. Mark the first snowfall with the homey comfort of Braised Pork Ribs with Polenta. Share a first Christmas together with Christmas Capon instead of goose, roast beef, or turkey. See in the New Year with Modena's zampone sausage and lentils, knowing the Modenese believe the lentils will bring a year of prosperity.

Herbed Seafood Grill
Pesce ai Ferri

This is home cooking and the food of *unpretentious restaurants along the Adriatic. Often those "restaurants" are no more than outdoor grills covered with canvas awnings set up on the beach. But the fish is always fresh, and always cooked over a wood fire. Do not let the lack of outdoor facilities stop you from making this simple dish. Cook it in winter and summer—over charcoal, on a stove-top griddle, and even in a sauté pan. Any firm-fleshed fish works in this recipe, from Spanish mackerel to bluefish, members of the bass family, triggerfish, sea trout, tilefish, swordfish, tuna, and a score of others. The most important ingredient in the fish is freshness. This recipe doubles easily.*

[Serves 3 to 4]

1 pound firm-fleshed fish fillets, about ¾ to 1 inch thick
1 large clove garlic
1 tablespoon minced Italian parsley
2 to 3 tablespoons minced fresh basil or fresh marjoram, or 1½ teaspoons dried whole-leaf basil or marjoram

2 tablespoons extra-virgin olive oil
Salt and freshly ground black pepper to taste
4 to 6 lemon wedges

Method

Working Ahead: *For the best flavor, season the fish, cover, and refrigerate 2 to 6 hours before cooking.*

Seasoning the Fish: Cut about four diagonal slashes in the fillets, about ⅛ inch deep and 1 inch long. Make a paste of the garlic, parsley, basil, and olive oil by pureeing in a food processor or grinding in a mortar. Rub it over both sides of the fillets. Place them on a platter, lightly cover with plastic wrap, and refrigerate 2 to 6 hours.

Grilling over Charcoal: Use real wood charcoal if possible, and burn it until the coals are covered with gray ash. Brush the grill with olive or vegetable oil to keep the fillets from sticking. If possible, place the grill about 6 inches from the coals. Add the fish with its seasoning rub. Cook it quickly, 2 to 4 minutes per side, browning on both sides. Check to be sure the fish is firm when pressed and opaque to the center, but not yet flaking and dry.

Stove-top Grilling: Heat a heavy griddle or gridded skillet over high heat. Brush it with a little olive oil, and arrange the seasoned fillets on it. Reduce the heat to medium and cook 3 to 4 minutes on one side, 2 to 3 minutes on the second side. Check for doneness as described above.

"Grilling" in a Sauté Pan: Film the bottom of a large sauté pan with olive oil. Heat it over high heat, taking care not to let the oil smoke. Add the fish with its seasoning rub, and turn the heat to medium. Cook 3 to 4 minutes on one side, 2 to 3 minutes on the second side.

Serving: Sprinkle the fish with a little salt and pepper. Serve hot, on a heated platter, garnished with lemon wedges.

Suggestions **Wine:** For delicately flavored fish, drink a crisp white like a Sauvignon from the hills of Bologna, a Sauvignon Blanc or Pinot Bianco from Friuli, or the elegant Cortese di Gavi of Piemonte. For tuna or bluefish, have a full-bodied white like Tuscany's Montecarlo, or a Vernaccia di San Gimignano.

Menu: Begin with Spring Salad with Hazelnuts (page 21), Maccheroni with Baked Grilled Vegetables (page 126), Linguine with Braised Garlic and Balsamic Vinegar (page 110) or Spaghetti with Anchovies and Melting Onions (page 130). For dessert, serve Torta Barozzi (page 395) or Iced Melon with Mint and Balsamic Vinegar (page 444).

Cook's Notes **Fresh Herbs:** For information on fresh herbs, see page 481.

A carrier of fresh fish from the Bologna banquet procession honoring the Swiss guard, Giuseppe Maria Mitelli, 1699

Fresh Tuna Adriatic Style
Tonno in Tegame

A *fast sauté of fresh herbs, tomato, and black olives sauces fresh tuna. Tuna used to be plentiful on the Adriatic coast of Romagna, especially in summer, when sautés like this one were popular. If tuna is not available, use yellowtail (also known as opah), halibut, or swordfish.*

[Serves 6]

4 tablespoons extra-virgin olive oil

1½ pounds fresh tuna, cut 1 inch thick and divided into 6 steaks

1 medium onion, minced

3 tablespoons minced Italian parsley

1 large clove garlic, minced

¼ cup minced fresh basil, or 1½ teaspoons dried whole-leaf basil

½ cup dry white wine

Salt and freshly ground black pepper

1 large vine-ripened tomato, cored, seeded, and diced, or 1 cup drained canned tomatoes, crushed

⅔ cup oil-cured black olives, pitted and coarsely chopped

Fresh basil leaves for garnish (optional)

Method

Working Ahead: *The fish cooks in almost no time, so serve the tuna straight from the sauté pan. But save last-minute fussing by chopping and measuring the ingredients well ahead of time.*

Sautéing the Tuna: Have a serving platter warming in a low oven. Heat the olive oil in a heavy 12-inch sauté pan over medium-high heat. Add the fish steaks in a single layer, sprinkling the onion and parsley over and around them. Sear the fish about 1 minute per side, so the flesh whitens and tightens. Slip a metal or wood spatula under the pieces to turn them without tearing. Turn the heat down to medium-low. Scatter the garlic, basil, and 3 tablespoons of the white wine around the fish. Sprinkle lightly with salt and pepper. Keep the fish uncovered as you cook it 2 to 3 minutes per side, or until still soft enough to have just a little "give" when pressed. If in doubt, slit into the center of a piece, checking that the meat is opaque but not dry or flaking.

Serving: Slip the steaks onto the heated serving platter. Turn the heat up to high, and add the remaining wine. Boil 30 seconds, scraping up any brown bits in the pan. Add the tomato and olives, and toss 20 seconds over high heat. Spoon the sauce over the tuna, and serve. A garnish of fresh basil leaves could be scattered over the tuna.

Suggestions   **Wine:** From the region, a young red Rosso del Bosco, or a white Pinot Bianco or Pinot Grigio from Friuli. A young red Sangiovese di Romagna or from Umbria is also good with the robust fish, as is a young red Cabernet Franc of Friuli.

Menu: Before the tuna, serve Linguine with Braised Garlic and Balsamic Vinegar (page 110) or Tagliatelle with Fresh Porcini Mushrooms (page 96). Follow it with a green salad, and then ripe peaches with Fresh Squaquerone Cheese (page 386) or Cardinal d'Este's Tart (page 417).

Cook's Notes **The Best Olives:** Taste olives before buying. Since wide selections of Italian olives are sometimes hard to find, do not hesitate to try olives from Greece, France, and other countries. The best oil-cured ones are tasty and rich without overwhelming saltiness. Better to use a good brine-cured black or green olive than a mediocre oil-cured one. The olive's nationality is far less important than its taste.

Parsley-Stuffed Shrimps
Gamberi Ripieni

Parsley, onion, and bread crumbs stuff big shrimp in this dish from Romagna's coast. They are usually sautéed in olive oil, but many grill the shrimps over charcoal.

[Serves 3 to 4 as a main dish, 4 to 6 as a first course]

Stuffing
1 tablespoon extra-virgin olive oil
⅓ cup dried unflavored bread crumbs
1 large clove garlic, minced
2 tablespoons minced Italian parsley
1 tablespoon minced onion
Salt and freshly ground black pepper to taste

Shrimps
1 pound raw jumbo shrimps (8 to 12 per pound)
Extra-virgin olive oil
Salt and freshly ground black pepper
2 large lemons, cut into wedges

Method   **Working Ahead:** *For the best flavor, make the filling and stuff the shrimps 4 to 8 hours before cooking. Keep them covered and refrigerated. Serve the shrimps immediately after broiling.*

continued

Making the Filling: Heat the 1 tablespoon olive oil in a small skillet over medium heat. Add the bread crumbs and garlic, and lower the heat to the lowest possible setting. Stir the crumbs constantly 3 minutes, or until they are golden brown. Turn the crumbs into a small bowl. Stir in the parsley and onion, and season with salt and pepper.

Stuffing the Shrimps: Shell the shrimps, leaving the tail section intact. Cut a long pocket into their undersides by making a deep slit down the length from the tail, stopping just short of slicing through the other end. Take care not to cut through the top side of the shrimps. Press a generous teaspoon of the stuffing into each pocket. Pile the shrimps on a plate, cover with plastic wrap, and refrigerate 4 to 8 hours.

Broiling and Serving: Preheat the broiler, and set a rack as close as possible to the flame. The shrimps should be about 5 inches from the flame when they cook. Arrange the shrimps on their sides in a single layer in a broiler pan or baking dish. Drizzle each one with a fine film of olive oil and sprinkle lightly with salt and pepper. Broil 2 minutes, or until bright pink on one side. Turn the shrimps over with tongs, and broil another 1 to 3 minutes, or until pink on the other side. They should be firm but not rubbery. Take care not to overcook them. Immediately remove them from the broiler.

Pile the shrimps on a heated serving platter, or serve right from their baking dish. Sprinkle with a little lemon juice. Arrange the remaining lemon wedges among them, and serve immediately.

Suggestions   **Wine:** Serve a dry white Albana di Romagna, Lombardy's fragrant Lugana, or Friuli's more aggressive Pinot Bianco.

Menu: Before the shrimps, have Spring Salad with Hazelnuts (page 21) or Tagliatelle with Caramelized Onions and Fresh Herbs (page 101). Green Beans with Balsamic Pesto (page 325) are excellent with the shrimps. Make dessert Cinnamon and Clove Custard (page 440) or Modena Rice Pudding (page 398).

Seafood Stew Romagna
Brodetto

<u>Brodetto</u> *is the king of Romagna's seafood stews. Making a proper one is almost a religious rite, with no two cooks ever entirely agreeing on method and ingredients. What sets apart this recipe is simmering onions in vinegar, then sautéing and stewing them with tomatoes and seafood. Instead of souring the <u>Brodetto,</u> the onions sweeten and enrich the stew. This is a singular dish unlike any other, a turn-of-the-century recipe shared by Gianni Quondamatteo.*

[Serves 6 to 8]

¾ cup red wine vinegar
2 large onions, finely chopped
9 tablespoons extra-virgin olive oil
Salt and freshly ground black
  pepper to taste
Two 3-inch strips of lemon zest
2 large cloves garlic, minced
2⅔ cups peeled, seeded, and
  chopped vine-ripened tomatoes,
  or 2⅔ cups canned tomatoes
  with their juice

4 cups dry white wine
3½ pounds combined filleted
  fresh fish, cut into bite-size
  pieces (such as bluefish,
  flounder, sea robin, sea trout,
  rockfish, cod, mullet, or shark)
  and shellfish (such as squid,
  cuttlefish, small clams, shrimps)

Method

Working Ahead: Brodetto *can be prepared several hours in advance, up to the point of adding the seafood. Chill until ready to continue, then bring the stew to a simmer, add the fish, and finish.*

Preparing the Onions: In a heavy 6- to 8-quart pot, bring the vinegar to a lively bubble over high heat. Add the onions, turn the heat to low, and partially cover the pot. Cook 15 minutes, or until the onions are soft and almost transparent. Stir occasionally. If the liquid threatens to evaporate totally, add about ¼ cup water. Once the onions are soft and rosy colored, uncover the pot and let the vinegar bubble gently, stirring frequently, until it evaporates. Add the oil, a little salt, and a generous sprinkling of freshly ground black pepper. Slowly sauté over medium-low heat, uncovered, 10 minutes, or until the onions turn golden. Stir frequently.

Making the Base: With the heat still at medium-low, stir in the lemon zest and garlic, and cook about 1 minute. Add the tomatoes, raise the heat to high, and boil, uncovered, 5 minutes, or until thick. Pour in the wine and bring the mixture to a boil.

continued

Boil over high heat 5 minutes, or until the mixture is reduced by about one third and no raw alcohol taste is left from the wine. The flavors should be slightly sweet from the tomato and onion, with a tart backdrop. Taste for seasoning.

Cooking the Seafood and Serving: Have soup dishes warming in a low oven. Use a tureen if available. If necessary, bring the *Brodetto* to a gentle bubble over medium to medium-high heat. If you are using squid or cuttlefish, cook it at a very gentle bubble about 20 minutes, or until tender, before adding the remaining seafood. Layer the firm-fleshed fish in the pot, topping it with the thinner, flakier fillets. Scatter the shrimps and clams on top of the fish. Using the back of a wooden spatula, gently press the fish into the sauce. Bring the liquid to a slow bubble. Cover, and cook 5 to 10 minutes, or until thickest pieces are firm and opaque to their centers. Ladle the *Brodetto* into the heated soup plates or tureen, and serve.

Suggestions **Wine:** A simple crisp white like a Sauvignon from Colli Bolognesi, a Trebbiano di Romagna, or a Verdicchio dei Castelli di Jesi.

Menu: Offer *Brodetto* as a one-dish main course, served with *Piadina* (page 384) or *Spianata* bread (page 367). Follow it with the Salad of Mixed Greens and Fennel (page 349) or the Salad of Spring Greens (page 350), then a dessert of Modena Crumbling Cake (page 400) or Meringues of the Dark Lake (page 421).

Cook's Notes **Olive Oil:** Use a fruity oil. See page 485 for information on selecting olive oils.

Brodetto

Even though there are almost as many different renditions of *Brodetto* as there are fishermen, all agree that tomato, olive oil, and wine are constants. The argument over what kind of seafood should go into the stew is not settled easily. Fish with pervading sweetness or hinting at lavishness are banned from *Brodetto*. This is fishermen's food, not a dish for the rich. Some make *Brodetto* with eel; others feel eel ruins the dish. In men's cafés up and down the Adriatic coast, the same arguments rage over almost every fish arriving on their boats.

Romagna folklorist Gianni Quondamatteo explains that the true *Brodetto* was defined years ago. At that time, supplies were meager when Romagna's fishermen went to sea, usually for seven and eight days at a time in small boats powered only by sail. A liter of olive oil, a small barrel of wine, and maybe some tomatoes had to last a week. Quondamatteo says that this was the foundation of *Brodetto*: seawater supplied the broth and the salt, and the unsalable fish they caught made the *Brodetto* a stew. It is still a part of traditions that have not changed in small coastal towns where men still mend nets at dockside and women still cook *Brodetto*.

Braised Eel with Peas
Anguille alla Comacchiese con Piselli

Once people get over the idea of eel, its mild taste wins over the most hesitant. Sweet peas, tomato, and a hint of vinegar all accentuate the nonfishy quality of this seafood. Because of their firm flesh, eels can be gently reheated, making them ideal for entertaining.

[Serves 4 to 6]

3 tablespoons extra-virgin olive oil

3 tablespoons minced Italian parsley

1 medium onion, minced

2 pounds eel, skinned and cut into 2-inch pieces (about 2 inches thick)

1 tablespoon red wine vinegar

3 tablespoons tomato purée, or 2 canned plum tomatoes, drained and crushed

3 tablespoons dry white wine

1½ pounds fresh sugar snap peas, shelled, or one 10-ounce package frozen tiny peas, defrosted

Salt and freshly ground black pepper

Method

Working Ahead: *This dish can be cooked 1 hour ahead, to the point of adding the peas. Keep it at room temperature, lightly covered. Reheat gradually over medium heat. Once the eels are hot, continue the recipe.*

Sautéing the Eel: Have plates warming in a low oven. Heat the oil in a 6-quart saucepan over medium heat. Add the parsley and onion. Sauté, stirring occasionally with a wooden spatula, 5 minutes, or until the onion is softened. Add the eel pieces and the vinegar, raising the heat to medium-high. Cook, turning gently, 10 minutes, or until the eel is seared. Turn the heat to medium-low, and add the tomato purée and white wine. Cook, uncovered, 10 minutes.

Adding the Peas and Serving: Stir in the fresh peas and cook another 5 to 8 minutes, or until they are tender. If you are using defrosted frozen peas, cook the eel, tomatoes, and wine 15 minutes instead of 10 over low heat, and then add the peas. Cook another minute, or long enough to heat the peas through. Season to taste, spoon onto the warmed dishes, and serve.

Suggestions

Wine: In the Comacchio, a local red, Rosso del Bosco, is drunk with eel. The wine is grapey and slightly acidic. Outside the area, drink the Veneto's Bardolino

Classico or Bardolino Classico Superiore, or a light-bodied red Merlot from the Friuli's Aquilea area.

Menu: As an introduction to the meal, have a plateful of steamed shrimps sprinkled with a little olive oil and black pepper. Serve the eel with boiled new potatoes in spring and summer, or later in the year with slices of Baked Polenta (page 353). Have a green salad, then finish with a plateful of Sweet Cornmeal Biscuits (page 422) and tiny cups of espresso, or Zabaione Jam Tart (page 415).

Cook's Notes **Buying Eel:** Most fish stores stock eel only occasionally but will special-order it. Ideally it should arrive live and be cleaned by your fishmonger. It must be as fresh as possible when cooked.

The Comacchio

The area where the Po River meets the Adriatic in Ferrara province is a vast and mysterious place called the Comacchio. It is the stillest place in all of Emilia-Romagna, with lagoons like sheets of glass. Villages of only a few houses cluster at intersections of long, straight roads. Stubs of ruins jutting up from mounds of sea grass mark the site of ancient Spina, the first Greek settlement along the Po River. The Ferrarese view the people of the Comacchio as a breed apart—reticent loners, a people of another world and time. The eels that are their livelihood came with the Romans, who designed the underwater traps that still secure the fish each year, when they migrate into the lagoons from their spawning grounds in the Sargasso Sea. Today the seafood is shipped throughout Italy. The Comacchio, naturally, boasts a multitude of local eel dishes. One favorite is simply to rub pieces of eel with olive oil and grill them over a wood fire. Another is this braising, a choice for spring and early summer.

Sage-and-Garlic-Scented Bluefish
Pesce Serra al Forno con Salvia

Sage is an unexpected seasoning for fish. It needs a bold partner, and bluefish is ideal. Although full-flavored by itself, bluefish tastes almost like meat when marinated with fresh sage, garlic, lemon, and olive oil. The first time I tasted sage and seafood in Romagna, the herb was combined with roasted fresh sardines. Finding fresh sardines in prime condition on this side of the Atlantic can be difficult. But the easily bought bluefish has a Mediterranean cousin (pesce serra) that is prepared almost the same way as the sardines. It shares some of the sardine's rich character and makes a good version of this dish.

[Serves 2 to 3]

About 3 tablespoons extra-virgin olive oil

12 ounces bluefish fillet, cut crosswise into 1-inch slices

1 large clove garlic, cut into paper-thin slivers

12 medium to small fresh sage leaves (do not use dried sage)

1 to 2 tablespoons fresh lemon juice

Salt and freshly ground black pepper

3 to 4 lemon wedges

Method

Working Ahead: *For the best flavor, season the fish 1 to 2 hours before cooking and keep it, covered, in the refrigerator. Serve the dish as soon as it has finished cooking.*

Seasoning the Bluefish: Use about ½ tablespoon of the olive oil to oil a large shallow gratin dish. I prefer an enameled cast-iron dish that can go from the refrigerator to the oven with no danger of cracking. Spread the pieces of fish in a single layer in the dish, spacing them about ½ inch apart. Dot the pieces with garlic slivers and sage leaves, then drizzle with a thin film of olive oil. Sprinkle with the lemon juice, and then with salt and pepper. Lightly cover the fish with plastic wrap, and refrigerate 1 to 2 hours.

Baking and Serving the Fish: Have dinner plates warming in a low oven. Preheat another oven to 450°F. Slip the gratin dish into the oven and bake 7 to 10 minutes, or until the bluefish is firm when pressed. Baste the fish with the pan juices after about 3 minutes. Do not overcook. Fish that flakes easily is overdone. If you are concerned about undercooking, cut into the thickest piece; it should be opaque all the way through, with no raw-looking center. Serve the bluefish directly from its baking dish, setting the pieces on the warmed dinner plates. Spoon the pan juices over the fish, and pass lemon wedges as the final seasoning.

Suggestions   **Wine:** From Romagna, drink a white Albana di Romagna. From Friuli, have a white Riesling Italico or Sauvignon Blanc.

Menu: The bluefish is excellent accompanied by steamed little red-skinned potatoes and the Salad of Spring Greens (page 350), or serve it with Roasted Beets and Onions (page 351). Before the fish, have Parsley Pasta with Tomato and Peas Villa Guidello (page 118). Make dessert Caramelized Almond Tart (page 409) or Zabaione Jam Tart (page 415).

Soup of Seafood and Chick-peas
Zuppa di Ceci e Pesce

Chick-peas may seem unusual in a seafood soup, but the combination dates back to at least the Medieval period, possibly to pre-Roman times. In this soup, their natural sweetness sharpens the taste of tomato and seafood. Sprinkling black pepper and olive oil over the soup at the table is an all-important finishing touch.

[Serves 4 to 6 as a main dish, 6 to 8 as a first course]

Chick-peas

1¼ cups (8 ounces) dried chick-peas, soaked overnight in cold water and drained

1 small to medium onion, minced

1 large clove garlic, minced

2 canned plum tomatoes, drained and crushed, or 1 large vine-ripened tomato, peeled, seeded, and chopped

10 cups Quick Stock (page 68)

Salt and freshly ground black pepper to taste

Soup

1 cup Winter Tomato Sauce (page 62)

About 3 cups Quick Stock

1 pound medium shrimp, shelled and halved

8 to 12 ounces mixed fillets of fish (bass, flounder, mullet, bluefish, sea trout, and/or rockfish), cut into bite-size pieces

Salt to taste

Final Seasoning

½ cup extra-virgin olive oil

Freshly ground black pepper

Method   **Working Ahead:** *The soup can be made 1 to 2 days ahead, up to the point of adding the seafood. Store it, covered, in the refrigerator. It needs only about 10 minutes to warm up to a gentle bubble. Cook in the seafood about 3 minutes, and the soup is ready to serve.*

Cooking the Chick-peas: In a 5-quart pot, stir together the drained and rinsed chick-peas, the onion, garlic, tomatoes, and 10 cups stock. Bring to a slow bubble, partially cover, and cook 3 hours, or until the chick-peas are tender. Season with salt and freshly ground pepper.

Making the Soup: Blend the tomato sauce and the 3 cups stock into the chick-peas, and simmer about 5 minutes. Taste for seasoning. The soup should have the consistency of heavy cream. Add water or more stock if necessary.

Cooking the Seafood and Serving: Have a tureen and soup dishes warming in a low oven. Set a pitcher of olive oil and a peppermill on the table. Heat the soup until it is bubbling quietly. Stir in the shrimps and seafood, and cook, uncovered, 3 minutes, or until the shrimps are firm and pink. Turn into the heated tureen or soup dishes, and serve. Drizzle a teaspoon to a tablespoon of olive oil over each serving, and grind enough pepper into the soup to give it an assertive snap.

Suggestions   **Wine:** From the region, a white Trebbiano di Romagna or a Sauvignon. If unavailable, have a white Sauvignon from Trentino–Alto Adige or Friuli.

Menu: Serve the soup as a main dish accompanied by *Spianata* (page 367) or *Piadina* bread (page 384). Follow it with a green salad. Make dessert Home-Style Jam Cake (page 401) or Strawberries in Red Wine (page 445).

From a Bologna banquet procession honoring the Swiss guard, by Giuseppe Maria Mitelli, 1699

Po River Catfish
Pesce Gatto in Umido

This is one of those dishes you can never get enough of. It is eaten up and down the banks of the Po on Emilia-Romagna's plain. As the catfish braises, it picks up the flavors of the rosemary, bay, wine, and vegetables. Plan on serving it with creamy baked polenta or wedges of steamed new potatoes.

[Serves 3 to 4]

1½ pounds thick catfish fillets
1 large clove garlic
2 teaspoons fresh rosemary leaves
Generous pinch of freshly ground
    black pepper
4 tablespoons extra-virgin olive oil
6 large celery leaves, finely minced
1 tablespoon finely minced celery
    stalk

2 tablespoons finely minced carrot
⅓ cup finely minced onion
1 California bay laurel leaf, broken
¼ cup dry white wine
1 canned plum tomato, drained
Salt

Method

Working Ahead: *For the best flavor, season the fish with its herb rub 2 to 4 hours before cooking. Once the fish is cooked, serve it immediately.*

Seasoning the Fish: Rinse the fish and pat it dry. Cut large fillets into quarters or halves so they are easy to turn with a spatula. Set them on a plate.

Combine the garlic, rosemary, pepper, and 1 tablespoon of the olive oil in a mortar or food processor. Crush to a coarse paste, or process until finely chopped. Rub the seasoning over the catfish, then cover it with plastic wrap and refrigerate 2 to 4 hours.

Cooking the Fish: Have a medium-size platter warming in a low oven. Make sure the vegetables are minced almost as fine as confetti. Heat the remaining 3 tablespoons olive oil in a large skillet over medium heat. Add the vegetables, including the celery leaves, and the bay leaf. Cook, stirring frequently with a wooden spatula, until the vegetables barely begin to pick up color, about 3 minutes. Lay the fillets in the skillet, keeping the heat at medium. Top them with any seasoning rub that might have remained on the plate. Take about 3 minutes to sear the fillets on both sides, turning them with two spatulas to avoid breaking them. They will pick up only a little color. To keep the vegetables from burning, pile them on the fish as it cooks. Add the wine to the skillet. Crush the tomato and add it. Turn the fish to coat it with the tomato and wine. Sprinkle lightly with salt. Pile the vegetables atop the fillets once again, and cover the skillet tightly. Cook 5 minutes, or until the fish is firm and opaque all the way through.

Serving: Transfer the fish to the heated platter. Pour the pan sauce over it. Serve immediately.

Suggestions   **Wine:** A white Trebbiano di Romagna or an Albana di Romagna. From other parts of Italy, have a Soave Classico from the Veneto or Sicily's white Corvo.

Menu: Serve with Baked Polenta (page 353) or potatoes, and the Salad of Mixed Greens and Fennel (page 349). As a prelude you could have small portions of Fresh Pears with Parmigiano-Reggiano and Balsamic Vinegar (page 30) or small portions of Modena's Spiced Soup of Spinach and Cheese (page 234). Have Baked Pears with Fresh Grape Syrup (page 442) or Chestnut Ricotta Cheesecake (page 452) for dessert.

Cook's Notes **Thick Fillets:** The thicker the fillets, the slower the fish cooks and the longer the time it has to absorb the sauce's flavors. If catfish is not to be had, use thick-cut halibut or cod steaks, or whole mullet.

Summer Clams with Balsamic Vinegar
Poveracce con Aceto Balsamico

*Balsamic vinegar is my own
addition to a popular Romagna recipe for local clams and mussels.
Colorful and easily prepared ahead, it doubles and triples with no effort.*

[Serves 2]

2 pounds small clams (tiny Manilas
or larger littlenecks are ideal)

2 quarts cold water

2 tablespoons salt (for ridding
clams of sand)

2 to 3 tablespoons extra-virgin
olive oil

3 tablespoons minced onion

1 clove garlic, minced

1 large vine-ripened tomato, cored,
seeded, and coarsely chopped, or
⅔ cup canned tomatoes with
their liquid

3 tablespoons chopped fresh basil
leaves

1 to 2 tablespoons commercial
balsamic vinegar

Salt and freshly ground black
pepper to taste

2 small clusters arugula, or small
romaine leaves, for garnish

Method

Working Ahead: *The clams and their juice can be cooked up to 8 hours ahead. Remove their top shells, arrange them on a platter, cover, and refrigerate them until about 10 minutes before serving. Be sure to purge the clams in salt water 30 minutes before cooking.*

Purging the Clams: Rid clams of any sand by first scrubbing them under cold running water. Then put them in a bowl, cover with the cold water, and sprinkle with the salt. Refrigerate no longer than 30 minutes. Drain and rinse.

Cooking the Clams and Sauce: Heat the oil in a 5-quart pot over medium heat. Sauté the onion 5 to 8 minutes, or until golden. Stir in the garlic and cook another minute. Add the clams to the pot, cover securely, and steam 8 minutes, or until the shells are open about an inch. Steam any clams that have not opened 1 more minute. If still unopened, discard. Keep the liquid simmering while you lift the clams onto a platter. Add the tomato and basil to the pot, and cook a few seconds. Remove the sauce from the heat. Stir in 1 tablespoon of the balsamic vinegar, and salt and pepper to taste. Let the clams and sauce cool to room temperature. Transfer the sauce to a sealed container. If desired, remove some of the top shells from the clams. Add any liquid from the plate to the sauce. Tightly cover the clams. Refrigerate the sauce and clams separately.

Serving: Take the sauce out of the refrigerator about 30 minutes before serving. Ten minutes before serving, remove the clams from the refrigerator and arrange them on individual plates. Taste the sauce for seasoning, stirring in the remaining tablespoon of vinegar if desired. Spoon the sauce over the clams. Arrange clusters of greens on each plate and serve.

Suggestions   **Wine:** A white Sauvignon from either the Colli Bolognesi or Friuli.

Menu: Serve with *Piadina* (page 384) or *Spianata* bread (page 367). Follow with a green salad, and have fresh fruit and Nonna's Jam Tart (page 413) or Modena Crumbling Cake (page 400) for dessert. If a first course is needed, have small portions of Tagliatelle with Caramelized Onions and Fresh Herbs (page 101).

Cook's Notes **Balsamic Vinegar:** These vinegars vary greatly in quality. See page 467 for guidelines in selecting a fine balsamic.

Substituting Mussels: Substitute 2 pounds mussels for the clams. Purge the mussels for 4 to 8 hours in cold water to cover, by first sprinkling the water with about ¼ cup cornmeal and then refrigerating them. Drain, scrub, and debeard. Cook as described above.

The Poor Little One

There is a small clam in Romagna called the "poor little one," or *poveracca*. For a long time the "poor little one" was scorned as too common for the gourmands who came to Romagna's coast to feast on fresh seafood. But the clam's exceptional flavor finally won out, and now its popularity equals that of its larger cousins. Eating *poveracce* is a treat for the ear as well as the palate. Served in mounds, the clam's thin, light shells tinkle and clatter as you fork each bit of meat. Although no two types of clam taste alike, and nothing quite matches the *poveracca*'s character, our small clams from both coasts hold their own in this recipe.

Erminia's Pan-Crisped Chicken
Pollo a Due Tempi Il Vecchio Molinetto

This chicken is the specialty of the house at Erminia Marasi's trattoria, Il Vecchio Molinetto, in Parma. Crackly on the outside, moist on the inside, with hints of rosemary, lemon, and black pepper, the dish is almost fat-free and easy to do. Two-step cooking makes good company food, since it needs little last-minute attention. First the chicken is sautéed; then hours later, just before sitting down to dinner, it is reheated and given a final crisping.

[Serves 4]

3½-pound frying or roasting chicken (organic free-range preferred)

1-inch sprig fresh rosemary, or ⅓ teaspoon dried rosemary leaves

1 small clove garlic

¼ teaspoon salt

⅛ teaspoon freshly ground black pepper

2 tablespoons fresh lemon juice

6 tablespoons extra-virgin olive oil

½ cup water

Salt and freshly ground black pepper

Garnish

2 to 3 sprigs fresh rosemary (optional)

Method

Working Ahead: *Season the chicken 18 to 24 hours before cooking. Do not refrigerate it between cooking and reheating. Cook the chicken about 2 hours before dining, keep it at room temperature, and then reheat as described below.*

Seasoning the Chicken: Rinse the chicken. Cut it into eight pieces, halving each side of the breast and eliminating the wings and backbone. Pat the pieces dry. Use a food processor or mortar and pestle to blend the rosemary, garlic, salt, pepper, and 1 tablespoon of the lemon juice into a paste, and rub it over the chicken. Set the pieces on a platter, cover lightly with plastic wrap, and refrigerate 18 to 24 hours.

First Cooking: The secret of the chicken's succulence lies in taking care not to overcook it. Follow the timing for the two-step cooking carefully, and you will have no difficulties. Heat the olive oil in a 12-inch sauté pan over medium-high heat. Slip in the chicken pieces, skin side down. Reduce the heat to medium and cook 1 minute to lightly sear them. Then turn the pieces to coat them with the oil. Arrange the pieces in the center of the pan. Set a 9-inch cake pan on top of the chicken, and weight it with several heavy cans.

Cook the weighted chicken, turning over the breast pieces after 8 minutes and the leg and thigh pieces after 10 minutes (put the weighted pan back on the chicken after each turning). Sprinkle the chicken with the additional 1 tablespoon lemon juice after turning the legs and thighs. Cook the breast pieces another 8 minutes and remove. Cook the leg and thigh pieces 10 minutes. Then crisp the chicken to a rich dark brown by reducing the heat to medium-low and arranging all the pieces back in the pan, skin side up. Cook under the weighted pan for another 2 minutes. With a slotted spoon or tongs, immediately remove the pieces to a platter. Let the chicken cool about 10 minutes, and then lightly cover with plastic wrap or foil. Pour away all the fat and replace the sauté pan over high heat. Swirl in the water, and take about 3 minutes to boil it down by half while scraping up the brown bits with a wooden spatula. Turn the pan juices into a small bowl, and put it in the freezer for 2 hours. Then lift off the hardened fat.

Second Cooking and Serving: Have a serving dish warming in a low oven. Film the bottom of a sauté pan with a little olive oil. Have the heat at medium when you slip in the chicken pieces, skin side down. Top with the cake pan and weights, and warm 5 minutes. Set aside the weighted pan. Turn the chicken pieces, moistening each piece with the reserved pan juices, and lightly cover with aluminum foil. Heat another 5 to 8 minutes. Pile the chicken pieces on the platter, and garnish with rosemary sprigs if desired (at Il Vecchio Molinetto there is no garnish). Serve hot or at room temperature.

Suggestions   **Wine:** Have young Barbera from the Piedmont's Asti area, or a flowery St. Magdalener of Trentino–Alto Adige.

Menu: Traditional Parma accompaniments are first courses of Tortelli of Ricotta and Fresh Greens (page 153), Cappellacci with Sweet Squash (page 145), or Tagliatelle with Prosciutto di Parma (page 94). For lighter dining, have Spring Salad with Hazelnuts (page 21) or a few pieces of Garlic Crostini with Pancetta (page 28), then the chicken accompanied by Green Beans Bolognese (page 327). End with Modena Rice Pudding (page 398). For picnics, team the chicken with Paola Bini's Potato Salad (page 19) and Marinated Baby Onions (page 16).

Dinner in a tavern from a 17th-century Bologna board game, by Giuseppe Maria Mitelli

Il Vecchio Molinetto

Il Vecchio Molinetto (The Old Mill) is an institution in Parma, typical of the simple *trattorie* and restaurants found throughout Emilia-Romagna and much of Italy. It shares the sense of timelessness found in most of these places. Its decor is unpretentious, and unchanged since it opened in 1954. Workingmen, businesspeople, and families dine here year after year on the Parma cuisine they have known since childhood. Whereas Americans often dine out on foods they do not cook at home, Italians most often dine out on the foods that mean home to them. Il Vecchio Molinetto serves the food of Parma's mothers and grandmothers. The pasta is always handmade, the local wines are straightforward, the cured pork comes from nearby farms, and the seasons dictate the menu.

These *trattorie* are usually the domains of women, and The Old Mill is no exception. Cook/owner Erminia Marasi may be shy and self-effacing, but she stubbornly holds the line in her kitchen, giving not an inch toward trend or fashion. Erminia's partner and sister-in-law, Anna Bertolazzi, is more than the Molinetto's waitress. She rules the dining room like a benevolent dictator. Regulars love her one-eyebrow-raised humor, her mothering, the reprimands when she feels you have ordered unwisely, and her approval of a new girlfriend or a new hairdo. The *vecchi molinetti* of Italy are not restaurants as we usually think of them. They are not removed from home life—they are an extension of it. Weddings, anniversaries, and birthdays are celebrated here. Everyone knows everyone by name. This is like a second living room for many Parmesans.

Maria Bertuzzi's Lemon Chicken
Il Pollo in Tegame di Maria Bertuzzi

Maria Bertuzzi shared this recipe at her Ristorante Grande in Rivergaro, along the Trebbia River in Piacenza province. She called it good _contadina,_ or farm food. I like the way fresh lemon finishes the dish's tomato sauce and the way the chicken easily reheats.

[Serves 4 to 6]

3½-pound frying or roasting chicken (organic free-range preferred), cut into 8 pieces
3 tablespoons extra-virgin olive oil
Salt and freshly ground black pepper
½ small carrot, minced
½ medium onion, minced
3 tablespoons minced Italian parsley
8 fresh sage leaves, or 8 dried whole sage leaves

Shredded zest of 1 large lemon
1 large clove garlic, minced
Pinch of ground cloves
¾ cup chopped ripe fresh tomatoes (peeled and seeded) or thoroughly drained chopped canned tomatoes
⅔ cup water or liquid from the canned tomatoes
5 to 6 tablespoons fresh lemon juice
Garnish
2 tablespoons minced Italian parsley

Method

Working Ahead: _The chicken can be made 1 day ahead and stored overnight, covered, in the refrigerator. Undercook by 10 minutes, and do not add the final 3 to 4 tablespoons lemon juice until just before serving._

Browning and Cooking the Chicken: Rinse and thoroughly dry the chicken pieces. Heat the oil in a heavy 12-inch sauté pan over medium-high heat. Slip in the chicken pieces, skin side down, arranging them so they do not touch. Brown over medium heat or lower, adjusting the heat so the chicken colors slowly, taking about 15 minutes to reach a rich amber color. Sprinkle the pieces with a little salt and pepper as they cook, turning them with two wooden spatulas. Remove the browned chicken to a platter. Pour off all but 2 tablespoons of the fat. Set the pan over medium heat and sauté the carrot, onion, parsley, and sage, 8 minutes, or until the onion starts to color. Stir in the lemon zest and continue sautéing, stirring often, 3 minutes, or until the onion is deep gold. Take care not to burn the brown glaze on the bottom of the pan. Blend in the garlic, cloves, tomatoes, and water, scraping up the glaze. Add the chicken and 2 tablespoons of the lemon juice. Bring to a gentle bubble. Cover the pan. Cook 15 minutes. Uncover and cook about 10 minutes, turning the chicken pieces to moisten them. The sauce should thicken and cling to the chicken.

Serving: Have a platter warming in a low oven. Sprinkle the remaining 3 to 4 tablespoons lemon juice over the chicken, and taste for salt and pepper. Pile the chicken on the platter, moistening the meat with the pan juices. Sprinkle with the parsley and serve.

Suggestions   **Wine:** From Piacenza, a local red Bonarda or Gutturnio. From other parts of Italy, have the Veneto's young red Merlot del Piave, a Chianti Classico of Tuscany, or a Santa Maddalena Classico from the Trentino–Alto Adige region.

Menu: Serve the chicken with freshly cooked Creamy Polenta (page 354), Basil and Onion Mashed Potatoes (page 345), or steamed green beans. Have an antipasto of Garlic Crostini with Pancetta (page 28) or a first course of Priest's Soup (page 227).

Tips for a Better-Tasting Chicken

- Trim away all fat, removing the skin if possible for the selected recipe.
- Use less oil in browning chicken, since it throws off so much fat of its own.
- Give chicken fuller flavor before cooking by rubbing it with a blend of minced garlic, fresh rosemary, and a little salt. Lightly cover the meat and refrigerate it overnight. (Across the Po plain from Ferrara, in Modena, the blend is called *aglione*.) When a recipe or personal preference calls for other herbs, substitute them for the rosemary.
- Leave the herb blend on chickens to be roasted if they are basted with some form of liquid. The addition of a little liquid keeps the blend from burning.

Protect the herb blend from burning and turning bitter by scraping it off chickens destined for pan-browning. Reserve the mixture and add it to the dish after browning is completed.

Riccardo Rimondi's Chicken Cacciatora
Pollo alla Cacciatora Riccardo Rimondi

Wedges of sweet pepper and slow-cooked onion flavor this chicken sauté. Serve the Cacciatora alongside boiled potatoes or over steaming polenta. Substituting rabbit here is also very successful. This recipe was given to me by Riccardo Rimondi, linguist and Ferrara historian. His trick of skinning and seasoning the chicken not only reduces fat but adds flavor. His suggestions for improving the chicken before it goes into the pot are invaluable for all chicken recipes. (see box, page 274).

[Serves 4 to 6]

3½-pound frying or roasting chicken (organic free-range preferred), skinned and cut into 8 pieces

1 large clove garlic, minced

3-inch sprig fresh rosemary, or 1 teaspoon dried rosemary leaves

¼ teaspoon salt

4 tablespoons extra-virgin olive oil

Freshly ground black pepper

4 medium Italian sweet frying peppers, or 3 medium red bell peppers, cut into 1-inch triangles

2 medium onions, cut into 1-inch triangles

1 medium vine-ripened tomato, peeled, seeded, and chopped, or ½ cup drained canned tomatoes

½ cup dry white wine

Salt and pepper to taste

Method

Working Ahead: *For the best flavor, season the chicken pieces 24 hours before cooking and refrigerate them, lightly covered. The finished Cacciatora mellows nicely when cooked 1 day ahead. Undercook it by about 10 minutes and rewarm gently in a covered sauté pan or in a 350°F oven in a covered oven-to-table dish.*

Seasoning the Chicken: Rinse and dry the chicken pieces. Combine the garlic, rosemary, and salt, either in a mortar and pestle or a food processor, and crush into a paste. Rub the paste into the chicken pieces, pile them on a platter, lightly cover with plastic wrap, and refrigerate for 24 hours. Wipe off the paste before browning, but reserve it in the marinating dish.

Browning the Chicken: Heat the oil in a 12-inch sauté pan over medium-high heat. Take about 25 minutes to slowly brown the chicken pieces until golden on all sides. Lower the heat if necessary. Occasionally slip a wooden spatula under the pieces to keep them from sticking. Sprinkle the chicken with freshly ground pepper as it browns. Remove the pieces to a platter.

continued

Finishing the Dish: Pour off all but a thin film of fat. Add the peppers and onions to the pan, and cook over medium heat until the onion begins to color. Take care not to burn the brown glaze on the bottom of the pan. Put the chicken back in the pan, and dab the reserved seasoning paste over it and add the tomatoes. Use two spatulas to tumble the chicken pieces with the vegetables. Sprinkle in the wine. Cook about 20 minutes over medium heat, at a gentle bubble, until the wine has evaporated. As the wine cooks off, scrape up the brown glaze on the bottom of the pan. Cover the pan and cook 20 more minutes over medium-low heat, or until the chicken is tender. Turn the pieces two or three times to check for sticking. Taste for salt and pepper before serving.

Suggestions   **Wine:** A lively red from Bosco Eliceo in Ferrara province is traditional with the *Cacciatora*. Or drink a Merlot from Lombardy or Trentino–Alto Adige, or a young Sangiovese di Romagna or of Umbria.

Menu: Serve with fresh-cooked Polenta (page 352) or Baked Polenta (page 353) and, if desired, Ferrara's *Coppia* bread (page 364). Begin the meal with a few slices of salami (page 501) or coppa (page 474) and Balsamic Vegetables (page 18). Make dessert fresh pears or peaches with Fresh Squaquerone Cheese (page 386).

Old Hen Sunday

In Romagna's countryside, Carnival begins with Old Hen Sunday, the Sunday before Lent. Tradition and superstition dictate that farmers and their families must eat the oldest hen in the barnyard that day to ensure good prices from the poultry buyer for the coming year. This is not as great a sacrifice as it may sound. The aged chicken can be tough and dry, but it is inevitably full of good flavor. Braising it with local wild mushrooms and a handful of olives is one of the many ways to begin the feasting of this boisterous holiday. By midnight of Fat Tuesday, two days later, every scrap of meat must be gone from the house. Ash Wednesday brings sobriety and denial.

VCELLI CHE VANO IN MANO
A CHI NE VVOLE, E GALINE
CHE FANNO TRENTA OVA
IL GIORNO

From the fantasy land of plenty, Cucagna, birds eating out of hand and hens laying thirty eggs a day. Bolognese artist Giuseppe Maria Mitelli, 1703.

Mardi Gras Chicken
Pollo di Carnevale

*T*his is the best kind of Romagna country food—chicken braised with wild mushrooms, herbs, vegetables, and olives. Although originally made in Romagna with a vintage barnyard hen, in the United States the dish is best prepared with a younger fryer or roaster. A free-range, organically fed chicken comes closest to the taste of Emilia-Romagna's home-raised poultry.

[Serves 6 to 8]

4- to 4½-pound frying or roasting chicken (organic free-range preferred), cut into 8 pieces

1 quart water

½ cup red wine vinegar

3 tablespoons (about ¼ ounce) dried porcini mushrooms

¾ cup hot water

4 tablespoons extra-virgin olive oil

8 large fresh sage leaves, or 8 whole dried sage leaves

2 ounces pancetta, minced

1 medium onion, minced

1 small carrot, minced

3 tablespoons minced Italian parsley

1 large clove garlic, minced

¾ cup dry white wine

1½ cups Poultry/Meat Stock (page 66) or Quick Stock (page 68)

1 tablespoon imported Italian tomato paste

⅓ cup black Ligurian or Niçoise olives

⅓ cup green Italian or Greek olives

Salt and freshly ground black pepper to taste

Method   **Working Ahead:** *The chicken can be cooked and served the same day, but mellowing the cooked chicken overnight in the refrigerator only makes it better the next day. Cut short the initial cooking time by about 10 minutes so reheating does not overcook the meat.*

Preparing the Chicken and Mushrooms: Trim all the fat from the chicken. If desired, the skin can be removed. In a large bowl combine the quart of water and the vinegar. Add the chicken pieces and soak about 20 minutes. Meanwhile, rid the porcini of sand by rinsing the pieces under cold running water. If they are small, drop them into a small bowl of cold water and swish them around a second. Let the particles settle to the bottom, and immediately scoop up the mushrooms. Repeat twice more. Then combine the rinsed mushrooms with the hot water, and let them soak while you brown the chicken.

continued

Cooking the Chicken: Pat the chicken pieces dry. Heat the oil in a large, heavy nonaluminum sauté pan over medium to medium-high heat. Take 20 minutes to slowly brown the chicken pieces on all sides, along with the sage leaves. Take care not to burn the crusty bits on the bottom of the pan. Remove the chicken and sage to a platter. Pour away all the fat in the pan. Set the heat at medium, and stir in the pancetta, onion, carrot, and parsley. Sauté, stirring frequently, 10 minutes, or until golden brown. Then stir in the garlic and drained mushrooms (reserving their liquid), and cook 1 to 2 minutes. Slip the chicken back into the pan. Line a sieve with a paper towel, and strain the mushroom liquid over the chicken. Cook at a gentle bubble, scraping the brown bits from the bottom of the pan with a wooden spatula, 8 minutes, or until all the liquid has evaporated.

Pour the wine over the chicken and take 8 to 10 minutes to simmer it down as above, turning the pieces every so often. Now add ½ cup of the stock and slowly bubble 8 minutes, or until there is only a fine film of moisture at the bottom of the pan. Stir in the remaining 1 cup stock and the tomato paste. Finish cooking the chicken, uncovered, in the sauté pan, bubbling the liquid gently 10 minutes, or until the sauce is rich in flavor and slightly thickened. Skim off any fat. Add the olives and cook 3 minutes, or just long enough to heat through. Taste the sauce for seasoning.

Serving: Have a shallow serving bowl heating in a low oven. Mound the chicken in the bowl, moistening it with its sauce. Serve hot.

Suggestions   **Wine:** A soft and full red Sangiovese di Romagna Riserva, a Barbarossa di Bertinoro, or a Salice Salentino Rosso from Apulia.

Menu: For a classic Romagnolo Sunday dinner, begin with a Platter of Cured Meats (page 14), then have cappelletti in broth, using one of the recipes on pages 134 to 136. Serve the chicken with carrots and green beans or with Garlic-Sautéed Cabbage (page 331). Finish the meal with Nonna's Jam Tart (page 413). For a simpler menu, begin with a few slices of salami (page 501). Accompany the chicken with freshly made Polenta (page 352) or boiled potatoes. End the meal with fresh fruits and unshelled nuts, accompanied by glasses of dry Marsala.

Cook's Notes   **Reading Poultry Labels:** Depending upon where you live and how your market labels poultry, a 4-pound chicken at one end of the meat case can be labeled "roaster" with the usual high price tag, while another 4-pound chicken down the aisle is marked "fryer" and priced lower. There is no difference between the two, so do save money and buy the fryer.

Selecting Olives: The small green olives from the Gard area of southern France are particularly fine in this dish. They resemble some of the locally cured olives found in Romagna. Ligurian and Niçoise black olives packed with herbs, oil, and brine are found in specialty food stores. The flavors of both types of olives should be mild, buttery, and not overly salty.

Balsamic Roast Chicken
Pollo al Forno con Aceto Balsamico

In Modena and Reggio cooks rub garlic and fresh rosemary into a chicken before roasting. At the table, the dish is finished with a few spoonfuls of the family's own balsamic vinegar. I do not exaggerate in saying that few sauces, no matter how intricate, can equal the distinction of a great balsamic. And few dishes equal the simple elegance of this one.

[Serves 4 to 6]

4- to 4½-pound frying or roasting chicken (organic free-range preferred)

1 tablespoon fresh rosemary leaves, or 1 teaspoon dried rosemary

1 large clove garlic

¼ teaspoon salt

2 tablespoons extra-virgin olive oil

Freshly ground black pepper

8 sprigs fresh rosemary

3 to 4 tablespoons artisan-made *tradizionale* balsamic vinegar, or a high-quality commercial balsamic blended with ½ teaspoon brown sugar

Method

Working Ahead: *Season the chicken and refrigerate 24 hours before cooking. Although leftovers are excellent, the chicken is best eaten hot from the oven.*

Seasoning the Chicken: Rinse the chicken under cold running water. Dry it thoroughly inside and out. Set it on a dinner plate. Mince together the rosemary leaves and garlic in the salt. Rub the olive oil over the chicken, then rub in the herb mixture. Sprinkle with pepper. Put two rosemary sprigs in the bird's cavity, and refrigerate 24 hours, lightly covered with plastic wrap. Keep the remaining rosemary sprigs for garnishing.

Roasting the Chicken: Preheat the oven to 350°F. Truss the chicken if desired. Rub into the chicken any of the seasoning that might have fallen onto the dinner plate. Use a small heavy roasting pan, and place the chicken in it breast side down. Roast 20 to 25 minutes per pound (about 1¼ to 1¾ hours), or until a thermometer tucked into the thickest part of the thigh or leg reads 170°F. Baste every 15 minutes or so with the pan juices. During the last 30 minutes of roasting, turn the chicken over to brown the breast. If the chicken is not deep golden brown when the cooking time is up, turn the heat to 475°F and brown it about 10 minutes, turning once.

Finishing with Balsamic and Serving: Transfer the chicken to a heated serving platter. Present it whole, drizzled with the balsamic vinegar, and carve at the table.

continued

Or use poultry shears to cut it into eight pieces in the kitchen. Spoon the balsamic vinegar over them, and scatter with the remaining rosemary sprigs. Serve immediately.

Suggestions **Wine:** Drink Bologna's Cabernet Sauvignon Colli Bolognesi, a Sangiovese di Romagna Riserva, or a fine Amarone Reciota della Valpolicella from the Veneto.

Menu: Traditionally Tortellini in Broth Villa Gaidello (page 134) is served at special dinners. Priest's Soup (page 227) or Modena's Spiced Soup of Spinach and Cheese (page 234) is lighter and excellent before the chicken. In Modena style, have Torta Barozzi (page 395) for dessert, or the old-style Frozen Zuppa Inglese (page 430).

Cook's Notes **Balsamic Vinegar:** For information on *tradizionale* and commercial vinegars, see page 467.

Variation with Capon: Even more festive than chicken is a 6- to 7-pound capon. Double the seasoning and the amount of vinegar. Season the capon as described for chicken. Roast it breast down at 325°F 20 to 25 minutes per pound, or until a thermometer inserted into the thigh reads 170°F. Turn the breast up during the last 30 minutes of roasting. Baste frequently with pan juices. Carve the capon as you would a turkey, then spoon the balsamic vinegar over it and serve.

Variation in Romagna: Rigging a new fishing boat is often celebrated with roast chicken made just like this one, but served without the balsamic vinegar.

Just a Few Drops of *Balsamico*

The little town of Spilamberto, near Modena, is home to the oldest of Modena and Reggio's three balsamic vinegar consortiums. The Consorteria dell'Aceto Balsamico is the spiritual mother to Modena and Reggio's organizations. Every year the Consorteria evaluates over a thousand of members' vinegars until one is singled out. On June 24, the festival of Saint John the Baptist, the highest honor a balsamic vinegar artisan can receive is awarded in Spilamberto. Before visiting a Spilamberto tasting, I dined with three men whose families had been making the vinegar for generations. As plates of vegetable fritters arrived, one of my hosts took a small silver flask bearing his family crest from his pocket. Removing the medicine-dropper top, he offered some of his private *balsamico* for my pleasure. With only a few drops of the brown liquid, that simple fritter became unforgettable. With each new course I waited in silent but eager anticipation, hoping he would again offer the special condiment. I was not disappointed. The final pleasure was droplets of the vinegar over small crocks of caramelized baked custard.

Christmas Capon
Cappone Natalizio

Since capon replaced swan and peacock as a favorite on 16th-century banquet tables, it gradually became the meat of holidays, especially Christmas. The original version of this dish from 19th-century Reggio had the capon turning on a spit over an open fire. In my version, the fire becomes an oven. I have remained true to the rest of the recipe, however, including flavoring the capon with sweet wine and prosciutto. Tucking a piece of prosciutto into the bird's cavity has been common practice since at least the days of Lucrezia Borgia. To eat the kind of roast capon gracing the table today in the region, substitute another ½ cup white wine for the Marsala.

[Serves 6 to 8]

6- to 7-pound capon (organic free-range preferred)	⅛ teaspoon freshly grated nutmeg
½ lemon	3-ounce piece of Prosciutto di Parma, coarsely chopped
Salt and freshly black ground pepper	½ cup dry white wine
	½ cup dry Marsala wine

Method

Working Ahead: *Season the capon 24 hours before roasting.*

Seasoning the Capon: Rinse the bird under cold running water. Pat it dry and trim away all visible fat. Rub it inside and out with the lemon half, gradually squeezing out the juice. Then sprinkle the cavity and all of the bird's skin with the salt, pepper, and nutmeg. Tuck the prosciutto into the cavity. Set the bird on a platter, lightly cover with plastic wrap, and refrigerate overnight.

Roasting the Capon: Preheat the oven to 325°F. Truss the capon if desired. Lay the bird, breast side down, in a shallow roasting pan just large enough to accommodate it. Roast 25 minutes to the pound (2½ to 3 hours), or until an instant-reading thermometer tucked into the thickest part of the thigh reads 170°F.

After the first hour, begin basting the capon with a third of the white wine. After 20 minutes, add another third. Wait another 20 minutes and baste the capon with the last of the white wine. Then begin basting with the Marsala, using a third at a time. Baste the capon every 20 minutes with the Marsala and spoonfuls of its own pan juices. If the juices threaten to dry or burn, add a little water to the pan. During the last 30 minutes of roasting, turn the bird over to brown the breast area.

continued

Serving: Warm a serving platter in a low oven. Carve the capon by slicing the breast meat into thick pieces and dividing the leg meat into three or four pieces. Arrange the pieces on the platter. Skim the fat from the pan juices and pour the juices over the capon. Scatter the prosciutto pieces from the cavity over the sliced meat, and serve hot.

Suggestions   **Wine:** An elegant red Amarone Recioto della Valpolicella of the Veneto, or Tuscany's Rosso di Montalcino.

Menu: At Christmas, serve after Tortellini (or cappelletti) in Broth Villa Gaidello (page 134 and pages 137 and 139). Accompaniments should be steamed broccoli or green beans, and Sweet-and-Sour Onions (page 333) or Sweet Fennel Jewish Style (page 335). Have Frozen Zuppa Inglese (page 430) or Duchess of Parma Torte (page 404). Serve the capon in the style of the 16th century by presenting it atop a platter of Tagliatelle with Caramelized Oranges and Almonds (page 188). Finish the meal in the spirit of the period with either Chocolate Christmas Spice Cake (page 458) or Marie Louise's Crescents (page 426). For lighter dining, begin with Fresh Pears with Parmigiano-Reggiano and Balsamic Vinegar (page 30), serve the capon with the above-mentioned vegetables, and finish the meal with Strawberries in Red Wine (page 445).

Cook's Notes **Substituting Turkey:** Leaner turkey is a fine stand-in for capon. The cooking time is shortened to 15 to 18 minutes to the pound.

Peacock being served at a 16th-century Ferrara court banquet

Pan-Roasted Quail
Quaglie in Tegame

*Pan-roasting keeps quail moist.
Gentle cooking with browned nubbins of onion, herbs, and pancetta gives
this dish its distinctive flavor. Be sure the herbs are fresh, as dried ones
do not achieve the same effect. Some Parma cooks deglaze the pan with
cream or a tomato sauce; both are worth doing. The recipe is good, too,
with breast of pheasant, wild duck, dove, or pigeon, and it doubles
easily. Eating quail with the fingers, one dainty bit at a time, is a simple
but sensual pleasure not to be missed.*

[Serves 6]

6 whole quail (about 22 ounces)

3 tablespoons extra-virgin olive oil

Salt and freshly ground black
    pepper

1 ounce pancetta, minced

3 tablespoons minced onion

4 cloves garlic, sliced paper-thin

2 tablespoons minced fresh
    marjoram

2 tablespoons minced Italian
    parsley

8 tablespoons minced fresh basil
    leaves

2 tablespoons grappa or brandy

¼ cup Poultry/Meat Stock (page
    66) or Quick Stock (page 68)

2 tablespoons dry white wine

¼ cup water

Sprigs of parsley, marjoram, and
    basil for garnish

Method
Working Ahead: *The quail can be cooked 1 hour or so ahead, up to the point of
adding the white wine to the pan. Cool and cover, keeping them at room temperature. Reheat
the quail over medium-low, raising the heat to medium and adding a bit of water to the pan
if scorching threatens.*

Cooking the Quail: Have a platter warming in a low oven. Trim away the dark
skin around the necks and the rear cavities. Rinse and pat dry inside and out.

Heat the olive oil in a 12-inch skillet over medium heat. Add the quail, placing
them on their sides, and take 8 to 10 minutes to slowly sauté them to golden brown
on all but one side. Sprinkle lightly with salt and pepper as they cook. Turn the birds
carefully with wooden spatulas. Hold back the quail as you pour off all the fat. Now
add the pancetta and onion, and cook over medium heat, 5 minutes, or until the
onion is golden and the fourth side of the birds has browned.

Sprinkle the garlic and herbs over the quail. Stir in the grappa or brandy and
the stock. Cook about 3 minutes, uncovered, over medium heat as you scrape up the

brown glaze from the bottom of the pan. Now turn the heat to low, cover the pan tightly, and cook 10 minutes. Add the wine, turning the quail to moisten them. Pile all the herbs and pancetta on top of the birds. Cover the pan snugly and cook another 10 to 15 minutes, or until a leg moves easily in its socket and the breasts give only a little when pressed. Add the ¼ cup water to the pan after about 5 minutes of cooking.

Serving: Pile the quail on the warm platter, spooning herbs, pancetta, and any cooking juices over each one. Tuck bouquets of fresh herbs here and there, and serve.

Suggestions   **Wine:** From the Trentino–Alto Adige, drink a lively young red St. Magdalener, or have the bigger red of Apulia, Salice Salentino Rosso.

Menu: The quail is light enough to follow Tagliatelle with Light Veal Ragù (page 100), Tagliarini with Fresh Figs Franco Rossi (page 107), or Fresh Garlic Soup Brisighella (page 222). Serve Sweet Fennel Jewish Style (page 335) with the quail. Dessert could be fresh pears with Parmigiano-Reggiano cheese, or Marie Louise's Crescents (page 326).

Giovanna's Wine-Basted Rabbit
Coniglio di Giovanna

Perhaps the most succulent rabbit I have ever eaten was made by Giovanna, the cook at Villa Gaidello. Moistened with bastings of wine, lemon, and butter, the meat crisps to a deep golden brown while sealing in every bit of its juices. For those who need to forgo butter, it can be replaced with olive oil. The flavors will change, but the dish is still irresistible.

[Serves 2 to 4]

2½- to 2¾-pound rabbit, in one piece
1 large clove garlic, split
8 tablespoons (4 ounces) unsalted butter, at room temperature, or 6 tablespoons extra-virgin olive oil

Salt and freshly ground black pepper
1-inch sprig fresh rosemary, or ½ teaspoon dried rosemary leaves
¼ cup dry white wine
3 tablespoons fresh lemon juice
3 or 4 sprigs fresh rosemary for garnish

Method   **Working Ahead:** *The rabbit is best roasted and eaten almost immediately. It will hold, lightly covered with foil, in a turned-off oven about 15 minutes while the rest of the meal is readied.*

Roasting the Rabbit: Preheat the oven to 325°F. Rinse and dry the rabbit thoroughly. Rub it all over with the split garlic, and reserve the garlic. Slather the entire surface of the rabbit with the butter or olive oil. Place in a shallow roasting pan just large enough to hold it comfortably. Sprinkle with salt and pepper. Add the reserved garlic and the rosemary to the pan. Roast the rabbit 30 minutes. Pour the wine and lemon juice over it, baste with pan juices, and cover loosely with foil. Roast 1 hour. Every 15 minutes, give the rabbit a quarter turn and baste with the pan juices. Turn the heat up to 450°F and uncover the rabbit. Roast another 15 minutes, or until golden brown. Baste often with the pan juices and turn once or twice for even coloring.

Serving: Have a serving platter warming in a low oven. Use poultry shears to cut the rabbit into serving pieces. Arrange on the platter and garnish with sprigs of rosemary. Drizzle the rabbit with its pan juices, if desired.

Suggestions   **Wine:** A white big in character and body, like a Gavi dei Gavi or Arneis di Roero from Piemonte, or a red Dolcetto d'Alba.

Menu: Serve as at Villa Gaidello, accompanied by wedges of steamed red and yellow peppers. Or with Paola Bini's Potato Salad (page 19). Garlic Sautéed Cabbage (page 331), or Basil and Onion Mashed Potatoes (page 345) make good side dishes. As a first course have the Villa's Parsley Pasta with Tomato and Peas (page 118) or small bowls of Priest's Soup (page 227). A fine old-style Modena dessert is Crumbling Cake (page 400) or Cinnamon and Clove Custard (page 440).

Cook's Notes   **A Whole Rabbit:** Special order through your butcher or market.

Doubling: The recipe doubles easily with 2 rabbits. Make sure the roasting pan is large enough to hold them without touching so the meat can brown easily.

Giovanna

Giovanna is retired now. I remember how shy she was during my first visit to Villa Gaidello. Her kitchen was in a corner of the 18th-century hay barn, now converted into the Villa's simple dining rooms. A few electric lights and a gas stove were the only additions to that kitchen in 200 years. Giovanna seemed to like it that way. As she cooked, her timidness fell away, but her eyes were always sad. I do not know what troubles kept that wounded look there. But if that was her dark side, her food was the light. It transcended a mere "good meal," often touching the heart. One night, tortellini from Giovanna's kitchen brought me to tears, rekindling an overwhelming sense of oneness with my own Italian heritage. And this rabbit, eaten on a bright Sunday afternoon when the hay barn was full of noisy families out for a spring jaunt, hushed my boisterousness for a moment. When people speak of soul food, I remember Giovanna's shy smile and those meals at Villa Gaidello.

Rabbit Dukes of Modena
Coniglio all' Aceto Balsamico alla Moda Estense

This recipe is at once homey and regal. It takes rabbit stew from the realm of everyday Modenese family cooking to a dish of nobility. It was inspired by the banquet dishes of the Este dukes, who held court in Modena from the end of the 16th century to the mid-1800s. Like so many court dishes of those times, the rabbit is flavored in several stages, creating superb depth of taste. But its final seasoning is its most important: balsamic vinegar is spooned over the cooked rabbit. In the days of the Este dukes, it would have been from the royal vinegar attics, the rarest of balsamics. Today artisan-made balsamico gives a splendid finish to the dish.

This recipe was originally done with rabbit, and I strongly urge you to try it that way. But chicken thighs and legs are also excellent here. The fact that it benefits from being cooked a day ahead makes the dish ideal for parties and important dinners. Credit for its interpretation goes to three Modenese: Italo Pedroni and Franca Prampolini of Osteria di Rubiara, and balsamic vinegar authority Renato Bergonzini.

[Serves 7 to 8]

Rabbit and Marinade

4 to 4½ pounds rabbit, each cut into 8 to 10 pieces

4 cups dry white wine

7 tablespoons wine vinegar

Tomato Sauce

3 tablespoons extra-virgin olive oil

1 medium onion, minced

1 stalk celery with leaves, minced

14- to 16-ounce can tomatoes with their liquid, or 1 pound vine-ripened tomatoes, peeled, seeded, and chopped

Aglione Seasoning

2 medium cloves garlic, minced

1 heaping tablespoon fresh rosemary leaves, or 1 heaping teaspoon dried rosemary leaves

¼ teaspoon salt

For Braising

3 tablespoons unsalted butter

1 tablespoon extra-virgin olive oil

Freshly ground black pepper

1 cup dry white wine

1 cup Poultry/Meat Stock (page 66) or Quick Stock (page 68)

6 tablespoons minced Italian
    parsley
5 tablespoons artisan-made
    tradizionale balsamic vinegar, or
    4 tablespoons top-quality
    commercial balsamic vinegar
    mixed with 1 teaspoon brown
    sugar

Method   **Working Ahead:** *The tomato sauce can be made 1 day before the rabbit is cooked. At the same time start marinating the rabbit, which needs 12 to 24 hours of steeping before cooking. The rabbit can be cooked 1 day before serving. Do not add the balsamic vinegar. Simply cool the dish, cover, and refrigerate it. Reheat the rabbit, covered, over moderate heat. Add the* balsamico, *cook for only a few seconds, and serve.*

Marinating the Rabbit: Twelve to 24 hours before cooking, place the rabbit pieces in a large stainless steel bowl. Add the 4 cups wine and 7 tablespoons wine vinegar. The pieces should be covered with liquid. If necessary, add a little more wine. Lightly cover with plastic wrap and refrigerate.

Making the Tomato Sauce: Heat the 3 tablespoons olive oil in a 3-quart saucepan over medium-high heat. Add the minced onion and celery, and sauté over medium heat, stirring frequently. Cook 15 minutes, or until the vegetables are a rich golden brown. Then stir in the tomatoes and cook at a lively bubble 5 minutes, or until thickened. Set aside.

Making the Aglione: Pile the minced garlic, rosemary, and salt on a cutting board. Mince until very fine. Or mash to a paste in a mortar and pestle.

Braising the Rabbit: Drain the meat (reserving the marinade), and pat the pieces dry. Heat the 3 tablespoons butter and 1 tablespoon olive oil in a 12-inch sauté pan over medium-high heat. Arrange the rabbit pieces in the pan so they barely touch. Take about 20 minutes to slowly brown on all sides over medium heat. Occasionally slip a wooden spatula under the pieces to keep them from sticking. Sprinkle with a little freshly ground black pepper as they cook. Once the rabbit pieces are a deep, rich golden brown on all sides, sprinkle with the *aglione*. Cook another minute, or until aromatic. Pour in 2 cups of the reserved marinade plus the 1 cup white wine. Bring the liquid to a simmer over medium heat, scraping up the brown bits from the bottom of the pan. Leave the pan uncovered and let the liquid bubble slowly 30 minutes. Adjust the heat if necessary. Remove the rabbit pieces to a platter.

Turn the heat up so the liquid boils. Continue boiling, stirring frequently with a wooden spatula, until the wine has totally evaporated. There should be a brown glaze on the bottom of the pan. Stir in the tomato sauce and the 1 cup of stock. Add the rabbit to the pan, turning the pieces to coat them with the sauce. Sprinkle 3 tablespoons of the parsley over the meat. Adjust the heat so the sauce bubbles only occasionally. Cover the pan tightly and cook over low heat 15 to 20 minutes, or until the rabbit is tender when pierced with a knife. Turn the pieces every so often. If the rabbit is particularly resilient, cook it longer, adding water to the pan if necessary. Once the meat is tender, uncover and continue cooking slowly another 15 minutes, or until the sauce thickens. Take care not to overcook the rabbit. Stir in the balsamic vinegar just before serving.

Serving: Have a heated serving platter ready. Spoon the rabbit onto the platter, moistening it with all the sauce. Sprinkle with the remaining 3 tablespoons parsley, and serve.

Suggestions   **Wine:** The fresh, grapey red made by Italo Pedroni and drunk with this dish rarely leaves his back garden, much less Italy. The Piedmont's Dolcetto d'Alba, a Merlot from Friuli, or a Grave del Friuli are also good with the rabbit.

Menu: As a first course, have Modena's Spiced Soup of Spinach and Cheese (page 234), made without egg, or Almond Spice Broth (page 237). Serve either boiled or Oven-Roasted Potatoes (page 344) with the rabbit. Dessert could be in true Este tradition with Lucrezia Borgia's Sweet Tagliarini Tart of Ferrara (page 194), or Frozen Zuppa Inglese (page 430).

Cook's Notes   **Substituting Chicken:** Eight large chicken thighs and drumsticks can be substituted for the rabbit. Remove the skin before marinating. Cooking time may be about 10 minutes shorter in the final simmering.

Balsamic Vinegar: Balsamic vinegars vary greatly in style and quality. See page 467 for information on selecting the best examples.

Rabbit Roasted with Sweet Fennel
Coniglio al Forno con Finocchio

Roasted onion and fennel bring out the best in rabbit, and make a main dish that cooks in a single roasting pan. The crushed fennel seeds seasoning the rabbit are not traditional in Emilia-Romagna, but they boost the flavor of our milder fennel, bringing it close to the wild fennels used in Italy.

[Serve 4 to 5]

2½- to 2¾-pound rabbit, cut into 8 pieces
1 large clove garlic
1½-inch sprig fresh rosemary
¼ teaspoon salt
⅛ teaspoon freshly ground black pepper
2 bulbs fresh fennel, cored and cut into 1½-inch wedges
1 large onion, cut into 1½-inch wedges
3 ounces pancetta, minced
3 cloves garlic, split
1 teaspoon fennel seed, coarsely ground
½ cup coarsely chopped fennel leaves
4 tablespoons extra-virgin olive oil
Salt and freshly ground black pepper to taste
½ cup dry white wine

Pan Sauce
¼ cup dry white wine
½ cup Quick Stock (page 68)

Method

Working Ahead: *The rabbit tastes best when seasoned 1 day ahead; leave it to mellow in the refrigerator overnight. The dish is best served shortly after roasting.*

Seasoning the Rabbit: The night before cooking, rinse and dry the rabbit pieces. Use a mortar and pestle or food processor to make a paste of the large garlic clove, rosemary, salt, and pepper. Rub it over the rabbit pieces. Put them on a plate, cover lightly with plastic wrap, and refrigerate.

Cooking the Rabbit: Preheat the oven to 350°F. Use a low-sided roasting pan large enough to hold the rabbit in a single layer, with spaces for the vegetables. Arrange the pieces in the pan. Dab the rabbit pieces with any seasoning rub that may have been left on the plate. Scatter the fennel, onion, pancetta, garlic pieces, fennel seed, and half the fennel tops over the rabbit. Sprinkle with the olive oil, salt, and pepper. Roast 30 minutes, basting often with the pan juices. Then pour in the wine and roast 1 hour. Baste often, turning the pieces occasionally. Add a little water to the pan if the juices threaten to burn.

Raise the heat to 450°F and cook 15 minutes, or until the rabbit is flecked golden brown. Turn the rabbit and vegetable pieces, and roast another 15 minutes, or until golden, basting once with the pan juices.

Serving: Transfer the rabbit and vegetables to a heated platter, and keep them warm in the turned-off oven with the door open. Quickly make a pan sauce by setting the roasting pan over two burners turned to high. Add the wine and stock. Scrape up the brown glaze from the bottom of the roasting pan as the liquids boil down by about half in 3 to 5 minutes. Scatter the remaining fennel leaves over the rabbit. Pour the sauce into a little sauceboat, and pass it along with the rabbit.

Suggestions   **Wine:** A white or red Rapitalà from Sicily, a Sangiovese di Romagna Riserva, or a Cabernet Sauvignon from the hills of Friuli or Bologna.

Menu: Begin with Tagliarini with Lemon Anchovy Sauce (page 112) or Tagliarini with Fresh Figs Franco Rossi (page 107). Have a simple dessert of Sweet Cornmeal Biscuits (page 422) or an elegant Frozen Hazelnut Zabaione with Chocolate Marsala Sauce (page 436). For lighter dining, dispense with the first course and serve the rabbit with boiled potatoes. Have Caramelized Almond Tart (page 409) for a special dessert.

Cook's Notes **Substituting Chicken:** Use 2½ to 3 pounds skinned large chicken drumsticks and thighs instead of the rabbit. Follow the recipe as written.

Porcini Veal Chops
Costolette di Vitello con Porcini

In Parma, at trattoria Il Vecchio Molinetto, large slices of fresh porcini mushrooms are slipped into pockets cut in these thick chops. Lacking the wild mushrooms in their fresh state, I use dried ones to make a great-tasting pan sauce. The secret of succulent veal chops is a quick searing on both sides, then a slow sauté until the chops are just blushed with pink inside.

[Serves 4]

3 tablespoons (½ ounce) dried
   porcini mushrooms
⅔ cup hot water
3 tablespoons extra-virgin olive oil
Four 1-inch-thick loin veal chops
Salt and freshly ground black
   pepper
¼ cup minced onion
1 small clove garlic, minced

¼ cup dry white wine
⅓ cup Meat Essences (page 61),
   or ½ cup Poultry/Meat Stock
   (page 66) or Quick Stock
   (page 68)
½ teaspoon fresh lemon juice
1 tablespoon unsalted butter, at
   room temperature

Method   **Working Ahead:** *The veal is best eaten right after it is cooked. Measure and chop the other ingredients early in the day; keep them covered at room temperature.*

Soaking the Porcini: Rinse the mushroom pieces under cold running water to rid them of sand. If the pieces are small, drop them into a small bowl of cold water, swish them around, and let the particles settle. Immediately scoop up the pieces. Repeat twice more. Soak the rinsed mushrooms in the hot water 30 minutes, or until softened. Then lift them out of the liquid and coarsely chop. Strain the liquid through a sieve lined with a paper towel, and set aside 3 tablespoons for the pan sauce. (The rest can be frozen for later use.)

Cooking the Chops: Have a serving platter warming in a low oven. Heat the olive oil in a 12-inch sauté pan over medium-high heat. Take 3 to 4 minutes to quickly brown the veal chops on both sides, sprinkling them with the salt, pepper, and minced onion as you turn them. Periodically slip a wooden spatula under each chop to keep it from sticking.

Once the chops are golden brown, lower the heat to medium-low and cook 8 to 12 minutes, turning once. Check for doneness at 8 minutes. Take care not to overcook them, or the veal will dry out. The interior of the chops should be blushed with pink and they should give a little when pressed with your finger. (Rare chops feel soft; well done, firm.) Once they are done, remove the chops to the heated platter and keep warm.

Making the Sauce and Serving: Spoon off all but about 2 tablespoons fat from the pan. Turn the heat to medium-high, and add the mushrooms and garlic. Stir and sauté 1 minute. Add the reserved mushroom liquid, and boil it down to nothing in about 2 minutes. Then turn the heat to high, stir in the wine, and boil it hard as you scrape up the brown bits from the bottom of the pan. Once the wine has evaporated (in about 1 minute), stir in the Meat Essences or stock. Bubble 1 minute. Stir in the lemon juice and cook just a few seconds, then pull the pan from the heat. Blend in the butter, and spoon the sauce over the chops. Serve immediately.

Suggestions   **Wine:** A Barbera or Gutturnio from Piacenza's Colli Piacentini, a Rosso Armentano of Romagna, or Tuscany's Chianti Classico Riserva.

Menu: Before the veal, have Garlic Crostini with Pancetta (page 28), Valentino's Pizza (page 29), or Tagliatelle with Balsamic Radicchio (page 98). Accompany the veal with Sweet Peas Parma (page 322), Oven-Roasted Radicchio (page 336), steamed asparagus, or Green Beans with Balsamic Pesto (page 325). Ugo Falavigna's Apple Cream Tart (page 411) or Marie Louise's Crescents (page 426) from Parma give the meal a fine finish.

Pan-Fried Veal Chops with Tomato Marsala Sauce
Costolette all'Emiliana

The pan-fried veal chop or cutlet with its golden crisp coating of bread crumbs and topping of cheese is an Italian favorite found throughout Emilia-Romagna. When the chop with its elegant long, curving rib bone appears on its own, it is in the Milanese style. When topped with prosciutto and/or Parmigiano-Reggiano, and possibly a pan sauce, it becomes the specialty of Emilia's and Romagna's cooks.

This lightened rendition is adapted from two similar dishes, one from Modena and the other from Bologna. Usually the chop is pounded, breaded, fried in butter, and then cooked in a butter-rich sauce. The Modenese often add Marsala and tomato. The Bolognese use only tomato and shavings of local truffle.

My version has the breaded chop cooked in oil, drained well on paper towels, and then topped with a quick, light pan sauce of Marsala and tomato. The chop keeps its crispness, while a single tablespoon of butter finishing the sauce gives a much more buttery taste than you might expect. The result is lighter, yet still robust and satisfying.

[Serves 4]

Veal

4 veal rib chops (with rib bone if possible), cut 1 inch thick, chine and feather bones trimmed away

2 eggs

1²⁄₃ cups dried bread crumbs (homemade preferred), ground very fine

Salt and freshly ground black pepper

3 tablespoons extra-virgin olive oil

3 tablespoons vegetable oil

Pan Sauce

1 tablespoon extra-virgin olive oil

¼ cup minced onion

Salt and freshly ground black pepper

¼ cup Poultry/Meat Stock (page 66) or Quick Stock (page 68)

¼ cup dry Marsala

1 cup well-drained canned tomatoes, crushed

1 tablespoon unsalted butter

4 ounces Italian Parmigiano-Reggiano cheese, shaved into furls with a vegetable peeler

Method   **Working Ahead:** *The veal chops can be pounded up to 8 hours before cooking. Refrigerate them, covered, until shortly before cooking. This dish is best eaten immediately after cooking. To make short work of the cooking, measure and chop all the ingredients ahead.*

Preparing the Veal: Trim away all fat from the chops and their bones. Make sure the bones are trimmed clean. Trim the chops so you are left with the large lean oval of meat. This is the eye of the rib, attached to the rib bone, or on its own in a boneless chop. Save any meat scraps for ragù sauces or the stockpot.

Using a meat pounder, pound the meat to half its original thickness, about ½ inch thick. Take care not to pull it away from the bone. Keep the chop from curling while cooking by lightly scoring a crosshatch pattern into one side of each chop: three long, very shallow cuts across the full width of the chop, and another three perpendicular to it. Unless you will be cooking the chops right away, set them on a platter, cover with plastic wrap, and refrigerate.

Cooking the Chops: Have a platter large enough to hold the chops in a single layer warming in a low oven, along with four dinner plates. Cover a cookie sheet with a triple thickness of paper towels for draining the fried chops. Beat the eggs in a shallow soup dish, and spread the bread crumbs on a platter. Remove the chops from the refrigerator, and lightly sprinkle the meat with salt and pepper.

In a sauté pan large enough to hold the chops in a single layer, heat the two oils over medium heat 4 to 5 minutes. Do not allow them to smoke. Test the temperature by dropping in a pinch of bread crumbs. If they sizzle and slowly begin to brown, the oil is ready. Dip the chops, one at a time, in the egg, letting any excess drip off. Then dip them in the crumbs, shaking off any excess. Slip the chops into the pan, making sure they do not overlap. Cook 2 to 2½ minutes on one side, or until a rich golden brown. Do not cook to dark brown, or the chops may dry out. Turn and cook to golden brown on the second side, about 2 minutes. Remove the chops from the pan, and drain them on both sides on the paper towels. Set them on the platter in the oven.

Making the Sauce and Serving: Immediately pour all the fat out of the pan, and wipe it clean with a thick wad of paper towels. Add the 1 tablespoon olive oil to the pan and heat it over medium-high heat. Add the onion and quickly stir until golden. Sprinkle them lightly with salt and pepper. Stir in the stock and cook down a minute or so to a moist glaze on the bottom of the pan. Then add the Marsala and cook down the same way. Stir in the tomatoes and simmer, stirring constantly, for 10 seconds, or until thick. Swirl in the butter, letting it melt only to a cream. Remove the pan from the heat.

continued

Place a veal chop on each heated dinner plate. Nap each chop with spoonfuls of the pan sauce, scraping the last bit of it from the pan. Divide the cheese among the chops, heaping the furls on top of the sauce. Serve immediately.

Suggestions　**Wine:** A soft red Merlot from the Colli Bolognesi, or a light-bodied Merlot from the Aquilea area of Friuli.

Menu: Serve in traditional style after a first course of Tagliarini with Lemon Anchovy Sauce (page 112) or Linguine with Braised Garlic and Balsamic Vinegar (page 110). Accompany the chops with steamed green beans or Oven-Roasted Radicchio (page 336). Have Home-Style Jam Cake (page 401) or Riccardo Rimondi's Spanish Sponge Cake filled with raspberry jam (page 433) for dessert. For lighter dining, begin with the "Little" Spring Soup from the 17th Century (page 232) before the veal with steamed potatoes, and make dessert Baked Pears with Fresh Grape Syrup (page 442).

Cook's Notes　**Extra-Fine Bread Crumbs:** Grind bread crumbs for a few seconds in a blender, reducing them to the texture of fine sand.

Lemon Roast Veal with Rosemary
Vitello al Forno

Scented with lemon and herbs, this veal roast gains extra succulence from a fine mincing of pancetta. Tucked into slits in the roast, it flavors and moistens the meat as it cooks. Some Emilia-Romagna cooks baste the veal with milk, but I prefer the equally traditional basting of white wine and the unusual finishing touch of fresh lemon, a favorite trick of a Modena friend. Moist veal is guaranteed by taking the meat only to the rosy stage. In Italy it would be more well done, a style that is delicious there but turns dry when done with most American veal.

[Serves 6 to 8]

3 to 4 pounds boneless loin of veal
2 ounces pancetta, minced
1 large clove garlic, minced
¼ cup minced Italian parsley
2 tablespoons fresh lemon juice
2 tablespoons extra-virgin olive oil
Salt and freshly ground black
　pepper

3-inch sprig fresh rosemary, or 1
　teaspoon dried rosemary leaves
⅔ cup dry white wine
½ cup Poultry/Meat Stock (page
　66) or Quick Stock (page 68)
Rosemary sprigs for garnish

Method   **Working Ahead:** *For the best flavor, season the roast with the pancetta mixture 1 day ahead. Refrigerate it, lightly covered, until about 1 hour before roasting. The roast is best eaten as soon as cooking is completed.*

Seasoning the Veal: Mince together the pancetta, garlic, and parsley. Turn into a bowl, stirring in 1 tablespoon of the lemon juice. Using a paring knife, make 15 or 16 deep slits into the roast, over its entire surface. Using your fingers, stuff the seasoning mixture into each slit. Set the roast on a platter, cover lightly with plastic wrap, and refrigerate 24 hours.

Roasting the Veal: Preheat the oven to 350°F. Rub the veal with the olive oil and sprinkle lightly with salt and pepper. Set it in a shallow roasting pan with the rosemary. The roast will take about 25 minutes to the pound (1¼ to 1¾ hours). Roast 20 minutes, then pour half the wine over the meat, basting with the pan juices. Continue roasting, basting and adding small amounts of wine, until an instant-reading thermometer inserted in the meat's center reads 150°F. Remove the roast to a warm platter and keep warm.

Making the Sauce: Skim the fat from the pan juices. Set the roasting pan on a burner over high heat. Bring the juices to a boil, stirring in the stock. Boil, scraping up the brown glaze in the pan with a wooden spatula, 2 minutes, or until the sauce has thickened slightly and is full-flavored. Season with salt and pepper, and stir in the remaining 1 tablespoon lemon juice.

Serving: Keep the sauce warm as you carve the meat into ¼-inch-thick slices. Garnish the platter with a few sprigs of rosemary, and pass the sauce separately.

Suggestions   **Wine:** A red Barbera from the Colli Bolognesi, a Barbera from Piemonte's Monferrato area, or a Barbera of Lombardia's Oltrepò Pavese. A young red Cabernet Sauvignon or Cabernet Franc from Friuli is also good with the veal.

Menu: The veal is excellent after any light first course made without lemon or balsamic vinegar. Have Tagliatelle with Caramelized Onion and Fresh Herbs (page 101), Fresh Garlic Soup Brisighella (page 222), or Priest's Soup (page 227). Accompany the veal with Green Beans Bolognese (page 327), Basil and Onion Mashed Potatoes (page 345), Grilled Winter Endives (page 337), or steamed broccoli. Finish the meal with Baked Pears with Fresh Grape Syrup (page 442) or Torta Barozzi (page 395).

Basil and Balsamic Veal Scallops
Scaloppine di Vitello a Basilico e Aceto Balsamico

Fresh basil and balsamic vinegar are an unbeatable seasoning for a sauté of veal, chicken, pork, or seafood. This recipe was inspired by vinegar expert Renato Bergonzini and is a Modenese favorite. Make it for a quick supper or for a menu where you need a fast-cooking main dish. The basil must be fresh (dried cannot be substituted here) and the balsamic vinegar a richly flavored one. In dishes like this, boneless pork loin is often substituted for veal.

[Serves 4]

1 pound veal scallops, or 1 pound top round of veal or boneless veal loin in a single piece, trimmed of fat

About 2 cups all-purpose unbleached flour (organic stone-ground preferred)

2 tablespoons extra-virgin olive oil

1 tablespoon unsalted butter

Salt and freshly ground black pepper

1½ tablespoons commercial balsamic vinegar blended with ⅓ teaspoon brown sugar, or 2 teaspoons artisan-made *tradizionale* balsamic vinegar

3 tablespoons minced fresh basil leaves

½ cup Poultry/Meat Stock (page 66) or Quick Stock (page 68)

1 tablespoon shredded fresh basil leaves for garnish

Method

Working Ahead: *The veal can be pounded and all ingredients measured up to 2 hours ahead. Keep the veal covered and stored in the refrigerator. Cook the veal just before serving.*

Preparing the Scallops: Check that your butcher or market cuts the scallops across the grain from a piece of veal free of connective tissue, like the top round or loin. If cut with the grain, the scallops will shrink in cooking. To cut them yourself, slice the veal across the grain into ¼- to ½-inch-thick pieces. Pound with a meat pounder to about ⅛ inch thick.

Cooking the Scallops: Warm a serving platter in a low oven. Spread the flour on another platter for dredging the meat. Heat the oil and butter in a 12-inch sauté pan over medium-high heat. Decide how many scallops will fit in the pan without touching. Dip those in the flour, dusting off any excess. Quickly brown the meat, taking only 20 to 30 seconds per side. Using a wooden spatula, transfer the scallops to the platter, and sprinkle with salt and pepper. Keep warm in the oven. Sauté the rest of the veal in batches, flouring the pieces just before they go into the pan. If necessary, add a little more oil to the pan. Keep the heat low enough so as not to burn the particles. Hold the meat in the warm oven.

Making the Sauce and Serving: Stir half of the commercial balsamic vinegar, if you are using it, and the 3 tablespoons basil into the sauté pan. Cook a few seconds, then stir in the stock and cook at a lively bubble 1 minute. Pour the sauce over the veal scallops. Sprinkle with the remaining commercial balsamic, or with all of the artisan-made balsamic if that is what you're using, and the shredded basil. Serve immediately.

Suggestions   **Wine:** From the Veneto, a young red Valpolicella Classico, or try a Santa Maddalena from Trentino–Alto Adige.

Menu: Begin with Modena's Spiced Soup of Spinach and Cheese (page 234). Have Oven-Roasted Potatoes (page 344) and steamed green beans with the veal. Make dessert Modena Rice Pudding (page 398).

Cook's Notes **Balsamic Vinegar:** See page 467 for information on balsamic vinegars.

— 8·30-01 - Excellent meal with veal. baked potatoes are OK.

Romagna Grilled Veal Chops
Costolette in Graticola

Grilled veal is the simplest and most satisfying kind of food. The irresistible aroma of meats grilling over a wood fire greets you in many Romagna restaurants, especially those in the hills near Verucchio. There, Ristorante Zanni has an old waist-high hearth as its grill. Chops of veal, pork, and the local castrato lamb turn brown and crusty over the hot coals while the fire warms the whole dining room. Make these chops as at Zanni, with either sage or rosemary. The recipe doubles easily.

[Serves 4]

4 veal loin or rib chops, cut 1 inch thick (about 1¾ pounds)

2 large cloves garlic, split

18 fresh sage leaves, or 4 or 5 sprigs fresh rosemary

3 tablespoons extra-virgin olive oil

Generous pinch of black pepper

Salt to taste

Fresh sage or rosemary sprigs for garnish (optional)

continued

Method   **Working Ahead:** *The veal is best flavored with the garlic, herbs, and oil about 24 hours ahead. Keep it covered in the refrigerator. Serve the veal hot from the grill or stove-top.*

Flavoring the Veal: Trim the chops of excess fat. Cut three shallow notches into the outer edge of the meat of each chop to keep it from curling in cooking. Place the chops in a shallow dish that holds them comfortably. Rub all the meat's surfaces with the split cloves of garlic. Then crush and rub the sage or rosemary into the meat, on all sides. Sprinkle the chops with the oil and pepper, slathering the oil over the meat. Tuck the garlic pieces and herb leaves among the chops, cover with plastic wrap, and refrigerate about 24 hours.

Cooking the Veal: Cook the chops over a charcoal grill, preferably using real wood charcoal, or use a stove-top grill or a sauté pan. Discard the garlic pieces before grilling.

Grilling over Charcoal: Heat the charcoal until a gray ash forms. Set the grill about 4 inches from the coals. Lift the chops from their dish, keeping the herbs on them, and set them on the hot grill. Quickly brown on both sides, lightly salting the chops before turning. Then slow down the cooking by covering the grill or by raising the rack several inches away from the fire. Cook a total of 10 minutes (including browning time), or until the chops are almost firm when pressed with the finger. If you have any doubt about doneness, make a small slit into the meat; it should be faintly blushed with pink.

Stove-top Grilling: Heat a gridded skillet or stove-top grill over medium-high heat. Brush the grill lightly with olive oil. Lift the chops from their dish, keeping the herbs on them. Take 2 to 4 minutes to quickly brown them on both sides, lightly salting the chops before turning. Immediately turn the heat to low and cook the chops 3 minutes per side, or until they are almost firm when pressed with a finger. Make sure the herbs are getting crisp without burning. If you have any doubt about doneness, check by making a small slit in the meat. It should be faintly blushed with pink.

"Grilling" in a Sauté Pan: Film the bottom of a 12-inch sauté pan with a little olive oil. Heat it over medium-high heat. Lift the veal chops from their dish, keeping the herbs on them. Take 2 to 3 minutes to quickly brown the chops on both sides, lightly salting them before turning. Lower the heat to low, and cook the chops about 3 minutes to a side, or until slightly firm when pressed. They should be faintly blushed with pink inside. Make sure the herbs are crisped but not burned.

Serving: Remove the chops to a platter and serve immediately. Garnish them with the grilled bits of herbs, and sprigs of fresh herbs if desired.

Suggestions   **Wine:** A young, medium-bodied red Sangiovese di Romagna or a soft red Barbera d'Alba or d'Asti from the Piedmont.

Menu: Have the chops as part of a traditional Romagna country dinner. Begin with a few slices of good salami (page 501) and *Piadina* flatbread (page 384). Have more *Piadina* with the veal chops and Oven-Roasted Potatoes (page 344), Garlic-Sautéed Cabbage (page 331), or Salad of Mixed Greens and Fennel (page 349). Enjoy Nonna's Jam Tart (page 413) or Sweet Cornmeal Biscuits (page 422) with fresh fruit for dessert. A traditional pasta course is small portions of tagliatelle with Country-Style Ragù (page 48).

Cook's Notes **Using Lamb or Pork:** Use loin or rib chops cut ¾ to 1 inch thick. Flavor and grill exactly as described above. Rosemary tends to be traditional with lamb, while either herb often flavors pork.

Romagna and the Romagnoli

The people of Romagna (*Romagnoli* in Italian), have a reputation for obstinacy and independence, for a keen critical eye and for openhearted hospitality. Their own poets call them arrogant and passionate, sloppy and kind, majestic and loving a practical joke. Writer Candido Bonvicini says, "Their dialect is wrought with roses, but teems with scorpions." And yet, doors are always open to passersby. Several of my Emilian friends say the people of Emilia will greet you with honest pleasure and warmth, and treat you well. But once you are gone, they will not think about you again. When you return, they will sincerely delight in having you back. A Romagnolo friend says *all* that is true of the people of Romagna, with one important difference. He says, "We will worry and wonder why you have not returned."

In Romagna, food is often more immediate, and flavors more primal than in Emilia. It has been said Romagnoli eat Homerian meals of food straight from the earth and the fire, washing them down with strong wine. Their wine is the red Sangiovese. Some say the Sangiovese stains the throat, labeling forever those who love it. It is part of their identity. The wine can be rough and aggressive. It can also be soft and velvety, almost seductive. Sangiovese always warms. Even at its most elegant, and it can achieve elegance, there is earthiness and vigor. White Albana is the other side of Romagna's nature. Even at its driest, this wine has a sweet nature; it is soft and winning. In its old sweet style, Albana is golden with scents of fruit trees in full blossom. The wine makers around Bertinoro say a glass of Albana and a May afternoon of watching spring come to Romagna's plain is the heaven of the Romagnoli.

Artusi's Delight
Polpette d'Artusi alla Villa Gaidello

In *Italy small meatballs are usually pan-fried and eaten as an antipasto, with or without sauce. But in this festive dish from Villa Gaidello, the larger meat patties are a second course. Their unique flavor comes from a blend of beef, chicken, cheese, herbs, pancetta, pine nuts, and currants. The dish is finished with a sweet/tart pan sauce of caramelized balsamic vinegar and garnished with small onions glazed to a golden turn.*

Villa Gaidello's creator, Paola Bini, explained that her family adapted this recipe from one by 19th-century cookbook author Pellegrino Artusi. The dish brings the tastes of another era to menus. Its long list of ingredients may appear daunting, but the patties go together quickly and can be prepared a day ahead.

[Serves 4 to 6]

Meat Patties

1 medium onion, quartered

¾ cup (3 ounces) Italian Parmigiano-Reggiano cheese, in chunks

⅓ cup tightly packed Italian parsley leaves

1 small clove garlic

1 large chicken thigh, skinned, boned, and cut into chunks

6 ounces lean pancetta, coarsely chopped

10 ounces lean ground chuck or sirloin beef

⅓ cup currants, soaked 10 minutes in hot water and drained

⅓ cup pine nuts, toasted

¼ cup dried bread crumbs

1 egg

1 teaspoon imported Italian tomato paste

⅛ teaspoon ground cinnamon

⅛ teaspoon salt

⅛ teaspoon freshly ground black pepper

Pinch of freshly grated nutmeg

Pinch of ground cloves

4 tablespoons extra-virgin olive oil

Glazed Onions (Optional)

2 tablespoons extra-virgin olive oil

16 pearl onions, boiled 10 minutes and peeled

½ teaspoon sugar

¾ cup Poultry/Meat Stock (page 66) or Quick Stock (page 68)

⅓ cup high-quality commercial balsamic vinegar

Sauce

3/4 cup Poultry/Meat Stock or Quick Stock

2 tablespoons unsalted butter

1/3 cup high-quality commercial
balsamic vinegar, or 3
tablespoons artisan-made
tradizionale balsamic vinegar

Salt and freshly ground black
pepper to taste

Method

Working Ahead: *The meat mixture can be blended and refrigerated up to 24 hours before cooking. You can cook the meat patties and sauté the onions up to the point of preparing the sauce. Hold the patties and onions at room temperature up to 2 hours. Reheat, and make the sauce shortly before serving.*

Preparing the Patties: Finely chop the onion, cheese, parsley, and garlic in a food processor fitted with the steel blade, using rapid on/off pulses. Add the chicken thigh and pancetta. Process until finely ground but not puréed. Turn into a medium bowl. Using a wooden spoon, blend in the beef, currants, pine nuts, bread crumbs, egg, tomato paste, cinnamon, salt, pepper, nutmeg, and cloves. Shape the patties with wet hands to form 1 1/2-inch-diameter balls. Flatten them to about 3/4 inch thick by gently pressing the balls with the palm of your hand.

Cooking the Patties: Line a cookie sheet with a triple thickness of paper towels. Heat the olive oil in a large sauté pan over medium heat. Arrange half the patties in the pan so they do not touch. Slowly brown on both sides, taking about 15 minutes. Turn them gently with two wooden spatulas, taking care not to break them. Drain them on the towels, and repeat with the remaining patties. Then pour off all the fat from the pan, but do not wash it.

Glazing the Onions: Use another skillet to sauté the onions. Heat the 2 tablespoons olive oil in the skillet. Sauté the onions over medium heat 5 minutes, or until they begin to color. Shake the pan as you sprinkle them with the 1/2 teaspoon sugar, and cook over medium heat 10 minutes, or until golden brown. Increase the heat to high, stir in the stock, and boil 3 minutes, or until reduced to almost nothing. Add the commercial balsamic vinegar and boil 1 minute. (If you are using artisan-made balsamic, add all of it in the next step.) Set aside.

Finishing and Serving: Have a serving platter warming in a low oven. Put the meatball sauté pan over medium-high heat. Stir in the 3/4 cup stock, and let it boil as you scrape up the brown bits in the pan. Cook 5 minutes, or until the liquid is reduced by two thirds. Stir in the 2 tablespoons butter and 1/3 cup commercial vinegar (artisan-made vinegar is added in a few moments). Cook at a slow bubble 2 minutes to thicken slightly. Season with salt and pepper. Add the meatballs and simmer over medium-low heat about 5 minutes to heat through. Turn them once to heat evenly. Rewarm the onions. If you are using artisan-made vinegar, stir it into the meat patty sauce just before transferring them to the heated platter. Spoon the meatballs onto the warm platter, and arrange the onions around them. Serve hot.

Suggestions   **Wine:** A Recioto della Valpolicella Amarone from the Veneto, or a Merlot from Colli Bolognesi.

Menu: Serve "Little" Spring Soup from the 17th Century (page 232) or Priest's Soup (page 227) in small quantities before, and a green salad after. Modena Crumbling Cake (page 400) with sweet wine for dunking is a perfect finish. For a buffet, have Mousse of Mortadella (page 22), Valentino's Pizza (page 29), and Garlic Crostini with Pancetta (page 28) as antipasti. Serve the meat patties with a green salad. Sweet Cornmeal Biscuits (page 422) with grapes is a fine dessert.

Seventeenth-century Bolognese banquet procession honoring the Swiss guard. Giuseppe Maria Mitelli, 1699.

Grilled Beef with Balsamic Glaze
Manzo alla Brace

As soon as spring weather warms, country <u>trattorie</u> and restaurants set out tables anywhere with a breeze and a little sun. At Osteria di Rubbiara outside Modena, the dining room is a grassy yard surrounded by the grain fields of the Po River plain. Scents of fresh-cut wheat mingle with the bouquet of tortellini in homemade broth. Next door are the Osteria's little grocery store, and inside dining rooms. Outbuildings house one of the area's most respected collections of artisan-made balsamic vinegars, the work of owner Italo Pedroni.

This crusty grilled beef basted with balsamic vinegar was inspired by a Pedroni dish. Blending a little brown sugar with a commercial balsamic brings it close to the character of the young artisan-made vinegars often cooked into dishes. If you have an older artisan-made <u>tradizionale</u> balsamic vinegar, drizzle a tablespoon over the finished beef at the table. Save the grilled beef for eating outdoors when it can be cooked over charcoal or over the especially fragrant fire made from hardwoods.

[Serves 6 to 8]

Marinade

Eight 3-inch sprigs fresh rosemary, or 3 tablespoons dried rosemary leaves

14 fresh sage leaves, or 14 dried whole sage leaves

4 large cloves garlic

4 tablespoons extra-virgin olive oil

⅓ cup dry red wine

3 pounds boneless beef chuck ribs (rib lifters), or boned chuck blade roast cut into chunks 1½ inches thick and about 4 inches long

Glaze

6 tablespoons commercial balsamic vinegar

1½ tablespoons brown sugar

Salt and freshly ground black pepper

1 tablespoon commercial balsamic vinegar blended with ½ teaspoon brown sugar, or 2 tablespoons artisan-made *tradizionale* balsamic vinegar

Bouquet of fresh sage and rosemary sprigs for garnish

Method   **Working Ahead:** *For the best flavor, start marinating the meat 24 hours ahead. The beef is best eaten hot off the grill. Once trimmed of fat, the leftovers make a fine salad: Dress*

with a little olive oil and balsamic vinegar, mounding the slices on a salad of mixed greens. Garnish with thin slices of red onion and Balsamic Vegetables (page 18).

Marinating the Meat: Do use fresh herbs if at all possible. Strip the rosemary leaves off their sprigs and mince them together with the sage and garlic. Blend with the olive oil and wine, and toss with the meat in a glass or stainless steel bowl. Lightly cover, and refrigerate 16 to 24 hours.

Cooking the Meat: For fine flavor, use the hot embers of a hardwood fire (oak, ash, nut, and fruitwoods are typically Italian) or the more available charcoal grill fired with real wood charcoal. These cuts of beef are best kept rare to medium-rare.

Grilling over Charcoal: Light the grill, using real wood charcoal if possible. As the coals burn to a coating of gray ash, set the meat on a platter at room temperature. Stir the 6 tablespoons balsamic vinegar and 1½ tablespoons brown sugar into the marinade left in the bowl. When the coals are ready, spread them out and top with another thin layer of unlit charcoal. Set the grill in place, letting it heat about 5 minutes. Place the meat pieces toward the center of the grill. When one side has browned, spoon marinade over the pieces and turn them to get crusty brown on the other side. Sprinkle lightly with salt and pepper. Continue basting. Once the meat is well browned, adjust the vents to lower the heat and cover the grill. Cook 5 to 10 minutes for rare, or 15 to 20 minutes for medium-rare, basting two or three times. Rare meat is barely firm when pressed with a finger; medium-rare is blushed with pink and just firm.

Grilling over Hardwood Embers: This is usually an open campfire. Have stones piled around the fire so a metal grill can be set about 6 inches above the red-hot embers. Brown the meat as directed above, adding a few small pieces of wood to the fire if it threatens to die. Instead of covering the charcoal grill to finish cooking the meat, tent a large piece of aluminum foil over the meat pieces to reflect heat back onto them. Cook, basting two or three times. Five minutes is all that is needed for rare meat, but do test it by pressing with your finger as described above. Six to 9 minutes produces medium-rare.

Serving: Transfer the meat from the grill to a heated platter, and cut it across the grain into diagonal ¼-inch-thick slices. Sprinkle the slices with the remaining balsamic vinegar, and serve hot. Garnish with herb sprigs if desired.

Suggestions   **Wine:** At the Osteria everyone drinks the local Lambrusco, which is dry, grapey, and refreshing. On this side of the ocean, pour a bigger Dolcetto d'Alba from the Piedmont, or a medium-bodied Chianti Classico from Tuscany.

Menu: Although also seasoned with balsamic vinegar, Paola Bini's Potato Salad (page 19) is perfect summer food with the meat. Make dessert fresh peaches and melon, or shales of Parmigiano-Reggiano cheese with pears.

Cook's Notes   **Other Meats:** Instead of beef, use chunks cut from the loin end of a leg of lamb, pork tenderloin, or boned chicken thighs.

Lamb with Black Olives
Agnello alle Olive

This is a company dish in Romagna and here in the United States. Cook it ahead, rewarm it for serving, and still have lamb that carves into moist, rosy slices. The technique of roasting with a small amount of liquid in a deep pot on top of the stove dates back to the days when ovens were scarce in many Emilia-Romagna homes. Flavors concentrate and intensify with this method of cooking, producing a pan sauce so rich in flavor that it rarely needs any further reduction.

[Serves 4 to 6]

Two 3-inch sprigs fresh rosemary, or 2 generous teaspoons dried rosemary leaves

1 large clove garlic

6- to 7-pound leg of lamb, trimmed of fat

Freshly ground black pepper to taste

2 tablespoons extra-virgin olive oil

Salt

½ medium red onion, chopped

⅔ cup dry red wine

½ cup well-drained canned tomatoes

3 tablespoons dry red wine

½ cup small black Ligurian or Niçoise olives, unpitted

½ cup Poultry/Meat Stock (page 66) or Quick Stock (page 68) (optional)

Method

Working Ahead: *For the best flavor, season the lamb with the garlic and rosemary 24 hours before cooking. Once cooked, the lamb can be cooled and held at room temperature, uncovered, about 2 hours. Rewarm over medium-low heat, taking care not to cook it beyond an internal temperature of 140°F.*

Seasoning the Lamb: Strip the rosemary leaves from the sprigs into a mortar. Add the garlic, and crush to a paste. To make the lamb fit snugly in the pot, have the butcher trim away the sirloin end of the piece up to the thick part of the leg. Set aside the sirloin end for another use. The shank bone should be cracked and tucked under the thick part of the leg, making a compact piece of meat of more or less even thickness. Final weight is about 5 pounds.

Use a paring knife to cut small slits in the leg of lamb. Fill them with the crushed herbs. Set the lamb on a plate, sprinkle it with pepper, lightly cover with plastic wrap, and refrigerate 8 to 24 hours.

continued

Cooking the Lamb: Select a heavy 4- to 5-quart saucepan large enough to hold the meat very snugly. Heat the oil in it over medium heat. Add the meat, salting it lightly, and take about 1 hour to slowly brown it on all sides. Turn the meat with wooden spatulas, lowering the heat if necessary to keep it from scorching. Add the red onion to the meat and brown it, still turning the meat so that it is crusty on all sides. Pour in the ⅔ cup wine and the tomatoes. Bring the liquid to the slowest of bubbles. Cover lightly with foil, but do not seal the foil to the pot. Cook over low heat 2 hours. Turn the lamb frequently as it cooks, basting it with the juices. At the end of 2 hours the sauce should be only a thick film at the bottom of the pan. Stir in the 3 tablespoons wine and the olives. Slowly bubble, uncovered, another 30 to 45 minutes. The lamb should reach an internal temperature of 140°F when tested with an instant-reading thermometer. Add the ½ cup broth if the pan juices threaten to dry up.

Serving: Have a serving platter warming in a low oven. Transfer the lamb to a cutting board, and carve it into ⅛- to ¼-inch-thick slices. Arrange the slices on the platter, and moisten them with the little bit of pan sauce. Spoon the black olives over the meat. Serve hot.

Suggestions   **Wine:** A soft red Sangiovese di Romagna Riserva, a Merlot from Trentino–Alto Adige, or Tuscany's Tignanello.

Menu: Begin the meal with Garlic Crostini with Pancetta (page 28) and Balsamic Vegetables (page 18). Serve boiled potatoes or Creamy Polenta (page 354) with the lamb. Have as dessert Baked Pears with Fresh Grape Syrup (page 442) or Caramelized Almond Tart (page 409).

Cook's Notes   Romagna is famous for its castrato, the meat of neutered young rams that grow plump grazing on the area's rich grass. Unlike mutton, castrato is not strong-tasting. It combines the delicacy of lamb with the full flavor of beef. Although lighter in character, American lamb can stand in for castrato in dishes like this one.

Lamb, Garlic, and Potato Roast
Agnello al Forno con Aglio e Patate

Roast lamb, garlic, and potatoes together until all are crusty and tender, and you have a favorite dish from the farmlands of Ferrara and Ravenna. Rubbing the lamb with sage and garlic and letting it rest overnight imparts depth. The real secret of its lovely taste, though, is the anchovies: just enough for body, not enough for anyone to identify. Spring in Piacenza brings a dish almost the duplicate of this one, with loin or leg of kid replacing the lamb. It is a delicious substitution, and a traditional one at Easter time.

[Serves 6 to 8]

3½- to 4-pound shank end leg of lamb or boneless shoulder, trimmed of fat and cut into 2-inch chunks

1 large clove garlic, minced

1 medium onion, chopped

3 tablespoons. extra-virgin olive oil

6 large fresh sage leaves, or 6 dried whole sage leaves

4 canned anchovy fillets, drained and chopped

8 large cloves garlic, halved

3 tablespoons. red wine vinegar

1½ cups dry white wine

Salt and freshly ground black pepper to taste

3 pounds red-skinned potatoes, unpeeled, cut into ½-inch-thick rounds

Method

Working Ahead: *The lamb should be marinated overnight, but do not cook it more than 2 hours ahead. Hold the cooked lamb, uncovered, at room temperature. (Refrigerating changes the quality of the dish, leaving it still good but tasting "reheated.") Rewarm the finished dish in a 350°F oven about 30 minutes.*

Seasoning the Lamb: In a glass or stainless steel bowl, combine the lamb with the first quantity of garlic, onion, olive oil, sage leaves, and anchovies. Toss, cover lightly with plastic wrap, and refrigerate 16 to 24 hours.

Cooking the Lamb: Total cooking time will be about 2½ hours. Preheat the oven to 450°F. Heat a large heavy metal roasting pan in the oven about 20 minutes. Turn the lamb pieces and their marinade into the hot pan, spreading them so they do not touch. Brown the meat on all sides in the oven, turning the pieces once or twice with wooden spatulas; this will take 20 to 30 minutes. Turn the heat down to 350°F. Stir the eight halved garlic cloves, vinegar, and half the white wine into the pan. Sprinkle with salt and pepper. Cook 45 minutes, basting the meat twice with the pan juices. Add the potatoes and the rest of the wine. Turn the potatoes to coat them with the pan juices. Lightly cover the pan with parchment paper or aluminum foil. Continue basting often with the pan juices as it roasts another 45 minutes, or until the potatoes are easily pierced with a knife. The meat should be equally tender. If it is not, continue cooking, covered, another 20 minutes. Warm a serving platter.

Final Browning and Serving: Turn off the oven and turn on the broiler, setting a rack so the roasting pan is about 3 inches from the flame. Slip the pan under the broiler and cook, turning the pieces and basting with the pan juices, 20 minutes, or until the potatoes are browned. Mound the lamb and potatoes onto the warmed platter, and serve hot.

Suggestions   **Wine:** The big, flavors of this dish are set off by a red Sangiovese di Romagna Riserva, a Barbarossa from Romagna, the Piemonte's Nebbiolo d'Alba, or Campania's red Taurasi.

Menu: For a traditional menu, begin with Priest's Soup (page 227) or Modena's Spiced Soup of Spinach and Cheese (page 234), made without eggs. Follow the lamb with a green salad, and then Ugo Falavigna's Apple Cream Tart (page 411) or Cardinal d'Este's Tart (page 417). For lighter dining, begin with Fresh Pears with Parmigiano-Reggiano and Balsamic Vinegar (page 30). Follow the lamb with Meringues of the Dark Lake (page 421).

From the fantasy land of plenty, Cucagna, a table always laden with everyone's favorite foods, by Giuseppe Maria Mitelli, 1703

Braised Pork Ribs with Polenta
Puntine di Maiale con Polenta

Mounding tender chunks of pork ribs over steaming polenta is a winter specialty from Ferrara. Tomato, olives, and basil add especially rich flavors to the meaty ribs. A thick beef chuck blade roast can be substituted with great success. With either meat, this dish evokes snug evenings in Ferrara farmhouses, when everyone gathers around the big kitchen table for hours of good talk and good food. Serve this on the first really cold night of winter, if possible in front of an open fire.

The Ferrarese claim that their pleasure in polenta comes from their proximity to the cornmeal-loving Veneto region. Just across the Po River, the Veneto is a long stone's throw from downtown Ferrara. Polenta with braisings like this one, often made with salt cod instead of pork, are eaten all across the Veneto plain.

[Serves 6 to 8]

5 pounds lean country-style pork spareribs (cut from blade end of pork loin) or beef chuck blade pot roast

3 tablespoons extra-virgin olive oil

1 large onion, minced

4 tablespoons minced Italian parsley

2 large California bay laurel leaves

1 large clove garlic

Generous pinch of ground cloves

Generous pinch of ground cinnamon

Generous pinch of ground allspice

⅛ teaspoon freshly ground black pepper

1 cup dry red wine

Two 14- to 16-ounce cans tomatoes, with their liquid

½ cup small Ligurian or Niçoise black olives, pitted

3 tablespoons chopped fresh basil leaves or 1½ teaspoons dried basil

Salt and freshly ground black pepper to taste

1 recipe Creamy Polenta (page 354)

Method

Working Ahead: *The pork or beef can be cooked 1 day ahead; cover and refrigerate overnight. Gently reheat before serving. A little water or broth may be needed to moisten the meat.*

Browning the Meat: Trim excess fat from the meat. If pork is in one piece, separate into pieces by cutting between the ribs. If you are using the beef roast, cut it into pieces about 1½ inches long and 1 inch thick. Heat the oil in a 12-inch sauté pan over medium-high heat. Add the meat in a single layer. Take about 20 minutes to brown it slowly, until dark brown and crusty on all sides. Remove the meat to a platter.

Braising: Keep the heat at medium as you stir in the onion and parsley. Cook 10 minutes, or until golden brown, taking care not to burn the brown glaze in the bottom of the pan. Stir frequently. Stir in the garlic, bay leaves, and spices. Return the meat to the pan, turning to coat it with the vegetables and seasonings. Pour in the wine, adjusting the heat so it bubbles slowly. As the wine cooks down over 10 to 15 minutes, use a wooden spatula to scrape up the brown bits on the bottom of the pan. Break up the tomatoes as you add them to the pan. Stir in the olives, and bring the mixture to a very slow bubble over low heat. Cover tightly and cook over low heat 1 hour. Add the basil, cover, and cook at a gentle bubble another 30 minutes, or until the meat is tender. Season with salt and pepper. Skim any fat from the surface of the sauce before serving.

Serving: Spoon over the hot polenta on a heated serving platter. Serve at once.

Suggestions **Wine:** This dish takes to a quaffing wine—generous in fruit, soft, and easy to drink. In Emilia-Romagna it would be a Barbera dei Colli Bolognesi di Monte San Pietro, or a Sangiovese di Romagna Riserva. From other parts of Italy drink a fruity Piemontese Gattinara, a Merlot from the Veneto, or a Salice Salentino Rosso of Apulia.

Menu: For lighter dining, let the meat and polenta stand on their own, followed by a dessert of fresh pears and grapes. For a fuller menu, serve small portions of Oven-Glazed Porcini (page 239) before the pork. Have Baked Pears with Fresh Grape Syrup (page 442) for dessert.

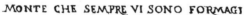

From the fantasy land of plenty, Cucagna, the mountain of cheeses, by Giuseppe Maria Mitelli, 1703

A Baked Pie of Polenta and Country Ragù
Polenta Pasticciata

Layering slices of polenta with meat ragù and Parmigiano-Reggiano cheese creates a lasagne-style casserole that is family food throughout Emilia-Romagna. The dish is ultimately practical, needing almost no last-minute effort. The polenta and ragù are best made ahead, and the assembled pie can wait a day before baking.

[Serves 6 to 8]

1 recipe Country-Style Ragù
(page 48)
Olive oil
1 recipe Polenta (page 352),
cooled in two oiled loaf pans

1 cup (4 ounces) freshly grated
Italian Parmigiano-Reggiano
cheese

Method   **Working Ahead:** *The polenta should be made at least 3 hours ahead so that it can be cool enough for slicing. It will keep, covered and refrigerated, 1 day. The ragù can be made and frozen up to a month in advance. The assembled dish can be covered and refrigerated up to 24 hours before baking. Bring it close to room temperature before baking.*

Assembling the Pie: Bring the ragù close to room temperature. Use olive oil to grease the bottom and sides of a shallow 3-quart baking dish. Cut the polenta into ¼- to ½-inch-thick slices. Spread a few spoonfuls of ragù over the bottom of the baking dish. Then entirely cover the bottom of the dish with a single layer of polenta slices. Spread half the ragù over the polenta, and sprinkle with ¼ cup of the cheese.

Add another layer of polenta, covering the ragù completely. Top with the rest of the ragù and another ¼ cup of the cheese. Finish the casserole with a final layer of polenta slices to cover the ragù. (There may be a few slices left over.) Spread about 1 tablespoon olive oil over the polenta, and then sprinkle with the remaining ½ cup Parmigiano-Reggiano. Cover the casserole with foil. Refrigerate if working ahead.

Baking and Serving: Preheat the oven to 350°F. The pie should be close to room temperature. Set it on a baking sheet. Bake for 1 to 1½ hours, covered, or until a knife inserted in the center of the casserole and left there about 30 seconds comes out quite warm. Once the casserole is heated through, uncover and bake another 5 minutes. The cheese topping should be melted but not leathery or dark brown. Cut the pie into squares, and serve on warmed dinner plates.

continued

Suggestions　**Wine:** A generous, quaffable red like a fine Sangiovese di Romagna, a Barbarossa from Bertinoro, Tuscany's Rosso di Montalcino, a young fruity Chianti Montalbano, or a young Rossese di Dolceacqua from Liguria.

　　　　　Menu: The pie is a one-dish meal, needing only a light antipasto, a salad, and dessert. Begin with small portions of Grilled Winter Endives (page 337), or a few slices of coppa (page 474) served with Marinated Baby Onions (page 16). Have the Salad of Mixed Greens and Fennel (page 349) with the pie or after it, then dessert of Ugo Falavigna's Apple Cream Tart (page 411) or Caramelized Almond Tart (page 409).

Cook's Notes　**Variations:** For polenta casseroles with a variety of fillings, including meatless ones, see the main polenta recipe on page 352.

January Pork
Arrosto con Bacche di Ginepro e Foglie di Alloro

Juniper berries and bay leaves bring soft spicy flavors to pork. In the days when the laborers and tenant farmers of Emilia-Romagna ate only what they could grow or barter for, fresh pork was a January treat. The family pig began its metamorphosis into salami, prosciutto, and other cured meats before or after a local January saint's day. In Piacenza, for instance, it was Saint Anthony's day, January 17. Almost every bit of pork was preserved in some way or other to sustain the family through the coming year. But the loin and ribs were set aside for immediate eating. Seasonings for this roast change from one part of the region to the other, but in the countryside old-timers still consider roast pork January's feast.

[Serves 6 to 8]

4 tablespoons extra-virgin olive oil

10 juniper berries

1 large clove garlic

1 whole clove

⅛ teaspoon freshly ground black pepper

4-pound boneless center loin of pork

Salt

1 large California bay laurel leaf

⅔ cup dry white wine

½ cup Poultry/Meat Stock (page 66) or Quick Stock (page 68) (optional)

Method   **Working Ahead:** *The pork must be marinated overnight, but do serve it right after roasting is completed.*

Seasoning the Pork: Combine the olive oil, juniper berries, garlic, clove, and pepper in a food processor. Process until finely chopped. Set the pork in a dish large enough to hold it snugly, and rub the entire surface with the spice mixture. Lightly cover the meat with plastic wrap, and refrigerate 18 to 24 hours.

Roasting: Preheat the oven to 325°F. Transfer the pork, with its marinade, to a shallow roasting pan. Spoon any remaining marinade over the pork. Sprinkle the meat lightly with salt, and set the bay leaf atop the meat. Roast 1 hour and 50 minutes, or until an instant-reading thermometer inserted in the roast's center reads 150°F. (Today's lean pork dries out if cooked beyond about 155°F. At 150°F the meat is safe, juicy, and barely blushed with rose pink.) As the meat cooks, baste it frequently with the pan juices and the wine. Add the wine in thirds: The first third goes over the pork after about 30 minutes of cooking. Add another third after 20 minutes. The last addition is poured over the meat after another 10 minutes. Add a little water if the pan juices threaten to burn.

Serving: Have a warm serving platter ready. Once the meat is done, remove it to the platter and keep warm. Degrease the pan juices and keep them hot. If the pan juices are skimpy, set the pan over high heat and stir in the broth. Simmer the juices as you scrape up the brown bits. Taste for seasoning and keep warm. Thinly slice the pork and arrange it on the warm platter. Moisten with the pan juices, and serve hot.

Suggestions   **Wine:** A soft red Dolcetto d'Alba from Piemonte, a red Bonarda of Piacenza, or the Trentino–Alto Adige region's red Teroldego Rotaliano.

Menu: Serve Almond Spice Broth (page 237) or Soup of Porcini Mushrooms (page 226) as a first course. Accompany the pork with Basil and Onion Mashed Potatoes (page 345) and Garlic-Sautéed Cabbage (page 331), Sweet Fennel Jewish Style (page 335), or steamed broccoli. Make dessert fresh pears and grapes with unshelled nuts for cracking, Paola Bini's Sweet Ravioli (page 424), or Nonna's Jam Tart (page 413).

From the fantasy land of plenty, Cucagna, dogs tied with strings of sausage and children born painlessly, as mothers dance and sing, by Giuseppe Maria Mitelli, 1703

Beef-Wrapped Sausage
Cotechino in Galera

Although cotechino sausage is found throughout the north of Italy, Modena claims it as its own. Rolling up cotechino in a big, thin slice of beef and simmering it in local wine makes an old-style Modena dish that everyone loves to call "Imprisoned Cotechino." It is traditionally served with mashed potatoes to sop up all the pan sauce.

[Serves 6 to 8]

3 quarts water

1½ pounds uncooked cotechino
  sausage

2 pounds beef top round steak, cut
  1¼ to 1½ inches thick, about 6
  inches wide by 10 inches long

Freshly ground black pepper to
  taste

½ medium onion, minced

2 tablespoons extra-virgin olive oil

1 large California bay laurel leaf

1 clove garlic, crushed

1 bottle Bardolino or other
  light-bodied red wine

3 cups Poultry/Meat Stock (page
  66) or Quick Stock (page 68)

Method

Working Ahead: *The cotechino sausage can be half-cooked 1 day before wrapping it in the beef. The finished dish mellows nicely if undercooked a little, then refrigerated overnight, covered. Gently rewarm it the next day for serving.*

Preparing the Cotechino: Bring the water to a gentle bubble in a 4-quart saucepan. Pierce the sausage in several places with a fork, and slip it into the water. Adjust the heat until the water quivers but does not bubble. Cook the cotechino 30 minutes, or until an instant-reading thermometer inserted into its center reads 120°F. Drain the sausage and set it aside to cool while you prepare its beef wrapping.

Wrapping the Cotechino: Butterfly the round steak along its long side, opening it up like a book. Season the inside with pepper and a tablespoon of the minced onion. Cut away the skin from the cotechino, and place the sausage on the beef. Roll it up, encasing the sausage completely in the beef with only its ends showing. Using cotton string, secure the roast by tying it at 1-inch intervals.

Cooking and Serving: Heat the oil in a 4-quart saucepan that will hold the meat snugly. Take about 35 minutes to brown the meat slowly over medium heat, until deep golden brown on three sides. Add the remaining onion and the bay leaf as you brown the last side. Remove the meat from the pan. Add the garlic and wine to the pan and bring to a gentle bubble. Scrape up the brown glaze from the bottom of the pan. Keep the pan uncovered as you boil off three quarters of the wine, taking about 15 minutes. Then add the meat and stock, bringing them to a gentle bubble again. Partially cover the pan. Cook over low heat 2 hours, or until an instant-reading thermometer inserted into the center of the cotechino reads 170°F. (If you are cooking this ahead, cool the meat in the liquid. Refrigerate, and lift the hardened fat from the surface before reheating.) Have a serving platter warming in a low oven. When you are ready to serve, skim the fat from the sauce. Transfer the cotechino to a heated platter and keep warm. Concentrate the sauce's flavors by boiling it, uncovered, 3 to 5 minutes, or until reduced by half. Once the sauce is reduced, return the meat to the pan. Bubble gently 20 minutes, covered, if the meat is cold. Warm only about 5 minutes if the meat is hot. Trim away the string, and cut into slices between ¼ and ½ inch thick. Overlap the slices on a heated platter, and moisten with the sauce. Pass the remaining sauce separately.

Suggestions   **Wine:** Modena's dry, fruity Lambrusco is drunk with the cotechino. From other parts of Italy, have a fuller red like Tuscany's Montescudaio, Sicily's red Rapitalà, or "La Monella" from Braida di Giacomo Bologna.

Menu: Serve with Baked Polenta (page 353) or fresh Polenta (page 352). Keep to the Modena theme with an antipasto of Balsamic Vegetables (page 18) served with a few slices of salami (page 501), or small portions of Salad of Tart Greens with Prosciutto and Warm Balsamic Dressing (page 26). For dessert, serve fresh pears with chunks of Parmigiano-Reggiano or Modena Crumbling Cake (page 400).

Cook's Notes   **Cotechino:** For information how to buy and use cotechino, see page 475.

Zampone of the Aristocrats
Zampone Nobile

The Modenese mark festive holidays and family celebrations with their legendary balsamic vinegar and their famed zampone sausage. Slices of the sausage are served over mashed potatoes or braised lentils. Their final seasoning is a drizzle of the best of balsamic vinegars. You could also serve the zampone and vinegar as Modenese aristocrats did years ago: with a <u>zabaione</u> custard, flavored with balsamic vinegar. According to Renato Bergonzini, "Old families exalted <u>zabaione</u> with spoonfuls of their best balsamic vinegars. Zampone and balsamic vinegar delight us Modenese—our two most extraordinary foods married on a single plate."

[Serves 8 to 10]

continued

1 zampone sausage (6 to 8
  pounds)
¼ cup balsamic vinegar
  (artisan-made *tradizionale* is
  preferred, but a fine commercial
  vinegar can be used)
  Potato Purée
5 pounds red-skinned potatoes
6 tablespoons (3 ounces) unsalted
  butter, or more to taste

About 1½ cups milk
Salt and freshly ground black
  pepper to taste
  **Zabaione Custard with Balsamic
  Vinegar**
8 egg yolks
3 tablespoons sugar
1 to 3 tablespoons artisan-made
  tradizionale balsamic vinegar or
  fine commercial balsamic vinegar

Method   **Working Ahead:** *The Modenese have a practical and easy way of preparing
zampone ahead. The zampone is prepared early in the day, but undercooked by about 30
minutes. Still in its cooking water, the sausage is refrigerated or put outside in the winter
cold. An hour and a half before serving, it is slowly brought to a bubble over medium heat.
Then the temperature is lowered, and the sausage is poached in water that is barely quivering
15 to 20 minutes to heat it through. The potato purée (or braised lentils) can be made 24
hours ahead and refrigerated, covered, in a shallow baking dish. Reheat, covered with foil,
30 minutes in a 350°F oven. The zabaione custard must be made shortly before serving.*

   Preparing the Zampone: Plan on cooking the zampone between 18 and 20
minutes per pound for a 7- to 8-pound sausage, about 25 minutes per pound for 4
to 6 pounds. Rinse and dry the zampone. Using a needle, pierce the skin in about
ten places. Wrap it tightly in cheesecloth or a kitchen towel, and secure it by tying
it with cotton string at 1½-inch intervals down the length of the sausage.

   Cooking the Zampone: Use a fish poacher long enough to hold the zampone
or a stockpot tall enough to immerse the sausage. Fill the pot with water and bring
it to a lively bubble. Slip in the zampone and adjust the heat so the water bubbles
every 20 seconds or so. If the top of the sausage protrudes above the top of the pot,
cover the pot with foil and seal it to the edges. Poach 18 to 25 minutes per pound
(about 2 hours), or until an instant-reading thermometer inserted into the sausage's
center reads 160°F.

   Making the Potato Purée: While the zampone is cooking (or a day ahead), boil
the potatoes in a 6-quart pot, 20 to 30 minutes, or until tender. Peel them, and pass
them through a food mill fitted with the fine blade into a large metal bowl. (Do not
use a food processor, as it makes gummy mashed potatoes.) While the potatoes are
still hot, blend in the butter and milk. Use enough milk to create a thick but creamy
consistency. Season with salt and pepper. If you will be serving the potatoes within
an hour or so, keep them warm by setting the bowl over a pot of simmering water.
Stir occasionally with a spatula. If preparing 24 hours ahead, butter a 2½-quart

baking dish. Spread the purée in the dish, cover with foil, and refrigerate. Reheat, covered, 30 minutes in a 350°F oven.

Making the Zabaione: Fill a 3-quart saucepan a third full with water. Bring it to a lively bubble over medium heat. In a large metal bowl, beat together the yolks and the sugar. (Use 2 tablespoons sugar for *tradizionale* vinegar, 3 tablespoons for commercial balsamic.) If you are using commercial vinegar, beat in half of it now. Set the bowl over the bubbling water, taking care that it does not touch the water. Whisk the custard 3 to 5 minutes. It should be foamy, but thick enough to leave a trail at the bottom of the bowl. Lift the bowl from the water, and beat in all the *tradizionale* vinegar or the remaining half of the commercial. Immediately turn the custard into a serving bowl, and serve warm.

Serving: Have a serving platter warming in a low oven. Remove the cooked zampone from the pot by hooking a large fork under the string and lifting the sausage to a cutting board. Carefully remove the string and cheesecloth. Slice half the zampone into ¼- to ½-inch-thick rounds. Spoon the hot potato purée onto the warm platter. Arrange the uncut portion of the sausage and the slices on the potatoes. If you are not serving the *zabaione,* drizzle the sausage with a few drops of balsamic vinegar, and serve hot. If you are serving the *zabaione,* omit the drops of balsamic. Pass the warm *zabaione* in a sauceboat. Only a spoonful of the custard is used on each serving. (Although the skin is vital to the sausage's juiciness, many diners trim it away, concentrating on the meat stuffing.)

Suggestions   **Wine:** In Modena, Lambrusco's grapey acidity cuts the zampone's richness and lightens its impact. From other parts of Italy, drink a red Freisa Secco or "La Monella" Braida di Giacomo Bologna from Piemonte, the Lombardia region's lively and fizzy red Sangue di Giuda, or a young Valpolicella Classico from the Veneto.

Menu: Before the zampone, offer nothing more than a cup of homemade broth with a few tiny pastas. Instead of the potatoes, zampone could be served with Lentils Modena Style (page 347). With either lentils or potatoes, serve Spiced Spinach with Almonds (page 330). A traditional dessert is Modena Crumbling Cake (page 400) for dipping into sweet wine, or Home-Style Jam Cake (page 401).

Cook's Notes **Zampone:** Modena's zampone are not imported into the United States as of this writing. American-made ones range in size from 3 to 8 pounds, depending upon their producer. Check the size before ordering. Also check if the sausage is pre-cooked, since then it needs only heating in water rather than the cooking described above. If zampone is unobtainable, substitute one or two cotechino sausages. See page 506 for information on buying zampone, and page 509 for Mail-Order Sources. If substituting cotechino, see page 475.

Balsamic Vinegar: For information on commercial and artisan-made vinegars, see page 467.

Treviso radicchio in the Bologna marketplace

VEGETABLE SIDE DISHES

No other element of Emilia-Romagna's cuisine heralds the seasons with such color and verve as the vegetable. In the region's marketplaces all foods change from month to month, but vegetables are a kaleidoscope of the passing year.

Spring brings every imaginable shade of green, accented with delicate browns and whites. There are asparagus, wild nettle, peas, artichokes, dandelion, fava beans, new garlic, wild mushrooms, and lettuces of every description.

Colors strengthen with summer, turning primary and sharp: eggplant; tomatoes; peppers in yellow, red and green; dark green lettuces; green beans; broccoli; onions of red, gold and white; carrots; celery; herbs; and zucchini with its sun-yellow flowers intact.

Autumn moves across the spectrum to golds and purples: huge cabbages in purple and green; dark spinach, chard and chicories; brown porcini; purple beets and long-leafed black cabbage. Squashes come in yellow, orange and brown. Chestnuts look like mahogany nuggets next to russet-and-cream-striped borlotti beans.

Winter cools to maroons, whites, and the icy greens of fennel, cauliflower, leeks, potatoes, braided garlic, kale, dried beans, truffles, and olives. Radicchio appears as long leaves, compact heads, or large roses.

Those forms of radicchio are among Emilia-Romagna's favorite vegetables, along with other tart greens, both wild and cultivated, to use for salads, grilling and sautéing. They are joined by sweet fennel, wild mushrooms, zucchini, cauliflower, beets, tomatoes, potatoes, colorful peppers, and onions, which serve not only as an ingredient but stand on their own as first courses and side dishes. Leafy chard, sweet squashes, cabbage, eggplant, asparagus and green beans are also especially popular.

Many of these vegetables are included in this chapter, which offers the simplest recipes in this book. They are purposely so—these are side dishes.

Italian vegetable recipes usually fall into one of two categories. There are dishes that are complex and assertive, standing on their own as first courses or antipasti. You will find them in the "The Antipasto Course" and in "Risotto, Soup, and Vegetable First Courses." Then there are dishes of more subtle or less complicated structure, meant to complement and bring out the best of poultry, seafoods, and meats. These are the side dishes you will discover in the following pages. Sometimes the dividing line blurs between a vegetable side dish and a vegetable first course. A number of the dishes collected here could happily be enjoyed on their own, but generally these are best as accompaniments to other foods.

This selection of recipes shares the wealth found in Emilia-Romagna's back gardens and bustling farms. Vegetables are precious, a link to the earth and to Italy's agricultural past that almost everyone I know there does not want to lose. Even if it means a tiny patch of earth behind a city apartment building, many of the people of Emilia-Romagna still grow their own vegetables. A corporate executive boasts of his spinach harvest, and of the green pasta his mother still makes with it. The mechanic who fills my car in a gas station outside of Ravenna tells me how he preserves his peppers each year, and how the family has Sunday dinner in his garden as soon as the weather turns warm.

The wisdom accumulated from centuries of cooking goes into preparing the precious produce. Vegetables are usually cooked in one of three ways. Boiling accents their pure, fresh flavors. Cooking them in any number of variations on the sauté/braise theme enlivens, mellows, or broadens their character. Baking and grilling add the dimension of caramelization and concentrated flavors.

I prefer steaming to boiling. This is where my American taste supercedes Italian tradition. Also I like my vegetables a little less cooked than my Italian relatives do. These recipes reflect those preferences.

Sautéing and braising do splendid things to vegetables. Browning onion in a little olive oil before sautéing cooked spinach, or another precooked vegetable, is a basic expression of the technique. Raw vegetables sautéed until cooked take on even more complex character—for example, green beans browned with onion and simmered in stock, with mortadella as their flavoring.

Build on the sautéing idea by adding herbs, tomatoes, and other aromatics. Small amounts of prosciutto, pancetta, or salt pork impart even more dimension to a dish.

Yes, there is fat, but usually in small quantities. Sautéing maximizes the fat's usefulness and flavor, giving far more depth and character than is had by merely dabbing butter or margarine on boiled vegetables.

Grilling is another example of small amounts of fat producing big results. Rubbing vegetables with a little olive oil before grilling ensures browning and deep caramelized flavors. Baking concentrates flavors with no fat at all.

In this collection of recipes from Emilia-Romagna, a middle ground is struck in the quantity of oils and fats. I have striven to keep the flavors authentic while cutting back on the generous amounts of fat traditional in many of Emilia-Romagna's dishes. If you wish to decrease the quantities even further, most can be cut in half. The dishes will change, but they will still make fine eating.

Sweet Peas Parma
Piselli con Prosciutto di Parma

This is an old and much-loved springtime dish from Parma. Freshly picked peas are best but frozen tiny peas substitute successfully when fresh ones are starchy and tough. Serve the peas as a side dish with roasted and grilled main dishes.

[Serves 6 to 8 as a side dish, 4 to 6 as a first course]

1 pound shelled sweet peas or frozen tiny peas, defrosted

2 tablespoons extra-virgin olive oil

1 tablespoon unsalted butter

1 clove garlic, lightly pressed with the blade of a large knife

2 ounces thinly sliced Prosciutto di Parma, coarsely chopped

3 tablespoons crushed canned tomatoes, or 1 medium vine-ripened tomato, peeled, seeded, and chopped

Salt and freshly ground black pepper to taste

Method   **Working Ahead:** *The prosciutto and tomato can be sautéed several hours ahead, just short of adding the peas. Cool, cover lightly, and keep at room temperature. Reheat and finish the recipe just before serving.*

Preparing the Peas: If using fresh peas, steam 4 to 8 minutes, or until lightly cooked, rinse under cold water to stop the cooking and set the color, and drain.

Preparing the Flavor Base: Heat the oil and butter in a large skillet over medium heat. Add the garlic and swirl it over the bottom of the pan, pressing on it to extract its oils. Once the garlic is golden (after about 3 minutes), discard it. Take care not to cook the garlic beyond golden, as it will turn bitter. Add half the prosciutto and sauté quickly 2 to 3 minutes, or until it begins to color. Stir in the tomato and simmer a few moments, or until it is thick and all the excess moisture has evaporated.

Serving: Have a serving bowl warming in a low oven. Stir the peas (steamed or defrosted) into the prosciutto mixture, and cook over medium heat only long enough to heat them through. Stir in the remaining prosciutto, season to taste, turn into the warmed bowl, and serve immediately.

Suggestions   **Menu:** At the height of the pea season, serve this as a first course. Offer it as a side dish with Balsamic Roast Chicken (page 279), Christmas Capon (page 281), Erminia's Pan-Crisped Chicken (page 270), Grilled Beef with Balsamic Glaze (page 303), or Giovanna's Wine-Basted Rabbit (page 284).

Cook's Notes **Prosciutto di Parma:** For information on selecting and using Parma ham, see page 497.

Fresh Fava Beans with Young Sheep Cheese

Fave con il Pecorino

May in Romagna means new green fava beans. Their grass-colored skins are stretched so taut over the plump beans, they squeak as you pick them out of their cottony pods. Along with the fava, May brings young sheep cheeses (pecorino) from hillside herds. Pairing these green and white symbols of spring goes back further than most Romagnoli can remember. Etruscan shepherds probably rested in Romagna's mountains, eating raw favas and new sheep cheese with coarse mountain bread.

In May and June, much of Italy shares this fondness for favas and pecorino. Restaurants usually offer the combination as a cheese course after the meat dish. But home cooks, especially in the country, still make it a meal unto itself.

[Serves 6 to 8]

3 to 4 pounds fresh unshelled fava beans

1½ pounds young sheep (pecorino) cheese (such as Pecorino Dolce, Lago Monate Pecorino, Fiore Sardo, and Pecorino Toscano)

1 loaf Modena Mountain Bread (page 388) or other rough country bread

Freshly ground black pepper to taste

Olive oil (optional)

Method

Working Ahead: *There is no last-minute concern here. Set out the cheese several hours ahead. The favas are best at room temperature.*

Serving: This is finger food. Set out the unshelled fava beans in a basket and the cheese on a board. Arrange the sliced bread in another basket. Set plates for everyone. Invite diners to shell their favas, eating the beans raw, and to help themselves to chunks of cheese and bread. Leisurely nibbling is the pleasure of this dish. Some like cheese and favas together, with bread as the chaser. Others eat cheese and bread with the occasional bean. Pepper is sprinkled on the beans and cheese according to individual taste. Romagnoli near the Tuscan border share Tuscany's penchant for drizzles of olive oil over the beans and cheese. Try it as a variation on the theme.

Suggestions

Wine: In Romagna a young red Sangiovese di Romagna is right with this combination—a simple local wine for simple local food. Other possibilities are a young white Vernaccia di San Gimignano of Tuscany, Sardinia's young Rosé di Alghero, or a young red Cabernet Franc from the Friuli region's Collio Goriziano.

Cook's Notes **Young Sheep Cheese:** At this writing, Romagna sheep cheeses are rare in the United States, but other young Italian sheep cheeses make fine substitutions. You can find them in cheese shops and specialty food stores. They are *not* grating cheeses like pecorino Romano. These are younger and moister cheeses, with round, tangy flavors. The cheeses will be firm but not hard, sliceable, and good to eat on their own. Taste whatever is available in your area to decide on the ones you like best.

Finding the Fava

Fava beans are also known as broad beans, horse beans, Windsor beans, or shell beans. They appear in different parts of the United States at different times from March to July. Depending upon your locale, favas may be as common as the green bean, or may be found only in specialty food stores and markets specializing in foods from Mediterranean countries. Look for bright green unblemished pods with no signs of wilting or withering. The amount of favas called for in a recipe may seem excessive, but much of the weight comes from the bean's thick pods.

Green Beans with Balsamic Pesto
Fagliolini al Pesto Modenese

If the cooks of Genoa who created pesto centuries ago had had balsamic vinegar, I am certain it would have been as vital to the sauce as basil. When summer green beans are tender and full of sweetness, this pesto sets them off as little else can. Renato Bergonzini, Modena food historian and balsamic vinegar expert, provided this recipe, which is excellent hot or at room temperature. The pesto is good over pasta, steamed or roasted sweet peppers, broccoli, fennel, potatoes, or peas.

[Serves 6 to 8]

4 tablespoons extra-virgin olive oil
1 large clove garlic
1⅓ cups tightly packed fresh basil
    leaves
¾ cup (3 ounces) freshly grated
    Italian Parmigiano-Reggiano
    cheese

Salt and freshly ground black
    pepper to taste
1½ pounds fresh green beans,
    trimmed
4 to 5 tablespoons commercial
    balsamic vinegar blended with
    ½ teaspoon dark brown sugar

Method

Working Ahead: *The flavors of this dish are best when it is served right after the pesto and beans are combined, or when it is left at room temperature no more than 4 to 5 hours before serving. The pesto can be prepared several hours before the beans are cooked. Cover and keep it at room temperature until ready to toss with the beans. The finished dish can be served at room temperature, but do toss the basil pesto with freshly cooked hot beans, then let them cool down. Keep the beans at room temperature, as refrigeration alters flavors.*

Making the Pesto: Combine the olive oil and garlic in a blender or a food processor fitted with the steel blade. Blend until almost smooth. Add the basil and Parmigiano-Reggiano, and blend until the basil is finely chopped but not puréed. Season with salt and pepper, and set aside.

Cooking the Beans: Pour about 2 inches of water into a 6-quart pot. Place a collapsible steamer in the pot, cover, and bring the water to a fierce boil. Pile the beans in the steamer, cover the pot, and steam 6 minutes, or until tender crisp.

Finishing the Dish: Turn the beans into a shallow serving bowl. Add the pesto to the beans, stirring in the vinegar and sugar mixture. Toss to thoroughly coat the beans. Taste for seasoning, and serve hot or at room temperature.

continued

Suggestions   **Menu:** Serve with Herbed Seafood Grill (page 254), Lemon Roast Veal with Rosemary (page 294), Riccardo Rimondi's Chicken Cacciatora (page 275), Lamb with Black Olives (page 305), Giovanna's Wine-Basted Rabbit (page 284), or Porcini Veal Chops (page 290). The beans are fine as an antipasto with a few slices of coppa (page 474) or salami (page 501) before Risotto of Baby Artichokes and Peas (page 209), Tagliatelle with Light Veal Ragù (page 100), or "Priest Stranglers" with Fresh Clams and Squid (page 124).

Cook's Notes   **Olive Oil:** A flowery oil from Liguria is excellent in this dish. See page 485 for information on olive oils.

Woman Taking Vinegar from Barrel from *Tacuinum Sanitatis in Medicina* (Tables of Health in Accordance with Medical Science), 14th century, Northern Italy

Green Beans Bolognese
Fagliolini alla Bolognese

This is a special-occasion food that melts away on the tongue. The beans taste so special, they could stand on their own as a first course. As a side dish, they are particularly good with lemon- or balsamic-flavored roasts or grills.

[Serves 6 to 8 as a side dish or first course]

2 to 3 tablespoons extra-virgin olive oil

1 small to medium onion, thinly sliced

1 pound green beans, trimmed and halved crosswise

2 ounces mortadella, minced

1 cup Poultry/Meat Stock (page 66) or Quick Stock (page 68)

Pinch of ground cloves

Salt and freshly ground black pepper to taste

Method

Working Ahead: *The beans can be cooked several hours ahead and reheated. Hold them, lightly covered, at room temperature.*

Sautéing the Beans: Heat the oil in a large skillet over medium heat. Add the onion and sauté over medium-high heat 4 minutes, or until wilted. Then add the beans and cook over high heat 8 minutes, or until the onions are deep golden brown. Stir frequently with a wooden spatula. Stir in the mortadella, stock, and cloves, and bring to a gentle bubble over medium-low heat. Cover and cook 15 minutes (checking for sticking), or until the beans are tender. If the beans threaten to stick or scorch, stir in about ¼ cup water.

Finishing and Serving: Have a serving bowl warming in a low oven. Concentrate the flavors by uncovering the pot and boiling off all the liquid. Keep turning and stirring the beans to protect them from burning. Once there is only a thick sauce clinging to the beans, turn them into the warmed bowl and serve.

Suggestions

Menu: Serve with Erminia's Pan-Crisped Chicken (page 270), Lemon Roast Veal with Rosemary (page 294), or Balsamic Roast Chicken (page 279). Have them as a first course before any of the above dishes, or before Tagliatelle with Caramelized Onions and Fresh Herbs (page 101) or Tagliarini with Lemon Anchovy Sauce (page 112).

Herb and Garlic Grilled Eggplant
Melanzane alla Graticola

Eggplant, so good on its own, is also a culinary chameleon, absorbing herbs and spices to become any number of different dishes. In Romagna palm-size slices are steeped in garlic, basil, parsley, and olive oil before being grilled over hot coals. Eaten either hot or at room temperature, this is one of those simple but supremely satisfying dishes that goes with almost anything and is good eaten on its own. It doubles easily.

[Serves 6 to 8]

2 medium eggplants (2 to 2¼ pounds), sliced vertically into ¼-inch-thick slices

About ⅔ cup extra-virgin olive oil

4 large cloves garlic, minced

¾ cup minced Italian parsley

¾ cup minced fresh basil leaves

⅛ teaspoon freshly ground black pepper

Salt to taste

Method

Working Ahead: *The eggplant is equally fine hot off the grill or at room temperature. Refrigeration throws off its balance of tastes and texture, so grill it no more than 4 hours before eating and keep at room temperature.*

Marinating the Eggplant: Lightly brush both sides of each eggplant slice with oil. Blend together the garlic, parsley, basil, and pepper. Spread a little of the herb blend on both sides of each slice. Lay the slices side by side on a large platter, stacking them if necessary. Lightly cover with plastic wrap and let stand at room temperature 2 to 4 hours.

Grilling Outdoors: Burn down a charcoal fire (using real wood charcoal briquets if possible) until a white ash has formed on the briquets. The heat should be moderate. Sprinkle the eggplant slices with salt. Grill the (undrained) eggplant slices 10 minutes, turning once, or until deep golden brown on each side and soft when pierced with a knife. Spoon any seasonings left on the platter over each slice after turning.

Grilling Indoors: Grill the (undrained) eggplant slices over medium heat on a gridded skillet or stove-top grill 8 minutes, or until deep golden brown on each side. Spread any seasonings left on the platter over each slice before turning. Do this in several batches unless your cooking surface is large enough to hold all the slices in a single layer. Or preheat the broiler, adjusting the rack so the eggplant will be about 4 inches from the flame. Spread any marinade left in the bowl over the slices, and arrange them on a broiler pan in a single layer. Broil slowly 8 minutes, or until the slices are deep golden brown on each side and the eggplant is soft when pierced.

Serving: Transfer the finished slices to a platter and serve.

Suggestions **Menu:** Serve with Erminia's Pan-Crisped Chicken (page 270), Herbed Seafood Grill (page 254), Fresh Tuna Adriatic Style (page 256), Grilled Beef with Balsamic Glaze (page 303), Balsamic Roast Chicken (page 279), January Pork (page 312), or Maria Bertuzzi's Lemon Chicken (page 273).

Cook's Notes **Using Zucchini:** Treat thick vertical slices of zucchini the same way, grilling them over higher heat and taking only 1 to 2 minutes per side. They should be browned and tender but not mushy.

First- or Main-Course Variation: To have the eggplant as a first course or main dish, top the warm slices with long furls of Parmigiano-Reggiano or young sheep cheese (cut with a vegetable peeler). The warm slices could also be topped with spoonfuls of bubbling Winter Tomato Sauce (pages 62), then finished with the cheese.

Spiced Spinach with Almonds
Spinaci in Padella del Settecento

Far more interesting than Italy's usual sauté of spinach and onion is Emilia-Romagna's 17th-century version of the recipe. In it spinach cooks with spices, nuts, currants, and cheeses. Serve the dish just as they did centuries ago, as a side dish, especially with roast capon, chicken, game, turkey, or rabbit. It makes a fine stuffing for pastas or for small roasted birds such as Cornish hens. In Romagna the sauté, made without nuts, spices, and ricotta, tops hot Piadina flatbread. My own inclination is to keep in the delicious ingredients, cut the hot Piadina into small wedges, top them with the spinach, and serve it as an antipasto or with drinks.

[Serves 4 to 6 as a side dish]

2 pounds fresh spinach, trimmed

3 tablespoons extra-virgin olive oil

½ cup minced onion

1 large clove garlic, minced

⅛ teaspoon ground cinnamon

Generous pinch of freshly grated nutmeg

5 tablespoons blanched almonds, toasted and coarsely chopped

2 tablespoons currants

½ cup (4 ounces) fresh ricotta cheese

Salt and freshly ground black pepper to taste

1 cup (4 ounces) freshly grated Italian Parmigiano-Reggiano cheese

Method

Working Ahead: *The spinach can be cooked up to 24 hours in advance. Squeeze out as much of its moisture as possible, wrap, and refrigerate. Sauté shortly before serving to keep the color bright.*

Cooking the Spinach: Rinse the spinach in a sink full of cold water. Lift the leaves right from the water into an 8-quart pot, without shaking off any of the water clinging to them. Set the pot over medium heat, cover, and cook 5 minutes, or until the leaves are wilted but still a bright dark green. Immediately turn the spinach into a colander. Briefly run cold water over the spinach to cool it down and stop its cooking. Then squeeze out the excess moisture and coarsely chop.

Finishing and Serving: Have a serving bowl warming in a low oven. Heat the olive oil in a large skillet over medium heat. Add the onion and sauté 8 minutes over medium to medium-high heat, or until golden brown. Stir in the garlic and cook another minute. Add the spinach, cinnamon, nutmeg, almonds, and currants. Stir while sautéing over medium heat 2 minutes, or until heated through and aromatic. Stir in the ricotta and heat a few seconds. Season with salt and pepper. Turn the spinach mixture into the serving bowl, and toss with the Parmigiano-Reggiano cheese. Serve hot.

Suggestions   **Menu:** Serve with zampone (page 506), as a topping for *Piadina* flatbread (page 384), as a filling for *Spianata* (page 367), or with sautéed, roasted, or grilled dishes such as Herbed Seafood Grill (page 254), Pan-Roasted Quail (page 283), Giovanna's Wine-Basted Rabbit (page 284), Lamb, Garlic, and Potato Roast (page 307), Balsamic Roast Chicken (page 279), Porcini Veal Chops (page 290), or Christmas Capon (page 281). Use it in place of the artichoke stuffing in tortelloni (page 141).

Cook's Notes **Using Other Greens:** Swiss chard, turnip greens, broccoli rape, beet greens, romaine, escarole, curly endive, and young dandelion greens are all excellent prepared this way. Cook the greens first as described above. They should be crisp-tender but still brightly colored. The tarter greens need longer sautéing with an additional tablespoon of olive oil.

Garlic-Sautéed Cabbage
Cavolo con Aglio

This old-fashioned dish from Romagna is a garlic lover's delight. Slow cooking in olive oil turns the garlic nutty and golden. Cooked cabbage is then browned in the garlic oil. Serve it with roasted meats and poultry. A dividend of the dish is how good it is tossed with fresh pasta.

[Serves 6 to 8]

1 large head green cabbage (about 2 pounds)

Salt (optional)

4 to 6 tablespoons extra-virgin olive oil

6 large cloves garlic, cut into ¼-inch dice

Salt and freshly ground black pepper

Method   **Working Ahead:** *The cabbage can be boiled early in the day, and the garlic can be sautéed then too. Refrigerate the cabbage, covered, until about 1 hour before sautéing. Keep the garlic covered at room temperature.*

continued

Cooking the Cabbage: Cut off any bruised outer leaves of cabbage. Trim away the tough base, but leave the core so the wedges remain intact. Cut the cabbage vertically into eight wedges. Bring a 6-quart pot of water to the boil (adding 1 tablespoon salt, if desired). Drop in the cabbage and boil, uncovered, 10 minutes, or until the core is barely tender when pierced with a knife. Drain in a colander, rinsing the wedges with cold water to stop the cooking. Then spread the wedges on paper towels to dry.

Sautéing the Garlic: Heat the olive oil in a large sauté pan over the lowest possible heat. Cook the garlic slowly, stirring frequently, 8 minutes, or until pale gold on all sides. Do not cook to dark brown, or it will turn bitter. Lift out the garlic with a slotted spoon and spread it on a plate. Reserve.

Finishing and Serving: Have a serving bowl warming in a low oven. Chop the cabbage into bite-size pieces. Turn the heat under the sauté pan up to medium-high. Add the cabbage and sauté about 10 minutes, turning with two wooden spatulas. Use higher heat if necessary to brown the pieces. Once it is browned, season with salt and pepper. Stir in the reserved garlic, and cook a few seconds to blend the flavors. Turn the cabbage into the warmed bowl, and serve hot.

Menu: Serve the cabbage with *Piadina* (page 384), Balsamic Roast Chicken (page 279), Pan-Roasted Quail (page 283), Lamb with Black Olives (page 305), Lemon Roast Veal with Rosemary (page 294), or Mardi Gras Chicken (page 277).

Cook's Notes **Pasta Variation:** Toss the hot cabbage with ¾ recipe Egg Pasta (page 80), cut for tagliatelle (page 90), or with 12 ounces imported boxed tagliatelle. Serve with 2 cups freshly grated Parmigiano-Reggiano cheese. Offer this either as a first course or as a supper main dish.

Sweet-and-Sour Onions
Cipolle alla Bolognese

Onions have their own special richness, and they absorb flavorings like few other vegetables. This lusty old Bolognese dish achieves its sweet-sour tastes in an unusual way. Instead of vinegar and sugar, the acid of the tomato and the sweetness of the unsalted butter create the flavors. The onions taste best after resting overnight in their sauce. This recipe doubles easily.

[Serves 6 to 8]

6 quarts water
2½ pounds white or yellow
    onions, 1½ to 2 inches in
    diameter, unpeeled
4 tablespoons (2 ounces) unsalted
    butter
Salt and freshly ground black
    pepper

½ cup drained canned tomatoes,
    crushed
¼ cup tomato purée
1 tablespoon sugar
2 tablespoons red wine vinegar
¼ cup water

Method

Working Ahead: *Prepare the onions 1 day ahead, taking care not to overcook them; cover and refrigerate. Rewarm in a covered sauté pan over medium-low heat about 20 minutes. Another ¼ to ½ cup of water may be needed in the pan to keep the onions from scorching.*

Precooking the Onions: Bring the water to a boil in a large pot. Cut a cross in the root end of each onion. Drop them into the boiling water, cook at a full boil 2 minutes, and immediately turn into a colander. Rinse with cold water. Peel by making a shallow slit down the side of each onion and slipping off the skin.

Braising the Onions: Heat the butter in a large skillet over medium heat. Sauté the onions, adding generous sprinklings of salt and pepper, 8 minutes, or until they begin to color and the butter is nut-brown. Keep turning the onions with wooden spatulas, adjusting the heat so the butter does not burn before the onions start to brown. Blend in the tomatoes and purée, and cook over medium-low heat 5 minutes, or until the tomatoes have thickened. Add the sugar, vinegar, and water. Keep the pan uncovered as you bring the liquid to a lively bubble and cook, turning the onions in the sauce, 3 minutes, or until the liquid has evaporated and the sauce is clinging to the onions. The onions should show only a little resistance when pierced with a knife. If they are still too firm, add another ¼ cup water and continue cooking, uncovered, at a slow bubble until tender. There should be enough sauce to generously moisten the onions. If you are rewarming them, add yet another ¼ cup water.

Serving: Have a serving bowl warming in a low oven. Turn the hot onions into the bowl, and serve.

Suggestions   **Menu:** Serve with Lemon Roast Veal with Rosemary (page 294), Christmas Capon (page 281), Romagna Grilled Veal Chops (page 297), Giovanna's Wine-Basted Rabbit (page 284), or any grilled meat or poultry.

Bologna onion seller, 17th century, by Giuseppe Maria Mitelli

Sweet Fennel Jewish Style
Finocchi alla Giudia

Emilia-Romagna's Jewish heritage dates back to the 11th century, when Jewish scholars, landowners, merchants, doctors, and teachers lived throughout the region. Over the centuries a treasury of Jewish recipes evolved, importing Jewish dishes from other places and providing Jewish interpretations of local specialties. In this old recipe, popular in Romagna but eaten throughout Italy, garlic seasons fresh fennel as it sautés in olive oil. It is a wonderfully gentle way of heightening fennel's delicate flavors. Either hot or at room temperature, the fennel complements roasted poultry and is especially good with game and lamb.

[Serves 6 to 8]

4 medium-size bulbs fennel (about 1½ pounds without tops), quartered and trimmed of stalks and leaves
4 tablespoons extra-virgin olive oil

3 large cloves garlic, cut into ¼-inch dice
½ cup water
Salt and freshly ground black pepper to taste

Method

Working Ahead: *The fennel can be prepared early in the day and stored, covered, at room temperature. Serve it reheated or at room temperature.*

Preparing the Fennel: Discard any hard or bruised outside layers of the fennel bulb. Trim away the darkened base of the fennel. Cut the bulb in half lengthwise, and then cut into julienne strips between ¼ and ½ inch wide.

Cooking the Garlic: Heat the oil in a large skillet over medium-low heat. Add the garlic, turn the heat to low, and cook 8 minutes, or until the pieces are pale blond. Take care not to cook beyond a golden color, or the garlic will turn bitter. Immediately scoop out the garlic with a slotted spoon and reserve.

Cooking the Fennel: Have a platter warming in a low oven. Turn the heat up to medium-high and add the fennel to the pan. Sauté about 10 minutes, turning the pieces so they become golden brown on all sides. Once the fennel is browned, add the water to the pan and sprinkle the fennel with salt and pepper. Cover the pan tightly and cook over medium-low heat 5 to 8 minutes, or until the fennel is tender. Uncover the pan and boil away any liquid left in it. Sprinkle the fennel with the reserved garlic. Serve on the heated platter.

continued

Suggestions   **Menu:** Serve with traditional Jewish dishes like poached or roasted chicken, cholent, or pot roast, as well as with non-Jewish ones—Balsamic Roast Chicken (page 279), Herbed Seafood Grill (page 254), Erminia's Pan-Crisped Chicken (page 270), Lamb with Black Olives (page 305), Pan-Roasted Quail (page 283), January Pork (page 312), or Thanksgiving turkey.

Oven-Roasted Radicchio
Radicchio al Forno

Brown, crisp, and tart, this unusual side dish contrasts richly flavored dishes like capon, roast chicken, lamb and pork. It is as good at room temperature as it is hot. When the weather is warm, people of the Po River plain roast radicchio outdoors over wood fires. This rendition makes roasted radicchio possible year-round by using the oven.

[Serves 6 to 8]

4 large heads (about 1½ pounds) radicchio	Additional olive oil
2 tablespoons extra-virgin olive oil	Salt and freshly ground black pepper

Method   **Working Ahead:** *The radicchio can be roasted early in the day. Allow it to cool, then cover lightly and keep at room temperature. Rewarm, uncovered, in a 300°F oven about 10 minutes, or serve at room temperature.*

Trimming the Radicchio: Remove any loose outer leaves from each head of radicchio (reserve them for Tagliatelle with Balsamic Radicchio, page 98). Using a paring knife, trim away any bruised or brown areas of the leaves. If there is a stem, peel away the surface but leave stem intact. If there is no stem, peel away any discolored portion of the core. Cut each head vertically into quarters so that the leaves are still attached to the core.

Roasting the Radicchio: Preheat the oven to 450°F. To speed up browning, use a large heavy roasting pan that measures about 12 by 24 inches and is 2 inches deep. Brush the bottom of the pan with the 2 tablespoons oil. Arrange the radicchio quarters, cut side down, in a single layer, with the pieces barely touching. Sprinkle generously with olive oil and then lightly with salt and pepper. Spread a sheet of aluminum foil over the top of the radicchio, slip the pan into the oven, and roast 20 minutes. Turn the heat down to 350°F and roast 1 hour to 1 hour and 20 minutes, or until the radicchio is wilted and beginning to crisp. It will be almost flattened like a fan, and dark red-brown. Uncover and turn the pieces over. Roast, uncovered, another 10 minutes, or until dark brown and quite crisp but not burnt. Serve hot or at room temperature.

Suggestions   **Menu:** The radicchio complements roasted, sautéed, or grilled main dishes. It pairs beautifully with Christmas Capon (page 281), January Pork (page 312), Rabbit Dukes of Modena (page 286), Balsamic Roast Chicken (page 279), Lamb, Garlic, and Potato Roast (page 307), Lamb with Black Olives (page 305), and Mardi Gras Chicken (page 277).

Cook's Notes **Selecting Radicchio:** To test for bitterness, always taste a little bit of the leaf from near the core before selecting a head.

Grilled Winter Endives
Cicorie alla Griglia

There are few vegetables that are not improved by grilling. Flavors intensify with browning. Many vegetables become so robust that they can easily stand in for meats as second courses. If you are looking for a meatless second dish that is light yet satisfying, a variety of grilled vegetables could be the answer. I like the touch of bitterness in grilled radicchio and Belgian endive. Other Emilia-Romagna favorites are eggplant, zucchini, peppers, onions, curly endive, and escarole. This recipe for oven and stove-top grilling stands in nicely when grilling out-of-doors is impossible.

[Serves 6 as a side dish, 4 as a main dish]

3 Belgian endives, split vertically
2 heads radicchio, each cut
   vertically into 3 wedges
⅓ cup extra-virgin olive oil
1 large clove garlic, minced
   (optional)

Salt and freshly ground black
   pepper to taste
3 tablespoons minced Italian
   parsley
1 cup (4 ounces) freshly grated
   Italian Parmigiano-Reggiano
   cheese (optional)

Method   **Working Ahead:** *The vegetables have more flavor when sliced and marinated several hours before cooking. They are good hot from the grill or at room temperature, and can be grilled several hours before serving.*

continued

Marinating the Endives: Toss the endives with the olive oil, garlic, and a little salt and pepper. Let stand at room temperature about 2 hours.

Oven Grilling: Preheat the broiler and set the oven rack so that when the endives are in their pan, they will be about 4 inches away from the flame. Trim away any wilted leaves from the endives and radicchio. If they have not been marinating in the oil ahead of time, rub each piece with a little oil. Cover a broiler pan with foil. Arrange the endives split side up and the radicchio wedges on their sides, all in a single layer in the pan. Sprinkle with the minced garlic (if you are using it) and a light dusting of salt and pepper. Broil 5 minutes, or until the endives are deep golden brown on one side and the radicchio is wilting and tinged with brown. Using tongs, turn the pieces and let them brown on the other side. The browning is the key: It must happen gradually, so the flavors are deep and rich. Do not let the vegetables burn. The radicchio will wilt, but the endive holds its shape nicely. When they are done, set the vegetables on a serving platter. Sprinkle with the parsley just before serving.

Stove-top Grilling: Prepare the endives and radicchio with olive oil as described above. Preheat a gridded skillet, griddle, or built-in stove-top grill over medium heat. Once it is hot, turn the heat to medium-high and arrange the vegetables in a single layer on the grill. Sprinkle with the garlic, salt, and pepper. Lower the heat if necessary so that it takes 8 to 10 minutes to cook the endives to a rich crusty brown on both sides.

Serving: Serve hot or at room temperature. Pass the cheese separately.

Suggestions **Menu:** Serve as a side dish with Fresh Tuna Adriatic Style (page 256), Herbed Seafood Grill (page 254), Lemon Roast Veal with Rosemary (page 294), Pan-Roasted Quail (page 283), or Maria Bertuzzi's Lemon Chicken (page 273). Serve as a second course after Spaghetti with Shrimps and Black Olives (page 132), Cappellacci with Sweet Squash (page 145), Classic White Risotto (page 201), Risotto of Baby Artichokes and Peas (page 209), or Ferrara's Soup of the Monastery (page 220). Make a light antipasto by serving the vegetables at room temperature, sprinkled with Parmigiano-Reggiano cheese.

Cook's Notes **Adding Balsamic Vinegar:** Balsamic vinegar and grilled vegetables are a superb pairing. See page 469 for information on selecting a good commercial vinegar. Drizzle 3 to 4 tablespoons over the hot or room-temperature grilled vegetables.

Zucchini, Peppers, and Onions Variation: Serve these individually or together. Slice 4 medium zucchini vertically about ¼ inch thick. Cut 4 large red and yellow bell peppers into large wedges. Cut 3 medium onions vertically into ¼-inch-thick slices. Toss each of the vegetables with ¼ cup extra-virgin olive oil, 1 minced garlic clove, and several grindings of black pepper (4 tablespoons chopped fresh marjoram or basil could be added). Let stand 1 to 2 hours. Grill 2 inches from the broiler flame, or over medium-high heat on a stove-top grill, until cooked to a rich deep brown color. Timing will vary from about 2 minutes per side for the zucchini to about 5 minutes per side for the onions. Serve the vegetables hot or at room temperature.

Sweet Squash for Yom Kippur
Zucca Disfatta

For centuries the sweet squash found in Ferrara has been cooked with sautéed onion and fresh citron to mark the last night of Yom Kippur. Butternut and a little baked yam come close to the sweet spiciness of Ferrara's squash. Fresh citron is difficult to find, but blanched lemon and orange zests flavored with a pinch of cinnamon do well in its place.

[Serves 6 to 8]

2½ to 3 pounds butternut squash
1 pound yams
3 tablespoons minced fresh citron
    rind, or 3 tablespoons mixed
    shredded lemon and orange zests
1 large onion, minced

3 tablespoons extra-virgin olive oil
4 cups water
¼ teaspoon ground cinnamon
Salt and freshly ground black
    pepper to taste

Method   **Working Ahead:** *The squash can be prepared up to 24 hours in advance; cover and refrigerate. Rewarm, covered, in the top of a double boiler.*

Baking the Squash and Yams: Preheat the oven to 400°F. Halve the squash vertically and scoop out the seeds. Lay a sheet of aluminum foil over a baking sheet, and lightly moisten the foil with olive oil. Set the squash halves on the foil, skin side up. Scrub and prick the yams. Set them on the pan with the squash. Bake both vegetables 1 hour, or until each is easily pierced with a knife. Cool for a short time, and then pass their pulp through a food mill into a large saucepan, or mash by hand. (A food processor makes the mixture too liquid.)

Preparing the Citron or Citrus Zests: Whether you are using the citron or the lemon and orange zests, bring the water to a boil in a small saucepan. Boil the rind or zests 3 minutes, and drain in a colander.

Finishing and Serving: Heat the olive oil in a medium skillet over medium heat. Take about 15 minutes to slowly sauté the onions until they are golden brown.

continued

Add the onions to the squash mixture, along with the citron rind or fruit zests and the cinnamon. Set over medium-low heat and cook slowly, stirring often with a wooden spatula to keep it from scorching, 15 minutes, or until most of the vegetables' excess moisture has evaporated. The mixture will be thick and full-flavored. Season with salt and pepper, and serve hot.

Suggestions **Menu:** In Italy the squash often accompanies poached turkey. Also serve it with roasted, sautéed, or grilled meats, or with poultry, such as Balsamic Roast Chicken (page 279), Christmas Capon (page 281), January Pork (page 312), or Mardi Gras Chicken (page 277).

Cook's Notes **Fresh Citron Rind:** Citron has been popular in Mediterranean cuisines for millennia. It shares lemon's sourness but is fragrant with spice and hints of resin. The fruit's rind is usually candied, but in this recipe it is used fresh. Since fresh citron is scarce in the United States, I have suggested the substitution of lemon and orange zests. Occasionally you will find fresh citron during the Jewish holiday of Sukkoth.

The Shop of Nuta

Ferrara's Jewish community began growing into one of Renaissance Italy's largest in 1275, when the ruling Este family guaranteed protection to the region's Jews in a time of rising anti-Semitism. By the second half of the 16th century, Ferrara had become a major Jewish center, opening its gates to Jews from Germany and those escaping the Spanish Inquisition. Today the community is diminished, but its traditions and foods are still part of the city.

One element still spoken of with longing is the shop of Nuta. Before World War II Nuta Ascoli kept a food shop and rooming house in the Jewish quarter. Caviar from Po River sturgeon was among Nuta's specialties. Certainly caviar is an unlikely food for Italy, but evidently it was one that Ferrara had quite a reputation for producing. She also made preserved mushrooms, turkey soup with *farro* grain, Passover cookies and her own extraordinary delicious renditions of goose prosciutto and salami. My very first meal in Ferrara began with a platter of thinly sliced goose-breast prosciutto prepared in Nuta's manner. It was moist, sweet and wonderfully rich. I was told that for centuries Jewish cooks had preserved goose as the rest of Italy preserved the pig. Every November Nuta had continued this tradition, rubbing fresh goose breast with salt, pepper and cloves. The meat cured and dried until April, when it was eaten in celebration of Passover. Nuta is gone now, but the Italian-Jewish tradition of curing goose continues.

Asparagus in the Style of Parma
Asparagi alla Parmigiana

Sprinkling a little Parmigiano-Reggiano cheese over almost any vegetable brings out unexpected nuances of taste. Parma cooks have given vegetables this classic treatment for centuries. Although not traditional in Parma, olive oil could replace the butter in this dish with good success. The recipe doubles easily.

[Serves 4 to 6]

1 to 1¼ pounds pencil-slim asparagus
2 to 3 tablespoons unsalted butter
Salt and freshly ground black pepper

¼ cup (1 ounce) freshly grated Italian Parmigiano-Reggiano cheese

Method

Working Ahead: *The asparagus can be precooked early in the day for serving at dinnertime. Store them in a plastic bag in the refrigerator. Sauté them just before serving.*

Precooking the Asparagus: Trim the tough ends from the asparagus stalks. These are so slender that peeling is unnecessary; just rinse the stalks and tips well. Have a large bowl of ice water handy. If you own a special asparagus cooker, cook the asparagus in it 3 to 5 minutes, or until the stalks are just turning tender (test by piercing with a paring knife). They should still be a little crunchy. Lacking an asparagus cooker, half-fill a large skillet with water. Bring the water to a fierce boil. Making sure all the asparagus tips are pointing in the same direction, spread the stalks out in the boiling water with the aid of two wooden spatulas. Boil over high heat, uncovered, 3 to 5 minutes, or until a stalk is crisp-tender when pierced with a knife. They should still be a little crunchy. Using the two spatulas to scoop under the stalks, quickly lift the asparagus from the pan and immerse them in the ice water. This stops the cooking. After about 10 minutes remove them from the ice water and drain well.

Sautéing and Serving: Have a serving dish warming in a low oven. About 10 minutes before serving, heat the butter in a large skillet over medium-high heat. Add the asparagus and sauté, turning gently with the spatulas, until heated through. Sprinkle with salt and pepper. Serve on warm platter, sprinkled with the cheese.

Suggestions

Menu: Serve with Erminia's Pan-Crisped Chicken (page 270), Pan-Roasted Quail (page 283), Basil and Balsamic Veal Scallops (page 296), Herbed Seafood Grill (page 254), Christmas Capon (page 281), Porcini Veal Chops (page 290), or Lemon Roast Veal with Rosemary (page 294).

Grandmother's Gratin
La Vecchia

This is Parma country food, a gratin of casseroled vegetables made by mothers and grandmothers for as long as anyone can remember. Many eat it as a main dish with no accompaniments. La Vecchia literally translates as "the old woman." In this case it not only refers to the grandmothers who often make this dish, but also is the name of the boiled poultry and meats left over from making broth. Those leftovers were stretched into one-dish meals by layering the meats with vegetables. Today many leave out the meat, as I have done in this recipe. Otherwise the dish is unchanged. Each layer of the casserole is dabbed with a battuto, a minced blend of garlic, onion, celery leaves and stalk, and salt pork.

This dish is indestructible: you can reheat it, chill it, reheat it again, and still it is good. The recipe is adapted from one in Guglielmo Capacchi's book on the home cooking of Parma, La Cucina Popolare Parmigiana.

[Serves 6 to 8 as a side dish, 4 to 6 as a main dish]

Battuto

3 ounces lean salt pork, in 1 piece

2 large cloves garlic, minced

6 tablespoons minced Italian parsley

1 medium onion, minced

Top half of a medium celery stalk with many leaves, minced

2 tablespoons extra-virgin olive oil

Salt and freshly ground black pepper to taste

Vegetables

2 medium vine-ripened tomatoes, thinly sliced

1½ pounds small red-skinned potatoes, sliced about 1/16 inch thick

2 medium to large red bell peppers, sliced into thin rings

1 large onion, sliced into thin rings

Salt and freshly ground black pepper to taste

Method

Working Ahead: *The gratin can be cooked early in the day. Let it rest at room temperature, lightly covered, and then reheat in a 350°F oven about 20 minutes before serving. It can also be made 1 day ahead. Refrigerate covered, and then rewarm. Serve it hot or warm.*

Making the Battuto: Blanch the salt pork by dropping it into a pan of boiling water and cooking at a full boil 5 minutes. Drain, rinse, and cool. Mince together the pork, garlic, parsley, onion, and celery until it is almost a paste. Use a food processor if desired, but do not purée the mixture. Beat in the olive oil, salt, and pepper.

Assembling the Gratin: Preheat the oven to 375°F. Use a 3- to 4-quart shallow baking dish that is both ovenproof and flameproof. An enameled cast-iron dish is ideal. Lightly oil the dish with olive oil. Set aside two or three slices of tomato for the topping. Spread one fourth of the potato slices over the bottom of the dish. Top with one third of the tomatoes, then spread on one third of the peppers and one third of the onions. Sprinkle lightly with salt and pepper, and dot with a quarter of the *battuto*. Repeat the layering exactly as before, and then repeat again. Top the last layer with slices of potatoes, a few onion rings, and the reserved tomato slices. Dot with the remaining quarter of the *battuto*.

Baking and Serving: Lightly cover the dish with foil and bake 50 minutes. Uncover, raise the heat to 425°F, and bake another 35 minutes. The edges of the potatoes should be crinkled and lightly browned. There will be a goodly amount of liquid in the dish. Set the dish over high heat on top of the stove and boil off the liquid, taking care not to burn the bottom of the gratin. Remove the dish from the heat and let it settle about 5 minutes before cutting the gratin into squares and serving.

Suggestions   **Menu:** If you are serving the gratin as a supper main dish, begin with Modena's Spiced Soup of Spinach and Cheese (page 234), Linguine with Braised Garlic and Balsamic Vinegar (page 110) or Salad of Tart Greens with Prosciutto and Warm Balsamic Dressing (page 26). End the meal with fresh pears and chunks of Parmigiano-Reggiano cheese, or fresh fruit and unshelled nuts for cracking. Offer as a side dish with Balsamic Roast Chicken (page 279), Lemon Roast Veal with Rosemary (page 294), January Pork (page 312), or Porcini Veal Chops (page 290).

INVESTITVRE DI
PARMA.

14.TA.

The cured pork of Parma from a 17th-century board game, by Giuseppe Maria Mitelli

Oven-Roasted Potatoes
Patate al Forno

Italy relishes the roasted potato, but few recipes achieve quite this degree of crispness and flavor. The key to success here is roasting the potato at high heat, covered with a light film of olive oil. Although the process requires attention, it can be done ahead; the potatoes reheat well just before serving.

[Serves 6 to 8]

4 pounds medium-size red-skinned potatoes

6 to 7 tablespoons extra-virgin olive oil

Salt and freshly ground black pepper

6 fresh sage leaves and/or 3-inch sprig of fresh rosemary

2 ounces pancetta, chopped (optional)

Method

Working Ahead: *The potatoes can be roasted early in the day. Leave them uncovered at room temperature; do not refrigerate. Reheat in a 400°F oven about 15 minutes. Finished potatoes can be held in a 200°F oven 20 minutes before serving.*

Precooking the Potatoes: Preheat the oven to 425°F. While the oven is heating, scrub the potatoes. Place them in a 6-quart pot, cover with cold water, and bring to a strong boil. Cook 8 minutes, or until barely tender. Drain them in a colander, and rinse with cold water to cool them down. Then quarter the potatoes but do not peel them.

Roasting the Potatoes: Use a thick metal roasting pan or a shallow enameled cast-iron baking dish large enough to hold the potatoes in almost a single layer. Spread the potatoes in the pan, and sprinkle them with 5 tablespoons of the olive oil and some salt and pepper. Turn the pieces with two wooden spatulas to coat with the oil. Slip the pan into the oven and roast the potatoes, turning them often but gently, 40 minutes, or until they begin to color. Sprinkle in the rest of the olive oil, the herbs, and the pancetta if desired. Turn the potatoes frequently as you roast them another 30 to 40 minutes, or until they are very crisp and cooked to a deep golden brown.

Serving: Keep the potatoes warm in a low oven before serving, but do not hold them more than 20 minutes. If you are making them ahead, remove them from the oven and cool, uncovered, to room temperature.

Suggestions   **Menu:** Serve with any roasted or grilled dish, as well as Pan-Roasted Quail (page 283), Maria Bertuzzi's Lemon Chicken (page 273), Porcini Veal Chops (page 290), Beef-Wrapped Sausage (page 314), or Lamb with Black Olives (page 305).

Basil and Onion Mashed Potatoes
Patate Mesce

In the mountainous border country between Piacenza province and the region of Liguria, creamy mashed potatoes become fragrant with a sauté of onion, parsley, fresh basil, and garlic. Fresh basil is vital here. The potatoes are especially good when they can sop up the sauces of country-style braisings like Beef-Wrapped Sausage or Maria Bertuzzi's Lemon Chicken. This recipe halves and doubles easily.

[Serves 8]

5 pounds small red-skinned
   potatoes
1 to 1½ cups milk
2 tablespoons unsalted butter
4 tablespoons extra-virgin olive oil
2 large onions, minced
½ cup minced Italian parsley
2 large cloves garlic, minced

½ cup minced fresh basil leaves
½ cup water
Salt and freshly ground black
   pepper
Olive oil
1 cup (4 ounces) freshly grated
   Italian Parmigiano-Reggiano
   cheese

Method   **Working Ahead:** *The potatoes can be prepared the day before serving, up to the point of baking the casserole. Cover and refrigerate. Bring to room temperature before the final baking.*

Cooking the Potatoes: Scrub the potatoes and place them in a 6-quart pot with cold water to cover. Put the lid in place, and set the pot over high heat. Bring the water to a lively bubble. Adjust the heat so the water does not boil over, and keep the pot partially covered. Cook the potatoes 15 to 20 minutes, or until easily pierced with a fork. Meanwhile pour 1 cup of the milk, the butter, and 1 tablespoon of the oil into a large bowl.

Sautéing the Flavorings: While the potatoes are cooking, heat the remaining 3 tablespoons oil in a 12-inch skillet over high heat. Add the onions and all but 2 tablespoons of the parsley. Turn the heat to medium-low and cover. Cook 15 minutes, or until the onions are soft and clear. Stir occasionally. Uncover and cook over medium-high heat, stirring frequently, 8 minutes, or until the onions are golden brown. Then stir in the garlic and basil, and cook another minute. Add the water and scrape up any brown bits in the skillet. Season with salt and pepper. Turn into the large bowl.

Mashing the Potatoes: When the potatoes are tender, drain and peel them. Pass the hot potatoes through the coarse blade of a food mill set over the large bowl, or mash them in the bowl with a potato masher. Blend the mashed potatoes with the ingredients at the bottom of the bowl. Season to taste. If the potatoes seem dry, add more milk. The mixture should be like very thick whipped cream, but not so loose that it will not hold a high mound on a spoon. Lightly oil a shallow 2½-quart baking dish. Spread half the potato mixture over the bottom of the dish. Top with half of the cheese, and then spread the remaining potatoes over the cheese. Sprinkle with the rest of the Parmigiano-Reggiano.

Baking and Serving: Preheat the oven to 350°F. Lightly cover the potatoes with aluminum foil, and bake 30 minutes, or until hot to the center. Just before serving, sprinkle with the reserved 2 tablespoons parsley. Serve hot.

Suggestions   **Menu:** In addition to the suggestions above, serve with Lamb with Black Olives (page 305), Giovanna's Wine-Basted Rabbit (page 284), Lemon Roast Veal with Rosemary (page 294), Christmas Capon (page 281), Balsamic Roast Chicken (page 279), and January Pork (page 312).

Lentils Modena Style
Lenticchie in Umido alla Modenese

Lentils, tomato sauce, and homemade stock make a dish that stands on its own as a first course or entree. In Modena, this recipe divides cooks into two camps. One side believes this is the only proper accompaniment to the town's famous zampone sausage, while the opposition argues that mashed potatoes are its only proper partner. Both sides agree, however, that eating lentils on New Year's Day brings prosperity through the year.

I like these as a buffet dish, easily fixed early in the day and reheated. The trick here is not to cook the lentils until they fall apart. They must be tender but still firm enough to hold their shape.

[Serves 12]

3 tablespoons extra-virgin olive oil

1 large clove garlic, split

2 medium onions, minced

1 large carrot, minced

1 small stalk celery with leaves, minced

3 to 4 fresh sage leaves, chopped, or 3 to 4 dried sage leaves, crumbled

2-inch sprig fresh rosemary, or ½ teaspoon dried rosemary leaves

2 large California bay laurel leaves

2 pounds dried green or brown lentils, rinsed (do not use red lentils, as they dissolve too quickly)

14- to 16-ounce can tomatoes with their juice

2 tablespoons imported Italian tomato paste

About 7 cups Poultry/Meat Stock (page 66) or Quick Stock (page 68)

Salt and freshly ground black pepper to taste

Method   **Working Ahead:** *The lentils can be prepared a day ahead, but slightly undercook them. Cover and refrigerate. To reheat, spread the lentils in a shallow baking dish, moisten with ½ cup stock, and cover securely with foil. Bake at 350°F 20 minutes, or until hot. Serve right from the baking dish.*

Making the Base: Heat the oil and garlic in a 12-inch sauté pan over medium heat. Rub the garlic over the bottom of the pan with a wooden spatula, cooking it 3 minutes, or until golden. Discard the garlic. Blend in the onion, carrot, and celery along with the sage, rosemary, and bay leaves. Stir frequently over medium heat 10 minutes, or until the onion turns a rich golden brown.

continued

Cooking the Lentils: Have a shallow serving bowl warming in a low oven. Stir the lentils into the sautéed vegetables, and cook about 2 minutes. Crush the tomatoes and add them to the pan. Stir in the tomato paste and 6 cups of the stock. Bring to a slow bubble. Cover the pan and cook very slowly, 30 minutes, or until the lentils are tender but still firm enough to hold their shape. Stir occasionally with a wooden spatula to keep them from sticking. Add another ½ cup stock if the lentils threaten to scorch.

Serving: Taste the lentils for seasoning. Turn them into the warmed bowl, and serve hot. (If serving with zampone or cotechino sausage, spread on a hot platter and arrange the sliced sausage over the lentils.)

Suggestions **Menu:** Serve with zampone (page 506) on New Year's Day as they do in Modena, or as a main dish after the Salad of Tart Greens with Prosciutto and Warm Balsamic Dressing (page 26). They are delicious accompanied by Grilled Winter Endives (page 337). Offer them, too, as part of a mixed antipasto platter along with Marinated Baby Onions (page 16), Platter of Cured Meats (page 14), Paola Bini's Potato Salad (page 19), and Garlic Crostini with Pancetta (page 28).

Cook's Notes **Special Lentils:** France's green lentils from Puy are particularly good in this dish. Find them in specialty food stores.

Bologna vegetable seller, 17th century, by Giuseppe Maria Mitelli

Salad of Mixed Greens and Fennel
Insalata Verde con Finocchio

Wine lovers advise serving salads of this kind after the main dish, when their vinegar and oil dressings cannot interfere with the wine. Yet many in Emilia-Romagna eat salad on the same plate with roasts and grills. The combination of hot and cool is enticing, especially when the wine is simple and not much damaged by vinegar.

[Serves 4 to 6]

1 small head Bibb lettuce
1 small head romaine lettuce
1 small head radicchio
1 bulb fresh fennel
3 to 4 tablespoons extra-virgin
olive oil

1 to 2 tablespoons red wine
vinegar
1 teaspoon commercial balsamic
vinegar (optional)
Salt and freshly ground black
pepper to taste

Method **Working Ahead:** *The greens can be washed and dried several hours ahead. Wrap them in paper towels, tuck the bundle into a plastic bag, and refrigerate until about 30 minutes before serving. Toss the salad just before dining.*

Preparing the Salad: Wash and dry the greens thoroughly. Discard any tough or bruised leaves. Tear into bite-size pieces, and place in a large bowl. Trim the fennel of any bruised areas and discard any tough portions. Thinly slice into sticks and add to the salad.

Dressing and Serving: Toss the salad first with the oil. Then sprinkle with the vinegar, including the balsamic if desired, and salt and pepper, and toss again to combine thoroughly. Taste for balance, adding a little more oil or vinegar as needed. Serve at once.

Suggestions **Menu:** Serve with Grilled Beef with Balsamic Glaze (page 303), Herbed Seafood Grill (page 254), Braised Eel with Peas (page 261), Lamb, Garlic, and Potato Roast (page 307), or Fresh Tuna Adriatic Style (page 256). Of course the salad is excellent after almost any second course, especially Thumb Pasta and Tomato Braised Beans Piacenza Style (page 229) or Rabbit Dukes of Modena (page 286).

Salad of Spring Greens
Insalata Verde

A *most traditional Italian salad bringing together all the greens of spring. Vary the lettuces according to what is available.*

[Serves 6 to 8]

About 14 cups mixed seasonal salad greens, combining tart and sweet greens of varying textures, such as dandelion, arugula, oak leaf, Bibb lettuce, mâche, and leaf lettuce

3 to 5 tablespoons extra-virgin olive oil
Salt and freshly ground black pepper
2 to 3 tablespoons red wine vinegar

Method　**Working Ahead:** *The greens can be rinsed and thoroughly dried up to 8 hours before serving. Roll them in paper towels and store in plastic bags in the refrigerator.*

Preparing the Salad: Discard any bruised or coarse leaves before thoroughly washing and drying the greens. Use a salad spinner to rid them of excess moisture. Tear the greens into bite-size pieces, and combine them in a large serving bowl. Toss with the olive oil and salt and pepper to taste. Then toss with vinegar to taste. Serve immediately.

Suggestions　**Menu:** Serve the salad with Braised Eel with Peas (page 261) or Christmas Capon (page 281). Serve it after Pan-Roasted Quail (page 283), Mardi Gras Chicken (page 277), or Artusi's Delight (page 300).

Roasted Beets and Onions
Bietole e Cipolle al Forno

Roasted beets and onions are sold in all the markets of Emilia-Romagna. These ready-cooked vegetables are taken home to become antipasti, side dishes, and salads. Combine them on a bed of romaine lettuce and dress with olive oil and a drizzling of balsamic vinegar for an easy first-course or third-course salad.

[Serves 6 to 8]

6 medium onions, unpeeled, but with roots trimmed away

8 medium beets, trimmed of tops and roots

Method

Working Ahead: *Roasted beets keep in the refrigerator, wrapped, 5 or 6 days. The onions are best kept at room temperature rather than chilled. Use them within a day of roasting.*

Roasting the Vegetables: Preheat the oven to 400°F. Wrap the beets individually in aluminum foil. Spread a sheet of foil over the oven rack. Place the onions on the foil and surround them with the wrapped beets. Roast 1 hour, or until the vegetables are easily pierced with a knife.

Serving: Offer the vegetables hot from the oven by slipping off the beet skins with the help of a fork and paring knife. Serve the onions by cutting a cross in their tops and seasoning with salt, pepper, and a little olive oil and/or vinegar. Or spoon a little balsamic vinegar into the onion and serve. If serving at room temperature or incorporating into a salad, trim away the onion skins. Cut the onions into wedges. Peel the beets and thickly slice or cut into wedges.

Serve as a salad by arranging the cut onions and beets on a bed of 10 to 12 romaine leaves. Sprinkle the entire arrangement with 4 tablespoons extra-virgin olive oil and 3 tablespoons good commercial balsamic vinegar. Add salt and pepper to taste.

Suggestions

Menu: Serve with Giovanna's Wine-Basted Rabbit (page 284), January Pork (page 312), Riccardo Rimondi's Chicken Cacciatora (page 275), or Beef-Wrapped Sausage (page 314).

Polenta Five Ways
Polenta

Grill it, fry it, sauté it, or roast it—polenta takes to all these methods. As an accompaniment, it absorbs meat juices and seasonings, while at the same time it brings to dishes the soft, gentle flavor of corn. Layer polenta as you would pasta in lasagne. Bake it with braised vegetables. Or layer it with nuts, fresh cheese, raisins, and honey. Even though the people of Emilia eat more polenta than do the Romagnoli, every part of Emilia-Romagna has its favorites, and every family has its own renditions.

Carlo Middione, author of *The Food of Southern Italy*, shared his easy method for making polenta. It is a revelation for those who hate the tedium of stirring 30 or 40 minutes, as the stiff porridge fights you every step of the way. I have simplified his approach a little further, so with almost no effort you have a smooth and velvety polenta, the goal of every aficionado.

[Serves 8 to 10]

2 teaspoons salt
10½ cups water

3½ cups (1 pound) organic stone-ground cornmeal

Method

Working Ahead: *Firm polenta for roasting, frying, and other uses can be made even a day ahead. After cooling on a plate or in a cake pan, cover and refrigerate it until ready to use. Creamy polenta can be cooked up to 4 hours ahead and kept in its bowl over a pot of gently simmering water. Just make sure the bowl is covered and sealed with foil. Stir every so often.*

Making the Polenta: Fill a 6-quart pot three-quarters full of water, and bring it to a strong bubble over high heat. Meanwhile, fill a kettle with the 10½ cups water, and set it to boil over high heat. Have at hand a large stainless steel bowl, a whisk, and a large heatproof glass measuring cup. Measure the salt into the bowl. Have the cornmeal in another bowl, ready to pour. When the kettle comes to a boil, pour the water into the large bowl. Using the whisk, stir the water into a whirlpool as you slowly pour in the cornmeal. Keep stirring in the same direction until the cornmeal is completely blended in and there are no lumps.

Cover the bowl with foil, sealing its edges securely. Set the bowl over the bubbling water in the 6-quart pot. Check that the bowl does not touch the water. If necessary, ladle off a little of the water. Cook 1½ hours, keeping the water bubbling at a moderate rate over medium heat. Three or four times during the cooking, use a rubber spatula to stir the polenta, scooping down to the bottom of the bowl to check for sticking. Do not worry if a little sticks to the bowl's surface. Reseal the foil after each stirring. After 1½ hours, the polenta with be thick, smooth, and have no suggestion of rawness in its taste. Use it immediately, or treat it in any of the following ways.

Baked Polenta

Turn the hot polenta out onto a board and allow it to cool. The polenta will make a spreading mound. It is usually sliced with a taut string to avoid sticky knives, or use a knife dipped in hot water. Arrange ½-inch-thick slices of the cooled polenta in a single layer in an oiled shallow pan. Bake in a 350°F oven 30 minutes, or until heated through.

Serve drizzled with a little melted butter or warmed olive oil and sprinklings of Parmigiano-Reggiano cheese. Or serve as a bed for braisings and stews, without the butter or oil and cheese. It is especially good with Mardi Gras Chicken (page 277), Rabbit Roasted with Sweet Fennel (page 289), and Riccardo Rimondi's Chicken Cacciatora (page 275).

The Polenta Eaters

For many in Emilia-Romagna, it took post–World War II affluence to finally banish polenta as the mainstay of their diet. Since the early 1700s polenta and beans had nourished peasants and laborers, especially in Emilia. The corn was brought from the New World and flourished on the Po River plain. Corn was cheap and plentiful when wheat was expensive and scarce. Before corn arrived in Italy from the Americas, thick porridges of water and ground grain were the food of laborers, foot soldiers, and farm workers. Buckwheat was popular along the Swiss/Italian border. The Romans ground dried beans and ancient strains of wheat and millet. So when cornmeal came upon the scene, its niche was already established. For many, it replaced wheat. Lamentably, corn lacked many of wheat's nutrients, and pellagra, a disease caused by niacin deficiency, became a major problem among polenta eaters. Polenta is so identified with northern Italy that southerners disparagingly call northerners *mangiapolenta,* "polenta eaters."

Grilled Polenta

Cool the polenta on a board or in a large cake pan. Slice it about ¼ inch thick, and then cut it into manageable squares. Brush with olive oil and grill over a barbecue, on a gridded skillet, or under the broiler, 8 minutes, or until browned on both sides. Serve with Piacenza Peppers Country Style (page 244), Garlic-Sautéed Cabbage (page 331), or Spiced Spinach with Almonds (page 330). Grilled Polenta is also excellent with Pan-Roasted Quail (page 283), Maria Bertuzzi's Lemon Chicken (page 273), and Balsamic Roast Chicken (page 279).

Fried Polenta

Cool the polenta on a board or in a large cake pan. Slice it about ⅛ inch thick, and cut into rectangles the size of a playing card. Deep-fry in vegetable oil at 375°F, 3 minutes, or until crusty and golden brown. Drain on paper towels and serve as a snack or with drinks.

Creamy Polenta

Add 2 cups water to the basic polenta recipe, and cook as described above. This can be held for 4 hours; see "Working Ahead." Serve Creamy Polenta with Braised Pork Ribs (page 309), Lamb with Black Olives (page 305), Braised Eel with Peas (page 261), Mardi Gras Chicken (page 277), or topped with Game Ragù (page 50).

Layered Polenta Casserole

For the traditional polenta baked with meat ragù, see A Baked Pie of Polenta and Country Ragù (page 311). Polenta pies or casseroles can be made without meat for a substantial main dish. Oil a 3-quart baking dish, cut cooled polenta into ½-inch-thick slices, and layer in the baking dish with any of the following:

Garlic-Sautéed Cabbage (page 331)
Spiced Spinach with Almonds (page 330)
Lentils Modena Style (page 347)
Winter Tomato Sauce (page 62)

Alternate three layers of polenta with two layers of filling, dusting each one with Parmigiano-Reggiano cheese. Bake at 350°F 45 minutes, or until hot all the way through.

Cook's Notes **Enrichments:** Poultry/Meat Stock (page 66) can be substituted for all or half the water. Milk can be used in the same way. With either liquid, 1 cup heavy cream can be stirred in just before serving.

The Old Way: Sweet Polenta

Until 40 or 50 years ago, polenta cooked with milk instead of water made a one-dish supper for mountain families. Slices of cooled polenta were arranged in layers in a shallow casserole. Each layer was spread with fresh ricotta and generous sprinklings of raisins and walnuts or almonds, then seasoned with cinnamon and generous drizzles of honey. Once the casserole was full, it was set to bake on the hearth in the embers, away from the hottest part of the fire. Although perhaps surprising to modern sensibilities, slivers of homemade lard were used to enrich the casserole. Where affluence took hold, butter replaced the lard and sugar stood in for honey, and more often meat dishes took the place of the cornmeal-based casserole. Then the polenta went from a main dish to a substantial winter dessert. For centuries cooked-down grape must (Fresh Grape Syrup, page 158) sweetened polenta casseroles like this one. It is still delicious poured over hot Creamy Polenta and eaten for breakfast.

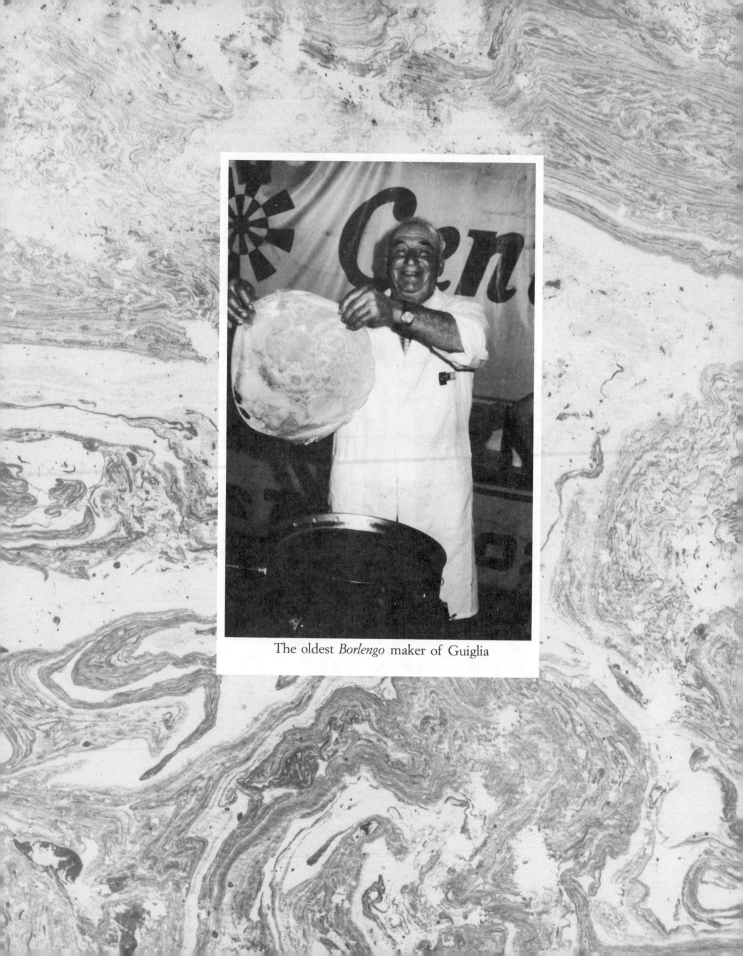

The oldest *Borlengo* maker of Guiglia

BREADS

Hearing Heaven in the Chimney

Bread and fire are inseparable. Bologna folklorist Piero Camporesi speaks of fire being at the heart of all food traditions. In peasant houses it rarely went out. Fire was too precious. The light beat back dark, and with it the evil associated with darkness. Darkness brought fear. Darkness was winter, when little grew, and winter meant cold. Fire was the warmth that kept life and nourished it. The hearth was the heart of the house, with its tall chimney linking the house and those who lived within it to the sky and to heaven.

Even embers were important. They gave nourishment. Chestnuts, beets, onions, potatoes, and field corn all cooked in the dying fire. Covered pots of food were buried to bake in the hot coals. Embers heated tiles for _Tigelle_ bread, pans for _Borlengo,_ and griddles for _Piadina._ Old people read fortunes in the embers and cinders. And people speak of the old peasant women who heard messages from heaven as winds moaned through the chimney.

For peasants the oven was a magical place, because it was here that food went from raw to cooked. They believed the same spirits that made bread rise so mysteriously also coagulated milk and fermented wine. Camporesi says those elfin spirits are part of Emilia-Romagna's Celtic heritage, buried deep in her civilization from long before the invasion of the ancient Romans.

What mystery bread must have been. In a pretechnological world, the rising of round loaves was associated with the sun rising in the sky, Christ rising to heaven, a woman's belly growing with child, with the oven becoming the womb. Going into the oven was passage. Bread dough passed through the entrance into the oven and changed forever.

Today the oven is still set apart, singled out. In the towns and villages of Emilia-Romagna, the sign marking bread shops reads "forno" ("oven"). There is no sign announcing "bakery." And while pastry and pasta makers take their titles from what they produce, often the man who bakes bread is not called a baker. He is il forno, "the oven." It is almost as though he is a part of the bread instead of its master.

The oven was the center of village life. Until the 1950s, many homes lacked ovens. The village baker made many people's bread, and they used his oven for their lasagne, savory pies, and sweet tarts.

Although most of Emilia-Romagna's breads are baked in ovens, some of her most unusual ones come from home hearths. In Romagna the crisp flatbread, Piadina, is still baked on griddles over hot coals.

Modena's hills have Borlengo—brittle and semi-transparent, cooked in shallow sauté pans over embers. Little round Tigelle bake between hot terra-cotta discs set on hearthstones. Twenty miles away these breads are unknown.

The region's different breads are usually highly localized. Bread itself, or merely its name, changes from place to place. Throughout Emilia bread doughs are fried into fritters. In the mountains chestnut flour becomes part of the fritter dough, while on the plain sometimes ricotta is added.

The bread baker or *fornaro* selling his wares in Bologna during the late 17th century, by Giuseppe Maria Mitelli

Romagna's hill bread, _Spianata_ is oven-baked or cooked atop a griddle in the fireplace. The name of this bread also changes as it gains toppings and fillings from Bologna to Ferrara.

During the Renaissance Ferrara's ducal court produced the region's most intricately sculpted bread, the Couple, or _Coppia._ Baked in an oven, it was made of expensive white flour, enriched with oil or lard and rolled into fanciful shapes. Throughout the region shapes change and the dough alters, but today this former bread of nobility is eaten by everyone.

In old documents, bread was either constantly praised or damned. Laws regulated its production, writers judged it, and peasants rioted for it. For rich and poor, it was the single most important food. Lauded for its purity, Parma's white bread of the 16th century was saluted with a saying considered old even then, "A good meal has the bread of Parma and the wine of Correggio."

Camporesi talks of how shapes were symbols of the forces of nature. Crescent-shaped breads were eaten at funerals, symbolizing the moon and rebirth. Round breads like _Spianata_ and so many others originated as pre-Christian sun symbols, rising again to bring warmth and growth.

Seeds, nuts and fruits in breads signify potency and fruitfulness. The long _Penza_ breads of Bologna swell with diced candied fruits like a penis swells with seed. There is the maleness of the long baguette, a shape common to so many places. The bread grows before entering the oven. Raisins in breads that rise were seen as seeds in the mother's swelling belly. How female is the bread oven itself, with its small opening and domed interior. It is the place of warmth, where bread is transformed before emerging as a completed being, like a child. Bread not only supported life; it was life.

When the elderly Guatelli brothers in Parma's farm country make their weekly bread, they continue the ritual of every baker in the area. They bless the flour by tracing into it a cross enclosed in a circle. Historian Guglielmo Capacchi explains that the making of the symbol may be Christian today, but it originated as old magic and a pagan rite long before Christ.

In Modena, food historian Renato Bergonzini remembers how his grandmother saved a piece of dough from one day's baking for leavening the next. As she put the dough in a bowl, she cut a cross into it and blessed herself. Renato was forbidden to touch it. But of course he did. He was fascinated by the living thing, and would lift the towel to take a peek. He said it was fantastical to a little boy, because the cross grew into a flower.

The Guatelli still mix, knead, and raise bread in their family's bread cupboard, or <u>madia.</u> Throughout the region, even the poorest of homes had this chest of drawers or cupboard topped with a covered trough. Here the bread was mixed, left to rise, and after baking, was stored.

Bergonzini recalls the time when his mother first added yeast to the bread. Before that the only leavening was dough saved from the last baking. After the advent of commercial yeast, the bread was never the same again. This sentiment is echoed by many home and professional bakers today. And many still use the old method.

The dough taken from one loaf to raise another keeps bread alive, continuously joining new loaves to those that came before. Flour, of course, is another constant. Since before the time of Christ, white flour, sifted free of bran and coarse fiber, has been highly prized. Sophocles praised Italy's wheat: "Favored Italy grows white with hoary wheat." Pliny, writing 2,000 years ago, called Italian wheat among the best in the world, the whitest and the heaviest in weight.

White flour was potent with meaning. Whiteness was God, pure, genuine—and expensive. Ferrara's white flour gained fame for its silky texture and purity of color. But poor crops and famine often made white flour an elusive commodity. In 15th-century Ferrara, even when harvests were plentiful, only the wealthy used white flour. The populace's bread was made from one third ground fava beans and two thirds coarse-ground wheat. Or they baked a blend of barley, rye, millet, spelt, and sorghum. And when famine struck, the aristocracy usurped the bread of the people as their own, leaving the populace to loaves made from ground acorns and even tree bark.

For the people of the plain, dark bread was for the less affluent. In the mountains, where little wheat grew, dark bread was even more prevalent. As little as a generation ago, mountain people made bread with home-ground flour, still flecked with bran and germ. For many today, those dark and fragrant breads are fond memories far more nurturing to both body and spirit than the elegant white loaves now available to all.

Harvesting Grain,
17th-century copper
engraving from a work by
Luigi Doria Romano

The recipes in this chapter express the range and variety of Emilia-Romagna's breads. Although not every one of the region's loaves is included, each type is represented: hearth cakes, pan breads, fritters and flatbreads, the elegant Couple bread, and a dark wheaten loaf created from the childhood memories of women who grew up in Modena's mountains. Most of these breads are best eaten with other foods. Ferrara's Couple bread could accompany any savory dish in this book. It is typical of the crusty, neutral-flavored white breads served throughout the region with antipasti, first dishes, and second courses. Its blandness is purposeful. Many in Emilia-Romagna believe that a bread of big or assertive flavors fights with the complex and often robust tastes of their savory dishes.

Tigelle, Spianata, and Piadina, on the other hand, are snack breads, usually eaten with toppings or fillings. Although Tigelle and Spianata often appear also as antipasti, I always think of these three, along with the unusual Borlengo, as Emilia-Romagna's Sunday-night breads. These are the snacks that become suppers for family and friends after a day of visiting and feasting on a big afternoon meal.

In this country, we might serve them at informal gatherings. Invite everyone into the kitchen, where they can scoop up the breads hot from baking, then help themselves to fillings and toppings. Each recipe offers menu suggestions and specific recommendations for accompaniments. Those suggestions also guide the cook in serving Emilia's favorite street food, her fritters of batter or bread dough.

These snack breads can become the heart and soul of a meal. Bring out a few vegetables, slices of salami, or a little cheese—and know that served exactly this way, these breads often sustained and nourished much of Emilia-Romagna.

Making Bread: Some Guidelines

Feeling bread come alive under our hands is such pleasure. It relaxes and comforts, while linking us to those basic forces that have touched bread bakers for centuries. Bread is the most forgiving of foods. As long as the yeast is alive, the bread will survive. Use these guidelines to ensure success every time:

♦ Build bread around your life, not your life around your bread. Slow risings fit easily into busy schedules and are the key to breads with full, mellow flavor.

I often make the sponge in the evening. (Usually a blend of all the yeast, liquid, and a part of the flour, the sponge ripens before being kneaded into the final bread dough.) The next morning I knead the sponge together with the rest of the ingredients and then leave it to rise for the rest of the day.

Even if a recipe instructs to "let rise 2 hours, or until doubled," leaving the dough for a few extra hours only deepens the bread's flavor. In the evening I shape the loaf, let it rise again, and bake it. The last rise is crucial. If the loaf overrises, the bread will be heavy. Deal with overrising by simply punching down the dough and letting it rise again, until it does not spring back when poked with a finger.

♦ Always check the date on the yeast package to make sure it is active. I prefer granulated yeast from the health food store, and I always store it in the freezer. Do not expose yeast to temperatures over about 110°F. And do not use fast-rising yeasts in these recipes. They may offer speed, but they sacrifice the mature flavor vital to most of these breads.

♦ Do use organic stone-ground flours. Their vitality adds much to breads. Store them in the refrigerator.

♦ Weighing ingredients gives the easiest and most accurate measure. Just pour the flour onto a scale, and there you are. One measuring cup of flour can vary from 3 to 6 ounces, depending upon how the cup is filled. My 4-ounce cup, called for in all these recipes, comes from spooning flour into a measuring cup and leveling it, without tamping or tapping. But even this method is not foolproof. If your flour is packed down in the sack, if the weather is humid, or if you spoon down deeper than I do, the measurement might be off. Weighing is the surest method. When working in very damp conditions, weigh out an additional ounce for every 8 ounces of flour.

◆ The sponge is traditional for most yeast breads. Sponges deepen flavors and come from the days when dough from the previous baking was the leavening agent. If you bake regularly, you might want to try the yeastless baking of long ago:

Take about 1½ cups of the dough from a yeast bread, such as *Spianata* or Modena Mountain Bread. Blend in ½ cup water, cover the bowl, and store it in a cool place or in the refrigerator. Within a week, use a cup as the sponge for your next loaf, saving a piece of that finished dough for leavening the next baking. Beat the piece of dough into the leftover chilled dough and keep cool. Do not use this technique with doughs high in butter, eggs, or sugar.

The Couple
Coppia

No other Ferrara food is as striking as her famous Couple bread. These single-serving breads are fashioned as long, leggy crosses, their four twirled "legs" resembling slender unicorn horns. Baking turns the Couple golden and creates a white bread of almost all crust. You break off pieces and eat them as you would a breadstick, with dishes from antipasto through the second course. The bread's flavor is neutral, some even say bland, making it the ideal partner for Ferrara's savory dishes. Translating as "the Couple" (ciupeta in Ferrara dialect; coppia in Italian), the bread and its unique shape spread to Modena and Bologna. Breads almost identical in flavor but shaped differently are eaten throughout Emilia-Romagna.

This recipe combines one from Ferrarese Luisa Picchietti and one from the Perdonati bakery in Ferrara. Luisa now bakes the Couple in her Highwood, Illinois, home. Perdonati makes some of Ferrara's most admired bread, and was one of the town's last bake shops to work with a wood-fired oven.

[Makes 6 breads, serving 6]

Sponge

¾ cup (3 ounces) all-purpose unbleached flour (organic stone-ground preferred)

⅛ teaspoon granulated yeast

3½ tablespoons warm water (110°F)

¼ cup water

1 teaspoon extra-virgin olive oil

¼ teaspoon salt

Dough

3 cups (12 ounces) all-purpose unbleached flour (organic stone-ground preferred)

1 teaspoon granulated yeast

1 cup warm water (110°F)

1 cup (4 ounces) cake flour

1 teaspoon salt

2 tablespoons extra-virgin olive oil

2 tablespoons lard or unsalted butter, at room temperature

2 tablespoons butter for greasing the pan

Method   **Working Ahead:** *Except for the shaping, this bread takes little actual effort. The long risings mean that life can go on as usual with just an occasional pause to take the bread to its next stage. The sponge matures over 18 to 24 hours. The finished dough takes 4 hours to rise before shaping and another 50 minutes to rise before baking. Baked breads freeze well 3 months.*

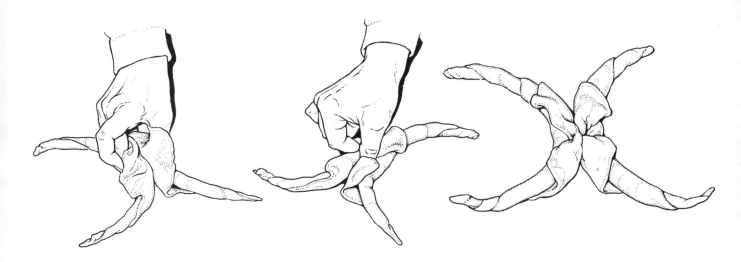

Making the Sponge: Start the sponge 18 to 24 hours before baking the bread. In a mixing bowl or food processor bowl, stir together 1 tablespoon of the flour, the yeast, and the 3 ½ tablespoons warm water. Allow 5 minutes for the yeast to bubble. Next, blend in the ¼ cup water (cold water if you are using a food processor, at 110°F if you are using an electric mixer or hand beating), olive oil, salt, and the rest of the ¾ cup of flour. Process or beat 30 seconds to 1 minute, or until the moist dough is very elastic. Turn into a large bowl, and seal the top with plastic wrap. Set aside at room temperature 18 to 24 hours. It will rise, looking blistered and bubbly.

Mixing the Dough: Put a spoonful of the flour in a bowl large enough for mixing the dough. Blend in the yeast and ¼ cup of the warm water. Let the mixture stand 5 minutes, or until the yeast is bubbly. Meanwhile, mix the flours and salt together in another bowl. Stir in the sponge, the rest of the water, the oil, lard or butter, and half the flour/salt mixture. Blend, using a heavy-duty electric mixer (about 3 minutes) or a food processor (about 30 seconds), until the dough is very elastic.

Work in the remaining flour mixture, switching to the dough hook if you are using an electric mixer. The dough should be lumpy and somewhat sticky. Knead the dough 5 minutes. If the dough is still sticky, work in another 1 to 2 tablespoons all-purpose flour. Resume kneading another 5 minutes. The dough will smooth out, lose some of its stickiness, and become elastic.

First Rising: Place the dough in an oiled bowl and seal the top with plastic wrap. Let it rise 4 hours, or until doubled in bulk, at room temperature.

Shaping: Divide the dough into six balls. Roll each one out to form a thin 8-inch square. Cut each square diagonally, forming two triangles. Use a rolling pin to elongate the top of each triangle. Then thin and extend the two side points. Starting at the wide base of each triangle, roll it up tightly, leaving about 2 ½ inches of the tip unrolled. They will look like long, thin, tightly twirled crescent rolls.

Make the Couple shape by turning the crescents so the two long flaps are facing away from each other, and the crescents arch away from each other starting at their centers. Pinch the unrolled tips together at their bases, along the line where they join the crescents. Then fold the tips away from each other, tucking their ends under to make two side-by-side hollow cylinders between the joined crescents. Push two fingers down into the center where the two cylinders meet. Pinch the cylinders together so they resemble two number 8's sitting side by side.

Second Rising: Grease two large or three standard baking sheets with the 2 tablespoons of butter, and arrange the breads on them. Cover with a kitchen towel, and let rest at room temperature 50 minutes. The breads will not rise perceptibly.

Baking and Serving: Preheat the oven to 325°F. Bake 10 minutes. Raise the heat to 350°F, and bake 30 minutes. Raise the temperature again to 375°F, and bake 5 to 10 minutes, or until light golden brown and very crisp. Cool the breads on a rack. The Couple is always served at room temperature.

Suggestions   **Menu:** This bread, in this or simpler forms, is traditionally served with all the region's savory dishes. Ferrara specialties are Domed Maccheroni Pie (page 180), Spaghetti with Anchovies and Melting Onions (page 130), Cappellacci with Sweet Squash (page 145), Rice of the Princes (page 211), Riccardo Rimondi's Chicken Cacciatora (page 275), and Rabbit Roasted with Sweet Fennel (page 289).

Cook's Notes   **Flours:** The use of cake flour may be surprising to bread bakers. But by tradition, this bread is made with the soft flour that made Ferrara famous. Mixing some cake flour into American all-purpose unbleached flour achieves a similar quality.

Bread of Life

It is impossible to resist speculating how the Couple came to have this singular shape. Some say it is the cross of Christianity. For others, the form is both male and female, depicting the anatomy of both sexes. Few in Ferrara can pinpoint its beginnings. Until the 13th century, breads there were either long or round. A document from 1287 mentions a decorative loaf, but gives no details of its shape. In the mid-1500s Christaforo di Messisbugo described each place setting at the banquets he arranged for the Cardinal d'Este in Ferrara as having a *pane intorto,* or twisted or bent bread. This sounds closer to the Couple's present-day shape. Perhaps no single baker invented the Couple. It may be a combination of symbols, some pre-Christian, and possibly coming from sources far from Ferrara. Many cultures depict bread as part of elemental life forces. Yeast comes to life; dough rises, falls, and rises again. The oven's nurturing warmth transforms the dough into food. It is easy to imagine the link with male/female, pregnancy, birth, and life. The Couple's strong visual statement is unmistakable.

Romagna Mountain Bread
Spianata

Much like an oversized <u>focaccia</u>, this big wheel of a bread is showered with leaves of dark green rosemary and browned to pale gold. <u>Spianata</u> is tender and chewy at the same time, and thoroughly satisfying whether eaten on its own or with meals. Throughout Romagna, bakers improvise with toppings and fillings for <u>Spianata</u>, making it a favorite snack bread and antipasto. In the tiny mountain town of Savignano di Rigo, Ristorante Ottavio presents a hot antipasto <u>Spianata</u> stuffed with browned onions. In Ferrara garlic, artichokes, and cheese are baked on the bread, turning it into a light lunch. At snack bars, a topping of sautéed spinach and cheese makes it a tasty hand-held meal.

Serve <u>Spianata</u> plain or stuffed as an antipasto before country-style dishes. Make it a main dish by adding any of the toppings that follow the basic recipe. Present it plain, sprinkled only with rosemary and coarse salt, as a dinner bread to accompany antipasti, first courses, and second dishes.

While greatly reducing the amount of fat called for in old <u>Spianata</u> recipes, this rendition still maintains the tender quality that sets the bread apart. Starting the bread with a sponge that ripens over 8 hours gives depth of flavor.

[Makes 1 large round loaf, serving 8 to 12]

Sponge

1 teaspoon granulated yeast

1 cup (4 ounces) all-purpose unbleached flour (organic stone-ground preferred)

1 cup warm water (about 110°F)

Dough

2 cups (8 ounces) all-purpose unbleached flour (organic stone-ground preferred), plus 2 tablespoons as needed

1½ teaspoons salt

2 tablespoons extra-virgin olive oil

2 tablespoons high-quality lard or unsalted butter, at room temperature

Topping

1½ tablespoons extra-virgin olive oil

About ¼ teaspoon coarse salt

1½ teaspoons chopped fresh rosemary leaves

Method   **Working Ahead:** *Although* Spianata *is made over a long time period, there is little actual effort. Arrange your schedule so you can spend a few moments at each of its stages.*

continued

The sponge must be started 7 to 11 hours before mixing the bread dough, and could be done the night before serving the bread. After the sponge is mixed with the rest of the ingredients, the dough's first rising takes about 3 hours, but it can be left for as long as 10 hours at this point. After shaping, count on another 2 to 3 hours of rising before baking. The finished bread holds, well wrapped, at room temperature or in the refrigerator several days. It freezes 3 months.

Making the Sponge: Start the sponge about 11 hours before baking the bread. Blend the yeast, 2 tablespoons of the flour, and ¼ cup of the warm water in a mixing bowl or a food processor bowl. Let stand 5 minutes, or until the yeast makes small bubbles. Beat in the rest of the flour and water, using an electric mixer, food processor, or wooden spoon. The batter should be very elastic. Scrape down the sides of the bowl, and seal it with plastic wrap. Let it stand at room temperature 7 to 8 hours. It could go as long as 12 hours without changing the character of the bread.

Making the Dough by Hand: Blend the 2 cups flour and the salt. Add half the mixture to the sponge, along with the olive oil and the lard or butter. Beat about 5 minutes, making a very elastic dough. Gradually beat in the rest of the flour mixture. Knead it by hand into a soft, but not sticky, dough. Add extra flour if necessary. Knead 10 minutes.

Making the Dough with a Heavy-Duty Mixer: Blend the 2 cups flour and the salt. Add half the mixture to the sponge, along with the olive oil and the lard or butter. Beat with the paddle attachment 5 minutes at lowest speed to develop the gluten. Then add the remainder of the flour and beat 1 minute. The dough should be soft but not sticky. If necessary, beat in the additional flour, keeping the dough soft. Switch to the dough hook and knead 10 minutes, or until very satiny and elastic. The dough will clean the sides and bottom of the bowl.

Making the Dough with a Food Processor: Process the sponge, oil, lard or butter, salt, and 2 cups flour with the plastic blade 30 seconds. Add the remaining flour and process 30 seconds. Let the dough rest 30 seconds. It should be soft but not sticky. Sprinkle with the additional 2 tablespoons flour if necessary. Then process 30 seconds.

First Rising: Place the dough in an oiled bowl, and seal the top with plastic wrap. Let it rise at room temperature 3 hours, or until 2½ times its original size.

Shaping the Dough: Lightly grease a 14- to 16-inch pizza pan. Punch the dough down. Thin and stretch the dough to fit the pan (a rolling pin helps). It should be between ¼ and ½ inch thick, and stretched all the way to the pan's edge.

Second Rising: Cover the pan with a kitchen towel, and let the dough rise 2½ to 3 hours. The dough should double in volume, and should not spring back when poked with a finger.

Baking and Serving: Preheat the oven to 400°F. Dimple the top of the loaf by poking it with your fingers. Spread the 1½ tablespoons olive oil over the top, and sprinkle with the salt and rosemary. Bake 10 minutes. Then lower the heat to 350°F and bake another 25 minutes. The bread is done when the bottom of the loaf sounds hollow when tapped. Serve hot, warm, or at room temperature, sliced into wedges.

Suggestions   **Wine:** Filled or topped, *Spianata* takes well to a young red Merlot, or to a white Pinot Grigio from Friuli's Aquilea area. Even simpler wines are a pleasure here, like a good California jug wine. Plain *Spianata* accompanies other foods, which will dictate the wine choice.

Menu: All of Romagna's dishes take to *Spianata*—for instance, Mardi Gras Chicken (page 277), Lamb with Black Olives (page 305), Seafood Stew Romagna (page 259), Summer Clams with Balsamic Vinegar (page 268). Filled or topped *Spianata* is delicious in small portions as an antipasto, or as a lunch or snack.

A Bread by Any Other Name

With only subtle variations, this flatbread takes on new flavorings and names from one area to the next throughout Emilia-Romagna. Kneading bits of chopped pancetta or salt pork into the dough makes Bologna's *la crescentina*. Enriching the dough with eggs, crackling, and the cooking broth of zampone sausage creates the *gnocco al forno,* or baked dumpling, a favorite snack bread of Emilia. A very similar bread in Romagna becomes *piadone*. The *torta salata* (or savory bread) of Modena, Ferrara, and Bologna is created when *spianata* is brushed with melted lard and sprinkled with coarse salt before baking.

Fillings and Toppings for *Spianata*

Onion Filling

1½ tablespoons extra-virgin
    olive oil
2 medium onions, thinly sliced into
    strips

Salt and freshly ground black
    pepper to taste
1 loaf *Spianata,* baked

Making the Filling: Heat the oil in a 12-inch skillet over medium-high heat. Quickly brown the onions, 4 to 5 minutes, stirring frequently. Season to taste. (The onions can be cooked ahead and rewarmed.)

Serving: Cut the loaf into eight to ten wedges, splitting each wedge horizontally into two pieces. Rewarm the bread, wrapped in foil, in a 350°F oven about 10 minutes. Stuff each wedge with a few spoonfuls of the warm onion filling, and serve.

Spinach and Cheese Topping

½ recipe Spiced Spinach with
    Almonds (page 330)
1 cup fresh whole-milk ricotta
    cheese (page 454)
2 tablespoons minced Italian
    parsley
2 tablespoons minced fresh basil
    leaves, or 1½ teaspoons dried
    basil

1 small clove garlic, minced
1 tablespoon minced onion
Salt and freshly ground black
    pepper to taste
1 recipe *Spianata* dough, shaped,
    risen, and ready to bake
2 tablespoons extra-virgin olive oil

Making the Topping: Mix together the cooked spinach, ricotta, herbs, garlic, and onion. Season with salt and pepper.

Baking: Preheat the oven to 400°F. Do not coat the dough with the basic topping (oil, rosemary, and salt). Bake the loaf 10 minutes. Reduce the temperature to 375°F, and bake another 10 minutes. Remove the loaf from the oven, and raise the heat to 400°F. Spread the spinach mixture over the partially baked loaf, and sprinkle with the 2 tablespoons olive oil. Bake 13 to 15 minutes, or until the bottom of the bread is crisp.

Serving: Serve hot from the oven, or cool on a rack and then rewarm about 10 minutes in a 350°F oven. The bread holds well, tightly wrapped, in the refrigerator about 2 days.

Fresh Artichoke and Cheese Topping

This topping can be made 1 day ahead, and it is worth every moment of the preparation. Serve the bread in small slivers as an antipasto, or in more generous portions as a supper or lunch main dish. I have adapted the bread from one tasted at Ferrara's Perdonati bakery.

2 large lemons
5 to 6 large artichokes
1½ tablespoons extra-virgin olive oil
¼ cup finely chopped onion
Salt and freshly ground black pepper to taste
1 small clove garlic, minced
3 tablespoons dry white wine
1½ cups fresh whole-milk ricotta cheese (page 454)
¼ cup freshly grated Italian Parmigiano-Reggiano cheese

2 tablespoons minced Italian parsley
2 tablespoons minced fresh basil leaves, or 1½ teaspoons dried basil
1 small clove garlic, minced
1 tablespoon minced onion
1 recipe *Spianata* dough, shaped, risen, and ready to bake
2 tablespoons extra-virgin olive oil

Making the Topping: Squeeze the lemons into a medium-size bowl of water. Peel the artichoke stems and slice them into ¼-inch-thick rounds. Add the cut pieces of artichoke to the bowl as you work. Cut away the leaves from around the bottom and sides of the artichokes. Then cut off the top two thirds of the leaves. Divide the artichoke hearts into eighths, and cut away their furry chokes. Heat the oil over medium heat in a 10-inch skillet. Add the artichokes (drained), ¼ cup onions, and salt and pepper. Brown slowly about 5 minutes. Stir often, turning the pieces of artichoke so they sear on all sides. Sprinkle with the first quantity of garlic and cook a few seconds longer.

Stir in the wine and bring to a simmer, scraping up any brown glaze on the bottom of the skillet. Cover and cook 3 to 5 minutes, or until the artichokes have softened. They should still have some firmness when pierced with a knife. Uncover the skillet, raise the heat, and cook off any liquid. Set the skillet aside.

Baking: Preheat the oven to 400°F. Do not coat the dough with the basic topping (oil, rosemary, and salt). Bake 10 minutes. Reduce the heat to 375°F, and bake another 10 minutes. Remove the bread from the oven, and raise the heat to 400°F. Blend together the ricotta, Parmigiano, parsley, basil, garlic, and onion. Spread the ricotta mixture over the partially baked loaf. Top with the artichoke sauté, including any of its pan juices. Sprinkle with the 2 tablespoons olive oil, and bake 13 to 15 minutes, or until the bottom of the bread is crisp.

Serving: Eat hot or warm from the oven, or cool on a rack. The bread will keep, well wrapped, 2 days in the refrigerator. Rewarm it about 10 minutes in a 350°F oven.

Spianata for the Madonna of August

A *traditional Romagna bread made in honor of the Madonna of the August harvest. In Romagna's countryside this ancient bread still celebrates the first wine grapes.*

2 cups wine or seedless red grapes
1½ tablespoons extra-virgin
   olive oil

2 tablespoons sugar
1 recipe *Spianata* dough, shaped,
   risen, and ready to bake

Preheat the oven to 400°F. Push the grapes into the top of the dough. Sprinkle with the oil and sugar. Bake 10 minutes. Then lower the heat to 350°F and bake another 25 minutes. The bread is done when the bottom of the loaf sounds hollow when tapped. Serve the bread warm or at room temperature as an antipasto, or with first and second courses.

Crispy Fritters
Gnocco Fritto

A *simple bread dough—in itself a rare treat for most of us these days—becomes irresistible when turned into golden fritters. For many in Emilia-Romagna bread fritters stretched precious dough (often watered down to make it go even further in the frying pan), satisfying hunger at little expense. A version of this fritter, fried and then soaked in a bowl of milk, was the dinner of Romagna's peasants until several decades ago.*

During an autumn polenta festival, I noticed that the fritter stand was even more popular than the table where mounds of golden polenta were being spooned out with a generous hand. As the local women rolled out their tender bread dough, they cut a small hole in the center of each round. The cooks called it the belly button (<u>ombelico</u> in Italian, <u>umbreghel</u> in local dialect), and insisted that it produced puffier fritters. After much testing I had to agree, and their trick is shared here.

[Makes 18 to 20 pieces]

4 cups (1 pound) all-purpose unbleached flour (organic stone-ground preferred)

2½ teaspoons (1 envelope) granulated yeast

½ cup warm milk (110°F)

3 tablespoons unsalted butter, at room temperature

1¼ teaspoons salt

½ cup plus 3 tablespoons milk

2 quarts vegetable oil for deep-frying

Method

Working Ahead: *The fritters are best fried and eaten as soon as possible, but the rising of the dough can be slowed down by putting it in the refrigerator overnight. Let it come to room temperature before rolling and cutting.*

Making the Dough by Hand: Pour the flour into a large mixing bowl. Transfer 1 tablespoon of the flour to a small bowl and blend it with the yeast. Add the warm milk and let it stand 10 minutes, or until the yeast is bubbly. While the yeast is proofing, add the butter and salt to the flour. Work the butter into the flour with your fingers or a pastry cutter. Using a wooden spoon, stir the yeast and the additional milk into the flour. Knead the rough dough in the bowl, or on a work surface, 10 minutes or until it is elastic. The dough starts out sticky, but kneading makes it smooth.

Making the Dough in a Food Processor: Place the flour in a food processor fitted with the steel blade. Transfer 1 tablespoon to a small bowl, and blend it with the yeast and the warm milk. Set aside 10 minutes, or until the yeast is bubbly. While the yeast is proofing, add the butter and salt to the flour, and process 30 seconds. Turn the yeast and the additional milk into the food processor. Process 30 seconds, stop a few seconds, and then process again 45 seconds. The dough should be smooth and elastic.

Rising: Place dough in a lightly oiled medium-size bowl. Cover with plastic wrap, and let stand at room temperature 2 to 2½ hours, or until doubled in bulk.

Shaping and Frying the Fritters: Divide the dough into eighteen to twenty balls. Roll them out as thin as possible, forming 7- or 8-inch circles (cut into 2- or 3-inch circles if serving as finger food with drinks). Cut out a ½-inch round from the center of each disc (the "belly button"). Let the dough relax 10 to 15 minutes. (Relaxing ensures a crisp and tender fritter, rather than a tough, chewy one.) Meanwhile, heat the oil in a deep-fryer or wok to 375°F. Spread a triple thickness of paper towels on a large baking sheet for draining the fritters. Heat the oven to 200°F. Fry one or two pieces at a time, turning and cooking them in the oil until golden brown on both sides (2 to 3 minutes total cooking time). Lift the fritters from the oil with a slotted spoon, and drain well on paper towels. Slip the fritters into the oven on a platter to keep warm while you continue frying the rest.

Serving: Serve hot, wrapped in a napkin-lined basket.

Suggestions   **Wine:** A crisp white such as a Sauvignon Blanc from Parma or Friuli, or a simple red Bardolino from the Veneto.

Menu: Serve as part of Antipasto Castelvetro (page 16), accompanied by a Platter of Cured Meats (page 14) and Marinated Baby Onions (page 16). Although often a first course in Emilia-Romagna, for modern appetites this trio is a complete supper. When serving as an antipasto, follow with Ferrara's Soup of the Monastery (page 220), Balsamic Roast Chicken (page 279), or Seafood Stew Romagna (page 259).

Lumpheads, or What's in a Name?

Although a fritter is delicious to eat, you do not want to be called one. *Gnocco* affectionately describes someone who is a little thick in the head—literally a lumphead. But *gnocco,* meaning bread fritter, is a perfect example of food names that change from one place to another. In Modena and Reggio's hills these are *gnocco fritto.* Rolled thicker and cut into haphazard rectangles, they become *cherseina* in those same hills. Minor variations in the dough make them Parma's *torta fritta.* In Castelfranco Emilia, the fritters are *crescentine fritte.* Go 20 miles down the road to Bologna, and *crescentine* is also a baked flatbread. In Ferrara fritters are *pinzino.* Romagna's *piadina fritta* of leavened bread dough are not to be confused with the flatbread called *piadina.*

Little Tile-Baked Hearth Breads
Tigelle

Tigelle are the size of an English muffin with a biscuitlike center and a crisp crust. They are best split open and brushed with olive oil and garlic, or slathered with a blend of minced salt pork, garlic, and rosemary called a <u>condimento.</u> Tigelle can be lunch, Sunday-night supper, a snack, or a first course. At mountain weddings and christenings, where trencherman dining still reigns, <u>Tigelle</u> and their <u>condimento</u> are served before a progression of pasta dishes.

In the Modena hills <u>Tigelle</u> are baked not in ovens but on hearthstones, with the bread sandwiched between hot terra-cotta discs <u>(tigelle)</u> the size of hockey pucks. Terra-cotta <u>Tigelle</u> tiles are unavailable in America, but the little breads bake successfully on top of the stove, on a griddle or even in a heavy skillet. The best way to bake them is on the type of baking stone normally used in the oven.

[Makes about 20 breads]

1½ teaspoons granulated yeast

½ cup warm water (110°F)

3¼ cups (13 ounces) all-purpose unbleached flour (organic stone-ground preferred), plus 2 tablespoons as needed

1 tablespoon unsalted butter, at room temperature

2 teaspoons salt

½ cup plus 2 tablespoons water

About 3 tablespoons extra-virgin olive oil (for griddle)

Condimento (optional)

8 ounces pancetta, minced very fine, or ½ cup extra-virgin olive oil

1 large clove garlic, minced

1 teaspoon fresh rosemary leaves, minced

½ cup (2 ounces) freshly grated Italian Parmigiano-Reggiano cheese (optional)

Method

Working Ahead: *The dough should be started about 4 hours before you intend to eat. Baked* Tigelle *hold well for several hours, wrapped in plastic wrap, and freeze successfully. Wrap them in a single layer of aluminum foil before freezing. Reheat them, defrosted, at 300°F, 20 to 30 minutes, or until hot to the center. If they are at all soggy, unwrap them and crisp them by baking another 5 to 10 minutes.*

Making the Dough by Hand: Combine the yeast and the warm water in a large mixing bowl. Stir in 1 tablespoon of the flour and let the mixture stand 5 minutes, or until the yeast is bubbly. Add the butter to the yeast mixture. Stir in the salt with a wooden spoon. Then blend in the rest of the water alternately with the remaining flour. You will have a lumpy, sticky dough. Knead the rough dough in the bowl or on a work surface 10 minutes, or until it is elastic. The dough starts out sticky, but kneading turns it smooth, soft, and elastic. If necessary knead in another 2 tablespoons flour.

Making the Dough in a Food Processor: Pour the yeast and the warm water into the bowl of a food processor fitted with the steel blade. Add about 1 tablespoon of the flour, and blend it into the yeast mixture. Let it stand 5 minutes, or until the yeast is bubbly. Add the butter, the rest of the flour, the remaining water, and the salt. Process 10 seconds, stop a few seconds, and process again 10 seconds. The dough should be smooth, soft, and elastic. If it is still sticky, blend in another 2 tablespoons flour.

Rising and Shaping: Lightly oil a medium bowl with olive oil. Place the kneaded dough in the bowl, cover it with plastic wrap, and let it stand at room temperature 2½ hours, or until almost tripled in bulk. Do not be concerned if the dough overrises at this point. Punch down the dough and shape it into twenty balls about 1½ inches in diameter. Roll them out into discs about 3½ inches in diameter and a little over ¼ inch thick. Cover them with a kitchen towel and let rest 40 minutes.

Making the Condimento: Blend together the pancetta or olive oil, garlic, rosemary, and cheese. Set aside at room temperature.

Baking the Tigelle: Heat the oven to 200°F. Heat a baking stone, metal griddle, or heavy sauté pan over a burner at the lowest heat, and gradually, over about 10 minutes, raise the heat to medium-low. Once the baking surface is hot, rub a little oil over it with a paper towel. Place three or four *Tigelle* on it so they are not crowded. Bake until speckled golden brown on both sides, about 6 minutes per side. Wrap them, several at a time, in foil and keep them in the warm oven. Continue baking batches until they are all in the warm oven.

Serving: Serve hot, wrapped in a napkin-lined basket, accompanied by minced garlic and olive oil or the *condimento*.

Suggestions   **Wine:** A fresh simple red with *Tigelle,* such as a young Sangiovese di Romagna or one from Umbria. The Piemonte's Campo Romano or a young Chianti Montalbano would be excellent too.

Menu: Have *Tigelle* as a casual meal, with or without their *condimento,* with coppa (page 474), salami (page 501), and Balsamic Vegetables (page 18). If desired, add nontraditional accompaniments of sliced radishes, tomatoes, scallions, cucumbers, celery, mozzarella, and fresh ricotta cheese (page 454). Serve the breads, along with the *condimento* and Balsamic Vegetables, as an antipasto before Giovanna's Wine-Basted Rabbit (page 284) or Erminia's Pan-Crisped Chicken (page 270).

Cook's Notes **Italian Salt Pork and Pancetta:** In Italy salt pork is used in the *condimento*. Italian salt pork is particularly satiny, not overly salty, and safe as well as delicious when eaten raw. It closest equivalent in the United States is not salt pork but pancetta. See page 486 for information on buying and using pancetta.

Borlengo
Borlengo alla Guiglia

*W*hat a delicious curiosity Borlengo is—a huge pan bread so thin it seems transparent, so crisp you expect it to shatter. Instead, Borlengo bends and folds, and tastes chewy and crisp at the same time. If its appearance is fascinating, its topping, called a condimento, is even more so. A liquid version of Tigelle's traditional filling, good pancetta or lard is melted with garlic and rosemary, then dabbed on the hot Borlengo. Just before folding it into quarters, the bread is showered with a handful of Parmigiano-Reggiano cheese. No wonder Borlengo is a favorite Sunday-night supper.

Ethnic food authority Cara De Silva not only shares my passion for Emilia-Romagna but also patiently perfected this recipe. I owe her a great debt. Borlengo is a prime example of how the simpler the dish, the more difficult the translation into another culture becomes. But do not be intimidated—Cara has made Borlengo easy for the home cook. It takes time but no special skill. Note, too, that olive oil can be substituted for the condimento's pancetta or lard. Although not traditionally used, it is a delicious low-cholesterol alternative.

[Makes 6 to 8 large discs]

Condimento
½ cup high-quality lard (page 483),
   or 8 ounces pancetta trimmed of meat,
   or ½ cup extra-virgin olive oil
2 tablespoons minced garlic
Two 3-inch sprigs fresh rosemary,
   or 2 teaspoons dried rosemary
   leaves
Salt and freshly ground black
   pepper to taste

Batter
1¼ cups plus 2 tablespoons (5½
   ounces) all-purpose unbleached flour
   (organic stone-ground preferred)
½ cup plus 2 tablespoons (2½
   ounces) cake flour
¾ teaspoon salt
2 tablespoons beaten egg
6 cups water

Topping
6 ounces Italian Parmigiano-Reggiano
   cheese, grated fine

continued

Method   **Working Ahead:** *The* condimento *will hold, covered, in the refrigerator 2 days. Grate the cheese shortly before serving. The* Borlengo *can be made several hours ahead, kept at room temperature, and then quickly reheated in the pan before topping with the* con-dimento *and cheese. Rewarm the* condimento *before using.*

Making the Condimento: Melt the lard or pancetta in a small saucepan over low heat. Keeping the heat very low, stir in the garlic, rosemary, and seasonings. Cook gently 15 minutes, or until the garlic is poached and soft. (Olive oil needs no melting; simply warm it with the flavorings.) Set aside.

Making the Batter: Blend the two flours, salt, and egg in a large bowl. Add 1½ cups of the water, and beat with an electric mixer 4 minutes, or by hand about 6 minutes. Stir in the remaining water. The batter should resemble slightly thickened milk. Add a little more water or flour if necessary. Let the batter stand 20 minutes.

Cooking the Borlengo: Heat two 10- to 12-inch nonstick or very well seasoned skillets over low heat. They are at the proper temperature when a few drops of water sprinkled on them hiss but do not skitter. Brush the skillets lightly with a little of the *condimento.* Film the skillets with batter, pouring off any extra and swirling to cover the bottoms completely. (This will take about ½ cup for a 12-inch skillet, ⅓ cup for a 10-inch one.) In Guiglia the *Borlengo* makers say, "*Borlengo* must be thin as a veil and transparent as glass."

Cook 30 minutes over low heat, or until the *Borlengo* no longer looks damp and raw on the upper side. It will still be unbrowned. Turn and cook another minute or so. During the cooking, the large semi-transparent bread will crater, blister, and possibly split. It behaves in a way you have rarely seen in anything made of flour. Don't worry. For a crisp bread that cooks a bit faster and is speckled with a little gold, use medium-low heat. Cook about 10 minutes on one side, then turn and cook another 5 minutes on the other. This *Borlengo* will have a brittle texture and taste "browner," but still be very good. Once the *Borlengo* is done, remove it from the pan and set aside at room temperature. They should not be covered.

Serving: Rewarm the *condimento.* Reheat the *Borlengo* in the same skillets over low heat 3 minutes, turning halfway through warming. Dab with a little of the warmed *condimento,* sprinkle with a tablespoon or a little more of the cheese, and fold into quarters.

Suggestions   **Wine:** In the Modena hills, fizzy local red or white wines are quaffed with *Borlengo.* You could also drink a simple Valpolicella or a young red Cellatica from Lombardy, or a fresh "La Monella" from Braida di Giacomo Bologna in the Asti area of Piemonte.

Menu: *Borlengo* is a fine Sunday-night supper. Plan on three or four per person. Follow it with either Baked Pears with Fresh Grape Syrup (page 442) or cool wedges of Cinnamon and Clove Custard (page 440).

Cook's Notes **Dainty Borlengo:** *Borlengo* can be cooked in 6-inch crêpe pans, using ¼ cup batter for each.

Fifteenth-century miniature of a woman making pan-cooked flatbread similar to *Borlengo* and *Gnocco Fritto*

A "Joke" of a Bread

Three hilltowns, Zocca, Vignola, and Guiglia, vie for the honor of being the true home of *Borlengo*. But it is perhaps Guiglia that has the strongest claim. The story of *Borlengo*'s beginnings goes back to a time long ago, when mountain lords clashed with great regularity. The old castle at Guiglia was ruled by Ugolino, a lord famous for his table. When his enemies laid siege, cutting off all food supplies, no one could imagine how Ugolino could continue to do battle. Fortunately the castle did have a large supply of flour. Bread and pasta doughs were continuously watered down. Finally thinned to batter, the transparent sheets were baked over fires to keep the troops fed. *Borlengo,* from the root *burla,* meaning "joke" in local dialect, was truly a joke of a bread, but the joke was on Ugolino's attackers. Another theory claims that *Borlengo* was born as the food of the poor. The oldest recipes call for only flour and water, with no expensive egg. Almost everyone had a fire, water, and a little flour. When all else failed, *Borlengo* could feed the family. Today the bread is a favorite Sunday-night snack after a day of dining in the country. Often only men make *Borlengo,* perhaps because they feel linked to Ugolino's soldiers, legendary for their courage and fortitude.

Stalking the Wild *Borlengo*

The bread sounded like no other that my friend Cara De Silva and I had ever heard of: a bread you can almost see through, as big as a cart wheel, dotted with cheese, garlic, and rosemary. Supposedly *Borlengo* was made in the hilltowns above Modena. Yet in Modena city and on the plain, few people had heard of it. Even in the hills *Borlengo* constantly eluded us. It was made in the winter; we were seeking it in the spring. Day after day, in town after town, we were told it was probably down the road or in the next village. The only constant was Rodiano. All agreed it was made in Rodiano. Of course, Rodiano was a mere pin speck on the map and finding it proved impossible. Every time we set out for Rodiano we lost our way on country roads no bigger than cow paths. Finally, we gave up the search and wandered the hills for pleasure. A blinding rainstorm brought us to a halt. Suddenly, the rain and mist cleared, and we were staring at a sign: "Welcome to Rodiano." Like Brigadoon, it appeared out of the mist.

We had been told that Rodiano had two *trattorie,* and that the one on the left made *Borlengo.* Of the four buildings making up Rodiano, sure enough, there side-by-side were two *trattorie.* We leapt gleefully out of the car, only to discover the sign on the left-hand trattoria: "Closed for vacation." Once again, *Borlengo* was not to be. We turned to the adjoining Trattoria Leonelli, crestfallen. Little did we know we were about to stumble upon yet another intriguing bread of the Modenese mountains. In the tiny back dining room, baskets holding small rounds of hot bread were served with platters of cured meats and pickled vegetables. With them came bowls of minced salt pork flavored with garlic and fresh rosemary. Our shy waitress called the breads *Tigelle.* We were shown how to split open the hot breads and spread them with the pork mixture, then eat the meats and vegetables as accompaniments. Instead of being heavy and overrich, the spread was sweet and clean-tasting. (Italian salt pork, *lardo,* is more delicately flavored than ours, and is cured to be safely eaten raw.)

Tigelle are not baked in ovens. In fact, they are not baked like any bread I know. They cook between hot terra-cotta discs or tiles. At Trattoria Leonelli the tiles, about 4 inches in diameter, are heated in a freestanding fireplace in the back garden. The hot discs are then hauled into the kitchen with its own open fire and piled on the heated hearthstone. Small rounds of risen bread dough are sandwiched between them. The bread bakes from the heat of the tiles, taking on the pattern of their sunburst embossing. It also takes its name from them: *Tigelle* is both the tile and the bread. When the Leonellis cater local weddings, 200 *Tigelle* are stacked on the hearth at a time. The bread is so old and so much a part of Modena mountain traditions that no one knows where or when it began.

The next day we had to move on to Bologna. But still resisting leaving the countryside, we decided to stop for coffee. Driving into the hilltop village of Guiglia, we almost went off the road. "Fifteenth Annual *Borlengo* Festival," proclaimed the banner strung over the street. We exploded with laughter. We were among the first to arrive. Chickens were still strutting across the town square. Under a yellow tent, the local men who make *Borlengo* were setting up. They worked with big round pans of hammered copper over gas-fired braziers.

Guiglia's oldest *Borlengo* maker demonstrated his technique. First he rubbed the hot pan with a chunk of home-cured pancetta. Then he ladled the milky batter into the pan, making a sheer film. It cooked to speckled gold on one side, then was turned and cooked on the other. More than two feet across, the *Borlengo* was crisp, parchmentlike. He dipped a brush into a pot of clear liquid flecked with green and white—homemade lard melted with garlic and rosemary. After dabbing the *Borlengo* with the brush, he showered it with a handful of Parmigiano-Reggiano cheese. We folded the *Borlengo* in quarters and ate it from a big napkin. We left the festival hours later—happy, full, and feeling like Stanley after he finally found Livingstone.

Piacenza's Great Fritter
Burtlêina

These rounds of crisp, golden, and cratered fritters are traditionally eaten as snacks with cured meats or jam. In Piacenza's farm country they were carried out to the farm workers as their lunch. The women stacked up three and four Burtlêina, tucked a salami and bottle of wine under their arms, and off they went. The original fritter consisted of a little flour and water fried in lard. For pure luxury, eggs were added to the batter.

Maria Bertuzzi shared this recipe and its traditions with me during a wonderful cooking lesson in the kitchen of her Ristorante Grande at Rivergaro, in the hills above Piacenza. Spiraling the Burtlêina batter into hot oil reminds me of the funnel cakes of our Pennsylvania Dutch country. While those are served with sweet syrup, Italy's fritters are lightly salted.

Welcome family and friends in from a winter's day outdoors with a snack of hot Burtlêina. Cut the rounds into wedges and accompany them with thin-sliced coppa, salami, or even some tart homemade jam. Offer a choice of wine or hot coffee.

[Makes 3 to 4 large fritters, serving 6 to 8]

1½ cups (6 ounces) all-purpose unbleached flour (organic stone-ground preferred)
½ cup (2 ounces) cake flour

2 eggs
2 teaspoons salt
2¼ cups water
6 cups vegetable oil for deep-frying

Method

Working Ahead: *Let the batter rest from 30 minutes to several hours. Once the fritters are fried, they are best eaten as soon as possible.*

Making the Batter: In Piacenza, mixing by hand literally means using your hand like a big spoon to beat and stretch the batter. A large spoon or whisk also works well. Blend together the flours, eggs, salt, and water into a smooth batter, the consistency of heavy cream. Let it stand at room temperature 30 minutes or longer. If the batter thickens in standing, stir in another ¼ cup water.

Frying the Burtlêina: Preheat the oven to warm. Lay out a triple thickness of paper towels for draining the *Burtlêina.* Pour the oil into a 12-inch sauté pan, and heat over medium-high heat to 370°F (use a deep-frying thermometer). Using a long-handled ladle, scoop up about 1⅓ cups of the batter. Stand back while you spiral the batter into the hot fat, making a large disc. Fry 4 to 5 minutes, or until golden on the bottom. Then carefully turn it, bracing the *Burtlêina* with two long metal spatulas. Continue frying until it is golden brown on the second side, 3 to 4 minutes. Lift the *Burtlêina* with a slotted spoon, and drain it well on both sides atop the paper towels. Then slip it onto a baking sheet and keep it warm in the oven. Repeat until all the batter is used up.

Serving: Serve *Burtlêina* hot on its own or accompanied by thin-sliced coppa and pancetta (pages 474 and 486). For lighter eating, serve Balsamic Vegetables (page 18). You could also offer it with a double recipe of Nonna's Homemade Tart Jam (page 413).

Suggestions   **Wine:** A simple red like a Bonarda from Piacenza, or a Sangiovese di Romagna or from Umbria.

Menu: For modern appetites serve *Burtlêina* as a snack. Or make it an antipasto, following the fritter with a light soup like Ferrara's Soup of the Monastery (page 220) or Modena's Spiced Soup of Spinach and Cheese (page 234). Have fresh fruit for dessert.

Romagna Griddle Bread
Piadina

A *bread for impatient appetites,
Romagna's hearty* Piadina *is semi-crisp and tender at the same time.
Resembling a flour tortilla, this simple bread tastes best when eaten with
its traditional toppings.* Piadina *is as much a part of Romagna's soul as
is her land. Poets compose odes to* Piadina, *historians chronicle its past,
and* Piadina *stands are almost as common as trees in Romagna's
countryside.*

Romagnoli eat Piadina *with meals as well as from the snack
stands throughout the region. Up until a few decades ago this ancient
bread was baked on griddles of unglazed terra-cotta over hot embers in
the fireplace. Today the bread is cooked on metal griddles on the stove
top, but hardware stores in Romagna still stock terra-cotta ones for those
who insist they impart irreplaceable flavor and crispness.*

*Traditional fillings are thin slices of prosciutto, salami, and sautéed
spinach, chard, or wild greens. Even more satisfying is Romagna's
squaquerone cheese, tangy and spoonable. It becomes memorable when
smeared on hot* Piadina *and topped with a few leaves of arugula. Make
an informal supper of* Piadina, *cooking them together so everyone can
enjoy their fragrance. Set out a variety of toppings, and invite diners to
try different combinations. This is more than a meal—it is a piece of
Romagna's rural heritage.*

[Makes 12 breads, serving 8 to 12]

4¼ cups (17 ounces) all-purpose unbleached flour (organic stone-ground preferred)	6 tablespoons (3 ounces) high-quality lard (page 483), chilled
1½ teaspoons salt	1 cup warm water
½ teaspoon baking soda	Additional lard or a little oil for the baking stone or pan

Method

Working Ahead: *The dough can be made early in the day; wrap and store it in the
refrigerator. Piadina are best baked and eaten warm, as soon as possible. They can be
wrapped in foil and kept warm in a low oven until you have finished cooking the entire
recipe. If they must be made several hours before serving, keep them tightly wrapped. Shortly
before serving, restore their pliability by lightly sprinkling each one with a little water,
restacking, and wrapping them in foil. Then reheat in a 325°F oven about 15 minutes.*

Making the Dough by Hand: Blend together all the dry ingredients in a large bowl. With your fingers, rub in the lard until the mixture resembles fine meal. Sprinkle the water over the mixture. Still using your hands, blend and knead 3 to 5 minutes, or until the dough is smooth, semi-soft, elastic, and not sticky. You can roll out the *Piadina* immediately, or cover the bowl with a towel and let the dough relax at room temperature about 30 minutes.

Making the Dough in a Food Processor: Combine the dry ingredients in a processor fitted with the steel blade. Run the machine about 5 seconds to thoroughly blend them. Add the lard, and process about 30 seconds to completely blend the lard with the flour. It should resemble fine meal. Sprinkle the water over the dough. Use the on/off pulse to blend in the water until the dough looks like large crumbs or clumps. Do not blend until it forms a ball. Turn the dough out on a work surface and knead three or four times to gather it into a ball. The dough will be smooth, elastic, semi-soft, and not at all sticky. Roll out the *Piadina* immediately, or wrap the dough in a kitchen towel and let it rest about 30 minutes at room temperature.

Shaping and Baking: Heat the oven to 200°F. Divide the dough into twelve balls. Use a rolling pin to roll each one out into a 7- to 7½-inch round. Make sure they are no bigger. If possible, cook the *Piadina* on a baking stone on top of the stove. If this is unavailable, it can be cooked in a heavy cast-iron skillet or griddle, or in a stainless steel–lined skillet with good, even heat distribution. I usually work with two stones or griddles to bake the breads quickly. Perfect *Piadina* are easily achieved by cooking them quickly without burning. They will be like a slightly stiffened flour tortilla, pliable enough to be torn or bent, but not so stiff that they are hard. Slow cooking produces a hard, crisp *Piadina*.

Heat the griddle or skillet over medium-high heat. If you are using a stone, heat it gradually, beginning at low and taking about 15 minutes to bring it up to medium. Usually the stone will be hotter than a metal skillet or griddle. Test the temperature by sprinkling the cooking surface with a few drops of water. They should fizzle and disappear in about 2 to 3 seconds. Rub the pan or stone with a little lard or oil. Bake the *Piadina* one at a time. It should take 30 to 45 seconds for the bottom to be speckled with deep golden brown. The uncooked side will look grainy and mottled. If this takes longer, raise the heat slightly. If the speckles are dark brown, the cooking surface is too hot. Lower the heat slightly. Using a metal spatula, flip the bread over and bake another 30 seconds. This second side will have fewer golden-brown speckles, and it will look slightly parched. Stack and seal the finished breads in a single layer of aluminum foil, and keep them warm in the oven.

Serving: Serve the *Piadina* hot, as rounds or cut in wedges, wrapped in a napkin-lined basket to keep them warm.

Suggestions   **Wine:** Young red Sangiovese di Romagna is traditional with *Piadina*. Umbria's Sangiovese is a good second choice.

continued

Menu: Serve *Piadina* hot with second courses like Seafood Stew Romagna (page 259), Mardi Gras Chicken (page 277), and Lamb with Black Olives (page 305). Enjoy it as a snack, casual supper, or first course by serving it hot with Spiced Spinach with Almonds (page 330) or simply sautéed spinach; prosciutto, coppa, or pancetta (pages 495, 474, or 486); or Fresh Squaquerone Cheese (below) and coarsely chopped fresh arugula. For a casual supper, offer it with all these accompaniments and any of the following that appeal.

An untraditional topping is squaquerone in combination with slices of vine-ripened tomato and chopped fresh basil, or fresh mozzarella and red onion. *Piadina* is also delicious with Piacenza Peppers Country Style (page 244) or topped with Garlic-Sautéed Cabbage (page 331).

Cook's Notes **Stuffed Variation:** Essentially stove-top calzone, these turnovers can be stuffed with any of the traditional fillings, or with about ¼ cup each tomato sauce and shredded mozzarella. Roll out a round of dough as thin as possible. Spread the filling over half of it. Fold over, and crimp the edges to seal. Bake on the griddle about 3 minutes per side over medium-low heat.

Fresh Squaquerone Cheese
Formaggio Squaquerone

A *fresh cow cheese originating in Romagna, squaquerone is tangy and creamy at the same time, a cross between yogurt and cream cheese. Sold from crocks in cheese stores throughout the area, it is spoonable and a little lumpy.*

I first tasted squaquerone slathered on hot <u>Piadina</u> flatbread and topped with arugula leaves—a perfect combination. Later I learned that a ripe tomato and thin slices of onion add even more goodness to the blend. The more I tasted squaquerone with different foods, the more captivating it became.

In Romagna, the method for making squaquerone is almost as old as milking cows. <u>Lactobacillus thermophilus</u> culture is added to raw or pasteurized milk. As the milk gains acidity, it thickens. After chilling about 36 hours, the typical texture of curds suspended in cream evolves. Attempts at approximating the cheese in the United States met with frustration. No matter what kinds of culture, milk, or temperature were used, the results were disappointing. One day, in total exasperation, I blended the elements that squaquerone reminded me of: yogurt, *buttermilk, sour cream, and cream cheese. The result was the closest I had come to the cheese as it is in Italy. This simple formula needs only a bowl, a spoon, and 10 minutes of effort.*

[Makes 2 to 2½ cups]

6 ounces cream cheese (preferably without guar gum), chilled
¼ cup sour cream, chilled
½ cup buttermilk, chilled

¾ cup plain low-fat yogurt with live cultures (preferably made without pectin and other additives), chilled
1 tablespoon fresh lemon juice
Salt (optional)

Method

Working Ahead: *Let the cheese mellow in the refrigerator 24 to 36 hours before using. It will keep, covered, 5 days in the refrigerator.*

Making Squaquerone: Use a fork to mash the cream cheese with the sour cream in a medium-size bowl until they are well blended. Gradually stir in the buttermilk, leaving pea-size lumps of the cream cheese mixture. Fold in (do not beat in) the yogurt and lemon juice until well blended. (If beaten in, the yogurt will liquify.) Add salt to taste if desired. Cover and refrigerate.

Using Squaquerone

- Spoon it over fruits (sweetening the cheese with honey, if desired).
- Spread it over sliced tomatoes.
- Mix with 2 cups chopped fresh herbs (basil, marjoram, parsley, and scallions) and use bread or crackers.
- Dab a few spoonfuls over the sautéed onions in *Spianata* stuffed with sautéed onions (page 370).
- Top *Piadina* with a salty prosciutto and spread with squaquerone. Or merely cover the bread with the cheese and top with thinly sliced red onion.
- Toss into hot pasta dressed with olive oil and garlic.
- Sauté a large chopped onion in olive oil until golden. Add a handful of fresh basil and a generous amount of minced garlic. Cook a few seconds. Toss with 1 pound tagliarini, spaghetti, or linguine and ½ cup squaquerone. Season with a generous amount of black pepper.
- Spoon the cheese over cucumber-onion salad.
- Spoon it over a whole roasted onion.
- Dab over potato salad dressed with olive oil, onion, and vinegar.
- Spread squaquerone on baked potatoes.

Modena Mountain Bread
Pane Montanaro

If I could make only one bread for the rest of my life, it would be this loaf. It is everything an old-style country bread should be; fragrant with wheat, dense with a crackled crust, and chewy with an interior that tugs at the tooth. Mixing whole-wheat and white flours, and letting the bread mellow through a long sponge and slow risings, bring out the deep, full flavor of the wheat. Crushed wheat berries mixed into the dough give the occasional crunch. The potato in the bread makes it moist. Both the potato and the small quantity of yeast keep the bread fresh a week.

[Makes 1 large loaf]

Sponge

2 tablespoons all-purpose unbleached flour (organic stone-ground preferred)

1½ teaspoons granulated yeast

¼ cup warm water (110°F)

2 cups (8 ounces) all-purpose unbleached flour (organic stone-ground preferred)

1 cup warm water (110°F)

Dough

5 to 6 ounces red-skinned potato(es)

Generous ½ cup (3 ounces) wheat berries

1 cup (4 ounces) whole-wheat flour (organic stone-ground preferred)

½ teaspoons salt

About 4½ cups (1 pound, 2 ounces) all-purpose unbleached flour (organic stone-ground preferred)

1½ cups organic stone-ground cornmeal (with baking stone)

1 tablespoon all-purpose unbleached flour (organic stone-ground preferred)

3 cups water (for steam)

Method

Working Ahead: *The bread takes about 1½ hours of actual effort, but it is spread over 2 days. The sponge works 12 to 18 hours. The potato and wheat berries can be cooked 1 day ahead and then refrigerated, covered. Have them at room temperature before blending them with the dough. The first rising takes 2 to 3 hours, the second 1½, and the bread bakes about 1¼ hours. It keeps, wrapped and refrigerated, 1 week and freezes well 3 months.*

Making the Sponge: Start the sponge 16 to 22 hours before baking the bread. In a medium-size bowl, stir together the flour, yeast, and ¼ cup water. Let the mixture stand 5 minutes, or until the yeast is bubbly. Beat in the remaining 2 cups flour and 1 cup warm water. If you are working with an electric mixer, beat 1 minute at medium speed. By hand, beat vigorously about 3 minutes. Scrape down the sides of the bowl. Cover the bowl tightly with plastic wrap, and set aside at room temperature 12 to 18 hours.

Preparing the Potato and Wheat Berries: Boil the unpeeled potato in water to cover 30 minutes, or until very tender. Cool and peel. Save 10 tablespoons of the potato cooking water, and purée it with the potato. Cool to room temperature. Cook the wheat berries in fiercely boiling water to cover 10 minutes, or until tender. Drain and cool. Use a blender, food processor, or mortar and pestle to lightly crush the berries. Set aside at room temperature.

Making the Dough in a Heavy-Duty Mixer: In the mixer bowl, combine the sponge, potato purée, wheat berries, whole-wheat flour, salt, and half the all-purpose flour. Beat with the paddle attachment at medium speed about 2 minutes. Beat in another 1 cup flour and switch to the dough hook. Gradually add more flour until you have a sticky dough. The dough will be soft but holding its shape around the dough hook while it cleans the bottom and sides of the bowl. If it puddles at the bottom, blend in another few tablespoons of flour. It will be very elastic, soft, and a little sticky. Knead 10 minutes in the mixer.

Making the Dough by Hand: In a large bowl, beat together the sponge, whole-wheat flour, potato purée, wheat berries, salt, and half the all-purpose flour. Beat 5 minutes, and then work in enough flour to make a soft, slightly sticky dough. Turn the dough out onto a work surface and knead 10 minutes. It will be very elastic, soft, and a little sticky. If necessary, knead in another few spoonfuls of flour.

First Rising: Lightly oil a large bowl. Add the dough, and seal the bowl with plastic wrap. Set aside to rise at room temperature 2 to 3 hours, or until the dough is two-and-one-half to three times its original size. It will look blistered and soft. No harm will come to the bread if you let the dough sit as long as 8 hours.

Preparing to Bake: Although a greased baking sheet can be used, I prefer to bake the bread on a baking stone or unglazed terra-cotta tiles. If you are using tiles or a stone, set them in the oven before preheating it. You will need a flat wooden peel, cookie sheet, or piece of heavy cardboard. (Once the dough is shaped, half the cornmeal is spread on the peel, cookie sheet, or cardboard to keep the dough from sticking, and the dough is set on the cornmeal to rise. Then you slip the bread from the peel, sheet, or cardboard onto the baking surface that has been covered with the rest of the cornmeal.) If you are using a cookie sheet, lightly oil it with a little olive oil. Whichever method you use, place a shallow pan, such as a jelly roll pan, on the floor of a gas oven or on the lowest rack of an electric one. This will hold the water that steams and is vital to the crust's dense texture.

Shaping and Second Rising: Punch down the dough, and knead it about 5 minutes. Shape the dough into a ball by stretching it down and under, tucking it under itself until you have a taut sphere. Spread half the cornmeal over the peel and set the dough on it, or set the dough on the oiled cookie sheet. Sprinkle it with the 1 tablespoon flour. Cover the dough with a kitchen towel and let it rise at room temperature 1½ hours, or until doubled in bulk. The bread is ready for baking when you poke it with a finger and it does not spring back.

Baking: Preheat the oven to 400°F. Make sure the rack is in the center of the oven. If you are using tiles or a stone, spread it with the rest of the cornmeal, and slip the bread onto it. If you are using a cookie sheet, merely slip it into the oven. Stand back as you pour the 3 cups water into the shallow pan at the bottom of the oven. Trap the burst of steam in the oven by closing the door immediately. Bake 1 hour. Then turn the bread upside down and bake another 10 to 15 minutes, or until the loaf sounds hollow when tapped. Put the loaf on a rack to cool. Although it is so tempting when it's hot, do let the bread cool 1½ to 2 hours before cutting it. It will be at its very best then.

Suggestions   **Menu:** Enjoy the bread on its own, or serve it with any first or second course. Modena Mountain Bread is splendid in Garlic Crostini with Pancetta (page 28), Mountain Soup with Garlic Croutons (page 235), and Fresh Garlic Soup Brisighella (page 222). Toast thin slices, rub them with garlic and olive oil, and spoon Piacenza Peppers Country Style (page 244) or Garlic-Sautéed Cabbage (page 331) over them. Toasted or not, the bread is excellent with Fresh Squaquerone Cheese (page 386) and fresh arugula or chopped Belgian endive.

Cook's Notes **Wheat Berries:** Wheat berries are found in the natural foods section of supermarkets, food co-ops, specialty food stores, and health food stores. They are sometimes labeled "Whole-Grain Wheat."

A Memory Bread

This is a bread of memory for the women of Highwood, Illinois, who emigrated to America from the Modena mountains. They remember breads of their childhood. Maria Picchietti and Giovanna Lamberti recall that wheat was sparse in the mountains. Families grew their own and ground it into flour, often leaving specks of the whole grain. The mothers of Sue Bernardi and Anna Mardini added potatoes to moisten the loaf. Instead of leavening with yeast, they carried on a tradition as old as bread itself by saving some dough from the last loaf to begin the next. In Modena, too, my elderly friends spoke of the same breads. Each family remembered the bread with slight differences, but its essence remained the same.

Approximating a Wood-Burning Oven

For the millennia before gas and electric stoves were dreamt of, brick and stone ovens heated with wood fires were the magical places where bread was cooked. Many artisan bakers still use these ovens, knowing that they impart a special flavor and vitality to bread. The scent of burning wood subtly impregnates the loaf, and somehow the life of the fire brings more vigor to the bread. You can approximate the old ovens by using soaked wood chips and a baking stone or tiles. Soak 3 cups of applewood, oak, walnut, or maple chips in water to cover for 1 hour. (Although I have not worked with them, grape vines and other fruit woods should work well here.) Drain, saving 1½ cups of the water. Return it to the chips. Set a large shallow pan on the lowest rack of the oven. Place a second rack, holding a baking stone or tiles, in the center of the oven. Then preheat the oven to the required temperature. When the dough is ready for baking, place it on the center rack. Pull out the lower rack holding the shallow pan. Stand back as you pour the wood and its liquid down the length of the pan. Immediately close the oven door. If the wood begins to smoke while the bread is baking, pour another ½ cup water over the chips and quickly close the oven door. Ideally, there will be a fragrant wood aroma but no smoke. Once the bread has baked, let the wood pan cool completely before removing it from the oven. The chips can be reused for flavoring foods on an outdoor grill.

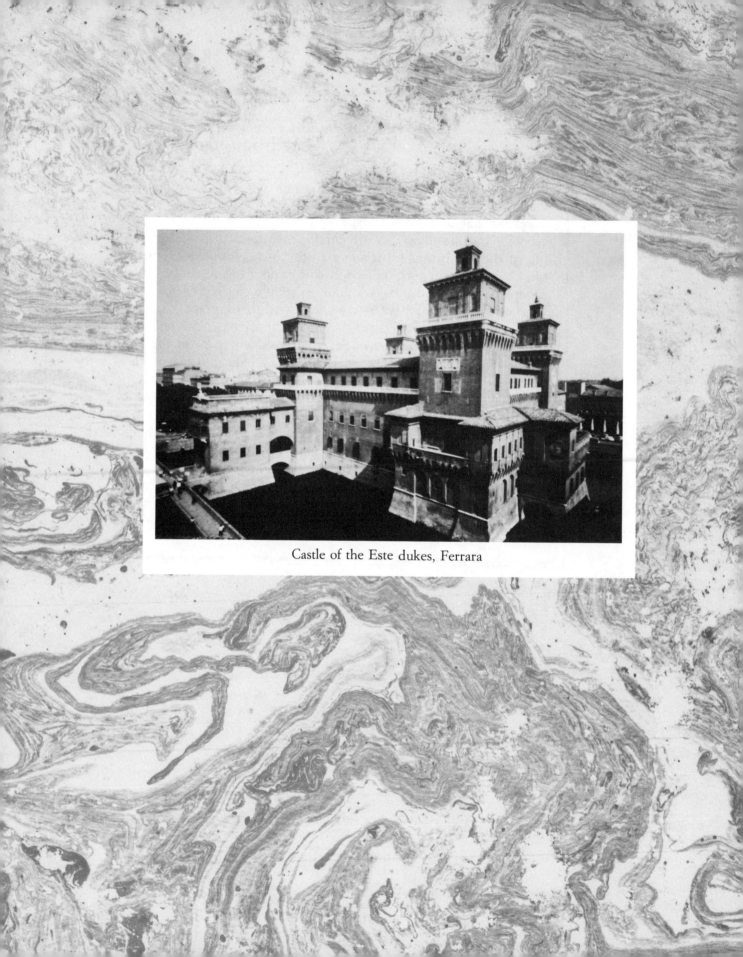
Castle of the Este dukes, Ferrara

DESSERTS

Cakes, Tarts and Pastries, Spoon Sweets, and the "Keeping Cakes" of Winter

his panorama of Emilia-Romagna's desserts spans both time and distance. It does not pretend to encompass the wealth of the region's sweets, but rather is a sampling of each area and period. Included here are 400 years of court food, beginning in the 1500s with Cardinal d'Este's Tart and weaving through the centuries to the contemporary Frozen Hazelnut Zabaione with Chocolate Marsala Sauce. I have borrowed as well from the vast collection of sweets marking feast days and festivals. And there are home dishes, their origins ranging from mountain villages to the farms of the Po River plain. Some are country desserts still baked in the hot coals of kitchen hearths, while others were created in the modern stainless steel kitchens of city restaurants.

Desserts in Emilia-Romagna possess almost as much diversity as do her pastas. The simplest of sweets, like fresh melon with balsamic vinegar and mint, exist side by side with the unrestrained excess of a frozen mousse of espresso, mascarpone cheese, and cream. The same pastry shop may produce the homey Ciambelle cake and sophisticated Duchess of Parma Torte. Desserts fall into several categories. Dolci is the all-inclusive term for sweets. A <u>torta</u> can be a cake, a tart, or a pudding in the shape of a cake.

"Keeping cakes" of winter is my own phrase for the spiced cakes of Christmas, baked in autumn and mellowed until the holidays. They are part of a category of sweets meant for long storage or maturing (<u>dolci di lunga conservazione</u>). Jams, conserves, cookies, candies, grape syrup, and liqueurs all fall into this group. Spoon sweets (<u>dolci al cucchiaio</u>) are literally spoonable custards and creams. For me, fruit dishes are part of this category, as are frozen desserts.

Chestnut dishes are under yet another heading. Although there are only three, they represent rich traditions from the hills and mountains of the region. These nuts were the flour, sweetener, and substance of many sweets in the past.

With each recipe you will find information on its traditions and ideas for serving the dish today. The menu suggestions at the end of each recipe get down to specifics, explaining how to serve the sweets with the rest of the dishes in this book.

A Note on Pastry: The tarts in this chapter share a similar pastry, a butter/sugar dough called <u>pasta frolla.</u> Some tarts demand a crust with more butter or sugar, and some less. In Nonna's Jam Tart, there is yet another possible interpretation of the pastry. The butter and sugar are whipped to a fluff with flour folded in later, creating a shortbread-style crust that is light and crisp.

Shorter, sweeter crusts may break apart as you transfer them to the tart pan. But remember, no one sees the bottom of your dessert. As long as the thickness of the crust is even for proper baking, there is nothing to worry about. Just press the pieces into the pan, joining the edges by pinching them together. These fragile crusts reward with melt-in-the-mouth tenderness.

Torta Barozzi
Torta Barozzi

> *A sensational specialty, made only in the castle town of Vignola outside Modena, Torta Barozzi is to chocolate cake what a diamond is to zircon. It looks like yet another flourless chocolate cake, but one mouthful banishes any sense of the mundane. This is a chocolate essence, moist and fudgy, with secret ingredients known only to the baker. Serve the rich cake cut in small wedges, and do tell the story of Modena's obsession with a seemingly conventional chocolate cake.*

[Makes 1 cake, serving 6 to 8]

½ cup (2 ounces) blanched almonds, toasted

2 tablespoons confectioner's sugar

4 tablespoons cocoa (not Dutch process)

1½ tablespoons unsalted butter

3 to 4 tablespoons all-purpose unbleached flour (organic stone-ground preferred)

8 tablespoons (4 ounces) unsalted butter, at room temperature

½ cup plus 2 tablespoons (4 ounces) sugar

4½ tablespoons smooth peanut butter

4 large eggs, separated

6 ounces bittersweet chocolate, melted and cooled

1 ounce unsweetened chocolate, melted and cooled

2½ tablespoons instant espresso coffee granules, dissolved in 1 tablespoon boiling water

1½ teaspoons dark rum

2 teaspoons vanilla extract

Decoration

1 tablespoon cocoa

½ tablespoon confectioner's sugar

Method

Working Ahead: *The Barozzi can be baked ahead and has admirable keeping qualities. It may be slightly better tasting in the first 24 hours after baking, but the cake keeps all its flavor when tightly wrapped and stored in the refrigerator up to 3 days. It freezes well 2 months. Serve at room temperature.*

Making Almond Powder: Combine the almonds, 2 tablespoons confectioner's sugar, and 3 tablespoons cocoa in a food processor fitted with the steel blade. Process until the almonds are a fine powder.

Blending the Batter: Butter the bottom and sides of an 8-inch springform pan with the 1 tablespoon of butter. Cut a circle of parchment paper to cover the bottom of the pan. Butter the paper with ½ tablespoon butter and line the pan with it, butter side up. Use the 3 to 4 tablespoons flour to coat the entire interior of the springform, shaking out any excess. Preheat the oven to 375°F, and set a rack in the center of the oven. Using an electric mixer fitted with the paddle attachment or a hand-held electric mixer, beat the butter and sugar at medium speed 8 to 10 minutes, or until almost white and very fluffy. Scrape down the sides of the bowl several times during beating. Beating the butter and sugar to absolute airiness ensures the *torta*'s fine grain and melting lightness. Still at medium speed, beat in the peanut butter. Then beat in the egg yolks, two at a time, until smooth. Reduce the speed to medium-low, and beat in the melted chocolates, the dissolved coffee, and the rum and vanilla. Then use a big spatula to fold in the almond powder by hand, keeping the batter light.

Whip the egg whites to stiff peaks. Lighten the chocolate batter by folding a quarter of the whites into it. Then fold in the rest, keeping the mixture light but without leaving any streaks of white.

Baking: Turn the batter into the baking pan, gently smoothing the top. Bake 15 minutes. Then reduce the oven heat to 325°F and bake another 15 to 20 minutes, or until a tester inserted in the center of the cake comes out with a few streaks of thick batter. The cake will have puffed about two thirds of the way up the sides of the pan. Cool the cake 10 minutes in the pan set on a rack. The cake will settle slightly but will remain level. Spread a kitchen towel on a large plate, and turn the cake out onto it. Peel off the parchment paper and cool the cake completely. Then place a round cake plate on top of the cake and hold the two plates together as you flip them over so the *torta* is right side up on the cake plate.

Serving: *Torta Barozzi* is moist and fudgy. Just before serving, sift the table-spoon of cocoa over the cake. Then top it with a sifting of the confectioner's sugar. (Or for a whimsical decoration, cut a large stencil of the letter "B" out of stiff paper or cardboard. Set it in the center of the cake before dusting the entire top with the confectioner's sugar. Carefully lift off the stencil once the sugar has settled.) Serve the *Barozzi* at room temperature, slicing it in small wedges.

Suggestions **Wine:** In Vignola, homemade walnut liqueur (*Nocino*) is sipped with the *Barozzi*. Here, the black muscat-based Elysium dessert wine from California does well with the cake's intense chocolate.

Menu: Serve after Modena dishes such as Giovanna's Wine-Basted Rabbit (page 284), Beef-Wrapped Sausage (page 314), Balsamic Roast Chicken (page 279), and Rabbit Dukes of Modena (page 286), or after light main dishes and first courses.

Cook's Notes **Chocolate:** Use a chocolate rich in deep fruity flavors, such as Tobler Tradition or Lindt Excellence.

Peanut Butter: Peanut butter is the surprise ingredient in the cake, and an important one. I use creamy Skippy, but no doubt other brands work well too.

Whipped Cream: Although not served this way in Vignola, the *Barozzi* is superb topped with dollops of unsweetened whipped cream. Count on whipping 1 cup of heavy cream to serve 6 to 8.

"It's All There on the Box"

Cracking the code of *Torta Barozzi* is Modena's favorite food game. For decades local cooks have tried to unravel its mystery, without success. When a Modenese dinner party gets dull, ask about *Torta Barozzi* and settle back. The heat of the debate will warm you for the rest of the evening. Eugenio Gollini invented the cake in 1897 at his Pasticceria Gollini in Vignola. The cake commemorated the birthday of Renaissance architect Jacopo Barozzi, a native son of Vignola who invented the spiral staircase. Today Gollini's grandsons, Carlo and Eugenio, still make *Barozzi* at the same *pasticceria*. Its recipe is secret, although its ingredients are stated on the cake's box. Family members have sworn never to reveal nor change the formula. But Eugenio Gollini smiles serenely when he tells you it is all there in plain sight.

Gollini offered no clue of how peanuts—a startling and definitely non-Italian ingredient—became part of the cake. I speculate that late 19th-century cooks considered these nuts, brought from Africa, to be exotic and intriguing. Perhaps in experimenting with them, the elder Gollini discovered how good they are with chocolate. Then he might have found that peanuts puréed into peanut butter ensured a smoother and even more melting *Torta Barozzi*. Historian Renato Bergonzini explained why the people of Vignola believe the cake's secret eludes discovery: "Barozzi left the last step of his spiral staircase unfinished. No one knows why, and no one would presume to finish it. To imitate the *torta* is like trying to finish Barozzi's staircase: impudent and foolish. Only the master himself can complete his work." I confess to both impudence and foolishness, but also to success. This recipe comes tantalizingly close to the original.

Modena Rice Pudding
Torta di Riso

The food of grandmothers, this baked rice pudding is scented with citron or almond. Baking burnishes it to a glowing gold and makes it firm enough to be sliced like a cake. Although made throughout the region, this rendition from Modena was shared by Catherine Piccolo of the Modena/St. Paul, Minnesota, Sister City Committee. This pudding is the dessert served after Sunday dinner in farmhouses on the Po River plain. It is pulled from the cold pantry for special guests, and is especially favored around Easter time.

[Serves 8 to 10]

3½ cups milk

1 cup (7 ounces) imported Superfino Arborio or Roma rice

1¼ cups (8¾ ounces) sugar

1½ tablespoons unsalted butter

5 large eggs, beaten

2 teaspoons grated lemon zest

¾ cup (4 ounces) high-quality candied citron, finely diced, or

¾ cup (3 ounces) blanched almonds, toasted and coarsely chopped

Method

Working Ahead: *The pudding can be made 1 day ahead. Wrap the dish and store it in the refrigerator until 1 hour before serving. It is equally good served warm from the oven or chilled.*

Cooking the Rice: In a heavy 3- to 4-quart saucepan, combine the milk and rice. Bring to a gentle bubble over high heat. Turn the heat down to low, cover tightly, and cook 20 to 25 minutes at a very slow bubble. Stir occasionally to check for sticking. When the rice is tender but still a little resistant to the bite (it will be a little soupy), stir in the sugar. Turn it into a bowl and allow it to cool.

Mixing and Baking the Torta: Butter a 9-inch springform pan with the 1½ tablespoons butter. Preheat the oven to 350°F. Stir the eggs, lemon zest, and citron or almonds into the cooled rice. Turn into the pan, and bake 55 to 65 minutes, or until a knife inserted 2 inches from the edge comes out clean.

Serving: To serve at room temperature, cool the pudding to room temperature on a rack, and then unmold. Refrigerate if you will be holding it for longer than 2 hours. Slice into narrow wedges. Serve warm by reheating the pudding in its mold at 325°F about 20 minutes. Then release the sides of the pan and set the *torta* on a round plate.

Suggestions   **Wine:** Usually no special wine accompanies the *torta,* just a little of the wine taken with dinner. On special occasions, I like small glasses of a chilled dry Marsala or a little Vin Santo from Tuscany.

    Menu: Have a few Garlic Crostini with Pancetta (page 28) as antipasto. Follow with Ferrara's Soup of the Monastery (page 220) as the main dish, and then the *torta.* The pudding is also a fine dessert after Riccardo Rimondi's Chicken Cacciatora (page 275) or Rabbit Roasted with Sweet Fennel (page 289).

Cook's Notes **Citron and Substitutions:** High-quality candied citron tastes sweet/tart and spicy. You can find it in large chunks in specialty food stores and Italian markets around Christmas time. If unavailable, substitute ¾ cup coarsely chopped candied pineapple, diced fine and blended with 2 teaspoons lemon juice, ⅛ teaspoon ground cinnamon, and a pinch of freshly ground black pepper. This substitution is successful in this dish, but not always in others calling for citron.

    My Own Variation: I like to pour hot Fresh Grape Syrup (page 158) over chilled slices of the *torta.*

Modena Crumbling Cake
Bensone di Modena

"Bensone always stains the tablecloth" declares an old Modena saying. Dunking the crumbling cake in glasses of sweet wine is a favorite way of eating Bensone. The cake breaks up in the wine and is eaten with a spoon.

Simple ingredients and even simpler technique create the S-shaped cake. Its crust is craggy, and the melting sugar on top looks like molten crystal. Bensone is never too sweet. It looks and tastes homemade—like a sweet, slightly crumbly biscuit.

[Makes 1 cake, serving 8 to 10]

1 tablespoon unsalted butter

2 cups (8 ounces) all-purpose unbleached flour (organic stone-ground preferred)

2 cups (8 ounces) cake flour

Pinch of salt

¾ teaspoon baking soda

¾ teaspoon baking powder

1 cup (7 ounces) sugar

2 teaspoons grated lemon zest

12 tablespoons (6 ounces) unsalted butter, chilled and cut into chunks

3 large eggs, beaten

1 teaspoon vanilla extract

¼ cup milk

1½ tablespoons pearl sugar (see Note) or granulated sugar

Method

Working Ahead: *The cake is best eaten within several hours of baking. It will keep, tightly wrapped, at room temperature 2 days.*

Blending the Dough: Preheat the oven to 350°F. Grease a large baking sheet with the 1 tablespoon butter. Set a rack in the center of the oven. Make the cake in the easiest and most traditional way—by hand. Put all the dry ingredients (including the lemon zest but not the pearl sugar) in a shallow bowl. Blend them with your hands or with a fork. Rub the chunks of butter into the dry ingredients, using your fingertips, until the mixture resembles coarse meal. Make a well in the middle of the mixture, and add all the liquids. Stir them with a fork to blend. Then gradually work in the dry ingredients, using a tossing motion rather than stirring to blend the dry and moist ingredients together. Thoroughly moisten the dough, but do not worry if it is lumpy. Avoid beating the dough, as that toughens it. The dough should be lumpy, sticky, and moist.

Shaping the Cake: Sprinkle a little flour on a work surface and turn the dough out on top of it. Lightly flour your hands. Protect the dough from being overworked by just patting and nudging it into shape. Create a long, slightly flattened cylinder 3 to 4 inches wide and about 1 inch thick. Twist it into an S shape. Transfer it to the baking sheet, and sprinkle it with the 1½ tablespoons sugar. (Some Modenese cooks first brush the dough with 3 tablespoons milk.) Slip the baking sheet into the oven.

Baking and Serving: Bake 25 minutes. Then lower the heat to 250°F and bake another 25 minutes, or until a tester inserted in the center comes out clean. Transfer the *Bensone* to a rack. Either let it cool about 20 minutes and serve it warm, or let it cool for about 1 hour and serve it at room temperature. Cut it into ½-inch-thick slices.

Suggestions   **Wine:** The Piedmont's Moscato d'Asti or Freisa di Chieri Amabile is a fine wine for sipping and dunking with the *Bensone*. In Modena it would be a fresh and sweet Lambrusco Amabile.

Menu: This is a simple, homey dessert, excellent after country dishes like Maria Bertuzzi's Lemon Chicken (page 273), Grilled Beef with Balsamic Glaze (page 303), Herbed Seafood Grill (page 254), Seafood Stew Romagna (page 259), or Rabbit Roasted with Sweet Fennel (page 289). Often *Bensone* is taken between meals with coffee.

Cook's Notes   **Pearl Sugar:** These pea-size pellets of white sugar are found in specialty food stores.

Home-Style Jam Cake
Ciambelle con Marmellata

Bake fruit jam in the center of Modena Crumbling Cake and you have a sweet called <u>Ciambelle</u> in Emilia-Romagna. This long, low cake tastes like a cross between a soft filled cookie and a sweet biscuit.

<u>Ciambelle</u> embodies the simple, direct quality of the homemade cakes of generations ago. Made by almost every grandmother in Emilia-Romagna, it is also found in every <u>pasticceria.</u> The cake greets youngsters after school, feeds neighbors dropping in for midmorning coffee, and makes a comforting finale to family dinners. In this country I take it on picnics and to potluck suppers, and serve it at casual dinners and buffets.

[Makes 1 cake, serving 6 to 8]

continued

Dough

1 tablespoon unsalted butter

1 cup (4 ounces) all-purpose unbleached flour (organic stone-ground preferred)

1 cup (4 ounces) cake flour

Pinch of salt

¼ teaspoon baking powder

¼ teaspoon baking soda

½ cup sugar

1 teaspoon shredded lemon zest

6 tablespoons (3 ounces) unsalted butter, chilled and cut into pieces

1 large egg

1 teaspoon vanilla extract

3 tablespoons milk

Filling

¾ cup Homemade Tart Jam (page 413) or high-quality store-bought plum, apricot, cherry, or strawberry preserves

Decoration

2 teaspoons pearl sugar (see Note, page 401) or granulated sugar

Method

Working Ahead: *Although the jam cake is best eaten within several hours of baking, it keeps 2 days if tightly wrapped and stored in the refrigerator.*

Blending the Dough: Preheat the oven to 350°F. Grease a baking sheet with the tablespoon butter, and set an oven rack in the center of the oven. Make the jam cake in the easiest and most traditional way—by hand. Put all the dry ingredients for the dough, including the lemon zest, in a shallow bowl. Blend them thoroughly with your hands or with a fork. Rub the butter into the dry ingredients, using your fingertips, until the mixture resembles coarse meal. Stir the egg, vanilla, and milk together. Make a well in the middle of the dry ingredients, and add the liquids. Gradually work in the dry ingredients, tossing them with a fork rather than stirring. The idea is to thoroughly moisten the dough but not beat it, as that makes it tough. Help with your hands. The dough should be lumpy, sticky, and moist.

Shaping and Filling the Dough: Generously flour a work surface, and turn the dough out onto it. Lightly flour your hands. Pat the dough out to form a rectangle about 8 inches wide and 13 inches long. Dab the jam down the center, in a ribbon about 2 inches wide. Fold the two flaps of pastry lengthwise over the filling, overlapping slightly. Pinch the seam together down the length of the cake. Pinch the ends together so the jam can't ooze out during baking.

Baking and Serving: Transfer the pastry to the baking sheet, and sprinkle with the 2 teaspoons sugar. Bake 25 minutes. Reduce the heat to 250°F and bake another 25 minutes. Serve the *Ciambelle* warm or at room temperature. Cut it into slices about ½ inch thick, and arrange them on a platter.

Suggestions   **Wine:** A cool white Moscato d'Asti or a dry Marsala Superiore or Ambra tastes fine with the *Ciambelle*. Many Emilians dip it in a local Lambrusco. "La Monella" from the Piedmontese vineyard of Braida di Giacomo Bologna is a fine stand-in for good Lambrusco.

Menu: Serve after Balsamic Roast Chicken (page 279), Giovanna's Wine-Basted Rabbit (page 284), January Pork (page 312), Artusi's Delight (page 300), Beef-Wrapped Sausage (page 314), or Lamb, Garlic, and Potato Roast (page 307).

Hawker selling *ciambelle* in Bologna's marketplace. Engraving by Giovanni M. Tamburini, from a picture by Francesco Curti, circa 1640.

Will the Real *Ciambelle* Please Stand?

Codifying *Ciambelle* defies all logic. It translates as "ring cake," yet this traditional recipe is for a long loaf that looks like a flattened baguette. In pastry shops throughout the region, you can find long loaves (with or without a jam filling) sitting side by side with the same pastry baked into rings. Even more confounding, some are like pound cakes while others resemble sweet buttery biscuits. Each is called *Ciambelle*. Seventeenth-century Bolognese engravings show street vendors hawking *Ciambelle* rings—they carried them strung like doughnuts on long poles. Early recipes describe sweet *Ciambelle* like this recipe, as well as savory ones baked without sugar. Every part of the region has its favorite version, and the name changes according to where you happen to be. What is the true *Ciambelle*? It is the one you are eating at that particular moment.

Duchess of Parma Torte
Torta Duchessa

Created in 1985 by pastry chefs Ugo Falavigna and Dino Paini, this torte honored the winners of Parma's Maria Luigia International Journalism Prize. If I die and go to heaven, I know I will be served this cake as my ultimate reward. Layers of hazelnut meringue separate two buttercreams, one a <u>zabaione</u> scented with Marsala, the other dark chocolate with rum and espresso.

[Serves 8 to 12]

Chocolate Buttercream

8 egg yolks

1 cup (7 ounces) sugar

6 tablespoons very strong brewed espresso

¼ cup dark rum

1 ounce unsweetened chocolate, melted

4 ounces bittersweet chocolate, melted

1 cup plus 6 tablespoons (11 ounces) unsalted butter, at room temperature

Method

Working Ahead: *The chocolate buttercream can be made 5 days ahead. Store it, covered, in the refrigerator. Bring it to room temperature before spreading on the meringues.*

Making the Chocolate Buttercream: In a metal electric mixer bowl or a medium metal bowl that works well with a hand-held electric mixer, combine the egg yolks, sugar, coffee, and rum. Whisk by hand over a pan of boiling water (not letting the bowl touch the water) 5 to 8 minutes, or until the custard is thick. It should read between 160° and 165°F on an instant-reading thermometer.

Once thickened, set the custard in its mixing bowl on the mixer, and beat it at medium speed 8 minutes, or until cool. If using a hand-held mixer, beat the same way. Then beat in the melted chocolates. Keeping the mixer at medium speed, beat in the butter, 1 tablespoon at a time, beating each addition until smooth. Scrape down the sides of the bowl from time to time. The final buttercream should be silken and fluffy. If it is too soft, chill 20 minutes and then beat to fluff it up. Keep the buttercream at room temperature if you will be using it within a couple of hours. Otherwise, cover and refrigerate.

Meringues

2 to 3 tablespoons unsalted butter

4 tablespoons all-purpose unbleached flour (organic stone-ground preferred)

2 cups (8 ounces) hazelnuts, toasted and skinned

¾ cup (5¼ ounces) sugar

3 tablespoons all-purpose unbleached flour (organic stone-ground preferred)

7 large egg whites (1 cup)

¼ teaspoon cream of tartar

Method

Working Ahead: *The nuts can be ground 1 day ahead. Once the whites are beaten, immediately fold in the nuts and bake. The baked and cooled meringues can be left on a rack at room temperature in a dry place 1 day before assembling the torte. If possible, avoid making meringues on humid days.*

Making the Meringues: Butter and flour three 9-inch round cake pans. Cut circles of parchment paper to fit the bottom of each pan, and set them in place. Preheat the oven to 350°F. Grind the nuts with half the sugar, and all the flour in a food processor. The mixture should be very fine but not turned to nut butter. Beat the egg whites with the cream of tartar to form soft peaks. Gradually beat in the remaining sugar, and beat to stiff peaks. Using a large spatula, fold in the nut mixture, keeping the meringue light. Spread the mixture in the pans. Bake the meringues 22 minutes. They should be golden and almost hard, but still have a little spring when pressed. If the weather is humid or the meringues are still soft, they may need another 5 minutes of baking. Cool them in the pans on a rack 1 hour. Then run a knife around the inside of the pans to loosen the meringues. Gently turn the layers out of their pans. Carefully peel away the parchment paper. Trim any ragged edges so all the layers are the same size. Leave the meringues on a rack at room temperature until ready to use.

Zabaione Buttercream

5 egg yolks

7 tablespoons dry Marsala

¼ cup sugar

1 teaspoon dark rum

12 tablespoons (6 ounces) unsalted butter, at room temperature

Method

Working Ahead: *The flavors of this cream are more fragile than the chocolate cream. So store it for no more than 24 hours, covered and refrigerated, before assembling the torte. Bring it to room temperature before spreading it on the meringues.*

Making the Zabaione Buttercream: Use a free-standing or a hand-held electric mixer for this buttercream. First, by hand whisk together the egg yolks, Marsala, sugar, and rum in the metal bowl of an electric mixer or a medium metal bowl that works well with a hand-held mixer. Set the bowl over a pan of boiling water, taking care that the water does not touch the bowl. Whisk 4 to 5 minutes, or until thickened. The custard should read about 160° to 165°F on an instant-reading thermometer.

Remove from the heat, and, with a mixer, whip at medium speed 8 minutes, or until cooled to room temperature. Keeping the mixer at medium speed, beat in 9 tablespoons of the butter, 1 tablespoon at a time, beating each addition until smooth. The buttercream may seem too soft, but do not worry. Add the last 3 tablespoons all at once, and beat until smooth. The buttercream should fluff up. If not, chill about 20 minutes and then beat until fluffy. Keep the buttercream at room temperature if you will be using it within a couple of hours. Otherwise, cover and refrigerate.

Chocolate Glaze
2½ ounces bittersweet chocolate

2½ tablespoons unsalted butter
2 teaspoons light corn syrup

Method

Working Ahead: *The glaze can be made several hours ahead and rewarmed over hot water. Since its sheen dims with refrigeration, it is best to leave the glazing for shortly before serving. Spread the glaze over the cold torte about 1 hour before presenting it at the table.*

Making the Glaze: Combine all the ingredients in a small bowl set over boiling water or a double boiler. Stir until it is a smooth cream. Set aside.

Assembling the Torte: Protect the borders of a flat round cake plate by covering them with 4 sheets of wax paper. Dab about 1 tablespoon of the chocolate buttercream in the center of the plate to hold the first layer of meringue in place. Place one meringue layer in the center of the plate. Spread chocolate buttercream ½ inch thick over the meringue layer, making it a little higher around the edges. (There will be enough left to frost the sides of the torte and decorate the top.)

Set the second meringue layer upside down on the buttercream. Press gently so it sits flat. Slather all the *zabaione* buttercream over the meringue, spreading it a little higher near the edges. Top with the last meringue, again upside down. Then, using your palms, press the center gently to make sure the layer is straight, not dipping down or bowing up. Firm the torte by chilling it in the refrigerator about 30 minutes. Using a long metal spatula, cover the sides of the torte with a thin coating of chocolate buttercream. Spoon the remaining chocolate buttercream into a pastry bag fitted with a wide serated tip. Pipe an undulating border around the outer edge of the torte's top layer. (There will be about ½ cup buttercream left over.) Refrigerate the torte at least 1 hour before topping it with the glaze.

Glazing and Serving: About 1 hour before serving, remove the torte from the refrigerator and carefully spoon the glaze on its top. Spread the glaze with the back of the spoon so it flows up to the buttercream border, completely covering the meringue. The glaze will harden to a bright sheen on the cold meringue. (If refrigerated, the sheen dims.) Using a wet knife, slice the torte while it is still cold. Then let it come to room temperature. To serve, slip the thin slices out of the cake and onto dessert plates.

Suggestions   **Wine:** Usually chocolate is not accompanied by wine in Italy, but California's Elysium dessert wine is a fine match to the torte.

   Menu: Reserve the torte for special occasions. Serve it after simple but elegant dishes like Christmas Capon (page 281), Pan-Roasted Quail (page 283), Giovanna's Wine-Basted Rabbit (page 284), Rabbit Dukes of Modena (page 286), Herbed Seafood Grill (page 254), or Lemon Roast Veal with Rosemary (page 294).

Cook's Notes **Chocolate:** My first choice is Tobler Tradition, with Lindt Excellence second.

Marie Louise, Duchess of Parma

The Duchess of Parma

There is only one. Although many women have held the title, in Parma when you say "Duchess of Parma," everyone knows you are referring to Marie Louise of Austria. She was the city's most beloved ruler, and her name is on everything suggesting refinement and excellence.

As princess of the Austro-Hungarian Empire and wife to Napoleon, she was forced to make a choice. She could either go into exile with Napoleon on Elba or rule Parma with the assistance of Austrian general Adam Albert Neipperg. A dashing military man, Neipperg was tall, intelligent, and strikingly handsome. The black patch over his eye only added excitement. Historical gossip claims they were lovers even before Marie Louise had to decide between Parma and Napoleon. She chose Parma, sharing her reign with Neipperg, and the next 30 years were some of the brightest in Parma's history. The city's elegant neoclassic opera house is one tangible legacy of Marie Louise's era. Some music experts say its audiences are even more demanding of singers than La Scala.

Another legacy is the city's identifying color, "Parma yellow." This soft golden yellow tinged with orange is always matte and velvety, never hard and flat. The opera house is Parma yellow, as are many of the town's buildings. The color is a melding of the Hapsburg yellow of Marie Louise's family crest and the yellow of France's Bourbon ruling family, who held Parma during the 18th century. (Modena has its yellow, similar to Parma's, stemming from Modena's own long relationship with Austria.) Pastry shops share another Marie Louise legacy: influences from France and Austria that make Parma pastries more refined and intricate than most.

Marie Louise (or Maria Luigia as she is known in Parma) is still a presence in the city. Her picture is found in shops, homes, and restaurants almost as often as portraits of native son Giuseppe Verdi. The portrait you see most often is the one I like the least. In it she is young, her long narrow head looks overbred, and the blue eyes are bland. In a later portrait, painted when she was in her fifties, she is far more compelling. Experience, intelligence, and passion speak out from the pale face. The jaw and cheekbones are strong, the eyes glow. This is a woman who could rule a duchy, a duchess worthy of Parma.

Caramelized Almond Tart
Crostata di Mandorle

*T*his tart from both Emilia and
Romagna is a big circle of shortbread covered with caramelized almonds
and tasting of lemon and almonds.

[Makes 1 tart, serving 8 to 10]

Pastry

1 cup (4 ounces) all-purpose unbleached
flour (organic stone-ground preferred)

1 cup (4 ounces) cake flour

6 tablespoons (2½ ounces) sugar

Shredded zest of 1 small lemon

8 tablespoons (4 ounces) unsalted
butter, chilled and cut into
chunks

1 large egg, beaten

1 tablespoon unsalted butter

Filling

¼ cup water

¾ cup (5¼ ounces) sugar

Shredded zest of 1 small lemon

5 tablespoons (2½ ounces)
unsalted butter

¼ cup heavy cream

3 tablespoons Anisette liqueur

⅓ cup water

3 cups (12 ounces) whole blanched
almonds, toasted and coarsely
chopped by hand

½ teaspoon almond extract

2 tablespoons Anisette liqueur

Method   **Working Ahead:** *The pastry shell can be baked 1 day ahead. The tart keeps well,*
tightly wrapped, in the refrigerator 2 to 3 days. Serve it at room temperature.

Making the Pastry in a Food Processor: Combine the dry ingredients, including the lemon zest, in a processor fitted with the steel blade. Blend 10 seconds. Then add the butter and process until the mixture looks like coarse meal. Add the egg and process only until the dough is crumbly. Gather it into a ball, wrap, and chill 30 minutes or overnight.

Making the Pastry by Hand: Stir the dry ingredients, including the lemon zest, together in a shallow bowl. Rub in the butter, using your fingertips or a pastry cutter, until there are just a few shales of solid butter left. Using a fork, toss in the egg to barely moisten the dough. Gather it into a ball, wrap, and chill 30 minutes or overnight.

Preparing the Crust: Preheat the oven to 400°F. Use the tablespoon of butter to grease an 11-inch fluted tart pan with removable bottom. Generously flour a work surface. Roll out the pastry to form a 14-inch round about ¼ inch thick (the pastry and filling are of equal thickness in this tart). Fit it into the tart pan. The dough is fragile, so do not worry if it breaks, just press the pieces together in the pan. No one sees the bottom of a tart shell. Prick it with a fork and chill 30 minutes. Line the crust with foil and weight it with dried beans or rice. Bake 10 minutes. Then remove the liner and weights, turn the temperature down to 350°F, and bake another 5 to 8 minutes, or until pale gold. Cool on a rack.

Making the Filling: Preheat the oven to 350°F. Combine the water and sugar in a 3-quart saucepan. Cook over medium heat 4 to 6 minutes, or until clear, brushing down the sides of the pan with a brush dipped in cold water. Raise the heat to high and bubble fiercely 9 to 12 minutes, or until the syrup is honey colored. Remove the pan from the heat, and stir in the lemon zest and butter. Once the butter has melted, stir in the cream, liqueur, $1/3$ cup water, and almonds. Set the pan over high heat a few seconds to dissolve the caramel. Stir in the almond extract, and pour the filling into the pastry shell.

Baking and Serving: Bake 30 minutes (do not worry when the filling bubbles and seethes). Just before removing it from the oven, brush with the 2 tablespoons liqueur. Cool the tart on a rack. Slice it in wedges for serving.

Suggestions   **Wine:** From the region, have a sweet red Cagnina of Romagna or the Veneto's white Torcolato. Or have small glasses of the same anise liqueur flavoring the tart.

Menu: The tart makes a fine finale to a menu featuring Tagliatelle with Caramelized Onions and Fresh Herbs (page 101), Spaghetti with Anchovies and Melting Onions (page 130), Mardi Gras Chicken (page 277), Lamb, Garlic, and Potato Roast (page 307), Fresh Tuna Adriatic Style (page 256), or Pan-Roasted Quail (page 283).

Ugo Falavigna's Apple Cream Tart
Torta di Mele Ugo Falavigna

Ugo *Falavigna, of Parma's*
Pasticceria Torino, sautés lemon-scented apples, spreads them in sweet
pastry, and naps the fruit in silky custard before baking. In this gentle
adaptation of his recipe, I have encouraged the apples to absorb even
more of the lemon, bringing out the fresh taste of the fruit and making
the custard seem creamier. Include the tart in any menu made without
lemon, but especially when pasta and ragù are offered as a main dish.

[Makes 1 tart, serving 6 to 8]

Pastry

¾ cup (3 ounces) cake flour

¾ cup (3 ounces) all-purpose
  unbleached flour (organic
  stone-ground preferred)

6 tablespoons (2½ ounces) sugar

Generous pinch of salt

6 tablespoons (3 ounces) unsalted
  butter, chilled and cut into
  chunks

1 large egg yolk

1 teaspoon vanilla extract

1 to 2 tablespoons cold water

½ tablespoon unsalted butter

Apples

5 medium Granny Smith apples

Juice of 1 large lemon

3 tablespoons unsalted butter

1½ tablespoons sugar

Custard

1 cup milk

1 vanilla bean, split lengthwise

6 tablespoons sugar

2 large eggs

2 large egg yolks

Garnish

¼ cup confectioner's sugar (optional)

Method

Working Ahead: *The pastry and custard can be made 1 day ahead. Cover and refrigerate them until you are ready to assemble the tart. The apples need to marinate in the lemon juice 3 to 4 hours. Serve the tart within 8 hours of baking.*

Making the Pastry by Hand: Blend the dry ingredients together in a bowl. Using a pastry cutter or your fingertips, cut in the butter until only a few shales of butter are visible. Using a fork, toss in the egg yolk, vanilla, and 1 tablespoon water, moistening the pastry only enough for it to hold together when gathered into a ball. If it is too dry, sprinkle with another tablespoon of water and toss. Do not stir or knead.

Making the Pastry in a Food Processor: Combine the dry ingredients in a food processor fitted with the steel blade. Add the butter and process 30 seconds, or until the mixture looks like coarse meal. Add the egg yolk, vanilla, and 1 tablespoon water.

continued

Process with the on/off pulse until the pastry begins to gather in small clumps. If it is dry, sprinkle with another tablespoon of water and process.

Chilling and Baking Pastry: Gather the dough into a ball, wrap it in plastic wrap, and chill 30 minutes. Meanwhile, use the ½ tablespoon of butter to grease a 9-inch tart pan with removable bottom. Sprinkle a work surface generously with flour. Roll out the dough to about ⅛ inch thick, and fit it into the tart pan. Chill at least 30 minutes. While the crust is chilling, preheat the oven to 400°F. Line the chilled pastry with aluminum foil, and weight it with dried beans or rice. Bake for about 10 minutes. Lift out the weights and liner. Continue baking another 5 minutes, or until it looks dry but not browned. Cool on a rack.

Sautéing the Apples: Peel and core the apples. Cut them into ½-inch-thick wedges, and toss them in a bowl with the lemon juice. Let the apples macerate with the lemon juice 3 or 4 hours at room temperature. Heat the 3 tablespoons of butter in a large sauté pan over medium-high heat. Turn the heat up to high as you add the apples. You want to cook off the apples' moisture without reducing them to mush. Sauté 5 to 6 minutes, or until they have given up their moisture and started to brown. Keep turning the pieces with a wooden spatula. Sprinkle with the sugar, and remove from the heat. Cool the apples by spreading them out on a large platter.

Making the Custard: Scald the milk in a 3-quart saucepan by heating it with the vanilla bean until bubbles appear around the edge of the pan. Remove it from the heat and cool for about 15 minutes. In a medium bowl, whip the sugar and the 2 whole eggs until the mixture sheets off the whisk. Then blend in the scalded milk and turn the mixture back into the saucepan. Have a sieve and a medium bowl handy for straining the custard once it has cooked. Using a wooden spatula, stir the custard continuously over medium-low heat 5 minutes, or until it reaches a temperature of 170°F and has thickened. Do not boil. Immediately pour it through a sieve into a bowl, removing the vanilla bean. (Rinse and dry the vanilla bean for use again.) Whisk in the remaining 2 egg yolks, and let the custard cool.

Assembling and Baking the Tart: Preheat the oven to 350°F. Fan out the apple slices on the pastry in a tight spiral pattern, forming a single layer. Pour the custard over the apples. Bake 40 minutes, or until a knife inserted midway between the center of the tart and the edge comes out clean. Cool the tart on a rack. Refrigerate if holding it more than 2 hours.

Serving: Serve the tart at room temperature, dusted lightly with confectioner's sugar if desired.

Suggestions   **Wine:** The tart's assertive lemon flavor does not complement wine.

Menu: The tart is excellent after any menu where lemon and apples are not used. I like it particularly after Christmas Capon (page 281), Tagliatelle with Light Veal Ragù (page 100), Lamb with Black Olives (page 305), Porcini Veal Chops (page 290), January Pork (page 312), and Pan-Roasted Quail (page 283).

Nonna's Jam Tart
Torta della Nonna

A cross between filled shortbread and fruit tart, <u>Nonna</u>'s (Grandmother's) dessert has a buttery crust and a homemade jam filling. It is a homey dessert, a favorite finish to Sunday dinners in Emilia-Romagna.

Jam tarts are found throughout Italy, but this particular one reminds me of Parma and Bologna. I first tasted the sweet/tart filling at the Atti bake shop, Bologna's favorite source for home-style sweets. There it is described as <u>brusca,</u> meaning tart and fresh. The crust was inspired by a dessert made by Parma hostess Elsa Zannoni.

I have taken some liberties with the recipe. By creaming the butter and sugar, and eliminating some flour in the bottom crust, the tart is shorter, crisper, and even more like shortbread. Flour added to the top crust makes it less fragile, so it can be woven into the traditional lattice. Absolutely essential to the tart's success is having the butter between 62° and 72°F so it can fluff to maximum volume and easily absorb all the flour.

[Makes 1 tart, serving 8 to 10]

Homemade Tart Jam (makes 2 cups)
1½ cups (12 ounces) dried apricots, peaches, or pitted prunes
6 tablespoons dry white wine
3 tablespoons sugar
Pastry
1 tablespoon unsalted butter
10 tablespoons (5 ounces) unsalted butter, at room temperature
¾ cup (5.25 ounces) sugar
2 teaspoons grated lemon zest
1 cup (4 ounces) all-purpose unbleached flour (organic stone-ground preferred)
1 cup (4 ounces) cake flour
Glaze
1 large egg, beaten

Method   **Working Ahead:** *The jam holds in the refrigerator 2 weeks and freezes 3 months. The dough can be made 24 hours ahead; wrap and chill it in the refrigerator. The finished tart keeps well, wrapped and chilled, 1 week.*

Making the Jam: In a saucepan, combine the dried fruit, wine, sugar, and enough water to cover the fruit. Let it stand 20 minutes to 1 hour. Then bring the liquid to a gentle bubble. Turn the heat to low, cover the pot securely, and cook 30 minutes, or until the fruit is very soft. Taste for sweetness, adding more sugar if desired. Set it aside to cool. *continued*

Making the Pastry: Use the 1 tablespoon butter to grease a 9-inch tart pan with a removable bottom. In a medium bowl, cream the butter, sugar, and lemon zest with an electric beater at medium speed. Take 8 to 10 minutes, fluffing the butter to three times its original volume.

Thoroughly mix the flours in another bowl. Measure out 1½ cups by spooning the flour into measuring cups and leveling it with a flat knife blade. Using a spatula, fold the 1½ cups into the creamed butter, and blend well. Take two thirds of the dough, roll it out quite thick (¼ to ½ inch), and then pat the dough into the tart pan, pressing it into the pan's sides. Work the remaining flour into the remaining dough. Pat it into a flattened ball. Refrigerate both portions of pastry at least 45 minutes.

Baking the Crust: Preheat the oven to 375°F, and place a rack in the center of the oven. Prick the crust in the tart pan with a fork. Set on a baking sheet, bake 20 minutes, or until pale gold. Remove it from the oven and cool on a rack.

Finishing the Tart: Meanwhile, roll out the remaining dough on a floured surface to form a 10-inch circle. Cut it into long strips about ¾ inch wide. Spread the fruit filling evenly over the cooled crust. Preheat the oven to 350°F.

Create a lattice top by laying five strips across the tart, parallel to each other and spaced about ½ inch apart. Use some of the beaten egg to seal them to the rim of the baked crust. Make a diagonal lattice with five more strips, spaced ½ inch apart. Press them into the rim of the baked crust. Brush all the pastry with beaten egg.

Baking and Serving: Bake the tart on the baking sheet 45 minutes to 1 hour, or until the top is golden brown. Cool it on a rack, and cut in narrow wedges.

Suggestions   **Wine:** On special occasions in Parma, the *torta* is served with the local sweet Malvasia wine. A Moscato from Sardegna or the Piedmont makes a fine stand-in. Usually the tart is eaten on its own after dinner, or in the afternoon with coffee.

Menu: Serve the tart after an elegant meal or an informal one, after Rabbit Dukes of Modena (page 286), Oven-Glazed Porcini (page 239), Seafood Stew Romagna (page 259), Riccardo Rimondi's Chicken Cacciatora (page 275), Beef-Wrapped Sausage (page 314), or Lamb, Garlic, and Potato Roast (page 307).

Zabaione Jam Tart
Torta La Greppia

Swirls of golden zabaione cream on top, tangy jam and crisp cookie crust underneath—from Parma's Ristorante La Greppia.

[Makes 1 tart, serving 6 to 8]

Jam Filling

1½ cups Homemade Tart Jam (page 413), made with pitted prunes and ½ teaspoon grated lemon zest

Pastry

½ cup plus 2 tablespoons (2½ ounces) all-purpose unbleached flour (organic stone-ground preferred)

½ cup plus 2 tablespoons (2½ ounces) cake flour

6 tablespoons (2⅔ ounces) sugar

¼ teaspoon baking powder

½ teaspoon grated lemon zest

Pinch of salt

6 tablespoons (3 ounces) unsalted butter, chilled and cut into chunks

1 large egg, beaten with 1 tablespoon cold water

½ tablespoon unsalted butter

Zabaione Cream

6 large egg yolks

½ cup plus 3 tablespoons dry Marsala

¼ cup sugar

¾ cup heavy cream, chilled, whipped until stiff

Method

Working Ahead: *The jam keeps, covered, in the refrigerator 2 weeks and freezes 3 months. The pastry can be baked 24 hours before assembling the tart, and the zabaione can be cooked, chilled, and refrigerated 1 day ahead. The finished tart is best served within 8 hours after it is assembled. Store it in the refrigerator.*

Making the Pastry in a Food Processor: Combine the flours, sugar, baking powder, lemon zest, and salt in a food processor fitted with the steel blade. Cut in the butter until reduced to a fine crumb. Add the egg and water, and process with the on/off pulse until the mixture begins to gather together in clumps. Turn the pastry out onto a piece of plastic wrap or wax paper. Gather it into a ball, wrap, and chill at least 30 minutes.

Making the Pastry by Hand: Combine the dry ingredients in a large shallow bowl. With a pastry cutter or your fingertips, work in the cold butter until only a few long shales of butter are visible. Sprinkle the pastry with the egg and water. Toss with a fork. Mix only long enough to barely moisten the flour. Gather the pastry into a ball, wrap, and refrigerate at least 30 minutes.

continued

Baking the Pastry: Use the ½ tablespoon butter to grease a 9-inch tart pan with removable bottom. Generously flour a work surface, and roll out the pastry to less than ⅛ inch thick. (If the weather is humid, roll the pastry between pieces of wax paper.) Fit the pastry into the tart pan, prick it with a fork, and chill at least 30 minutes. Preheat the oven to 375°F. Line the crust with aluminum foil, and weight it with dried beans or rice. Bake 10 minutes. Remove the weights and foil, and continue baking another 5 to 8 minutes, or until golden brown. Cool on a rack.

Making the Zabaione: Bring a saucepan half full of water to a boil. In a large metal bowl, whisk together the egg yolks, Marsala, and sugar. Set the bowl over the boiling water and whisk 5 minutes, or until the mixture is thick and reads 165°F on an instant-reading thermometer. Turn the *zabaione* into a storage container, and cool it to room temperature. Cover and chill in the refrigerator several hours or overnight. (The *zabaione* must be cold when the cream is folded into it.) Fold in the stiffly beaten cream shortly before assembling the tart.

Assembling and Serving the Tart: Evenly spread the jam over the crust. With a long spatula, swirl on the *zabaione* cream, covering the jam completely. Chill the tart until about 20 minutes before serving. Cut it into wedges.

Suggestions   **Wine:** Small glasses of lightly chilled sweet *(semi-secco* or *dolce)* Marsala Superiore Riserva are excellent with this. This is a fine sipping Marsala that can rival a port or Madeira.

Menu: Serve after Porcini Veal Chops (page 290), Pan-Roasted Quail (page 283), Erminia's Pan-Crisped Chicken (page 270), or main-dish portions of Tagliatelle with Prosciutto di Parma (page 94) or Tortelli of Ricotta and Fresh Greens (page 153), followed by a green salad.

Cardinal d'Este's Tart
Torta di Farro Messisbugo

This tart is edible time travel from the 16th century, when Ferrara bakers created the sweet in the palace kitchens of Cardinal Ippolito d'Este. Inside a sweet saffron crust plumped barley, cream cheese, orange zest, and spices bake into a subtle pudding. During the Cardinal's time, sweets like this often appeared at the beginning of a meal with prosciutto, salads, and marzipan biscuits. Even though it is a dessert today, the tart's grain and cheese make it nourishing enough to follow a simple main-dish salad.

[Makes 1 tart, serving 6 to 8]

Pastry

⅔ cup (2⅔ ounces) all-purpose unbleached flour (organic stone-ground preferred)

½ cup (2 ounces) cake flour

2 tablespoons sugar

3 tablespoons unsalted butter, chilled

⅛ teaspoon saffron threads, soaked in 1 tablespoon cold water

1 large egg yolk

½ tablespoon unsalted butter

Filling

⅓ cup (2 ounces) whole-grain spelt or pearl barley

Generous pinch of salt

3 cups water

8 ounces fresh Italian cheese (Casatella, Raviggiolo, or Robbiola) or American cream cheese (preferably without guar gum)

⅔ cup plus 1 tablespoon (5 ounces) sugar

2 large eggs, beaten

4 tablespoons (2 ounces) unsalted butter, melted

Pinch of salt

⅛ teaspoon freshly ground black pepper

1 tablespoon grated orange zest

1 teaspoon ground cinnamon

1 cup (5 ounces) raisins or coarsely chopped dried apricots, soaked in hot water to cover

Topping

2 tablespoons unsalted butter, melted

1¼ teaspoons sugar

¼ teaspoon ground cinnamon

Generous pinch of freshly ground black pepper

2 tablespoons candied melon seed, candied anise seed, or toasted pine nuts

continued

Method   **Working Ahead:** *The crust and grain can be cooked 1 day in advance. Cover both and store in the refrigerator. The finished tart is best eaten at room temperature within 8 hours after baking, but it holds well in the refrigerator 1 or 2 days.*

Making the Pastry by Hand: Combine the dry ingredients in a shallow bowl. Rub the butter in with your fingertips until there are only a few crumbly shales visible. Make a well in the center of the mixture, and pour in the saffron water and the egg yolk. Use a fork to blend the liquids, and then gradually scrape in flour from the well's walls. A pastry cutter helps blend in the last of the dry ingredients. Work the dough only long enough for it to gather into a ball. Wrap, and chill 30 minutes.

Making the Pastry in a Food Processor: Combine the dry ingredients in a food processor fitted with the steel blade. Blend in the butter. Then add the egg yolk and saffron water. Use the on/off pulse to blend the dough only long enough for clumps to form. Turn the pastry out onto a sheet of plastic wrap or wax paper. Gather it into a ball, wrap, and chill 30 minutes.

Baking the Crust: Generously flour a work surface. Butter a 9-inch tart pan with removable bottom and fluted sides with the ½ tablespoon butter. Roll out the pastry very thin, and fit it into the pan. If the weather is humid, roll it out between sheets of wax paper. Trim the excess dough leaving a 1½-inch overhang. Fold that over to the inside of the pan so the crust stands at least ¼ inch above its rim. Chill 30 minutes to overnight. Preheat the oven to 400°F. Prick the pastry with a fork. Line it with aluminum foil and weight with dried beans or rice. Bake 10 minutes. Remove the liner and weights, and bake another 5 minutes, or until pale gold. Cool on a rack.

Making the Filling: If you are using spelt, soak it overnight in cold water, then drain and turn it into a 2-quart saucepan. Cover with 2 inches of cold water. Cover the pan, and bubble gently 2 hours, or until the grain is tender. Drain well and cool. Barley needs no soaking. Simply cover it with the 3 cups water and cook, covered, at a gentle bubble 1¼ hours, or until very tender. Drain well and cool. Preheat the oven to 350°F, and set a rack in the lower third of the oven. Have a baking sheet handy. Beat the cheese and sugar until creamy. Beat in the eggs until smooth. Then blend in the 4 tablespoons melted butter and the salt, black pepper, orange zest, and cinnamon. (Eliminate the salt if the cheese is at all salty.) Stir in the drained raisins or apricots and the cooked and well-drained grain.

Baking and Serving: Set the pastry shell on the baking sheet. Pour in the filling. Spread the 2 tablespoons melted butter over the top. Slip the baking sheet into the oven, and bake 20 minutes. Sprinkle the sugar, cinnamon, pepper, and seeds or nuts over the top. Bake another 35 minutes, or until a knife inserted in the center comes out clean. Cool on a rack and serve at room temperature, sliced into small wedges.

Suggestions   **Wine:** From Ferrara's Bosco Eliceo wine area, drink a sweet red Fortana Amabile or from Romagna have a sweet red Cagnina or the sweet white Moscato wines of Sardinia.

Menu: For the simplest dining, have the Salad of Tart Greens with Prosciutto and Warm Balsamic Dressing (page 26) as the main dish and serve the tart for dessert. The tart is excellent after any light menu not flavored with cinnamon. Ferrara's Rabbit Roasted with Sweet Fennel (page 289), Fresh Tuna Adriatic Style (page 256), and Giovanna's Wine-Basted Rabbit (page 284), are particularly good choices. For menus suggestive of the tart's origins, have Rabbit Dukes of Modena (page 286), Artusi's Delight (page 300), or Christmas Capon (page 281).

Cook's Notes   **Fresh Italian Cheeses:** A creamy full-fat cheese, sweet with freshness, is needed in this tart. The ones listed come from Emilia-Romagna and are in their prime during their first 10 days of life. Taste available imports (whether from the region or not) for sharpness, bitter undertones, or excess salt. Better to use a fine domestic cream cheese than an import past its prime.

Old engraving of Ferrara

Farro and Spelt

Although nothing can be exactly as it was, dishes like this give us a glimpse into the past. Pastry crusts with saffron were common in the 16th century, and cinnamon, pepper, and orange flavored sweet as well as savory dishes. Typical of the period, too, was the pound *each* of butter and sugar that I have eliminated in this modern version. The original recipe calls for either wheat kernels, *farro,* or rice—a choice that appears in many recipes of the era. *Farro* is spelt, or emmer, two very old strains of wheat used by the ancient Romans and still found in central Italian dishes today. Although there are slight differences between the two grains, in Italy *farro* refers to them both. After discovering that wheat grains bake into hard kernels, I turned to spelt. Surprisingly, it closely resembles barley in flavor. See Mail-Order Sources (page 509) to find spelt in the United States. But the even more readily available barley makes a fine alternative. The homey-sounding tart turns exotic with its topping of either candied melon seeds or anise seeds, which suggest the Arab influences on the sweets of the Renaissance. Toasted pine nuts are the third choice offered in the original recipe.

Meringues of the Dark Lake
Mandorlini del Ponte

These are meringues with a difference. The egg whites are cooked before baking, making the meringue crackly instead of chewy. Chunks of toasted almond add even more crunch. This is an heirloom recipe from the village of Pontelagoscuro (Bridge of the Dark Lake) in Ferrara province. Serve the meringues whenever a light sweet is needed to round out a menu.

[Makes 30 cookies]

½ tablespoon unsalted butter
3 tablespoons all-purpose
   unbleached flour (organic
   stone-ground preferred)
4 large egg whites
1 cup plus 2 tablespoons
   (8 ounces) sugar

⅔ cup (2⅔ ounces) all-purpose
   unbleached flour (organic
   stone-ground preferred)
2 cups (8 ounces) blanched
   almonds, toasted and coarsely
   chopped

Method

Working Ahead: *The meringues are at their best eaten within a day or two of baking, but they are still very good up to 1 week later. Store them at room temperature in an airtight container.*

Making the Meringues: Preheat the oven to 350°F. Use the ½ tablespoon butter to grease a cookie sheet. Sprinkle it with 3 tablespoons flour and discard the excess. Bring a saucepan half filled with water to a boil over medium heat. Using a hand-held electric mixer, whip the egg whites to soft peaks in a metal bowl. Slowly beat in the sugar. Put the bowl over the bubbling water, taking care that it does not touch the water. Beat 5 minutes at high speed, or until the whites become thick and shiny, coating the bottom of the bowl. Beat in the flour until just blended. Remove the bowl from the heat, and fold in the almonds. Drop the batter by tablespoonfuls onto the baking sheet. Bake 30 minutes, or until pale gold. Remove them immediately to a rack, and allow to cool.

Suggestions

Menu: Serve the cookies with fruit or after-dinner coffee, or as dessert after a robust menu.

Sweet Cornmeal Biscuits
Gialetti di Romagna

Cornmeal and polenta have been part of Emilia-Romagna's repertoire since corn first came from the Americas via Spain. These crunchy cookies are found throughout the southern part of Emilia-Romagna, as well as in the neighboring Veneto region. Homey looking and fragrant with cornmeal, they are superb with fresh fruit or just by themselves with espresso.

[Makes about 50 cookies]

1 cup (4 ounces) cornstarch

1 cup (5 ounces) coarse yellow cornmeal

2 cups (8 ounces) all-purpose unbleached flour (organic stone-ground preferred)

Generous pinch of salt

1 cup (8 ounces) unsalted butter, at room temperature

1 cup (7 ounces) sugar

3 large eggs

1 tablespoon water

1½ teaspoons grated lemon zest

1 teaspoon vanilla extract

Generous ½ cup (2½ ounces) raisins, soaked in hot water for 15 minutes and drained

½ cup (2 ounces) pine nuts, toasted

½ tablespoon unsalted butter

Method

Working Ahead: *The cookie dough can be mixed and refrigerated, tightly wrapped, overnight. The baked biscuits store well in a sealed tin about 1 week and freeze 3 months.*

Making the Dough: Blend the cornstarch, cornmeal, flour, and salt in a bowl until well mixed. Combine the butter and sugar in the bowl of an electric mixer. Beat at medium speed with the paddle attachment 8 minutes, or until pale and very fluffy. A hand-held electric mixer can also be used. Beat in the eggs, one at a time, making sure the mixture is fluffy before adding the next egg. Then beat in the water, lemon zest, and vanilla. Keeping the speed at medium, beat in about 1½ cups of the dry ingredients until just blended. Then blend in another cup until barely mixed. Add the rest of the dry ingredients, along with the raisins and nuts. The dough will be thick, sticky, and soft. Cover the bowl and refrigerate 30 minutes.

Shaping and Baking: Preheat the oven to 350°F. Use the ½ tablespoon butter to lightly grease a 14 by 18-inch cookie sheet. The cookies will bake in three batches. Drop the chilled cookie dough by teaspoonfuls onto the baking sheet, spacing them 1 to 1½ inches apart. Make a crosshatch pattern on top of each biscuit by dipping a dinner fork in a glass of water, then pressing the back of the fork gently into the cookie dough, flattening it slightly. Wet the fork again, and press it into the dough at right angles to the first impression. Chill the unused dough. Bake the biscuits 20 minutes, or until they are pale blond with golden brown edges. Remove the cookie sheet from the oven, and use a metal spatula to remove the biscuits to a rack to cool. Drop another batch of the chilled dough by teaspoonfuls onto the baking sheet, and press and bake as before. Repeat with the third batch. Make sure the dough is cold when the cookies go into the oven.

Serving: Pile the *Gialetti* on a colorful plate, and serve.

Suggestions   **Wine:** In Bologna, a local Lambrusco is a fine dipping medium for *Gialetti.* In the United States, serve them with lightly chilled dry Marsala or with espresso.

Menu: The *Gialetti,* served with or without fruit, are a fine finish to a rich meal. Also serve them after Romagna seafood dishes like Fresh Tuna Adriatic Style (page 256), Herbed Seafood Grill (page 254), or "Priest Stranglers" with Fresh Clams and Squid (page 124); and after main dishes like Grilled Beef with Balsamic Glaze (page 303), Lamb with Black Olives (page 305), or Lamb, Garlic, and Potato Roast (page 307). They pair beautifully with Baked Pears with Fresh Grape Syrup (page 442).

Cook's Notes **Using Cornstarch:** I have found that adding cornstarch to the traditional blend of cornmeal and flour gives the cookies a pleasing tenderness.

Paola Bini's Sweet Ravioli
Ravioli Dolci di Paola Bini

Tender pastry turnovers filled with winter fruits, sweet squash, and chestnuts are a specialty of Villa Gaidello, near Modena. They originated in Medieval convent kitchens. There, fresh grape syrup and fruits were cooked into a conserve called savor. *Often chestnuts were blended in, just as Villa Gaidello does today. And now, as then, the ravioli are excellent with sweet wine.*

Throughout Emilia-Romagna variations on this theme crop up at Christmas, just before Lent, and on local saints' days. Each area gives the pastries its own name; tortelli, tortellini, cappelletti, or ravioli, even though their shapes seldom change. Some cooks bake the turnovers, as in this recipe, while others fry them.

Whatever the name, their sugarless fillings always recall the days when sugar was dearly priced. Then, spiced fruits and cooked-down grape syrup satisfied most sweet tooths. Today, present the ravioli at the end of special dinners, especially at Christmas time.

Pastry

1 cup (4 ounces) all-purpose unbleached flour (organic stone-ground preferred)

1 cup (4 ounces) cake flour

½ cup plus 2 tablespoons (4 ounces) sugar

¼ teaspoon baking powder

2 teaspoons grated lemon zest

6 tablespoons (3 ounces) unsalted butter, chilled and cut into chunks

1 large egg beaten with 2 tablespoons cold water

Filling

2 cups Fresh Grape Syrup (page 158), or 1¼ pounds seedless red grapes, stemmed

½ large quince or Granny Smith apple, cored and chopped

½ medium Bosc pear, cored and chopped

½ medium Winesap or Rome Beauty apple, cored and chopped

½ cup diced peeled butternut squash

½ cup water

2 teaspoons grated orange zest

1 teaspoon grated lemon zest

½ cup peeled roasted or canned chestnuts, crumbled

⅓ cup golden raisins

¼ cup pine nuts, toasted

1 tablespoon Strega liqueur

1 tablespoon unsalted butter

Glaze

1 large egg, beaten

Method

Working Ahead: *The pastry and filling can be made up to 3 days before assembling the ravioli. Once baked, the ravioli freeze well 1 month and hold in the refrigerator, well wrapped, 4 days. Reheat 5 minutes at 350°F before serving.*

Making the Pastry by Hand: Combine the dry ingredients, including the lemon zest, in a bowl. Cut in the butter with a pastry cutter until the mixture resembles coarse meal. Using a fork, toss in the egg/water mixture until the dough can be gathered into a ball. If it is too dry, sprinkle with another tablespoon of water, toss, and then gather into a ball. Wrap, and chill at least 2 hours.

Making the Pastry in a Food Processor: Combine the dry ingredients, including the lemon zest, in a food processor fitted with the steel blade. Process 10 seconds. Add the butter and process until the mixture looks like coarse meal. Sprinkle with the egg mixture, and use the on/off pulse until the dough gathers in clumps. Turn it out onto a board, gather into a ball, and wrap in plastic wrap. Chill at least 2 hours.

Making the Filling: In a saucepan combine the grape syrup or fresh grapes, quince, pear, apple, squash, water, and citrus zests. Bring to a lively bubble and partially cover. Reduce the heat so the fruit is bubbling slowly, and cook 2 hours, stirring frequently, until the pieces are breaking down and very soft. Check for sticking, adding a little water if necessary. Pass the fruit through a food mill fitted with the coarse blade. Turn it back into the saucepan and cook over medium heat, uncovered, 45 minutes. Stir frequently and check for scorching. The fruit should thicken and reduce but not burn. It is ready when it thickly coats a wooden spoon. Cool, and set aside ½ cup for another use. Stir in the chestnuts, raisins, pine nuts, and Strega.

Assembling and Baking: Preheat the oven to 350°F. Use the tablespoon of butter to grease two cookie sheets. Roll out the dough on a floured board to less than ⅛ inch thick. Use a scalloped biscuit cutter to cut out 3-inch rounds. Place a teaspoon of filling in the center of each round and fold it in half, sealing the edges with a little of the beaten egg. Reroll and fill the scraps of dough. Arrange the ravioli on baking sheets, and brush them with the egg glaze. Bake the ravioli, a sheet at a time, 20 minutes or until golden brown. Cool on a rack.

Serving: Serve the ravioli piled on a colorful platter. At Christmas we arrange them on a bed of fresh pine. Some cooks moisten the ravioli with Fresh Grape Syrup (page 158).

Suggestions

Wine: A sweet white Albana Amabile or Passito from Romagna is heavenly with the ravioli. Try also Malvasia delle Lipari from Sicily, or Torcolato of the Veneto.

Menu: The ravioli pair well with old-style dishes like Christmas Capon (page 281), Artusi's Delight (page 300), Giovanna's Wine-Basted Rabbit (page 284), and Rabbit Dukes of Modena (page 286), or after a main course of tagliatelle with Piacenza's Porcini Tomato Sauce (page 64).

Marie Louise's Crescents
Torte Maria Luigia

Few ever guess the secret ingredient of these pastries from Parma. Enveloped in the sweet crust are tastes of vanilla, citron, and almond. The mystery lies in their filling. Cooking fresh spinach in sugar may come as a surprise to many, but sweet spinach tarts are found in Reggio, in France, and even in 18th-century England. I suspect if we could stroll through the markets of ancient Persia and India, we would find them there too. Ugo Falavigna, of Parma's Pasticerria Torino, believes the original of this recipe came from Austria to Parma in the early 19th century. He claims it came from the court cook to Marie Louise, Duchess of Parma. Whatever their origins, the turnovers are absolutely delicious and elegant enough to end the most important of dinners. I often serve them after a frozen or fruit-based dessert with coffee in the living room.

[Makes 50 pastries]

Pastry

2½ cups (10 ounces) cake flour

2¼ cups (9 ounces) all-purpose unbleached flour (organic stone-ground preferred)

1 cup (7 ounces) sugar

Pinch of salt

1 cup plus 4 tablespoons (10 ounces) unsalted butter, cut into chunks

2 to 5 tablespoons dry white wine

1 large egg, beaten

Filling

12 ounces fresh spinach, trimmed

1⅓ cups (9½ ounces) sugar

1 teaspoon dark rum

1½ cups (6 ounces) blanched almonds, toasted and finely chopped

Generous ¼ teaspoon ground cinnamon

⅛ teaspoon freshly ground black pepper

⅓ cup (1½ ounces) candied citron, finely minced

1½ teaspoons vanilla extract

½ tablespoon unsalted butter

Glaze

1 large egg, beaten

¼ cup sugar

Method **Working Ahead:** *The filling and pastry can be made 1 day ahead. Cover both and refrigerate. The pastries are best eaten within a few days of baking. Store them in a sealed tin. They also freeze well. Rid them of any sogginess after defrosting by crisping them in a 400°F oven about 10 minutes before serving.*

Making the Pastry in a Food Processor: In smaller food processors, this recipe is best done in two batches. Combine the flours, sugar, and salt in a food processor fitted with the steel blade. Process a few seconds. Add the butter, processing until the mixture looks like coarse meal. Blend together 2 tablespoons of the wine and the egg. Add this to the pastry, processing with the on/off pulse only until the dough begins to gather into small crumbs. If it is too dry to be gathered into a small ball, sprinkle with another tablespoon or two of wine and process a few seconds. Wrap, and chill 30 minutes or as long as 24 hours.

Making the Pastry by Hand: Combine the flours, sugar, and salt in a large shallow bowl. With your fingertips or a pastry cutter, work in the butter until there are just a few large shales visible. Beat together 2 tablespoons of the wine and the egg. Using a fork, toss the pastry with the egg mixture. Do not overmix. Just blend until the pastry barely holds together when gathered into a ball. If it is too dry, sprinkle with another 1 or 2 tablespoons of wine and toss. Wrap, and chill 30 minutes or as long as 24 hours.

Cooking the Spinach: Fill a sink with cold water, and rinse the spinach well. Measure the sugar into a 4- to 6-quart pot. Lift the spinach out of the water and transfer it right to the pot. Set the pot, uncovered, over high heat and cook, stirring occasionally, 5 to 8 minutes. The spinach should be wilted but still bright green. Set a colander in a bowl and drain the spinach, reserving its cooking liquid. Set the spinach aside to cool. Once it is cool, squeeze out the excess moisture and finely chop.

Making the Filling: Turn the spinach cooking liquid back into the spinach cooking pot and set it over high heat. Boil, uncovered, 8 to 10 minutes, or until the bubbles are big and shiny. This means all the water has evaporated and now the sugar is totally liquified and boiling on its own. This liquid will be pale celery green and will thicken. Turn off the heat. Put the chopped spinach in the bowl that held the cooking liquid. Pour in the hot syrup from the pot, taking care that it does not spatter. Let the mixture cool. Then stir in the rum, almonds, spices, citron, and vanilla.

Shaping and Baking: Have a small bowl of water handy. Use the ½ tablespoon butter to grease a large baking sheet. Preheat the oven to 375°F. Generously flour a work surface, and roll out half the dough to a little less than ⅛ inch thick. (In humid weather roll the dough out between sheets of wax paper.) Cut it into rounds with a 3½-inch fluted biscuit cutter or a glass. If time allows, chill the rounds 30 minutes before filling them. Dip your finger in the water and moisten the edges of the rounds. Place a generous teaspoonful of filling in the center of each round. Fold the dough over so it forms a half moon, and seal the edges. Set the crescents on the baking sheet. Brush the pastries with beaten egg and sprinkle lightly with sugar. Bake in the center of the oven 25 minutes, or until the edges are golden brown. Cool the pastries on a rack, and repeat with the remaining dough.

continued

Suggestions   **Wine:** Serve the pastries with a sweet Malvasia or a Moscato d'Asti.

Menu: In keeping with their heritage, offer the pastries after a period meal of Almond Spice Broth (page 237), Christmas Capon (page 281), and chunks of Parmigiano-Reggiano cheese with fresh fennel. They are also excellent after His Eminence's Baked Penne (page 170) or Lasagne Dukes of Ferrara (page 168).

Espresso and Mascarpone Semi-Freddo
Semi-Freddo di Espresso e Mascarpone

<u>Semi-freddo</u> (partially frozen) always suggests to me a cross between soft ice cream and the richest of frozen mousses. In this one, Italian meringue helps aerate the espresso cream. But mascarpone intensifies the taste and gives the espresso depth.

This style of dessert is a contemporary addition to Emilia-Romagna's home repertoire. There, egg whites are beaten with a little sugar and folded into the mousse. But now that raw eggs are a concern in the United States, I have cooked the whites with a hot sugar syrup, creating Italian meringue. The result is even more elegant than the original. Serve partially frozen in wine glasses, or unfrozen over wedges of rum-soaked Spanish Sponge Cake.

This recipe is particularly generous. Making a smaller amount can be tricky, as electric mixers often have difficulty beating only a few egg whites. If you need only half this amount, make the entire recipe and divide it in half, freezing the other half for another time.

[Serves 10 to 12]

Espresso Custard

6 tablespoons very strong brewed espresso, or 3 tablespoons instant espresso granules and boiling water

4 large egg yolks

4 tablespoons (1⅓ ounces) sugar

2 tablespoons dark rum

2 teaspoons vanilla extract

1 pound mascarpone cheese

¼ cup heavy cream

Italian Meringue

4 large egg whites, at room temperature

¾ cup (5¼ ounces) sugar

¼ cup water

Garnish

2 ounces bittersweet chocolate, shaved

Method   **Working Ahead:** *The semi-freddo freezes well 1 month. Serve it partially defrosted. It is also excellent served merely chilled within an hour or so of making. After that, the meringue begins to break down and the mousse becomes too soft.*

Making the Custard: If you are using coffee granules, pour them into a glass measuring cup. Add enough boiling water to make ⅓ cup. Stir and let cool. In a large metal bowl, whisk together the egg yolks, sugar, coffee, rum, and vanilla. Set the bowl over a pan of boiling water, taking care that the bowl does not touch the water. Whisk 3 minutes, or until thick. The custard should reach 160°F on an instant-reading thermometer. Scrape it into a small bowl, cool, cover, and chill in the refrigerator. Soften the mascarpone with the cream. Fold it into the chilled custard, blending completely but keeping the mixture light.

Making the Italian Meringue: In an Italian meringue hot sugar syrup is poured into egg whites as they are beaten, cooking and stabilizing them so they will not break down when folded into desserts. The key to success is in not overbeating the whites before the sugar reaches its proper temperature of 248° to 250°F. Starting to beat the whites as the sugar syrup comes close to its final temperature guards against overbeating.

Have a candy thermometer handy. Put the whites in the bowl of an electric mixer. Pour the ¾ cup sugar and ¼ cup water into a tiny saucepan, and set over medium heat. Cook at a lively bubble 3 minutes, or until the syrup is clear. Wash down the sides of the pan frequently with a brush dipped in water. Once the syrup is clear, turn the heat to high and put the thermometer in the pan. When the syrup reaches 245°F, turn on the mixer at medium speed. Wait a few seconds and then turn the machine to high speed. By the time the syrup is at 248° to 250°F, the whites should be beaten to stiff but moist peaks and should look smooth (if they are gathering together into clumps, they are overbeaten). Continue beating the whites as you immediately pour the hot syrup into the bowl. Keep beating on high speed about 3 minutes. Then turn the mixer down to medium, and beat until the whites cool to room temperature.

Finishing and Serving: Fold the whites into the custard, keeping it light. Spoon the mixture into a container and freeze. Three hours before serving, transfer it to the refrigerator. Serve the semi-freddo in wine glasses, or scoop ovals of the mousse onto dessert dishes. Sprinkle with the chocolate shavings. To serve without freezing, spoon the mixture into an attractive serving-dish or wine glasses, and refrigerate. Serve within an hour, garnished with the chocolate shavings.

Suggestions   **Wine:** A dry Marsala with the semi-freddo.

Menu: Serve after Pan-Roasted Quail (page 283), Lemon Roast Veal with Rosemary (page 294), Erminia's Pan-Crisped Chicken (page 270), or other dishes made with lemon or balsamic vinegar.

Cook's Notes   **Mascarpone:** Mascarpone comes in two consistencies: a thick cream and a solid cheese. For this recipe, seek out the thick cream.

Frozen Zuppa Inglese
Zuppa Inglese di Vincenzo Agnoletti

Here frozen layers of almond mousse and chocolate cream are sealed between slivers of light sponge cake. This sumptuous dessert is easily prepared ahead (and can be doubled) and is impressive enough for the most important of dinners. Covered in swirls of whipped cream, the cake's finishing touch is a gilding of green and red from crushed pistachios and slivers of candied cherry. Parma's Duchess Marie Louise dined on a dessert very similar to this one in the early part of the last century. Today there is a sense of timelessness to the dish. Serve it when a menu needs a classical, polished finish.

[Serves 8]

Filling

¼ cup water

6 tablespoons (2⅔ ounces) sugar

8 large egg yolks

6 tablespoons almond syrup
(see Note)

1 teaspoon vanilla extract

2½ ounces bittersweet chocolate,
melted

⅓ cup shelled green pistachio
nuts, crushed

1 cup heavy cream, whipped and
chilled

Cake

⅓ cup dark rum

3 tablespoons sugar

One 9-inch square Spanish Sponge
Cake (page 433)

Frosting

1½ cups chilled heavy cream, whipped
until stiff

2 candied red cherries, each cut
into 8 slivers

¼ cup shelled green pistachio nuts

Method

Working Ahead: *The sugar syrup holds, covered, in the refrigerator at least 1 month. The fillings can be made 1 day ahead; store them, covered, in the refrigerator. Freeze the finished dessert up to 1 month. Unmold it, frost, and serve.*

Making the Filling: Combine the water and the 6 tablespoons sugar in a tiny saucepan. Bring to a gentle bubble over medium heat. Once the liquid is clear and the sugar is melted (about 3 minutes), cook over medium heat another 2 minutes. Allow to cool. Strain the cooled syrup into a large stainless steel bowl. Whisk in the egg yolks and 3 tablespoons of the almond syrup. Set the bowl over a pot of boiling water, making sure it does not touch the water. Whisk until the custard is very thick, 2 to 5 minutes. It will reach about 165°F on an instant-reading thermometer. Whisk in the last 3 tablespoons almond syrup and the vanilla. Immediately turn the custard into the bowl of an electric mixer, and beat at medium-low speed 5 minutes. Then beat at low speed 10 minutes, or until cooled to room temperature. Scoop half the mixture into another bowl. Thoroughly blend the melted chocolate into that custard. Stir the crushed pistachios into the remaining custard. Fold half the whipped cream into the chocolate mixture. Fold the remaining cream into the almond custard. Chill the custards 3 hours or as long as 24.

Preparing the Rum Syrup: Combine the rum and 3 tablespoons sugar in a tiny saucepan. Boil 10 seconds, and allow to cool.

Assembling the Zuppa Inglese: Although Agnoletti suggests lining a mold with Spanish Sponge Cake, filling it, and then burying it in the snow, there is another method that makes unmolding a little easier. Line an 8¼ by 4¼-inch loaf pan with plastic wrap, leaving a generous overhang. Slice the cake in half vertically. Using a long serrated knife, divide each half horizontally into three very thin sheets of cake. Trim two pieces to fit the long sides of the loaf pan, and another two smaller pieces to slip into the short ends. Before fitting them into the loaf pan, barely moisten the cake with rum syrup by lightly brushing each slice. Do not cover the bottom of the loaf pan with cake.

Fill the mold half full with the almond custard, smoothing with a spatula. Any extra custard can be frozen for later use. Trim a slice of cake to fit over the custard, completely covering it. Set it in place, pressing gently with the palm of your hand. Sprinkle it with a little liqueur. Spread all the chocolate custard over the cake, and completely cover it with another trimmed slice of cake. Do not sprinkle this slice with liqueur. Use scissors to trim and even out the side slices of cake. Pull up the overhanging plastic wrap to cover, and seal the mold. Freeze from 12 hours to 1 month.

Decorating and Serving: About 30 minutes before serving, remove the mold from the freezer. Use four pieces of wax paper to cover the sides of an oval or rectangular serving dish. Turn the mold out onto the dish. First lift off the pan, then gently pull away the plastic wrap. Thickly frost the top and sides with the whipped cream, using a long narrow spatula and circular motions to create lavish swirls. Lightly crush the pistachios with the side of a large knife. Arrange them in a row about ¾ inch wide down the center of the cake, then down the two narrow ends to the platter. Stud the slivers of red cherry here and there among the green nuts. Refrigerate the cake up to 30 minutes, then cut into ½-inch-thick slices.

Suggestions   **Wine:** A festive wine with this elegant dessert—a sweet sparkling Asti Spumante from the Piedmont, or a Recioto di Soave of the Veneto.

Menu: Serve after Pan-Roasted Quail (page 283), at the end of a Christmas menu including Christmas Capon (page 281), or after Rabbit Dukes of Modena (page

286), Giovanna's Wine-Basted Rabbit (page 284), or Lemon Roast Veal with Rosemary (page 294).

Cook's Notes **Almond Syrup:** This sweet syrup is white to pale gold and made of sweet and bitter almonds. Imported from Italy as *latte di mandorle* and from France as *orgeat,* you can find it in specialty food stores and liquor shops. Once opened, the syrup keeps for up to a year in the refrigerator. Use it as sweet almond flavoring in coffee and milk drinks, and in desserts.

An English Soup

The provenance of this unusual *zuppa inglese* may seem more French than Italian, even though the name means "English Soup." But according to its 19th-century creator, Vincenzo Agnoletti, cook to the Duchess of Parma, *zuppa inglese* did originate in Italy. Writing sometime shortly before 1834, he claims the *zuppa* came full circle from Italy through France and England, then back into contemporary fashion in Italy. The custard in this dish is made with a sugar syrup rather than the more usual milk or cream. The French use this same technique today for frozen parfaits. Agnoletti offered it as one of his many variations on making custard. He suggested varying flavorings with vanilla, coffee, or fruit purées. Change the custards to your own taste as desired. Modern *zuppe inglese* in Emilia-Romagna and throughout Italy differ slightly from this one. They are not frozen. Rather, most are a custard trifle molded in a loaf or dome shape. Layers of liqueur-soaked cake enclose dense pastry creams in assorted flavors. Rum syrup often moistens the cake. But Emilia-Romagna shares Tuscany's taste for Alchermes, the liqueur of spices, flowers, and red cochineal brought to Italy by Arab invaders many centuries ago. Alchermes is often used to soak the cake of the region's *zuppe inglese,* turning the dessert a startling crimson. There are few restaurant dessert tables in Emilia-Romagna without a *zuppa inglese,* and most of them are Alchermes red.

Riccardo Rimondi's Spanish Sponge Cake
Pan di Spagna

A feathery light, butterless sponge cake with a fine crumb. Translating literally as "Spanish bread," throughout Italy this cake is filled with creams, custards, or jams, layered into trifle-like zuppe inglese, *or simply moistened with liqueur and topped with fresh berries.*

My recipe departs slightly from the traditional method, making it easier to mix and guaranteeing fine results. Usually only egg yolks are beaten with the sugar. Adding one whole egg to the mixture eases the crucial folding together of ingredients and creates a more velvety cake. I substitute cake flour for the potato starch or cornstarch used by many bakers. The cake is the lighter for it. This recipe doubles easily.

[Makes one 8- or 9-inch round or square sponge cake, serves 6 to 8]

½ tablespoon unsalted butter

3 tablespoons all-purpose unbleached flour (organic stone-ground preferred)

7 tablespoons (1¾ ounces) all-purpose unbleached flour (organic stone-ground preferred)

7 tablespoons (1¾ ounces) cake flour

1 large egg

3 large egg yolks

½ cup plus 2 tablespoons (4½ ounces) sugar

1 teaspoon grated lemon zest or vanilla extract

4 large egg whites

Method
Working Ahead: *The cake can be baked 2 days ahead. Cool it completely, wrap airtight, and refrigerate. Or freeze up to 3 months.*

Making the Batter: Have all the ingredients at room temperature. Butter and flour an 8- or 9-inch round or square cake pan. Place a rack in the center of the oven. Preheat the oven to 425°F. Sift the measured flours into a bowl, and then stir them to blend thoroughly. Pour the flour back into the sifter. Use a medium-size mixing bowl and a hand-held electric mixer to beat the whole egg, yolks, sugar, and lemon zest or vanilla at medium speed about 8 minutes. The mixture will be pale, fluffed to about five times its original volume, and very creamy. Set it aside.

Whip the egg whites until they form stiff, but not dry, peaks. With a large spatula, gently fold a quarter of the whites into the egg mixture, using big round scooping motions down to the bottom of the bowl, then up and around over the top of the batter. Fold in the rest of the whites, leaving a few streaks of white. Sift a quarter of the flour mixture over the eggs, and gently fold it in. Repeat the sifting and folding until all the flour is completely incorporated. Work quickly in order to keep the batter as airy as possible.

Baking: Immediately turn the batter into the cake pan, slip it into the oven, and turn the heat down to 325°F. Bake about 40 minutes (check a square cake pan after 35 minutes). The cake should be golden brown. Its center should spring back when pressed with a finger, and a knife inserted in the center should come out clean. Let it cool about 5 minutes in the pan, and then turn it out on a rack to cool.

Suggestions   **Menu:** Top Spanish Sponge with fresh strawberries or raspberries after a main course of Fresh Tuna Adriatic Style (page 256), Balsamic Roast Chicken (page 279), Herbed Seafood Grill (page 254), Lamb, Garlic, and Potato Roast (page 307), "Priest Stranglers" with Fresh Clams and Squid (page 124), Seafood Stew Romagna (page 259), or Lasagne of Emilia-Romagna (page 165). Use it in Frozen Zuppa Inglese (page 430) and with Espresso and Mascarpone Semi-Freddo (page 428).

For a fast and light dessert, split the cake into two layers and fill it with a high-quality fruit jam (raspberry, apricot, wild blueberry, and peach are several personal favorites). Dust the top with a little confectioner's sugar. Serve it after any of the dishes mentioned above, or others of your own choosing.

Mandan di Lombardia, e di Romagna Per comprare da queste Pan di Spagna.

A nun of the Abbey of Saints Nabbore and Felice slices Spanish sponge or bread, 18th century. Caption reads: "They come from Lombardia and Romagna to buy this Spanish bread."

A Little History

What the basic butter cake is to America, Spanish Sponge is to Italy. For centuries Emilia-Romagna's court and convent kitchens turned out the cake. A Bolognese recipe from the early 1600s instructs the cook to beat the eggs and sugar for an hour and a half before adding flour! The cake appears again in the 18th century as a specialty of the Bolognese Abbey of Saints Naborre and Felice. There it was cut into long slices and eaten plain. Although many believe Spanish Sponge entered Italy through Naples, where the Spanish ruled, I would not discount Emilia-Romagna's strong Spanish connections. During the Medieval and Renaissance periods, Ferrara's court and Bologna's university were international centers. Parma had a long relationship with Spain, culminating in the early 18th century when Duchess Elisabetta Farnese married King Philip V of Spain. No doubt Parma gained recipes as well as intrigues, politics, and fashions through that alliance.

Frozen Hazelnut Zabaione with Chocolate Marsala Sauce
Biscotto allo Zabaione con Cioccolato

If Paradise could be mounded on a spoon, it would be this posh cream—a melding of ice cream and mousse, warmed with the toasty flavors of Marsala and hazelnuts. Bittersweet chocolate sauce, spiked with Marsala and coffee, offers a perfect contrast. During the 19th century, creams similar to this, frozen in fancy molds, were chic dining for the upper classes of Emilia-Romagna. This recipe doubles easily.

[Serves 6 to 8]

Zabaione

1 cup heavy cream, chilled

1 tablespoon sugar

4 tablespoons water

3 tablespoons sugar

1¼ cups (4½ ounces) hazelnuts, toasted and skinned

2 tablespoons sugar

6 large egg yolks

¼ cup dry Marsala

¼ teaspoon vanilla extract

Chocolate Marsala Sauce

1½ tablespoons instant espresso coffee granules

½ cup boiling water

⅓ cup dry Marsala

4 ounces bittersweet chocolate

5 teaspoons sugar

2 tablespoons unsalted butter

Garnish

⅓ cup (1 ounce) hazelnuts, toasted, skinned, and coarsely crushed

Method   **Working Ahead:** *The sugar syrup can be prepared up to 3 weeks ahead; cover and refrigerate. The zabaione can be made up to 1 month ahead and frozen. The chocolate sauce holds nicely in the refrigerator up to 24 hours. Stir in the butter as you heat the sauce for serving.*

Making the Zabaione: Combine the cream and the 1 tablespoon sugar in a medium bowl, and whip to soft peaks. Refrigerate until ready to use. Combine the water and 3 tablespoons sugar in a tiny saucepan, and bring to a simmer over medium heat. Once the sugar has dissolved and the liquid is clear, simmer another 2 minutes. Set the sugar syrup aside and allow it to cool. Then refrigerate until needed. Combine the hazelnuts and the 2 tablespoons sugar in a food processor or blender, and grind to a paste. Set aside.

Turn the cooled sugar syrup into a large metal bowl, and whisk in the egg yolks and Marsala. Set the bowl over a pan of boiling water, making sure the bowl does not touch the water. Whisk 3 minutes, or until the custard is thick, leaving a clear trail at the bottom of the bowl when stirred with a spoon. It will be between 160° and 165°F on an instant-reading thermometer. Do not let the mixture boil, or the yolks will curdle. Immediately turn the custard into a mixing bowl, and beat with a hand-held or freestanding electric mixer at medium speed until cool, 8 to 10 minutes. Beat in the ground hazelnuts and the vanilla until well incorporated. Using a large spoon, fold in about a quarter of the whipped cream to lighten the mixture. Then add the remaining whipped cream, folding until it is thoroughly blended. Spoon into six to eight small ramekins that have been rinsed with cold water (but not dried). Set them on a small tray, cover with plastic wrap, and freeze. (The mousse can also be frozen in a 1½-quart shallow dish or deep soufflé dish, and then scooped into individual servings at the table.)

Making the Sauce: Combine the coffee granules with the boiling water, and stir until dissolved. Turn into a small bowl, and add the Marsala, chocolate, and sugar. Set over a pan of hot water, and stir until the chocolate has melted. If necessary, rewarm over hot water before serving. Stir in the butter just before serving.

Serving: If you used individual ramekins, spread a pool of the warm chocolate sauce on each dessert plate. Dip the molds in a bowl of hot water, loosening the edges with a small knife. Turn each mousse out onto the sauce or next to it. Sprinkle with the crushed hazelnuts, and serve. If you used one large dish, you can serve the mousse partially defrosted and creamy. Transfer it from the freezer to the refrigerator about 4 hours before serving. At serving time, use two large spoons to scoop out ovals of the mousse and place them on dessert plates. Spoon a band of warm chocolate sauce across each oval, and sprinkle with crushed hazelnuts.

Suggestions   **Wine:** A still Malvasia from Emilia or a Torcolato from the Veneto.

Menu: Serve after Lemon Roast Veal with Rosemary (page 294), Giovanna's Wine-Basted Rabbit (page 284), Herbed Seafood Grill (page 254), or Balsamic Roast Chicken (page 279).

Cook's Notes   **Chocolate:** My first choice is Tobler Tradition, with Lindt Excellence as a second.

Frozen Chocolate Pistachio Cream
with Hot Chocolate Marsala Sauce
Crema di Cioccolata da Eletta

This may be my favorite frozen chocolate mousse. It is intensely fudgy, with the unexpected touches of pistachio and Marsala. I also like the hint of coffee in the chocolate sauce, and the ease of making everything ahead. Eletta Violi shared this recipe from her trattoria in the Parma hills. A blooming rose of a woman, Eletta is as generous as her food. Present the chocolate cream as the finale of a menu of simple but elegant dishes. It is especially good after anything flavored with lemon or balsamic vinegar.

[Serves 8 generously]

5½ ounces bittersweet chocolate, melted

1 ounce unsweetened chocolate, melted

4 tablespoons (2 ounces) unsalted butter

5 tablespoons dry Marsala

2 large egg yolks

4 large egg whites, at room temperature

⅛ teaspoon cream of tartar

½ cup (3½ ounces) sugar

¼ cup water

1 cup cold heavy cream, whipped with 1 teaspoon vanilla extract

¾ cup shelled pistachios, chopped

1 recipe Chocolate Marsala Sauce (page 436)

Method

Working Ahead: *The chocolate cream holds well in the freezer 1 month. The chocolate sauce can be made up to 24 hours before serving, but do not add the butter. Rewarm the sauce over boiling water, whisking in the butter just before serving.*

Making the Chocolate Cream: Set aside the melted chocolates to cool. Combine the butter and Marsala in a medium bowl, and set it over boiling water. Once the mixture is bubbling, remove the bowl from the heat and allow it to cool for a few moments. Then beat in the egg yolks. Set the bowl over boiling water again, and stir with a whisk 2 minutes, or until thickened. Remove it from the heat and stir in the melted chocolates. Set aside to cool. Once the chocolate mixture has cooled, beat the egg whites with the cream of tartar, beginning at low speed, until soft peaks form. Have the sugar and water bubbling in a tiny saucepan. Using a candy thermometer, quickly bring the syrup to 248° to 250°F. Make sure the whites are to the soft-peak stage. Then beat at high speed as you pour in the boiling sugar syrup. Beat at high 3 minutes, then at medium speed until the mixture reaches room temperature. Keep the mixture light as you fold the whites, whipped cream, and all but 3 tablespoons of the chopped pistachios into the chocolate mixture. Turn the mixture into a storage container and freeze at least 4 hours. Slightly soften the cream by transferring it from the freezer to the refrigerator several hours before serving.

Preparing the Sauce: Warm the sauce, whisking to combine, in a stainless steel bowl set over a saucepan of simmering water. (If you prepared the sauce ahead, whisk in the butter now.)

Serving: Using a small ice cream scoop, place several balls of the mousse in each of eight wine glasses. Drizzle with the hot sauce. Top with the remaining pistachios, and serve.

Suggestions   **Wine:** Chocolate and wine usually do not mix, but a sweet Marsala Superiore Riserva is fine here.

Menu: Serve after light dishes like Linguine with Braised Garlic and Balsamic Vinegar (page 110), Giovanna's Wine-Basted Rabbit (page 284), Erminia's Pan-Crisped Chicken (page 270), Herbed Seafood Grill (page 254), Braised Eel with Peas (page 261), Balsamic Roast Chicken (page 279), or Lamb, Garlic, and Potato Roast (page 307).

Cook's Notes **Chocolate:** My first choice is Tobler Tradition, with Lindt Excellence as a second.

Reducing the Recipe: If you are serving fewer than eight people, do not make half a recipe. I find it easier to make the full amount, divide it in half, and freeze it in two separate containers. The second quantity will hold 1 month in the freezer, ready whenever you need a dessert on short notice.

The glass seller, 17th century, by Giuseppe Maria Mitelli

Cinnamon and Clove Custard
Budino all'Emiliana

*What a surprise this custard is.
Creamy on the tongue, it tastes of cinnamon, vanilla, and clove. Yet this
old recipe from Emilia's farmland has no added fats. The secret to its
richness is in boiling down and concentrating the milk before adding the
eggs and sugar.*

*Farm women used to pour the custard into a covered pan and bury
it in the hot coals of the kitchen hearth, where it baked while they went
to work in the fields. At dinner the custard was often eaten as a main
dish, napped with the farm's own concentrated grape syrup. Today the
custard bakes in home ovens and is usually taken as a dessert. But it
still tastes especially fine with grape syrup. This sweet has such a
polished, almost urbane quality that it is equally at home on a rustic
menu of country-style foods or with more sophisticated dishes. The recipe
doubles easily.*

[Serves 4 to 6]

2¼ cups milk

4-inch strip lemon zest

6 whole cloves

5-inch stick cinnamon, broken

1 vanilla bean, split lengthwise

½ cup (3½ ounces) sugar

2 teaspoons unsalted butter

4 large eggs

1 large egg yolk

2½ cups Fresh Grape Syrup,
    warmed (page 158) (optional)

Method   **Working Ahead:** *The milk can be concentrated early in the day. Keep it covered
and refrigerated until about 1 hour before baking the custard. The finished custard is best
served lightly chilled, and holds well overnight.*

Concentrating the Milk: In a 3-quart saucepan, combine the milk, lemon zest,
cloves, cinnamon stick, and vanilla bean. Bring to a boil, and cook at a lively bubble
10 minutes, taking care that the milk does not boil over. The milk should be reduced
by about one fifth. Remove the pan from the heat, add the sugar, and stir until it
melts. Let the milk cool to room temperature.

Blending and Baking the Custard: Preheat the oven to 350°F. Use the 2
teaspoons butter to grease a 2¼-cup baking dish with a diameter of about 7 inches
and sides about 1½ inches high. Set out a slightly larger baking pan to use for a water

bath. Baking in a water bath shields the custard from the toughening effects of direct heat. Shield it further by folding a kitchen towel in half and laying it over the bottom of the larger pan. The custard dish will be set on the towel and then the boiling water poured in. (The custard could also be divided among five ½-cup buttered ramekins. Use a baking pan large enough to hold them without touching, and set them on a towel in the pan as described above.)

Bring about 2 quarts water to a boil in a kettle. Give the cooled milk a stir, and then pour it through a strainer into a mixing bowl. Thoroughly whisk in the eggs and yolk. Pour into the custard dish, and cover the dish (or each ramekin) with foil. Set the custard dish (or ramekins) in the towel-lined baking pan, and set the pan on the center rack of the oven. Carefully pour boiling water into the water pan, to within ½ inch of the top of the custard dish (or ramekins). Bake 50 minutes, or until a knife inserted halfway between the center of the custard and its edge comes out clean. The center will still be creamy. (If baking in ramekins, test them after 25 minutes.) Turn off the oven, open the door, and let the custard sit in the water bath about 15 minutes. Then remove it from the bath and cool it on a rack.

Serving: Turn the custard out onto a round dinner plate (or on individual dessert dishes). Cover and chill. Serve cool, not cold, cut in wedges. If desired, accompany it with spoonfuls of warm Fresh Grape Syrup (page 158) or fresh berries.

Suggestions   **Wine:** In Emilia, homemade wine—simple, slightly sweet, and quaffable—is taken with the custard. Do not gentrify this dessert with fancy wines. Have a simple Moscato d'Asti, or serve the custard on its own, followed by coffee.

Menu: Serve after country dishes like Erminia's Pan-Crisped Chicken (page 270), Lamb, Garlic, and Potato Roast (page 307), Riccardo Rimondi's Chicken Cacciatora (page 275), Grilled Beef with Balsamic Glaze (page 303), Pappardelle with Lentils and Parmigiano-Reggiano (page 120), or Tagliatelle with Ragù Bolognese (page 93). On the elegant side, offer after Christmas Capon (page 281), Pan-Roasted Quail (page 283), Artusi's Delight (page 300), or Rabbit Dukes of Modena (page 286).

Baked Pears with Fresh Grape Syrup
Pere al Forno con Sapa

Baked pears caramelized in rich grape syrup have been enjoyed in Italy's wine areas for centuries. This dish evokes harvesttime and autumn winemaking, when the air is filled with the sweet, spicy scents of crushed grapes. The syrup brings depth to the fruit and eliminates any need for sugar. Serve the pears warm, cool, or at room temperature. Pouring a little fresh cream over the fruit is traditional.

[Serves 6 to 8]

Pears

6 large Bosc pears, peeled, cored, and halved

Juice of 2 large lemons

1 tablespoon unsalted butter

Grated zest of 1 large lemon

½ teaspoon ground cinnamon

1 recipe Fresh Grape Syrup (page 158)

Garnish

1 large bunch red grapes (optional)

Method   **Working Ahead:** *Fresh Grape Syrup is made 2 days before the dessert is made, and can be made 5 days ahead and refrigerated. The syrup freezes well 2 to 3 months. The pears are best served on the same day they are baked. Offer them warm, cool, or at room temperature.*

Baking the Pears: Preheat the oven to 375°F. Protect the peeled pears from darkening by moistening them with the lemon juice. Use the butter to grease a 10- or 11-inch round baking dish or a shallow 9 by 13-inch baking dish. Arrange the pears in a starburst pattern in the round dish or side by side, spoon fashion, in the rectangular dish. Sprinkle with the lemon zest and cinnamon. Bake the pears about 1 hour, basting every 20 minutes with ⅓ cup of the grape syrup, using a total of 1 cup (reserve the rest for spooning over the pears at the table). When the pears are easily pierced with a knife, remove them from the oven. If the pan juices are runny, tip the baking dish and spoon the juices into a saucepan. Cook at a fierce bubble 5 minutes, or until thick and caramelized. Pour the juices over the pears.

Serving: Serve the pears warm, cool, or at room temperature. Arrange them on a platter in a sunburst pattern, or serve directly from the baking dish. Use a tablespoon to drizzle a little Fresh Grape Syrup in a zigzag pattern over the pears. Pass the remaining syrup in a bowl for those who wish more on their pears. Garnish by tucking small clusters of red grapes around the pears.

Suggestions   **Wine:** A simple sweet red like Aleatico from Elba or a Lambrusco Amabile.

Menu: Serve the pears with country-style dishes or in any menu where a light dessert is needed. They are excellent after Braised Pork Ribs with Polenta (page 309), Baked Maccheroni with Winter Tomato Sauce (page 173), Maria Bertuzzi's Lemon Chicken (page 273), Lasagne of Wild and Fresh Mushrooms (page 171), or January Pork (page 312).

Bologna fruit seller, 17th century, by Giuseppe Maria Mitelli

Iced Melon with Mint and Balsamic Vinegar
Melone con Aceto Balsamico

Perfect hot-weather food from Reggio and Modena. Save this recipe for high summer, when melons are at their best. The sweetest of melons are made even more delicious with a few drops of rich balsamic vinegar.

[Serves 6 to 8]

1 medium Crenshaw, honeydew, cantaloupe, or casaba melon
About 1 tablespoon sugar (optional)

2 tablespoons artisan-made balsamic vinegar or high-quality commercial balsamic vinegar
8 to 9 sprigs fresh mint

Method   **Working Ahead:** *The dish can be prepared 1 hour or so before serving.*
Serving: Cut the melon into eight wedges, peeling and seeding each wedge. Arrange in a sunburst pattern on a large round platter. Sprinkle with the sugar (if desired), vinegar, and mint. Serve lightly chilled.

Suggestions   **Wine:** If you are using a rich, sweet balsamic vinegar, drink a delicate white Moscato d'Asti. More acidic vinegars will overwhelm wines.
Menu: The melon is light and refreshing enough to end any menu not using balsamic vinegar. Have the melon after Herbed Seafood Grill (page 254), Riccardo Rimondi's Chicken Cacciatora (page 275), Tagliatelle with Caramelized Onions and Fresh Herbs (page 101), *Piadina* bread with accompaniments (page 384), Spaghetti with Shrimps and Black Olives (page 132), or bowls of Seafood Stew Romagna (page 259).

Cook's Notes   **Balsamic Vinegar:** See page 467 for information on commercial and artisan-made balsamic vinegars.
Variations: For the melon, substitute strawberries, peaches, nectarines, apricots, or pears.

Strawberries in Red Wine
Fragole al Vino Rosso

When strawberries are in their prime, make this simple dessert from Ferrara. The berries and a good red wine exchange fragrances with fine results. Take the dish along on picnics, and serve it with a summer buffet as an alternative to richer sweets (the recipe doubles easily).

Marinate the berries in the same red wine you will sip with them later. The wine need not be grand or expensive, but must have lots of fruity flavor.

[Serves 6 to 8]

2 cups fruity red wine (Merlot, Santa Maddalena, Valpolicella, or Zinfandel)
1 teaspoon fresh lemon juice
1/4 cup sugar, or to taste

2 pints ripe strawberries, rinsed and hulled
1 1/2 cups heavy cream, whipped, or 6 to 8 sprigs fresh mint (optional)

Method

Working Ahead: *Steep the berries in wine 1 hour before briefly chilling. Keeping them much longer than 2 hours softens the fruit too much.*

Marinating the Berries: Combine the wine, lemon juice, and sugar to taste in a deep bowl. Add the strawberries, cutting larger ones in half. Let stand 1 hour at room temperature. Then refrigerate 30 minutes to 1 hour before serving.

Serving: Spoon the berries, with some of their juices, into small bowls. Pass the whipped cream separately. (In Ferrara, cream is not usually taken with the berries. They can also be garnished with sprigs of fresh mint.)

Suggestions

Wine: The same wine used to marinate the berries.

Menu: The berries are a fine finish to full-bodied menus as well as lighter ones. For example, serve them after Artusi's Delight (page 300), Domed Maccheroni Pie (page 180), Riccardo Rimondi's Chicken Cacciatora (page 275), Tagliatelle with Caramelized Onions and Fresh Herbs (page 101), or Lasagne Dukes of Ferrara (page 168), all from the Ferrara/Modena plain.

A Passion for Watermelon

Peaches, apples, strawberries, and kiwi may flourish in Ferrara's countryside, but watermelon provokes mischief and mayhem. On a May afternoon, Nicola Gigli, of Ferrara's tourist board, joined me for a drive through the province's farmland. Gigli pointed to a field of green corn and asked, "What do you think that is?"

"A field of corn," I replied.

He grinned. "Yes and no." He went on: "Here in Ferrara, country people leave their houses unlocked, keys in their cars. We trust each other and usually have no reason not to. Except about watermelon. We have a passion for it, and stealing melons is a favorite pastime. When I was a kid we would roam the farms, hunting melons. When we found them, we sat right there in the field and feasted. The farmers were furious. Hiding watermelon patches is a fine art here. All kinds of tricks are used. For instance, that cornfield is just a cover. In its center, hidden from sight, is a big watermelon patch."

Raising his eyes to the sky, he murmured, "Ah, to be young again!"

Chestnut Desserts

Chestnuts used to be the wheat of Italy's mountain people. Land for growing wheat is scarce in the hills, but there is room enough for chestnut trees to flourish. Flour ground from the dried nuts made pastas, breads, cakes, and fritters. Even the aromatic dried leaves were saved. Moistened with water, they became flavorful wrappings for cushioning flatbreads baked on stone griddles, and for protecting vegetable patties cooking between clay tiles or under heated clay domes. But the biggest treats of chestnut season were the newly harvested nuts of October and November. Everyone reveled in their sweetness.

Even today, hot roasted chestnuts are sold on street corners in towns and cities, and autumn chestnut festivals thrive in mountain villages throughout Emilia-Romagna. At Castel del Rio, in the mountains of Bologna province, crowds gather on October weekends for the town's annual chestnut festival. In front of the village's Medieval castle, local men roast chestnuts over blazing fires.

The nuts are traditionally cooked in giant-size black pans that are suspended over the flames by chains hooked up to iron tripods. The pans' long handles are the levers used to flip the chestnuts into the air. The nuts hover for a moment over the sparks and flames. There is an intake of breath. Will they fall back into the pan or disappear into the fire? Invariably the nuts land safely and continue roasting until their shells are brittle and almost charred.

The festival-goers buy little bags of the hot nuts and plastic cups of the season's new red wine. Sloughing off the black shells with one hand, they sip from the cup in the other. Sweet and meaty, the chestnuts taste the way their burning leaves smell—of forests, honey, and sweet hay.

In the marketplace, freshly gathered chestnuts glow like polished mahogany nuggets in large baskets. Marring their beauty with cooking seems a sin, until you reach into the bag of still-warm roasted nuts, rub off more shell, and eat. The sin is venial rather than mortal.

Chestnut desserts are loved today, but in the old days they were special indeed. Years before prosperity and transportation brought sugar and sweets to the mountains, dried chestnuts made most of the desserts. Dried and left whole, or ground into flour, the nuts became the cakes, breads, fritters, and winter puddings. Whole nuts are still reconstituted into soups, stews, pastas, and fillings. One mountain valley in Parma celebrates the New Year by stuffing turkey with nothing but fragrant chestnuts.

Fresh chestnuts always mean Christmas in Emilia-Romagna. No matter how many elaborate desserts crowd the table, hot chestnuts roasted over an open fire are still treasured. Rushed from the hearth, they are shelled hot and dropped into glasses of sweet red wine. The wine changes from place to place, but the tradition is always the same.

Fortunately, some of these desserts can be made in our kitchens. Each of the recipes shared here emphasizes a different dimension of the chestnut and another facet of its traditions. Sweet chestnut flour becomes fritters like the ones sold in Castel del Rio's town square. An old dish from Parma's mountains emphasizes the goodness of freshly roasted chestnuts with a flamboyant flambé. The special quality chestnuts bring to cakes and baked puddings is illustrated in Chestnut Ricotta Cheesecake, adapted from traditional recipes found throughout Emilia and Romagna.

If you are lucky enough to live in an area with Italian markets, you will find fresh chestnuts in good supply during November and December. The freshest ones are plump, fragrant, and shiny, looking like polished wood. Taste them in all their natural sweetness, just as they are eaten in Emilia-Romagna after special winter meals. Simply roast the chestnuts as described on page 451, and serve them with sweet red wine for dunking. Of course these are excellent, too, in the recipes that follow.

Since most of the United States' chestnut trees were destroyed by blight in the early part of this century, imported chestnuts stock our stores. Sometimes it takes a long while for them to reach their final destination. If the chestnuts you can find are starting to dry out, turning dark and matte in appearance, don't worry—once roasted they can still be quite flavorful. But if the nuts are really withered and exhausted, use the respectable substitutes found in jars and cans.

Whether made with fresh or good-quality preserved chestnuts, these recipes are edible souvenirs of those mountain festivals and of the centuries of heritage that keep them alive and well.

Sweet Chestnut Fritters Castel del Rio
Gnocchi di Castagne Castel del Rio

A *taste of mountain tradition from the Apennine hills of Bologna province. I first ate these fritters in the mountain village of Castel del Rio, above Imola, where the ripening of the local chestnuts in October launches a month of fairs and markets. Today they are sweet treats, but years ago these fritters were often the main meal of the day. They are not light, or delicate, but they are satisfying on a cold day. The recipe doubles easily.*

Fresh sweet chestnut flour makes the fritters utterly delicious, but stale flour produces only disappointment. When buying chestnut flour (see page 509 for Mail-Order Sources), check that it is from the new crop. The nuts are dried in autumn, and the flour is usually ground from December through February. Keep chestnut flour fresh by storing it in the freezer.

[Makes about 14 fritters, serves 6 to 10]

1 large egg yolk
1 teaspoon extra-virgin olive oil
½ cup water
1 cup (3½ ounces) chestnut flour
  (see Note)

¼ cup sugar
1 to 2 quarts vegetable oil for
  deep-frying
2 large egg whites
½ cup confectioner's sugar

Method   **Working Ahead:** *The fritters are best fried and eaten immediately. However the batter, minus the egg whites, is prepared 3 hours ahead. Blend in the whites shortly before frying.*

Making the Batter: In a bowl, blend together the egg yolk, olive oil, water, chestnut flour, and sugar, making a smooth batter. Cover and let the batter rest at room temperature about 3 hours.

Frying and Serving: Pour 2 inches of oil into a frying pan or wok, and heat to 375°F (use a deep-frying thermometer). Cover a baking sheet with a triple thickness of paper towels. Preheat the oven to 175° to 200°F. Just before frying, whip the egg whites to stiff peaks. Lighten the chestnut batter by stirring in a quarter of the whites. Then, using big round strokes, fold the remaining whites into the batter, keeping the mixture light. Drop the batter by tablespoonfuls into the oil, trailing the spoon over the oil so the batter spreads out into a thin sheet. (This keeps the fritters from being too dense and heavy.) Fry no more than two or three at a time, turning them after about 90 seconds. They will brown and crisp on both sides in about 3 minutes. Lift the fritters out of the fat with a slotted spoon, drain well on the towels, and slip onto a platter and into the warm oven.

Serving: Eat the fritters as soon as possible after frying. Use a sifter to dust them with the confectioner's sugar just before serving.

Suggestions   **Wine:** A sweet red from Romagna, the delicious Cagnina, a sweet Lambrusco, or a fresh young red like a new Chianti.

Menu: Have the fritters on their own as snacks, or as dessert after bowls of Mountain Soup with Garlic Croutons (page 235), Ferrara's Soup of the Monastery (page 220), or Fresh Garlic Soup Brisighella (page 222).

Cook's Notes   **Chestnut Flour:** You can find chestnut flour in specialty food stores, Italian groceries, and shops specializing in Mediterranean food products. If at all possible, check its aroma before buying. The flour should smell sweet and woodsy, with no sense of staleness or any smoky aromas that suggest bacon. If there is even a hint of an off odor, do not buy the flour.

Capacchi's Blazing Chestnuts
Le Castagne alla Vampa di Capacchi

In this old-time dessert from the Parma mountains, roasted chestnuts are soaked in sweet lemon syrup. Flaming them with homemade grappa or pear brandy gives them their name (vampa means blaze). According to Guglielmo Capacchi, who shared this recipe from his book on Parma's home cooking, La Cucina Popolare Parmigiana, when ricotta was available, people topped the chestnuts with it. Today whipped cream is often used.

Seek out the shiniest, plumpest chestnuts available. If you can roast them over an open fire, they will pick up appealing smokiness, giving the dish greater authenticity. Either of the following techniques produces roasted chestnuts delicious eaten on their own, still hot from cooking.

[Serves 6 to 8]

2 pounds fresh chestnuts
2 cups (14 ounces) sugar
1 cup water
Zest of 2 large lemons, in strips
¼ cup fresh lemon juice

⅓ cup grappa or pear eau-de-vie (such as Pear William)
1 pound high-quality or Homemade Ricotta Cheese (page 454), or 1¼ cups heavy cream, whipped

Method   **Working Ahead:** *The sugar syrup keeps, covered, in the refrigerator 1 week or more. Roast the chestnuts several hours before dining. Let them soak up the lemon syrup before heating them in the oven and flaming.*

Roasting Chestnuts over a Fire: Have a good bed of coals built up in a fireplace or a large grill. Cut a slit two thirds of the way around each nut. Spread the chestnuts in a special chestnut roasting pan (which has a perforated bottom and a long handle) or a shallow heavy roasting pan. Holding the pan over the hot coals, roast the nuts 40 minutes, or until the shells loosen. Turn them often, and occasionally rest the pan directly on the coals. (If you are using a heavy roasting pan, set it directly on the coals and use a long-handled spoon to turn the nuts as they cook.) Take care not to burn the chestnuts. As soon as they are cool enough to handle, slip off the shells and all the inner skin under the shell.

Roasting Chestnuts in the Oven: Preheat the oven to 400°F. Cut a slit two thirds of the way around each nut, and spread them out in a roasting pan. Bake 45 minutes to 1 hour, or until the shells loosen and the nuts are tender. As soon as they are cool enough to handle, slip off the shells and all the inner skin under the shell.

Soaking the Chestnuts: Spread the chestnuts in a shallow baking dish. Combine the sugar, water, and lemon zest in a medium saucepan. Bring to a lively bubble over medium heat. Cook at a fast bubble, 2 minutes, or until the syrup is clear. Add the lemon juice to the hot syrup, and immediately pour it over the chestnuts. Let them stand at room temperature several hours.

Flaming and Serving: Slip the chestnuts into a 350°F oven and bake about 10 minutes. Have the ricotta or whipped cream at the table. Pour the liquor over the hot chestnuts. Immediately take the dish to the table. Stand back as you light the liquor and it blazes up.

Suggestions   **Wine:** A little of the grappa or pear eau-de-vie with the chestnuts.

Menu: In keeping with the Parma theme, serve Erminia's Pan-Crisped Chicken (page 270), Porcini Veal Chops (page 290), or Pan-Roasted Quail (page 283) as a prelude to the chestnuts.

Cook's Notes **Keeping Chestnuts:** Store fresh uncooked chestnuts in the refrigerator.

Chestnut Ricotta Cheesecake
Budino di Castagne e Ricotta

This rich crustless cheesecake studded with chestnut chunks is scented with the unbeatable combination of vanilla and dark rum. That flavoring brings unexpected elegance to the cake, which originated as a simple country pudding. Creamy, smooth ricotta is crucial here. You can find it in cheese shops, specialty food stores, and Italian markets, or you can make your own. The grainy ricotta sold in most supermarkets won't give you a melting texture. Do use fresh chestnuts if they are available. If not, use the best-quality prepared ones you can find. Present the cake at the end of a celebration dinner, or take it along to a party. It can be baked well in advance and travels well.

[Makes 1 cake, serving 8 to 12]

Chestnuts

1 pound fresh chestnuts, or 1 pound bottled chestnuts (see Note)

½ cup (3½ ounces) sugar

1 vanilla bean, split lengthwise

½ cup dark rum

1 to 2 tablespoons water if needed

1 tablespoon unsalted butter

Pudding

2 pounds high-quality whole-milk or Homemade Ricotta Cheese (page 454)

4 large eggs, beaten

2 teaspoons vanilla extract

½ cup (3½ ounces) sugar

4 tablespoons (2 ounces) candied citron, minced

Method

Working Ahead: *The chestnuts can be roasted and flavored 1 day in advance. Store them, covered, in the refrigerator. The cake is best still a little warm from the oven, or cooled and eaten within 24 to 36 hours of baking. Wrap it well and store it in the refrigerator.*

Roasting the Chestnuts: Preheat the oven to 400°F. Cut a slit two thirds of the way around each nut. Spread the nuts out in a roasting pan, and bake 45 minutes to 1 hour, or until they are tender. Cool about 10 minutes. Then slip off the shells and the inner skin just under the shell.

Flavoring the Chestnuts: Combine the peeled chestnuts, sugar, vanilla bean, and rum in a 4-quart saucepan over high heat. Cook at a lively bubble 5 to 8 minutes, stirring often with a wooden spatula, until very thick. Add a little water if the chestnuts threaten to scorch. The chestnuts should be almost whole. Cool the mixture and remove the vanilla bean. Crush the chestnuts against the side of the pan until broken into bite-size pieces.

Finishing and Baking: Use the tablespoon of butter to grease the bottom and sides of a 10½-inch springform pan. Preheat the oven to 350°F. In a medium bowl, stir the ricotta with the eggs, vanilla, sugar, and citron until well blended. Lace the chestnuts through the ricotta mixture, creating streaks like a marble cake. Do not overmix. Turn the batter into the springform pan, smoothing the top. Bake in the center of the oven 1 hour. Then reduce the heat to 325°F and bake another 15 minutes, or until a knife inserted about 2 inches from the edge comes out clean. The center of the cake will still be a little creamy. Remove the cake from the oven and let it cool.

Serving: Unmold the cake by releasing the sides of the springform pan. Serve warm or cool, but not cold. To serve it cool, let it come down to room temperature, then wrap and refrigerate. Let the slices sit at room temperature about 15 minutes before serving.

Suggestions **Wine:** Typically wine is not taken with the cake, but a fresh fruity white Malvasia or Moscato is lovely with it.

Menu: Serve the cheesecake after second courses like Herbed Seafood Grill (page 254), Balsamic Roast Chicken (page 279), Pan-Roasted Quail (page 283), Mardi Gras Chicken (page 277), Christmas Capon (page 281), or Rabbit Roasted with Sweet Fennel (page 289).

Cook's Notes **Chestnuts:** If fresh chestnuts are unavailable, the best prepared chestnuts I have found are roasted and packed without liquid in glass jars. They are imported from France under the brand name Minerve.

Homemade Ricotta Cheese
Ricotta

Emilia-Romagna's ricotta is
particularly creamy and sweet. Those qualities make all the difference in
the region's pasta fillings and desserts—not to mention how satisfying
good ricotta is, just eaten on its own or with fruit. The ricottas available
to most of us in supermarkets are grainy on the tongue and spare in
flavor. Although Italian groceries, cheese shops, and specialty food stores
carry sweet, creamy ricotta, making your own is worth the time.

There is a knack to cheesemaking. It takes some care and patience.
But follow this recipe closely, and I think you will be pleased with the
results. All you need is a 6-quart saucepan with a stainless steel, tin,
nickel, or enamel interior, an instant-reading thermometer, a wooden
spatula, a colander, and a large piece of cheesecloth. The finished cheese
keeps 4 days in the refrigerator. You can double the recipe; use two
saucepans if you do so.

[Makes about 1 pound]

2½ quarts whole milk
¾ cup less 1 tablespoon heavy
  cream, pasteurized but not
  ultrapasteurized or sterilized

5 tablespoons plus 1 teaspoon
  fresh lemon juice
⅛ teaspoon salt (optional)

Method   **Working Ahead:** *The cheese must be made in one session from start to finish; count
on about 1½ hours. Much of this time is semi-unattended cooking. You should be in the
kitchen, but you don't need to be hovering over the stove.*

Cooking the Milk into Curd: This recipe may seem daunting in its detail, but
it is really quite easy. Because cheesemaking is unfamiliar to many, the instructions
lead you through the process step by step. Keep in mind that slowly heating the milk
mixture develops a soft ricotta curd. Fast heating hardens the curd, producing a very
different cheese.

Stir together all the ingredients except the salt in a heavy 6-quart saucepan with
a nonreactive interior. Set the pan over medium-low heat. Cook 40 minutes, or until
the milk reaches 170°F on an instant-reading thermometer. Keep the heat at medium-low. To keep the curd large, do not stir more than three or four times. If you
lift it with the spatula, you will see sandlike particles of milk forming as the clear whey
begins separating from the curd. As the milk comes close to 170°F, the curds will be

slightly larger, about the size of an uncooked lentil. When the temperature reaches 170°F, turn the heat up to medium. Do not stir. Take 6 to 8 minutes to bring the mixture to 205° to 208°F when measured at the center of the pot. The liquid whey will be almost clear. By the time the cheese comes to 205°F, the curd should mound on the spatula like a soft white custard. At 205°F to 208°F, the liquid will be on the verge of boiling, with the surface looking like mounds about to erupt. Turn off the heat and let the cheese stand 10 minutes.

Draining the Cheese: Line a colander with a double thickness of dampened cheesecloth. Turn the mixture into it, and let it drain 15 minutes, or until the drained cheese is thick. Turn the cheese into a covered storage container, add salt if desired, and refrigerate the ricotta until needed.

Cook's Notes **Using Ricotta:** For snacks and lunches, mound cool ricotta on wedges of warm *Piadina* bread (page 384). Use ricotta in pasta fillings: Piacenza's Tortelli with Tails (page 162), Tortelli of Ricotta and Fresh Greens (page 153), "Little Hats" Faenza Style (page 137), and Christmas Cappelletti (page 138). For desserts, in addition to Chestnut Ricotta Cheesecake (page 452), see Capacchi's Blazing Chestnuts (page 450) and Cardinal d'Este's Tart (page 417).

The "Keeping Cakes" of Winter

"Keeping cakes"—dense cakes full of spices and fruit—were first created in Medieval convents and monasteries, where they were baked in the autumn and stored away to mellow until Christmas.

In Emilia-Romagna, as in all of Italy, each area has its own traditional keeping cake. The three shared in this chapter stand out for their popularity in their respective provinces. They also illustrate the sometimes subtle and often intriguing differences in keeping cakes. Shadings of taste are dictated by tradition and built flavor by flavor, with nuances coming from unexpected ingredients like red wine, chocolate, or black pepper. For those of us who know only the American/British fruitcake, these could be fine additions to a holiday repertoire.

Parma's and Reggio's Spongata honey cake seems more like a pastry than a cake. Its disc of golden crust encloses a filling of nuts, fruits, and bread crumbs, held together with honey. The round dark loaves of Pampepato from Ferrara taste of spices, chocolate, citron, and orange. Bologna's spice and honey cake, the Certosino, is distinguished by candied fruits not only in the cake but decorating its top as well.

Although each of these cakes seems quite different, they are all variations on a theme shared with keeping cakes found throughout Italy and much of Europe. Baked into the cakes are the preserved treasures of the autumn harvest; fruits, nuts, and sweeteners. Everything precious was employed in celebrating Christmas, the most important moment of the Christian year.

Each cook used the best ingredients he or she could afford. Candied fruits expressed the ultimate wealth of processed sugar, an expensive commodity until the 19th century. In the Middle Ages, topping Bologna's Certosino cake with its big chunks of candied fruits was like displaying emeralds and rubies.

Honey was more easily had and much less expensive than sugar. Honey still sweetens Certosino and Spongata. Poorer convents and monasteries substituted honey for sugar. In wine-growing areas, cooked-down grape syrup was the least expensive sweetener of all. Even today, grape syrup and dried fruits (rather than candied ones) separate Modena's Christmas cake from the honey-and-candied-fruit-sweetened Certosino of neighboring Bologna.

Spices traveled long distances from exotic places. Stored under lock and key, they were used with great care. They were thought to cure ills and to preserve food against spoilage, as well as giving incomparable flavor to all sorts of dishes. What a treat it must have been to eat a cake flavored with precious cinnamon, nutmeg, clove, and pepper. It was the spices, not the sugar or the fruit, that gave these cakes their names. A common name for a keeping cake is _pan speziale,_ meaning spiced bread; the _speziale_ was the spice seller or pharmacist. Peppered bread, _pamp_ or _pan pepato,_ evolved into Ferrara's _Pampepato._

As time passed, spices and sugar became more affordable. But a new treasure entered the Christmas cakes: chocolate. A 17th-century Bolognese recipe describes making chocolate from the cocoa bean. Bologna's aristocrats of the early 1600s sipped hot chocolate scented with cinnamon, jasmine, and ambergris. But most likely, chocolate was not baked into Christmas cakes until the 19th century. Today chocolate sets apart Ferrara's _Pampepato_—not only is it a flavoring, but a full cloak of chocolate seals the cake. Even Bologna's _Certosino,_ created by the Medieval Carthusian monks, received its measure of chocolate during the 1800s.

Flavorings may shift slightly with evolving tastes, but the cakes' role never changes. They still mean Christmas for all of Emilia-Romagna, welcoming unexpected guests through the holidays and always appearing as the finale of Christmas dinner.

Chocolate Christmas Spice Cake
Pampepato

Crumbly but wonderfully moist, this cake has enough surprises of fruity chocolate, nuts, and spice to set it far apart from ordinary Christmas fruitcakes. Taste it at its best by baking the Pampepato *several days before serving. One loaf could become a holiday house gift while the other is kept for celebrating Christmas with the family.*

Pampepato was created at the monastery of Corpus Domini during the 15th century. A century later the monastery achieved further distinction by becoming the burial place of one of Ferrara's most illustrious duchesses, Lucrezia Borgia d'Este. Some believe the cake's original name was pan del pape, *or bread of the pope, while others say it was* pan pepato, *or peppered bread.*

Pampepato was first cloaked in chocolate during the late 19th century. The crisp coating not only singles out Pampepato *from the Christmas cakes of Emilia and Romagna but also seals the cake, keeping it moist through the entire holiday season.*

Ferrarese Riccardo Rimondi shared this recipe with me. He tells of Christmas in Ferrara, when every pasticceria *makes its own* Pampepato, *packing it in golden cellophane or gilded boxes. On Christmas Eve every shop displays platters of sliced* Pampepato. *Shoppers are invited to share the Christmas tradition as they collect the last-minute supplies for the next two days of feasting.*

[Makes 2 cakes, serves 6 to 8 each]

½ tablespoon unsalted butter

3 tablespoons all-purpose unbleached flour (organic stone-ground preferred)

1½ cups (6 ounces) cake flour

1½ cups (6 ounces) all-purpose unbleached flour (organic stone-ground preferred)

6 tablespoons (2½ ounces) candied citron, cut into very fine dice

¾ cup plus 2 tablespoons (5 ounces) candied orange rind, cut into very fine dice

2 small dried figs, finely minced

1¾ cups (7 ounces) whole blanched almonds, toasted and coarsely chopped

¼ teaspoon baking powder

½ teaspoon baking soda

1 cup plus 3 tablespoons water

1½ cups (10½ ounces) sugar

¼ cup (1¾ ounces) ground sweet chocolate (see Note)

1 cup (2½ ounces) cocoa (not Dutch process)

Generous ½ teaspoon ground cloves

Generous pinch of freshly ground black pepper

1 teaspoon ground cinnamon

Icing

8 ounces bittersweet chocolate, melted

Method　　**Working Ahead:** Pampepato *must be made at least 12 hours in advance. Ideally it should ripen 3 to 4 days. Keep it tightly wrapped at room temperature.*

Making the Cakes: Butter and flour a cookie sheet using the ½ tablespoon butter and 3 tablespoons of flour. Preheat the oven to 300°F. In a large shallow bowl, thoroughly mix the flours, candied fruits, figs, almonds, baking powder, and baking soda. In a small saucepan over medium heat, blend the water, sugar, ground chocolate, and cocoa to a creamlike consistency. Do not let it boil. Cool about 15 minutes, and then stir in the spices. Make a well in the dry ingredients, and fill it with the chocolate mixture. Stir with a wooden spoon to combine everything, taking care not to overmix. It will be a very sticky dough. Use a rubber spatula to make two round mounds of the dough on the cookie sheet, spacing them about 3 inches apart. Each should be no more than 6 to 7 inches in diameter. Smooth the mounds.

Baking, Mellowing, and Icing: Bake the cakes 1 hour and 25 minutes, or until a tester inserted in the center of one comes out clean. Cool them to room temperature on the baking sheet. Then wrap the two cakes airtight in plastic wrap and let them ripen at room temperature 12 hours to 4 days.

Set the cakes upside down on a rack, and spread an almost transparent film of melted chocolate over the bottom of each. Once it has hardened (after an hour or so), flip the cakes over and spread a slightly thicker film over the top and sides of the cakes. When the chocolate hardens, rewrap the cakes and store them at room temperature.

Serving: Slice *Pampepato* not in wedges but like bread, across the width of the loaf, into long, thin slices. Arrange on a platter. Serve *Pampepato* with a sweet wine or with after-dinner coffee.

Suggestions　　**Wine:** Drink Malvasia delle Lipari from Sicily, or sip a Vin Santo of Tuscany.

Menu: Of course this is Christmas food and so is fine after Christmas Capon (page 281), but *Pampepato* is also excellent after any special dinner, especially menus featuring fine balsamic vinegar, so prized by the Este Dukes of Ferrara. Do serve it after Balsamic Roast Chicken (page 279), Rabbit Dukes of Modena, (page 286) and Artusi's Delight (page 300).

Cook's Notes　**Ground Chocolate:** Sold in boxes like cocoa, ground chocolate is sweetened and contains more cocoa butter than cocoa does.

Spiced Christmas Cake of Bologna
Certosino

*E*aten right after baking and cooling, this cake is packed with surprise pockets of melted chocolate and the flavor is spicy with clove, cinnamon, and nutmeg. Age the cake as they do in Bologna, tightly wrapped for 1 week or even a month, and it becomes dense and chewy as the honey glaze sinks deep into its interior.

Certosino takes its name from the Bolognese Abbey of Certosa, where it was first made by monks—no one knows exactly when, but most agree that chocolate was not used in the cake until the 19th century.

[Makes 1 cake, serving 10 to 12]

½ tablespoon unsalted butter
2 tablespoons all-purpose unbleached flour (organic stone-ground preferred)
1¼ cups honey
3 tablespoons red wine
1½ cups (8 ounces) mixed candied fruits (orange rind, citron, lemon rind, pineapple), cut into small dice
1½ cups (6 ounces) all-purpose unbleached flour (organic stone-ground preferred)
1⅓ cups (5½ ounces) cake flour
½ cup (3½ ounces) sugar
2½ ounces bittersweet chocolate, finely chopped
1 cup (4 ounces) blanched almonds, toasted and coarsely chopped

¼ cup (1 ounce) pine nuts, toasted
¼ teaspoon baking soda
6½ tablespoons Dutch process cocoa
¼ teaspoon ground cloves
½ teaspoon ground cinnamon
⅛ teaspoon freshly grated nutmeg
Generous pinch of freshly ground black pepper
Grated zest of ½ large lemon
Decoration
5 long wide strips candied citron
5 long narrow strips candied orange peel
10 candied cherries
5 tablespoons honey, melted

Method   **Working Ahead:** Certosino *can be baked and served immediately. But to experi-ence it as they do in Bologna, bake it 1 to 3 weeks before Christmas. Store, tightly wrapped, in a cool place or in the refrigerator.*

Making the Batter: Preheat the oven to 325°F. Butter and flour a 9-inch cake pan. Melt the 1¼ cups honey in a 2-quart saucepan over medium heat. Stir in the wine. Set aside to cool about 10 minutes. Meanwhile, in a large bowl, thoroughly blend the candied fruits, the flours, and the sugar, chopped chocolate, nuts, baking soda, cocoa, spices, and lemon zest. Make a well in the center of the dry ingredients, and pour in the honey. Gradually stir the dry ingredients into the honey, taking care not to overmix the dough. The dough will be sticky. Turn it into the cake pan, patting it to form a domed round loaf. Only the bottom edge of the cake should be resting against the sides of the cake pan.

Decorating: Decorate the top with a sunburst pattern of citron, tucking the orange peel between the larger citron pieces. Top each strip of orange peel with a candied cherry. Cluster the remaining cherries in the center of the cake.

Baking: Bake 55 minutes, or until a knife inserted in the center comes out with only a few traces of melted chocolate. Let the cake cool 5 minutes in the pan, then turn it out onto a rack. Pour the hot honey over the top. Cool, then wrap tightly and store at cool room temperature 1 to 3 weeks before cutting.

Serving: Use a long sharp knife to cut the *Certosino* into thin wedges, or slice it like bread into thin slices.

Suggestions   **Wine:** A rich dessert wine like Sicily's white Malvasia delle Lipari or Vin Santo of Tuscany.

Menu: *Certosino* is synonymous with Christmas. Serve it after Christmas Capon (page 281) or roasted turkey at holiday time. Make it part of a Christmas sweet tray, along with Paolo Bini's Sweet Ravioli (page 424), Marie Louise's Crescents (page 426), and Home-Style Jam Cake (page 401).

Cook's Notes **Candied Fruits:** The best candied fruits are candied in large, recognizable pieces. They look like fruits, not cubes. Their flavors are a revelation. Find them at holiday time in Mediterranean and Italian markets, and at specialty food stores.

Honeyed Christmas Cake
Spongata di Berceto

Throughout Parma, Reggio, and parts of Piacenza, <u>Spongata</u> means Christmas. Born in the mountains, this unusual cake with its honey, nut, and fruit filling is baked between sweet crusts of butter pastry.

Parma food historian Guglielmo Capacchi remembers his grandmother making <u>Spongata</u> at her mountain farm in November. She always wrapped it and set it to mellow for Christmas in mounds of freshly gathered chestnuts. How delicious the cake must have been, having absorbed all the woodsy perfume of the chestnuts. Even without that fragrance, this recipe creates a fine <u>Spongata</u> for holiday meals and winter entertaining.

<u>Spongata</u> and composer Giuseppe Verdi are inseparable. The cake is strongly identified with Verdi's birthplace and home of many years, the village of Busseto, out on the Parma/Piacenza plain. Verdi is more than the local boy who made good; he is truly beloved. And people in Busseto say he doted on <u>Spongata.</u> To ensure that no one forgets the connection, Verdi's picture appears on the wrapped <u>Spongate</u> sold in nearly every pastry shop in the area.

[Makes 1 cake, serving 8 to 10]

Pastry

1¼ cups (5 ounces) cake flour

1 cup plus 2 tablespoons (4½ ounces) all-purpose unbleached flour (organic stone-ground preferred)

½ cup (3½ ounces) sugar

Pinch of salt

8 tablespoons (4 ounces) unsalted butter, chilled and cut into chunks

1 to 3 tablespoons dry white wine

1 large egg, beaten

Filling

1 tablespoon dried bread crumbs, toasted

Generous ½ cup (2 ounces) walnuts, toasted

Generous ¾ cup (3 ounces) blanched almonds, toasted

½ cup plus 2 tablespoons honey

⅓ cup raisins

¼ cup pine nuts, toasted and coarsely chopped

¼ cup candied citron, cut into fine dice

⅛ teaspoon ground cloves

½ teaspoon ground cinnamon

⅛ teaspoon freshly grated nutmeg

1 large egg, beaten

Method   **Working Ahead:** *The pastry can be made 1 day ahead. The finished cake must mellow at least 3 days at room temperature. It will keep, tightly wrapped, in the refrigerator 3 weeks.*

    Making the Pastry in a Food Processor: Blend the flours, sugar, and salt in a food processor fitted with the steel blade. Add the butter and process until the mixture resembles coarse meal. Stir 1 tablespoon of the wine into the beaten egg, and sprinkle over the dough. Process with the on/off pulse until the mixture begins to form small crumbs. If it is still dry and will not gather into a small ball, sprinkle it with another tablespoon or two of wine, and process another few seconds. It will form small crumbs, but should hold together when you try to form a small ball. Gather it into two balls, one slightly larger than the other. Wrap and chill at least 30 minutes.

    Making the Pastry by Hand: Mix the dry ingredients together in a large shallow bowl. Using a pastry cutter or your fingertips, work in the butter until it looks like coarse meal. Stir 1 tablespoon of the wine into the beaten egg, and sprinkle the mixture over the dough. Toss it with a fork, mixing only long enough to barely moisten the flour. The pastry is ready if you can gather it into a ball. If the dough is too dry, sprinkle it with another tablespoon or two of wine, and toss. It will look like small crumbs and should hold together when you make a small ball. Gather the pastry into two balls, one a little larger than the other. Wrap and refrigerate at least 30 minutes.

    Making the Filling: Combine the bread crumbs, walnuts, and almonds in a food processor and mince to a coarse powder, using the on/off pulse. Set the honey in a medium-size metal bowl over boiling water, and let it melt. Remove the bowl from the heat and blend in the nuts, raisins, pine nuts, citron, cloves, cinnamon, and nutmeg.

    Assembling and Baking: Butter and flour an 8-inch pie pan. (If the weather is humid, roll out the pastry between two pieces of wax paper.) Roll out the larger ball of dough to form a round 3/16 inch thick. Line the pie pan with it, leaving a 1 1/2- to 2-inch overhang. Roll out the smaller ball to the same thickness, and cut out an 8-inch round. Place it on a sheet of foil spread over the back of a cake pan or on a flat dish. Refrigerate the two pieces 30 minutes to 2 hours. Preheat the oven to 400°F. If the pastry is very stiff from chilling, let it become pliable at room temperature. Then spread the filling over the bottom of the pastry-lined pie pan, forming it into an 8-inch disc that is about an inch thick. Gather the edges of the overhanging pastry over the filling.

    Brush the folded-over dough with beaten egg and top it with the round piece. Set the round of pastry in place atop the cake, gently pressing it down to seal it to the egg-washed and folded over pastry. The *Spongata* should look like a large thick disc. Bake 15 minutes. Then reduce the heat to 350°F and bake 45 to 50 minutes, or until the crust is golden brown and crisp. Let the *Spongata* cool in the pie pan. Then turn it out onto a plate, wrap it securely in plastic wrap, and set it aside at room temperature to mellow 3 days.

Serving: Slice the *Spongata* into thin wedges and serve at room temperature.

Suggestions **Wine:** From the region, drink a sweet Malvasia, or have Sicily's Malvasia delle Lipari.

Menu: Serve the cake with traditional Christmas dishes like Christmas Capon (page 281). It is also excellent after Pan-Roasted Quail (page 283), Erminia's Pan-Crisped Chicken (page 270), Beef-Wrapped Sausage (page 314), January Pork (page 312), Lemon Roast Veal with Rosemary (page 294), and Rabbit Dukes of Modena (page 286).

The *Spongata* cake of Reggio from a
17th-century board game, by Giuseppe Maria Mitelli

In the Land of Giuseppe Verdi

Along the Po River on Emilia-Romagna's plain, you can still find towns where life is little changed. In his book *The Po of Mysteries (Un Po di Misteri),* Enzo Sermasi writes about the country at the Parma/Piacenza border, where composer Giuseppi Verdi was born, lived, and died, and where he remains a living entity. There village men gather in wine taverns where "plastic and Coca-Cola have not passed through the door." They drink wine in the old way—from small white bowls, not as a beverage but as a food. The men dance together, and they sing Verdi as easily as they make conversation. Shaking his head, one old man says, "Young people don't like Verdi. No, no, I know it sounds impossible, but they do not." Then he adds with a grin, "But when they grow up it changes. It is inevitable."

In shops and homes throughout Parma province, pictures of Verdi replace the usual portraits of political leaders. There are the local specialties that have become Verdi foods—Christmas *Spongata* cake and the cured pork shoulder of San Secondo. So famous for creating exquisite eating from every part of the pig, Parma has a saying: "The pig is like the music of Verdi—there is nothing left to throw away."

The Parma plain feels timeless, its green pastures and small farms unchanged in centuries. Verdi country is addictive. Does anyone here *not* eat well? At Trattoria Vernizzi in Frescarolo di Busseto, there is a collection of Verdi memorabilia and wonderful culatello. This small local ham, cured solely on this tiny stretch of plain, rarely leaves Parma province and is prized even above Parma ham. Dinner at Vernizzi is filled with laughter, as we win the owner's approval by nearly swooning over the quality of his culatello. Even the butter is extraordinary in its sweetness. La Buca, in Zibello, is another jewel on the Verdi plain, where mothers and daughters have cooked for three generations. It is a small house with two rooms opening off a wide entry hall. On the left is the room for diners, on the right, the bar. Neither has changed much in 80 years.

Smart diners from Mantua, Parma, and Piacenza come to eat handmade tagliatelle and pastas filled with sweet squash, the local cured pork shank with piquant apple conserve, and vegetables grown within shouting distance. In the bar village life continues, seemingly untouched by anything known to the diners across the hall. Men play cards around the one big table. Only dialect is spoken, and although we are noted with amiable nods, we know not to intrude; this is not of our life. But we do touch in a subtle way. Verdi's *Aida* plays on a radio in the background. As I unconsciously sway to the music, some of the agreeable nods become warm smiles. For a moment Verdi is our link. Then the men turn back to their cards. I turn to follow my hostess, who wants to show me how to make culatello.

Emilia-Romagna countryside of vineyards, pastures and farmland

A GUIDE TO INGREDIENTS

Find guidelines for selecting and using ingredients at the beginning of each entry. The food's traditions, folklore and its production are shared after the guidelines.

Balsamic Vinegar
Aceto Balsamico

Buying, Storing, and Using Balsamic Vinegar

Buying balsamic vinegar poses all the hazards of Russian roulette. Grab the first thing you find on the market shelf and you might end up with a mellow, rich example or a vinegar so raw and poorly balanced that it will turn you off to any future encounters. Also, since price is no indicator of quality (and in the United States ranges from $3 to well over $100 for a small bottle), it is important to know what you are buying.

This vinegar originated in Emilia-Romagna's provinces of Modena and Reggio nearly a thousand years ago. Today, it not only continues to be a vital part of the culture there, but no other area has

succeeded in reproducing high-quality balsamics. Exported balsamic vinegars fall into three categories: vinegars made in the provinces of Modena and Reggio by the traditional artisan method and tested by the balsamic consortiums of Modena and Reggio; commercially produced vinegars from Modena and Reggio; and imitations produced outside the provinces of Modena and Reggio.

The Imitations: Balsamic vinegar production has become highly profitable. Imitations from as far away as Naples are now common, as well as vinegar shipped in bulk from Italy and bottled in the United States. These vinegars rarely equal Modena and Reggio's products. (There is a rumor at the time of this writing of American-made balsamic vinegars, too.) Each balsamic vinegar bottled in Italy bears a code indicating its place of origin. Check labels for API MO, indicating Modena, or API RE for Reggio.

Artisan-Made Balsamic Vinegar of Modena and Reggio: Members of Modena's consortium of producers of traditional balsamic vinegar are combating the Russian roulette aspect of buying

balsamics by instituting a DOC, or domain of origin control, for Modenese vinegars.

A vinegar bearing the Modena consortium seal and the words *Aceto Balsamico Tradizionale di Modena* must be made by the traditional artisanal method, have been aged for a minimum of 12 years, and have been produced within the confines of Modena province. It cannot contain any wine vinegar or caramel.

No vinegar receives that seal until a critical evaluation and tasting is completed by five experts. The accepted balsamic is bottled by the consortium. Once a vinegar producer delivers his barrel of balsamic to the consortium for evaluation, he never touches it again, until it is either sealed in bottles or the rejected barrel is returned to him.

Approved vinegars are identified by a distinctive bottle. Although molded in one piece, it resembles a glass globe set in a rectangular stand.

Reggio's own *balsamico* consortium has instituted similar restrictions on their vinegars. Look for a curvaceous vase-shaped bottle with a round seal stating "Consortium of Producers of Aceto Balsamico Tradizionale di Reggio Emilia." They offer three different quality levels indicated by colored labels, with gold being the highest designation, silver the next, and then red.

There is a third consortium based in Spilamberto, not far from the city of Modena. This group, Consorteria dell'Aceto Balsamico Tradizionale, is considered the spiritual mother of Modena's and Reggio's organizations and inspired their formations. Although the Spilamberto group has no commercial function, it trains and qualifies the master tasters that evaluate Modena's and Reggio's consortium vinegars. The Spilamberto consorteria came together with the goal of revitalizing balsamic traditions and helping families reestablish vinegar attics destroyed during World War II. Membership is open to all balsamic vinegar makers (whether they sell their vinegars or make them only for personal pleasure) and now numbers over 1,900 members. Throughout the year, members submit their vinegars for evaluation, hoping that their balsamic will be the winner of Spilamberto's coveted Palio di San Giovanni award for the best vinegar of the year, presented on San Giovanni's Day, June 24.

Whether from Modena or Reggio, these vinegars are the Rolls-Royces of balsamics. The best examples are luscious and complex. They should have a luster or glow and be sable brown or brown-black in color. When the bottle is tipped, the vinegar should look viscous and coat the glass.

To me, the taste of a good artisan-made balsamic is that of a fine liqueur rather than anything you would put on a salad. It resembles a mixture of old port and a full-flavored brown sauce, backed by a little acid. A good one changes on the palate from a dark noncloying sweetness with a suggestion of caramel and wood to a subtle backtaste of acid accenting the vinegar's complex character.

Although these vinegars are expensive (from $40 to over $100 a bottle), they will last a long time if used as they are in Reggio and Modena. They taste best sipped as liqueurs or drizzled in small quantities over finished dishes. Cooking would diminish this vinegar's special quality. Use only a small spoonful for seasoning simple pastas and risotti, grilled or roasted meats, seafood, poultry, vegetables, fritters and frittatas, or fresh berries, melons, pears, peaches or nectarines.

See Mail-Order Sources (page 509).

Commercial Balsamic Vinegar from Modena and Reggio: These are the vinegars most readily available in the United States and the ones used for testing recipes in this book. In Italian they are called *industriale.* They are acidic and straight-forward, begging to be blended *into* dishes.

Commercial balsamics are made in a variety of ways. The most desirable are a blend of high-quality wine vinegar, cooked-down grape must, young balsamic vinegar, and possibly some caramel. Aging in balsamic barrels is favored. The least desirable combine raw-tasting wine vinegar with caramel and herbs, with no balsamic vinegar or cooked must at all.

At their best they are less complex renditions of artisan-made vinegar, with finely balanced sweetness and acidity melded together as a unified whole. Poor examples seem to break apart on the palate, first tasting sweet and then, after a pause, hitting hard with raw acidity. A well-made commercial balsamic has sweetness accentuated by tartness and a deep brown taste. Add these to sauces, soups, stews, salads and marinades. Like their older counterparts, these vinegars are fine drizzled over almost anything deep-fried, as well as summer fruits.

Since there is such a difference from brand to brand, suggesting a specific commercial vinegar is important to the success of the recipes in this book. Fini is a sound example, available by mail order and in shops throughout the country. (Fini

was purchased by a large American food company in 1990. It is too soon to tell if the quality of the vinegar will be diminished by the change in management.) Other brands of good quality are Giuseppe Giusti, Elena Monari Federzoni, Cavalli, or Cattani.

Storing: Store all balsamic vinegars in a cool, dark place like a kitchen cupboard away from the stove or oven.

Cooking with Balsamic Vinegar

Balsamic vinegar appears in recipes from antipasto to dessert (see Index for specific dishes). Here are some additional ideas for enjoying it in traditional as well as nontraditional ways. In Reggio and Modena, it is not a vinegar but a *condimento,* or seasoning.

Using commercial balsamic:

♦ Enrich commercial balsamic vinegars by adding a little dark brown sugar: a generous pinch per tablespoon of vinegar.

♦ Because of its intense flavor, balsamic vinegar is an excellent substitute for salt on cooked meats, fish, poultry, and vegetables.

♦ Sprinkle on baked new potatoes in place of butter or sour cream.

♦ Drizzle it over stir-fried vegetables.

♦ Grill wedges of sweet red and yellow peppers and onion over a hot fire. Sprinkle with fresh oregano leaves or chives, black pepper, and balsamic vinegar. Serve at room temperature. (See Grilled Winter Endives, page 337.)

♦ Add a few spoonfuls to potato salad or cole slaw, or to any vinaigrette dressing. (See Paola Bini's Potato Salad, page 19.)

♦ Drizzle some into bean or vegetable soups.

♦ Rub a few tablespoons into bluefish, salmon, swordfish, tuna, lamb, chicken, beef, or pork, along with some garlic and fresh coriander. Then broil, grill, or roast.

♦ Blend with a little brown sugar and baste roasting duck, pork, or goose with the mixture. (See Grilled Beef with Balsamic Glaze, page 303.)

♦ Blend a few spoonfuls with juniper berries, onion, red wine, and olive oil as a game marinade.

♦ Sprinkle over slices of Grilled Polenta (page 354).

- Try a spoonful in your favorite pesto. (See Green Beans with Balsamic Pesto, page 325.)
- Sprinkle a tablespoon or two over tomato salad with mozzarella and fresh basil.
- When sautéing chicken, chops, or steaks, use 3 tablespoons combined with ½ cup broth to make a quick pan sauce. Slices of fresh ginger work well here.

Using artisan-made balsamic vinegar of Modena and Reggio:
- Sip after dinner as a liqueur.
- Use a few drops to top grilled poultry, meats, or seafoods. Salmon, scallops, and lobster are particularly complemented by this type of vinegar.
- A few drops of balsamic vinegar bring out the sweetness and character of fresh fruit. (See Iced Melon with Mint and Balsamic Vinegar, page 444.)
- Scatter a few drops of aged *balsamico* over a simple apple tart that has been flavored with sugar, cinnamon, and a little butter.

How Balsamic Vinegar Is Made

If you could climb up into the attics of the old palazzos and farmhouses in Modena and Reggio provinces, you would discover rows of wooden barrels filled with a vinegar produced nowhere else in the world. Imitations are attempted outside the area, but none duplicate true balsamic's unique qualities. Some call it a nectar, others a condiment. For nearly 1,000 years it was so precious that Europe's royalty tasted it before commoners outside Emilia even knew it existed. Until about 25 years ago, old, artisan-made balsamics were never sold, they were shared as gifts to visiting dignitaries and treasured friends and relatives. To this day well-born brides of Modena and Reggio accept nothing less than a tiny cask as their dowry. That cask could well hold a balsamic aged over a century and resounding with such deep, rich flavor that it is reserved for sipping as a liqueur on special occasions.

This vinegar was first created about 1,000 years ago in the provinces of Modena and Reggio. Balsamic tastes like no other vinegar. Its flavor is sweet, tart, layered with woods and caramel undertones. The artisanal process that produces it is unique in all Italy, and possibly in the world.

Every autumn in Modena and Reggio provinces, the Trebbiano grape is harvested at the height of its sweetness. Its sugars are intensified by first setting out closed boxes of the fruit on the sunny porches of homes for several days. Then the freshly pressed juice, or "must," is simmered down to a sweet concentrate. (Trebbiano grapes are favored but the law allows for other regional varieties—Lambrusco, Occhio di Gatto ("cat's eye"), Berzemino, and Spergola—to balance the vinegar's character where necessary.) During 24 or more hours of cooking, the grape's sugar lightly caramelizes, creating one of the many flavor elements that give balsamic vinegar its unique taste. Unlike wine vinegar, which is made by converting alcohol to acid, balsamic is produced by converting sugar to acid.

The cooled, settled liquid is drawn off and mellowed in rows of progressively smaller wooden barrels set out in airy, sun-filled attics (called *acetaia,* or vinegar attic). Strong debate wages over whether or not the barrels should contain a "mother," the gelatinous bacterial substance that attacks alcohol or sugars and oxidizes them to form acetic acid or vinegar. Some makers throw it away as it forms, claiming it harms the balsamic, while others nurture the "mother" with great care. Those who discard the "mother" combine the cooked must with balsamic vinegar to create the fermentation necessary to turn the must into *balsamico.*

Yet another factor is the wood itself. A different wood (chestnut, oak, cherry, mulberry, or ash) might form each cask, imparting its own particular color and flavor to the balsamic. Every barrel has holes in its top, encouraging evaporation and concentration of flavors, an important dimension of the vinegar's complex character. Modena's and Reggio's climate of steamy hot summers and icy winters gives the vinegar its needed rhythm of aging: fermentation and later evaporation in the heat, with long rests in the cold.

As vinegar is taken from the smallest or end barrel (about once a year), the barrel is refilled from the next larger one. Each barrel is topped off from the next larger one until the biggest is reached. That is replenished with the cooked must.

Decanting and topping up in a typical Modenese balsamic vingar set.

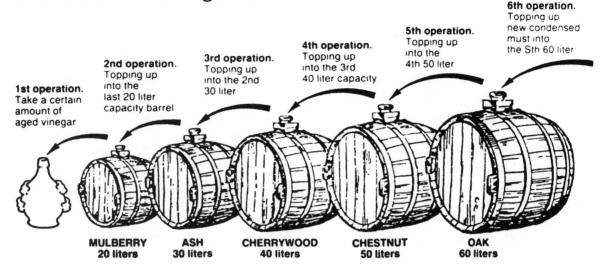

1st operation. Take a certain amount of aged vinegar

2nd operation. Topping up into the last 20 liter capacity barrel

3rd operation. Topping up into the 2nd 30 liter

4th operation. Topping up into the 3rd 40 liter capacity

5th operation. Topping up into the 4th 50 liter

6th operation. Topping up new condensed must into the 5th 60 liter

| MULBERRY | ASH | CHERRYWOOD | CHESTNUT | OAK |
| 20 liters | 30 liters | 40 liters | 50 liters | 60 liters |

There is no set number of barrels, but according to balsamic vinegar maker and research scientist Dr. Claudio Biancardi, there must be a minimum of three. The first is where the fermentation begins converting the balsamic's sugars to acid. In the second barrel, enzymes work on the developing vinegar, giving it many nuances of aroma, taste and color. Dr. Biancardi says the slower the enzymes work, the more complex the vinegar. He explains that in the third barrel the enzyme action continues, but at an even slower rate, along with evaporation and concentration of flavors.

Vinegar from the end of a row of casks is often transferred to tiny barrels or open jugs for further maturing. There the *balsamico* could rest for several generations, becoming viscous, intensely aromatic, sweet and silky, as its acidity is muted with each passing decade. This is the stuff of dowries and coveted gifts, passed from one generation to the next. In Modena it is said, "One generation makes balsamic for the next."

Variables are infinite in this system; the result is that no two balsamic vinegars are alike. Each maker might use a different combination of woods. (Old barrels, seasoned by decades or even centuries of use, are treasured. When they deteriorate, new casks are built around them, or chunks of their woods are added to other barrels, guaranteeing the vinegar's constant contact with the aged wood.) No two sets of barrels produce the same vinegar.

I experienced a vivid example of this when Modenese producer Giuseppe Giusti invited me to taste old vinegars. He led me up into the rambling vinegar attics of his home. Countless rows of ancient barrels were everywhere, many first filled with vinegar by his family in the 16th century. Every Giusti since then has made balsamic vinegar.

We settled in the largest attic, flooded with sun and banked with shelves of the smallest casks. With a long glass pipette he drew some liquid from a little cask at the end of a row of barrels and filled a goblet no bigger than a thimble. The vinegar looked brown, thick, and shiny. I sniffed a little hesitantly. No sharpness, only rich round smells. The taste swept me away—flavors of browned meats, old port, wood, herbs, and only enough acid to give depth. This could not be called vinegar; its deep resonance all but hummed.

Then Giusti dipped into a barrel from another row and filled a second glass. Startling. All I could think of was wild flowers and new hay. The vinegar was as thick and aromatic as the first, but it tasted young and fresh, with all the delicacy of a spring meadow.

Giusti explained that both vinegars had been started at the same time by his great-grandfather, 120 years before. Their taste difference came from the barrels, some of which dated back two centuries.

In the Beginning

Vinegar makers speculate over how the multiple barrel system and its variety of woods came into being. One theory is that it started with an old practice of mellowing vinegars for different uses in barrels of different woods. Vinegar for pickling or flavoring meats was often aged in oak. Vinegar for preserving fruits was stored in cherry barrels, while vinegars for pickling the nut harvest or saucing game frequently matured in chestnut.

Ordinary vinegar had been a favorite preservative and seasoning of Mediterranean peoples since before Christ. According to balsamic expert Renato Bergonzini, during the Middle Ages, vinegar making in some parts of of Italy was a coveted process performed by guilds whose members swore oaths of secrecy. In modern Italian, *tenere il segreto dell'aceto* ("to keep the secret of vinegar") means tenaciously holding to a confidence.

In Modena and Reggio, however, anyone with land and vines could have made balsamic vinegar. It might have begun when boiled-down grape juice (known as *saba* or *sapa* and popular as a sweetener since Roman times; find its recipe on page 158) was stored in a barrel that had held wine or guild-made vinegar. The wine or vinegar's residue encouraged acetic acid to develop, yielding a sweet/tart vinegar.

Another approach was the ancient and common practice of tempering a very acid tasting vinegar with sweet grape syrup, which perhaps led to a barrel of the mixture being forgotten and aging long enough to make a new kind of vinegar. For centuries families produced different-style balsamics, using many variations on these methods. Since 1878 the multiple-barrel technique using only boiled-down grape must has been favored, and in the late 1970s it became the legal definition of Modena's and Reggio's "traditional" artisan-made balsamic vinegar (*Aceto Balsamico Tradizionale di Modena*).

First a Medicine, Then a Seasoning

Balsamic's name derives from "balm," or curative. Earliest records tell of the vinegar's medicinal powers, not its culinary uses. Balsamic is credited with aiding everything from colds to heart conditions. During the plague of 1630, the Duke of Modena refused to leave his castle without an open jug of balsamic vinegar purifying the air in his carriage. Lucrezia Borgia, in one of Italy's first product testimonials, declared it an invaluable balm for the discomforts of childbirth. Composer Gioacchino Antonio Rossini claimed it bolstered his spirits when life became oppressive. Many still believe small sips produce tranquility and restore failing health. And I know balsamic makers who always carry little flasks of it, diluting a few drops in water to soothe a sore throat, inhaling it to clear the head, or seasoning a veal chop with an eyedropperful at the dinner table. In rural parts of Modena and Reggio housewives still place an open cask of their homemade balsamic on a stand in the stair landing below the vinegar attic. Its aromas fill the house, freshening the air and hopefully warding off ills, while at the same time displaying the balsamic-making skills of the family matriarch.

Butter
Burro

Selecting and Storing Butter

Use Grade AA unsalted butter—the sweeter the better. If available, you might want to try the new Plugra butter. Produced to equal European butters, it contains 10.88 percent less water than American butters. Because of its higher butter fat and lower water content, about 10 percent less is needed in sautéing and sauce making. In baking, do not reduce the quantity of butter called for, but Plugra makes slightly lighter pastries and fluffier buttercreams. It has good flavor.

Storing: Since butter absorbs flavors, keep it well wrapped when storing it in the refrigerator. Check its package for an expiration date. Use up within several days of that date. Butter freezes well; seal it in a plastic bag and freeze up to 3 months.

A New Way to Use Butter

In the past, Emilia-Romagna's unsalted, often intensely sweet-tasting butter was second only to pork as the area's cooking medium. Olive and seed oils tied for third place. For health reasons, today many regional cooks reserve butter for where its flavor really counts.

Like cooks in Emilia-Romagna, I too have decreased the quantity of butter in the recipes. Wherever possible, it is used sparingly as a flavoring agent rather than as the sole cooking medium. For instance, in a dish such as Tagliatelle with Prosciutto di Parma (page 94), which traditionally calls for large amounts of butter in the sauce, a reduction of tasty poultry stock finished with a little butter achieves a similar effect. Use the same trick when saucing any filled pastas calling for melted butter and cheese: Cut the butter back to 1 to 2 tablespoons, and blend it with 1 cup stock that has been boiled down to ½ cup.

Browning the meat patties of Artusi's Delight (page 300) in olive oil instead of butter sacrifices nothing in flavor and very little in authenticity.

Finishing the pan sauce by swirling in a little butter at the last minute makes it taste much richer than it actually is. The natural sweetness of the unsalted butter balances beautifully with the tart tang of the balsamic vinegar. These techniques are repeated in many of the dishes. For instance, just 1 tablespoon of butter tossed with a pound of pasta and Winter Tomato Sauce (page 62) brings out still more of the tomato's natural sweetness.

Butter in Emilia-Romagna

Until recently, butter was a status symbol in Emilia-Romagna, and in much of Italy. Until the late 1940s it was available only to those with enough land to graze cattle or with enough money to buy butter ready-made. Parmigiano-Reggiano cheese expert Dr. Mario Zannoni explains that during the 19th century many parts of Italy were fat-poor, lacking any form of the nutrient.

Emilia-Romagna's rich grazing land set it apart from much of Italy. Its wealthy citizens fared better than many of their counterparts in other areas. Historic recipes of Emilia-Romagna's affluent call for butter to be lavished over roasts of lean game. Pounds of it were used in pasta fillings during the Renaissance. Sixteenth- and 17th-century vegetable dishes often featured broccoli, fennel, cauliflower, or spinach simmered in butter the way we boil vegetables in water today.

Butter was so dear to the region's peasants and artisans, on the other hand, that it was actually a form of payment for some. To this day, part of the wage paid to a Parmigiano-Reggiano cheesemaker is all the butter and ricotta he can use and sell. (Both are by-products of the cheese's production.)

If you drive along the country roads of Parmigiano-Reggiano cheese country, look for signs—often delightful three-dimensional ones—depicting whole Parmesan cheeses, marking the *caseificio,* or cheesemaking dairy. Tacked underneath will be notices of butter for sale. Local bread, some of that butter, and a wedge of Parmigiano-Reggiano make a fine picnic.

Coppa
Cured Pork Shoulder

Buying, Using, and Storing Coppa

At this time, Italian coppa is not exported to the United States. But fine coppe are produced here—so good, in fact, that I often prefer them to domestic prosciutti. In seeking them out, look for a solid piece of meat marbled with a moderate amount of fat. The meat should be rosy, never dark brown, never blackish, and never dried out.

Often shops carry pieces of identical-looking meat, one labeled *coppa* and the other called *capocollo.* The capocollo's seasoning often includes fennel and hot pepper. Domestic coppa's flavorings usually are similar to the milder seasonings of Emilia-Romagna: a mixture of salt, pepper, and perhaps a mild spice like clove, cinnamon or nutmeg.

Always taste before buying. Look for a meaty flavor with no one spice standing out and only a quiet backdrop of salt. There should be a pleasingly complex aftertaste with no suggestion of rancidity. The texture is compact, but not dry or stringy. Well-aged coppa feels supple on the tongue. Some brands to seek out are Rapelli and Volpi.

Coppa is sliced a bit thicker than prosciutto. It is excellent on antipasto platters (use ¼ to ½ ounce per person). Use it in cooking when you cannot get a high-quality prosciutto.

Storing: Sliced coppa will keep, well sealed, in the refrigerator for about 4 days. A whole piece, unwrapped, will keep under refrigeration about 2 weeks. If it dries out too much, wrap it in a clean dish towel that has been dampened with white wine and store it in the refrigerator about 24 hours. Slice off the dry end piece before using.

Coppa in Italy

Coppa is one of the overlooked gems of Italian cured meats. Admirers of this aromatic charcuterie call it the poor man's prosciutto.

Coppa is a solid mass of meat cut from the shoulder of the pig. After being seasoned, it is rolled into a compact cylinder, stuffed into a casing, and hung to cure in dry, airy rooms. Because of local dialects and changing names for cuts of meat, in some parts of Italy coppa is also called *capocollo* ("top of the neck"). It can be seasoned with hot pepper, or as in the Marche region of central Italy, with salt, sweet spices (nutmeg, cloves, cinnamon, and the like), orange zest, almonds, and pine nuts. There is also a *coppa d'inverno* ("coppa of winter"), which resembles head cheese.

Emilia-Romagna's rendition is a solid piece of pork shoulder cured with salt, pepper, and occasionally, subtle sweet spices. Its success depends on leisurely aging and the region's own particularly flavorful pork.

Piacenza's coppa is especially admired. It is aged at least 6 months, instead of the more usual 3 or 4. When dried out by summer heat, the coppa is remoistened by wrapping it in wine-soaked cloths; the meat takes on a lovely aroma from the wine. A fine coppa has some of prosciutto's depth and sweetness but is more robust in character.

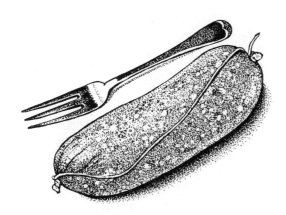

Cotechino
Pork Sausage

Buying, Cooking, and Storing Cotechino

Cotechino is a large, lightly cured pork sausage 2 inches in diameter in Italy (closer to 3 in the United States) and usually 10 to 12 inches long. Even though cotechino cures for several days, it is still a fresh sausage and is always cooked before serving.

Buy cotechino fresh from local specialty food stores, pork stores and Italian groceries. (See Mail-Order Sources, page 509.)

Cotechino is cooked exactly the same way as zampone (page 315), and it can replace the harder-to-find zampone in many recipes.

It is traditionally poached or steamed and eaten hot—often with mashed potatoes, lentils (a New Year's tradition in much of Italy), braised beans, and/or spinach. Beef-Wrapped Sausage (page 314) is a substantial winter specialty of both Modena and its neighbor Ferrara, in which partially cooked sausage is wrapped in a thin slice of beef and then braised with herbs, wine, and stock.

Less traditional but equally tempting is the holiday turkey created by my stepfather, Arthur Fulvini, a sausage-maker and native of Emilia's northernmost province, Piacenza. After partially cooking a whole cotechino, he tucks it into the center of a stuffed turkey before roasting. Its fragrance permeates both stuffing and breast meat. Eaten together, cotechino and turkey breast are delectable.

Storing: Store fresh cotechino, unwrapped, in the refrigerator up to 5 days.

Cotechino in Emilia-Romagna

Like the more famous zampone, cotechino was first made in Modena. Both sausages are cooked and served hot, and both now share a similar coarsely ground and spiced filling. Zampone is the more regal, as its filling goes into a plump pig's foot. Cotechino's juicy and slightly chewy filling is merely stuffed into a large sausage casing.

The word *cotechino* derives from *cotenna,* or skin. In the past the skin made up two thirds of its filling, giving cotechino its poor-relation status as compared to the mostly meat-filled zampone. The rest of the filling was pork taken from many parts of the pig, spices, garlic, and, in Ferrara, generous amounts of red wine. Just over the Po River in Cremona, cotechino is still flavored with vanilla. Mantova adds a little sweet-tart *sapa,* the syrupy reduction of fresh-pressed wine grapes, while Romagna makes a bullet-shaped version with a turkey crop as casing.

All this is evidence of cotechino's origins: it was born of *la miseria,* or great poverty. After almost every bit of the pig was put by, given over to a landlord, or sold, the last scraps became cotechino. Occasionally even all the casings had been used, so a cleaned turkey crop would be substituted. Like France's andouillette sausage of tripe and intestine, cotechino went beyond mere sustenance to become enticing eating.

Today cotechino is made with more luxurious ingredients. In the United States, lean pork shoulder, some skin, and spices constitute a cotechino.

Cream
Panna

Buying Cream

Cream in Emilia-Romagna rarely exceeds 40 percent butterfat, which is the same as our heavy or heavy whipping cream (the label changes from one part of the United States to another). Beware of plain "whipping" cream, which can be so thin that it is nearly impossible to whip. Also avoid ultrapasteurized or sterilized creams, or ones "stabilized" with additives. Flavor is the issue here. If you are going to cook with a liquid containing about 35 calories a tablespoon and 40 percent fat, it had better taste good.

Often co-op markets, health food stores, and specialty food shops carry a local dairy's heavy cream that is simply pasteurized, not cooked and stabilized into tasteless oblivion. Please seek it out. Its sweet, luscious flavor will repay any effort.

Cooking with Cream

Savory dishes laden with large amounts of cream are not Emilia-Romagna's style. If cream is used at all, it is usually as an accent to a recipe, not as a main ingredient. Passionate traditionalists abhor the growing practice of saucing filled pastas like tortellini and tortelli with cream rather than small amounts of butter. In fact, cream is considered too sweet for these preparations. Desserts and cream are, however, another matter. Mousses, *semi-freddi,* and filled pastries, all made silken with whipped cream, are popular.

Culatello

One of Parma province's most remarkable pork products is rarely exported beyond its borders. A small ham of complex taste and great finesse cut from the rear leg of the pig, culatello is successfully cured only in a small area of Parma's plain, and to this day is still produced almost exclusively by local farmers and artisans.

My introduction to culatello must have been orchestrated by the god of unforgettable dining experiences. It was my first trip to Parma, and the consortium overseeing the production of Parmigiano-Reggiano cheese invited me to lunch at La Filoma. Under the guidance of its now-retired creators, Ursula and Sergio Ravazzoni, the restaurant had become a Parma institution—simple, gracious and comfortable. Long established in an old palace near the cathedral, Parma businessmen had been lunching there for decades.

Just beyond the entrance was the customary table artfully displaying vegetable antipasti, salami, Prosciutti di Parma, great mounds of fruits, platters of desserts, and a tumble of large pear-shaped pieces of what looked like oversize salami.

Sergio Ravazzoni asked me what I would like as an antipasto. Ah, did he by any chance have culatello? I'd heard it was very good.

My companions laughed out loud. Signore Ravazzoni merely smiled knowingly. Certainly he had culatello. La Filoma, it turned out, was famous for its culatello. Indeed Signore Ravazzoni was one of Parma's culatello connoisseurs, and had been buying his hams from the same family for more than 20 years. For me he would open a new one. (I later learned that in Parma a culatello is not cut, it is opened.)

A service table was set up next to ours, supplied with a cutting board and a long thin-bladed knife. Signore Ravazzoni placed on the board one of those pear-shaped "salami" from the entry display. It was about 18 inches long, rounded at the bottom, narrow toward the top, and about 7 inches wide at its broadest. Ravazzoni trimmed away a few remnants of the dusty white exterior. By now the whole room's attention was focused on us. Then he cut into the culatello. The buzz of talk ceased.

The little ham exuded fragrances—grassy meadows, dried hay, that nutty quality of damp autumn leaves. I could almost see the aromas floating around the room. I could hear the entire room inhaling and then, after a few beats, the prolonged sighs of contented exhaling. All around men were smiling at me. From a neighboring table one leaned over, gestured toward the culatello, and whispered, "You will like this—it's very good here." I felt as though I were being initiated into a secret society.

A platter of four slices of russet-rose meat was set at my place. It was thinly cut, but not as thin as Prosciutto di Parma. Barely any outer fat rimmed the slices, and the lean meat was moderately marbled. Fragrances had intensified; grass and wild flowers, bubbling yeast, and black earth wet after a rain now sprung to mind.

The meat tasted moist, yet felt like silken leather on the tongue. It was sweet and salty at the same time, with an intensely meaty flavor reminiscent of old-time beef steaks that used to be aged for weeks. It was like a grand old Bordeaux translated into ham.

Culatello became obsession. I tasted it wherever I could find it—in the *trattorie* of towns no bigger than a large farmyard; in little bars with two or three tables for dining; at elegantly napped tables of smart restaurants; and from white paper packets bought at general stores and pork stores on the plain and in Parma city. At those shops it sold for almost double the price of Prosciutto di Parma (about $25 to $30 a pound). In some places people made their own; in others they bought from artisans and farmers. Culatello was always presented as an antipasto, accompanied only by Parma's uncomplicated bread and occasionally curls of intensely sweet butter.

My La Filoma experience was never repeated. None of the restaurants sliced culatello tableside, nor did life stop each time a platter of it was served. But no one was ever blasé about the ham. Almost every time I ate it, someone would point out, "You lose a whole prosciutto just to make a little culatello." They always told of how rare and precious it was, how it could be made only in a small part of Parma's plain. They would talk on about how its full, ripe character and its sweetness are unequaled even by the finest Prosciutto di Parma (this I could debate).

Rarely was it ever compared to any other cured meat from anywhere else in Emilia-Romagna. When I once mentioned culatello in the same breath as ham from another region, I was treated with all the gentle and polite solicitude accorded to someone who has obviously lost her senses.

No two culatelli are exactly alike, but for all their individuality, they fall into basic categories: *stagionata,* meaning fully seasoned, ripe, even strong, and aged up to 18 months; and *dolce,* literally translated as "sweet," but also meaning mild, young, and fresh, usually about 12 months old. The former is favored by many Parmesans but can be an acquired taste for neophytes. I realized Ravazzoni's wisdom in selecting a sweet ham of medium age for my initiation to culatello instead of an older, stronger example that might have put me off.

Culatello inspires strong opinions. Factory-made examples are generally held in low regard. Few Parmesans I know would eat them, and some speculated that they are all shipped out of the province. Several connoisseurs were adamant about culatello being eaten at the source, claiming that away from its home, it quickly loses its unique taste and aroma.

The fact is, little culatello ever leaves the area. Most of it is eaten in Parma province. Milan is the other main consumer, with some going to Rome. The Milanese connection is an old one, dating back to the 1400s, when the Pallavincos, the then ruling family of Busseto (a town in the ham's zone), used gifts of culatello as a political pacifier in their dealings with the land-hungry Duke of Milan. During the 18th and 19th centuries, the Visconti ruled Milan and culatello territory. Noble tributes of the ham were constantly demanded for consumption at the Milanese court.

How Culatello Is Made

As I learned more about culatello, each piece of information generated more questions: Why was this ham made only here? How did it evolve? How was it made? In an era of meat "cured" by 10-minute chemical injections, how had such artisanship survived?

Luck and good friends brought me to Ettore Grisendi, whose official title then was public relations director of the consortium of producers of Prosciutto di Parma. He is an impassioned living encyclopedia of Parma's gastronomy. Grisendi unraveled the mysteries of culatello in a day of intense exploration.

We drove across the green Parma plain toward the Po River, where villages and farms seem to lean against the embankment. The air was still, soft, moist, smelling of hay and of the roses that dappled every garden. This was culatello country, the *basse Parmense,* or Parma lowlands, an area about 6 by 8 miles along the Po River, where embankments built up against flooding hold in morning fogs, increasing the humidity and warmth that led to culatello's creation. In this microclimate airborne organisms combine with lightly salted meat, and at least a year of aging, to make a singular ham. Try curing the special cut outside this area and the result lacks culatello's fragrance, savor, and moisture.

Grisendi emphasized that culatello evolved here from very practical needs. "Imagine you are a peasant. Your one pig has to feed the family for an entire year. The big, meaty rear leg is most prized. Try to cure a whole leg or prosciutto in the warm, moist climate of the plain as it's done up in the mountains (where Prosciutto di Parma is made) with minimal salt, and you'd have spoiled meat. So either you use excessive salt (and we Parmesans don't like that) or you divide the leg into smaller cuts that need only moderate salting to keep for a year or more. Now it is a delicacy, but it came from *la miseria,* from being poor."

"But also from being picky," I added.

"Surely, but remember, if you need money, good culatello is easy to sell. Salt meat is not."

My firsthand lesson in culatello making was given by Grisendi's old friends, a mother-and-son team of artisans, who work in a garage-style extension to their small house. Grisendi acted as commentator.

He showed how the leg is boned, defatted, and divided into three parts. The largest muscles (top and bottom round) become culatello (out of a 24-pound leg, there will be only a 6- to 7-pound culatello). The next largest portion, from right next

to the round (on the other side of the leg bone), is the fiocchetto, which is cured like culatello. The triangular shank piece is boned, but with fat and skin left intact, salted, pressed in a wooden frame, hung, and cured. Although some call this *zampetto* or *jambetta* (meaning foot or shank), Grisendi explained that old-timers call it *il prete* (the priest), because it always went to the parish priest.

Once cut, culatello is rubbed with coarse sea salt twice during about 15 days of refrigeration.

"The goal is the same as for Prosciutto di Parma," explained the son. "Use just enough salt to keep the meat from turning, yet not so much as to overwhelm its natural sweetness."

Once the salting period is completed, the meat is carefully nudged into a casing of semi-transparent pig bladder. Then the ham is "spanked" with a tack-studded wooden paddle to release any air bubbles under the casing.

After a few days of chilling to dry out the moist casings, each ham is coaxed into a pear shape by being tied with wet hemp, which tightens as it dries. A spiderweb of intricate hemp lacing is worked at the meat's base and woven into a fancy fishnet up the sides. It looks like fine crochet. Even after decades of experience, an artisan needs at least a quarter of an hour to weave the netting.

Now the culatelli are hung in a ground-level room with large open windows. Grisendi explained that because the air is humid both in summer and in winter, with few breezes, they dry very slowly and their centers stay moist and tender.

After a year, a fine white mold covers most of the hams, which means they are ready for testing. Grisendi illustrated by poking the meat with a sharpened horse bone (the same test used for Parma ham), going in about an inch, withdrawing it, and sniffing the end. If there is an off aroma, the culatello has spoiled and is discarded. The hole is always sealed with fat. Air around a ham is desirable; air *in* a ham is disastrous. Depending upon demand, culatelli that are ready can be used immediately or aged another 2 to 6 months.

Before it is cut the culatello's white surface is scrubbed off. Its exterior is remoistened during 7 or 8 days of soaking in red or white wine. The wine's acidity cuts some of the salt and adds another dimension to the meat's taste.

At this time, Parma's culatello is not available in the United States. I would be dubious about any that are, since they would probably be factory-produced and possibly not of high quality. Also I tend to believe those purists who say that culatello loses its special character when taken away from its home. That character seems more fragile than those of Parma ham or Parmigiano-Reggiano cheese. Away from the humid air of the Po embankments, culatello's unique qualities might suffer. Like certain wines, some foods should be left to flourish in their place of origin.

The best places to taste culatello are where restaurateurs do their own curing or obtain the ham from skilled farmers and artisans. These will not be tourist places. The territory encompasses the small townships of Zibello, Polesine Parmense, Busseto, and Soragna, and parts of San Secondo, Colorno, Roccabianca, and Sissa. Culatello on a menu in this area is worth sampling. In Parma city the restaurant scene changes with alarming speed these days, so check up-to-date sources before dining. A *salumeria* (where all-pork products are sold) is always a fine place to start. Try to begin tastings with *dolce,* moving on to *piu stagionata* (more ripened or aged) as your palate matures.

The grain sifter, 17th century, by Giuseppe Maria Mitelli

Flour
Farina

Selecting American Flours for Italian Recipes

Italy's flour falls into two categories. *Grano tenero* is a tender wheat flour with a modest protein content, similar to our all-purpose flour. *Grano duro* is a flour of hard durum wheat with a high protein content. The degree of sifting, indicating how much of the bits of bran and grain has been eliminated, is marked on the package: "00" for the finest sift, "0" for a slightly coarser flour, "1" for yet coarser, and "2" for coarser still.

Gluten is the mixture of proteins in flour that makes doughs elastic when worked. How much gluten a flour contains is an important question when deciding which type to use for a recipe. The more gluten or protein in a flour, the more elastic the dough and the more water it will absorb. Higher-protein flours yield chewy and resilient pastas and breads. Grano duro (hard wheat) is extremely low in starch and high in gluten; this is the durum flour used for commercial pastas.

Flours very low in gluten and high in starch, like American cake flour, come from soft wheats. They make velvety cakes and tender pastries, but heavy breads and pastas.

Grano tenero, with its medium levels of starch and gluten, is used in most breads and fresh handmade pastas in Emilia-Romagna. The best American equivalent is an all-purpose unbleached flour with a protein content at the high end of the spectrum, between 11 and 14. Flours for pasta making are explored in detail in the Pastas chapter (page 71).

When making cakes and pastries, I imitate a grano tenero that is on the soft or starchy side by blending American all-purpose unbleached flour with cake flour. Recipes give specific proportions.

To find out the protein content of a flour, check the bag for the nutritional information, which states the grams of protein per 4 ounces of flour. Cake flour is about 8, all-purpose (a blend of soft and hard wheats) ranges from 9 to 12, all-purpose unbleached goes from about 10 to 14, and bread flour is 13 to 15. These amounts vary slightly from brand to brand and from one part of the United States to another.

Using Organic Flour: In attempting to reproduce the flour of Emilia-Romagna, there is more to consider than just gluten content. Many of the region's flours have a vitality, a liveliness of taste and texture, born of different strains of wheat, soil, and perhaps even processing. In Emilia-Romagna it is said that this quality is a pale reflection of what existed 100 years ago.

Before the Industrial Revolution, with its bleaching, bromating, and roller-milling that stripped away every bit of bran and germ, the best of the region's flour is said to have had enormous vigor, flavor, and bouquet. Today there is a budding Italian organic food movement that is trying to bring back the wholesome, flavorful wheats and the limited processing of long ago. In the United States, we can attempt to replicate that flour by using stone-ground organically raised wheat. In addition to retaining nutrients, the absence of excessive processing and additives allows the natural wheat flavors to emerge.

In the interest of using ingredients everyone can find, I have tested my recipes with commercially processed flours. The dishes are even better, of course, if you use organic stone-ground grain. Just be sure to store these flours, well sealed, in the refrigerator or freezer, because the very factors that make them more nutritious and tasty also cause them to become stale quickly.

Measuring Flour: One level measuring cup of flour can hold between 3½ and 6 ounces of flour, depending upon how it is filled. These variations in quantities make tremendous differences in pasta and can have disastrous results in baking. Imagine if the writer of your favorite cake recipe measured

flour averaging 4 ounces per cup and you measure in a way that yields 6 ounces—a heavy cake is unavoidable.

Margins for error disappear when you use a scale: an ounce is an ounce no matter how you measure it. Although weighing ingredients may seem cumbersome, I find it much easier to set a bowl or paper bag on the scale and fill it with flour until the gauge reads the required weight than to measure out cup after cup.

But if only measuring cups are available, you will get 4 ounces of flour, or enough for "one egg of my pasta," in 1 cup of flour measured by lightly spooning the flour into the cup and leveling. Do not tap or tamp. Scooping into the canister with a measuring cup is less exact—usually 4 ounces equals a scant cup.

Wheat Flour in Emilia-Romagna

Wheat was the glamour grain of the Mediterranean. Since the verge of prehistoric times battles have been fought, treaties made and broken, and piracy has flourished to control the production and transport of wheat from Constantinople to Gibraltar.

Wheat flour played a vital role in the survival of so many. Bread was indeed the staff of life for peasants and, during times of famine, for nobility as well. Wheat had remarkable qualities attributed to it. For instance, Emilia-Romagna's Ferrara area produced a flour renowned for its fragrance, silken texture and special properties essential to making Ferrara's famed Couple bread, *Coppia* (page 364). Understanding the flours of Emilia-Romagna, so vital to its pastas, pastries and breads, means exploring a little of its past.

One of the most significant factors in the wealth of Emilia-Romagna has been the fertile plain created by the Po River, where wheat has flourished since at least the 14th century. The moist climate and rich soil nurtured a soft wheat. (Hard durum wheat, first introduced to Sicily by Arab invaders in the 9th century, thrived in southern Italy's hot, dry climate and eventually became the foundation of Italy's commercial dried pasta industry.)

Renaissance cookbooks refer to the "flower of the flour" (*fiore di farina*)—the silkiest, whitest, most unadulterated of flours, reserved for the most exquisite and delicate dishes. It was rich man's food, associated with purity and wealth. In Emilia-Romagna the flower of the flour, taken from grain grown locally, was often used not only for pastries and breads but also in local pasta recipes. Those recipes marked the beginning of the region's reputation for outstanding pasta.

Ferrara's early agricultural records show that the peasant, on the other hand, had coarse dark flour, bulked with bran, wheat germ, oats, rye, barley, millet, and even ground beans. Of course nutritionally he made out better than his wealthy counterpart, but usually he had little else to eat. Today we might hail such loaves as being high in fiber and all sorts of nutrients (and probably pay a premium for them), but in those days no one was delighted at the prospect of such heavy bread, no matter how nutritious.

As wheat became more affordable, the peasant loaf grew lighter in color and consistency. It evolved into the mixed-grain breads still baked high in Emilia and Romagna's Apennine mountains, where life changes more slowly than on the plain. Although the breads contain only locally available ingredients, as they did four centuries ago, what is available has changed. Modena Mountain Bread (page 388) is an example of this living tradition and those changes. With its whole-wheat flour, crushed wheat kernels, and potato for added moisture, it not only satisfies and satiates but it reflects the greater affluence of today's populace.

The traditional use of white flour in many of the region's breads (especially those of the Po plain) speaks of Emilia-Romagna's agricultural wealth, especially since the Industrial Revolution, when new milling techniques made white flour more affordable. Even *Piadina* (page 384), the humble quick bread of Romagna, has been made with white flour for at least a century.

Soft, silky flours make the finest pastries, and Emilia-Romagna's native supply of soft wheat has given it a generous share of dishes prepared in a crust. They have evolved from elaborate court dishes like An Unusual Tortellini Pie (page 175) and Domed Maccheroni Pie of Ferrara (page 180), to convent-made desserts like Riccardo Rimondi's Spanish Sponge Cake (page 433) and the unusual turnovers honoring the Duchess of Parma (page 404), to a vast collection of home-style tarts that crowd pastry shop windows from Rimini to Piacenza. Local flours may have changed over the centuries, but the rich baking traditions born in the kitchens of palaces and convents during the Medieval and Renaissance periods still flourish throughout the region.

Herbs
Erbe, Odori

The foundation of many of Emilia-Romagna's dishes is the slow browning of meats and vegetables, with herbs used only as a soft accents. Rarely does any one herb dominate a dish. Special care is needed when using rosemary, sage, thyme, juniper, and bay. Too much of these fragrant but powerful accent herbs can overwhelm a dish. In contrast, basil is a prime blending herb that melts into a pleasing backdrop for most recipes. Marjoram falls somewhere between the two extremes and is best used in small quantities.

Fresh Herbs

Fresh herbs taste brighter, truer, and more alive than dried. They impart vitality and depth to dishes, as Tagliatelle with Caramelized Onions and Fresh Herbs (page 101) vividly illustrates. Now that so many markets carry them year-round, cooking with them no longer requires an extra effort. Think about growing your own or stocking up at farmers' markets in the summer, when herbs are inexpensive and in their prime, then freezing them for use in winter.

Freezing: To freeze fresh herbs, harvest them just before they flower (when the flavor is best), rinse them, and roll them up in paper towels to absorb the moisture; then strip the leaves into plastic bags, seal well, label, and freeze. Tiny-leafed herbs like thyme, savory, and young marjoram can be frozen on their stems. Use the herbs without defrosting; simply break off what you need. The leaves will have darkened, but the flavors will be bright and fresh.

Dried Herbs

If dried herbs are your only choice, select whole-leaf varieties instead of the stale-tasting powdered examples. Buy only enough to last about 3 months and store them in a cool, dark place. Before adding dried herbs to a dish, activate flavors by rubbing herbs between your palms.

Garlic

I prefer to buy heads of large-cloved garlic. Big cloves mean less fiddling with peeling and are usually the amount I need for a dish.

Whenever people tell me they cannot or will not eat garlic, I suspect two things; burning or a garlic press. Mincing is favored over a press, as the press releases too many of garlic's volatile oils.

Burning is responsible for much of the dislike of garlic. Burnt garlic is bitter, can upset some digestive systems, and is generally inedible. Thoughtlessly written recipes are often the culprit. So many read, "Heat the oil or butter, add the chopped onion, carrot, celery, and garlic, and cook until browned." By the time the onion is browned, those little bits of garlic are burnt. Always add garlic after the browning is completed. Let it sauté for a few moments until it releases its aroma or is pale gold (never dark brown), and then add whatever liquid is called for to stop the browning process.

Buying and Storing: Buy clean-looking large-cloved heads that are firm when pressed and show no sign of yellowing or drying out. Store garlic in an open basket at room temperature. It will generally keep in good condition about 2 weeks.

Herbs in Emilia-Romagna

As you travel through Emilia-Romagna, you will find subtle differences in the herbs flavoring the region's dishes. Basil is favored in tomato-growing Parma and Piacenza, perhaps because of Piacenza's close neighbor Liguria, where basil is all but worshiped. Along Romagna's Adriatic coast, basil seasons grilled fish and seafoods, like Summer Clams with Balsamic Vinegar (page 268). On the slopes of the region's Apennine mountains, juniper perfumes local game. A few stalks of thyme or leaves of bay laurel are added only occasionally to meats, poultry and game in Emilia. Marjoram is favored over its cousin, oregano. You will find marjoram in the cooking of Modena and Bologna, and in Romagna's seafood dishes, such as Spaghetti with Shrimps and Black Olives (page 132).

Garlic is used with a gentle hand throughout the region. The bulb's curative powers have been acclaimed since ancient times. An old saying councils, "Where you find garlic, you find health." In Emilia-Romagna and much of Italy, garlic infusions treat many illnesses and children eat toasted bread rubbed with garlic and olive oil to ward off parasites.

Rosemary and sage (either separately or together) season foods throughout the region. *Aglione* is a blend of fresh rosemary, garlic, and salt rubbed into meats, poultry, and fish and stirred into stews throughout Modena's countryside. And whether in Piacenza, Bologna, or Ferrara, sage often flavors dried beans.

Italian, or flat-leaf, parsley is the region's most popular flavoring, not as a decorative garnish over finished dishes but cooked into them as a seasoning. Italian parsley evokes for me a blend of celery leaf, sweet basil, and black pepper. It is distinctive, assertive, and very different from the curly variety. Balance the sweet onions and salty anchovies in Spaghetti with Anchovies and Melting Onions (page 130) with Italian parsley. Its green herbal quality intensifies the browned beef tastes of Grilled Beef with Balsamic Glaze (page 303). Those green leaves bring flavor to most of the region's savory dishes. If Italian parsley is hard to find in your area, plant some into the garden or grow it on a sunny windowsill. Its hardiness and good taste will reward your efforts.

Lard
Strutto

Selecting the Best

Much of the lard used in Emilia-Romagna's dishes can successfully be replaced with olive oil without sacrifice in taste or authenticity. But there are a few regional recipes that lose their special goodness when oil is substituted for lard. To taste them at their best, you must use the very best lard. Flavorful lard free of chemicals is sometimes hard to find in the United States. Making your own takes almost no time, and a batch will hold in the refrigerator several weeks or 8 months in the freezer.

Ask your butcher to set aside some fresh pork fat for you. The creamy and fragrant fat around the kidney is the prized "leaf" lard. The hard layer from either side of the pig's spinal column (known as fatback) is also prime material, but almost any blend of fresh fat will yield worthwhile results.

To Make 1 Cup Lard: Trim away any meat and connective tissue from 12 ounces of pork fat. Pour about ¼ inch of water in the bottom of a deep heavy saucepan. Add the fat and cook very slowly over medium-low to low heat until it has melted. Do not let the fat brown.

Storing: Pour the melted fat through a strainer into a glass or stainless steel container, and chill. (Or pour the fat into a square cake pan, harden it in the refrigerator, and then cut it into 12 cubes. After freezing the cubes on a baking sheet, turn them into a plastic bag. These are ideal when small quantities are needed as each equals about 2 tablespoons.)

Lard in Emilia-Romagna

Until post–World War I affluence made butter affordable, lard was the most popular cooking fat in Emilia-Romagna. It was inexpensive (all but the

Lard and sausage shop from a 1698 board game, by Giuseppe Maria Mitelli

poorest families had a pig, and lard could be made from leftover scraps of fat) and delicious. Today olive oil is beginning to replace much of the lard traditionally used in Emilia-Romagna's cookery.

Aromatic lard, redolent with the natural sweetness of pork, is still vital to a few of Emilia-Romagna's dishes. It gives the deep, full flavor and fluffiness that sets apart Romagna's pizza-style mountain bread, the *Spianata* (page 367). *Piadina* (page 384), the simple flatbread eaten from one end of Romagna to the other, needs lard for tenderness and taste. A small amount of lard creates the crispest of crusts in the pastry enclosing Reggio's spinach and cheese tart, *Erbazzone* (page 247).

Consider these dishes special treats. Enjoy them as they have been made for centuries, rather than compromising their goodness and authenticity with substitutions.

Mortadella

Buying, Using, and Storing Mortadella

This famous Bolognese sausage is unmistakable in appearance; it looks like a big squat torpedo encased in a dark red sheath. Italian mortadella is not exported to the United States at this writing, but good ones are produced on this side of the ocean.

A fine mortadella is a smooth purée of soft pink pork stuffed into a natural casing. It is studded with cracked peppercorns and cubes of creamy fat (the Bolognese do not like pistachios in their mortadella). The flavor is delicate, so subtly spiced that no one seasoning stands out except the pepper. Two domestic brands worth seeking out are Primo and Santa Maria. Always taste before buying.

When you find a sausage you like, offer it as it is done in Bologna—as an antipasto. Buy a thick slice, cut it into bite-size cubes, and spear them with long bamboo skewers. In Bologna, the local Lambrusco wine always accompanies mortadella. In the United States, try "La Monella" from the Piemontese vineyard of Braida di Giacomo Bologna, or a young, fresh Valpolicella or fizzy red Sangue di Giuda from Lombardia, or a dry white sparkling Pinot di Pinot. Once you have enjoyed mortadella on its own with no embellishments, then try a Mousse of Mortadella (page 22) and taste it as a seasoning in Green Beans Bolognese (page 327).

Storing: Tightly wrap sliced mortadella and refrigerate up to 4 days. With a whole sausage, cover only the cut end with plastic wrap and refrigerate up to 1½ weeks.

Mortadella in Emilia-Romagna

The early Romans ate mortadella. It is mentioned favorably in a diary from 1376, and by the 16th century several styles were popular. According to food writers of the time, Scappi and Messisbugo, mortadella of liver (which is still made today), yellow mortadella of pork, cheese, spices, and saffron, and the ancestor of Bologna's sausage were all served at banquets.

There are three theories of how mortadella got its name. The first has mortadella coming from *mortaio,* for the mortar in which the pork meat was transformed into a smooth paste. Another says it derives from *mirtatum,* the word for myrtle berries, centuries ago sometimes used in place of expensive peppercorns. The third claims it originated from *mortarium,* a kind of salted meat used by the

Mortadella seller in 17th-century Bologna, engraving by Giovanni M. Tamburini, from a picture by Francesco Curti, circa 1640

Romans. Early mortadella recipes salt the meat for several days before blending it with black wine, pepper, and spices, and pounding it into sausage stuffing.

In the 14th century Bologna gained her reputation for mortadella because of the succulence of the local pork. Then the pork meat was pounded into a smooth cream and whipped with cinnamon, nutmeg, pepper, salt, and pieces of pork fat until light and airy. After stuffing the mixture into a large casing, the sausage was cured in a cool dry area for a short time and then cooked. It is still made that way today, with seasonings changing only slightly from one producer to the next. The stuffed sausages are hung on revolving racks in room-size ovens where they slowly roast.

Mortadelle range from 1-pound bullets to man-size sausages, 6 feet long and 1½ feet wide. In 1989 a sausage from the town of Correggio-Emilia (not far from Modena and Reggio) made the *Guinness Book of World Records*. The Veroni company created a 2,864-pound mortadella that was over 19 feet long.

Although mortadella is made throughout Italy, to my mind the best ones are still to be found in Bologna and Modena, where a sixth sense guides sausage makers in their work.

Olive Oil
Olio d'Olive

Selecting, Tasting, and Storing Olive Oils

Since olive oils vary so much in character and since price is no indication of quality, consider finding your favorite oils by joining forces with like-minded friends. Together buy five or six oils that seem to be good candidates, and taste for your favorites.

Olive oils are graded according to how much acidity they contain and whether they are processed with or without solvents. As yet, the United States has no standard for imported Italian oils. The following designations are those of the International Olive Oil Council, of which Italy is a member. These definitions cover all Italian olive oils exported to the United States.

Extra-virgin *(extra vergine)* oils are the premium ones, with not more than 1 percent acidity. They are pressed and processed without heat or solvents. The color ranges from gold to deep green, according to where and with which olives the oil is made. One color is not preferred over another. Clouded unfiltered oils are prized by many for their sometimes fuller flavor. Extra-virgin is my choice for salads and cooking. But the label is not a guarantee of a good-tasting oil, as they vary greatly in style and flavor. You must sample before settling on an oil.

Fine virgin *(sopraffino vergine)* cannot exceed 1.5 percent acidity and is pressed and processed without heat or chemicals. Its flavor is more subdued than extra-virgin. Many cooks use this type of oil for cooking, saving extra-virgin for seasoning and salads.

Semi-fine virgin *(fino vergine)* cannot exceed 3.3 percent acidity and is pressed and processed without heat or chemicals. This is rarely seen in the United States.

Olive oil replaces what used to be called pure olive oil. Its acidity is under 4 percent but is not specifically stated. This is refined olive oil (oil treated with solvents that are steamed off after they have removed undesirable acid levels and tastes), blended with enough virgin olive oil to give it color and flavor. Refining has no effect on the nutrients in olive oil.

Light is an American marketing title with no official meaning, except it usually describes refined oil with little flavor or color. Its caloric count is the same as all other olive oils, 120 calories a tablespoon. There is no reason to use these oils in cooking, as they contribute nothing to a dish.

Pomace olive oil is made by heating the paste left after olives are crushed to produce all the virgin oils. Heating and processing extracts the last remaining oil from the paste, which is then blended with virgin oil.

Once you have collected likely candidates, taste by taking a small spoonful and "chewing" it, letting the oil work on your palate. Then suck air through the oil and see how distinctive flavors come through. Finally, swallow and wait for the aftertaste. At each step the oil should *not* be bland, fatty, flat, highly acidic, bitter, or too peppery. It can be anything and everything from delicate, sweet, flowery, and almost spritzy on the tongue to very fruity or even meaty with olive character, and it can have pleasant tastes of nuts, herbs, fruits, or vegetables. There is no one paragon of oils. Flavors are determined by climate, location, weather, and production techniques. Each olive-producing area of Italy has its own style(s) of oil.

In Emilia-Romagna the preference is for oils tasting of rich olives with sweet, lush overtones and a little pepper. The best candidates for this style are from Tuscany, Umbria, the Veneto, and Liguria. Some brand names to look for are Amoretti & Gazzano, Ardoino, Raineri, Guerrieri-Rizzardi, C.A.B. (Cooperativa Agricola Brisighellese), Biondi Santi, Roselle, Col d'Orcia, Carapelli, Mancianti, and Regina Sibilla.

Storing: Once you find an oil or oils that please, buy several bottles. Store them in a cool dark place and use them within a year.

Olive Oil in Emilia-Romagna

In Emilia-Romagna olive oil is native only to Bologna, a small part of Romagna in the Apennine foothills around Brisighella, and a tiny area of Parma province. It was the third most popular cooking medium in the region after butter and pork. Seed oils from sunflower, rapeseed, and corn are used only occasionally when their neutral character is needed. Originally they were favored for fueling oil lamps, not cooking.

Until recently, the pairing of olive oil with butter, pancetta, or prosciutto characterized a small part of Emilia-Romagna's cuisine. With each passing year, however, more olive oil is used and less of the saturated fats. Two tradition-bound Bolognese gastronomes exclaimed recently, "Soon we'll be eating like the Tuscans!" But in fact, neighboring Tuscany is responsible for Emilia-Romagna's preference for fruity olive oils with hints of pepper. For centuries Emilia-Romagna's grain was traded for Tuscany's olive oil.

One poignant story of that exchange was shared by Parma's Renzo Cattabiani, Parma director of the consortium of Parmigiano-Reggiano cheese, in

trying to communicate to me what life was like when he was a boy during World War II.

"There was so little food. Emilia was richer than the other regions—at least we had a little wheat. But Tuscany, for instance, had nothing. It all went to the army. I remember the Tuscan women would come over the high Apennines pulling wagons because their farm animals had been eaten. They were like donkeys in the traces, pulling wagons of olive oil to trade for wheat. That's how we lived. We loved that oil. Lard, butter—no one ever saw that—but the oil meant we could cook and burn it in our lamps for light, and the wheat meant those women could live."

Olive oil no longer means sustenance. With prices in America as high as $30 or $60 a bottle, it has become a symbol of luxury. Boutique oils are now big business, with a dizzying array on the market, and price is not always an indicator of quality. Learn to trust your palate.

Pancetta
Rolled and Dry-Cured Italian Bacon

Buying and Storing Pancetta

Although Italian pancetta is not imported into the United States, you can find good domestic examples in Italian groceries and specialty food stores. Two good brands are Rapelli and Volpi. Because of its special cure, pancetta is safe (and delicious) to eat uncooked. In Emilia-Romagna pancetta is not smoked.

Look for cylinders about 4 inches in diameter that are spiraled with equal amounts of fat and lean. The meat should range from rosy pink to deep red. Avoid pancetta with dry or brown-looking meat or yellowish fat; the fat must be white. Have the pancetta thinly sliced, just a little thicker than you would prosciutto.

Fine pancetta is sweet, meaty, and not oversalted. Its texture should be melting and tender. The slow curing creates fat that is pleasingly creamy and flavorful, and somehow never tastes or feels fatty.

Sample before buying. Taste first for excess salt. Then, after swallowing, wait a few moments. If there is any suggestion of gaminess or rancidity, pass it by.

Storing: Although freezing is never ideal, pancetta can be frozen. And considering that usually only an ounce or two is used at a time, and that in much of the country it is available only in specialty food stores, stocking up makes sense. Divide a pound or more into 1-ounce portions, put them into airtight plastic bags, and freeze up to 3 months.

Refrigerated sliced pancetta will keep, well wrapped, about 1 week.

Using Pancetta

Today's health concerns mean that pancetta is used only in small quantities as a flavoring agent, but rarely is it totally eliminated, simply because its taste is irreplaceable.

◆ Make the antipasto of Garlic Crostini with Pancetta (page 28).

◆ Sauté chopped vegetables and herbs with 1 to 2 ounces of pancetta and a few spoonfuls of olive oil to create the base of a vegetable or bean soup.

◆ An ounce of pancetta cooked with a spoonful of olive oil makes a rich flavor base for tomato, meat, and mushroom sauces.

◆ One or two slices draped over game birds and game roasts will moisten and flavor the lean meat during cooking.

◆ Use pancetta instead of bacon to make wilted salads with hot bacon dressing.

◆ Cook away all of pancetta's fat in a sauté pan over medium-low heat. Drain off the fat, and then sprinkle the browned bits over steamed broccoli, fennel, cauliflower, Brussels sprouts, green beans, or potatoes.

Nothing matches the flavor of pancetta. If it is unobtainable in your area, order some by mail (see Mail-Order Sources, page 509) and freeze it.

Pancetta in Emilia-Romagna

In Emilia-Romagna and the United States, pancetta lacks snob appeal, which may be why the pleasures of eating it by itself are often overlooked. Many know its fine cooking properties, but few realize how good pancetta is on its own.

This bacon cut of the pig is rubbed with salt, pepper, and occasionally mild spices, and left to cure about 2 weeks. Then the piece is rolled into a compact cylinder of spiraling lean meat and snowy white fat and stuffed into a casing. After slow curing in cool, airy rooms another 2 months or more, pancetta develops a big meaty taste and satiny texture.

Although in some parts of Italy pancetta's robust character is emphasized with smoking, Emilia-Romagna generally uses only the unsmoked variety. As with all regional cured meats, each area produces its own version. Every farmer's *cantina* (wine cellar) has a few homemade *pancette* hanging from the rafters. Two of the most prized styles are Piacenza's, aged 2 to 3 months, with a particularly creamy texture, and Parma's, scented with red wine and a hint of garlic.

Pancetta is everyday food in the homes of Emilia-Romagna, where it is used for sandwiches and snacks. Even those who claim it is not quite fine enough for company will never deny what pancetta's full flavor and silken melting qualities can do for regional dishes. Italy's classic little antipasto meatball owes its succulence to generous amounts of ground pancetta worked into the blend of meats, cheese, and seasonings (see An Unusual Tortellini Pie, page 175). Modena's old recipe for pasta and lentils (page 120) is lackluster without its crusty bits of browned pancetta. And many vegetable sauces, soups, and side dishes begin with sautéing a little pancetta in olive oil, like Tagliatelle with Balsamic Radicchio (page 98) and Ferrara's Soup of the Monastery (page 220).

Parmigiano-Reggiano Cheese
Parmesan Cheese

The cheese most identified with Italy, and most imitated, is Parmigiano-Reggiano, which can be made only in Emilia and a small part of the Lombardy region's Mantua province. It is a part skim milk cheese, aged 18 months to 3 years, and comes in old gold-colored 80-pound wheels. Parmigiano-Reggiano is a *grana* (meaning grain)-style cheese. This is the generic term for aged hard Italian cheeses whose interiors are speckled with grain-shaped white flecks of crystallized amino acids that often crackle in the mouth, as a grain might.

Selecting, Storing, and Using Parmigiano-Reggiano Cheese

Because it is so often imitated, the identity of Parmigiano-Reggiano is subject to great confusion in the United States. To quote ethnic food authority and Parmigiano-Reggiano expert Cara De Silva, "Here the word *Parmesan* has come to be used as the generic, rather like the way Kleenex is used for tissues. But Parmigiano-Reggiano is not a kind of Parmesan; it *is* Parmesan cheese, the only Parmesan." There are countless imitations and other kinds of grana cheeses, but only one Parmigiano-Reggiano. Its flavor and consistency are unequaled by any other cheese. Because it is an artisan-made product, no two Parmesans are the same, although all meet a minimum standard established by the Parmigiano-Reggiano cheese consortium. Many surpass that standard, and those are the ones to seek out.

Appearance

On the rind, check for "parmigiano-reggiano" stenciled repeatedly in a vertical pattern around the cheese in lower-case letters. Make sure the oval "Export" seal is branded into the cheese, an assurance that the cheese has been double tested for soundness. Then check for age: In an open area on the rind the oval consortium mark is branded into the cheese. Near it are two other brands, one of which indicates the year in two figures (89, 90, 91), the other, in three letters, the month of production (most are clear, such as NOV for November, DEC for December; but GEN is January, MAG is May, GIU is June, and LUG is July—shortened forms of the Italian).

How Old: Older is *not* better. Today's Parmigiano-Reggiano usually reaches its peak at about 2 years. Before World War II, when different cows gave Parmigiano-Reggiano milk, the cheese successfully aged longer.

Some connoisseurs prefer winter cheeses for their more intense flavor and velvety texture, the result of their higher concentrations of proteins and fats. Others like the lighter, more flowery qualities of late spring or summer cheeses.

When to Buy: To get Parmigiano-Reggiano at its absolute prime, try to buy from a freshly opened cheese. Ask your favorite cheese dealer to call when a new Parmesan is about to be opened. Aside from getting a first cut, the rush of fragrance as the wheel splits apart is utterly intoxicating.

In Italy the cheese is broken open with a series of small cuts from a stubby almond-shaped Parmigiano-Reggiano knife and a longer arrow-shaped blade. The knives do not cut into the cheese (which would compact it under the blade) as much as they break it apart, releasing its scaly, granular structure. Shops in Emilia's cheesemaking areas that sell premium Parmigiano-Reggiano are awarded a big golden replica of the almond-shaped knife mounted on an oval plaque. It is always prominently displayed.

An open or cut cheese should have no more than 1/4 to 1/2 inch of dryness next to the rind.

The cheese's interior is scaly or flakey when broken, with white dots resembling grain kernels. The color should be uniform. It can range from pale cream to a deep yellow straw color, depending on when the cheese was made. Holes in a cheese are major flaws. Do not buy Parmigiano-Reggiano with holes.

If the cheese looks oily or has a moist sheen, it has been stored at too high a temperature and should be passed over.

Aroma: It should be inviting, fragrant with scents of earth, herbs, flint, hay, cream, and sometimes flowers or fruit. There should be no suggestion of sharpness or acid.

Flavor: Although no two Parmigiano-Reggianos are exactly alike, a superb one has big, deep flavors. The cheese turns creamy and crackly on the tongue, and the taste gets deeper as you chew. Most telling is the aftertaste. It should create a desire for more. Saltiness, sharpness, bitterness, tartness, shallow flavor, or an annoying tang are all signs of careless handling or an inferior cheese. When you find a fine cheese, buy what you can use over 4 weeks.

Storing: Vacuum packing is the ideal way to store the cheese. Or wrap it tightly in plastic wrap. Store it in the vegetable area of the refrigerator. If vacuum packed, it will keep about 3 months. Otherwise the cheese keeps about 1 month. If it dries out, wrap it in a lightly moistened towel, and then loosely in foil or plastic wrap. Refrigerate a day, then remove the towel and wrap it up again airtight. (Freezing Parmigiano-Reggiano breaks down its structure and alters its taste.) Grate the cheese as you need it.

How to Use: The most familiar way of using Parmigiano-Reggiano is grated or shaved, as a seasoning or condiment. Grated Parmigiano-Reggiano and pasta are synonymous in Emilia-Romagna—except in seafood dishes, where the cheese competes with the fish. Most *risotti* need finishing with a handful of Parmigiano to bring their flavors into full focus (see pages 201 to 214). A bowl of grated cheese is always passed with soups, whether they be of vegetables, beans, pasta, or simple broths. The cheese brightens other ingredients and seasonings without overpowering them. Shave Parmigiano-Reggiano into dishes when a more mouth-filling sense of the cheese is needed, such as the Salad of Tart Greens with Prosciutto and Warm Balsamic Dressing (page 26), or over chunky pastas.

Parmigiano-Reggiano is unparalleled as a table cheese. After a main course, serve it in a large piece at room temperature, passing the almond-shaped Parmesan knife for each diner to help him- or herself. Or break it into chunks before serving it. In Modena, chunks of Parmigiano-Reggiano sometimes are moistened with a drop or two of aged balsamic vinegar.

During the Renaissance, court banquets in Emilia-Romagna, and as far away as Rome, featured pieces of the cheese served with fresh fennel or accompanied by platters of truffles in pomegranate sauce, roasted chestnuts, pears and apples, and vegetable tarts. Today in Parma, nothing distracts you from the pleasures of Parmigiano-Reggiano. It is served only with bread and a soft red wine. In the United States, a Barbarossa or Sangiovese Riserva from Romagna complements the cheese, as does Barbera, Dolcetto d'Alba, or a fruity Zinfandel.

Nothing matches a fine Parmigiano-Reggiano; there is no substitute.

Origins

Artisans have been making Parmigiano-Reggiano for seven centuries. They gather annually in each province where the cheese is produced to celebrate their craft and the fellowship that unites them. It is always a night to remember—as I know from one hot evening in May when Parma's 34th annual Cheesemaker's Ball was starting to loosen up. Toasts had been drunk. The almost 500 cheesemakers, dairymen and their families had applauded the awards and speeches. The two young apprentices who had saved hundreds of cheeses from a dairy fire had been given a special accolade. Liveried waiters had served up an elegant meal. And now everyone was ready to relax.

Gradually the jokes in Parma dialect began, with women laughing discreetly behind their hands. Jackets were doffed, ties loosened, veneers of aloofness allowed to fall away. A microphone was loosed from the band as officials on the dais spontaneously formed a zany quintet. Across the ballroom, I was given a serenade worthy of La Scala by two dairy farmers.

That quintet of cheese consortium officials was the hit of the evening, with each soloing a newly made-up verse satirizing the cheesemaker's life. Finally, everyone joined in for old folk songs sung with much laughter and sentiment. Laughing with those Parmesans (who are jokingly known as "little cheeses" in much of Italy), I marveled over the power of heritage; how the quality of that cheese and its traditions were as important to their identities as their own individuality.

Although to many Americans Parmesan means an imitation of the real thing sprinkled on pasta from a jar or can, Parmigiano-Reggiano is an eating cheese experts rank as one of the three or four finest cheeses on earth. Once a great one is tasted, it is not likely to be forgotten. Each mouthful embodies the spirit of those cheesemakers and their 700 years of tradition.

Records from the 13th century attest to the rave notices Parmigiano-Reggiano received from Italians and other Europeans as well. Because of its large size, tough crust and lengthy aging, the cheese shipped well and held up under the vagaries of poor storage. This, in addition to its appealing character, may be why we find Parmesan part of the cuisine from Sicily to England. Parmigiano-Reggiano cheese expert Dr. Mario Zannoni says it was shipped even to Constantinople during the 18th century, where it was highly favored by the Pasha's court.

Although the cheese has been a prime export for centuries, it has never been successfully duplicated outside of Emilia. By law Parmigiano-Reggiano can be made only in the Zona Tipica, the provinces of Parma, Reggio-Emilia, Modena, part of Bologna (on the left bank of the Reno River), and in a small piece of the Lombardy region's Mantua province that juts over the Emilia side of the Po River. Try to produce the cheese with milk from outside this area and it will not age as well, nor have quite the same depth and complexity of taste. Grana-style cheeses produced on the Po River plain outside Parmigiano-Reggiano's zone are usually called *grana padano,* meaning grana of the Po plain.

Parmigiano-Reggiano was first made in the Enza River valley, which separates what are now the provinces of Reggio-Emilia and Parma. For the past 500 years Reggio was part of Ferrara and later Modena's holdings, while the cheese was strongly identified with Parma. Hence the old reference to the cheese simply as "Parmigiano." When an official consortium was formed in 1934 by cheese producers and dairymen to define the zone and to control quality, Reggio finally got what she felt was her due, and the cheese officially became Parmigiano-Reggiano.

Although speculation exists about the ancient Etruscans making a Parmesan-like cheese in Emilia, the first references to a cheese called *Parmigiano* did not appear until the 1300s. Most famous was Boccaccio's description in the *Decamaron* of the luscious-sounding land of Bengodi. In that mythical land of plenty, he described a mountain of grated Parmigiano where ravioli makers perched, fashioning the little squares of pasta and rolling them down the slopes so they arrived at the bottom coated in savory cheese, ready to eat.

Agriculture exploded in Emilia-Romagna during the late 13th and early 14th centuries, when the marshes of the vast Po plain were drained and irrigation systems developed. Cows and oxen brought in to plow the new fields grew fat on the rich grazing land. The cows gave more milk than could possibly be drunk, so cheese was made. Because of those lush pastures, the milk was especially high in the proteins, fats, and other substances necessary for a cheese to age well. And so a large cheese that kept for a long time was born.

Parmigiano-Reggiano was prized far beyond Italy's borders, as proved by Samuel Pepys, the gossipy 17th-century English diarist. On September 14, 1666, he wrote that he had saved his important papers, wine, and "Parmazan" cheese from the Great Fire of London by burying them in the back garden. And British gentlemen of the time who took the then-required Grand Tour consistently wrote of Italy's best cheese, Parmigiano.

Cheese seller by Giuseppe Maria Mitelli,
17th century

Mountain climbers to this day depend on Parmigiano's easily digested proteins to produce quick and long-lasting energy. The cheese's nutrients sustained French dramatist Jean-Baptiste Molière, who lived on it and little else through much of his old age. He may have initiated a fad, for in Molière's day the Parmigiano diet was fashionable—three glasses of port and 12 ounces of Parmigiano per day—in Parisian theatrical circles.

Thomas Jefferson was captivated by the cheese on his visits to Italy, and asked that it be shipped to him in the Colonies.

Robert Louis Stevenson carried a piece of Parmesan in his snuff box, claiming it was very nutritious as well as pleasingly aromatic. In Stevenson's *Treasure Island,* Dr. Livesey filled his snuff box in the same way.

Pepys, Jefferson, and Molière valued Parmigiano for its flavor, but today its great

monetary worth makes the cheese business collateral for development loans. Wheels of Parmigiano-Reggiano are often aged in secured "banks." Cheese bank robberies, when Parmigianos valued at six and seven figures disappear, are reported in the international press. Considering that one wheel is worth about $800 on the retail market, the disappearance of a truckload is a major loss.

How Parmigiano-Reggiano Is Made

In over 1,000 small cheese dairies, or *caselli,* throughout the zone, Parmigiano-Reggiano is made by artisans every day of the year. Until 1984, cheese made between April 1 and November 11 bore the name Parmigiano-Reggiano, while winter cheese was called *Vernengo* (from *inverno,* winter). Today, because of changes in calving practices, Parmigiano-Reggiano is produced all year round.

To become a master cheesemaker, or *casaro,* of Parmigiano-Reggiano requires an apprenticeship of 10 to 14 years, followed by a life making cheese 7 days a week, 52 weeks a year, with no holidays until retirement. As one master told me: "The cows give milk twice a day no matter what. They don't stop because it's Christmas."

The cheesemaker receives little scientific training and often might have only 5 years of formal schooling. Yet consortium scientists who research the hows and whys of Parmigiano-Reggiano all bow to the cheesemaker's instincts and skill. This skill is constantly challenged as the milk's levels of acid, fat, and protein vary throughout the year. This means few batches of cheese are made exactly the same way. One scientist, Dr. Leo Bertozzi, observed, "In my opinion, fine cheese is 30 percent the milk and 70 percent the skill of the cheesemaker."

In payment, the cheesemaker receives a generous salary, a home attached to the dairy, and all the ricotta and butter he chooses to make and sell from the skimmed cream and whey. Frequently he keeps pigs, which are fattened on whey from the cheese, becoming, among other delicacies, Prosciutto di Parma.

The master and his assistant work each morning at big copper vats shaped like inverted bells. They blend skimmed milk from the previous evening's milking with whole milk from that morning's milking. Whey from the previous day's cheesemaking and rennet (the stomach lining of suckling calves) are added as the milk is heated, cooled, and reheated. Newly formed curd is carefully broken up and cooked by the cheesemaker until it is finally time to shape a Parmesan.

Forming the curds into a wheel of cheese is a two-man operation. Heavy curds from the bottom of the 4-foot-deep kettle are scooped with a wooden paddle into a large cheesecloth. Once hefted up to the kettle's rim, the soft white curd is drained in cheesecloth sacks and then pressed into round wooden forms. After most of the whey has drained off, a metal perforating stencil is slipped around each cheese, marking it with the repeating "parmigiano-reggiano" logo.

The cheeses rest for several days in their wooden forms before being unmolded and placed in salt brine 20 to 25 days. After a brief drying, their long aging begins, either at the cheese dairy or at one of the huge communal aging rooms throughout the zone. There each one is brushed, turned, and tested regularly during its 18- to 24-month maturation. A cheese that meets the consortium standards, that is, has no holes and is not soured or spoiled in any way, receives an oval Consorzio della Formaggio Parmigiano-Reggiano brand and is also marked with the month and year of its birth. As negotiants buy cheeses for resale, they add their brands and metal identification discs.

A problem with a cheese is quickly traced to its source. Each cheese is marked with a production date and vat number and, as each vat in the *casello* always contains the same farm's milk, problems can be tracked instantly. Part of the cheesemaker's expertise is knowing every dairy and every cow.

Every person connected with Parmigiano-Reggiano labors with relentless regularity—except the cows. Known in cheese country as *mucce* (pronounced "mookey"), the cows lounge away their lives in spacious stalls. It is the farmer, not the *mucce,* who trudges out to pasture, collects precious grass, trudges back, and then all but hand-feeds it to the animals.

Driving through Emilia's lush countryside and never seeing a cow was disconcerting to me until it was explained that the natural and material wealth of the area was the cheese's greatest asset and its worst liability. The region's wealth from agriculture and trade made expensive animal proteins like meat and Parmigiano-Reggiano affordable to many, leading to more production of these products. At the same time, that wealth led to burgeoning towns and growing industry swallowing up grazing land. Now the grass in those diminishing pastures is too precious to allow trampling by grazing cows. And so dairy farmers have become grass cutters.

The Parmigiano-Reggiano Cheese Song

Verdi's achievements will not be threatened by this playful piece, but how many cheeses can claim a song dedicated to their greatness? And how fitting that the cheese born in the land of Toscanini, Pavarotti and Verdi should have a musical tribute.

Il Grana Parmigiano-Reggiano
Arciere dell'Amore parole di Agrafe*

Forestiera che vieni in Emilia,
non scherzare con facile gioco.
Dai caselli di Reggio e di Parma
nasce il grana, ch'è figlio del fuoco.
Se lo assaggi, ti sciogli in elogi,
in domande ridenti e stupite:
« Chi vi diede una tal meraviglia?
Me lo sposo, o Sindaco, sì! »

Stai attenta, ha più d'un millennio,
ma il suo colpo non sbaglia la mira.
Quando Rambo era ancora nel limbo,
percorreva le strade del mondo,
e mieteva in castelli e capanni
i più ambìti successi d'amor!

Forestiera, non scherza il formaggio
battezzato da queste contrade.
Solo latte, poi latte, poi latte,
e poi fiamma, e poi fiamma e poi fiamma.
Solo latte, e poi fiamma. E' sincero.
Di vigore nutrito, d'ardor,
o gli cedi, con grazia disposta,
o ti prende per forza d'amor.

Stai attenta, ha più d'un millennio.
. . . .
Quando il grana passava la leva
s'inchinava al coscritto, ammirato,
il tenente e s'alzava cortese:
« Il campione è venuto fra noi! ».
Non ostenta blasoni o corone,
esso è figlio di campi e di stalle.
Forestiera che vieni in Emilia,
se lo sposi non esci di qui.

Stai attenta, ha più d'un millennio.
. . . .

Grana Parmigiano-Reggiano—
Archer of Love
by Agrafe
Translated by Anna Teresa Callen

Foreign lady coming to Emilia
do not think of playing an easy game.
From Reggio's and Parma's farms
the son of fire, Grana, is born.
You melt in praises if you taste Him,
curious and smiling questions will arise,
"Who gave you such a marvel?
I want to marry Him,
call the Mayor, oh, yes!"

But be careful, He is a thousand years old
and he doesn't miss the aim.
When Rambo was still in limbo
the roads of the world He roamed,
the most sought-after loves
among castles and shacks He won.

Foreign lady, the cheese baptized in these
surroundings is not a joke.
Only milk, and milk, and more milk.
And then fire, and fire, and fire; milk and fire only.
Sincerity is His name.
Nourished with vim and vigor,
either you graciously succumb to Him
or He will take you by force of love.

But, be careful, He is a thousand years old.

When Grana went to be drafted,
the tenent bowed to the conscript,
"The champion is among us," he shouted.
He does not flaunt coats of arms or crowns,
a son of the stables and the fields is He.
Foreign lady coming to Emilia,
if you marry Him, you will never escape.

Be careful, though, for He is a thousand years old.

*Printed with the kind permission of Aedes Muratoriana, publisher, Modena. Excerpted from *Storia del Formaggio di Grana "Parmigiano-Reggiano"* (1200–1990) by Mario Iotti.

Porcini Mushrooms

The porcino reigns as Italy's king of wild mushrooms because of its meaty character and versatility in the kitchen. Both fresh and dried porcini are prized in everything from salads, pastas, soups, and side dishes to main dishes of poultry, meats, and game.

Selecting, Storing, and Using Dried and Fresh Porcini Mushrooms

Dried porcini stand in when fresh are not available, but the two are used in different ways. Tasting so intensely of beef, earth, and woods, dried porcini often function as a seasoning, not a main ingredient.

Dried porcini are sold both loose and in plastic bags ranging from ½ ounce to 2 pounds. If you are purchasing them in Italy, always check the package for the expiration date, which should be at least 6 months in the future. On either side of the Atlantic, make sure "porcini" is stated on the label, not simply "wild mushrooms."

Look for large pieces, colored from beige to dark brown (pale mushrooms are usually more delicate in taste, dark ones more robust), with only a little dust and crumbled mushroom at the bottom of the package. Then turn the package upside down so the dust falls past the transparent plastic window found on almost every bag. If the dust is weblike or if it moves on its own, do not buy the mushrooms.

The aroma should be appealing, with strong scents of earth, beef bouillon, and aromatic woods.

If the mushrooms smell stale or musty, do not buy them.

Storing: Dried porcini hold well 6 to 8 months if kept dry, cool, and away from light. Store them in sealed plastic bags or glass jars in a cool closet or cabinet. If you stocked up on more than you will use in 8 months, freeze the mushrooms in well-sealed plastic bags.

Preparing Dried Porcini: You must remove all sand and soften dried porcini before cooking them. To wash them, drop the pieces into a bowl of cold water, swish them around vigorously, and pause a few seconds, letting the particles of grit settle to the bottom of the bowl. Then quickly scoop out the mushrooms with your hands, and repeat the process two to three times, or until very few particles appear. Alternately, large pieces can be rinsed under cold running water.

Soften the mushrooms by covering them with hot water and soaking them about 30 minutes. Remove them from the liquid (if more sand particles have appeared, rinse the mushroom pieces again), and use as directed in recipe.

The mushrooms' soaking liquid is almost as prized as the porcini themselves. Often it is strained through a paper-towel-lined sieve into the dish being cooked, as in Meat Ragù with Marsala (page 56) or Porcini Veal Chops (page 290). If it is not called for in the dish you are making, strain the liquid anyway and freeze it. Porcini liquid gives a meaty accent to soups, stews, sauces, and sautés.

Cooking with Dried Porcini: The mushroom adds a robust flavor, invaluable in meatless dishes like Lasagne of Wild and Fresh Mushrooms (page 171).

Dried porcini are particularly good with tomatoes, as illustrated in Piacenza's Porcini Tomato Sauce (page 64). Try sautéing a small quantity of softened porcini with fresh champignon-type mushrooms as a side dish to meat and poultry dishes.

Porcini blend well with most herbs, and they shine with garlic and onion. So many dishes of poultry, meat, and game gain depth and richness from just a few dried porcini added to their cooking juices; see Mardi Gras Chicken (page 277) and Ragù of Giblets (page 54).

Fresh Porcini

Look for fresh porcini in specialty markets during the spring and fall. Small to medium-size mushrooms (3 to 5 inches tall) have less chance of being woody or coarse than larger ones. The coloring on the caps ranges from beige to yellow to dark brown. Avoid any that are moist, discolored, or bruised. The mushrooms should be firm and unwrinkled, and should smell of the earth.

Storing: To store fresh porcini, wrap them loosely in paper towels and refrigerate no more than 2 days.

Cooking with Fresh Porcini: Clean fresh porcini by wiping off particles of sand or debris with a damp cloth. Do not immerse them in water.

The flavor of fresh porcini is far more subtle than that of its dried counterpart. Use them the same way, in simple preparations where the natural flavor of the mushroom stands out. Cooked or raw fresh porcini taste marvelous with shavings of Parmigiano-Reggiano cheese. The caps of large porcini are often grilled with olive oil, garlic, and parsley, and eaten as a second course.

Slip a few slices of sautéed fresh porcini inside a veal chop, as in the original version of Porcini Veal Chops (page 290). Sautéed fresh porcini become a sauce for pasta; see Tagliatelle with Fresh Porcini Mushrooms (page 96).

Thinly slice one or two mushrooms, arrange on each salad plate, and drizzle lightly with olive oil and a little lemon juice. Top with shavings of Parmigiano-Reggiano cheese. You can approximate the taste of fresh porcini by using a combination of dried ones and fresh cultivated mushrooms, as in Oven-Glazed Porcini (page 239).

Porcini in Emilia-Romagna

Scientifically, the porcino is *Boletus edulis.* In France they are called *cèpes.* But Italy is more playful, dubbing them *porcini,* or "little pigs." Imagining a mushroom as a well-fed piglet is easy once you see the porcino's plump domed cap and its stout stem.

Fresh porcini appear first in March or April and continue through July. They return in greater abundance from September to November. Their flavor and aroma call up veal cooked in white wine and the loamy scents of deep forests. Throughout Emilia-Romagna the mushroom season is celebrated with simple dishes like grilled porcini caps, salads of raw porcini with shavings of Parmigiano-Reggiano cheese, pastas sauced with buttery porcini sautés, porcini cooked into risotto, porcini gratins finished with balsamic vinegar, and soups of porcini.

In areas where the mushrooms flourish, restaurants often give over their whole menu to wild mushroom dishes, with the porcino as star. Each province has its own source of especially fine mushrooms. For instance, Parma prizes the porcini of Borgo Val di Taro, in her province's Apennine foothills. Until a few years ago, there was a restaurant in the hills of Reggio that opened only in the spring and autumn mushroom seasons. There was no written menu, only dish after dish made with porcini that the cook, a woman well into her eighties, had gathered herself. Lamentably, the old cook had passed away and the restaurant closed.

All over Italy, people still hunt for and dry their own mushrooms. Once, while interviewing the owner of a Parma food shop, I noticed several brands of dried porcini on display. I asked him which he thought were the most flavorful. Not realizing I was referring to the packaged mushrooms, he enthusiastically replied, "There is a hillside on your right just as you go out on the western road. My family always finds the best porcini there." Obviously those packages were for the uninitiated.

Prosciutto
Ham

Since Roman times the term *prosciutto* (from *prosciugare,* meaning to lose water, to dry up) has applied to a cured rear leg of pork as well as wild boar, deer, chamois, wild goat, and sometimes even breast of goose. But today *prosciutto* generally means ham of pork.

There are two kinds of prosciutto: *crudo,* or raw, and *cotto,* or cooked. Prosciutto crudo is cured and aged raw ham, requiring no cooking before serving. Prosciutto cotto is mildly cured ham that is precooked by roasting or steaming, much like American boiled ham, but with no water added.

At this time, Prosciutto di Parma (Parma ham) from Emilia-Romagna is the only Italian prosciutto crudo allowed to be imported into the United States. Prosciutto cotto from several areas in Italy is also imported.

Selecting, Using, and Storing Prosciutto

Prosciutto crudo is usually served as an antipasto, accompanied only by bread and wine, and occasionally fruit. In Modena it is offered along with coppa and salami, a platter of marinated vegetables, and a basket of hot bread fritters (see Antipasto Castelvetro, page 16). Romagnoli snack on their prosciutto by stuffing it into folded rounds of warm *Piadina* (page 384). Throughout Italy prosciutto is a favorite sandwich filling. It can be wrapped around asparagus or bread sticks, or speared on long picks with chunks of cheese.

Flavoring dishes with ham goes back at least as far as the Roman period. Today prosciutto is cooked and/or blended into sautés, sauces, soups, stews, and pasta fillings.

Selecting Prosciutto: To serve as an antipasto, seek out imported Italian Prosciutto di Parma whenever and wherever possible. I know of no domestically cured *prosciutti* that can match its flavor (see page 497).

If Parma ham is unavailable, there are two *prosciutti* that can replace it in cooking: San Pietro from Switzerland, and Columbo from Canada. *Always* sample hams before buying, tasting for the least salty example.

If prosciutto cotto is unavailable, substitute a high-quality boiled ham with no water added. Use it to flavor sauces and stews and in sandwiches.

Storing: Tightly wrap sliced prosciutto crudo or prosciutto cotto in plastic wrap and store in the refrigerator at temperatures between 42° and 46°F no more than 2 days. Do not freeze.

Prosciutto in Emilia-Romagna

Emilia-Romagna produces one of Europe's most highly regarded hams—the Prosciutto di Parma (page 497), famed for its fragrance and concentrated natural sweetness. It can be cured only in Parma province.

However, prosciutto of all kinds is made in the region's hills and mountains. Although often coarser than Parma ham, each prosciutto has its own appeal. They are as different as the people who make them, whether they be mountain farmers who cure just enough hams to sustain themselves and to sell for next year's animal feed, the regional artisans who fiercely guard their curing secrets and supply only a handful of restaurants and shops, or the executives of large meat factories that ship thousands of hams throughout Italy and Europe.

At Bertinoro, the Medieval mountain village sitting on a balcony-like cliff over Romagna's vineyards and plain, you can taste a prosciutto from higher up in the hills, near Tuscany. It is moist and salty, with a bold, meaty character, and is perfect with the area's Griddle Bread (page 384).

In Piacenza's Gutturnio vineyards, the local winemaker's home-cured prosciutto is lean and pleasantly gamey.

Castelvetro's castle restaurant near Modena serves a countrified salty ham that pairs wonderfully with their sweet/sour Marinated Baby Onions (page 16).

Modenese say their prosciutto is special because it has *il bacio del Cimone,* "the kiss of Mount Cimone's cold, dry air." Reggio, Bologna, and Imola, of course, all make similar claims about the individuality of their hams.

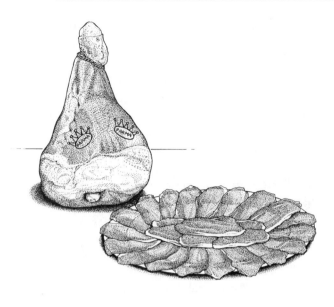

Prosciutto di Parma
Parma Ham

Fragrant and sweet, Prosciutto di Parma is one of the world's most sought-after hams. It can be produced only in the hills of Parma province in an area designated by law. Cured solely with salt and aged 10 months to 2 years, each step of the process is dictated by law and overseen by the Parma Ham Consortium (Consorzio del Prosciutto di Parma). To qualify as a true Parma ham, the meat must have the brand of Parma's five-pointed ducal crown seared into its side.

Selecting, Storing, and Using Parma Ham

Although every ham bearing the Parma crown meets the consortium's standard, some exceed it. Those are the hams to look for. You will find them in shops specializing in high-quality Italian foods and catering to a demanding clientele. Always examine and taste before selecting a prosciutto.

No two Parma hams are alike. They are made by artisans and reflect the individuality of their creators. Older hams often taste earthy, with a pleasant mustiness or ripeness and more assertive saltiness. Younger hams taste of pork's natural sweetness and can have scents of fresh-cut hay. For the uninitiated, the younger ham is more accessible; the older is more of an acquired taste. No hams

under 400 days old enter the United States. In Italy, Parma hams must attain a minimum of 10 months and can be aged up to 2 years.

When buying, check first for the Parma crown branded into the side of the ham. Then look for large hams or pieces of large hams, as the denser the muscle the sweeter the meat. Check meat and fat color, aroma and always taste. The ham has two major sets of muscles. The thicker will always be more generously marbled, and have the milder and sweeter flavor. The shallower muscle will be more mature and intense in character, often saltier.

Prosciutto is often shipped in vacuum packing. Once the original wrapper is removed, the meat must breathe and should not be sealed airtight. Make sure the first slice of an already cut ham is discarded, as it will be dry.

The meat should be soft pink to deep rose, with a fine marbling of fat running through the lean. The fat should be rose-toned where it touches meat and white farther away—never yellow. A thick fat covering on untrimmed ham is desirable.

The ham should be fragrant, with scents of hay, roasted meat, sweetness, and yeastiness. Any suggestion of ammonia or rancidity indicates a poor ham. The flavor, depending on age, should be sweet or like well-ripened fruit, with some earthiness; delicate but round, with intensely meaty undertones. Salt should be a backdrop. Wait a few beats after swallowing. If there is a rancid aftertaste, the ham has been stored improperly; do not buy it.

Prosciutto is always sliced paper-thin. Slices must lie side by side, never stacked. If you are slicing a whole unboned ham, set it on its side with the shank bone pointing downward. Slice the top muscle horizontally, parallel to the femur bone. Remove the bones and then slice the thicker muscle vertically. If you are working with boned ham, slice across the grain (vertically) throughout. Slice the ham as close to serving time as possible, and keep the slices covered.

Storing: Presliced prosciutto should be purchased as close to serving time as possible. Keep it sealed and chilled until about an hour before dining. It will hold in decent condition up to 2 days if stored in the refrigerator at 42° to 46°F. The prosciutto must be well wrapped and sealed in its original wrapper to protect the slices from drying out.

Wrap large chunks of prosciutto in porous fabric, such as cheesecloth or a kitchen towel, allowing the ham to breathe, and store it in the refrigerator at 42° to 46°F (the vegetable crisper is an ideal location). Freezing ruins Prosciutto di Parma, diminishing its flavor and changing its texture.

Serving: Always serve the ham at room temperature. For a classic antipasto, serve as in Parma. Arrange three to four slices side by side on a plate, accompanied not by fruit but simply by bread (see page 14). Drink a lively, fruity white wine. In Parma it will be a dry, slightly spritzy Malvasia from the same hills where the prosciutto is made. Here drink a crisp white Portuguese Vinho Verde, or a Galestro from Tuscany.

If the only available Parma ham is full-flavored but salty, serving it with ripe melon, fresh figs, or pears will help blunt the salt's impact. Hot Caramelized Pears with Prosciutto (page 31) is another way of enjoying these hams.

Parma ham is never served cooked and hot, as you would a steak or chop. It is cooked only when it seasons dishes—for example, in Tagliatelle with Prosciutto di Parma (page 94), Parsley Pasta with Tomato and Peas Villa Gaidello (page 118), or Sweet Peas Parma (page 322).

When cooking with Prosciutto di Parma, I usually cook a little chopped ham into the base sauté of a dish, building a foundation of flavor, and then sprinkle slivers of uncooked ham over the finished recipe for impact.

Parma Ham in Emilia-Romagna

Eating the ham in Parma is a purist's paradise. It is always an antipasto with three or four semi-transparent slices draped over a plate. I have never seen fruit, sauces or garnishes served with the prosciutto there. Bread and the fizzy white Malvasia wine from the same hills that the ham comes from are its only accompaniments. Even butter with the bread is debated. Some Parmesans declare it an affectation.

The rosy red meat with its edging in white fat tastes like someone infused the flavors of nuts, cream, ripe fruit and meat essence into a ham.

If the taste is memorable, the prosciutto's texture will equal it. The meat is supple, concentrated rather than dried, and feels silky on the tongue. But to me, most startling is the vitality of taste. The ham is still evolving, like a good wine. And that sense comes through in every mouthful.

Three ingredients are necessary to make Parma ham: salt, air, and time. The list of what is *not* allowed is much longer: no sugar, spices, smoke, water, nitrites, nor any of the dubious substances often associated with modern ham production. Salt is allowed, and .035 ounces of sodium nitrate per 2.2 pounds salt is legal, but few producers employ nitrates.

If the ingredients are simple, the process is intricate. Producers of Prosciutto di Parma share one goal: to cure a leg of pork with an absolute minimum of salt in order to keep the meat as sweet-tasting and as supple as possible while retarding spoilage. Maintaining a good balance is the challenge. The maker's skill is also challenged by the exacting process that produces the ham's silky texture.

Parmesans have had 2,000 years to perfect their ham and to take advantage of a unique combination of resources.

According to the Parma Ham Consortium, it was a hundred years before Christ when Cato first mentioned ham in Parma in his *Architecture of Agriculture*. He speaks of curing legs of wild Parma pig by layering them in barrels with salt. Prized for their taste, they became favorite Roman banquet fare and were shipped south regularly.

Salt was a precious commodity, as it was vital to preserving and seasoning so many foods, and each time it crossed a boundary, the Romans imposed heavy duties. Luckily, what is now Parma province (then a Roman military post) had its own supply.

Parma's near neighbor, Salsomaggiore, had natural salt deposits, which contained important components that may have gone a long way in shaping Parma's taste for delicately cured pork products. Salsomaggiore's salt contained boric carbonate and boric acid, which soften and sweeten meat while imbuing it with a rainbow-colored iridescence. Today their use is banned, and that tender sweetness is achieved by other methods. But sweetness and tenderness still single out modern Parma ham from coarser prosciutti.

As Salsomaggiore's salt supply dwindled, the microclimate in and around the village of Langhirano in the foothills of the Apennines was discovered. Breezes from the east and west sweep the area constantly. Ham makers claim they contribute mightily to the ham's special flavor. Salt air from the Ligurian and Tuscan coasts to the west dries out during its passage over the mountains. Moist air from Parma's Po plain to the east is sweetened with scents of orchards, wheat fields, hay bales, vineyards, and farms. Cool temperatures, low humidity, and the primal elements of salt and sweet created an ideal setting for prosciutto.

At first, producing ham was literally a cottage industry, with prosciutto hung in homes from attic to cellar. By the end of the 19th century Langhirano's architecture was dominated by long, narrow, multistoried buildings where the hams are still cured. These "apartment houses for hams" are situated on an angle to catch the breezes from the mountains and the plain. Movable shutters on their tall windows protect the hams from the direct sun while allowing the air to flow freely.

How Prosciutto di Parma Is Made

The pigs, of course, were the other vital ingredient. Until about six centuries ago, Parma's stretch of the Po River plain was thickly forested in chestnut and oak. Those forests gave the local wild pigs forage that was so lush, it was unequaled in all Italy. So Parma's pig was fat—all the better to produce a velvety, succulent ham. Contemporary Parma ham producers insist that lean meat does not make great prosciutto.

The Parma ham consortium and its member producers make a strong distinction between salted meat and prosciutto. One expert, Ettore Grisendi, says, "It is easy to preserve meat with large amounts of salt. But skill and patience are required to maintain the natural sweetness of the meat while using little salt."

A vital part of the process is drying and gradually remoistening the hams by slowly bringing them from high, airy attics down to moist cellars. This may have first occurred centuries ago by accident, but today it is vital to Prosciutto di Parma's character.

Each and every step is like that, with one minute detail after another finally adding up to a good prosciutto. The ham is helpless and needs constant attention. Ham people say the prosciutto wants care like a baby. They describe the creation of a Parma ham as "Si da prosciutto balia," "To give the ham to a wet nurse."

Prosciutto pigs come from crossing five approved breeds. They must spend at least the last 4 months of their lives on the Po plain in the regions of Emilia-Romagna, Lombardy, Piedmont, or the Veneto. The pigs feed on a prescribed diet of grains and whey from cheese production (in Parmigiano-Reggiano country, in fact, every cheese factory has its own band of pigs).

Animals mature to at least 1 year and must weigh between 352 and 440 pounds. *"Molto fatto,"* or "well made," describes the ideal pig with a firm, well-developed muscle structure containing a minimum amount of water.

Water and acid are the enemies of Parma ham. Younger, less developed meat contains more water. More water means more salt absorbtion which can block the fermentation process. That process helps develop the simple proteins necessary to the ham's velvety texture and complex flavor.

Acid content is controlled by the method of slaughter. If the animal is stressed, PH rises and so does salt absorbtion. Today all pigs meet their demise in a calm state.

Legs are trimmed to the shape of a chicken drumstick, and after rigid inspection are marked with the acceptance symbol "PP." Large legs with a thick fat cover are preferred. They absorb less salt during curing because of their greater maturity and denser, drier muscle.

At the factory, *la salagione* (the salting) marks the pork's first contact with salt, when coarse sea salt is massaged into the meat. During the following 25 days of refrigeration a second salting is done. Most crucial at this first step is controlling the intake of salt by making daily adjustments in temperature and humidity. With high humidity more salt is absorbed; with low humidity, less salt. The challenge is to avoid spoilage yet slow down the penetration of salt as much as possible.

Fluctuating humidity and temperature continues during *il riposo* (the rest), when the hams hang for 2 months, still in refrigerated rooms. The meat is now dull brown. It will return to its original rosy color without any additives aiding the process by the end of the curing and aging.

Il riposo ends with *la toletta* (the cleaning and trimming), when the meat is trimmed away from the femur bone's knob and the protruding aitch bone is cut to lie flat against the ham's surface. After removing excess salt with a wash of warm water, the hams are hung to dry 3 to 6 days.

Pre stagionatura (the pre-aging) marks the hams' gradual 4-month journey from dry, airy attics, where they are perfumed by aromatic breezes as the salt finishes permeating the meat, to moist half-cellars. By the end of 4 months, the meat's surface is sealed by drying and hardening. At this point the legs of pork are merely salted meat, not yet Prosciutti di Parma. *La toletta secca* (the covering of exposed meat with softened suet) helps the ham remoisten itself. It initiates *la stagionatura,* the aging and fermenting process that creates Parma ham.

As the round, bare meat area on the ham gets coated with suet, a fine line is left uncovered at the join between the lean meat and the covering of fat. Now the ham hangs another 4 or 5 months while the moisture in the heart of the prosciutto seeks escape through that uncovered line of meat. The moisture spreads gradually throughout the entire ham. This remoistening marks the beginning of fermentation. Fermentation takes the salted leg of pork across that crucial line to become Prosciutto di Parma.

Enzymes and biochemical reactions work at the meat's structure by breaking down its proteins. Over 4 or 5 months, complex proteins break down to simple proteins, giving the prosciutto its singular

texture and making it easier to digest than fresh pork. Slowly the color changes back to the original soft rose. At about 10 months Prosciutto di Parma comes into full flower. Some prefer it aged more; but all agree that these final months are vital to the distinctive character of the ham. (For U.S. export, 400 days are required.)

When the United States government tested Parma ham for reentry after a 20-year absence, another aspect of the curing process was discovered. Parma ham is self-sterilizing. The 400-day process annihilates pork's four most potent diseases (hog cholera, African swine fever, hoof and mouth disease, and viscular disease), leaving not even any residue to give evidence of their demise.

Branding with the five-pointed ducal crown of Parma completes the exacting process. No ham is branded unless inspected by the consortium, and a ham without a crown is not a Prosciutto di Parma. Using a horse bone, consortium inspectors perform *la puntatura* (the puncturing) by piercing every ham at five crucial points and inhaling the scent of each. The bone whittled from a horse's femur has no odor of its own and little porosity. It releases aromas quickly, so that an inspector can move from ham to ham with surprising speed.

Fatal flaws in a ham are rancidity and oversalting. Each place on the ham gives up a different scent, ranging from the aroma of roasted meat to floweriness to old straw.

Because the ham's proteins have been broken down during fermentation, they are absorbed quickly by the body and offer a fast, sound source of energy. In Italy you always hear of mountain climbers and other sportsmen touting the benefits of Prosciutto di Parma.

This is no news to Emilians. They knew that over 1,000 years ago, when Hannibal of elephants-crossing-the-Alps fame paused in the valley of the Trebbia, north of Parma. There he fortified himself and his army with the local bread, the local wine, and the ancestor of today's Prosciutto di Parma. At that moment the military genius became a gastronome.

La Salama da Sugo
Ferrara's Juicy Salame

This Ferrara specialty can be seen hanging from the rafters of every meat market and delicatessen in the province, looking like clusters of cannonballs and radiating aromas of meat ripened with wine and spices. *Salama da sugo* translates literally as "juicy or sauced salame" because of its moist center. It is made and served like no other salame in Emilia-Romagna.

Although now controlled by a consortium, salama da sugo's production has not changed much in 500 years. For all that time it has appeared at banquets, holidays, and festivals.

The *salama,* or *salamina* (little salame), as it is known affectionately, is made with a collection of ingredients that reads like the shopping list for a Medieval dinner party. Meat is taken from at least five areas of the pig; liver, tongue, and sometimes heart are added. Then nutmeg, salt, clove, pepper, and cinnamon are blended in. Once the mixture has mellowed overnight, it gets a generous dose of red wine.

Everything is stuffed into a round casing and tied to emulate the jewel cases and decorative jars of centuries ago that were round, lobed and shaped like melons. One poet in the 1700s called the salama "a jewel case filled with love."

What the salama really is full of is moist, aromatic meat. After 6 months to a year of careful curing, the globe is soaked overnight in water and then steamed or poached with great care. It is always a main course, served hot on a platter of potato purée. The favorite way of presenting it at home is with the top cut away and a spoon plunged into its center, where the piquant meats are at their best.

For outlanders salama da sugo can be an acquired taste—its pungency often overwhelms the palate. But if you are in Ferrara, you must sample this holdover from the feasts of the Este court, because it is available nowhere else in Italy, nor in the United States.

Salami
Dry Cured Sausage

Technically speaking, a *salame* (the singular of *salami*) is a blend of chopped meat, seasonings, salt, and possibly an additional preservative, all stuffed into a casing and dry-cured for up to 6 or 7 months. It is eaten uncooked (the curing process rids the meat of any harmful organisms).

Selecting, Storing, and Using Salami

As of this writing, Italian salami are not imported into the United States. Seek out good domestic ones that are seasoned as closely as possible to the style of Emilia-Romagna. Most of the salami in Emilia-Romagna are coarsely ground. Big, meaty tastes dominate them, with garlic and black pepper only as accents, along with hints of wine, clove, cinnamon, or nutmeg—no heavy doses of hot pepper or fennel.

The sausage casing should be natural, not plastic. The label should list meat, salt, spices, possibly dry milk, and one or two preservatives. In cured meats, less is most certainly more. Long lists of chemicals, and the addition of water and sweeteners, are not found in well-made naturally cured salami. Types to look for are Cacciatore (hunter's salami in short links), Toscano, and Veneto.

Taste for a pleasant balance of seasonings, lack of chemical overtones, and a good meaty flavor. Let the aftertaste blossom by waiting a few moments. If there is any sense of rancidity or unpleasant flavor, do not buy the salami.

Storing: If you are using the salami within about 24 hours, you can buy it presliced. Store it in the refrigerator, well sealed in its original wrapper. Store chunks of unsliced salami, unwrapped, in the refrigerator (sealing them airtight encourages spoilage). They will keep for a month or more, continuing to dry and ripen. Trim away dry end pieces before slicing.

Serving: Salami is a fine antipasto on its own or served with prosciutto and coppa as in much of Emilia-Romagna (see Antipasto Castelvetro, page 16). If you are serving it alone, count on about ¼ to 1 ounce per person.

Salami is cut on the diagonal, forming ovals. The thickness is a matter of personal taste. Slender salami are often cut about ⅛ inch thick, while plumper or drier ones are sliced thinner. Serve the salami at room temperature, with Crispy Fritters (page 373), Modena Mountain Bread (page 388), or chewy store-bought bread. Simple but full red wines are the best foils for salami. In much of Emilia, a dry local Lambrusco is favored. In the United States, drink a lively red Sangue di Giuda from Lombardy, a young Sangiovese from Romagna, or light-bodied Cabernet from Friuli.

Salami in Emilia-Romagna

In Italy, the kind of salami you eat speaks of who you are. For many Italians their area's salami, along with the innumerable other forms of preserved pork, are part of their identity. Ask a Florentine about his city's fennel-flavored *finocchiona,* or a Neapolitan to explain the elements of lightly smoked *salame di Napoli,* and be prepared for a passionate discourse on the salami. It will range over regional and family history as well as artisanship, all laced with fierce personal opinions on where, when, and how to eat them.

In Emilia-Romagna, pork has reigned in supreme succulence since before the days of the Caesars. Parmesans feast proudly on their *salame Felino,* claiming its special sweetness is garnered from the hay and grass-scented air of Felino's countryside. In Ferrara, a slick Armani-clad young man, seemingly with no interest in food much less culinary traditions, overhears my questions in a shop. He proudly volunteers that his mother and grandmother still make *zantil* (Ferrara's chewy garlic-and-wine-scented salame that looks like a wizened baseball bat). I ask, "You eat it because it's of your family, right?" "Well, yes" is the shrugged response, "but if you are Ferrarese, you eat zantil. In Piacenza *salame Piacentino* must be tasted, but that is for the Piacentini. I am of Ferrara."

The artisan- and family-made salami still found in some of the region's shops and restaurants (ask for *salame artisanale*) are often a revelation. The concentration of pure meat taste is always memorable. A superb salami gives the sense that someone separated each component of taste and texture and accented each one, making the reassembled whole greater than the sum of its individual parts.

Emilia-Romagna's seasoning philosophy is "keep it subtle." Blends of salt, pepper, spices, and some wine let the character of the meat shine through. But as you travel from town to town, you will find subtle shadings of taste—an herbal or flowery quality picked up from the local air; the touch of clove, cinnamon, pepper, or coriander; lacings of garlic; the enrichment of rich red wine. And occasionally, especially in Romagna, hot pepper provides a little punch.

Years ago the Romagnoli called salami slices "gold pieces." Although Emilia-Romagna has always had a wealth of meat compared to much of Italy, before World War II many peasants and laborers ate meat only on Christmas and Easter. Usually it was boiled to stretch it as far as possible. A few slices of salami was the roast of the poor. Made from pieces of pork that could not be successfully preserved whole, it was more affordable than solid cuts of cured shoulder or prosciutto.

Prize-winning pigs at the Veroni family salumeria in Correggio, early 20th century. Photograph copyright © Studio Manzotti, Correggio.

And it was almost all meat, unlike the mostly fat pancetta and pork jowl that provided flavoring in dishes of the day. Pieces of gold, indeed. A salami would be doled out tenderly, savored small bit by small bit.

Today salami is a snack food and is prized as an antipasto. It is held dear when well made, but salami as celebration food or as sustenance is a fading memory.

Some of the region's best-known examples are Parma's *Felino,* with its own DOC, or controlled area of production; Ferrara's garlic-flavored zantil (also known as *gentile*); and the rare *salame d'oca,* goose meat scented with clove, a remnant of Ferrara's large Jewish community. West of Ferrara province, Romagna produces another gentile, seasoned with salt and pepper. Connoisseurs claim that garlic in this gentile is a sign of sloppy craftsmanship. Salame Piacentina of Piacenza is spiced with a secret blend that always suggests clove, cinnamon, and garlic to me. The Po delta is proud of its plump balls of red-wine-and-garlic-

flavored *la bondiola,* which are often encased in well-washed turkey crops or pigs' bladders and smoked in the big chimneys of delta homes.

Salume
Cured Pork

What *charcuterie* is in France, *salume* is in Italy. This general term describes all preserved or cured pork products, like prosciutto, salami, coppa, and pancetta. *Salume* derives from *sale,* or salt, the primary ingredient in any recipe for preserving pork. Salume is sold in a *salumeria,* or pork store, where sausages, mortadelle, hams, and salami hang over counters like great stalactites.

Emilia-Romagna's salume is held in high regard throughout Italy. The region's fine cured pork products began long ago when Emilia-Romagna's exceptionally fertile land created lush foraging for the wild pigs that predated any domesticated animals. During the Roman period, salted wild boar from Emilia-Romagna rivaled the best cured meats from throughout the Empire.

As agriculture and domestication took hold, preserving a pig to last through the year became a form of artisanship. Sheep and goats were as economical to keep as the pig (the cow required expensive grazing land, so it was not as popular) but lacked the sweet-tasting fat that gave pork such succulence. It was fat that kept the meat moist and palatable even when the sometimes crude salting methods produced meat so salty that it was barely edible. And pigs grew fatter in Emilia-Romagna than in most other parts of Italy. Until the late 1940s, for many Emilia-Romagna families survival often depended on the successful curing of each and every part of the animal, so that there would always be at least a little meat or fat to eat.

There is a rhythm to salume that is deeply ingrained in the culture of Emilia-Romagna. It begins with the ritual winter slaughter of the pig and builds through the year as each part becomes ready to eat.

According to Gianni Quondamatteo, chronicler of Romagnolo foodways, in Romagna, slaughter must take place between Saint Andrea's Day, November 30, and January 17, the day of Saint Antonio Abate.

Quondamatteo explains how the pig joins with the life of the peasants and farmers in le nozze del porco, "the wedding of the pig." This is the 8- to 10-day period when all of the animal is cured and "married" into the natural and ancient rhythms of gathering food, preserving it for winter, and taking nourishment and sustenance from it. In the process the pig gives itself entirely to the people, wedding them symbolically, and in this, literally sustaining them through the year. At the end of each day of work, families gather to celebrate the "wedding" with fresh sausages, blood puddings and even fresh roasted meat—a great luxury years ago.

Whether in Emilia or Romagna, the first parts of the pig ready for eating are the fresh sausage, the lard (strutto), and the ciccioli (hard pork fat cooked down into golden shales that are crunchy and savory). The marriage continues with any number of interpretations of cotechino and zampone, ready after a week or so. Within several months pancette (salted cheeks and bacon) and salami finish curing. Depending on their density, some salami cure even longer. After 6 months the coppe are ready and the spalla (shoulder) can be eaten. At about 11 months the most prized piece, the prosciutto, will be cut. And then it is time for another nozze del porco.

Spalla di San Secondo
Cured Pork Shoulder from San Secondo

This specialty from the Parma plain around the little town of San Secondo is a boned pork shoulder (spalla) cured in salted white wine, with some producers adding pepper, cinnamon, and sodium nitrate. Once it is stuffed into a large casing, the spalla resembles an oversized pear. Spalla is always poached or steamed before being eaten as an antipasto. Its flavor reminds me of corned beef.

Part of spalla di San Secondo's appeal in Emilia-Romagna is its connection to the much-loved composer Giuseppe Verdi, who was born and lived much of his life near San Secondo. He relished spalla and supposedly left oft-quoted directions for soaking, poaching and serving it.

What is thought to be Verdi's own recipe for curing this speciality was passed from his gardener's son to Giovanni Tamburini, owner of Tamburini, Bologna's lavish food emporium. There was quite a stir on the day the first spalla di Verdi was tasted back in 1986. Everyone agreed it was one of the best they had eaten, even if it did contain a little too much salt. Today spalla di San Secondo is still made only around the town in Parma province and at Tamburini in Bologna. It is not exported to the United States.

Tomatoes and Tomato Paste
Pomodori e Concentrato di Pomodoro

Selecting and Using Tomatoes

Fresh Tomatoes: When you find a vine-ripened tomato so good you want to eat it like an apple, you have discovered the intense lushness that characterizes much of Emilia-Romagna's tomatoes. This is the sort of tomato that regional cooks merely warm in a little butter or oil with a few leaves of fresh herbs and then toss with pasta. The fruit's joyous flavor explodes on the palate.

Haunt farmers' markets and organic and heirloom vegetable vendors for this kind of quality. Taste before you buy. The fact that a tomato is vine ripened does not necessarily mean the flavor is wonderful. Great-tasting tomatoes are often older varieties, with skins too thin to ship thousands of miles and eccentric growing habits that do not encourage mass production. They are out there, however, and in season you should accept nothing less.

The Peel and Seed Question: Interestingly, peeling is rarely mentioned in old Italian cookbooks. Certainly peeling is not always necessary today, especially when a recipe is a country dish in which skins would add texture, or when the mixture will be passed through a food mill. Perhaps peeling is required in modern dishes because the newer tomato varieties have thicker skins, developed for long-distance shipping.

To seed or not to seed is a personal and textural preference. A tomato high in acid or unbalanced in flavor will be bitter with or without seeds and skin.

To peel a tomato, blister it over a gas burner, grill, or under the broiler rather than dropping it in boiling water. Water dilutes the flavor, whereas quick searing intensifies it. Use a long fork to hold the fruit over the heat, and blister the skin quickly without cooking the tomato. Then let the tomato cool for a few seconds and slip off the skin. If peeling many tomatoes, arrange them on your oven's broiler pan and sear them as close to the broiler as possible.

Canned Tomatoes: Canned tomatoes are my first choice when the only fresh ones available are the American winter tomatoes.

Italy's San Marzano or San Marzano–type canned tomatoes do not always possess superior flavor. Quality varies with alarming unevenness from one imported brand to the next. Often a domestic brand is better.

Recommending specific brands is difficult, since the selection varies greatly from one part of the country to the next. Try a tomato tasting with some similarly minded friends. Collect all the brands of canned tomatoes available in your area, and sample them for deep, rich tomato character with enough acid to set off the ripe sweet flavors. Make a big pot of tomato soup as the finale.

Cooking with Canned Tomatoes: For recipes in this book calling for canned tomatoes, use peeled whole plum or round tomatoes. Do not use crushed, ground, or puréed tomatoes. They lack the clean, light quality of whole canned ones and they usually are heavily dosed with thick purée, which intensifies strong acid flavors.

Tomato Paste: Tubes of imported tomato paste (ideally from Parma) do get my vote over the domestic canned variety. The concentration is often stronger, so the flavor is rounder and deeper.

Tubes also win over cans for convenience. Everyone has had the experience of opening a can of tomato paste in order to use 1 tablespoon and then finding it has turned into something resembling a laboratory experiment after a couple of weeks in the refrigerator. Refrigerated tubes will hold for 4 to 5 weeks with no spoilage.

The Tomato in Emilia-Romagna

Although most of us think of Italy's tomato canning industry as being concentrated in the south, Parma is a major northern center, especially for tomato paste. Why Parma? Ideal climate is one important factor, and old alliances may be another.

According to Parma historian and linguistic authority Professor Guglielmo Capacchi, it is likely that Parma's first tomatoes arrived from France during the late 1700s along with a glittering contingent from the Bourbon court of Louis XV. Capacchi also points out that earlier writings mention the *tomacle* being offered with maccheroni during the mid-1500s on the Po plain.

The widespread pairing of tomato and pasta was still 300 years away. But Spain (which brought the tomato from the Americas) had spread the fruit to her large holdings in southern Italy, where it was being eaten, with some hesitancy, by the 1600s. Parma's strong alliance with Spain at that time makes it easy to create an unrecorded historical scenario: A Spanish ambassador presents the Duke of Parma with a basket of this bright red curiosity from the New World. The Duke politely takes a bite, likes it, and the tomato is initiated into Parma cuisine. Highly unlikely. But what is likely is that the tomato may have been a botanical curiosity for a long time and then gradually gained acceptance as food.

Certainly by the early 19th century, when Marie Louise of Austria, wife of the exiled Napoleon, reigned as the Duchess of Parma, a collection of stuffed tomato recipes were part of the court cook's repertoire. In 1887 Carlo Rognoni and Lodovico Pagani launched Parma's commercial tomato production with their perfected Riccio strain, which is still the foundation of the area's industry today.

While the gentry were eating fresh and canned tomatoes, Emilia-Romagna's peasants preserved the harvest by drying as well as bottling. Strings of dried tomatoes festooned the beams of country kitchens in the region.

Gianni Quondammatteo, historian of Romagna's gastronomic past, claims that tomatoes gained popularity in Romagna only in the 1800s. Household lore dictated that flasks of preserved tomatoes be hung from rafters, and conserved tomatoes were always added to the liquid of the poaching Christmas capon.

The tiny dried tomatoes of Rimini were and still are thought to give noble dimension to broths. The area's folklore claims tomato skins helped heal insect bites and keep away flies and mosquitoes. A nutritious tomato marmalade still strengthens babies and sufferers of anemia.

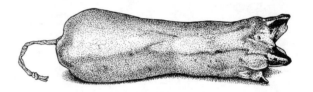

Zampone
Sausage of Stuffed Pig's Foot

Zampone is Modena's most distinctive cured pork product. Coarsely ground pork, pork skin, and spices are blended and stuffed into the boned and cleaned front foot (*zampa,* the root of *zampone,* means "pig's foot"). The sausage is lightly cured and then cooked. A good zampone makes your lips lusciously sticky with gelatinous juices, is pleasantly pebbly on the tongue, tastes of rich pork and mild spicing, and is an appealing dark amber.

Buying, Storing, and Using Zampone

Zampone is produced in the United States mostly during the winter, especially at Christmas. Order it from Italian purveyors (see Mail-Order Sources, page 509). Some producers encase the filling not in the foot but in rind from other parts of the pig and call it zampino.

Uncooked zampone holds well, unwrapped, in the refrigerator about 4 days. Cooked, it will keep 5 to 7 days. Check the producer's directions for whether or not soaking is recommended before cooking. I prefer not to freeze zampone.

See page 316 for cooking directions. Leftover zampone slices make a robust, homey supper, simply reheated and sprinkled with balsamic vinegar. Or cut slices into small pieces, reheat them with browned onions, and toss with a stubby maccheroni or maltagliati pasta (page 88) and grated Parmigiano-Reggiano.

Cotechino (page 475) can be used if zampone is unavailable.

Zampone in Emilia-Romagna

Modena's passion for zampone, its famous hallmark sausage, knows no bounds. At the first chill of autumn, zampone makers set to work creating rotund clubs of sausage. They hang in amber-colored clusters, decorating shop windows and tempting passersby.

One can be put off by a stuffed pig's foot, but for the people of Modena there is not a second's hesitation. Slices of zampone, hot and juicy from their cooking liquid, have been captivating hungry Modenese since at least the 1500s.

Modena's zampone and cotechino, *cappello da prete* (priest's hat), and *sassolino* (named for the village the sausage comes from) all share a similar stuffing and are always served hot. The Modenese say these sausages are a celebration of the pig with "a taste of everything." The filling comes from many parts of the animal and no doubt originated as a way of using up what was left after curing larger, more desirable pieces of pork.

Combining meat from the shoulder, neck, shank, cheek, and sirloin creates rich flavor, as each part contributes its own character. Succulence and body come from a balance of lean with fat and a little gelatinous pork rind. Salt, pepper, nutmeg, clove, and cinnamon add subtle spicing.

Preparing zampone used to be a lengthy affair. It was heavily salted and needed long soaking. Then a cross-shaped incision was made in the side of the sausage. After wrapping it in a heavily oiled cloth, it was steamed for about 1½ hours per pound on a raised rack in a special oval casserole, the *zamponiera.*

Today much less salt is used and some zampone are sold precooked, needing only reheating before serving.

Christmas, weddings, and parties without zampone are unthinkable. To leave zampone out of Modena's traditional *Bollito Misto* (mixed poached meats) is heresy. When not part of the *Bollito,* with

Old Modena postcard touting the town's three main attractions—the Ghirlandina bell tower, Lambrusco wine and zampone sausage

its capon, beef, calf's head, and veal roast, zampone is sliced and served hot over mashed potatoes, accompanied by sautéed spinach, and moistened with balsamic vinegar or a green herb sauce. Modenese debate the authenticity of substituting lentils or braised white beans for the potatoes, a penchant of some local cooks.

Although the Modenese are sure zampone was born in their territory, no one has yet found solid documentation of exactly where and when. One legend has its creation set in 1511 at Mirandola, out on Modena's plain. The town was under siege by Pope Giulio II. Starvation was a reasonable prospect. The few pigs left in town had been slaughtered. The question was, how to preserve the scraps of meat left after all the sausage casings had been used up? Why not cure it in its own skin?

This predecessor to zampone was called *manicotto,* meaning stuffed muff or sleeve.

Firm proof of zampone's existence in the 1600s can be seen in a period painting showing the plumped pig's feet being sold in Modena's Piazza Grande. The same year the United States was born, Milan's governor, Duke Francesco III, demanded that "twenty-four zampetti of the finest stuffing" be sent to him post haste. By the 19th century, Modena postcards illustrated the town's three main tourist attractions: its famed cathedral tower, Lambrusco wine, and zampone. At the same time zampone was praised and sought by non-Modenese. Composer Gioacchino Antonio Rossini and Italy's liberator, Garibaldi, both doted on it. The sausage was even sold in Paris, where Emile Zola called it "delicious and divine."

A Note on Wine

Over the years of gathering information for this book I have enjoyed and learned about many of Emilia-Romagna's wines, but wine is not where my expertise lies. I have always believed a competent food expert should have a working knowledge of wines, but professionally you give your life either to food or to wine.

While Emilia-Romagna's wines bring me great pleasure, the challenge of her foods, history, and folklore have occupied most of my research. Far better that you should read the works of Burton Anderson, Victor Hazan, and other experts on Italian wines.

In the wine suggestions accompanying most of the recipes, I include as least one from the region. These are my own favorites, and they are usually

LA BOTTE DA DEL VINO, CH' ELL' HA.

Suol conforme a la causa esser l'effetto,
Ne d'infetto liquor l'urna ripiena
Vale à sominiſtrar balſamo eletto.

Good wine from a good barrel gives good health. Giuseppe Maria Mitelli, 17th century.

from the same area as the dish. If a first choice is not from the area, it is because my personal preference dictates otherwise. Because Emilia-Romagna's wines are not broadly exported to the United States at this time, included also are suggestions for more readily available wines from other parts of Italy.

Mail-Order Sources

California

Vivande
2125 Fillmore Street
San Francisco, CA 94115
(415) 346-4430

Vivande will ship all their Italian products, including artisan-made balsamic vinegar, commercial balsamics, olive oils, cured meats, cheeses, fancy durum flour, canned foods, olives, prepared dishes, fresh meats, and sausages. Write for a catalog.

Williams-Sonoma
100 North Point
San Francisco, CA 94133
(800) 541-2233

Williams-Sonoma's free catalog offers equipment and selected foods, including olive oils and Fini's balsamic vinegar.

Domingo's
17548 Ventura Boulevard
Encino, CA 91316
(818) 981-4466

There is no catalog, but Domingo's ships customer's requests for Italian foods. Telephone or write.

Sorrento Market
5518 Sepulveda Boulevard
Culver City, CA 90230
(213) 391-7654

This small market is stocked to the ceiling with imports. No catalog, but Sorrento will ship all but the most perishable goods.

Bristol Farms
606 Fair Oaks Avenue
South Pasadena, CA 91030
(818) 441-5588

837 Silver Spur Road
Rolling Hills Estates, CA 90274
(213) 541-9157

1570 Rosecrans Avenue
Manhattan Beach, CA 90266
(213) 643-5229

There is no catalog, but they will ship most Italian ingredients including Perfect Addition Rich Stock (see page 69), olive oils, porcini mushrooms, pastas, olives, artisan and commercial balsamic vinegars, canned goods, cured meats, and cheeses. Telephone or write to any of their three locations, all in the Los Angeles area.

Illinois

Convito Italiano
11 East Chestnut Street
Chicago, IL 60611
(312) 943-2983

Catalog available for Christmas holidays. They ship pastas, seasonings, cured meats, cheeses, canned goods, olive oils, porcini mushrooms, balsamic vinegars, frozen and prepared foods, breads, and wines.

Missouri

Purity Foods, Inc.
2871 West Jolly Road
Okemos, MI 48864-3547

Purity Foods are processors of spelt grain. Write them for information on where spelt can be purchased in your area.

New Jersey

D'Artagnan, Inc.
399–419 St. Paul Avenue
Jersey City, NJ 07306
(800) 327-8246 or (201) 792-0748

D'Artagnan are specialists in fresh meats, game, foie gras, and confit. They ship fresh rather than frozen products. Their list of products is impressive and includes quail, pigeon, squab, rabbit, hare, and organic poultry, including capon. A catalog is available.

New York

Balducci's
424 Sixth Avenue
New York, NY 10011
(212) 673-2600
(800) 822-1444 for catalog, from out of
New York State
(800) 247-2450 for catalog, from within
New York State

Balducci's carries all Italian products, including artisan-made and commercial balsamic vinegars, zampone, chestnut flour, a broad range of imported pastas, and cured meats. Their catalog features mainly prepared foods, but they will ship all ingredients carried in the shop.

Dean & DeLuca
560 Broadway
New York, NY 10012
(800) 221-7714 or (212) 431-1691

Dean & DeLuca carries a vast array of Italian products, including artisan-made balsamic vinegars, cheeses, and cured meats.

Todaro Brothers
555 Second Avenue
New York, NY 10016
(212) 679-7766

Like Balducci's and Dean & DeLuca, Todaro will ship all but the most fragile items. Their selection of Italian goods is vast.

A Partial Bibliography

Agnoletti, Vincenzo. *Manuale del Cuoco e del Pasticciere*. 3 vols. (1832). Bologna: reprint Arnaldo Forni, 1983.

Ascoli Vitali-Norsa, Giuliana, editor. *La Cucina nella Tradizione Ebraica*. 3rd ed. Padova: Adei Wizo Publishers, 1984.

Baruzzi, Marina, and Massimo Montanari, editors. *Porci and Porcari nel Medioevo, Paesaggio Economia Alimentazione*. San Marino di Bentivoglio Museo della Civilta Contadina: Villa Smeraldi, 1981.

Bassani, Aureliano and Giancarlo Roversi. *Eminenza, il pranzo e servito*. Bologna: Aniballi Edizioni, 1984.

Bellei, Sandro, and Ugo Preti. *Cosa Bolle in Pentola a Modena*. 4 vols. Modena: Modena Libri, 1980.

Bentini, Jadranka; Alessandra Chiappini; Giovanni Battista Panatta; and Anna Maria Travagli. *A Tavola con il Principe, Materiali per una Mostra Su Alimentazione e Cultura nella Ferrara degli Estensi*. Ferrara: Amministrazione Provinciale di Ferrara, 1988.

Bergonzini, Renato. *L'Aceto Balsamico nella Tradizione e nella Gastronomia*. Modena: Mundici Zanetti Editori, 1979.

———. *Il Nocino*. Modena: Mundici Zanetti Editori, 1978.

———. *A Tavola con i Cibi Tradizionali della Nostra Montagna*. Edito a cura del Comune di Pavulla e della Comunita Montana del Frignano.

Bernardi, Adria. *Houses with Names*. Urbana and Chicago: University of Illinois Press, 1990.

Camporesi, Piero. *Alimentazione Folclore Societa*. Parma: Pratiche Editrice, 1980.

Capacchi, Guglielmo. *La Cucina Popolare Parmigiana*. Parma: Artegrafica Silva Parma, 1985.

Chiappini, Luciano. *La Corte Estense alla Meta del Cinquecento*. Ferrara: Beriguardo, 1984.

Consorzio Produttori di Aceto Balsamico Naturale Modena. *Aceto Balsamico Tradizionale di Modena*. Modena: Camera di Commercio Industria Artigianato Agricoltura, 1981.

Contoli, Corrado. *Guida alla Veritiera Cucina Romagnola*. Bologna: Edizioni Calderini, 1972.

da la Riva, Bonvesin. *Le Cinquanta Cortesie da Tavola*. Edited by Mario Cantella and Donatella Magrassi. Milan: La Spiga, 1985.

Dalli, Antonio Maria. *Piciol Lume di Cucina* (1701). Edited by Marzio Dall'Acqua and M. Margherita Ghini. Parma: reprint Antigraphus, 1987.

Dall Olio, Enrico. *Il Prosciutto di Parma*. Parma: Grafiche Step Editrice, 1989.

———. *Tradizioni Parmigiane*. Vols. 1 and 2. Parma: Grafiche Step Editrice, 1989.

Faccioli, Emilio, editor. *L'Eccellenza e il Trionfo del Porco*. Comune di Reggio Emilia, Assessorato alla Cultura Mazzotta, 1982.

Ghinato, Angela; Italo Marighelli; Marcella Marighelli; Renato Sitti; Gianni Varani; Claudio Borri; and Ervardo Fioravanti. *Cucina e Folclore Ferrarese*. Ferrara: Edizione Ferraria Libro, 1985.

Longhi, Giuseppe. *La Cucina Ferrarese (Piu Storia che Leggenda)*. Bologna: Edizioni Calderini, 1979.

Maioli, Giorgio, *Civilta della Tavola a Modena*. Bologna: Aniballi Edizioni, 1985.

———. *I Racconti della Tavola a Reggio Emilia*. Bologna: Mario e M. Pia Aniballi–Edizioni Ges, 1980.

Maioli, Giorgio, and Giancarlo Roversi. *Civilta della Tavola a Bologna*. Bologna: Mario e M. Pia Aniballi–Edizioni Ges, 1981.

Mantovi, Franco. *Folklore e Gastronomica fra Secchia e Panaro*. Modena: Editrice Cooptip, 1968.

Messisbugo, Christofaro. *Libro Novo nel Qual s'Insegna a Far d'Ogni Sorte di Vivande Secondo la Diversita de i Tempi Cosi di Carne Come di Pesce*. Venetia, 1557. Bologna: reprint Arnaldo Forni Editore, 1982.

Nascia, Carlo. *Li Quatro Banchetti Destinati per le Quatro Stagioni dell'Anno*. Preface and notations by Massimo Alberini. Bologna: reprint Arnaldo Forni, 1981.

Paglia, Gianni, *Breviario della Buona Cucina Bolognese*. Bologna: Edizioni Calderini, 1959.

Paltrinieri, Gabriella, and Renato Bergonzini, editors. *L'Aceto Balsamico di Modena, Cenni Storici Tecnici e Didattici*. Modena: Comune di Modena Assessorato alla Cultura, 1981.

Quondamatteo, Gianni. *Grande Dizionario (e Ricettario) Gastronomico Romagnolo*. Imola: Grafiche Galeati, 1978.

———, editor. *E'Luneri Rumagnol, Antologia di Cultura Romagnola*. Imola: Grafiche Galeati, 1980.

———, and Giuseppe Bellosi. *Romagna Civilita*. Vols. 1 and 2. Imola: Grafiche Galeati, 1977.

———; Luigi Pasquini; and Marcello Caminiti. *Mangiari di Romagna*. Bologna: Guidicini e Rosa Editori, 1979.

Razzetti, Fausto, editor. *Parma a Tavola*. Parma: Accademia Italiana della Cucina, Delegazione di Parma, 1990.

Rossetti, G. B. *Dello Scalco*. Ferrara: 1584.

Roth, Cecil. *The History of the Jews of Italy*. Philadelphia: The Jewish Publication Society of America, 1946.

Roversi, Giancarlo. *La Tavola Imbandita da Giuseppe Lamma*. Bologna: Grafis Edizioni, 1988.

Scappi, Bartolomeo. Presentazione di Giancarlo Roversi. *Opera dell'Arte del Cucinare* (Venezia, 1570). Bologna: reprint Arnaldo Forni, 1981.

Solmi, Angelo. *Maria Luigia, Duchessa di Parma*. Milan: Rusconi Libri, 1985.

Stefani, Bartolomeo, Cuoco Bolognese. *L'Arte di Ben Cucinare* (Mantova, 1662). Bologna: reprint Arnaldo Forni, 1983.

Westbury, Lord. *Handlist of Italian Cookery Books*. Firenze: Leo S. Olschki Editore, 1963.

Zamboni, Aniello. *La Maniera con cui Vengono Cucinati i Pesci Diversi in Comacchio e Presso le Famiglie di Valle*. Comacchio: Libreria Marino Rizzati, 1988.

Photo Credits

When no attribution is given, the article in the color photographs is either from the author's own collection or was obtained from commercial sources.

Tagliatelle with Ragù Bolognese. White pasta bowl courtesy of Pottery Barn, New York City.

Soups of Tortellini, Garganelli and Anolini. Antique silver cheese bowl and spoon courtesy of The Tudor Rose, 28 East 10th Street, New York City.

Maccheroni with Grilled and Baked Vegetables. Photographed at Alice Ross's Cooking Studio, 15 Prospect Street, Smithtown, New York.

Linguine with Braised Garlic and Balsamic Vinegar. Photographed at Alice Ross's Cooking Studio, 15 Prospect Street, Smithtown, New York.

Lasagne Dukes of Ferrara. Antique silver candlestick and candelabrum courtesy of Nelson & Nelson, 1050 Second Avenue, New York City. Antique spoon, fork and knife with enamel handles courtesy of Michael's Antiques, 1050 Second Avenue, New York City. Tablecloth imported from Umbria, Italy, courtesy of Ceramica, 59 Thompson Street, New York City. Handblown small wine glass courtesy of Maria Guarnaschelli.

Pan-Fried Veal Chops with Tomato-Marsala Sauce. Handblown wine goblet from Simon Pearce, 385 Bleecker Street, New York City.

Balsamic Roast Chicken with Modena Mountain Bread and Asparagus in the Style of Parma. Copper vase courtesy of Cara De Silva.

Romagna Grilled Veal Chops with Piadina Flatbread.

Photographed at Alice Ross's Cooking Studio, 15 Prospect Street, Smithtown, New York. Round ceramic serving platter from Ceramica, 59 Thompson Street, New York City.

Christmas Capon on a bed of Tagliatelle with Caramelized Orange. Renaissance-style round ceramic plates, small ceramic pedestal and oval ceramic serving platter courtesy of Ceramica, 59 Thompson Street, New York City. Large antique marble pedestal compote and small antique Venetian glass pedestal compote courtesy of Barr-Gardner Associates, 125 East 57th Street, New York City.

Rabbit Roasted with Sweet Fennel. Photographed at Alice Ross's Cooking Studio, 15 Prospect Street, Smithtown, New York. Ceramic serving platter courtesy of Ceramica, 59 Thompson Street, New York City.

Three Polenta Dishes. Photographed at Alice Ross's Cooking Studio, 15 Prospect Street, Smithtown, New York.

Grilled Winter Endives. Photographed at Alice Ross's Cooking Studio, 15 Prospect Street, Smithtown, New York.

Frozen Zuppa Inglese. Antique picture frames courtesy of Anna Teresa Callan.

Chestnut Ricotta Cheesecake. Photographed at Alice Ross's Cooking Studio, 15 Prospect Street, Smithtown, New York.

Three Christmas Cakes. Hammered copper cake plate courtesy of Maria Guarnaschelli.

Grateful acknowledgment is made to the following for permission to use black-and-white illustrations:

Il Collectionista, Milan: pages 15, 23, 57, 74, 95, 115, 140, 164, 184, 187, 196, 200, 221, 282, 326, 343, 361, 379, 435, 464, and 507.

Casa di Risparmio, Bologna: pages xiii, 43, 47, 133, 108, 169, 233, 235, 255, 265, 271, 276, 302, 308, 310, 313, 334, 348, 358, 403, 439, 443, 479, 483, 484, 491, and 508.

Consorzio Produttori di Aceto Balsamico Tradizionale di Modena: page 471.

Index

Spiced spinach with almonds, 330–331

Spinach:
and cheese filling for *spianata*, 370–371
egg pasta, 81
Marie Louise's crescents, 426–428
Modena's spiced soup of cheese and, 234–235
Piacenza's tortelli with tails, 162–164
Reggio's tart of garden greens, 247–249
spiced, with almonds, 330–331

Spinaci in padella del settecento, 330–331

Spongata di Berceto, 462–464

Spuma di fegato con tartufi, 24–25

Spuma di mortadella, 22–23

Squab, braised, dome of rice stuffed with, 216–218

Squaquerone cheese, fresh, 386–387
"little hats" Faenza style, 137

Squash, 147
Paola Bini's sweet ravioli, 424–425
sweet, cappellacci with, 145–147
sweet, for Yom Kippur, 339–340

Squid:
"priest stranglers" with fresh clams and, 124–126
seafood stew Romagna, 259–260

Stews:
rabbit dukes of Modena, 286–288
seafood, Romagna, 259–260

Stocks, 59–60
poultry/meat, 66–67
quick, 68
store-bought, 69

Strawberries:
iced, with mint and balsamic vinegar, 444
in red wine, 445

Strepponi, Giuseppina, 122

"Stretching the pot," 53

Stricchettoni, 78, 89

Stricchettoni Villa Gaidello, 118–119

Stringhetti, 78, 89

Strozzapreti, *see* "Priest stranglers"

Strozzapreti con poveracce e le seppie, 124–126

Strutto, 483

Sugo di carne, il, 61–62

Sweet-and-sour onions, 333–334

Swiss chard:
Piacenza's tortelli with tails, 162–164
Reggio's tart of garden greens, 247–249
spiced, with almonds, 331
tortelli of ricotta and fresh greens, 153–154

Tagliarini, 78, 90
egg pasta for, 80
with fresh figs Franco Rossi, 107–109
with lemon anchovy sauce, 112–113
tart of Ferrara, sweet, 194–196, 197

Tagliarini ai fichi Ristorante Franco Rossi, 107–109

Tagliarini con bagnabrusca, 112–113

Tagliatelle, 78–79, 90, 97
with artichokes and mascarpone sauce, 144
with balsamic radicchio, 98–100
with caramelized onions and fresh herbs, 101–103
with caramelized oranges and almonds, 188–189
egg pasta for, 80
with fresh porcini mushrooms, 96–97
with fresh tomatoes and balsamic vinegar, 105–106
garlic-sautéed cabbage with, 332
with light veal ragù, 100
with prosciutto di Parma, 94–95
with radicchio and two beans, 103–105
with ragù Bolognese, 93

Tagliatelle:
con arance e mandorle, 188–189
con cipolle e erbucce, 101–103

e fagioli con radicchio, 103–105
con funghi porcini, 96–97
con pomodori e aceto balsamico, 105–106
al prosciutto di Parma, 94–95
con radicchio e aceto balsamico, 98–100
con ragù bolognese, 93
con ragù Vecchio Molinetto, 100

Taglioline, 78

Tardura, la, 136

Tarts:
apple cream, Ugo Falavigna's, 411–412
caramelized almond, 409–410
Cardinal d'Este's, 417–419
of fresh artichokes, 245–247
of garden greens, Reggio's, 247–249
jam, Nonna's, 413–414
sweet tagliarini, of Ferrara, 194–196, 197
zabaione jam, 415–416

Tebaldi, Renata, 122

Thumb pasta and tomato braised beans Piacenza style, 229–231

Tigelle, 375–377, 380–381

Tomato(es), 505–506
braised beans and thumb pasta Piacenza style, 229–231
Ferrara's soup of the monastery, 220–221
fresh, tagliatelle with balsamic vinegar and, 105–106
Grandmother's gratin, 342–343
light veal ragù with, 52–53
light veal ragù with, tagliatelle with, 100
Marsala sauce, pan-fried veal chops with, 292–294
parsley pasta with peas and, Villa Gaidello, 118–119
porcini sauce, baked maccheroni with, 174
porcini sauce, Piacenza's, 64–65
porcini soup, 67
sauce, winter, 62–63
sauce, winter, baked maccheroni with, 173–174

A Note About the Author

Lynne Rossetto Kasper is a native of the New York area, born in Englewood, New Jersey, in February, 1943. After majoring in theater and art in college, Lynne's food career began during the late 1960s, in New York City where she taught, wrote and consulted. Upon moving to Denver, Colorado, in 1976, she created a cooking school that became the largest in the state. In 1981 her career took new directions as she began a nearly five-year stay in Europe. There she worked with chefs, home cooks, scientists, folklorists, and historians. She researched food history and sought out the culinary artisans still producing traditional foods in the old ways.

As a food writer, Lynne's work has appeared in The New York Times, Newsday, The Washington Post, Bon Appétit, Cuisine and The Journal of Gastronomy. For three years (1978–1981) Lynne wrote a weekly food column, "Epicure at Large," for Denver's Rocky Mountain News. She is featured in Time-Life's "Great Meals in Minutes" series as part of the Italian Menus volume. She was awarded the Maria Luigia, Duchess of Parma Prize for International Journalism.

She has lectured on northern Italian food and culture at The Smithsonian Institution, Washington, D.C., and for academic and professional groups in the United States and Canada. Her five-part Smithsonian lecture on Emilia-Romagna was a "first" for the institution and met with high acclaim.

Lynne is a professional cooking teacher with over 20 years experience. She began teaching as a generalist with extensive training under leading chefs and teachers in Europe and the United States. Lynne has run cooking schools in New York, Denver, and Brussels. The James Beard Foundation named Lynne one of the twelve best American cooking teachers of 1988.

Elected to L'Accademia Italiana della Cucina (one of Italy's leading gastronomic societies), Lynne is also a member of the American Institute of Wine and Food, and a founding and certified member of the International Association of Culinary Professionals.

Her husband, Frank Kasper, is a native New Yorker, a lover of wine and food, and is president of an international export firm. They live in St. Paul, Minnesota.

Verdi, Giuseppe, 122, 462,
465
Verdure sott'aceto, 18
Vermicelli pancake, sweet,
190–191
Villa Gaidello, 20
Artusi's delight, 300–302
egg pasta with
Parmigiano-Reggiano
cheese and nutmeg,
81
parsley pasta with tomato and
peas, 118–119
tortellini in broth, 134–137
Vitello al forno, 294–295

Watermelon, 446
Wine, 508
Wine, red:
fresh grape syrup, 158–159
risotto of rosemary and,
205–206
strawberries in, 445
see also Marsala

Wine, white:
-basted rabbit, Giovanna's,
284–285
-braised sausage, gramigna
with, 114–115
pasta, 82
Wood-burning oven,
approximating, 391

Yams:
cappellacci with sweet squash,
145–147
sweet squash for Yom Kippur,
339–340

Zabaione:
Duchess of Parma torte,
404–407
frozen hazelnut, with
chocolate Marsala sauce,
436–437
jam tart, 415–416
zampone of the aristocrats,
315–317

Zampone, 506–508
of the aristocrats, 315–317
buying, storing and using of,
506–507
in Emilia-Romagna, 507–508
Zampone nobile, 315–317
Ziti with wine-braised sausage,
115
Zucca disfatta, 339–340
Zucchini:
grilled peppers, onions and,
338–339
herb and garlic grilled, 329
Zuppa:
di aglio fresco, 222–223
di cavolo nero, 235–237
di ceci e pesce, 264–265
dei frati cappuccini, 220–221
di funghi porcini, 226–227
inglese di Vincenzo Agnoletti,
430–432
Zuppa Inglese, frozen, 430–432

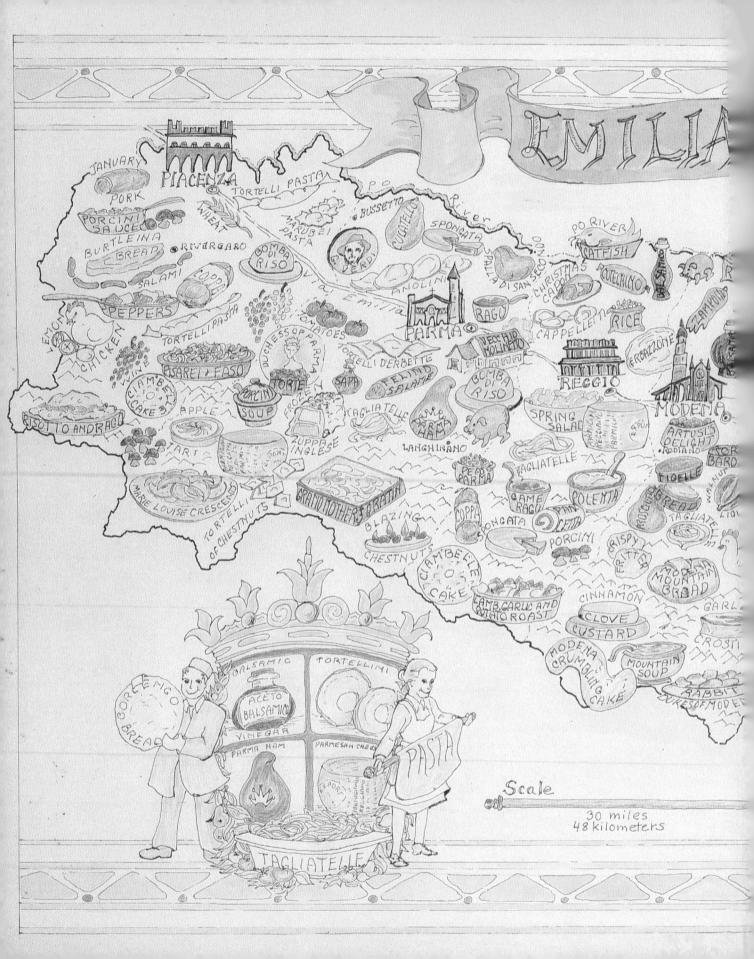